THE POETICAL WORKS
OF
ROBERT BROWNING

General Editor: MICHAEL MEREDITH

THE OXFORD ENGLISH TEXTS
EDITION OF THE POETICAL WORKS
OF ROBERT BROWNING

Vol. I: PAULINE, PARACELSUS

Vol. II: STRAFFORD, SORDELLO

Vol. III: PIPPA PASSES, KING VICTOR AND KING CHARLES, DRAMATIC LYRICS, THE RETURN OF THE DRUSES, A BLOT IN THE 'SCUTCHEON, COLOMBE'S BIRTHDAY (*Bells and Pomegranates* i–vi)

Vol. IV: DRAMATIC ROMANCES AND LYRICS, LURIA and A SOUL'S TRAGEDY (*Bells and Pomegranates* vii–viii), CHRISTMAS-EVE AND EASTER-DAY

Vol. V: MEN AND WOMEN

Vol. VII: THE RING AND THE BOOK (Books I–IV)

Vol. VIII: THE RING AND THE BOOK (Books V–VIII)

THE POETICAL WORKS OF
ROBERT BROWNING

Volume IX

THE RING AND THE BOOK

Books IX–XII

EDITED BY

STEFAN HAWLIN

AND

T. A. J. BURNETT

CLARENDON PRESS · OXFORD

OXFORD
UNIVERSITY PRESS

Great Clarendon Street, Oxford OX2 6DP

Oxford University Press is a department of the University of Oxford.
It furthers the University's objective of excellence in research, scholarship,
and education by publishing worldwide in
Oxford New York

Auckland Bangkok Buenos Aires Cape Town Chennai
Dar es Salaam Delhi Hong Kong Istanbul Karachi Kolkata
Kuala Lumpur Madrid Melbourne Mexico City Mumbai Nairobi
São Paulo Shanghai Taipei Tokyo Toronto

Published in the United States
by Oxford University Press Inc., New York

First published 2004

British Library Cataloguing in Publication Data
Data available

Library of Congress Cataloging in Publication Data
Data available

ISBN 0-19-818671-1

1 3 5 7 9 10 8 6 4 2

Typeset by Kolam Information Services Pvt. Ltd, Pondicherry, India
Printed in Great Britain
on acid-free paper by
Biddles, King's Lynn

PREFACE AND ACKNOWLEDGEMENTS

IT is a pleasure to record our obligations and thanks to friends, colleagues, and scholars. Our principal debt is to Michael Meredith, the General Editor, for his continuous encouragement, and for going through the typescript so carefully, making many suggestions. At the end of this volume we are pleased to include his 'Afterword' about the real Franceschini case, based on his researches with Simonetta Berbeglia in the Arezzo archives. Simonetta Berbeglia must be thanked in her own right, for valuable suggestions on a number of points in relation to Arezzo and Italian history. We should also like to thank again Dr Scott Lewis and Dr Philip Kelley for access to the *Brownings' Correspondence* Database, and for searches on the Database in relation to the commentary here. The gift of a full set of *Studies in Browning and His Circle* from Rita S. Patteson, Manuscripts Librarian of the Armstrong Browning Library, has greatly aided our work.

Marcella McCarthy read the typescript and made shrewd observations and corrections. John Drew, John Clarke, Adam Roberts, Richard Finn OP, and Eamon Duffy have kindly answered inquiries. Obviously, we have learnt greatly from the work of others scholars: in this instance, from Roma A. King, Jun. and Susan Crowl, and from the textual work of Thomas J. Collins. In this volume, as on earlier volumes, Leofranc Holford-Strevens of OUP has shared his erudition in a very generous way.

We should like to thank the staffs of the libraries where most of our research was done: the Bodleian Library, the British Library, and the University of Buckingham Library. Lastly, we should like to thank each other, for a long and happy collaboration.

S. H., T. A. J. B.

11 March 2003

CONTENTS

TEXTUAL NOTE TO BOOKS IX–XII

THE primary sources provide evidence of the growth of Browning's text, as follows:

1. *The Printer's copy manuscript.* The ninth book of the poem is heavily revised in manuscript. In the course of a sample five pages (144–8), for instance, there are five revisions to accidentals, but seventy-two revisions to substantives. The revisions are predominantly in order to improve the rhythm, as in line 617, where 'the inapprehensive husband' becomes 'inapprehensive Guido', or to make the language more vivid, as well as more euphonious, as in line 616, where 'Marched bag and baggage forth, at beat of drum' is changed to 'March out of door, spread flag at beat of drum'. Book X is more lightly revised, a sample five pages (233–7) yielding but one revision to the accidentals, and thirty-eight revisions to substantives. Again, the revisions are for the most part to tighten up the sense, to make the language more vivid, and to improve the rhythm—as in 1713, where the line was revised three times, from the somewhat leaden 'And what I saw fit, strove the world should see' to 'And what I saw, I taught the world to see' to 'And what I loved, I taught the world to love' and, finally, to the beautifully balanced and rhythmic 'And what my heart taught me, I taught the world'. Similarly, 1674 progresses from 'The outward product men may estimate' to 'The outward product all may estimate' to 'The outward product we may praise or blame' until it is recast as 'It is the outward product we appraise:'. Book XI, too, is more lightly revised than Book IX, a sample five pages (270–4) revealing three revisions to the accidentals and forty-four to the substantives. The revisions are chiefly intended to improve the rhythm of the lines, as in 709, where 'Born, bred and baptized' becomes 'Born, baptized and bred', or to make the sense more specific, as in 715, where 'Who at this moment pay the Maker thus' is changed to 'Who pay the Maker in this speech of mine'. In 732, where 'And God's too, I feel certain:' first becomes 'As mine,

so God's too, I feel:', and then finally 'Mine and God's also, doubtless,' the last version is far more powerful, and more characteristic of Guido than its predecessors. Book XII is lightly revised, a sample five pages (338–42) showing only four revisions to accidentals and eleven to substantives. The revisions achieve a more vivid image, as in 145, where 'at the Mannaia' becomes 'at Mannaia's foot', or 173, where 'addressed' becomes 'harangued'. In the next line, 174, 'Entreated pardon' is changed to 'He begged forgiveness', a more down to earth expression and thus more telling. Line 182 was originally almost the same as 187, but was then altered radically in order to introduce the *umbilicus*. It is interesting, therefore, that lines 737–50, where Bottini recounts Arcangeli's pun on '*Ad umbilicum sic perventum est!*', are not found in the manuscript. Book IX has had eighty lines added to the text (including the first sixteen lines of the book), and Book X forty-eight, while Book XI has had a mere fourteen added, though they include the important line 2426. Book XII has had but one; line 84.

2. *The First Edition*. The revisions made to the text at proof stage reveal a significant difference as between Books X and XI of the poem and Books IX and XII. In the course of four sample pages of the manuscript of Book IX there are four substantive variants from the text of the first edition, and thirty-five variants in the accidentals. In the case of Book X four sample pages of the manuscript reveal twenty substantive variants and ninety-two accidental variants. In the case of Book XI four pages of the manuscript reveal twenty-four substantive variants and fifty accidental variants, while in the case of Book XII four sample pages of the manuscript reveal seven variants in the substantives and twenty-six variants in the accidentals. In the course of the whole of Book IX thirteen lines have been added at proof stage; of Book X fifty-seven; of Book XI sixty-two; and of Book XII forty-five. In the Yale proofs, however, there is little difference between the three books that they cover. The proofs of Books IX, X, and XI are corrected galleys, together with corrected but deleted page proofs of Book XI, pp. 193–5. There are no corrected proofs of Book XII. Very few of the changes made by RB are corrections of inaccurate type-setting or

broken sorts; most are revisions. Book IX has twenty-nine substantive changes, fifty-seven accidental, five corrections, three paragraph changes and one line added. Book X has forty-five substantive changes, sixty-two accidental, and four corrections, while Book XI has thirty-eight substantive changes, ninety accidental and five corrections. These figures give an average of one revision per eighteen lines in the case of Book IX, and per nineteen lines in the cases of Books X and XI. Further revision must have been carried out between the galley proof stage and the first edition since there are instances where the text found in the proof has not been adopted in the first edition.

3. *The Second Edition.* The text of Books IX–XII was revised for the second edition in 1872 (see the introduction to Volume Seven of this edition) when a significant number of revisions were made. In the course of 1579 lines, Book IX has two hundred and forty-six variants between the first and second editions, while in the course of 2135 lines Book X has two hundred and thirty-nine. In the course of 2427 lines Book XI has two hundred and eighty variants, while in the course of 874 lines Book XII has eighty-one. Book IX is therefore the most heavily revised with an average of one revision every six lines, while Books X and XI are similar with an average of one revision every nine lines, while yet again Book XII is the most lightly revised with an average of one revision every eleven lines.

Emendations to the text

Accidentals

Book IX: 16, 164, 429, 716, 717, 841, 850, 868, 919, 977, 1108, 1163, 1287. Book X: 29, 37, 130, 372, 480, 659, 669, 695, 698, 701, 737, 741, 832, 872, 949, 1041, 1100, 1159, 1205, 1507, 1790, 1989, 1990, 2090. Book XI: 22, 48, 217, 236, 456, 495, 507, 602, 669, 830, 884, 920, 1074, 1219, 1226, 1358, 1390, 1410, 1417, 1432, 1437, 1440, 1497, 1610, 1618, 1824, 1836, 1864, 2013, 2029, 2071, 2134, 2276, 2361. Book XII: 3, 53, 141, 153, 337, 368, 405, 458,

494, 647–51, 652, 653, 654–734, 661, 710, 734, 735, 736–44, 745, 746, 747–9, 797.

Substantives

Book IX: 21, 549, 723, 742. Book X: 181, 360, 385, 728, 921, 977, 987, 1883, 2080. Book XI: 279, 622, 2072, 2194. Book XII: 774, 819.

Restored paragraphs

Book IX: 213, 239, 290, 610, 643, 720, 888, 1506. Book X: 965, 1430, 1791, 1955. Book XI: none. Book XII: 118, 318, 492, 672, 868.

Accidentals

Of the eighty-nine emendations which we have made to accidentals, thirty-six result from revisions made by Browning in the Dykes Campbell copy of *The Poetical Works*, 1888–9, and the list of revisions in RB's hand to vols. iv–x of *The Poetical Works*, 1888–9, preserved at Brown University. All these revisions were adopted in *1889*. In only two cases (Book X, line 737, where *1889* follows *DC*, and Book XI, line 1497, where *1889* follows *BrU*) do the two witnesses differ, and in both we have adopted the version found in the Brown University list, as we have in Book XI, 1437, where only *BrU* has an emendation, and this is adopted in *1889*. The remainder of the emendations result for the most part from editorial correction of inaccurate typesetting in the editions of 1888–9 and 1889, or from supplying missing characters caused by broken sorts found in the printing of those two editions. Of these twenty-two are of significance: Book IX, line 919, where the substitution of 'Such' for 'such' makes sense of the punctuation; Book X, lines 29, where the substitution of 'how' for 'How' also makes sense of the punctuation, 480, where a full stop at the end of the line strengthens the question in the next line, 659, where the restoration of the commas strengthens the distance which ought to exist between priest and wife, 737, where the deletion of the full stop allows lines 736 and 737 to form one passage with lines 738–40, and 1790, where the restoration of the question mark found in the earlier witnesses refers back to the question which begins in line 1781; Book XI, lines 602, where a question mark is required at the end of the line, 669, where a comma was not required at the end of the line, 1219, where the question mark needs to follow the quotation, 1226, where a comma is required at the end of the line to make clear that three separate actions are expected, 1410, where the comma after 'soprano' needlessly interrupted the flow of Guido's question, 1417, where quotation marks are needed at the end of the line, 1618, where a question mark is required after 'escape', 2013 and 2134, where the line must end with the colon found in the earlier witnesses for the passage to make sense syntactically; and Book XII, lines 53, where the hyphen is needed to ensure that the main stress falls on 'Naples', 337, where a quotation mark is required after 'thanks!', 368, where a comma is needed after '"*Quod*', 405, where we restore the question mark after 'Eh' of the earlier witnesses, 458, where quotation marks are needed after 'do!' to mark the end of the first part of Bottini's letter, 647–750, where Browning fails to use quotation marks when Bottini's letter resumes, and 710, where we restore the comma after 'Pompilia'.

Substantives

We have made nineteen emendations to substantives. To deal with the simple cases first, Book IX, line 21, Book X, lines 385 and 728, and Book XI, lines 279 and 2072 result from deliberate changes made by RB in both the Dykes Campbell copy and the Brown University list, while Book IX, lines 723 and 742, Book X, lines 360 and 977, Book XI, line 2194 and Book XII, line 819 are typographical errors similarly corrected by RB. That leaves eight cases where the text found in *1888* and *1889* can be improved by critical examination of the witnesses. In Book IX, line 549, we have emended 'sunk' to 'sank', the correct form of the verb, and moreover that which is found in the manuscript. In Book X, lines 181 and 921, we have corrected the spelling of 'license' and 'unsheath' respectively to that found in the earlier witnesses. In Book X, line 1883, we emend 'that', clearly a typographical error, to 'than', also the form that is found in the earlier witnesses. Similarly, in line 2080 we emend 'make' to 'made', which not only corrects the tense (the accomplices are already dead) but also is the reading found in the manuscript and the first edition. In Book X, line 987, we have inserted 'me' after 'under', thus restoring sense and giving the line ten feet. All the earlier witnesses have 'me' after 'under'. In Book XI, line 622, we have emended 'made' to 'make', thus putting it into the same tense as 'wave', and restoring the reading found in all the earlier witnesses. Finally, in Book XII, line 774, we have emended 'account' to 'accounts', the more usual form found in this expression, and the reading found in the manuscript and the first edition.

REFERENCES AND ABBREVIATIONS

Note: the place of publication is given if it is not London or Oxford.

ABL The Armstrong Browning Library, Baylor University, Waco, Texas.

Allingham *William Allingham: A Diary*, ed. Helen Allingham and Dollie Radford (1907).

Altick Richard D. Altick (ed.), *The Ring and the Book* (Harmondsworth, 1971).

Altick and Loucks Richard D. Altick and James F. Loucks, II, *Browning's Roman Murder Story: A Reading of 'The Ring and the Book'* (University of Chicago Press, Chicago and London, 1968).

Aurora Leigh *Aurora Leigh*, ed. Margaret Reynolds (University of Ohio, Athens, 1992).

Biographie universelle *Biographie universelle, ancienne et moderne*, 52 vols. (Paris, 1811–28).

BIS *Browning Institute Studies*, annual volumes, 1973–90.

BN *The Browning Newsletter* (Armstrong Browning Library, Waco, Tex.), 1968–72.

Brady Ann P. Brady, *Pompilia: A Feminist Reading of Robert Browning's 'The Ring and the Book'* (Ohio University Press, Athens, 1988).

Buckler William E. Buckler, *Poetry and Truth in Robert Browning's The Ring and the Book* (New York and London, 1985).

BSN *Browning Society Notes* (Browning Society of London), 1971–

Carlyle: *Works* (Centenary ed., 30 vols., 1896–9).

Catholic Encyclopedia: 15 vols. (Robert Appleton Co., New York, 1907–12)

Checklist *The Brownings' Correspondence: A Checklist*, compiled by Philip Kelley and Ronald Hudson, The Browning Institute and Wedgestone Press (Winfield, Kan., 1978; supplements in later vols. of BIS).

Conclaves W. C. Cartwright, *On Papal Conclaves* (Edinburgh, 1868)

Cook A. K. Cook, *A Commentary Upon Browning's 'The Ring and the Book'* (1920).

Correspondence *The Brownings' Correspondence*, ed. Philip Kelley and Ronald Hudson (to vol. viii), ed. Philip Kelley and Scott Lewis (Wedgestone Press, Winfield, Kan., 1984–).

Curious Annals Beatrice Corrigan (ed.), *Curious Annals: New Documents Relating to Browning's Roman Murder Story* (University of Toronto Press, Toronto, 1956).

Dearest Isa: *Robert Browning's Letters to Isabella Blagden*, ed. Edward C. McAleer (Austin, Tex. and Edinburgh, 1951).

EBB Elizabeth Barrett Browning

EPD English Poetry Database (Chadwyck-Healey, Ann Arbor, Mich., 1992–5)

Everyman *The Old Yellow Book: Source of Robert Browning's The Ring and the Book*, translated and edited by Charles W. Hodell (Everyman Library series, 1911).

Gest John Marshall Gest, *The Old Yellow Book, Source of Browning's The Ring and the Book: A New Translation with Explanatory Notes and Critical Chapters upon the Poem and Its Source* (University of Pennsylvania, Philadelphia, 1927).

Griffin and Minchin *The Life of Robert Browning*, by William Hall Griffin, completed and edited by Harry Christopher Minchin, 3rd ed., revised and enlarged (1938; 1st ed., 1910).

Griffin Collections William Hall Griffin, biographer of Robert Browning, 'Collections for his *Life* of Robert Browning', 7 vols., British Library, Additional MSS 45558–45564.

Hawthorne Nathaniel Hawthorne, *The French and Italian Notebooks*, ed. Thomas Woodson (Ohio State University, Columbus, 1980), vol. xiv of the *Centenary Edition of the works of Nathaniel Hawthorne*, 23 vols. (1964–).

Hodell Charles W. Hodell, *The Old Yellow Book, Source of Browning's The Ring and the Book, in Complete Photo-Reproduction, with Translation, Essay, and Notes*, 2nd ed. (Carnegie Institution of Washington, 1916; 1st ed., 1908).

Honan Park Honan, *Browning's Characters: A Study in Poetic Technique* (Yale University Press, New Haven and London, 1961).

Hudson *Browning to his American Friends*, ed. Gertrude Reese Hudson (1965).

It. Italian.

Jack Ian Jack, *Browning's Major Poetry* (1973).

James Henry James, 'The Novel in "The Ring and the Book"', in *Notes on Novelists* (1914).

Johnson Samuel Johnson, *A Dictionary of the English Language*, Times Books facsimile of the 1755 text (1979).

Kelley and Coley *The Browning Collections: A Reconstruction with Other Memorabilia*, compiled by Philip Kelley and Betty A. Coley, Armstrong Browning Library, Baylor University, Texas (1984).

Kelly John N. D. Kelly, *The Oxford Dictionary of Popes* (1986).

L. Latin.

Landis *Letters of the Brownings to George Barrett*, ed. Paul Landis and R. E. Freeman (Urbana, Ill., 1958).

Learned Lady: *Letters from Robert Browning to Mrs Thomas FitzGerald*, ed. Edward C. McAleer (Cambridge, Mass., 1966).

Letters *Letters of Robert Browning Collected by Thomas J. Wise*, ed. Thurman L. Hood (1933).

Letters of EBB *The Letters of Elizabeth Barrett Browning*, ed. Frederic G. Kenyon, 2 vols. (1898).

Life *Life and Letters of Robert Browning*, by Mrs Sutherland Orr, new ed. rev. by Frederic G. Kenyon (1908; 1st ed., 1891).

Miller Betty Miller, *Robert Browning: A Portrait* (1952).

MLR *Modern Language Review.*

New Letters *New Letters of Robert Browning*, ed. William Clyde DeVane and Kenneth Leslie Knickerbocker (1951).

ODEP *Oxford Dictionary of English Proverbs*, 3rd ed., ed. F. P. Wilson (1970).

OED^2 *Oxford English Dictionary*, 2nd ed., ed. J. A. Simpson and E. S. C. Weiner, 20 vols. (1989).

Ogilvy *Elizabeth Barrett Browning's Letters to Mrs. David Ogilvy 1849–1861*, ed. Peter N. Heydon and Philip Kelley (1974).

Ohio *The Complete Works of Robert Browning*, ed. Roma A. King, jun., *et al.* (Ohio University Press, Athens, Ohio, 1969–). *The Ring and the Book* comprises vols. vii (1985), viii (1988), and ix (1989).

OYB Old Yellow Book. In references in the style 'OYB lxxi (78)' the roman numeral refers to Hodell's complete facsimile and translation (see Hodell), and the arabic numeral to the more widely available Everyman reprint of Hodell's translation (see Everyman). Quotations have been freshly translated, and do not necessarily correspond exactly with Hodell's translation.

Pastor Ludwig Pastor, *The History of the Popes*, ed. F. I. Antrobus *et al.*, 40 vols. (1891–1953)

Pettigrew and Collins *Robert Browning: The Poems*, ed. John Pettigrew, supplemented and completed by Thomas J. Collins, 2 vols. (Penguin English Poets, Harmondsworth; Yale University Press, New Haven, 1981).

R&B *The Ring and the Book.*

RB Robert Browning

Roba di Roma William Wetmore Story, *Roba di Roma*, 2 vols. (1863).

Rossetti Letters *Letters of Dante Gabriel Rossetti*, ed. Oswald Doughty and John Robert Wahl, 4 vols. (1965–7).

Rossetti Papers *Rossetti Papers, 1862 to 1870*, compiled by William Michael Rossetti (1903).

SBC *Studies in Browning and his Circle* (Armstrong Browning Library, Waco, Tex.), 1973–

SS Secondary Source: Browning's secondary source for the poem, the Italian manuscript 'Morte dell'Uxoricida Guido Franceschini Decapitato'. References in the style 'SS 12' are to the paragraph numbers in the reprint and translation in our Vol. VII, Appendix B.

Story Henry James, *William Wetmore Story and his Friends*, 2 vols. (1903).

Sullivan Mary Rose Sullivan, *Browning's Voices in The Ring and the Book* (University of Toronto Press, Toronto, 1969).

Thomas Charles Flint Thomas, *Art and Architecture in the Poetry of Robert Browning* (Troy, NY, 1991).

Tilley M. P. Tilley, *A Dictionary of the Proverbs in England in the Sixteenth and Seventeenth Centuries* (Ann Arbor, Mich., 1950).

TLS *Times Literary Supplement.*

Treves Frederick Treves, *The Country of 'The Ring and the Book'* (1913).

Trumpeter *Browning's Trumpeter: The Correspondence of Robert Browning and Frederick J. Furnivall 1872–1889*, ed. William S. Peterson (Washington, DC, 1979).

Vasari *Lives of the Most Eminent Painters, Sculptors, and Architects*, trans. from the Italian of Giorgio Vasari by Mrs Jonathan Foster, 5 vols. (1850–2)

VP *Victorian Poetry* (Morgantown, W.Va.)

Wedgwood *Robert Browning and Julia Wedgwood*, ed. Richard Curle (1937).

Note: references to Shakespeare are to *The Riverside Shakespeare*, ed. G. Blakemore Evans, *et al.* (Houghton Mifflin Company, Boston, 1974).

Abbreviations and signs used in the text and textual notes

*	An emendation by the editors.
. . . .	Omission by the editors.
{ }	Comment by the editors.
>	Substitution by RB of the word or passage preceding the symbol with the word or passage following the symbol (e.g.

	this>that means that RB has substituted 'that' for 'this' in the MS, proof, or printed work).
^ ^	Additions within the body of the text (e.g. ^decent^ means that RB inserted 'decent' between 'as' and 'wrappage' after he had written 'as wrappage' in order to make the text read 'as decent wrappage').
⟨ ⟩	Deletion in manuscript.
[ ]	Text which is illegible in the MS. The distance between the brackets represents the length of the illegible portion of text; dubious readings are contained within square brackets and preceded by a question mark.
|	Division between lines.
[—]	In the main text, a paragraph-break obscured by the pagination.
BrU	List of revisions in RB's hand to vols. iv–x of *Poetical Works*, 1888–9, preserved at Brown University Library, Providence, RI.
DC	Copy of *Poetical Works*, 1888–9, formerly belonging to James Dykes Campbell, and containing revisions by RB, preserved in the British Library.
MS	The autograph printer's copy MS for *The Ring and the Book*, 1868–9, preserved in the British Library.
Yale 1	Proofs for *The Ring and the Book*, 1868–9. Corrected page proofs of Books I–VI (with the exception of quires H and I of Book II, lines 415–1032, which are from the second edition, and carry no corrections), and corrected galley proofs of Books VII–XI, together with corrected but deleted page proofs of Book XI, pp. 193–5, and uncorrected page proofs of Book XII. Preserved in the Beinecke Library, Yale University, as 1p / B821 / 868a.
1868	*The Ring and the Book*, 1868–9.
1872	*The Ring and the Book*, 1872, [1882], [1883].
Yale 2	Sheets from the Second Edition, vols. I, III, and IV, revised by RB but mislaid so that the revisions never appeared in print. Preserved in the Beinecke Library, Yale University, as 1p / B821 / 868c.
1888	*The Poetical Works of Robert Browning*, 16 vols., 1888–9.
1889	*The Poetical Works of Robert Browning*, second impression, 16 vols., 1889.

THE RING AND THE BOOK

Books IX–XII

INTRODUCTION TO BOOK IX

JURIS DOCTOR JOHANNES-BAPTISTA BOTTINIUS

THE speaker of Book IX is Giovanni Battista Bottini, 'Advocate of the Fisc and of the Reverend Apostolic Chamber', the prosecution lawyer. In Book VIII the lawyer Arcangeli defended Guido against the death-penalty on the grounds of injured honour. Now we have a portrait of the lawyer charged with maintaining Pompilia's innocence and bringing Guido to book for her murder.

The sources only provided Browning with hints; the substance of this character is his own invention. In OYB there is a real Bottini, who made formal depositions to the court (pamphlets 6, 13, and 14). Pamphlet 13 is a careful working out of the argument that there was insufficient evidence to prove Pompilia's adultery, and therefore no justification for her murder; it is formally expressed and legalistic, a careful examination of evidence and points of law. It provided the poet with some clues to the character he here creates, but Browning's high farce and caricature leave it a long way behind.

Bottini is one of Browning's most brilliant comic creations, a truth obscured—for some—by his extensive use of allusion. His monologue is a high-flown comedy, what Donald Davie (in another context) calls 'high-spirited', 'good-tempered' comedy, the pure spirit of joke, neither falling to the anger of satire on one side, nor the frivolity of absurdity on the other.[1] In the first place, Bottini's argument is a comedy of concessions. 'If', 'Suppose', 'Concede', 'Admit': these are the words that embody his favoured strategy. He claims to be painting a picture of Pompilia as a near saint, a paragon, but he proceeds to 'concede' or 'admit' many of the charges brought against her by the defence, apparently only for the sake of argument, but actually establishing them in his listeners' minds. Inadvertently, he creates an image of Pompilia as a flagrant, cheeky adulteress, who paradoxically (somehow) has done nothing serious to provoke Guido's rage or warrant her own death.

[1] Donald Davie, 'Ed Dorn and the Treasures of Comedy', *Vort*, *1* (Fall, *1972*), *24*.

Bottini contrasts with Arcangeli. The latter (in Book VIII) was so mired in his concern with food, family, wealth, and the connoisseurship of fine Latin, that he was barely able to concentrate on writing his deposition for Guido's defence. Bottini is more focused, more self-centred, more professional. Unlike Arcangeli, the proudly married man, he is single: 'a rigid bachelor', Cook calls him, 'with no unprofessional cares or interests'.[2] Sullivan draws attention to Arcangeli's unsympathetic description of him as a 'lean-gutted hectic rascal', a 'pale-haired red-eyed ferret' (VIII. 224–5). Other critics note that while Arcangeli only works on a first draft, Bottini gives us a finished (or all but finished) speech, which he delivers, as if in final rehearsal. Arcangeli can barely wait to leave his desk to get to his son's birthday party, and the delicious food and society it promises. Bottini is without family, and describes himself heroically as the 'son' of 'mother' Law (1507–8, 1525, 1563), the servant of her concerns and of his own brilliance. Unlike the socially expansive Arcangeli, he is alone in his 'modest studio' (I. 1202), fantasizing (in onanistic fashion) the triumph of professional skill. He wants to be allowed to deliver his speech theatrically before the court, rather than, as he is obliged to, submitting it in printed form.

In these circumstances, the performance is excessive and over-reaching, showing a 'pompous, inflated style' within which 'no Latinate polysyllabic word or phrase is too outrageous'.[3] Perhaps (in Susan Sontag's sense) the speech is also 'camp' in its ingenuity and bravura, its compulsion to 'astonish, outsmart, upstage any conceivable listener or reader'. Bottini seeks effects that help to achieve this, and 'revels' in his successes.[4]

In the character sketch of him in Book I Browning describes him (after Chaucer's Chauntecleer) as a straining cockerel:

> The tall wight stands a-tiptoe, strives and strains,
> Both eyes shut, like the cockerel that would crow,
> Tries to his own self amorously o'er
> What never will be uttered else than so
>
> (I. 1203–6)

Bottini prefers to see himself (in self-aggrandizing fashion) as a master painter, an epic poet, or one of the orators of antiquity (17–18, 217,

[2] Cook, 179. [3] Sullivan, 117.

[4] Susan Sontag, *Against Interpretation and Other Essays* (1967), 275–92. The quotation here is from Donald Davie's paraphrase of her idea, in *Two Ways Out of Whitman* (2000), 122.

1573). His speech begins with an exordium comparing his work and the making of it to the practice of the master painter, a conceit that becomes so elaborate and extended that he almost loses control of it (17–118). Other passages show ludicrous rhetorical heightening. In one instance he tells himself that he is so overcome with the brilliance of Pompilia's pure image that he must 'paint' her all at once or not at all (191–212). In another case, simply explaining how (after the departure of the Comparini) Pompilia and Guido might have settled to ordinary married love, he crowds together allusions to Revelation, Virgil, and the Song of Solomon (280–9).

This straining is also enacted through his use of allusion, particularly to the classics, but also to the Bible. In Pamphlet 13, the real Bottini refers just once to the classics, to Ovid's *Heroides* (i. *12*).[5] Browning develops this into an addiction: there are over fifty classical allusions, to Virgil, Anacreon, Catullus, Ovid, Persius, Moschus, Homer, Cicero, Suetonius, Thucydides, Sophocles, and (most often) Horace. Here, indeed, is a love of exaggeration, an emphasis on style that 'slights content', a sensibility alive to 'pure artifice' at the expense of meaning,[6] and the particular worship of Horace seems bound up with this aspect of his sensibility. The allusion at *566–82* shows clearly how argumentative style triumphs over content, to such an extent that clarity of meaning is virtually lost. In another instance (*1338–413*) allusions to the *Eclogues* and *Georgics*, the *Fasti*, and then again the *Eclogues* are drawn into an argument that, at first sight, would seem impossible to illustrate in these terms. The whole process is 'too much', 'self-amorous' indeed, for the reader (not Bottini) hugely comic.

The contrast between married and single men has occurred before. 'Half Rome', the sadist of Book II, was married, and sought to exert a dominant control over his wife, the highly confined 'angel of the house'. 'Half-Rome' is contrasted with 'Other Half-Rome', the speaker of Book III, a bachelor with a kitsch view of female saintliness. But both cruelty and sentimentality drain 'the other' of content. Both characters diminish, in different ways, the real 'other' of the feminine, or appropriate it to their own ends. Now, between Books VIII and IX, Browning repeats the pattern, with profounder (or at least multiplied) effect. In VIII the lawyer Arcangeli does not mention his wife often, but she is at the centre of his worship of 'home-sanctitudes' (VIII. 1774), primarily the mother of the son who represents his own egoism. In the closing lines of VIII, Arcangeli

[5] OYB clxxvii (184)   [6] Sontag, 279, 277, 281.

makes a wonderful slip in quoting Horace, conflating the pearls (*bacis*) he has cunningly purchased for his wife with his wife's breasts. This botched allusion draws together 'his solid satisfaction in the comforts of married sexuality and his pride and complacency in his middle-class wealth'.[7] While Arcangeli's imagination is over-invested in bosomy domesticity, Bottini shows what Sullivan calls 'a leering attitude to women',[8] a salacious eye. Needless to say, this is little noted by early critics, and later critics are often still coy.

Perhaps some aspects of Bottini's franker, un-Victorian address to sexuality have been inspired by his classical reading, but really there is something particular here: his text fairly buzzes with euphemism, *double entendre*, sexual innuendo, and images of nakedness. At the most innocent level this manifests itself in slightly lavish vocabulary, or phrases with a hint of innuendo: 'bosom uberous' (*53*), 'olent breast' (*313*), 'sweets of wifehood' (*334*), 'the garb of truth' (*891*)—a euphemism for nakedness. It progresses to more explicit sexual innuendo—the naked Phryne smiling 'smooth' (*174*), 'a super-sweet makes kiss seem cold' (*536*)—to the open image of Pompilia and Caponsacchi caught *in flagrante* like Venus and Mars (*868–77*), and the real naughtiness of Archimedes stabbed by the soldier (Pompilia penetrated by Caponsacchi) (*759–65*). This last has been called, somewhat hyperbolically, 'the most audacious sexual scene in Victorian literature',[9] but it is all of a part with Bottini's particular way of noticing nude statues, short skirts, and obscene Renaissance texts (*804*, *1186–7*, *1204*).

The ironic pattern set up here shows moral nuance. In Book VIII Arcangeli is veritably lost in the world of the body, so that his besetting vice is simple greed, overindulgence in food. He is a fat man, devoted to the pleasures of the table, a fact that the austere, thin Bottini notes with disgust. 'Thou Archangelic swine' (949) he puns on his opponent's name, jokingly placing archangels and pigs side by side. In another place he refers to Arcangeli as 'gross pamperer of the flesh / And niggard in the spirit's nourishment' (1401–2). What, quite, he means by 'spirit' here might be matter for debate, but in these insults he relies on a traditional opposition of body and soul, which helps to point to his own inadequacy. Where Arcangeli's mode is a distorted investment in the bodily realm, Bottini's mode is a distorted investment in the 'spiritual', one that ends in a particular kind of emotional narrowness and a mildly pornographic

[7] See our note to VIII. 1805–7.
[8] Sullivan, 113.
[9] Altick and Loucks, 180.

sensibility; that is to say, he creates images provocative of sexual arousal while himself seemingly being uninterested in any idea of sexual love. Bottini's thinness goes with his 'hectic', high-strung temperament. In contrast to Arcangeli, he certainly shows 'spirit'—the high ambition of his whole speech—but his artificial, denatured style is the appropriate accompaniment to his narrowed, denatured spirit, in particular his attitude towards women. He is a much fuller examination of the lecherous eye of the speaker of 'Soliloquy of the Spanish Cloister'—'Can't I see his dead eye glow' (30). He has under-invested in the warmth and intimacy of human love, just as (by contrast) Arcangeli has distorted that realm to his own greedy instincts.

THE RING AND THE BOOK.

1868–9.

IX.

JURIS DOCTOR JOHANNES-BAPTISTA BOTTINIUS,

FISCI ET REV. CAM. APOSTOL. ADVOCATUS.

HAD I God's leave, how I would alter things!
If I might read instead of print my speech,—
Ay, and enliven speech with many a flower
Refuses obstinate to blow in print,
As wildings planted in a prim parterre,—
This scurvy room were turned an immense hall;
Opposite, fifty judges in a row;
This side and that of me, for audience—Rome:
And, where yon window is, the Pope should hide—

MS {fo. 123. At the head of the page is the title '*9. Juris Doctor Johannes-Baptista Bottinius, Fisci et Rev.* <*cam.*> *Cam. Apostol. Advocatus.*' in RB's hand} 1–16 *MS* {lines added later. The lines were originally written parallel with the edge of the page in the right-hand margin of fo. 123 *(version 1)*, and then deleted. They were then rewritten on fo. 124, a half-leaf of paper inserted following fo. 123 *(version 2)*} 1 *MS (version 1)* {line added later} 3 *MS (version 1)* {line added later} *MS (version 1)* Ay, and add flowers of speech refuse in print 4 {not found in *MS (version 1)*} *MS (version 2) 1868 1872* obstinately blow *MS (version 2) 1868* {no comma} 5 *MS (version 1)* To blow, like wildings in a prim parterre,— *MS (version 2)* barren planted in parterre,—>planted in a prim parterre,— 6 *MS (version 1)* little>sorry *MS (version 2)* sorry>scurvy *MS (version 1)* ^turned^ 7 *MS (version 1)* Opposite,— *MS (version 1)* row,—>row; 8 *MS (version 1)* me for audience,—Rome; *MS (version 2)* Rome 9 *MS (version 1)* And where the *MS (version 1)* be>watch *MS (version 2) 1868* be—

---

2 *If . . . speech*: Bottini is frustrated that he is not allowed to deliver his speech in defence of Pompilia personally (and dramatically) before the court; it can only be submitted in printed form.

3 *flower*: figure of rhetoric.

4 *blow*: bloom.

5 *As . . . parterre*: i.e. as wild flowers in a neat, ornamental garden.

6 *scurvy*: shabby, contemptible.

Watch, curtained, but peep visibly enough.
A buzz of expectation! Through the crowd,
Jingling his chain and stumping with his staff,
Up comes an usher, louts him low, "The Court
"Requires the allocution of the Fisc!"
I rise, I bend, I look about me, pause
O'er the hushed multitude: I count—One, two—

Have ye seen, Judges, have ye, lights of law,—
When it may hap some painter, much in vogue
Throughout our city nutritive of arts,
Ye summon to a task shall test his worth,
To manufacture, as he knows and can,
A work may decorate a palace-wall,
Afford my lords their Holy Family,—
Hath it escaped the acumen of the Court
How such a painter sets himself to paint?
Suppose that Joseph, Mary and her Babe
A-journeying to Egypt, prove the piece:
Why, first he sedulously practiseth,
This painter,—girding loin and lighting lamp,—

10 *MS (version 1)* Curtained—but somehow visible the same!>Curtained—but somehow visible no less. *MS (version 2) 1868* but yet visibly 11–14 *MS (version 1)* {lines added later} 11 *MS (version 1)* expectation: thro' *MS (version 2)* expectation: thro'>expectation! Thro' *Yale 1* Thro'>Through 12 *MS (version 1)* [ ]>staff *MS (version 1)* {no comma} 13 *MS (version 1)* bends 14 *MS (version 1) MS (version 2)* {no quotation mark at beginning of line} *MS (version 1)* Fisc"— 15 *MS (version 1)* I look around me,—calmly pause>I bow, I look around me,—[ ]>I bow, I look around me,—pause 16 *MS (version 1)* people; I>multitude: **MS (version 1)* One, two, three— *1868 1872* two— *1888 1889* two—— 17 *MS* {New paragraph indicated by 'New Par.' in left-hand margin} 19 *MS* such,>arts, 20 *MS* and>shall *21 *MS 1868 1872 1888* And *DC BrU* And>To *1889* To 25 *MS* paint>paint? 26 *MS* That>Suppose that *etc.* 27 *MS 1868* {no comma} *MS* prompt>prove 28 *MS* practiseth

---

13 *louts him low*: bows obsequiously; cf. VI. 439 n.

14 *allocution*: formal address, from L. *alloqui*, to address, speak to.

19 *nutritive*: nourishing.

26–7 *Joseph ... Egypt*: the 'Flight into Egypt', from Matt. 2: 12–14, a common subject for Renaissance painters. Browning himself seems to have been particularly fond of one such painting in the Uffizi: see IV. 323–6 n.

29 *girding ... lamp*: i.e. getting ready: cf. Luke 12: 35.

On what may nourish eye, make facile hand;
Getteth him studies (styled by draughtsmen so)
From some assistant corpse of Jew or Turk
Or, haply, Molinist, he cuts and carves,—
This Luca or this Carlo or the like.
To him the bones their inmost secret yield,
Each notch and nodule signify their use:
On him the muscles turn, in triple tier,
And pleasantly entreat the entrusted man
"Familiarize thee with our play that lifts
"Thus, and thus lowers again, leg, arm and foot!"
—Ensuring due correctness in the nude.
Which done, is all done? Not a whit, ye know!
He,—to art's surface rising from her depth,—
If some flax-polled soft-bearded sire be found,
May simulate a Joseph, (happy chance!)—
Limneth exact each wrinkle of the brow,
Loseth no involution, cheek or chap,

30 *MS* hand, 31 *MS* studies, styled *MS* so, 32 *MS* Of wh>From *etc.* 33 *MS* to cut and carve,—>he cuts and carves,— 34 *MS* This Luca, or this Carlo>This Federigo, Luca,>This Luca or this Carlo *MS* like:— *1868* like: 36 *MS* Their use, each notch and nodule signify,>Each notch and nodule signify their use, *1868* use, 38 *MS* {line added later} *MS 1868* man,— 40 *MS* leg arm 41 *MS* nude[ ]>nude. 43 *MS* He, *MS* from>to *Yale 1* He to>He—to 44 *MS* {no comma} *Yale 1* soft-beared> soft-bearded 45 *MS* Joseph,—happy chance!— *1868 1872* chance!) 46 *MS* {beginning of fo. 125}

31 *studies . . . so*: 'careful preliminary sketches for a work of art, or (more usually) for some detail or portion of it': OED², which gives the following example (1822): 'Of this piece there are extant . . . more fragments and original sketches, or, as a painter would call them, *studies*, than of any other of Mr. Home's productions.' Browning himself studied drawing twice a week, with a Mrs Emma McKenzie, in Rome in the winter of 1858–9. Either then, or subsequently, he also studied anatomy in relation to art: see XI. 291–2 n. This passage uses specialist vocabulary: see ll. 36, 47, 56 nn.

33 *Molinist*: i.e. heretic. References to Molinos and Molinism are an important element in the poem as a whole: cf. I. 307 n., and Vol. VIII, Appendix A. The Catholic Church was against dissection at this time, hence the need for the corpse to be non-Christian.

36 *nodule*: a knot of bone, an anatomical term in Browning's day: see l. 31 n.

44 *flax-polled*: with a head (poll) with flax-like hair, i.e. straight and silver grey. Cf. Polonius and Sir Andrew Aguecheek: *Hamlet*, IV. v. 195–6, *Twelfth Night*.

47 *involution*: (an anatomical term) a rolling, curling, or turning inwards.

Till lo, in black and white, the senior lives!
Is it a young and comely peasant-nurse
That poseth? (be the phrase accorded me!)
Each feminine delight of florid lip,
Eyes brimming o'er and brow bowed down with love,
Marmoreal neck and bosom uberous,—
Glad on the paper in a trice they go
To help his notion of the Mother-maid:
Methinks I see it, chalk a little stumped!
Yea and her babe—that flexure of soft limbs,
That budding face imbued with dewy sleep,
Contribute each an excellence to Christ.
Nay, since he humbly lent companionship,
Even the poor ass, unpanniered and elate
Stands, perks an ear up, he a model too;
While clouted shoon, staff, scrip and water-gourd,—
Aught may betoken travel, heat and haste,—
No jot nor tittle of these but in its turn

50 *MS* poseth,—be *Yale 1* poseth,> poseth? *MS* me,— *Yale 1* me,>me! 53 *MS* uberous?>uberous,— 55 *MS* Mother-Maid— *1868* Mother-Maid: 65 *MS* No tittle of these but ministers in turn,>No jot nor tittle of these but, in its turn,

---

50 *be . . . me!*: i.e. 'let me be allowed this phrase'. The meaning of 'poseth' here, 'places herself in an attitude, as an artist's model', was a new sense in the mid-nineteenth century; Bottini's hedge draws attention to this slightly modish turn of phrase. See OED².

53 *Marmoreal . . . uberous*: i.e. 'white (marble-like) neck and milk-filled breasts'. This is pretentious vocabulary from Bottini. 'Uberous', nonetheless, was a favourite word of Francis Quarles, whose works Browning knew well. Cf., in this instance, *Emblems*, I. xii. 7–8: 'The ub'rous breasts, when fairly drawn, repast / The thriving infant with their milky flood.' For Browning's knowledge of Quarles, see *Life*, 30, and John Maynard, *Browning's Youth* (Cambridge, Mass., 1977), 315, 449.

55 *Mother-maid*: i.e. the Virgin Mary.

56 *stumped*: rubbed down, blurred. A 'stump' was a soft pointed instrument (of indiarubber or other material) 'used for rubbing down hard to produce a uniform tint, and for other similar purposes': OED².

57 *flexure*: grace, curve.

61 *unpanniered*: unloaded (of his baskets); hence he is 'elate' because he now has the easy job of posing for the painter.

63 *clouted . . . water-gourd*: i.e. worn shoes, walking-stick, satchel, and water container. 'Clouted shoon' is from Milton's *Comus*, 634.

Ministers to perfection of the piece:
Till now, such piece before him, part by part,—
Such prelude ended,—pause our painter may,
Submit his fifty studies one by one,
And in some sort boast "I have served my lords."

But what? And hath he painted once this while?
Or when ye cry "Produce the thing required,
"Show us our picture shall rejoice its niche,
"Thy Journey through the Desert done in oils!"—
What, doth he fall to shuffling 'mid his sheets,
Fumbling for first this, then the other fact
Consigned to paper,—"studies," bear the term!—
And stretch a canvas, mix a pot of paste,
And fasten here a head and there a tail,
(The ass hath one, my Judges!) so dove-tail
Or, rather, ass-tail in, piece sorrily out—
By bits of reproduction of the life—
The picture, the expected Family?
I trow not! do I miss with my conceit
The mark, my lords?—not so my lords were served!
Rather your artist turns abrupt from these,
And preferably buries him and broods
(Quite away from aught vulgar and extern)
On the inner spectrum, filtered through the eye,
His brain-deposit, bred of many a drop,
E pluribus unum: and the wiser he!

66 *MS* piece,— 71 *MS* {New paragraph indicated by 'New Par' in left-hand margin} 72 *MS* required— 73 *MS* {no comma} 75 *MS* {beginning of fo. 126} *MS* mid 76 *MS* {no comma} *Yale 1* this then>this, then 78 mix [ ]>mix 79 *MS* {no comma} 81 *MS* (Or,>Or, *MS* in,— *MS* out 82 *MS* life,— *Yale 1* life,>life— 84 *MS* not— *Yale 1* not—>not! 85 *MS* Not 86 *MS* from these, abrupt>abrupt from these, 87 *MS* broods, *Yale 1* broods,>broods 88 *MS* Quite *Yale 1* Quite>(Quite *MS* all>aught *MS* externe, *Yale 1* extern,>extern)

77 "*studies,*": cf. l. 31 n. : the quotation marks are to emphasize that these are only preliminary sketches.

91 *E pluribus unum*: i.e. 'one [image] emerging from many' (L.). The phrase is from *Moretum*, a poem ascribed to Virgil, l. 102, where, during the mixing of a garlic relish, one colour emerges from several.

For in that brain,—their fancy sees at work,
Could my lords peep indulged,—results alone,
Not processes which nourish such results,
Would they discover and appreciate,—life
Fed by digestion, not raw food itself,
No gobbets but smooth comfortable chyme
Secreted from each snapped-up crudity,—
Less distinct, part by part, but in the whole
Truer to the subject,—the main central truth
And soul o' the picture, would my Judges spy,—
Not those mere fragmentary studied facts
Which answer to the outward frame and flesh—
Not this nose, not that eyebrow, the other fact
Of man's staff, woman's stole or infant's clout,
But lo, a spirit-birth conceived of flesh,
Truth rare and real, not transcripts, fact and false.
The studies—for his pupils and himself!
The picture be for our eximious Rome
And—who knows?—satisfy its Governor,
Whose new wing to the villa he hath bought
(God give him joy of it) by Capena, soon
('T is bruited) shall be glowing with the brush
Of who hath long surpassed the Florentine,

92 *MS* brain, *MS* which>their 93 *MS* indulged, 94 *MS 1868 1872* the result, 95 *MS* life, 96 *MS* digestion not *MS* the>raw 101 *MS* say,— 102 *MS* Than>Not 104 *MS* {beginning of fo. 127} *MS* not the fact 106 *MS* flesh— 107 *MS* G[ ]>Truth *MS* transcript fact.>transcripts, fact and fact>transcripts, fact and false.

---

97 *chyme*: semi-liquid food, i.e. food after it has been digested.

105 *stole*: long robe.

clout: swaddling clothes; usually pl. 'clouts'.

109 *eximious*: distinguished, eminent. Bottini uses this pretentious Latinism to sound impressive. As OED[2] notes, though common in the seventeenth century, by the nineteenth century the few examples 'are humorously bombastic or pedantic'. Cf. 'Jochanan Hakkadosh', 12.

112 *by Capena*: i.e. near the site of the Porta Capena, the gate that used to exist at the beginning of the Appian Way. Since the gate was long destroyed, Bottini is simply indicating the pleasant, green area about 1/3 mile south of the Coliseum.

114 *the Florentine*: Michelangelo (1475–1564), brought up in Florence.

The Urbinate and . . . what if I dared add,
Even his master, yea the Cortonese,—
I mean the accomplished Ciro Ferri, Sirs!
(—Did not he die? I'll see before I print.)

End we exordium, Phœbus plucks my ear!
Thus then, just so and no whit otherwise,
Have I,—engaged as I were Ciro's self,
To paint a parallel, a Family,
The patriarch Pietro with his wise old wife
To boot (as if one introduced Saint Anne
By bold conjecture to complete the group)
And juvenile Pompilia with her babe,
Who, seeking safety in the wilderness,
Were all surprised by Herod, while outstretched
In sleep beneath a palm-tree by a spring,
And killed—the very circumstance I paint,
Moving the pity and terror of my lords—
Exactly so have I, a month at least,
Your Fiscal, made me cognizant of facts,
Searched out, pried into, pressed the meaning forth

115 *MS 1868 1872* and . . 116 *MS* him the 117 *Yale 1* sirs!>Sirs! 118 *MS* {line added later} *MS* {no brackets} *1868* I'll 119 *MS* {New paragraph indicated by 'New Par.' in left-hand margin} 122 *MS* Family 123 *MS* Pietro— 124 *MS* boot, as>boot, (as 125 *MS* group—>group)— 126 *MS* babe— 134 *MS* {beginning of fo. 128}

115 *The Urbinate*: Raphael (1483–1520), born in Urbino.

116 *the Cortonese*: Pietro Berrettini, known as Pietro da Cortona (1596–1669), the baroque painter already mentioned at v. 488–91: see n.

117 *Ciro Ferri*: (1634–89), the chief pupil and assistant of Pietro da Cortona. Bottini's suggestion that Ferri is a better painter than Michelangelo, Raphael, and Pietro da Cortona shows him to be a slave of fashion.

119 *End . . . ear*: i.e. 'Apollo tells me to end the formal opening of my speech.' The phrasing imitates Virgil, *Eclogues*, vi. 3–4: 'Cynthius [= Phoebus] aurem / vellit et admonuit': 'Cynthius pulled my ear and warned me.' Cf. Milton, 'Lycidas', 77.

124 *Saint Anne*: the mother of the Virgin Mary. Bottini's 'Family' of Pietro, Violante, Pompilia, and Gaetano is of course an awkward fit for the real Holy Family fleeing to Egypt. It is not clear if we should imagine 'patriarch Pietro' as St Joachim, the father of the Virgin Mary, or as St Joseph.

133 *Fiscal*: man of the fisc, public prosecutor.

Of every piece of evidence in point,
How bloody Herod slew these innocents,—
Until the glad result is gained, the group
Demonstrably presented in detail,
Their slumber and his onslaught,—like as life.
Yea and, availing me of help allowed
By law, discreet provision lest my lords
Be too much troubled by effrontery,—
The rack, law plies suspected crime withal—
(Law that hath listened while the lyrist sang
"*Lene tormentum ingenio admoves*,"
Gently thou joggest by a twinge the wit,
"*Plerumque duro*," else were slow to blab!)
Through this concession my full cup runs o'er:
The guilty owns his guilt without reserve.
Therefore by part and part I clutch my case
Which, in entirety now,—momentous task,—
My lords demand, so render them I must,
Since, one poor pleading more and I have done.
But shall I ply my papers, play my proofs,
Parade my studies, fifty in a row,
As though the Court were yet in pupilage,

139 *MS* onslaught:>onslaught,— 142 *MS* effrontery, *Yale 1* effrontery,>effrontery,— 143 *MS* {no comma} *MS* she>Law 145 *Yale 1* "*Leno*>"*Lene* 147 *MS* budge!)— 148 *MS* o'er— 151 *MS* Which in 152 *MS* and>so *MS* [ ]>them 156 *MS 1868 1872* {no comma}

---

136 *Herod . . . innocents*: cf. Matt. 2: 1–18. Here Guido is Herod the Great, and Pietro, Violante, and Pompilia are the 'holy innocents' whose slaughter he ordered.

143 *The rack*: the instrument of torture. Guido confessed to the murders under torture (or so Browning assumed from his study of OYB). See Vol. VIII, Appendix C for a detailed account of the actual torture proposed for Guido.

145–7 "*Lene . . . duro*": 'You bring to bear a gentle rack on those normally resistant': Horace, *Odes*, III. xxi. 13–14. Bottini supplies his own translation. Horace is speaking about wine, saying that the tough-minded, resistant to physical torture, are powerless before the assault of wine, which gets them talking. Bottini wittily applies the lines to the effects of the rack.

148 *my . . . o'er*: cf. Ps. 23: 5.

154 *ply*: wield vigorously (as a weapon).

play: fire off, deploy.

Claimed not the artist's ultimate appeal?
Much rather let me soar the height prescribed
And, bowing low, proffer my picture's self!
No more of proof, disproof,—such virtue was,
Such vice was never in Pompilia, now!
Far better say "Behold Pompilia!"—(for
I leave the family as unmanageable,
And stick to just one portrait, but life-size).
Hath calumny imputed to the fair
A blemish, mole on cheek or wart on chin,
Much more, blind hidden horrors best unnamed?
Shall I descend to prove you, point by point,
Never was knock-knee known nor splay-foot found
In Phryne? (I must let the portrait go,
Content me with the model, I believe)—
—I prove this? An indignant sweep of hand,
Dash at and doing away with drapery,
And,—use your eyes, Athenians, smooth she smiles!
Or,—since my client can no longer smile,
And more appropriate instances abound,—

157 *MS 1868 1872* And 161 *MS* evil was not>vice was never 162 *MS* Pompilia,"—for>Pompilia"!—(for 163 *MS* {beginning of fo. 129} *MS* Family *164 *MS* life-size,—>life-size)— *1868 1872 1888 1889* life-size.) 165 *MS* thy>the *MS* Fair 170 *MS* Phryne,—I>Phryne?—(I *MS*{no comma} 171 *MS* believe,—>believe)— 172 *MS* I 174 *MS* Why,>And,—

169 *splay-foot*: an ugly, outward-turned foot.

170–4 *Phryne . . . smiles*: the notorious courtesan, who inspired Apelles' Venus Anadyomene and Praxiteles' Cnidian Venus. Her unblemished beauty is supposed to have been an index of her moral innocence in the famous incident referred to here, where her lawyer asked her to expose herself in court: 'The orator Hyperides was one of her lovers, and he defended her when she was accused by Euthias on one occasion of some capital charge; but when the eloquence of her advocate failed to move the judges, he bade her uncover her breast, and thus ensured her acquittal': *Dictionary of Greek and Roman Biography and Mythology*, ed. by William Smith, 3 vols. (1844–9), iii. 359. A famous contemporary painting, 'Phryne before the Areopagus' (1861) by Jean-Léon Gérôme, shows Hyperides himself sweeping off Phryne's 'drapery' to reveal her nakedness. In the following lines Bottini fantasizes that his speech will accomplish some similar exposure of beauty and innocence, though, of course, his choice of image suggests one aspect of his own salacious mindset: see Introduction.

What is this Tale of Tarquin, how the slave
Was caught by him, preferred to Collatine?
Thou, even from thy corpse-clothes virginal,
Look'st the lie dead, Lucretia!
Thus at least
I, by the guidance of antiquity,
(Our one infallible guide) now operate,
Sure that the innocence thus shown is safe;
Sure, too, that, while I plead, the echoes cry
(Lend my weak voice thy trump, sonorous Fame!)
"Monstrosity the Phrynean shape shall mar,
"Lucretia's soul comport with Tarquin's lie,
"When thistles grow on vines or thorns yield figs,
"Or oblique sentence leave this judgment-seat!"

A great theme: may my strength be adequate!
For—paint Pompilia, dares my feebleness?
How did I unaware engage so much
—Find myself undertaking to produce
A faultless nature in a flawless form?
What's here? Oh, turn aside nor dare the blaze
Of such a crown, such constellation, say,

177 *MS* tale>Tale 178 *MS* {no comma} 179 *MS* virginal corpse-clothes> corpse-clothes virginal 182 *MS* antiquity 183 *MS* sole sure guide) forthwith would>one infallible guide) now 184 *MS* innocence once shown> innocency shown *1868 1872* innocency shown *MS* safe— 188 *MS* com>with Tarquin's trick comport>comport with Tarquin's trick 190 *MS* leaves *MS* Judgment-seat!" 191 *MS* {beginning of fo. 130} *MS* {New paragraph indicated by 'New Par.' in left-hand margin} *MS* theme. May>theme,—may 193 *MS* much?>much 197 *MS* [ ]>such *MS* say

177–80 *What . . . Lucretia!*: i.e. 'what is this outrageous story blackening the name of Lucretia (Pompilia)?' The tale told by Tarquin, to cover his rape of Lucretia, was that he had found her in bed with a slave, whom she had preferred to Collatine, her husband. He then killed them both: see Livy, I. 58. Cf. VIII. 1684 n.

187 *Monstrosity*: physical deformity or abnormality.

188 *comport with*: bear with, endure.

189 *When . . . figs*: i.e. when the impossible happens. Cf. Luke 6: 44: 'For of thorns men do not gather figs, nor of a bramble bush gather they grapes.' Here, and in the following passage, Bottini's style has a bombastic intensity.

As jewels here thy front, Humanity!
First, infancy, pellucid as a pearl;
Then childhood—stone which, dew-drop at the first,
(An old conjecture) sucks, by dint of gaze,
Blue from the sky and turns to sapphire so:
Yet both these gems eclipsed by, last and best,
Womanliness and wifehood opaline,
Its milk-white pallor,—chastity,—suffused
With here and there a tint and hint of flame,—
Desire,—the lapidary loves to find.
Such jewels bind conspicuously thy brow,
Pompilia, infant, child, maid, woman, wife—
Crown the ideal in our earth at last!
What should a faculty like mine do here?
Close eyes, or else, the rashlier hurry hand!

Which is to say,—lose no time but begin!
Sermocinando ne declamem, Sirs,
Ultra clepsydram, as our preachers smile,

199 *MS* First infancy, *MS* pearl— 200 *MS* Then Childhood—>Then childhood— *1868 1872* Then, 201 *MS* {no commas} 202 *MS* heavens *MS* so,— 206 *MS* fire,>flame,— 210 *MS* Ideal 212 *MS* or,>or else, *213 *MS* {New paragraph indicated by 'New Par:' in left-hand margin} *1868 1872* {new paragraph. Paragraphing obscured in *1888* and *1889* by this line's being at the head of the page} *MS* begin— 214 *Yale 1* sirs,> Sirs, 215 *MS* sage man says,>the preachers say, *1868 1872* say,

198 *front*: forehead.

200–2 *stone . . . so*: this seems to be a version of the old belief that pearls, diamonds, and other gems grow from dew. Cf. *Mandeville's Travels*, ch. xiv (xviii): 'I have often tymes assayed that if a man kepe hem [small gems] with a lityll of the roche, and wete hem with May dew oftesithes, thei schull growe everyche year; and the smale wole wexen grete. For right as the fyn perl congeleth and wexeth gret of the dew of hevene, right so doth the verray dyamand.'

204 *opaline*: (adj.) having the colour or irridescence of an opal. Cf. *Fifine at the Fair*, 1191, 'Goldoni', 7.

207 *lapidary*: jeweller, expert in gems.

212 *Close . . . hand!*: i.e. Either close one's eyes at the brilliance of Pompilia (i.e. not even attempt to paint her), or else set to work painting fast (in a desperate attempt to capture her beauty).

214–15 *Sermocinando . . . clepsydram*: 'Don't let me go on delivering my speech beyond the clepsydra' (L.). The ancient clepsydra, or water-clock, shaped like an

Lest I exceed my hour-glass. Whereupon,
As Flaccus prompts, I dare the epic plunge—
Begin at once with marriage, up till when
Little or nothing would arrest your love,
In the easeful life o' the lady; lamb and lamb,
How do they differ? Know one, you know all
Manners of maidenhood: mere maiden she.
And since all lambs are like in more than fleece,
Prepare to find that, lamb-like, she too frisks—
O' the weaker sex, my lords, the weaker sex!
To whom, the Teian teaches us, for gift,
Not strength,—man's dower,—but beauty, nature gave,
"Beauty in lieu of spears, in lieu of shields!"
And what is beauty's sure concomitant,

217 *MS* we>I 218 *MS* marriage: 219 *MS* {beginning of fo. 131} *MS* :>, 220 *MS* of>o' *MS* girl and girl>lamb and lamb, 221 *MS* differ, know>differ? Know 222 *MS* she— 224 *MS* like lamb,>lamb-like, 225 *MS* sex—

hourglass, measured time by letting water drip through a small aperture. According to Pliny, it was Pompey who first used it to limit the speeches of the Roman orators. It had been standard in Athens long before: hence the invitation to one's opponent to answer an embarrassing question 'in my water' (ἐν τῷ ἐμῷ ὕδατι), i.e. in my own time-allowance.

217 *Flaccus . . . plunge*: a pompous piece of wit: Bottini compares himself with the epic poet. In the *Ars Poetica*, Horace (Q. Horatius Flaccus) suggests that the epic poet should plunge 'in medias res', into the middle of his story: *Ars Poetica*, 148–9. The first scene of the *Iliad* is set in the tenth year of the siege of Troy. In the *Aeneid*, Virgil plunges into the middle of the narrative with 'vix e conspectu Siculae telluris in altum / vela dabant laeti . . .': *Aeneid*, I. 34–5.

219 *arrest your love*: engage your interest.

224 *frisks*: jumps gaily—but with the innuendo of 'is sexually flirtatious'.

226–8 *Teian . . . shields*: 'the Teian' is the Greek lyric poet Anacreon (*c.* 570–485 BC), born in the Ionian city of Teos in Asia Minor. The full distinction between the *Anacreontea* [poems in the manner of Anacreon] and genuine Anacreon was only emerging in the nineteenth century: see *Correspondence*, X. 141. Browning would have known the poem alluded to here, no. 24 in the Loeb *Anacreontea*, as Anacreon's second ode 'On Women'. Browning's affection for the *Anacreontea* is shown in his unpublished translations of eleven of them. 'On Women' he translates thus: 'Horns to bulls, gave nature, / Likewise hooves to horses: / Hares their footed swiftness, / Lions—teeth wide-yawning: / To the fishes—swimming, / To the birds their plume-play. / Women—no more had she! / What then? She gives Beauty.' He abbreviates the ending, which runs: '. . . Beauty; instead of all shields, instead of all spears: for she, who is beautiful, subdues both iron and fire.' For Browning's translation, and his love of Anacreon, see Pettigrew and Collins, ii. 947, 1135.

Nay, intimate essential character,
But melting wiles, deliciousest deceits,
The whole redoubted armoury of love?
Therefore of vernal pranks, dishevellings
O' the hair of youth that dances April in,
And easily-imagined Hebe-slips
O'er sward which May makes over-smooth for foot—
These shall we pry into?—or wiselier wink,
Though numerous and dear they may have been?

For lo, advancing Hymen and his pomp!
Discedunt nunc amores, loves, farewell!
Maneat amor, let love, the sole, remain!
Farewell to dewiness and prime of life!
Remains the rough determined day: dance done,
To work, with plough and harrow! What comes next?
'T is Guido henceforth guides Pompilia's step,
Cries "No more friskings o'er the foodful glebe,
"Else, 'ware the whip!" Accordingly,—first crack

233 *MS* dishevelings 235 *MS* []>easily- 236 *MS* over smooth 237 *MS* wink,— 238 *MS* proved,>been. *239 *MS* {New paragraph indicated by 'New Par' in left-hand margin} *1868 1872* {new paragraph. Paragraphing obscured in *1888* and *1889* by this line's being at the head of the page} 240 *MS* [ ]>Loves, 241 *MS* *amor—* 242 *MS* the>to 245 *MS* step— 246 *MS* no>"No *MS* oer

235 *Hebe-slips*: youthful slips, i.e. sexual indiscretions. Hebe, daughter of Hera and Zeus, was a personification of adolescence. She was the joyful cupbearer of the gods (*Iliad*, IV. 2), pouring out their nectar for them, until, in tradition, it was said that one day she slipped and was so ashamed that she refused to appear in their presence again. Hence Ganymede took over this office.

240–1 *Discedunt . . . amor*: 'Love-affairs depart . . . Let love remain.' No obvious quotation corresponds with this. Hodell calls it 'a medieval adaptation of Catullus', but gives no source. It is probably intended as a paraphrase of Catullus 61: 119–43, verses that present a topos of Greek origin: marriage as the renouncing of all illicit love-affairs to concentrate on the one love. Catullus refers to various parts of the Roman marriage ceremony—the fescennines (ritual licentious verses), the giving-up of the favourite slave, etc.—to emphasize how the bridegroom must now 'serve Talassius' (the god of marriage). In this context, l. 239 is in the spirit of the preceding verses of Catullus, 61: 114–18: 'Raise high the torches, boys: / I see the bridal veil approaching. Come, sing in unison / "O Hymen Hymeneal O, / O Hymen Hymeneal!' (trans. Gould).

O' the thong,—we hear that his young wife was barred,
Cohibita fuit, from the old free life,
Vitam liberiorem ducere.
Demur we? Nowise: heifer brave the hind?
We seek not there should lapse the natural law,
The proper piety to lord and king
And husband: let the heifer bear the yoke!
Only, I crave he cast not patience off,
This hind; for deem you she endures the whip,
Nor winces at the goad, nay, restive, kicks?
What if the adversary's charge be just,
And all untowardly she pursue her way
With groan and grunt, though hind strike ne'er so hard?
If petulant remonstrance made appeal,
Unseasonable, o'erprotracted,—if
Importunate challenge taxed the public ear
When silence more decorously had served
For protestation,—if Pompilian plaint
Wrought but to aggravate Guidonian ire,—
Why, such mishaps, ungainly though they be,
Ever companion change, are incident
To altered modes and novelty of life:
The philosophic mind expects no less,
Smilingly knows and names the crisis, sits
Waiting till old things go and new arrive.

248 *MS* {beginning of fo. 132} 251 *MS* I? 252 *MS* I *MS* [ ]>to see>there should 253 *MS* king, 254 *MS* The 255 *MS* Only I 256 *MS* hind, 257 *MS* nay— 258 *MS* {no comma} *Yale 1* just>just, 259 *MS* And, *Yale 1* And, all>And all *MS* untoward[ ]>untowardly *MS* ways 260 *MS* strike husband>though hind strike *MS* hard?— 265 *MS* Pompilia's>Pompilian 266 *MS* her lord's chagrin,—>Guidonian ire,— 272 *MS* and new things come,> new things arrive,>and new arrive.

249–50 *Cohibita . . . ducere*: 'was restrained from leading her life with greater freedom': OYB ix (11). These words are near the opening of Arcangeli's first pleading.

251 *brave*: challenge, disobey.

hind: agricultural labourer.

256 *deem you*: do you think that.

259 *untowardly*: stubbornly resisting, perversely.

272 *old . . . arrive*: cf. 2 Cor. 5: 17. Cf. l. 282 n.

Therefore, I hold a husband but inept
Who turns impatient at such transit-time,
As if this running from the rod would last!

Since, even while I speak, the end is reached:
Success awaits the soon-disheartened man.
The parents turn their backs and leave the house,
The wife may wail but none shall intervene:
He hath attained his object, groom and bride
Partake the nuptial bower no soul can see,
Old things are passed and all again is new,
Over and gone the obstacles to peace,
Novorum—tenderly the Mantuan turns
The expression, some such purpose in his eye—
Nascitur ordo! Every storm is laid,
And forth from plain each pleasant herb may peep,
Each bloom of wifehood in abeyance late:
(Confer a passage in the Canticles.)

[—]

273 *MS* for>but 274 *MS* transit-time— 276 *MS* {New paragraph indicated by 'New Par.' in left-hand margin} *1868* reached 277 *MS* {beginning of fo. 133} *MS 1868* man, 279 *MS 1868* intervene, 280 *MS* object,— 281 *MS* to see— 282 *MS* is new again,>again is new, 283 *MS* [ ]>gone *MS* {no comma} 288 *MS* late—

274 *transit-time*: i.e. time of change.

281 *Partake . . . see*: a euphemism for sexual intercourse between husband and wife.

282 *Old . . . new*: cf. Rev. 21: 4–5.

284–6 *Novorum . . . ordo!* : 'Of new things . . . the order is being born', adapting Virgil ['the Mantuan'] *Eclogues*, iv. 5, 'magnus ab integro saeclorum nascitur ordo'. The *Fourth Eclogue*, the famous Messianic eclogue, is one of the most heightened and enigmatic pieces of classical verse; in early times, and still in the nineteenth century, it was often read as referring to the birth of Christ. In this quotation Virgil speaks of a new temporal order, a Golden Age of peace, heralded by the birth of a mysterious child. In his pretentious way, Bottini applies (or misapplies) this weight of implication to the simple possibility of marital harmony commencing between Guido and Pompilia. For a balanced discussion of the Eclogue, see Ronald Syme, *The Roman Revolution* (1939), 218–20.

289 *Confer . . . Canticles*: i.e. 'add in a reference to a passage in the Song of Solomon'. Bottini makes a mental note to add in a biblical passage to elaborate the image he has developed in the three preceding lines. Probably he is thinking of S. of S. 2: 11–12: 'For, lo, the winter is past, the rain is over and gone; the flowers appear on the earth; the time of the singing of birds is come, and the voice of the turtle is heard in our land.'

But what if, as 't is wont with plant and wife,
Flowers,—after a suppression to good end,
Still, when they do spring forth,—sprout here, spread there,
Anywhere likelier than beneath the foot
O' the lawful good-man gardener of the ground?
He dug and dibbled, sowed and watered,—still
'T is a chance wayfarer shall pluck the increase.
Just so, respecting persons not too much,
The lady, foes allege, put forth each charm
And proper floweret of feminity
To whosoever had a nose to smell
Or breast to deck: what if the charge be true?
The fault were graver had she looked with choice,
Fastidiously appointed who should grasp,
Who, in the whole town, go without the prize!
To nobody she destined donative,
But, first come was first served, the accuser saith.
Put case her sort of... in this kind... escapes
Were many and oft and indiscriminate—
Impute ye as the action were prepense,

*290 *MS* {New paragraph indicated by 'New Par:' in left-hand margin} *1868 1872* {new paragraph. Paragraphing obscured in *1888* and *1889* by this line's being at the head of the page} *MS* the way with flower>'tis wont with plant 294 *MS* Of>O' *MS* lord and>good-man 296 *MS* [ ] [ ]>shall pluck *MS* prize. >increase. 298 *MS* [ ] alleged,>foes allege, 302 *MS* case were altered> fault were graver 304 *MS* grace>prize! 305 *MS* Nobody destined to such>To nobody she destined donative, 306 *MS* {beginning of fo. 134} *MS* First>But, first *MS* saith the accuser here,—>the accuser saith: *1868* saith 307 *MS 1868 1872* of . . *MS* kind,>kind . . *1868 1872* kind . . 308 *MS* often>oft 309 *MS* not>ye

---

294 *good-man*: yeoman, master; cf. III. 423 n.

295 *dibbled*: used a dibble or dibber (i.e. a hoe) to make holes for bulbs or young plants.

299 *feminity*: femininity; cf. VI. 1446 n.

305 *donative*: gift, present (of herself).

307 *escapes*: small sins, minor transgressions, 'applied especially to breaches of chastity'. OED^2 cites, for example, Lodge (1596): 'The escapes of Jupiter, the wanton delights of Venus, and the amorous deceits of Cupid'. But the word is clearly intended ambiguously and euphemistically: it suggests also 'escapades', and 'evasions' of the law: see OED^2, I.a.

309 *Impute ye as*: do you make the charge that.

prepense: deliberate, planned (stress on the second syllable). The legal phrase 'malice

The gift particular, arguing malice so?
Which butterfly of the wide air shall brag
"I was preferred to Guido"—when 't is clear
The cup, he quaffs at, lay with olent breast
Open to gnat, midge, bee and moth as well?
One chalice entertained the company;
And if its peevish lord object the more,
Mistake, misname such bounty in a wife,
Haste we to advertise him—charm of cheek,
Lustre of eye, allowance of the lip,
All womanly components in a spouse,
These are no household-bread each stranger's bite
Leaves by so much diminished for the mouth
O' the master of the house at supper-time:
But rather like a lump of spice they lie,
Morsel of myrrh, which scents the neighbourhood
Yet greets its lord no lighter by a grain.

Nay, even so, he shall be satisfied!
Concede we there was reason in his wrong,
Grant we his grievance and content the man!
For lo, Pompilia, she submits herself;
Ere three revolving years have crowned their course,
Off and away she puts this same reproach

310 *MS* so!>so? 311 *MS* denizen>butterfly 315 *MS* company, *Yale 1* company,>company; 316 *MS* a>its 317 *MS* the liberal bounty here,—>such bounty in a wife, 319 *MS* the eye,>eye, 320 *MS* wife>spouse, 321 *MS* household bread *Yale 1* household bread>household-bread 323 *MS* good man>master *MS* supper-time,— 324 *MS* likened>like 327 *MS* {New paragraph indicated by 'New Par.' in left-hand margin} *MS* so,— 329 *MS* man!— 330 *MS* Pompilia— *MS* herself— 331 *MS* []>crowned

prepense' (echoed here—see 'malice' in the next line) means 'malice premeditated or planned beforehand; wrong or injury purposely done': OED^2.

313 *olent*: sweet-smelling, fragrant, from L. *olere* to smell. OED^2 gives only two earlier uses, and we have been unable to trace any others. It suits Bottini, however, on two counts: as a pretentious Latinism, and as a word whose sensuousness has an air of innuendo. The more usual word, with the same meaning, is 'redolent'.

318 *advertise*: inform, warn (in a formal way). Cf. Ruth 4: 4.

Of lavish bounty, inconsiderate gift
O' the sweets of wifehood stored to other ends:
No longer shall he blame "She none excludes,"
But substitute "She laudably sees all,
"Searches the best out and selects the same."
For who is here, long sought and latest found,
Waiting his turn unmoved amid the whirl,
"*Constans in levitate,*"—Ha, my lords?
Calm in his levity,—indulge the quip!—
Since 't is a levite bears the bell away,
Parades him henceforth as Pompilia's choice.
'T is no ignoble object, husband! Doubt'st?
When here comes tripping Flaccus with his phrase
"Trust me, no miscreant singled from the mob,
"*Crede non illum tibi de scelesta*
"*Plebe delectum,*" but a man of mark,
A priest, dost hear? Why then, submit thyself!
Priest, ay and very phœnix of such fowl,
Well-born, of culture, young and vigorous,
Comely too, since precise the precept points—
On the selected levite be there found

334 *MS* Of>O' *MS* ends,— 335 *MS* {beginning of fo. 135} 337 *MS* same:"— 338 *MS* this,>here, 340 *MS* *levitate,*— *MS* indulge the quip!—>Ha, my lords? 341 *MS* quip,— *Yale 1* quip,—>quip!— 342 *MS* away the bell>the bell away 347, 348 *MS* {no quotation marks at beginnings of lines}

---

340 "*Constans in levitate,*": 'constant in inconstancy, or lack of seriousness' (L.). The phrase is from Ovid, *Tristia*, v. viii. 18, and applies to the Goddess Fortune, here to Caponsacchi.

342 *levite*: deacon, priest—but with a bad pun on 'levity'.

bears . . . away: = comes first, wins the prize; a proverbial phrase: see ODEP, 44. Cf. 'The Two Poets of Croisic', 27; 'With George Bubb Dodington', 17. Browning easily associated together 'levite' and 'bell' because of his coining of the phrase 'Bells and Pomegranates': see *Correspondence*, xi. 129, 131.

347–8 "*Crede . . . delectum,*": 'Trust me, you've picked a man who isn't from the wretched multitude', from Horace ['Flaccus'], *Odes*, II. iv. 17–18, substituting *illum . . . delectum* (masculine) for the original *illam delectam* (referring to a girl).

350 *phœnix*: best kind, paragon.

352 *precept*: rule.

353–4 *On . . . blemish*: cf. Lev. 21: 16–24, the ancient Jewish law that a man chosen to be a priest must not be physically marked or disabled in any way. Bottini uses the biblical text in a mischievous way to suggest how handsome Caponsacchi is.

Nor mole nor scar nor blemish, lest the mind
Come all uncandid through the thwarting flesh!
Was not the son of Jesse ruddy, sleek,
Pleasant to look on, pleasant every way?
Since well he smote the harp and sweetly sang,
And danced till Abigail came out to see,
And seeing smiled and smiling ministered
The raisin-cluster and the cake of figs,
With ready meal refreshed the gifted youth,
Till Nabal, who was absent shearing sheep,
Felt heart sink, took to bed (discreetly done—
They might have been beforehand with him else)
And died—would Guido have behaved as well!
But ah, the faith of early days is gone,
Heu prisca fides! Nothing died in him
Save courtesy, good sense and proper trust,
Which, when they ebb from souls they should o'erflow,
Discover stub, weed, sludge and ugliness.
(The Pope, we know, is Neapolitan
And relishes a sea-side simile.)

354 *MS* {no comma} 355 *MS* out>all *MS* flesh. 356 *MS* sleek 357 *MS* way— 358 *MS* {no comma} 359 *MS* deftly danced>danced 360 *MS* [ ]>smiled 361 *MS* {line added later} 362 *MS* [ ]>The *MS* meal, 365 *MS* {beginning of fo. 136} 366 *MS* but>had *1868* had 369 *MS* graceful>proper *MS* trust— 372, 373 {not found in *MS*} 372 *Yale 1* {Beginning of new paragraph moved from 372 to 374} *1868 1872* you

---

355 *uncandid*: i.e. defiled, corrupted.

356–66 *son of Jesse . . . well!*: these lines conflate and adapt—in ludicrous manner—three biblical passages in order to create a tale of amorous love in the style of Boccaccio. The passages are 1 Sam. 16: 12, 2 Sam. 6: 14–16, and 1 Sam. 25. The son of Jesse, the dashing David (Caponsacchi) meets the wife of Nabal, the beautiful Abigail (Pompilia), and they fall in love. The grumpy husband Nabal (Guido) conveniently dies, leaving David and Abigail free to marry—only, of course, Guido (unlike Nabal) does not die.

365 *They . . . else*: they might have got to bed before him (i.e. commenced their sexual relationship).

368 *Heu prisca fides!*: 'Alas for old-world honour!': Virgil, *Aeneid*, VI. 878.

371 *Discover*: reveal.

372–3 *Pope . . . simile*: in his fantasy of the circumstances in which he would like to deliver his speech, Bottini has imagined the Pope listening in on the court proceedings from behind a curtain: see ll. 9–10. Innocent XII, a Neapolitan aristocrat, was

Deserted by each charitable wave,
Guido, left high and dry, shows jealous now!
Jealous avouched, paraded: tax the fool
With any peccadillo, he responds
"Truly I beat my wife through jealousy,
"Imprisoned her and punished otherwise,
"Being jealous: now would threaten, sword in hand,
"Now manage to mix poison in her sight,
"And so forth: jealously I dealt, in fine."
Concede thus much, and what remains to prove?
Have I to teach my masters what effect
Hath jealousy, and how, befooling men,
It makes false true, abuses eye and ear,
Turns mere mist adamantine, loads with sound
Silence, and into void and vacancy
Crowds a whole phalanx of conspiring foes?
Therefore who owns "I watched with jealousy
"My wife," adds "for no reason in the world!"
What need that, thus proved madman, he remark
"The thing I thought a serpent proved an eel"?—
Perchance the right Comacchian, six foot length,

374 *MS* {New paragraph indicated by 'New Par.' in left-hand margin} 376 *MS* man>fool 377 *MS* {no comma} 381 *MS* silently>manage to 383 *MS 1868* the fact and 385 *MS 1868* jealousy and *MS* [ ]>men, 387 *MS* Feels> Turns *MS 1868* the mist 391 *MS 1868* {no comma} *MS* world".> world"! 392 *MS 1868* that who says "madman" should remark *1872* that who says "Madman" should remark 393 *MS 1868* he *Yale 2* I>he *MS 1868 1872* eel?"— 394 *MS* —Perchance

Cardinal-Archbishop of his native Naples when elected to the papacy in 1691. Browning makes a feature of his love of the sea: see X. 486–510 and 1440–50, where he does employ 'sea-side similes'.

380–1 *now . . . sight*: cf. OYB lxxxiv (92) (Pompilia's Deposition): 'he said that he wished to kill me. . . . he pointed a pistol at my breast . . . I feared that if Guido did not slay me with weapons he might poison me.'

394 *Comacchian*: an eel from Comacchio, near Ravenna, a famous delicacy, particularly good to eat in Lent when meat was forbidden. Eels lived naturally in the lagoon district around Comacchio, but they were also farmed there, in fish ponds. In Browning's day the lagoons were famous as the place where, after the fall of the Roman Republic in 1849, Garibaldi came nearest to being captured by the Austrians. Here, in Bottini's sexually heightened imagination, Pompilia is the lithe, good-to-eat eel, 'the luscious Lenten creature'.

And not an inch too long for that rare pie
(Master Arcangeli has heard of such)
Whose succulence makes fasting bearable;
Meant to regale some moody splenetic
Who, pleasing to mistake the donor's gift,
Spying I know not what Lernæan snake
I' the luscious Lenten creature, stamps forsooth
The dainty in the dust.

Enough! Prepare,
Such lunes announced, for downright lunacy!
Insanit homo, threat succeeds to threat,
And blow redoubles blow,—his wife, the block.
But, if a block, shall not she jar the hand
That buffets her? The injurious idle stone
Rebounds and hits the head of him who flung.
Causeless rage breeds, i' the wife now, rageful cause,
Tyranny wakes rebellion from its sleep.
Rebellion, say I?—rather, self-defence,
Laudable wish to live and see good days,

395 *MS* Not inch>And not an inch *MS* same dainty>illustrious>same *1868 1872* same 396 {not found in *MS*} 397 *MS* {beginning of fo. 137} *MS* bearable, 398 *MS* the>some 399 {not found in *MS*} *1868* Who pleases 400 *MS* Who spies— *1868* And spies— 403 *MS* {New paragraph indicated by 'New Par.' in right-hand margin} 404 *MS* My Judges>His *etc. 1868* His *MS* read right the>for downright 405 *MS homo,—* 406 *MS* blow redoubles blow: 'tis>blow to blow: but is his wife a block.>blow to blow: but is his wife the block.>blow redoubles blow, his wife the block. 407 *MS* []>But, 409 *MS* breaks>fits *1868* fits *MS* flung: 411 *MS* calls rebellion into life,>brings rebellion into life,>wakes rebellion from its sleep, 413 *MS* Praiseworthy>Laudable

398 *splenetic*: bad-tempered person.

400 *Lernæan snake*: i.e. monster. The multi-headed poisonous water-snake which ravaged the country of Lernae near Argos. If one of its heads was cut off, it grotesquely spouted two new ones. The killing of the beast was one of the Labours of Hercules. Cf. 'Aristophanes' Apology', 3991–3, where Browning is translating Euripides' *Herakles*: 'the Lernaian snake / He [Hercules] burned out, head by head, and cast around / His darts a poison thence.'

404 *lunes*: mad fits, jealous rages. Cf. *Merry Wives*, IV. ii. 21–2: 'Why, woman, your husband is in his old lunes again.'

405 *Insanit homo*: 'the man is insane' (L.), from Horace, *Satires*, II. vii. 117. At VIII. 1183–4 Arcangeli refers to the immediately preceding lines in Horace: see n.

408 *injurious*: i.e. capable of inflicting hurt.

413 *live . . . days*: cf. 1 Pet. 3: 10; Ps. 34: 12.

Pricks our Pompilia now to fly the fool
By any means, at any price,—nay, more,
Nay, most of all, i' the very interest
O' the fool that, baffled of his blind desire
At any price, were truliest victor so.
Shall he effect his crime and lose his soul?
No, dictates duty to a loving wife!
Far better that the unconsummate blow,
Adroitly baulked by her, should back again,
Correctively admonish his own pate!

Crime then,—the Court is with me?—she must crush:
How crush it? By all efficacious means;
And these,—why, what in woman should they be?
"With horns the bull, with teeth the lion fights;
"To woman," quoth the lyrist quoted late,
"Nor teeth, nor horns, but beauty, Nature gave!"
Pretty i' the Pagan! Who dares blame the use
Of armoury thus allowed for natural,—
Exclaim against a seeming-dubious play
O' the sole permitted weapon, spear and shield
Alike, resorted to i' the circumstance
By poor Pompilia? Grant she somewhat plied
Arts that allure, the magic nod and wink,

414 *MS* Impels>Pricks our *MS 1868* on to fly the foe 415 *MS* more,— 416 *MS* in the true>i' the very 417 *MS 1868* Of the foe 418 *MS 1868* is *MS* so— 419 *MS* Let him>Shall he 420 *MS* [ ]>Who *MS* dictates such a duty to a wife? *Yale 1* What dictates>[?How],— *Yale 1* wife?>wife. *1868* wife. 421 *MS* {no comma} *Yale 1* blow>blow, 422 *MS* baulked, I say, *Yale 1* baulked, I say,>baulked by her, *MS* again 423 *MS* rebound to> admonish 424 *MS* {New paragraph indicated by 'New Par:' in left-hand margin} *MS* me? we>me?—we *MS 1868 1872* crush; 427 *MS* {beginning of fo. 138} *MS* {New paragraph indicated by 'New Par.' in left-hand margin} *MS 1868 1872* fights, 428 *MS* woman" 429 *MS* nature **MS 1868 1872* gave!" *1888 1889* gave. 430 *MS* pagan! *MS* shall>dares 431 *MS 1868 1872* the armoury *MS* he finds but natural,>thus allowed for natural,— 432 *MS* Except against>Cry out upon>Exclaim against *MS* single dubious>seeming-dubious *Yale 1* seeming dubious>seeming-dubious

421 *unconsummate*: unachieved, unfulfilled.

427–9 "*With . . . gave!*" : referring again to Anacreon's 'On Women': see ll. 226–8 n.

The witchery of gesture, spell of word,
Whereby the likelier to enlist this friend,
Yea stranger, as a champion on her side?
Such man, being but mere man, ('t was all she knew),
Must be made sure by beauty's silken bond,
The weakness that subdues the strong, and bows
Wisdom alike and folly. Grant the tale
O' the husband, which is false, were proved and true
To the letter—or the letters, I should say,
Abominations he professed to find
And fix upon Pompilia and the priest,—
Allow them hers—for though she could not write,
In early days of Eve-like innocence
That plucked no apple from the knowledge-tree,
Yet, at the Serpent's word, Eve plucks and eats
And knows—especially how to read and write:
And so Pompilia,—as the move o' the maw,
Quoth Persius, makes a parrot bid "Good day!"
A crow salute the concave, and a pie

438 *MS* the>this 439 *MS* Nay,>That *1868 1872* Yet *MS* side,>side? 440 *MS* Who being>Such, being *1868* Such, being *MS* man,> men, *MS* {no brackets} 441 *MS* [ ]>by 443 *MS* folly: grant>folly. Grant 444 *MS* Husband, *MS* were proved>for proved *1868* for proved 445 *MS 1868* letter,— 446 *MS* The abomination>The abominations *1868* The abominations 448 *MS* [? this] hers—>them hers— 450 *MS* plucks *MS* knowledge-tree,— 451 *MS* serpent's 452 *MS* write, 453 *MS* at the spur>at the move *Yale 1* at>as *MS* taste>maw *Yale 1* maw>maw, 454 *MS* {line added later} *MS* Which Persius found would make a parrot speak,>Quoth Persius, makes a parrot bid "Good Day!" 455 *MS* {line added later} *MS* pie>a pie

441 *beauty's silken bond*: cf. Pope, *Rape of the Lock*, ii. 28.

453–8 *as . . . scribe*: i.e. as movements of the maw (the stomach), i.e. hunger, provoke birds to speech, so Pompilia's 'hunger after fellowship' may have provoked her to learn to write. The allusion is to Persius, the Prologue to the *Satires*, 8–11: 'quis expedivit psittaco suum "chaere" / [corvos quis olim concavum salutare] / picamque docuit nostra verba conari? / magister artis ingenique largitor / venter, negatas artifex sequi voces': 'Who taught the parrot his "hello", [taught the crow to salute the concave], trained the magpie to try our words? Stomach—master of art, bestower of genius, expert at eliciting speech when nature refuses it.' The line in square brackets here is spurious, but is noted in some early nineteenth-century editions. In the original context Persius is scolding the way lucre provokes second-rate poets to write.

455 *concave*: i.e. the arch of the sky (from L.: see previous n.).

Endeavour at proficiency in speech,—
So she, through hunger after fellowship,
May well have learned, though late, to play the scribe:
As indeed, there's one letter on the list
Explicitly declares did happen here.
"You thought my letters could be none of mine,"
She tells her parents—"mine, who wanted skill;
"But now I have the skill, and write, you see!"
She needed write love-letters, so she learned,
"*Negatas artifex sequi voces*"—though
This letter nowise 'scapes the common lot,
But lies i' the condemnation of the rest,
Found by the husband's self who forged them all.
Yet, for the sacredness of argument,
For this once an exemption shall it plead—
Anything, anything to let the wheels
Of argument run glibly to their goal!
Concede she wrote (which were preposterous)
This and the other epistle,—what of it?
Where does the figment touch her candid fame?
Being in peril of her life—"my life,

456 *MS* {line added later} *MS* Strain to attain>Endeavour at 457 {not found in *MS*} *Yale 1* {line added So she, through hunger after fellowship,} 460 *MS* {beginning of fo. 139} *MS* Declares explicitly to be the case *Yale 1* Declares explicitly to be the case.>Explicitly declares did happen here. 462 *MS* skill, 464 *MS* learned— *Yale 1* learned>learned, 465 *MS* *voces*"!— 467 *MS* {line added later} *MS* Lies in *MS* {no comma} 468 *MS* the same,—>them all,— 472 *MS* goal[ ]>goal! 473 *MS* wrote . . which *MS* preposterous . . 475 *MS* fleck *Yale 1* fleck>touch

461–3 "*You . . . see!*": slightly adapting the alleged 'Letter of Pompilia, written in the prison of Castelnuovo, to her parents' (3 May 1697): 'I sent you word of them [Guido's suspicions of me] on purpose, but you did not believe the letters sent you were in my own hand. But I declare that I finished learning how to write in Arezzo': OYB clv f. (160).

465 "*Negatas . . . voces*": 'skill at imitating the words she was unable to form for herself': see ll. 453–8 n.

467 *lies i'* : shares.

475 *figment*: fiction, invention.

candid: pure, spotless (from L. *candidus*, white); cf. l. 355 n.

476–7 "*my. . . purchase,*": 'la mia vita era a hora' (It.), a quotation from the same letter: see ll. 461–3 n.

"Not an hour's purchase," as the letter runs,—
And having but one stay in this extreme,
Out of the wide world but a single friend—
What could she other than resort to him,
And how with any hope resort but thus?
Shall modesty dare bid a stranger brave
Danger, disgrace, nay death in her behalf—
Think to entice the sternness of the steel
Yet spare love's loadstone moving manly mind?
—Most of all, when such mind is hampered so
By growth of circumstance athwart the life
O' the natural man, that decency forbids
He stoop and take the common privilege,
Say frank "I love," as all the vulgar do.
A man is wedded to philosophy,
Married to statesmanship; a man is old;
A man is fettered by the foolishness
He took for wisdom and talked ten years since;
A man is, like our friend the Canon here,
A priest, and wicked if he break his vow:
Shall he dare love, who may be Pope one day?
Despite the coil of such encumbrance here,
Suppose this man could love, unhappily,
And would love, dared he only let love show!
In case the woman of his love, speaks first,
From what embarrassment she sets him free!

479 *MS 1868* And out *MS 1868* world a 480 *MS* [?How]> What 481 *MS* so? 482 *MS* What modesty shall bid 485 *MS 1868* Save by the magnet moves the *MS* mind— *Yale 1* mind—>mind? 486 *MS* Most *MS 1868* {no comma} 490 *MS* {beginning of fo. 140} 492 *MS* statesmanship, *MS* old, 494 *MS* since, 496 *MS* vow, 497 *MS* And dare to love—he may be Pope one day! *1868* He dare to 498 {not found in *MS 1868*} 499 *MS 1868* love, though, all the same— 500 {not found in *MS 1868*} 501, 502 {order reversed in *MS 1868*} 501 *MS* Should you, a woman he could love, speak first— *Yale 1* Should you, a woman he could love, speak first—>Should one, a woman he could love, speak first— *1868* Should one, a woman he could love, speak first— 502 *MS* you set *Yale 1* you set>she sets *MS 1868* free

487 *athwart*: against, contradicting.

498 *coil*: difficulty, confusion.

"'T is I who break reserve, begin appeal,
"Confess that, whether you love me or no,
"I love you!" What an ease to dignity,
What help of pride from the hard high-backed chair
Down to the carpet where the kittens bask,
All under the pretence of gratitude!

From all which, I deduce—the lady here
Was bound to proffer nothing short of love
To the priest whose service was to save her. What?
Shall she propose him lucre, dust o' the mine,
Rubbish o' the rock, some diamond, muckworms prize,
Some pearl secreted by a sickly fish?
Scarcely! She caters for a generous taste.
'T is love shall beckon, beauty bid to breast,
Till all the Samson sink into the snare!
Because, permit the end—permit therewith
Means to the end!

How say you, good my lords?
I hope you heard my adversary ring
The changes on this precept: now, let me
Reverse the peal! *Quia dato licito fine,*
Ad illum assequendum ordinata
Non sunt damnanda media,—licit end

504 *MS* And confess—Whether>Confess that, whether *MS* not,>no, 507 *MS* roll,>bask, 508 *MS* cover of mere>the pretence of 509 *MS* {New paragraph indicated by 'New Par.' in left-hand margin} *MS* deduce the 514 *MS 1868* Or 515 *MS* taste: 517 *MS* Sampson 518 *MS* In fine,>Because, 519 *MS* Means to the end! *Quia dato licito fine,* *MS* {no new paragraph} 520–3 {not found in *MS*} 524 *MS* {beginning of fo. 141}

513 *muckworms prize*: i.e. which muckworms value. Muckworms = (lit.) worms that live in 'muck' or dung, (fig.) misers, money-grubbers. Cf. *Strafford*, I. i. 63; and Pope, 'To Mr. John Moore', 23: 'Misers are Muckworms.'

514 *pearl . . . fish*: cf. IV. 310.

517 *Samson*: i.e. strong man. Pompilia's soliciting of Caponsacchi is compared to Delilah's seduction of Samson: cf. Judges 16.

523–5 *Quia . . . media*: 'If the end is lawful, the means ordered towards carrying it out cannot be condemned': OYB clxxvii (184): pam. 13, Bottini. In OYB, the real Bottini does use the argument advanced in this passage, but Browning tips it over into the ludicrous: see next n.

Enough was found in mere escape from death,
To legalize our means illicit else
Of feigned love, false allurement, fancied fact.
Thus Venus losing Cupid on a day,
(See that *Idyllium Moschi*) seeking help,
In the anxiety of motherhood,
Allowably promised "Who shall bring report
"Where he is wandered to, my winged babe,
"I give him for reward a nectared kiss;
"But who brings safely back the truant's self,
"His be a super-sweet makes kiss seem cold!"
Are not these things writ for example-sake?

To such permitted motive, then, refer
All those professions, else were hard explain,
Of hope, fear, jealousy, and the rest of love!
He is Myrtillus, Amaryllis she,
She burns, he freezes,—all a mere device
To catch and keep the man, may save her life,

526 *MS* Enough was the escape from death, I hope: *1868* Enough was the escape from death, I hope, *1872* Enough in the escape from death, I hope, *Yale 2* Enough in the>Enough is in *Yale 2* hope,>trust, 527 *MS* Which legalized the *1868 1872* the means 528 *MS* fact— 530 *MS Moschi*, masters mine!) *Yale 1 Moschi*, masters mine!)>*Moschi*) seeking help, 531 *MS* {no comma} 532 *MS* brings>shall bring 533 *MS* is>he 534 *MS* "Shall have for recompense>"I give him for reward 535 *MS* "Who brings the truant's self in safety back—>"But who brings safely back the truant's self, 536 *MS* "An ambrosial 537 *MS* To such>Are not 538 *MS* {New paragraph indicated by 'New Par.' in left-hand margin} 540 *MS* jealousy and 542 *MS* He>She *MS Yale 1* she>he 543 *MS* sole man saves>man may save *1868* man may

530–6 *Idyllium . . . cold!*: Moschus, *Idylls*, i. 3–5. The Greek bucolic poet Moschus, of Syracuse (fl. *c.*150 BC) is known for a few elegant extant poems. In this one, 'Eros on the Run', Venus posts a kind of 'wanted' notice for her lost boy. Browning is extravagantly witty in giving this allusion to Bottini: at l. 536 he makes more vivid the sexual innuendo of the original, in keeping with Bottini's salacity.

537 *Are . . . example-sake*: cf. 1 Cor. 10: 11: 'Now all these things happened unto them for ensamples: and they are written for our admonition, upon whom the ends of the world are come.'

541 *Myrtillus, Amaryllis*: type-names of amorous lovers, from Giambattista Guarini's *Il Pastor Fido*. The alleged love letters between Caponsacchi and Pompilia are signed with these type-names: see OYB xcii–xcix (99–106). In this passage Bottini is alluding to the exaggerated love language of these letters.

Whom otherwise nor catches she nor keeps!
Worst, once, turns best now: in all faith, she feigns:
Feigning,—the liker innocence to guilt,
The truer to the life in what she feigns!
How if Ulysses,—when, for public good
He sank particular qualms and played the spy,
Entered Troy's hostile gate in beggar's garb—
How if he first had boggled at this clout,
Grown dainty o'er that clack-dish? Grime is grace
To whoso gropes amid the dung for gold.

Hence, beyond promises, we praise each proof
That promise was not simply made to break,
Mere moonshine-structure meant to fade at dawn:
We praise, as consequent and requisite,
What, enemies allege, were more than words,
Deeds—meetings at the window, twilight-trysts,
Nocturnal entertainments in the dim
Old labyrinthine palace; lies, we know—
Inventions we, long since, turned inside out.

544 *MS* Who>Whom   545 *MS 1868* is best   *MS* for good ends, we feign: 547 *MS* and thing she plays!>and thing she feigns! *1868 1872* is what   548 *MS* What   *549 *MS* sank *1868 1872 1888 1889* sunk   *MS* his private>particular   550 *MS* ^hostile^   551 *MS* What   *MS* [ ] daintily>first had   552 *MS* squeamish>dainty   553 *MS* {beginning of fo. 142}   554 *MS* {New paragraph indicated by 'New Par.' in left-hand margin}   *MS* And, more than>Hence, beyond   *MS* applaud when>praise each   555 *MS 1868* break,—   556 *MS* [ ]>No *1868* No   *MS* moonshine>moonlight>moonshine   *MS* fabric>[?phantom]>structure   *MS* day>dawn: 557 *MS 1868* So call—(proofs consequent and requisite)—   558 *MS 1868* What enemies allege of—more   559 *MS 1868* twilight-tryst,   560 *MS 1868* entertainment   561 *MS* And   *MS* palace,—   562 *MS* we have long>we, long since,

---

548–50 *Ulysses . . . garb*: this tale of Ulysses' cunning is told in *Odyssey*, IV. 240–58 and alluded to in Euripides, *Hecuba*, 239–44.

551–2 *boggled . . . clack-dish*: 'baulked at this rag, grown squeamish at that beggar's bowl'. A clack-dish was a beggar's bowl with a wooden lid that could be 'clacked' to attract the attention of passers-by: cf. *Measure for Measure*, III. ii. 126. For 'boggled' cf. VI. 282 n.

554–6 *Hence . . . dawn*: i.e. we praise her not only for making such promises, but also for keeping them: Cook, 187.

Must such external semblance of intrigue
Demonstrate that intrigue there lurks perdue?
Does every hazel-sheath disclose a nut?
He were a Molinist who dared maintain
That midnight meetings in a screened alcove
Must argue folly in a matron—since
So would he bring a slur on Judith's self,
Commended beyond women, that she lured
The lustful to destruction through his lust.
Pompilia took not Judith's liberty,
No faulchion find you in her hand to smite,
No damsel to convey in dish the head
Of Holophernes,—style the Canon so—
Or is it the Count? If I entangle me
With my similitudes,—if wax wings melt,
And earthward down I drop, not mine the fault:
Blame your beneficence, O Court, O sun,
Whereof the beamy smile affects my flight!

563 *MS* Does *1868* Would 564 *MS 1868* must lurk 565 *MS* contain>disclose 566 *MS* dare[ ]>dared 568 *MS* Should>Must 569 *MS* does he 570 *MS 1868* {no comma} 573 *MS 1868* smite,— 574 *MS 1868* the head in dish, 577 *MS* similitudes, and wax-wings>similitudes,—if wax-wings 578 *MS* earth-ward *MS* down I drop, like Icarus,>Icarus comes tumbled down,> down I drop,—not mine the fault,— 579 *MS* Court and>Court, my 580 flight—

564 *perdue*: hidden; cf. III. 1233 n.

566 *Molinist*: cf. I. 33 n.

569 *Judith's self*: cf. the apocryphal Book of Judith, ch. 13. The devout Jewish widow Judith pretended to seduce the Assyrian commander Holofernes, and then, alone with him in his tent, cut off his head.

573 *faulchion*: scimitar; from Judith 13: 6 (AV).

574–5 *No . . . Holophernes*: in the AV, Judith and her maid smuggle Holofernes' head out of the camp in a 'bag of meat.' Here, however, Browning is recalling Botticelli's portrayal of this scene in his 'Return of Judith to Bethulia' (*c.*1470), in the Uffizi. This shows Judith bearing the sword, and her maid carrying Holofernes' head, wrapped in material, on a dish balanced on her head.

577–82 *wax . . . Icarus*: Bottini presents himself as an over-reaching Icarus, the boy who in Greek mythology flew too near the sun with wings held together with wax. The wax melted, the wings collapsed, and Icarus plunged to his death: see Ovid, *Metamorphoses*, VIII. 182–235.

What matter, so Pompilia's fame revive
I' the warmth that proves the bane of Icarus?

Yea, we have shown it lawful, necessary
Pompilia leave her husband, seek the house
O' the parents: and because 'twixt home and home
Lies a long road with many a danger rife,
Lions by the way and serpents in the path,
To rob and ravish,—much behoves she keep
Each shadow of suspicion from fair fame,
For her own sake much, but for his sake more,
The ingrate husband's. Evidence shall be,
Plain witness to the world how white she walks
I' the mire she wanders through ere Rome she reach.
And who so proper witness as a priest?
Gainsay ye? Let me hear who dares gainsay!
I hope we still can punish heretics!
"Give me the man" I say with him of Gath,
"That we may fight together!" None, I think:
The priest is granted me.

Then, if a priest,
One juvenile and potent: else, mayhap,
That dragon, our Saint George would slay, slays him.

581 *MS* —What *MS* since>if *MS* revives>revive 582 *MS* {beginning of fo. 143} 583 *MS* {New paragraph indicated by 'New Par.' in left-hand margin} 584 *MS* quit>leave *MS* home>house 585 *MS* Of 589 *MS* her>fair 591 *MS 1868* husband! *1872* husband: *MS* must speak—>shall be, 592 *MS* A>Some *1868 1872* Some 593 *MS* be reached.>she reach. 594 *MS* that witness but a priest? Ha,>so proper witness as a priest? 596 *MS* {line added later} 599 *MS* me:>me. 600 *MS* {New paragraph indicated by 'New Par:' in right-hand margin} *MS* then,>Then, 601 *MS* potent— 602 *MS* The>That

595 *Gainsay ye?*: Do you deny this?

597–8 "Give . . . together!": the 'man of Gath' is the Philistine giant Goliath. These are Goliath's words of defiance to the Israelite army: 1 Sam. 17: 10. This is another instance of Bottini's over-reaching rhetoric.

602 *our Saint George*: i.e. Caponsacchi. Cf. 1. 585 n.

And should fair face accompany strong hand,
The more complete equipment: nothing mars
Work, else praiseworthy, like a bodily flaw
I' the worker: as 't is said Saint Paul himself
Deplored the check o' the puny presence, still
Cheating his fulmination of its flash,
Albeit the bolt therein went true to oak.

Therefore the agent, as prescribed, she takes,—
Both juvenile and potent, handsome too,—
In all obedience: "good," you grant again.
Do you? I would you were the husband, lords!
How prompt and facile might departure be!
How boldly would Pompilia and the priest
March out of door, spread flag at beat of drum,
But that inapprehensive Guido grants
Neither premiss nor yet conclusion here,
And, purblind, dreads a bear in every bush!

603 *MS* And if>And should *MS* stout>strong 605 *MS* Praiseworthy work> Work else praiseworthy 606 *MS* workman,—>worker,— 607 *MS* ^check o' the^ 608 *MS* [ ]>Cheating *MS* fulmination of its>fulminations of their 609 *MS* the bolt went true enough>each bolt therein went true *610 *MS* {New paragraph indicated by 'New Par:' in left-hand margin. Paragraphing obscured in *1868* and *1872* by this line's being at the head of the page} *MS* [ ]>as *MS* takes 611 {not found in *MS*} *1868* A priest, juvenile, potent, 613 *MS* {beginning of fo. 144} *MS 1868* ye 614 *MS* easy would departure be!>facile had departure been! 615, 616 *MS* {lines added later} 615 *MS* had>would *MS* Priest 616 *MS* Marched bag and baggage forth,>March out of door, spread flag 617 *MS* the inapprehensive husband> inapprehensive Guido 618 *MS* here,—>here, 619 *MS* Purblind, he>And, purblind,

606–7 *Saint Paul . . . presence*: St Paul's enemies noted that, while his letters 'are weighty and powerful . . . his bodily presence is weak, and his speech contemptible': 2 Cor. 10: 10. In the apocryphal 'Acts of Paul and Thecla' he is described as 'a man small of stature, with a bald head and crooked legs, in a good state of body, with eyebrows meeting and nose somewhat hooked, full of friendliness; for now he appeared like a man, and now he had the face of an angel': *New Testament Apocrypha*, ed. W. Schneemelcher, 2 vols. (Cambridge and Louisville, Ky., 1991), ii. 239.

608 *fulmination*: (lit.) thundering; (fig.) denunciation.

617 *inapprehensive*: stupid, slow-witted.

619 *dreads . . . bush!*: cf. *Midsummer Night's Dream*, v. i. 21–2: 'Or in the night, imagining some fear, / How easy is a bush suppos'd a bear!'

For his own quietude and comfort, then,
Means must be found for flight in masquerade
At hour when all things sleep.—"Save jealousy!"
Right, Judges! Therefore shall the lady's wit
Supply the boon thwart nature baulks him of,
And do him service with the potent drug
(Helen's nepenthe, as my lords opine)
Which respites blessedly each fretted nerve
O' the much-enduring man: accordingly,
There lies he, duly dosed and sound asleep,
Relieved of woes or real or raved about.
While soft she leaves his side, he shall not wake;
Nor stop who steals away to join her friend,
Nor do him mischief should he catch that friend
Intent on more than friendly office,—nay,
Nor get himself raw head and bones laid bare
In payment of his apparition!

[—]

621 *MS* to fly>for flight *MS* privacy,—>[ ] masks>masquerade 622 *MS* By night>At hour *MS* Jealousy!" 623 *1868* judges! 624 *MS* balks 625 *MS* Do his [ ]>And do him *MS* drug— 626 *MS* the skilled>my lords *MS* opine)— 627 *MS* Brings blessed respite to>Gives blessed respite to> Shall respite blessedly *1868* Shall respite *MS* each frittered nerve,>each frittered nerve *1868* frittered 628 *MS* And keeps the frightened man would harm himself,>And holds the frightened man would harm himself,>Accordingly, there lies he, sound asleep,>O' the much-enduring man: accordingly, 629 *MS* {line added later} 630 *MS* all woes, raved about or real,>woes, or real or raved about, *1868 1872* woes, 631 *MS* —While *MS* side; *MS* wake 632 *MS* And stop her as she steals to join the priest,—>Nor stop who steals away to join her friend, 633 *MS* her>him 635 *MS* Obtain a bloody head and broken bones> Nor get himself the raw head and bones laid bare>Nor get himself raw head and bones laid bare 636 *MS* interference:—No!>apparition!

---

624 *thwart*: (adj.) perverse, obstinate.

626 *Helen's nepenthe*: the special drug, inducing forgetfulness of all grief and trouble, given by Helen to Telemachus and Menelaus in *Odyssey*, IV. 220–2: 'into the bowl that their wine was drawn from she threw a drug that dispelled all grief and anger and banished remembrance of every trouble.' Bottini's sly wit is also at work here. Pompilia is cast as the utterly beautiful but ambiguous Helen, who eloped with Paris, but then (after the Trojan war) was reconciled to her husband Menelaus. 'Helen's nepenthe' would be an appropriate drug to cover over adultery or induce forgetfulness of it.

636 *apparition*: appearance; showing himself.

Thus
Would I defend the step,—were the thing true
Which is a fable,—see my former speech,—
That Guido slept (who never slept a wink)
Through treachery, an opiate from his wife,
Who not so much as knew what opiates mean.

Now she may start: or hist,—a stoppage still!
A journey is an enterprise of cost!
As in campaigns, we fight but others pay,
Suis expensis, nemo militat.
'T is Guido's self we guard from accident,
Ensuring safety to Pompilia, versed
Nowise in misadventures by the way,
Hard riding and rough quarters, the rude fare,
The unready host. What magic mitigates
Each plague of travel to the unpractised wife?
Money, sweet Sirs! And were the fiction fact
She helped herself thereto with liberal hand

637 *MS* {line added later} *MS* {New paragraph indicated by 'New Par' in right-hand margin} 638 *MS* Thus would I justify—>Would I defend the step, 640 *MS* That Guido got an opiate from his wife.>That Guido slept (who never slept a wink) 641, 642 *MS* {lines added later} *643 *MS* {New paragraph indicated by 'New Par' in left-hand margin} *1868 1872* {New paragraph. Paragraphing obscured in *1888* and *1889* by this line's being at the head of the page} *MS 1868* but hist,— 644 *MS* a thing which costs, which costs!> an enterprise which costs! *1868* which costs! 645, 646 *MS* {lines added later} 645 *MS* and others pay: *1868* and others 646 *MS militat!* 650 *MS* {beginning of fo. 145} 651 *MS* host,—what 652 *MS* Our>Each *MS* []>wife? 653 *MS* sirs! *Yale 1* sirs!>Sirs! *MS 1868 1872* fact,

643 *hist*: a sibilant exclamation, equivalent here to 'Listen!' or 'Think!'

646 *Suis . . . militat*: 'No one serves as a soldier at his own expense', adapting 1 Cor. 9: 7.

653–6 *were . . . to?* : the argument is a fair burlesque; it was not actually used by Bottini. A long list of heavy valuables which Pompilia was charged with carrying off is given in the 'Sentence of the Criminal Court of Florence': OYB vi, vii (6). Pompilia said in her deposition (OYB lxxxv (93)): 'I took some little things in my use (*robbicciuole di mio uso*), a box with many trifles (*bagattelle*) in it, and some money, I don't know how much it was, from a strong-box (*sgrigno*). They were, too, my own, as appears from the note both of the things and of the money made by the Registrar of Castelnuovo.' With this Caponsacchi's deposition agrees: Cook, 189.

From out her husband's store,—what fitter use
Was ever husband's money destined to?
With bag and baggage thus did Dido once
Decamp,—for more authority, a queen!

So is she fairly on her route at last,
Prepared for either fortune: nay and if
The priest, now all a-glow with enterprise,
Cool somewhat presently when fades the flush
O' the first adventure, clouded o'er belike
By doubts, misgivings how the day may die,
Though born with such auroral brilliance,—if
The brow seem over-pensive and the lip
'Gin lag and lose the prattle lightsome late,—
Vanquished by tedium of a prolonged jaunt
In a close carriage o'er a jolting road,
With only one young female substitute
For seventeen other Canons of ripe age
Were wont to keep him company in church,—
Shall not Pompilia haste to dissipate
The silent cloud that, gathering, bodes her bale?—

655 *MS 1868* her>the 657 *MS* thus did>did [ ]>thus did 658 *MS* Decamp: why we have that queen's authority.>Decamp so,—for our more authority.>Decamp,—for more authority, a queen! 659 *MS* {New paragraph indicated by 'New Par.' in left-hand margin} *MS* are we>is she *MS* our>her *MS* last— 661 *MS* ardent in the>all a glow with 665 *MS* [ ]>Though *MS* brilliance— 666 *MS* [ ]>seem *MS* over-[ ]>over-pensive 667 *MS* [ ]>lag *MS* play was pleasant late—>prattle [ ] late—>prattle lightsome late— 668 *MS* Though but through>Induced by *MS* lengthy>prolonged 669 *MS* {no comma} 670 *MS* companion [ ]>companion to replace>young female substitute 671 *MS* The>For 673 *MS* by all her means>by might and main>to dissipate 674 *MS* To dissipate the cloud that bodes her bale,—>The silent cloud that, gathering, bodes her bale,—

657–8 *Dido . . . queen*: a ludicrous epic comparison, supposedly providing 'authority' or precedent for Pompilia's booty-laden escape. Queen Dido uncovered the treasure of her husband Sychaeus and fled with it from Tyre to north Africa, where she founded Carthage. Dido's circumstances were different from Pompilia's. In her case, her wicked brother Pygmalion had secretly murdered Sychaeus out of jealousy at his wealth. Sychaeus' ghost then appeared to Dido and revealed the crime and the location of the treasure. She dug it up and fled. The story is told in *Aeneid*, I. 340–68.

674 *bale*: mischief, trouble.

Prop the irresoluteness may portend
Suspension of the project, check the flight,
Bring ruin on them both? Use every means,
Since means to the end are lawful! What i' the way
Of wile should have allowance like a kiss
Sagely and sisterly administered,
Sororia saltem oscula? We find
Such was the remedy her wit applied
To each incipient scruple of the priest,
If we believe,—as, while my wit is mine
I cannot,—what the driver testifies,
Borsi, called Venerino, the mere tool
Of Guido and his friend the Governor,—
Avowal I proved wrung from out the wretch,
After long rotting in imprisonment,
As price of liberty and favour: long
They tempted, he at last succumbed, and lo
Counted them out full tale each kiss and more,
"The journey being one long embrace," quoth he.
Still, though we should believe the driver's lie,
Nor even admit as probable excuse,
Right reading of the riddle,—as I urged
In my first argument, with fruit perhaps—

675 *MS* irresolution>irresoluteness 677 *MS* both! Use>both?—use *1868* both?—use 678 *MS* Those means the Court allows her,—what>(Since means to the end, are lawful) what>Since means to the end, are lawful? What 679 *MS* {beginning of fo. 146} 680 *MS* administered— 682 *MS* salve her wit applied to [?care]>remedy her wit applied 683 *MS* {line added later} *MS* priest,— 685 *MS* I shall not,—>I cannot,— *MS* half>what 686, 687 *MS* {lines added later} 688 *MS* *1868* The avowal 691 *MS* succumbed,— 692 *MS* *1868* kiss required,— 693 *MS* {line added later} *MS* The journey was *Yale 1* The>"The *1868* was *MS* embrace, quoth he: *Yale 1* embrace,>embrace", 695 *MS* excuse— 696 *MS* riddle—what *Yale 1* riddle,>riddle,—

675 *irresoluteness*: lack of enthusiasm or decision.

681 *Sororia . . . oscula*: 'at least sisterly kisses'; cf. Ovid, *Metamorphoses*, IV. 334, IX. 539. 'Some of this high-comedy paragraph (684–707) is based upon the records, which are full of arguments for and against the driver's story about the kissing; the rest is caricature': Cook, 189. See next nn.

That what the owl-like eyes (at back of head!)
O' the driver, drowsed by driving night and day,
Supposed a vulgar interchange of lips,
This was but innocent jog of head 'gainst head,
Cheek meeting jowl as apple may touch pear
From branch and branch contiguous in the wind,
When Autumn blusters and the orchard rocks:—
That rapid run and the rough road were cause
O' the casual ambiguity, no harm
I' the world to eyes awake and penetrative.
Say,—not to grasp a truth I can release
And safely fight without, yet conquer still,—
Say, she kissed him, say, he kissed her again!
Such osculation was a potent means,
A very efficacious help, no doubt:
Such with a third part of her nectar did

698 *MS* this,>what 700 *MS* [?passionate] vulgar [ ]>vulgar interchange of love, *1868* love, 701 *MS* an>but 703 *MS* In>On orchard-boughs>From branch and branch 704 *MS* {line added later} *MS 1868* rocks. 705 *MS 1868* The *MS* course>run 706 *MS* ambiguity,— 708 *MS* Yet, shall I>Yet,—not to *1868* Yet,— *MS 1868* forego 709 *MS 1868* without and *MS* still?>still,— 710 *MS* and he kissed her again,—>and he again kissed her,—>and he kissed her again,— *1868* and he 711, 712 *MS* {lines added later} 711 *MS* means— 713 *MS 1868* This

698 *owl-like*: (lit.) 'able to see at night', (fig.) 'seemingly wise, but really stupid': cf. II. 216, VI. 1786 nn. The sardonic phrasing 'owl-like (at back of head!)' encapsulates two points that the real Bottini makes in his 'first argument': that the court must discount the driver's testimony about the kissing because (1) how could he see this at night? and (2) how could he see what was happening behind him, when he was supposedly driving the carriage forwards at break-neck speed? : OYB lxxv (82), Bottini, pam. 6.

701–7 *innocent jog . . . penetrative*: the real Bottini makes this point, but Browning tips it into comedy with the florid addition of ll. 702–4. 'Furthermore, there is the possibility to be considered that the jostling together of those sitting in the carriage might have happened from the high speed; and from this fact an overcurious witness might believe that they were kissing each other, although in fact the nearness of their heads and faces to one another might indeed be by mere chance, and not for the purpose of shameful and lustful kisses. Because whenever an act may be presumed to be for either a good or a bad end the presumption of the evil end is always excluded': OYB clxxix (185), Bottini, pam. 13.

711 *osculation*: kissing; in English a pompous Latinism, but taken straight from the source: see OYB lxxv (82), clxxix (185).

713–14 *Such . . . imbue*: Such [osculation] . . . The allusion is the description of Lydia's lips in Horace, *Odes*, I. xiii. 14–16: 'dulcia . . . oscula, quae Venus / quinta

Venus imbue: why should Pompilia fling
The poet's declaration in his teeth?—
Pause to employ what—since it had success,
And kept the priest her servant to the end—
We must presume of energy enough,
No whit superfluous, so permissible?

The goal is gained: day, night and yet a day
Have run their round: a long and devious road
Is traversed,—many manners, various men
Passed in review, what cities did they see,
What hamlets mark, what profitable food
For after-meditation cull and store!
Till Rome, that Rome whereof—this voice
Would it might make our Molinists observe,
That she is built upon a rock nor shall
Their powers prevail against her!—Rome, I say,
Is all but reached; one stage more and they stop
Saved: pluck up heart, ye pair, and forward, then!

[—]

714 *MS* [] []>why should *MS* []>fling 715 *MS* {beginning of fo. 147} *MS* {line added later} *MS* teeth,— *716 *MS 1868 1872 1888* what,— *DC BrU* what,—>what— *1889* what— *717 *MS 1868 1872 1888* end,— *DC BrU* end,—>end— *1889* end— 718 *MS* no whit>enough, 719 *MS* Superfluous, so permissible? Pass we on!>No whit superfluous, so permissible? *720 *MS* {New paragraph indicated by 'New Par.' in right-hand margin} *1868 1872* {New paragraph. Paragraphing obscured in *1888* and *1889* by this line's being at the head of the page} *MS* []>yet a *723 *MS 1868 1872* review *1888* view *DC BrU* view>review *1889* review 725 *MS* store, 726 *MS* Till, Rome— *MS 1868* voice, 729 *MS* her,— 730 *MS* reached,— 731 *MS* Saved,— *MS* ^ye pair,^

parte sui nectaris imbuit': '[Lydia's] sweet lips, which Venus has imbued with the fifth part of her nectar'. Venus is imagined touching Lydia's lips with nectar, the mysterious drink of the gods, so making the lips (and the kisses they give) especially intoxicating and irresistible. Bottini, characteristically carried away by his own erotic reference, exaggerates 'quinta parte' (fifth part) to 'third part'. These lines also refer back to 534.

722–3 *many . . . see*: echoing *Odyssey*, I. 3–4, and Horace's Latin version, *Ars Poetica*, 142: 'qui mores hominum multorum vidit et urbes'. Again, Bottini strains towards the epic mode: cf. l. 217 n.

727 *Molinists*: cf. l. 33 n.

728–9 *built . . . her*: cf. Matt. 16: 18, the classic text on the founding of the Catholic Church.

Ah, Nature—baffled she recurs, alas!
Nature imperiously exacts her due,
Spirit is willing but the flesh is weak:
Pompilia needs must acquiesce and swoon,
Give hopes alike and fears a breathing-while.
The innocent sleep soundly: sound she sleeps,
So let her slumber, then, unguarded save
By her own chastity, a triple mail,
And his good hand whose stalwart arms have borne
The sweet and senseless burthen like a babe
From coach to couch,—the serviceable strength!
Nay, what and if he gazed rewardedly
On the pale beauty prisoned in embrace,
Stooped over, stole a balmy breath perhaps
For more assurance sleep was not decease—
"*Ut vidi*," "how I saw!" succeeded by
"*Ut perii*," "how I sudden lost my brains!"
—What harm ensued to her unconscious quite?
For, curiosity—how natural!
Importunateness—what a privilege
In the ardent sex! And why curb ardour here?
How can the priest but pity whom he saved?
And pity is so near to love, and love
So neighbourly to all unreasonableness!

732 *MS* {New paragraph indicated by 'New Par.' in left-hand margin} *MS* nature— *Yale 1* nature—>Nature— *MS* alas!— 734 *MS* Pompilia's soul is> Spirit is *MS* willing, *MS 1868* weak, 736 *MS* Lay>Give *MS* breathing-while: 737 *MS 1868* sleeps. 738 *MS* There>So 739 *MS* charm> mail, 740 *MS* had>have *742 *MS 1868 1872* couch,— *1888* coach,— *DC BrU* coach,—>couch,— *1889* couch,— *MS 1868* man! 744 *MS* by>in 745 *MS* {beginning of fo. 148} *MS* [?perchance]>perhaps 747 *MS vidi*"— 748 *MS perii*"— *MS* wits,">head>brains!" 749 *MS* inconscious 752 *MS* whence the>why want 753 *MS* saved,—>saved?— 754 *MS 1868* how near 755 *MS 1868* How *MS* to unreasonableness— *1868* to unreasonableness!

732 *Nature . . . recurs*: partly proverbial, from Horace, *Epistles*, I. x. 24: 'Naturam expelles furca, tamen usque recurret': 'You can boot out Nature, but she'll always return.'

734 *Spirit . . . weak*: cf. Matt. 26: 41.

747–8 "*Ut . . . perii*,": cf. Virgil, *Eclogues*, viii. 41: 'ut vidi, ut perii, ut me malus abstulit error!': 'I saw, I was lost, madness swept me away!'—a lover describing the first impact of seeing his beloved. Virgil in turn was imitating Theocritus ii. 82.

As to love's object, whether love were sage
Or foolish, could Pompilia know or care,
Being still sound asleep, as I premised?
Thus the philosopher absorbed by thought,
Even Archimedes, busy o'er a book
The while besiegers sacked his Syracuse,
Was ignorant of the imminence o' the point
O' the sword till it surprised him: let it stab,
And never knew himself was dead at all.
So sleep thou on, secure whate'er betide!
For thou, too, hast thy problem hard to solve—
How so much beauty is compatible
With so much innocence!

Fit place, methinks,
While in this task she rosily is lost,
To treat of and repel objection here
Which,—frivolous, I grant,—my mind misgives,
May somehow still have flitted, gadfly-like,
And teased the Court at times—as if, all said

756 *MS 1868* And for *MS* Pompilia,>love's object, *MS* he was>love were 757 *MS* care *Yale 1* care>care, 758 *MS* [?so]>still 759 *MS* immersed in> absorbed by 760, 761 *MS* {lines added later} 760 *MS* Archimedes busy *MS* book, 763 *MS* [ ] sword>sword till it 765 *MS* betide— 769 *MS* {New paragraph indicated by 'New Par.' in right-hand margin} 772 *MS* know,—>grant,— *MS* but, why misgives *1868* but, still misgives 773 *MS* My mind, may still>My mind, it may *1868* My mind, it may 774 *MS 1868 1872* teazed *MS* said and done,>said

760–4 *Archimedes . . . all*: high sexual innuendo: just as the soldier stabbed Archimedes, killing him, so Caponsacchi perhaps penetrated sexually the 'sleeping' Pompilia, and took her innocence! Altick calls this, somewhat hyperbolically, 'the most audacious sexual scene in Victorian literature': Altick and Loucks, 180. The extravagance of the innuendo comes from the remoteness and ingenuity of the parallel. The mathematician and inventor Archimedes (*c.*287–212 BC), absorbed in a mathematical problem, was oblivious when the besieging Romans finally broke into his native city of Syracuse. He was killed by one of the sacking soldiers, who did not recognize him, even though the Roman general Marcellus had given express orders he should be spared. The ancient version of the story says he was intent on a diagram he had drawn in the sand, not (as Bottini imagines) 'busy o'er a book': see Livy, xxv. 31, Cicero, *de Finibus*, v. 50.

And done, there seemed, the Court might nearly say,
In a certain acceptation, somewhat more
Of what may pass for insincerity,
Falsehood, throughout the course Pompilia took,
Than befits Christian. Pagans held, we know,
Man always ought to aim at good and truth,
Not always put one thing in the same words:
Non idem semper dicere sed spectare
Debemus. But the Pagan yoke was light;
"Lie not at all," the exacter precept bids:
Each least lie breaks the law,—is sin, we hold.
I humble me, but venture to submit—
What prevents sin, itself is sinless, sure:
And sin, which hinders sin of deeper dye,
Softens itself away by contrast so.
Conceive me! Little sin, by none at all,
Were properly condemned for great: but great,
By greater, dwindles into small again.
Now, what is greatest sin of womanhood?
That which unwomans it, abolishes
The nature of the woman,—impudence.
Who contradicts me here? Concede me, then,
Whatever friendly fault may interpose
To save the sex from self-abolishment

775 *MS 1868* there still seemed, one might *MS* ^nearly^ 777 *MS* {beginning of fo. 149} *MS* [ ]>pass 778 *MS* took 779 *MS* Christian: 780 *MS 1868* We *MS* a good and,>good and truth, 781 *MS* ^put^ 783 *MS Debemus*: but *MS* light: 784 *MS* exacter>the exacter 785 *MS* ye say.>ye hold. *1868* ye hold. 786 *MS* reply— 789 *MS* so: 794 *MS* unwomans, and> unwomans, which>unwomans it, 795 *MS* [ ]>The *MS* virtue>nature *MS* impudence>[ ]>impudence 796 *MS* [ ] [?a step]:—>Concede me, then, 797 *MS* [ ]>fault 798 *MS* [ ]>from *MS* self-abolishment,

776 *acceptation*: received sense, perspective.

782–3 *Non . . . Debemus*: Cicero, *Epistulae ad Familiares* ('Letters to Friends'), I. ix. 21: 'We are not bound always to hold the same language, but we are bound to be constant in our aims.'

784 "*Lie . . . bids*: imitating Christ's formula in Matt. 5: 21–2, 27–8, etc.

790 *by*: compared with.

795 *impudence*: shamelessness, loose morals.

Is three-parts on the way to virtue's rank!
And, what is taxed here as duplicity,
Feint, wile and trick,—admitted for the nonce,—
What worse do one and all than interpose,
Hold, as it were, a deprecating hand,
Statuesquely, in the Medicean mode,
Before some shame which modesty would veil?
Who blames the gesture prettily perverse?
Thus,—lest ye miss a point illustrative,—
Admit the husband's calumny—allow
That the wife, having penned the epistle fraught
With horrors, charge on charge of crime she heaped
O' the head of Pietro and Violante—(still
Presumed her parents)—having despatched the same
To their arch-enemy Paolo, through free choice
And no sort of compulsion in the world—
Put case she next discards simplicity
For craft, denies the voluntary act,
Declares herself a passive instrument
I' the husband's hands; that, duped by knavery,

799 *MS* rank: 800 *MS 1868* Now, *MS* ^here^ *MS* [ ],>duplicity, 801 *MS* [ ]>Feint, 802 *MS* other do they than thus interpose,>other do they [ ] than interpose,>worse do one and all than interpose, 806 *MS* {beginning of fo. 150} 807 *MS* an>a point *1872* let *Yale 2* let>lest 808 *MS* Husband's *MS* put case>allow 809 *MS* Pompilia,>That the wife, *MS* which>fraught 810 *MS 1868* crime, 811 *MS* Violante—>Violante—(812 *MS* parents—>parents)— *MS* and despatched ^the^ thing *1868* and despatched the thing *1872* dispatched 815 *MS* She,—taking thought,>Put case that she,— *1868* Put case that she 818 *MS 1868* hands of Guido; duped *MS* the dull brain,—>knavery,—

803 *deprecating*: defensive, averting.

804 *in . . . mode*: in the manner of the Venus de' Medici (in the Tribune of the Uffizi at Florence). This famous antique sculpture shows a naked but modest Venus, her right hand covering her breasts, her left hand covering her genitals. EBB's maid was shocked on first seeing it (see *Correspondence*, xiv. 248), though for EBB it was an exemplary instance of female purity: cf. *Aurora Leigh*, III. 703–6: ' "I comprehend a love so fiery hot, / It burns its natural veil of august shame, / And stands sublimely in the nude, as chaste / As Medicean Venus." ' Bottini's tone is very different from this.

809–10 *epistle . . . horrors*: OYB lv (56–7). Bottini and Arcangeli have already jousted concerning the authenticity of this letter: see VIII. 157–99.

She traced the characters she could not write,
And took on trust the unread sense which, read,
And recognized were to be spurned at once:
Allow this calumny, I reiterate!
Who is so dull as wonder at the pose
Of our Pompilia in the circumstance?
Who sees not that the too-ingenuous soul,
Repugnant even at a duty done
Which brought beneath too scrutinizing glare
The misdemeanours,—buried in the dark,—
Of the authors of her being, as believed,—
Stung to the quick at her impulsive deed,
And willing to repair what harm it worked,
She—wise in this beyond what Nero proved,
Who when folk urged the candid juvenile
To sign the warrant, doom the guilty dead,
"Would I had never learned to write," quoth he!
—Pompilia rose above the Roman, cried
"To read or write I never learned at all!"
O splendidly mendacious!

[—]

819 *MS* Traced charactery, [ ]>She traced the characters, *1868* characters, she 820 *MS* ^unread^ 821 *MS 1868* Were *MS* [ ] [ ] [ ]>but to be *1868* but to be *MS 1868* once. 822 *MS* calumny for truth, I say:>calumny, I reiterate,— 823, 824 *MS* {lines added later} 823 *MS* [ ]>[ ]>pose 827 *MS* before>beneath *MS* a>too *MS* [ ]>glare 829 *MS* [?so]>she *1868* she 830 *MS* own righteous>impulsive 831 *MS* {line added later} 833 *MS* in his youthful candour—called one day>when needs were the candid juvenile *1868* Who, when needs were *1872* Who, when folks 834 *MS* To> Should *1868* Should *MS* dooming>doom 836 *MS* Roman— 838 *MS* {beginning of fo. 151}

823 *pose*: attitude, posture.

825 *too-ingenuous*: overly frank, totally straightforward.

826 *Repugnant . . . at*: even rejecting, even being opposed to.

832–5 *Nero . . . write*: when the teenage Nero became emperor (AD 54) and was first asked to sign a death-warrant, he is reputed to have said 'Quam vellem nescire litteras' ('How I wish I had never learnt to write!'). This story is told in Suetonius, *Nero* 10, as an instance of the promising start of Nero's reign. *candid* = open, fair.

838 *splendidly mendacious*: cf. Horace, *Odes*, III. xi. 35–6: Pompilia is 'splendidly untruthful' like the virtuous Hypermnestra: 'splendide mendax et in omne virgo / nobilis aevum': 'splendidly untruthful, a maiden noble for all time to come'. Hypermnestra put loyalty to her husband before all else, and was 'splendidly untruthful' to her

But time fleets:
Let us not linger: hurry to the end,
Since flight does end, and that disastrously.
Beware ye blame desert for unsuccess,
Disparage each expedient else to praise,
Call failure folly! Man's best effort fails.
After ten years' resistance Troy succumbed:
Could valour save a town, Troy still had stood.
Pompilia came off halting in no point
Of courage, conduct, her long journey through:
But nature sank exhausted at the close,
And, as I said, she swooned and slept all night.
Morn breaks and brings the husband: we assist
At the spectacle. Discovery succeeds.
Ha, how is this? What moonstruck rage is here?
Though we confess to partial frailty now,
To error in a woman and a wife,
Is't by the rough way she shall be reclaimed?
Who bursts upon her chambered privacy?

839 *MS* {New paragraph indicated by 'New Par:' in right-hand margin} *MS* fleets,— 840 *MS* I linger not but *Yale 1* I linger not but>Let us not linger: *MS* close>end, *841 *MS* End does our flight and all>Since end does flight and all *1868* Since end does flight and all *1872 1888* end and that, *DC BrU* end and that, >end, and that *1889* end, and that 842 *MS* unsuccess— 843 *MS* the expedients> each expedient 845 *MS* fell flat— *1868* fell flat: 846 *MS* city>town, *MS* she>Troy 847 *MS* proved deficient>came off halting 848 *MS 1868* the long *MS* through,— *850 *MS 1868 1872* And, as *1888 1889* And as {? broken sort} *MS* night: 853 *MS* [ ]>rage *MS* have we?>is here? 854 *MS* {line added later} *MS* here, 855 *MS* When we confess to error in a wife,>To error in a woman and a wife,

---

father who wanted her to kill her husband. While her forty-nine sisters, the Danaids, stabbed their husbands to death, she refused to carry out her father's plan, warned her husband, and got him to flee. To Horace she is the type of the virtuous, mature wife. Pompilia is 'splendidly untruthful' *to her husband*, perhaps a further irony.

842 *Beware . . . unsuccess*: be careful not to blame merit simply because it is unsuccessful.

847 *halting*: (lit.) limping, walking lamely, (fig.) deficient. Browning may well be recalling Falstaff's use of 'to come halting off', which occurs in a bawdy context: cf. *2 Henry IV*, II. iv. 48–9.

852 *succeeds*: follows, comes next.

853 *moonstruck rage*: insane anger; cf. *Paradise Lost*, XI. 486: 'moon-struck madness'.

What crowd profanes the chaste *cubiculum?*
What outcries and lewd laughter, scurril gibe
And ribald jest to scare the ministrant
Good angels that commerce with souls in sleep?
Why, had the worst crowned Guido to his wish,
Confirmed his most irrational surmise,
Yet there be bounds to man's emotion, checks
To an immoderate astonishment.
'T is decent horror, regulated wrath,
Befit our dispensation: have we back
The old Pagan licence? Shall a Vulcan clap
His net o' the sudden and expose the pair
To the unquenchable universal mirth?
A feat, antiquity saw scandal in
So clearly, that the nauseous tale thereof—
Demodocus his nugatory song—
Hath ever been concluded modern stuff
Impossible to the mouth of the grave Muse,
So, foisted into that Eighth Odyssey

858 *MS* her>the *MS cubiculum*— 860 *MS* ^to^ *MS* ministry>ministrant 861 *MS* O' the>Good 864 *MS* []>checks 865 *MS* astonishment,— 866 *MS* []>'Tis *868 *MS 1868 1872* licence? *1888 1889* license? 869 *MS* {beginning of fo. 152} 870 *MS* quenchless>unquenchable *MS* mirth?—a feat>mirth?— 871 *MS* Antiquity itself>A feat, antiquity 875 *MS* muse>Muse 876 *MS* {no comma} *MS* in>into

858 *cubiculum*: bedchamber (L.).

861 *commerce*: communicate.

868–77 *Vulcan . . . pickthank*: the 'Song of Mars and Venus' is sung by the bard Demodocus to entertain the Phoenicians, in *Odyssey*, VIII. 266–369. It tells how Vulcan, the blacksmith god, catches his wife Venus and her lover Mars naked in the act of adultery with the use of a fine metal net, and then, to vindicate his anger, invites along the other gods to see. Early critics sometimes questioned the Song's genuineness because of its humour and licentiousness, and many, like Bottini, saw it as 'nugatory' (worthless, trivial). Plato saw 'scandal' in its presentation of adultery (*Republic*, 390 C). Rapin, the French critic, censured its 'lowness' (rather than its immorality), seeing its comedy as contrary to the seriousness necessary for epic ('the grave Muse', as Bottini calls it). In Browning's time, Gladstone, while clearly troubled by its 'licentiousness' and 'indelicacy', conceded its authenticity, the modern view: see W. E. Gladstone, *Studies in Homer and the Homeric*, 3 vols. (1858), ii. 461–5. Bottini gets worked up here, with the exaggerated alliteration of 'nauseous' and 'nugatory'. Cf. III. 1450–5, VI. 1459 nn.

By some impertinent pickthank. O thou fool,
Count Guido Franceschini, what didst gain
By publishing thy secret to the world?
Were all the precepts of the wise a waste—
Bred in thee not one touch of reverence?
Admit thy wife—admonish we the fool,—
Were falseness' self, why chronicle thy shame?
Much rather should thy teeth bite out thy tongue,
Dumb lip consort with desecrated brow,
Silence become historiographer,
And thou—thine own Cornelius Tacitus!

But virtue, barred, still leaps the barrier, lords!
—Still, moon-like, penetrates the encroaching mist
And bursts, all broad and bare, on night, ye know!
Surprised, then, in the garb of truth, perhaps,
Pompilia, thus opposed, breaks obstacle,
Springs to her feet, and stands Thalassian-pure,

877 *MS* Still, despite>O thou fool *Yale 1* fool>fool, 878 *MS 1868* were gained 879 *MS 1868* thy shame thus *1872* secrets 880 *MS* in waste?>a waste— 882 *MS* "Why, say my wife"—admonishes the sage, *1868* Why, say 883 *MS* "Were false, and I bid chronicle *1868* Were false, and thou bid chronicle *MS* the fact,>my shame, *1868* shame, 884 *MS* "Much *MS* my . . . my 885 *MS* "Dumbness>"And dumbness>Dumb *MS* brow,— 886 *MS* "Silence *MS* were sole>become 887 *MS* "And I—mine *MS* Tacitus!" *888 *MS* {New paragraph indicated by 'New Par:' in left-hand margin. Paragraphing obscured in *1868* and *1872* by this line's being at the head of the page} *MS* lords [?!]>lords, 889 *MS* ^, moon-like,^ *MS* cloud>mist 890 *MS* And, all the [?prouder], peeps through>And, bursts, all broad and bare, on 891 *MS* {line added later}

877 *pickthank*: busybody.

885 *desecrated brow*: i.e. cuckold's horns.

887 *Cornelius Tacitus*: the Roman historian (*c.*55–120), proverbially wise and grave. A double pun, picking up l. 885: Guido should be 'horn quiet', i.e. tacit (silent) about Pompilia's adultery and tacit about his own horns (*Corn*elius).

891 *in . . . truth*: i.e. naked. The phrase is perfectly poised between an innocent figurative meaning, and salacious innuendo: the implication that Pompilia is literally naked, caught in the act of adultery. With these lines generally, and the image of truth breaking through veils or mists to stand sublimely naked, cf. *Aurora Leigh*, III. 703–6, which they seem to parody. Cf. 804 n.

893 *Thalassian-pure*: 'marriage-pure' or 'pure as the sea', 'pure as someone freshly washed by the sea', (?)'pure as the new-born Venus'. Talassius or Thalassius was the Roman marriage god, the personification of the ritual cry 'Talassio' when the bride is

Confronts the foe,—nay, catches at his sword
And tries to kill the intruder, he complains.
Why, so she gave her lord his lesson back,
Crowned him, this time, the virtuous woman's way,
With an exact obedience; he brought sword,
She drew the same, since swords are meant to draw.
Tell not me 't is sharp play with tools on edge!
It was the husband chose the weapon here.
Why did not he inaugurate the game
With some gentility of apophthegm
Still pregnant on the philosophic page,
Some captivating cadence still a-lisp
O' the poet's lyre? Such spells subdue the surge,
Make tame the tempest, much more mitigate
The passions of the mind, and probably
Had moved Pompilia to a smiling blush.
No, he must needs prefer the argument

896 *MS* own ag>lesson back, 897 *MS* the true and>this time the *MS* way *Yale 1* way>way, 899 *MS* {beginning of fo. 153} 901 *MS* weapons here—*Yale 1* weapons>weapon 904 *MS* [ ]>Still *MS* [ ]>pregnant *MS* in>on *MS* page?>page,— 905 *MS* artful>captivating 906 *MS* ^spells^ *MS* [ ]>subdue *MS* sea,>surge, 907 *MS* tempest— 908 *MS* mind— *MS* most of all>probably 909 *MS* rosy *Yale 1* rosy>smiling 910 *MS* No,— *MS* preferred brute force,>must needs prefer

escorted to the groom's house. But there is also a typical Bottini undertone. The literal meaning of 'Thalassian' is 'of or pertaining to the sea', so the meaning would again be respectable: 'pure as the sea', 'pure as someone fresh washed by the sea'. But it was Venus who was born pure and naked from the sea (as in Botticelli's painting of *The Birth of Venus*), and there is just the hint of this third meaning. This is certainly an unusual word, but Browning might be remembering its use in a lyrical passage of Henry Taylor's *Philip Van Artevelde*, Pt. II: 'Colour, to wit—complexion;—hers was light / And gladdening . . . her skin elsewhere / White as the foam from which in happy hour / Sprang the Thalassian Venus': III. ii. 430–4.

897–8 *Crowned . . . obedience*: i.e. did *not* crown him with the cuckold's horns, but with the glory of obeying him exactly. Cf. Prov. 12: 4: 'A virtuous woman is a crown to her husband: but she that maketh ashamed is as rottenness in his bones.'

902–6 *Why . . . lyre?*: 'Why didn't Guido begin the encounter with Pompilia by graciously using some proverb, still having force from its context in a learned book, or why didn't he use some lovely phrase or piece of poetry still soft-sounding or whispering as though it has just come off the poet's lyre?' 'A-lisp' seems to be an adjective, and is Browning's invention.

O' the blow: and she obeyed, in duty bound,
Returned him buffet ratiocinative—
Ay, in the reasoner's own interest,
For wife must follow whither husband leads,
Vindicate honour as himself prescribes,
Save him the very way himself bids save!
No question but who jumps into a quag
Should stretch forth hand and pray us "Pull me out
"By the hand!" Such were the customary cry:
But Guido pleased to bid "Leave hand alone!
"Join both feet, rather, jump upon my head:
"I extricate myself by the rebound!"
And dutifully as enjoined she jumped—
Drew his own sword and menaced his own life,
Anything to content a wilful spouse.

And so he was contented—one must do
Justice to the expedient which succeeds,
Strange as it seem: at flourish of the blade,
The crowd drew back, stood breathless and abashed,
Then murmured "This should be no wanton wife,
"No conscience-stricken sinner, caught i' the act,
"And patiently awaiting our first stone:
"But a poor hard-pressed all-bewildered thing,

911 *MS* ^she^ 912 *MS* the>him 917 *MS* that>but *MS* sinks>jumps 918 *MS* Stretches a hand forth and cries>Should stretch a hand forth and bid>Should stretch forth hand and pray one *1868 1872* pray one *919 *MS* hand:" such>hand!" Such *1868 1872 1888 1889* hand!" such 920 *MS* cry,>bid, *MS* alone— 921 *MS* head.>head, *1868* head, 922 *MS* [ ]>by *MS* rebound—">rebound!" 924 *MS* {line added later} 926 *MS* {New paragraph indicated by 'New Par:' in left-hand margin} 929 *MS* {beginning of fo. 154} 930 *MS* wife— 931 *MS 1868* creature, 933 *MS* {no comma}

---

912 *buffet ratiocinative*: the hard 'blow' or punch of rational argument.

917 *quag*: marsh. The image that follows, of Guido floundering in a marsh, begging Pompilia to jump on top of him, is high farce.

930 *should be*: i.e. must be.

932 *patiently . . . stone*: i.e. quietly waiting to be stoned to death for adultery: see John 8: 7.

"Has rushed so far, misguidedly perhaps,
"Meaning no more harm than a frightened sheep.
"She sought for aid; and if she made mistake
"I' the man could aid most, why—so mortals do:
"Even the blessed Magdalen mistook
"Far less forgiveably: consult the place—
"Supposing him to be the gardener,
" 'Sir,' said she, and so following." Why more words?
Forthwith the wife is pronounced innocent:
What would the husband more than gain his cause,
And find that honour flash in the world's eye,
His apprehension was lest soil had smirched?

So, happily the adventure comes to close
Whereon my fat opponent grounds his charge
Preposterous: at mid-day he groans "How dark!"
Listen to me, thou Archangelic swine!
Where is the ambiguity to blame,
The flaw to find in our Pompilia? Safe
She stands, see! Does thy comment follow quick
"Safe, inasmuch as at the end proposed;

934 *MS* far— *MS* perhaps— 936 *MS* help;>aid; 937 *MS* help best,>aid most, *MS* chose>why— *MS* err:>do: 939 *MS* forgiveably:> forgivably: 940 *MS* " 'Supposing>"Supposing 941 *MS* " 'Sir," *MS* what follows on.">so following." *MS* {New paragraph indicated at "Why" by 'New Par.' in right-hand margin and then cancelled} 944 *MS* white> flash 945 *MS* His>Which *MS* besmirched?>had smirched 946 *MS* {New paragraph indicated by 'New Par:' in left-hand margin} 947 [?great]> fat 948 *MS* Preposterous— *MS* groans>he groans 949 *MS* {line added later} *MS* [ ]>thou *MS* Arcangelic 950 *MS* blame? 951 *MS* find? See, Venus-like she stands,>find in our Pompilia?—Safe 952 *MS* Pompilia, she stands, [?then]. Does a>She stands, see! Does thy 953 *MS* "Safe— *MS* proposed

938–41 *Magdalen . . . following*: Mary Magdalene mistook the resurrected Jesus for a gardener in John 20: 15.

944 *flash in*: i.e. shine brightly, dazzle.

949 *Archangelic swine*: referring to Arcangeli's piggish love of food, and the fact that he is overweight: see 1. 1132, 1151 n.

953 *inasmuch . . . proposed*: i.e. in the sense that she had reached her desired objective—her personal safety.

"But thither she picked way by devious path—
"Stands dirtied, no dubiety at all!
"I recognize success, yet, all the same,
"Importunately will suggestion prompt—
"Better Pompilia gained the right to boast
" 'No devious path, no doubtful patch was mine,
" 'I saved my head nor sacrificed my foot!'
"Why, being in a peril, show mistrust
"Of the angels set to guard the innocent?
"Why rather hold by obvious vulgar help
"Of stratagem and subterfuge, excused
"Somewhat, but still no less a foil, a fault,
"Since low with high, and good with bad is linked?
"Methinks I view some ancient bas-relief.
"There stands Hesione thrust out by Troy,
"Her father's hand has chained her to a crag,
"Her mother's from the virgin plucked the vest,
"At a safe distance both distressful watch,

954 *MS* "But, [?sure],>"But thither *MS* her path>way *MS* []>path— 955 *MS* "Dirtied beyond>"Dirtied with []>"Is dirtied, no 956 *MS* We>I 957 *MS* th[]>will *MS 1868 1872* prick— *Yale 1* prick>prick,— 958 *MS 1868* "What, had *MS* boast— 959 *MS* {beginning of fo. 155} *MS* were 960 *MS* foot:'>foot?' *1868* foot?' *1888 1889* {! is damaged but legible} 965 *MS* ^but still^ *MS* fault— 966 *MS* {no comma} *Yale 1* high and>high, and 967 *MS* we>I *MS* bas-relief— 969 *MS* rock,> crag, 970 *MS* [?the]>[?her] plucked the vest and veil,—>the virgin plucked the vest,—

961–2 *Why . . . innocent?*: i.e. why didn't she trust that God would rescue her?

968–80: *Hesione . . . trick!*" the story of Hesione is essentially another version of the St George and the dragon or Perseus and Andromeda myth, which fascinated Browning: see I. 585 n. When King Laomedon broke a promise to the gods, they afflicted Troy with a plague and a sea-monster; the latter had to be placated with virgin sacrifice. Eventually Hesione, Laomedon's own daughter, was set out for the monster, but she was rescued by Hercules: see Ovid, *Metamorphoses*, XI. 194–220, for one version of the story. As a young man Browning had a copy of 'Perseus and Andromeda' by Polidoro da Caravaggio over the desk where he worked. The description here may owe something to the engraving, particularly in its details of a man and woman lurking behind the rock where the naked Andromeda is chained, and in the image of the dragon with its forepaws 'paddling' the waves: see l. 990. For the engraving, see John Maynard, *Browning's Youth* (Cambridge, Mass., 1977), 160–2.

"While near and nearer comes the snorting orc.
"I look that, white and perfect to the end,
"She wait till Jove despatch some demigod;
"Not that,—impatient of celestial club
"Alcmena's son should brandish at the beast,—
"She daub, disguise her dainty limbs with pitch,
"And so elude the purblind monster! Ay,
"The trick succeeds, but 't is an ugly trick,
"Where needs have been no trick!"

My answer? Faugh;
Nimis incongrue! Too absurdly put!
Sententiam ego teneo contrariam,
Trick, I maintain, had no alternative.
The heavens were bound with brass,—Jove far at feast
(No feast like that thou didst not ask me to,
Arcangeli,—I heard of thy regale!)
With the unblamed Æthiop,—Hercules spun wool
I' the lap of Omphale, while Virtue shrieked—
The brute came paddling all the faster. You
Of Troy, who stood at distance, where's the aid

972 *MS* near and near *Yale 1* near comes>nearer comes 974 *MS* [ ]>some *977 *MS 1868 1872* "She *1888 1889* ' She [broken sort] *MS* daubs, disguises her pure>daub, disguise her dainty 978 *MS* eludes>elude 979 *MS* tis 981 *MS 1868* Faugh! 982 *MS* absurd a speech.>absurdly put! 983 *MS contrariam—* 984 *MS* Maintain that trick>Trick, I maintain, 986, 987 *MS* {lines added later} 989 *MS* virtue>Virtue 990 *MS* {beginning of fo. 156} *MS* And the>The 991 *MS* the earth,>Troy,

972 *orc*: ferocious sea-monster. Not the modern sense, but so used in medieval and Renaissance texts. Browning may well be remembering the terrifying *orca* of *Orlando furioso*, Canto X, which intends to attack Angelica, who is also chained naked to a rock. Cf. 'Caliban upon Setebos', 177, 274.

976 *Alcmena's son*: Hercules: see l. 968 n.

978 *purblind*: dim-sighted, partially blind.

982–3 *Nimis . . . contrariam*: 'Exceedingly incongruous! . . . I hold the opposite opinion': these phrases are from the OYB: cii (110), clxxxii (188).

985–8 *Jove . . . Æthiop*: cf. *Iliad*, I. 423–5: Zeus cannot be contacted because he is far away feasting 'with the blameless Ethiopians'.

987 *regale*: choice repast, feast, from It. *regalo*.

988–9 *Hercules . . . Omphale*: i.e. there was no hero available to rescue Pompilia. Hercules was effeminized when he became the slave of Omphale, queen of Lydia. This picture of him spinning wool while lying in her lap is from Ovid, *Heroides*, IX. 73–100.

You offered in the extremity? Most and least,
Gentle and simple, here the Governor,
There the Archbishop, everywhere the friends,
Shook heads and waited for a miracle,
Or went their way, left Virtue to her fate.
Just this one rough and ready man leapt forth!
—Was found, sole anti-Fabius (dare I say)
Who restored things, with no delay at all,
Qui haud cunctando rem restituit! He,
He only, Caponsacchi 'mid a crowd,
Caught Virtue up, carried Pompilia off
Through gaping impotence of sympathy
In ranged Arezzo: what you take for pitch,
Is nothing worse, belike, than black and blue,
Mere evanescent proof that hardy hands
Did yeoman's service, cared not where the gripe
Was more than duly energetic: bruised,
She smarts a little, but her bones are saved
A fracture, and her skin will soon show sleek.
How it disgusts when weakness, false-refined,

993 *MS* Governor 994 *MS* mob *Yale 1* mob,>friends, 998 *MS* Was *MS* anti-Fabius,—dare I say,— 999 *MS* To restore things with *1868* To restore 1000 *MS 1868 Qui,* *MS 1868 1872 cunctando,* 1001 *MS* mid 1002 *MS* virtue>Virtue 1003 *MS 1868* Thro' the 1004 *MS* stains>what 1005 *MS* ^worse,^ 1006 *MS* An 1008 *MS* energetic— *MS* skin>bruised 1009 *MS* Might smart>She smarts *MS* the>her *MS* were>are 1010 *MS* breaking,>fracture, *MS* the skin would soon grow>her skin will soon show 1011 *MS* me when the>when weakness, *MS* false-refined

998 *anti-Fabius*: i.e. an active, heroic man, who leapt into battle. Q. Fabius Maximus Verrucosus (d. 203 BC) was known as 'Fabius Cunctator' (Fabius the Delayer) because of his policy of caution and attrition against Hannibal during the Second Punic War: he followed Hannibal's army but avoided pitched battles. In describing Caponsacchi as an 'anti-Fabius' Bottini again delights in his own elaborate wit.

1000 *Qui . . . restituit*: 'who by *not* delaying restored the thing'. Bottini wittily turns upside-down Ennius's praise of Fabius by adding *haud* (not) to the original statement *unus homo nobis cunctando restituit rem* ('one man's delay alone restored our state'). This line from Ennius is quoted in Cicero's *De Senectute*, 10, where (in the context) Cato is praising Fabius' 'patient endurance' as against Hannibal's 'boyish impetuosity': see previous n.

1004 *ranged*: i.e. gathered round as spectators, on-looking. Cf. 'Childe Roland', 199.

Censures the honest rude effective strength,—
When sickly dreamers of the impossible
Decry plain sturdiness which does the feat
With eyes wide open!
Did occasion serve,
I could illustrate, if my lords allow;
Quid vetat, what forbids I aptly ask
With Horace, that I give my anger vent,
While I let breathe, no less, and recreate,
The gravity of my Judges, by a tale?
A case in point—what though an apologue
Graced by tradition?—possibly a fact:
Tradition must precede all scripture, words
Serve as our warrant ere our books can be:
So, to tradition back we needs must go
For any fact's authority: and this
Hath lived so far (like jewel hid in muck)
On page of that old lying vanity
Called "Sepher Toldoth Yeschu:" God be praised,
I read no Hebrew,—take the thing on trust:

1012 *MS* Bla[m]>Censure>Censures 1013 *MS* And *MS* [?wea]kly>sickly 1014 *MS* the sturdiness *Yale 1* the sturdiness>plain sturdiness *MS* did>does 1016 *MS* {New paragraph indicated by 'New Par:' in right-hand margin} 1017 *MS* illustrate . . would my lords allow?>illustrate if my lords allow? 1018 *MS 1868* forbids, 1019 *MS* Flaccus, 1020 *MS* {beginning of fo. 157} *MS 1868* recreate 1021 *MS* Judges?>Judges, *MS* by a a tale— *1868* by a tale— 1023 *MS 1868* tradition,— *1868* fact? 1025 *MS* Must be>Serve as 1027 *MS* best authority,—and this I cite>any fact's authority,—and this 1029 *MS 1868* O' the page 1030 *MS* "Sephir Toldos Jeschu": *Yale 1* "Sephir Toldos Jeschu":> "Sepher Toldoth Yeschu":

1018 *Quid vetat*: 'what forbids'—part of a quotation from Horace: 'quamquam ridentem dicere verum / quid vetat': 'though what forbids me from telling the truth with a laugh?': *Satires*, I. i. 24–5.

1022 *apologue*: moral story.

1029 *lying vanity*: cf. Ps. 31: 6: 'I have hated them that regard lying vanities: but I trust in the Lord.'

1030 *Sepher Toldoth Yeschu*: (Browning's transliteration of the Hebrew) 'The Book of the History of Yeshu'. The usual modern transliteration is *Toledot Yeshu*. This is a Jewish mock Gospel, a compilation of scurrilous oral traditions about Yeshu (or Jesus), probably put together in the tenth century, which deliberately debunks and parodies

But I believe the writer meant no good
(Blind as he was to truth in some respects)
To our pestiferous and schismatic . . . well,
My lords' conjecture be the touchstone, show
The thing for what it is! The author lacks
Discretion, and his zeal exceeds: but zeal,—
How rare in our degenerate day! Enough!
Here is the story: fear not, I shall chop
And change a little, else my Jew would press
All too unmannerly before the Court.

It happened once,—begins this foolish Jew,
Pretending to write Christian history,—

1033 *MS* {line added later} *MS* Blind *MS* respects, 1034 *MS* schismatic: . .>schismatic . . *1868 1872* schismatic . . 1035 *MS* is>be 1038 *MS* How all>How rare 1039 *MS 1868* story,— *MS* [ ] not me, who>fear not I shall 1040 *MS* since else>else 1042 *MS* {New paragraph indicated by 'New Par:' in left-hand margin} 1043 *MS* {line added later}

the Christian Gospels. Here Jesus, the illegitimate son of a Roman soldier, lives a life devoted to blasphemy and magic, and is eventually hanged, a fate he fully deserves. Judas steals Jesus' body from the tomb, and buries it at the bottom of a riverbed, hence starting the false rumours of the Resurrection. As one authority tactfully remarks, 'the work is an expression of vulgar polemics written in reaction to the no less vulgar attacks on Judaism in popular Christian teaching and writing': *The Oxford Dictionary of the Jewish Religion*, ed. by R. J. Zwi Werblowsky and G. Wigoder (1997), p. 695.

This anti-Christian propaganda is quite a rare text before the second half of the nineteenth century, and it is hard to see where Browning would have read it. J. C. Wagenseil produced a parallel Hebrew–Latin edition in 1681. There was only one English-language version available before the 1870s, *The Gospel According to the Jews, Called Toldoth Jesu, The Generations of Jesus* (London: Carlile, 1823). Perhaps Browning only knew the text by reputation: he lets Bottini describe it as 'muck' (i.e. scurrilous), which it certainly is, but he also lets Bottini imply that there is some genuine religious 'zeal' in it—something hard to see from either a Jewish or Christian perspective. The important point here is that the anecdote of the disciples, the dream, and the chicken (1042–1108) is *not* in the *Toldoth*. The way in which here St Peter, St John, and Judas all appear ridiculous makes it bear some resemblance to the satirical style of the *Toldoth*, but actually it is rather more genial than anything in the original. Rowena Fowler suggests the anecdote may be Browning's invention, 'for it does not appear in any versions of the *Toldoth*, nor among compilations of Talmudic or modern Jewish folk tales': VP 35 (1997), 261. Presumably Browning intends Bottini's knowledge of the *Toldoth*, an anti-Christian text, to add to our sense of his dubious character.

1034 *schismatic* . . . : schismatic [clergy? Papacy? Church?]. Perhaps sensing he is on dangerous ground, or simply being diplomatic, Bottini does not fill in the blank here.

That three, held greatest, best and worst of men,
Peter and John and Judas, spent a day
In toil and travel through the country-side
On some sufficient business—I suspect,
Suppression of some Molinism i' the bud.
Foot-sore and hungry, dropping with fatigue,
They reached by nightfall a poor lonely grange,
Hostel or inn: so, knocked and entered there.
"Your pleasure, great ones?"—"Shelter, rest and food!"
For shelter, there was one bare room above;
For rest therein, three beds of bundled straw:
For food, one wretched starveling fowl, no more—
Meat for one mouth, but mockery for three.
"You have my utmost." How should supper serve?
Peter broke silence: "To the spit with fowl!
"And while 't is cooking, sleep!—since beds there be,
"And, so far, satisfaction of a want.
"Sleep we an hour, awake at supper-time,
"Then each of us narrate the dream he had,
"And he whose dream shall prove the happiest, point
"The clearliest out the dreamer as ordained
"Beyond his fellows to receive the fowl,
"Him let our shares be cheerful tribute to,
"His the entire meal, may it do him good!"
Who could dispute so plain a consequence?
So said, so done: each hurried to his straw,
Slept his hour's-sleep and dreamed his dream, and woke.
"I," commenced John, "dreamed that I gained the prize

1046 *MS* thro' *Yale 1* thro'>through 1047 *MS* {no comma} 1048 *MS* heresy in the [ ]>Molinism i' the bud: 1049 *MS* {line added later} *MS* Foot-sore, 1050 *MS* And>They 1051 *MS* they knocked>so knocked 1052 *MS* {beginning of fo. 158} *MS* food and rest!" *Yale 1* food and rest!">rest and food!" 1053 *MS* above, 1054 *MS* straw, 1056 *MS* a>but 1058 *MS 1868* silence. 1059–1067 *MS* {no quotation marks at beginnings of lines} 1059 *MS* sleep,>sleep!— 1060 *MS* for>of 1064 *MS* to>out 1067 *MS* meal— 1071 *MS* "I" commenced John "dreamed

1068 *so . . . consequence*: i.e. so logical a conclusion. A 'consequence' in this sense is the logical result of a process of reasoning: see OED[2], 3.

"We all aspire to: the proud place was mine,
"Throughout the earth and to the end of time
"I was the Loved Disciple: mine the meal!"
"But I," proceeded Peter, "dreamed, a word
"Gave me the headship of our company,
"Made me the Vicar and Vice-gerent, gave
"The keys of heaven and hell into my hand,
"And o'er the earth, dominion: mine the meal!"
"While I," submitted in soft under-tone
The Iscariot—sense of his unworthiness
Turning each eye up to the inmost white—
With long-drawn sigh, yet letting both lips smack,
"I have had just the pitifullest dream
"That ever proved man meanest of his mates,
"And born foot-washer and foot-wiper, nay
"Foot-kisser to each comrade of you all!
"I dreamed I dreamed; and in that mimic dream
"(Impalpable to dream as dream to fact)
"Methought I meanly chose to sleep no wink
"But wait until I heard my brethren snore;
"Then stole from couch, slipped noiseless o'er the planks,
"Slid downstairs, furtively approached the hearth,
"Found the fowl duly brown, both back and breast,
"Hissing in harmony with the cricket's chirp,

1072–1074 *MS* {no quotation marks at beginnings of lines} 1075 *MS* "But I" proceeded Peter "dreamed a word 1076–1079 *MS* {no quotation marks at beginnings of lines} 1077 *MS* I was>Made me *MS* Viceregent, *1868 1872* Vice-regent, *MS* [?held]>gave 1078 *MS 1868* Heaven and Hell 1081 *MS* {beginning of fo. 159} 1082 *MS* his eyes>each eye 1083 *MS* Yet [?l]>With long-drawn *MS* sigh— *Yale 1* sigh—>sigh, *MS* smack— *Yale 1* smack—>smack, 1085 *MS* {no comma} 1086 *MS* [ ]>foot-washer 1091 *MS* [?snore]>breathe; *1868 1872* breathe; 1092 *MS 1868 1872* to the door, 1094 *MS* on>both

1074 *Loved Disciple*: one of St John's traditional titles; cf. John 19: 26.

1075–9 *word . . . dominion*: i.e. made him leader of the disciples and first head or pope of the Church. Cf. Matt. 16: 18–19.

1081 *The Iscariot*: Judas.

1086 *foot-washer . . . foot-wiper*: hypocritically recalling Jesus' actions and sayings in John 13: 1–17.

1089 *Impalpable to dream*: as insubstantial with regard to a dream.

"Grilled to a point; said no grace but fell to,
"Nor finished till the skeleton lay bare.
"In penitence for which ignoble dream,
"Lo, I renounce my portion cheerfully!
"Fie on the flesh—be mine the ethereal gust,
"And yours the sublunary sustenance!
"See that whate'er be left ye give the poor!"
Down the two scuttled, one on other's heel,
Stung by a fell surmise; and found, alack,
A goodly savour, both the drumstick bones,
And that which henceforth took the appropriate name
O' the Merry-thought, in memory of the fact
That to keep wide awake is man's best dream.

So,—as was said once of Thucydides
And his sole joke, "The lion, lo, hath laughed!"—
Just so, the Governor and all that's great
I' the city, never meant that Innocence

1096 *MS* point,— 1097 *MS* bones lay picked and bare.>skeleton lay bare. 1100 *MS 1868 1872* etherial *MS* [ ]>gust, 1102 *MS* See, *1868* "See, *MS 1868* left, *MS* {no quotation mark at end of line} 1103 *MS* scuttled, on on 1104 *MS* too late>alack, 1105 *MS 1868* drumstick-bones, 1107 *MS 1868* merry-thought, 1108 *MS* the best>our best *1868 1872* our best **MS 1868 1872* dream. *1888* dream *DC BrU* dream>dream. *1889* dream. 1109, 1110 {not found in *MS*} 1111 *MS* {New paragraph indicated by 'New Par' in left-hand margin} 1112–14 *MS* {lines added later} 1112 *MS* {beginning of fo. 160} *MS* City, *MS* she should starve—>Innocence

1100 *ethereal gust*: impalpable (or heavenly) enjoyment—a circumlocution for 'smell'. Cf. 'Christmas-Eve', 904.

1102 *whate'er . . . poor*: alluding to Judas' self-righteous comment at John 12: 5.

1107 *Merry-thought*: the wishbone, the forked bone between the neck and breast of the chicken.

1109–10 *Thucydides . . . laughed*: the great Greek historian Thucydides (*c.*460–*c.*400 BC) was famous for his brooding gravity. Yet an ancient commentator, responding to the Kylon digression in *Histories*, I. 126, detected humour in the style (if not the subject-matter): 'Some, admiring the perspicuity of the narrative about Kylon, have said "here the lion smiled".' Bottini is having some difficulty integrating his anecdote about the apostles into his larger argument. What he appears to be saying is that the Governor's and the Archbishop's vague intentions of helping Pompilia were dreams, whereas Caponsacchi, like Judas, lived and acted in the real world; which might appear to invert the moral point, hence the injunction 'grant the parallel' in 1124, cf. 1130.

Should quite starve while Authority sat at meat;
They meant to fling a bone at banquet's end:
Wished well to our Pompilia—in their dreams,
Nor bore the secular sword in vain—asleep.
Just so the Archbishop and all good like him
Went to bed meaning to pour oil and wine
I' the wounds of her, next day,—but long ere day,
They had burned the one and drunk the other, while
Just so, again, contrariwise, the priest
Sustained poor Nature in extremity
By stuffing barley-bread into her mouth,
Saving Pompilia (grant the parallel)
By the plain homely and straightforward way
Taught him by common sense. Let others shriek
"Oh what refined expedients did we dream
"Proved us the only fit to help the fair!"
He cried "A carriage waits, jump in with me!"

And now, this application pardoned, lords,—
This recreative pause and breathing-while,—
Back to beseemingness and gravity!
For Law steps in: Guido appeals to Law,
Demands she arbitrate,—does well for once.
O Law, of thee how neatly was it said
By that old Sophocles, thou hast thy seat

1113 *MS* [?Amid]>Should starve thus *etc.* *1868* Should starve thus *MS* meat *1868* meat. 1114 *MS 1868* end, 1116 *MS 1868* asleep: 1119 *MS* but long ere dawned the day,>next day,—but long ere day, 1120 *MS 1868* other: 1121 *MS* [ ],>contrariwise, 1122 *MS* nature 1123 *MS* {line added later} 1124 *MS* (Pompilia—if you grant the parallel)>Saving Pompilia (grant the parallel) 1127 *MS* "Oh, *Yale 1* "Oh,>"Oh 1128 *MS* [ ]>us 1129 *MS* {line added later} *MS* cried— 1130 *MS* {New paragraph indicated by 'New Par' in left-hand margin} [ ]>lords,— 1131 *MS* breathing while,— *Yale 1* breathing while,—>breathing-while,— 1133 *MS* steps,>steps *MS* in,— *MS* law, *Yale 1* law,>Law 1135 *MS* Oh, Law—

1116 *Nor . . . vain*: i.e. nor wielded their civil authority uselessly. The phrasing is from Rom. 13: 4.

1118–19 *pour . . . her*: i.e. meaning to act like a Good Samaritan: cf. Luke 10: 34.

1136–7 *thou . . . throned*: roughly translating Sophocles, *Oedipus at Colonus*, 1382: Δίκη ξύνεδρος Ζηνὸς ἀρχαίοις νόμοις: 'as sure as Justice, as declared of old, sits sharing Zeus' throne'.

I' the very breast of Jove, no meanlier throned!
Here is a piece of work now, hitherto
Begun and carried on, concluded near,
Without an eye-glance cast thy sceptre's way;
And, lo the stumbling and discomfiture!
Well may you call them "lawless" means, men take
To extricate themselves through mother-wit
When tangled haply in the toils of life!
Guido would try conclusions with his foe,
Whoe'er the foe was and whate'er the offence;
He would recover certain dowry-dues:
Instead of asking Law to lend a hand,
What pother of sword drawn and pistol cocked,
What peddling with forged letters and paid spies,
Politic circumvention!—all to end
As it began—by loss of the fool's head,
First in a figure, presently in a fact.
It is a lesson to mankind at large.
How other were the end, would men be sage
And bear confidingly each quarrel straight,
O Law, to thy recipient mother-knees!
How would the children light come and prompt go,

1137 *MS* [?meaner]>meanlier 1140 *MS* way 1142 *MS 1868* "lawless," means men 1143 *MS* help themselves through simple>extricate themselves through *MS* mother-wit[?!]>mother-wit 1145 *MS* {beginning of fo. 161} *MS* wife—>foe— 1146–8 *MS* {lines added later} 1146 *MS* Whoever 1148 *MS* law *Yale 1* law>Law 1149 *MS* cocked— 1150 *MS* piddling 1151 *MS* circumvention,— *MS* to what>all to *MS* [?end?]> end, 1152 *MS* {no comma} 1153 *MS* For a figure first and a fact presently.> In a figure first and a fact presently.>First, in a figure, presently in a fact. 1154 *MS* {line added later} 1155 *MS* [?wise]>sage 1157 *MS* law, *MS* mother-lap>mother-knees,— 1158 *MS* How happy>How would the human children come and go,>How would the children light come and prompt go,

1149 *sword . . . cocked*: cf. ll. 380–1 n.

1153 *First . . . fact*: i.e. first by rash action, and soon by the result of that action: beheading.

1158 *light*: lightly (adv.). The phrasing here adapts the proverbial 'light come, light go'.

This with a red-cheeked apple for reward,
The other, peradventure red-cheeked too
I' the rear, by taste of birch for punishment.
No foolish brawling murder any more!
Peace for the household, practice for the Fisc,
And plenty for the exchequer of my lords!
Too much to hope, in this world: in the next,
Who knows? Since, why should sit the Twelve enthroned
To judge the tribes, unless the tribes be judged?
And 't is impossible but offences come:
So, all's one lawsuit, all one long leet-day!

Forgive me this digression—that I stand
Entranced awhile at Law's first beam, outbreak
O' the business, when the Count's good angel bade
"Put up thy sword, born enemy to the ear,
"And let Law listen to thy difference!"
And Law does listen and compose the strife,

1159 *1868 1872* This, 1160 *MS* The other red-cheeked too by taste of birch> The other peradventure red-cheeked too 1161 *MS* For punishment. No foolish murders more!>By gentle taste of birch for punishment. 1162 *MS* {line added later} *MS 1868* murders 1163 *MS* What peace in>Peace for *MS* household!>household, **MS* pratice *1868 1872* practice *1888 1889* practise 1165 *MS* for>in *MS* life:>world: 1166 *MS* Perhaps: since,>Who knows? Since, *MS* wherefore>why should *MS* [ ]>enthroned 1167 *MS* world,>tribes, *MS* judged,>judged? 1168 *MS* come?>come: 1170 *MS* {New paragraph indicated by 'New Par' in left-hand margin} *Yale 1* disgression>digression *MS* stood 1171 *MS* as law's first beam outbroke>as first law's beam outbroke>at Law's first beam, outbroke *Yale 1* outbroke>outbreak 1172 *MS* business and >business, when 1174 *MS* law>Law 1175 *MS* law>Law *MS* did *Yale 1* did>does

---

1166–7 *Twelve . . . tribes*: i.e. the twelve disciples throned in heaven to judge the twelve tribes of Israel. Cf. Matt. 19: 28: 'And Jesus said unto them, Verily I say unto you, That ye which have followed me, in the regeneration when the Son of man shall sit in the throne of his glory, ye also shall sit upon twelve thrones, judging the twelve tribes of Israel.'

1168 *'t is . . . come*: cf. Matt. 18: 7.

1169 *leet-day*: day appointed for court session. A leet was originally 'a special kind of court of record which the lords of certain manors were empowered by charter or prescription to hold annually or semi-annually': OED². Here Bottini imagines his idea of heaven: a kind of eternal day in court.

1173 *Put . . . ear*: playing on Matt. 26: 51–2.

Settle the suit, how wisely and how well!
On our Pompilia, faultless to a fault,
Law bends a brow maternally severe,
Implies the worth of perfect chastity,
By fancying the flaw she cannot find.
Superfluous sifting snow, nor helps nor harms:
'T is safe to censure levity in youth,
Tax womanhood with indiscretion, sure!
Since toys, permissible to-day, become
Follies to-morrow: prattle shocks in church:
And that curt skirt which lets a maiden skip,
The matron changes for a trailing robe.
Mothers may aim a blow with half-shut eyes
Nodding above their spindles by the fire,
And chance to hit some hidden fault, else safe.
Just so, Law hazarded a punishment—
If applicable to the circumstance,
Why, well! if not so apposite, well too.
"Quit the gay range o' the world," I hear her cry,
"Enter, in lieu, the penitential pound:
"Exchange the gauds of pomp for ashes, dust!
"Leave each mollitious haunt of luxury!

1176 *MS* Settled *Yale 1* Settled>Settle *MS* suit— 1178 *MS* She>Law 1179 *MS* {beginning of fo. 162} *MS* her value of a perfect white>her value of a perfect pure>the worth of perfect chastity, 1180 *MS* fancy of the speck>fancying the flaw *MS* find,>find. 1181 *MS* —Superfluous 1182 *MS* Tis 1183 *MS* sure— 1186 *MS* leap, 1187 *MS* robe: 1188 *MS* Wise mothers [ ] thus much>Mothers should risk thus much *1868* Mothers may risk thus much 1190 *MS* {line added later} *MS 1868* On the *MS* missed.> safe. 1191 *MS Yale 1* law>Law 1193 *MS 1868* well— *Yale 1* opposite,> apposite, 1194 *MS* world," methinks I hear the voice>range o' the world, I hear the voice— *Yale 1* voice—>cry, 1195 *MS* ^,in lieu,^ 1196 *MS 1868* dust:— 1197 *MS* "Thine old mollitious haunts of luxury,>"Leave the> "Leave each mollitious haunt of luxury, *1868* luxury,

---

1184 *toys*: amusements, flirtations. Cf. *Paradise Lost*, IX. 1034.

1186 *curt*: short.

1194 *range*: ranging expanse, the plain.

1196 *ashes, dust*: symbols of penitence and death.

1197 *mollitious*: sensuous, lovely, from L. *mollis*, soft. Browning first came on this very rare word in the poetry of Francis Quarles, where it occurs several times: in *Barnabas & B* there is 'mollicious rest' (79), and in *Argalus and Parthenia* 'the dainty and

"The golden-garnished silken-couched alcove,
"The many-columned terrace that so tempts
"Feminine soul put foot forth, extend ear
"To fluttering joy of lover's serenade,—
"Leave these for cellular seclusion! mask
"And dance no more, but fast and pray! avaunt—
"Be burned, thy wicked townsman's sonnet-book!
"Welcome, mild hymnal by . . . some better scribe!
"For the warm arms were wont enfold thy flesh,
"Let wire-shirt plough and whipcord discipline!"
If such an exhortation proved, perchance,
Inapplicable, words bestowed in waste,
What harm, since Law has store, can spend nor miss?

And so, our paragon submits herself,
Goes at command into the holy house,
And, also at command, comes out again:

1200 *MS* "Thy feminine foot to step forth, give [?thine] ear>"Feminine soul put foot forth, nor stop ear *1868* nor stop ear   1201 *MS* "[?The]>"To fluttering   *MS* [ ],>serenade, *1868* serenade,   1202 *MS 1868* seclusion;   1203 *MS 1868* pray;   1204 *MS* Thy>"Be burned, thy   *MS* Sonnet-book!   1205 *MS* [?chaste]>mild   *MS* by>by . . .   *MS* [ ]>some   *MS* [ ]>scribe!   1206 *MS 1868 1872* arms,   *MS* waist, *Yale 1* waist,>flesh,   1207 *MS* plague>plough   *MS 1868 1872* whip-cord *1868* disclipine " [broken sort]   1208 *MS* {beginning of fo. 163}   1210 *MS* matter,>harm, since   *MS* law>Law *1868 1872* law   *MS* miss!   1211 *MS* {New paragraph indicated by 'New Par' in left-hand margin} *Yale 1* {New paragraph indicated by 'New P.' in left-hand margin}   *MS* so our   1212 *MS 1868* {no comma}

---

mollitious ayre' (I. 489) and 'sweet mollitious ayres' (III. 129). Subsequently, citing Quarles, he deploys it in RB to EBB, 19 Jan. 1846: *Correspondence*, xii. 6. Given the presence of 'alcove' in the next line, his most immediate memory is his own earlier use in *Sordello*, III. 129–30, where he describes the palace of the decadent Friedrich II: 'mollitious alcoves gilt / Superb as Byzant domes'. Cf. 53 n.

1202 *cellular*: characterized by cells, i.e. monastic. Cf. Charles Lamb, *Elia*, Ser. II, xi: 'A poor Carthusian, from strict cellular discipline'.

1204 *wicked . . . sonnet-book*: the *Sonetti lussuriosi* ('Lewd Sonnets') of 1524, by Pietro Aretino (1492–1556), so called because he was a native of Arezzo. This erotic, uncompromisingly plain-spoken sonnet sequence (mocking Petrarchan conventions of love) was written to accompany illustrations by Giulio Romano showing various sexual positions. In 1527 Pope Clement VII condemned and suppressed the book. Here we may note Bottini's lubricious implication that Pompilia had been enjoying the book, and his inability, off the cuff, to think of any pious poets in l. 1205. Cf. X. 654.

For, could the effect of such obedience prove
Too certain, too immediate? Being healed,
Go blaze abroad the matter, blessed one!
Art thou sound forthwith? Speedily vacate
The step by pool-side, leave Bethesda free
To patients plentifully posted round,
Since the whole need not the physician! Brief,
She may betake her to her parents' place.
Welcome her, father, with wide arms once more,
Motion her, mother, to thy breast again!
For why? Since Law relinquishes the charge,
Grants to your dwelling-place a prison's style,
Rejoice you with Pompilia! golden days,
Redeunt Saturnia regna. Six weeks slip,
And she is domiciled in house and home
As though she thence had never budged at all.
And thither let the husband,—joyous, ay,
But contrite also—quick betake himself,
Proud that his dove which lay among the pots
Hath mued those dingy feathers,—moulted now,
Shows silver bosom clothed with yellow gold!

1214 *MS* Could>For, could 1217 *MS* whole>sound 1218 *MS* by the>by 1219 *MS* plentifully>there in plenty>plentifully 1221 *MS* The law>She may 1223 *MS* Receive>Motion 1224 *MS 1868* The law relinquishes its 1226 *MS 1868* But gives you back Pompilia; 1227 *MS 1868* *regna*! 1230 *MS 1868* husband, joyous—ay, 1231 *MS* also quick *MS* himself— 1234 *MS* gold: *1868* gold.

1215–16 *Being . . . matter*: cf. Mark 1: 45. As Jesus healed the leper, so Pompilia has been cleansed of sin by her stay in the convent.

1218–19 *step . . . round*: cf. John 5: 2–4.

1220 *whole . . . physician*: cf. Matt. 9: 12, etc.

1225 *prison's style*: i.e. *domus pro carcere*, house arrest (L.). Cf. II. 1342 n.

1227 *Redeunt . . . regna*: 'the reign of Saturn returns', i.e. the Golden Age comes back: Virgil, *Eclogues*, IV. 6. Cf. ll. 284–6, 1376–7 nn.

1232–4 *lay . . . gold*: cf. Ps. 68: 13: 'Though ye have lien among the pots, yet shall ye be as the wings of a dove covered with silver, and her feathers with yellow gold.' Modern versions translate 'sheepfolds' instead of 'pots'. 'Mued' is a variant spelling of 'mewed': of a bird 'to moult, shed, or change (its feathers)': OED². Pompilia has been renewed from degradation, to a new brightness.

So shall he tempt her to the perch she fled,
Bid to domestic bliss the truant back.

But let him not delay! Time fleets how fast,
And opportunity, the irrevocable,
Once flown will flout him! Is the furrow traced?
If field with corn ye fail preoccupy,
Darnel for wheat and thistle-beards for grain,
Infelix lolium, carduus horridus,
Will grow apace in combination prompt,
Defraud the husbandman of his desire.
Already—hist—what murmurs 'monish now
The laggard?—doubtful, nay, fantastic bruit
Of such an apparition, such return
Interdum, to anticipate the spouse,
Of Caponsacchi's very self! 'T is said,
When nights are lone and company is rare,
His visitations brighten winter up.
If so they did—which nowise I believe—
(How can I?—proof abounding that the priest,
Once fairly at his relegation-place,
Never once left it) still, admit he stole
A midnight march, would fain see friend again,
Find matter for instruction in the past,

1235 *MS* [ ]>Quick, *MS* let him>he shall *1868* Quick, he shall *MS* back to>to the *MS* fled— 1236 *MS* {beginning of fo. 164} *MS 1868* back! 1237 *MS* {New paragraph indicated by 'New Par.' in left-hand margin} *MS 1868* O let 1239 *MS* [?Is>Once] *MS* you! 1240 *MS* ye>field with corn ye fail 1241 *MS* thistle-seed>thistle-beards 1245 *MS* murmur[ ]>murmurs *MS* monish 1248 *MS* spouse,— 1249 *MS 1868* {no comma} 1252 *MS* [?it be so]>so they did— *MS* scarcely>nowise 1253 *MS* With evidence> How can I?—proof *1868* How 1254 *MS 1868 1872* {no comma} 1255 *MS 1868* it—

1240 *preoccupy*: fill beforehand.

1242 *Infelix . . horridus*: 'unfruitful darnel, rough thistle', adapted from Virgil, *Georgics*, I. 151–4.

1245 *hist*: listen! (an exclamation).

1246 *bruit*: rumour, report.

1248 *Interdum*: sometimes, occasionally, now and then (adv.).

Renew the old adventure in such chat
As cheers a fireside! He was lonely too,
He, too, must need his recreative hour.
Shall it amaze the philosophic mind
If he, long wont the empurpled cup to quaff,
Have feminine society at will,
Being debarred abruptly from all drink
Save at the spring which Adam used for wine,
Dreads harm to just the health he hoped to guard,
And, trying abstinence, gains malady?
Ask Tozzi, now physician to the Pope!
"Little by little break"—(I hear he bids
Master Arcangeli my antagonist,
Who loves good cheer, and may indulge too much:
So I explain the logic of the plea
Wherewith he opened our proceedings late)—
"Little by little break a habit, Don,
"Become necessity to feeble flesh!"
And thus, nocturnal taste of intercourse
(Which never happened,—but, suppose it did)
May have been used to dishabituate
By sip and sip this drainer to the dregs

1259 *MS* fireside? *MS* too— 1260 *MS* hour[ ]>hour. 1261 *MS 1868* Should 1262 *MS 1868 1872* If one, was wont 1263 {not found in *MS*} *Yale 1* (His>Have *Yale 1* home)>will, 1265 *MS* wine— 1266 *MS* {beginning of fo. 165} *MS 1868* Dread *MS* consequence>harm *MS* ^just the^ *MS* [ ]>hopes *Yale 1* hopes>hoped 1267 *MS* {no commas} *MS 1868 1872* meaning *MS 1868* gain 1268 *MS* {no comma} *Yale 1* Tozzi now> Tozzi, now 1269 *MS* little" break— *MS* he bids>him bid 1271 *MS 1868* cheer— *MS 1868* much— 1272 *MS* that>the 1273 *MS* the>our 1274 *MS* friend! *Yale 1* friend!>Don! *1868* Don! 1276 *MS* {no comma} 1277 *MS* {line added later} *MS* Which *MS* did, 1278 *MS* Might>May

1262 *empurpled cup*: i.e. a cup of wine. Bottini again shows himself a master of euphemism and innuendo in this contrast between wine (sexual intercourse) and the spring-waters of Eden (sexual abstinence).

1268 *Tozzi*: Luca Tozzi (1638–1717), Innocent XII's main physician, the successor of Marcello Malpighi of Bologna. His name is prominent in the historical record because, in Sept. 1700, he treated the Pope during his final illness. Cf. XI. 2333, XII. 40.

1276 *intercourse*: 'conversation', but also 'sexual intercourse'. Cf. V. 1219.

O' the draught of conversation,—heady stuff,
Brewage which, broached, it took two days and nights
To properly discuss i' the journey, Sirs!
Such power has second-nature, men call use,
That undelightful objects get to charm
Instead of chafe: the daily colocynth
Tickles the palate by repeated dose,
Old sores scratch kindly, the ass makes a push,
Although the mill-yoke-wound be smarting yet,
For mill-door bolted on a holiday:
Nor must we marvel here if impulse urge
To talk the old story over now and then,
The hopes and fears, the stoppage and the haste,—
Subjects of colloquy to surfeit once.
"Here did you bid me twine a rosy wreath!"
"And there you paid my lips a compliment!"
"Here you admired the tower could be so tall!"
"And there you likened that of Lebanon
"To the nose of the beloved!" Trifles! still,

1280 *MS* Of>O' 1281 *MS* That brewage>Brewage which, *1868* which broached 1282 *MS 1868* o' the *Yale 1* sirs!>Sirs! 1283 *MS* Such is the second-nature *MS* use *Yale 1* Such is the second-nature>Such is the second-nature, *Yale 1* use>use, *1868* Such is the second-nature, *1287 *MS 1868 1872* push, *1888* push *DC BrU* push>push, *1889* push, 1288 *MS* {line added later} *MS* mill-yoke wound is 1289 *MS* the bolted mill-door>mill-door bolted *MS 1868* holiday— 1290 *MS 1868* And *MS* marvel if the impulse pricks *Yale 1* prick>urge *1868* marvel if the 1293 *MS 1868* once? 1295 *MS* the>a 1296 *MS 1868* "There 1297 *MS* {beginning of fo. 166} 1298 *MS* {no quotation mark at beginning of line} *MS* nose of>the nose o' *MS* beloved!"—Trifles— *MS* yet>still, *1868* o' the beloved!"—Trifles—still,

1280 *conversation*: 'relaxed talk', but again with the innuendo 'sexual intercourse or intimacy'. Cf. IV. 876 n.

1283 *use*: custom, habit.

1285 *colocynth*: a bitter medicine, used as a purgative, made from the fruit of the plant *Citrullus Colocynthis* or 'Bitter-apple'. Cf. *Othello*, I. iii. 347–9: 'The food that to him now is luscious as locusts, shall be to him shortly as acerb as the coloquintida.'

1297–8 *And . . . beloved*: Pompilia (at least in Bottini's fantasy) recalls a teasing comment by Caponsacchi, complimenting her on her beautiful nose by playfully referring to a passage from the Song of Solomon, 7: 4: 'thy nose is as the tower of Lebanon which looketh toward Damascus.' Caponsacchi is remembering one of the most erotic passages: cf. the preceding verses: 'Thy navel is like a round goblet . . . Thy two breasts are like two young roes that are twins.'

"*Forsan et hæc olim*,"—such trifles serve
To make the minutes pass in winter-time.

Husband, return then, I re-counsel thee!
For, finally, of all glad circumstance
Should make a prompt return imperative,
What in the world awaits thee, dost suppose?
O' the sudden, as good gifts are wont befall,
What is the hap of our unconscious Count?
That which lights bonfire and sets cask a-tilt,
Dissolves the stubborn'st heart in jollity.
O admirable, there is born a babe,
A son, an heir, a Franceschini last
And best o' the stock! Pompilia, thine the palm!
Repaying incredulity with faith,
Ungenerous thrift of each marital debt
With bounty in profuse expenditure,
Pompilia scorns to have the old year end
Without a present shall ring in the new—
Bestows on her too-parsimonious lord
An infant for the apple of his eye,
Core of his heart, and crown completing life,
True *summum bonum* of the earthly lot!
"We," saith ingeniously the sage, "are born

1299 *MS* some such may>if such may>such trifles 1301 *MS* {New paragraph indicated by 'New Par:' in left-hand margin} *MS* recounsel 1304 *MS* in>i' *1868* i' 1306 *MS* the inconscious *1868* the unconscious 1308 *MS* jollity— 1313 *MS* due *Yale 1* due>debt 1314 *MS* bounteous [?and]>bounty 1315 *MS 1868* will not have 1317 *MS 1868* upon her parsimonious 1319 *MS* the crown *Yale 1* the crown>and crown 1320 *MS 1868* The *MS* [ ]>earthly 1321 *MS* "[?Men],">"We,"

1299 *Forsan . . . olim*: 'perhaps even this one day . . . ', the beginning of the *sententia* 'forsan et haec olim meminisse iuvabit': 'perhaps even this one day will be a joy to recall': Virgil, *Aeneid*, I. 203.

1306 *hap . . . unconscious*: luck . . . unsuspecting.

1311 *the palm*: i.e. the victory.

1313 *thrift . . . marital debt*: i.e. withholding of sexual intercourse. Cf. VIII. 954–6 n.

1320 *summum bonum*: highest good (L.).

1321–2 "*We . . . us.*": we have been unable to identify this quotation.

"Solely that others may be born of us."
So, father, take thy child, for thine that child,
Oh nothing doubt! In wedlock born, law holds
Baseness impossible: since "*filius est*
"*Quem nuptiæ demonstrant*," twits the text
Whoever dares to doubt.

Yet doubt he dares!
O faith, where art thou flown from out the world?
Already on what an age of doubt we fall!
Instead of each disputing for the prize,
The babe is bandied here from that to this.
Whose the babe? "*Cujum pecus?*" Guido's lamb?
"*An Melibœi?*" Nay, but of the priest!
"*Non sed Ægonis!*" Someone must be sire:
And who shall say, in such a puzzling strait,
If there were not vouchsafed some miracle
To the wife who had been harassed and abused
More than enough by Guido's family
For non-production of the promised fruit
Of marriage? What if Nature, I demand,
Touched to the quick by taunts upon her sloth,
Had roused herself, put forth recondite power,
Bestowed this birth to vindicate her sway,

1322 *MS* us"— 1323 *MS* child— 1325 *MS 1868* impossible, 1326 *MS* {beginning of fo. 167} *MS* {no quotation mark at beginning of line} *MS* *demonstrant,—* 1328 *MS* {New paragraph indicated by 'New Par:' in right-hand margin} 1329 *MS 1868 1872* {no comma} 1330 *MS* On>Already on *MS* doubt is this>doubt 1331 *MS* {line added later} 1332 *MS* this 1333 *MS* lamb—G>babe? 1341 *MS* marriage. *MS* nature, *Yale 1* nature,>Nature, 1343 *MS* [?Have]>Had *MS* unusual>recondite 1344 *MS* [ ]>sway *Yale 1* sway,>sway? *1868* sway?

1325–6 "*filius . . . demonstrant,*": 'the son is whom the marriage points to': Bottini adapts Ulpian, at Digest L. xvi. 195: 'mater semper certa est: pater est, quem nuptiae demonstrant.'

1326 *twits*: upbraids, rebukes.

1333–5 "*Cujum . . . Ægonis!*": 'Whose the flock? . . . Is it Meliboeus's? . . . No, it belongs to Aegon!': a witty deployment of Virgil, *Eclogues*, iii. 1–2. In the original context this is the dialogue of two shepherds establishing who owns a flock of sheep. Virgil writes 'verum Aegonis' rather than 'sed Aegonis'.

Like the strange favour, Maro memorized
As granted Aristæus when his hive
Lay empty of the swarm? not one more bee—
Not one more babe to Franceschini's house!
And lo, a new birth filled the air with joy,
Sprung from the bowels of the generous steer,
A novel son and heir rejoiced the Count!
Spontaneous generation, need I prove
Were facile feat to Nature at a pinch?
Let whoso doubts, steep horsehair certain weeks
In water, there will be produced a snake;
Spontaneous product of the horse, which horse
Happens to be the representative—
Now that I think on't—of Arezzo's self,
The very city our conception blessed:
Is not a prancing horse the City-arms?
What sane eye fails to see coincidence?

1345 *MS* Ay, put the favour,>Repeat the favour,>Like to the favour, *1868* Like to the favour, *MS 1868* memorized, 1346 *MS 1868* Was 1347 *MS 1868* swarm, 1348 *MS 1868* house— 1350 *MS* steed, *Yale 1* steed,>steed! *1868* steed! 1351 *MS* Just as a *1868* Just so a 1353 *MS* [?A]>Were *MS* nature *Yale 1* nature>Nature 1354 *MS* days>weeks, *1868 1872* weeks, 1355 *MS* snake: 1356 *MS 1868* A second product *MS* horse—which 1357 *MS* {beginning of fo. 168} 1358 *MS 1868* {no comma} 1359 *MS* where>our *etc.* *MS 1868* blessed! 1360 *MS* city's arms?>City-arms? 1361 *MS 1868* sees not such

---

1345–50 *Maro . . . steer*: Maro (Virgil) memorized (i.e. recorded, perpetuated the memory of) this 'strange favour' in *Georgics*, IV. 281–314, 528–58. The bees of the shepherd Aristaeus had all died because he had offended the gods. Cyrene, his mother, taught him how to make reparation: he made a sacrifice of four bulls and four heifers, draining the sacrificial blood from their throats. Returning nine days later, he saw bees swarming from the decomposing carcasses. Bottini appears to be suggesting that Gaetano was also conceived by 'spontaneous generation', but actually the *double entrendre* of 1350 implies that he may have 'sprung from the bowels' of that 'generous' young bull Caponsacchi.

1350 *steer*: young ox or bull.

1352 *Spontaneous generation*: i.e. without the action of sexual intercourse. There is a topical point in that the theory of organisms' spontaneous generation, which might have passed for true in Bottini's day, had been called into question by Browning's.

1354–5 *horsehair . . . snake*: an old superstition.

1360 *City-arms*: a fact long known to Browning: see EBB's *Casa Guidi Windows*, where she describes how 'Arezzo's steed pranced clear from bridle-hold': Part I, 509.

Cur ego, boast thou, my Pompilia, then,
Desperem fieri sine conjuge
Mater—how well the Ovidian distich suits!—
Et parere intacto dummodo
Casta viro? Such miracle was wrought!
Note, further, as to mark the prodigy,
The babe in question neither took the name
Of Guido, from the sire presumptive, nor
Giuseppe, from the sire potential, but
Gaetano—last saint of our hierarchy,
And newest namer for a thing so new!
What other motive could have prompted choice?

Therefore be peace again: exult, ye hills!
Ye vales rejoicingly break forth in song!
Incipe, parve puer, begin, small boy,
Risu cognoscere patrem, with a laugh
To recognize thy parent! Nor do thou
Boggle, oh parent, to return the grace!
Nec anceps hære, pater, puero

1364 *MS* language>distich 1366 *MS 1868* but language baffles here. *1872* a miracle 1367 *MS* And>Note, 1369 *MS* Guido from *Yale 1* Guido from> Guido, from 1370 *MS* Giuseppe from *Yale 1* Giuseppe from>Giuseppe, from 1371 *MS* the hierarchy:>the hierarchy, *1868* the hierarchy, 1372 *MS* {line added later} *MS 1868* new: 1374 *MS* {New paragraph indicated by 'New Par.' in left-hand margin} 1376 *MS puer,—* *MS* poor>small 1377 *MS 1868* smile 1378 *MS* recognise *MS* parent: nor>parent! Nor 1379 *MS* o Parent, *MS 1868* grace—

1362–6 *Cur...viro?*: this couplet (distich) is from Ovid, *Fasti*, v. 241–2: (Juno's words) 'Why should I despair of becoming a mother without a husband, and of bringing forth without contact with a man, always supposing that I am chaste?' These are the words of Juno to Chloris: she wants to imitate Jupiter's action of giving birth to Minerva on this own, without the agency of a lover.

1373 *What...choice?*: Browning himself had wondered why exactly Pompilia called the child Gaetano, but had not found a satisfying explanation: see our Vol. VII, p. xxvii.

1375 *Ye...song!*: adapting Isa. 55: 12.

1376–7 *Incipe...patrem*: 'Begin, baby boy, to recognize your father with a smile', adapting Virgil, *Eclogues*, iv. 60, which has 'matrem' instead of 'patrem'. Cf. ll. 284–6, 1227 nn.

1379 *Boggle*: hesitate (through fear or scruple). Cf. ll. 551–2.

1380–1 *Nec...prayer!*: 'And do not doubtful hesitate, father, in recognizing your child!': Bottini 'ekes out' or extends the prayer from Virgil's *Eclogue*: see ll. 1376–7 n.

Cognoscendo—one may well eke out the prayer!
In vain! The perverse Guido doubts his eyes,
Distrusts assurance, lets the devil drive.
Because his house is swept and garnished now,
He, having summoned seven like himself,
Must hurry thither, knock and enter in,
And make the last worse than the first, indeed!
Is he content? We are. No further blame
O' the man and murder! They were stigmatized
Befittingly: the Court heard long ago
My mind o' the matter, which, outpouring full,
Has long since swept like surge, i' the simile
Of Homer, overborne both dyke and dam,
And whelmed alike client and advocate:
His fate is sealed, his life as good as gone,
On him I am not tempted to waste word.
Yet though my purpose holds,—which was and is
And solely shall be to the very end,
To draw the true *effigies* of a saint,
Do justice to perfection in the sex,—
Yet let not some gross pamperer of the flesh
And niggard in the spirit's nourishment,
Whose feeding hath offuscated his wit

1381 *MS 1868* might *MS* phrase:>prayer! 1383 *MS 1868* drive; 1384 *MS* Whither>Because *MS* {no comma} 1385 *MS* And>He, 1386 *MS* They hurry there, and>Must hurry thither, 1387 *MS* {beginning of fo. 169} *MS* last end far worse than the first.>last worse than the first, indeed! 1388 *MS* are: no>are. No *MS* word>blame 1389 *MS* On>O' *MS* murder: they>murder! They 1390 *MS* [ ]>heard 1391 *MS* My full mind on the matter, [ ] outpouring>My mind on the matter, which, outpouring full, 1392 *MS* Had>Has *MS* like the surge i'>swept, like surge i' *1868* swept, like surge i' 1394 *MS* [ ]>And 1399 *MS effigies>effigiem 1868 effigiem* 1400 *MS* [ ]>Do 1401 *MS* Still *1868* Yet, *MS* of flesh *1868* o' the flesh 1402 *MS* ^spirit's^

1384–7 *Because . . . indeed!*: cf. Matt. 12: 43–5.

1392–3 *simile / Of Homer*: cf. *Iliad*, v. 87–92. A ludicrous imitation of Homer's heroic image of Diomedes scattering the Trojan lines like a river in flood.

1399 *effigies*: likeness, drawn or painted image (now archaic, but current for Browning).

1403–4 *Whose . . . lose*: i.e. overindulgence has fuddled Arcangeli's intelligence, not his legal knowledge, which he never had in the first place.

Rather than law,—he never had, to lose—
Let not such advocate object to me
I leave my proper function of attack!
"What's this to Bacchus?"—(in the classic phrase,
Well used, for once) he hiccups probably.
O Advocate o' the Poor, thou born to make
Their blessing void—*beati pauperes!*
By painting saintship I depicture sin:
Beside my pearl, I prove how black thy jet,
And, through Pompilia's virtue, Guido's crime.

Back to her, then,—with but one beauty more,
End we our argument,—one crowning grace
Pre-eminent 'mid agony and death.
For to the last Pompilia played her part,
Used the right means to the permissible end,
And, wily as an eel that stirs the mud
Thick overhead, so baffling spearman's thrust,
She, while he stabbed her, simulated death,
Delayed, for his sake, the catastrophe,
Obtained herself a respite, four days' grace,
Whereby she told her story to the world,
Enabled me to make the present speech,
And, by a full confession, saved her soul.

[—]

1406 *MS* business>function 1407 *MS* in>(in 1408 *MS* once,>once) 1409 *MS* prove>make 1410 *MS* Th[ ]>Their *MS* null—>void— *MS* *pauperes*!— 1411 *MS 1868* sin, 1412 *MS* the pearl I *Yale 1* the pearl I> the pearl, I *1868* the pearl, I *MS 1868* the jet, 1413 *MS* And through *MS* [ ]>crime. 1414 *MS* {New paragraph indicated by 'New Par' in left-hand margin} 1415 *MS* a crowning 1417 *MS* {beginning of fo. 170} 1420 *MS* spear-man's *MS* stroke,>thrust, 1423 *MS* thereby>herself *MS* good days>days' grace, 1424 *MS* Wherein>Whereby 1425 *MS* this>the

1407 "*What's . . . Bacchus?*": i.e. what's the relevance of this?: a Greek proverb. 'Greek tragedy had its origin in choruses which danced and recited in honour of Dionysus (Bacchus). As time went on its original purpose was more and more ignored, and conservative critics exclaimed τί ταῦτα πρὸς Διόνυσον ("Where does Bacchus come in?"); which phrase became proverbial': Cook, 195.

1410 *beati pauperes!*: 'Blessed are the poor', one of the beatitudes (Luke 6: 20).

1411 *depicture*: depict, paint in words; cf. VIII. 754 n.

Yet hold, even here would malice leer its last,
Gurgle its choked remonstrance: snake, hiss free!
Oh, that's the objection? And to whom?—not her
But me, forsooth—as, in the very act
Of both confession and (what followed close)
Subsequent talk, chatter and gossipry,
Babble to sympathizing he and she
Whoever chose besiege her dying bed,—
As this were found at variance with my tale,
Falsified all I have adduced for truth,
Admitted not one peccadillo here,
Pretended to perfection, first and last,
O' the whole procedure—perfect in the end,
Perfect i' the means, perfect in everything,
Leaving a lawyer nothing to excuse,
Reason away and show his skill about!
—A flight, impossible to Adamic flesh,
Just to be fancied, scarcely to be wished,
And, anyhow, unpleadable in court!
"How reconcile," gasps Malice, "that with this?"

1427 *MS* {New paragraph indicated by 'New Par.' in left-hand margin} *MS* spent malice leers>would malice leer 1428 *MS* Gurgles>Gurgle *MS 1868 1872* choaked *Yale 2* remonstrance:>remonstrance! *Yale 2* snake,>Snake, 1430 *MS* that>as, 1431 *MS* Of—not confession but what followed close,>Of both confession and what followed close, *1868* and, *1868* close, 1435 *MS* That talk is>As this were *MS* tale— 1436 *MS* Falsifies>Falsified 1437 *MS* Admits not one poor>Admitted not one 1438 *MS* Pretends to a>Pretended to 1441 *MS* [?my]>a 1443 *MS* —[ ]>—A 1445 *MS* And certainly not pleaded in a court!>And, anyhow, unpleadable in court! 1446 *MS* {beginning of fo. 171} *MS 1868 1872* {no commas} *MS* this with that?">that with this?"

1428 *remonstrance*: representation, protest.

1429–42 *Oh . . . about*: an anacoluthon, perhaps intended to suggest Bottini's exasperation. He starts with the intention of saying 'as [= 'as if', like imperial Latin *tamquam* of an allegation], in the very act of confession, she gave me the lie', but expands the confession to include peripheral conversation, loses the thread, and starts anew, but gradually slips back from predicates appropriate to 'all this' into those more suited to 'she'.

1435 *As*: as if.

1443 *flight*: i.e. a flight from human imperfection into divine perfection, which none born of Adam can achieve and which would be accounted exaggeration if pleaded in court.

1446 *that . . . this*: i.e. Bottini's presentation of Pompilia as only ambiguously innocent and Pompilia's death-bed claim to be *wholly* innocent.

Your "this," friend, is extraneous to the law,
Comes of men's outside meddling, the unskilled
Interposition of such fools as press
Out of their province. Must I speak my mind?
Far better had Pompilia died o' the spot
Than found a tongue to wag and shame the law,
Shame most of all herself,—could friendship fail
And advocacy lie less on the alert:
But no, they shall protect her to the end!
Do I credit the alleged narration? No!
Lied our Pompilia then, to laud herself?
Still, no! Clear up what seems discrepancy?
The means abound: art's long, though time is short;
So, keeping me in compass, all I urge
Is—since, confession at the point of death,
Nam in articulo mortis, with the Church
Passes for statement honest and sincere,
Nemo presumitur reus esse,—then,
If sure that all affirmed would be believed,
'T was charity, in her so circumstanced,
To spend the last breath in one effort more
For universal good of friend and foe:

1447 *MS* {New paragraph indicated by 'New Par:' in left-hand margin} 1448 *MS* [?mere]>men's 1453 *MS* if friendship failed,>should friendship fail, *1868* did *1868 1872* fail, 1454 *MS* lay>lie *1868* alert. 1455 *MS 1868* Listen how these protect 1456 *MS* trust to>credit 1457 *MS* Did she speak falsely> Lied our Pompilia, 1458 *MS* no;— *MS* explain [ ]>clear up discrepancy>clear up what seems discrepancy? *1868* Still, no;—clear 1459 *MS 1868* abound,— *MS* long;>long, *MS* but>though *MS 1868* short, 1462 *MS* {line added later} *MS* [ ]>*Nam* 1463 *MS* truth, in simple charity,>statement honest and sincere, 1466 *MS* How fitting>What charity, *MS 1868* in one 1467 *MS 1868* her last 1468 *MS* the universal>universal *MS* foe— *1868* foe,

---

1459 *art's . . . short*: adapting the famous aphorism *Ars longa, vita brevis*, originally coined by Hippocrates of Cos.

1462–4 *Nam . . . esse*: 'For at the moment of death . . . no one is presumed guilty.' This exact phrasing is not from OYB, though the real Bottini makes the same point in different words at lxxxvi (83) and clxv (173).

And,—by pretending utter innocence,
Nay, freedom from each foible we forgive,—
Re-integrate—not solely her own fame,
But do the like kind office for the priest
Whom telling the crude truth about might vex,
Haply expose to peril, abbreviate
Indeed the long career of usefulness
Presumably before him: while her lord,
Whose fleeting life is forfeit to the law,—
What mercy to the culprit if, by just
The gift of such a full certificate
Of his immitigable guiltiness,
She stifled in him the absurd conceit
Of murder as it were a mere revenge
—Stopped confirmation of that jealousy
Which, did she but acknowledge the first flaw,
The faintest foible, had emboldened him
To battle with the charge, baulk penitence,
Bar preparation for impending fate!
Whereas, persuade him that he slew a saint
Who sinned not even where she may have sinned,
You urge him all the brisklier to repent
Of most and least and aught and everything!
Still, if this view of mine content you not,

1469 *MS* [?So]>And,— 1471 *MS* simply>solely 1472 *MS* [?same]>like 1473 *MS 1868* Whom the crude truth might treat less *MS* courteously: *1868* courteously, 1474 *MS* Indeed, expose to danger or cut short>Indeed, expose to peril, abbreviate *1868* Indeed, 1475 *MS 1868* The life and long 1476 *MS* him,— 1477 *MS* {beginning of fo. 172} *MS* life will soon be>fleeting life is 1478 *MS* kindness>mercy *MS* if thereby>if by just *Yale 1* if by>if, by 1479, 1480 *MS* {lines added later} 1481 *MS* that>the 1482 *MS* just>mere *MS* revenge— *1868* revenge! 1483 *MS* That satisfaction of the violence>Stopped confirmation of that jealousy 1484 *MS* if>had *1868* had *MS 1868* acknowledged 1485 *MS 1868* might embolden 1486 *MS* his fate,>his judge, *1868* his judge, *MS* bar>baulk 1487 *MS* And fail prepare himself for what impends.>Bar preparation for impending fate. *1868* fate. 1488 *MS* Whereas— *MS 1868* him he has slain 1489 *MS 1868* not in the little she did sin, 1490 *MS* likelier>brisklier 1492 *MS 1868* Next,— *MS* ^of mine,^ *1868* mine, *MS 1868* ye

1471 *Re-integrate*: = redintegrate = restore, renew (to a previous condition). For the source of this word, see XII. 692 n.

Lords, nor excuse the genial falsehood here,
We come to our *Triarii*, last resource:
We fall back on the inexpugnable,
Submitting,—she confessed before she talked!
The sacrament obliterates the sin:
What is not,—was not, therefore, in a sense.
Let Molinists distinguish, "Souls washed white
"But red once, still show pinkish to the eye!"
We say, abolishment is nothingness,
And nothingness has neither head nor tail,
End nor beginning! Better estimate
Exorbitantly, than disparage aught
Of the efficacity of the act, I hope!

Solvuntur tabulæ? May we laugh and go?
Well,—not before (in filial gratitude

1493 *MS* {line added later} 1494 *MS* We>'Tis *1868* 'Tis *MS 1868* resource, 1495 *MS* Fall back upon>We fall back on 1496 *MS* [ ]>Submit *MS* Submit that>Submit you,— *1868* Submit you,— 1497 *MS* That sacrament>The Sacrament *MS* all>the 1498 *MS* Why then, what is not, clearly never was,>What is not,—was not, in a certain sense. *1868* in a certain sense. 1499 *MS* "What is white>"Souls grown white 1500 *MS* {no quotation mark at beginning of line} *MS* Was>Were *1868* "Were *MS* shows>show 1501 *MS* nothingness *Yale 1* nothingness>nothingness, *1868* nothingness 1502 *MS 1868* {no comma} 1503 *MS* beginning;—else a doubt be cast>beginning;—better trust>beginning;—better estimate *1868* beginning;—better 1504 *MS* {line added later} 1505 *MS* On>Of *MS* act. How, lords?>act. {How, lords? made new line at beginning of new paragraph}>act, [ ]?>act, I hope! *1506 *MS* {New paragraph indicated by 'New Par.' in left-hand margin} *1868 1872* {new paragraph} *1888 1889* {no new paragraph. Paragraphing obscured by this line's being at the head of the page} 1507 *MS* before,—in

---

1493 *genial falsehood*: i.e. the well-meaning pretence of Pompilia's death-bed confession.

1494 *We . . . Triarii*: 'We come to our third rank (i.e. our last resource)': a Latin proverb. In the early Roman army the third rank was comprised of the oldest and most experienced soldiers; if the *hastati* and *principes* failed, they fell back on the *triarii*: 'from this arose the saying, "to have come to the *triarii*", when things are going badly': Livy, VIII. viii. 11–12. Cf. 'George Bubb Dodington', 327.

1496–8 *confessed . . . sense*: this ludicrous and theologically incorrect argument was not made by the real Bottini, but is used at OYB cliii (156), in the pro-Guido anonymous pamphlet: 'We should notice, further, that the declaration made by the wife in the face of death may be doubtful in itself, in the sense that after confession and absolution one's sin is cancelled as if it had never been committed, so that in a court of justice she would no longer have any need of pardon.'

1499 *Molinists*: i.e. heretics: cf. l. 33 n.

1506 *Solvuntur tabulæ?*: 'Are the tablets resolved?', i.e. 'Is the case closed?', adapting

To Law, who, mighty mother, waves adieu)
We take on us to vindicate Law's self!
For,—yea, Sirs,—curb the start, curtail the stare!—
Remains that we apologize for haste
I' the Law, our lady who here bristles up
"Blame my procedure? Could the Court mistake?
"(Which were indeed a misery to think)
"Did not my sentence in the former stage
"O' the business bear a title plain enough?
"*Decretum*"—I translate it word for word—
"'Decreed: the priest, for his complicity
"'I' the flight and deviation of the dame,
"'As well as for unlawful intercourse,
"'Is banished three years:' crime and penalty,
"Declared alike. If he be taxed with guilt,
"How can you call Pompilia innocent?
"If both be innocent, have I been just?"

Gently, O mother, judge men—whose mistake
Is in the mere misapprehensiveness!
The *Titulus* a-top of your decree
Was but to ticket there the kind of charge

1508 *MS* adieu,— 1509 *MS 1868* self— 1510 *MS* {beginning of fo. 173} *MS* oh>yea, *Yale 1* sirs,—>Sirs,— *MS* curb [ ]>curb the *MS* restrain> curtail 1511 *MS* apologise 1512 *MS* lady of us all, who>Law, our lady who here 1513 *MS 1868* "And *MS* Did I then>Did the Court *1868* Did 1514 *MS* {no quotation mark at beginning of line} 1517 *MS* recite> translate 1521 *MS* years': *1888 1889* {' in years:' is damaged but legible} *MS* p>crime *etc.* 1522 *MS 1868* {no comma} 1524 *MS* "If he *1868* "If they 1525 *MS* {no new paragraph} *Yale 1* {New paragraph indicated by 'New Par.' in left-hand margin} *MS* men! *1868* men!— *MS* Their>—whose 1526 *MS 1868* poor misapprehensiveness. 1527 *MS* atop *Yale 1* a top>a-top

Horace, *Satires*, II. i. 86, 'Solventur risu tabulae': 'The case will be laughed out of court.'

1517 *Decretum*: decree, legal decision: see next n.

1518–21 '*Decreed . . . years*': translating the *Decretum Relegationis Amasii* ('Decree of banishment of the lover') issued by the court on 24 Sept. 1697: OYB xcix (106). Guido argued that it proved Pompilia and Caponsacchi's guilt, Caponsacchi that it did no such thing: see V. 1218–25, VI. 2009–10 nn.

1527 *Titulus*: title.

1528 *ticket*: set down, indicate.

You in good time would arbitrate upon.
Title is one thing,—arbitration's self,
Probatio, quite another possibly.
Subsistit, there holds good the old response,
Responsio tradita, we must not stick,
Quod non sit attendendus Titulus,
To the Title, *sed Probatio*, but the Proof,
Resultans ex processu, the result
O' the Trial, and the style of punishment,
Et pœna per sententiam imposita.
All is tentative, till the sentence come:
An indication of what men expect,
But nowise an assurance they shall find.
Lords, what if we permissibly relax
The tense bow, as the law-god Phœbus bids,
Relieve our gravity at labour's close?
I traverse Rome, feel thirsty, need a draught,
Look for a wine-shop, find it by the bough
Projecting as to say "Here wine is sold!"
So much I know,—"sold:" but what sort of wine?

1532 *MS Subsistit*— *MS* {no commas} *Yale 1* response>response, 1533 *MS* mind,>stick, 1535 *MS* the>to *MS* proof,>Proof, *1868* to Proof, 1536–9 *MS* {These lines and the first two words of 1540 have been written out again for the sake of clarity by RB on the verso of fo. 172} 1536 *MS* through the Cause>and result *1868* and result 1537 *MS* Yet to be tried: simply tentative,>Yet to be tried: and style of punishment,>O' the Trial and the style of punishment,>O' the Trial and the style of punishment, 1538–41 *MS* {lines added later} 1538 *1868 imposita*; 1539 *MS* Simply>—Simply *MS* come,—>come, *1868* come, 1540 *MS 1868* Mere 1541 *MS* Nowise assurance>And nowise an assurance *1868* And 1542 *MS* {beginning of fo. 174} *MS* Just so—that>Lords, [ ]>Lords, what if 1543 *MS* bids[?—]>bids *MS* {no commas} 1544 *MS* the close of [ ],—>close of speech?— *1868* close of speech? 1547 *MS* tell>say 1548 *MS* know, then:>know,—"sold":

1532–8 *Subsistit . . . imposita*: from OYB clxvii (175): pam. 13, Bottini. The argument here was made by the real Bottini, though not (of course) with the ludicrous illustration of the wine-shop at 1545–61.

1542–3 *relax . . . bids*: i.e. no longer be like Apollo in his role as the angry archer-god, dealing out sudden death, but rather take up his role as the god of the lyre and music. This elegant allusion is to Horace, *Odes*, II. x. 19–20: 'At times Apollo wakes with the lyre his slumbering song, and does not always stretch the bow.'

Strong, weak, sweet, sour, home-made or foreign drink?
That much must I discover by myself.
"Wine is sold," quoth the bough, "but good or bad,
"Find, and inform us when you smack your lips!"
Exactly so, Law hangs her title forth,
To show she entertains you with such case
About such crime. Come in! she pours, you quaff.
You find the Priest good liquor in the main,
But heady and provocative of brawls:
Remand the residue to flask once more,
Lay it low where it may deposit lees,
I' the cellar: thence produce it presently,
Three years the brighter and the better!

Thus,
Law's son, have I bestowed my filial help,
And thus I end, *tenax proposito;*
Point to point as I purposed have I drawn
Pompilia, and implied as terribly
Guido: so, gazing, let the world crown Law—
Able once more, despite my impotence,
And helped by the acumen of the Court,
To eliminate, display, make triumph truth!
What other prize than truth were worth the pains?

1549 *MS* —Strong, 1551 *MS* we>is *MS* sold" *MS* bough "but 1552 *MS* Find out and tell>Find, and inform *MS* lips"! 1553 *MS* I hang my Title> law hangs her Title>Law hangs her Title 1554 *MS* I entertain>she entertains *MS* a case>such Case 1555 *MS 1868* crime: come *MS* in, I pour [?it],>in, she pours, you [?treat]>in, she pours, you quaff. 1556 *MS* We>You 1557 *MS* brawls:— *1868* brawls. 1558 *MS* Rem[ ]>Remand 1559 *MS* [ ]>low 1560 *MS* cellar,— *MS* presently 1561 *MS* better. 1562 *MS* {no comma} 1563 *MS* a>my 1564 *MS proposito*— 1565 *MS* I have>have I 1567 *MS* Guido,— *MS* praise>crown *MS* Law 1568 *MS* Assisting, even through>Able, despite>Able once more, despite 1569 *MS* {line added later} 1570 *MS* To eliminate, and clarify the truth—>To eliminate, display, make triumph truth— 1571 *MS* {line added later} *MS* were worth the pains? I have said.>than truth were worth the pains?

1564 *tenax proposito*: 'tenacious of my purpose', from Horace, *Odes*, III. iii. 1, part of the definition of the just and determined man that begins that ode.

There's my oration—much exceeds in length
That famed panegyric of Isocrates,
They say it took him fifteen years to pen.
But all those ancients could say anything!
He put in just what rushed into his head:
While I shall have to prune and pare and print.
This comes of being born in modern times
With priests for auditory. Still, it pays.

1572 *MS* scarce exceeds 1573 *MS* P>famed *etc.* *MS 1868* Panegyric 1574 *MS* vaunt>say 1575 *MS* But he—those Pagans>But he—those Ancients *Yale 1* he—>all *MS* anything; 1576 *MS* all that>just what *MS 1868* head, 1577 *MS* pare. Well, well—>pare and print. 1578 *MS* This> [?It]>This

1573 *panegyric of Isocrates*: the 'Panegyricus', published in or after 380 BC, by the great Athenian orator Isocrates (436–338 BC), is a massive, ornate speech praising Athens as the leading Greek state, urging unity on the Greeks as a whole, and a war against Persia. Though it is in prose—so it is hard directly to compare lengths—it is significantly longer than Bottini's panegyric of Pompilia. Quintilian says it took ten years or more to write; it is [Plutarch], *Lives of the Ten Orators*, 837 F, who says that 'he laboured upon his Panegyric oration ten years, or, as some tell us, fifteen': see Plutarch, *Moralia* (Loeb), x, p. 376.

Bottini ends his monologue with this comically strained comparison, yet one that reflects his aspirations: '[Isocrates] represents Attic prose in its most elaborate form .... His periods are artistic and elaborate; the structure of some of the longer sentences is so complex that he overreaches himself'; 'Ancient criticism already noticed in him too constant and too ostentatious an effort to heighten the grandeur of his themes. In the time of the Roman satirist Lucilius ... Isocratic style meant pretentiousness': *Oxford Classical Dictionary*, 3rd ed. (1996), p. 771; Peter Levi, *A History of Greek Literature* (1985), p. 369.

INTRODUCTION TO BOOK X

THE POPE

THE speaker of Book X is Pope Innocent XII, Antonio Pignatelli (1615–1700), an aristocratic cardinal from southern Italy who had been elected pope in July 1691. Browning presents him speaking on the evening of 21 February 1698. It is one month and nineteen days since the brutal attack on Pompilia. Different opinions of the rights and wrongs of the case have been circulating through Rome (Books II–IV). The protagonists themselves have spoken (Books V–VII). In late January and early February, lawyers for the defence and prosecution have prepared their cases (Books VIII and IX). Now, Guido has been found guilty of murder. In a last bid to avoid the death-penalty, his lawyers have appealed for a stay of execution on account of the clericate (the minor orders he holds in the Church), and so it is Pope Innocent who has the final earthly say on the 'coil' of the legal case.

Most critics see Pope Innocent as essentially Browning's spokesman, the vehicle for his own judgements on the different characters. Browning's Pope is eighty-six years old (actually the real Innocent was eighty-two), and he is the magisterial, humble sage who makes the final assessment of all the legal documents, confessions, witness-statements, and other depositions cast in front of him. In Book I the poet describes him as 'simple, sagacious, mild yet resolute' (1222), and this view has been echoed by critics assessing the monologue: 'The Pope's soliloquy, mellow with the experience of a long life of action and contemplation, is marked throughout by a rare dignity and elevation'; 'he shows himself to be . . . a man of deep humility and strong religious sense'.[1]

The monologue's setting is the Pope's private study, somewhere in the Vatican, at the end of a cold, rainy day. There is something of the sad, exhausted atmosphere of 'Andrea del Sarto', except that the Pope, despite his age and his sense of the world's depravity, still has inner vitality and enthusiasm for good. The real Pope Innocent probably had little to do with the Franceschini trial. The evidence suggests that his *chirograph* (personal writ), commanding Guido's death, was a simple denial of the

[1] Cook, 198; Sullivan, 120.

relevance of the clericate, a legal formality, and not an extended judgement. In fact, when Browning poured over the Old Yellow Book he had all the legal pleadings for and against Guido, but little indication of the outcome of the case, no official judgement or adjudication. There are, besides, only three brief mentions of Pope Innocent.[2] Browning took the decision to make Innocent his great Judge, offering a 'Day of Judgement' on the whole court proceedings.

To do this, he had to do research into the real Innocent XII. Sometime in 1865 he wrote to his friend W. C. Cartwright asking for 'any particulars of the private life and character of Innocent XII: and of the Jubilee he instituted in 1694'.[3] In March 1866, he wrote to Antony Panizzi also asking for 'any particulars of the Pope's private life, the persons, resident or foreign, remarkable at Rome: the Jubilee of 1694 or 5: anything illustrative of the social life there, in short'.[4] Probably these were early enquiries, for the Jubilee of 1694 did not become a major feature in the poem.[5] Cartwright had lived in Rome for extended periods, and was fascinated by ecclesiastical history, so he was a good person to ask: in this same period he wrote a learned book *On the Constitution of Papal Conclaves* (*1868*); in the next decade he would write *The Jesuits: Their Constitution and Teaching* (*1876*). Only a rather inconsequential reply from Panizzi survives, and no reply from Cartwright, so we do not know what, specifically, they may have contributed to the poem. The historical allusions in the poem itself, however, provide insight into the nature of Browning's research.

The Pope's personal austerity, his love for the poor, and his Bull against nepotism and papal corruption (of June 1692) are facts displayed in earlier Books. Browning knew about Miguel de Molinos (1627–96), the Spanish priest who had become the focal point for a large circle in Rome, and how he had been censured and imprisoned in 1687: as Browning imagines it, the reverberations of this controversy must still have been going on under Innocent XII. Now he found out a welter of other information that he wove into the fabric of the poem. He understood the general political situation: the rivalry of France and Austria played out at the papal court, and the Turkish threat (now receding).[6] He knew of doctrinal

[2] OYB ccxxxv (235), ccxxxvii (237), ccxxxix (238).

[3] RB to Cartwright, [n.d.]: Berg Collection, New York Public Library. The letter begins: 'Dear Cartwright—this is the *memorandum* . . .'.

[4] RB to Panizzi, 19 Mar. 1866: ABL.

[5] It does feature, of course, as the inspiration for Violante's confession concerning Pompilia's birth.

[6] XII. 81–4; XI. 1807–9.

disputes: the argument over the Divine Names in missionary China, and the adjudications on Quietist or semi-Quietist theology.[7] He found out about papal practices and ceremonies: the blessing of the Hat and Rapier, the 'Fisherman's ring', the blessing of the Golden Rose on Laetare Sunday, the ceremonies connected with a pope's death.[8] He knew something of different ecclesiastical positions at the papal court (Cardinal Camerlengo, and the Cardinal Referendary); and something about the buildings the Pope had ordered to be erected.[9] It can be conjectured that he made lists of names: the Pope's physicians (Malpighi, Tozzi), the various ambassadors to Rome (Martinitz, Bouillon, and Contarini), and prominent cardinals (Colloredo, Altieri, Albano, Spada).[10] Browning's use of all this was largely impressionistic, to give 'colour' (rather than any exact or scholarly verisimilitude). None the less, the quantity of this detail, deployed here and in Books IX, XI, and XII, shows the trouble he went to to get inside the period.

In a sense this is ironic, for the Book as a whole is historically anachronistic. Much of what the Pope says is Browning's own liberal-Protestant thinking transplanted back into a seventeenth-century context. This starts at the beginning of the Book, with the Pope's extended reading from the papal chronicle about the events of January 897, the so-called 'cadaver synod' and its aftermath. This evil episode would have been of no interest to the real Innocent XII; for Browning, however, it was ideal material to examine the fallibility of all human judgement, the impossibility (as he saw it) of truth ever residing within an institutional context. In fact, Browning took over his interest in the cadaver synod from his father.[11] Rather than being the excuse (as it could easily have been) for anti-Catholic satire, it became his means of establishing the Pope's character: Innocent looks soberly at the madness, cruelty, and egoism so evident in the cadaver synod, and so articulates (with touches of black humour) his sense of his own limitations and vulnerability. Being God's 'Vice-gerent' on earth weighs heavily on him; he trembles before the judgement he has to make—to free Guido, or to confirm the death sentence. It is a moment of calm before the 'passion' (like Christ's passion) of the terrible decision (199–200).

[7] X. 1589–1604; XII. 64–7.

[8] VIII. 1085–7; X. 92, 1097–9, 2060–1.

[9] VIII. 1084; XI. 638; XII. 52–3.

[10] XII 39, IX. 1266, XI. 2331, XII. 40; XI. 2346–7, XII. 112, XII. 117; XI. 2346–7, XI. 2337, XII. 42–3.

[11] See Appendix A.

None the less, he goes ahead. Lines 399–1238 give his judgements on all the characters, major and minor. Guido receives the longest and darkest analysis (399–868), followed by brief depictions of the people who, in one way or another, seconded him: Girolamo, Abate Paolo, Guido's mother, the Governor of Arezzo and its Archbishop. Then there is superb praise for Pompilia, a saint, 'First of the first' (1004). And then a complex portrait of Caponsacchi, by no means perfect in the Pope's eyes, a mixture of instinctive goodness and worldly confusion, but, on balance, the knightly champion of truth, the gladiator defending Pompilia (the Christian martyr) from the wild beast (Guido). This section ends with a characterization of the Comparini, worldly Laodiceans, who have evaded the necessary choice between good and evil, and paid a terrible price.

It is in the next part of the monologue (1239–1850) that anachronism clearly surfaces again. Viewing the terrible history of the Franceschini case—the suffering of Pompilia, the near triumph of evil in the person of Guido—the Pope begins a long examination of the basis of his religious faith, and whether such a faith can be justified in the face of the 'darkness' of these events. The passages that follow are rooted in Browning's particular problems as a nineteenth-century liberal-Protestant, responding to currents of thought within his own time. In fact, within the framework of his philosophical and theological presuppositions, and his cultural perceptions, it was difficult for Browning to establish his faith on any kind of secure intellectual basis. Three issues predominate in this section of the monologue, and can be usefully separated out (for these passages are sometimes dense and elliptical, at the extreme end of Browning's manner).

First, there is Browning's anti-institutionalism: Truth and religious faith cannot (he argues) be effectively passed down through a community or institution developing and changing over time (i.e. a Church). The Pope is horrified by the way in which Pompilia was completely failed by the institutional Church as represented by its priests, its archbishop, and the Roman convent that harboured her (1440–1630). Second, there is Browning's address to the issue of historical-critical readings of Scripture (the impact of thinkers like D. F. Strauss and Ernest Renan). Historical-critical biblical scholarship was beginning to have a popular impact in the mid-nineteenth century, and seemed (through reason) to be undermining both more traditional and more literalistic ways of reading Scripture. The authoritative, revelatory Gospels that Browning had grown up with seemed to be undermined: a historical Christ appeared to be disappearing into myth, and the Gospels seemed to be only provisional humanly-developed documents. Could they still be read as 'a fact, / Absolute, abstract, independent truth, / Historic'? Probably not. Maybe they had to be read instead as 'only truth reverberate, changed, made pass / A spectrum into mind, the narrow eye' (1388–92).[12] Scripture, in other words, like institutions, was no sure grounding for faith. Here Browning stands at the beginning of a mindset that (at its extreme) would lead to atheism (though he did not know this), and of course he was separated from some of the theological traditions of his time that would have given him answers.

Third, Browning (or the Pope) is preoccupied with the 'apostolic age', the gloriously heroic time when the early Christians, filled with certitude, full of heroism, could die for their faith: the specific evocation of the Neronian persecutions of the 60s AD (1829–33) is something echoed elsewhere in the poem, but also (in this Book) it lies at the centre of a wider frame of reference. Here was the blessed time of the pristine origins, uncontaminated by tradition, or institutional development, or Enlightenment rationality. Faith was fresher and easier. The clear implication is that people of the seventeenth (or nineteenth century) have a harder and nobler job to discern faith than the first Christians (1825–50). Clearly this emphasis (not really historical) has everything to do with Protestant theological commitments deeply engrained in Browning's viewpoint, but again (as here expressed) it is another source of doubt for the Pope: the remote past shines with faith, which only throws into relief present doubts and difficulties. Without any back-up or grounding from institutions and tradition, and with Scripture such a problematic evidence of the Incarnation, faith becomes a very lonely assertion indeed, but nonetheless one that is made here in spirited and moving terms (1631–60).

Perhaps the most vital part of the monologue is its ending, for though it is no more nor less anachronistic than what has gone before, Browning is able to feel his way back into the dramatic texture of the writing. The Pope becomes upset, almost angry, as he contemplates what will succeed his own times: the receding 'sea of faith' and its consequences. In religious terms, the seventeenth century (as he sees it) has been a kind of masque, a pageant still upholding a coherent and ordered religious worldview, one maintained (only just perhaps) within institutional structures, passed

[12] For a scholarly, modern account of the problem Browning is wrestling with here, the relationship between the Gospels and history, see Luke Timothy Johnson, *The Real Jesus* (New York, *1996*).

down reasonably through the generations. Now, he senses an 'anti-masque' of confusion about to descend on the world, something partly comic and partly grotesque: a world in which the individual (rather than inheriting a coherent religious vision) will have to find the path to virtue and truth by instinct only. Caponsacchi is 'the first experimentalist / In the new order of things' (1910–11). He has danced the complex 'morrice' of virtue aright, but how easily he could have gone wrong, how easily he could have been like Abate Paolo. Pompilia and her parents are perhaps the first victims of this crazy new world 'disorder': 'The world's first foot o' the dance is on their heads' (1954). The monologue's penultimate passage is even more overtly pessimistic: the Pope sees a sophisticated spirit of 'culture' and 'civility', really a form of secularization, overwhelming the rough, older beliefs in a supernatural worldview. His writing and signing Guido's death-warrant becomes his last act of defiance to the unbelieving eighteenth century that is about to dawn.

A few critics want to see some dramatic distance between Browning and his Pope here: in other words, they would like to say that Browning does not follow the Pope into this deep kind of pessimism, particularly when (of course) the Pope's predictions of an age of unbelief and confusion so clearly apply to what Browning might have feared about religious faith in his own age. Browning, though, is clearly in this somewhere: on the brink of old age himself, he has something invested in this jeremiad against the worldly spirit.

X.

THE POPE.

LIKE to Ahasuerus, that shrewd prince,
I will begin,—as is, these seven years now,
My daily wont,—and read a History
(Written by one whose deft right hand was dust
To the last digit, ages ere my birth)
Of all my predecessors, Popes of Rome:
For though mine ancient early dropped the pen,
Yet others picked it up and wrote it dry,
Since of the making books there is no end.
And so I have the Papacy complete

{fo. 176. At the head of the page is the title '10. The Pope.' in RB's hand} 3 *MS* history 4, 5 *MS* {lines added later} 4 *MS* Written>(Written 5 *MS* {no comma} *MS* birth,>birth) 6 *MS* Rome; 7–10 *MS* {lines added later} 7 *MS* drops *MS* {no comma} 8 *MS* pick *MS* write 9 *MS* end:

---

1 *Ahasuerus*: King of Persia, often identified as Xerxes (486–465 BC). The allusion is to Esther 6:1: 'On that night could not the king [Ahasuerus] sleep, and he commanded to bring the books of records of the chronicles; and they were read before the king.' Pope Innocent's association of himself with this worldly absolutist, who was defeated by the Greeks at Marathon and Salamis, is self-deprecating. Ahasuerus was 'shrewd' enough to have the chronicles of Persia read to him, and so (providentially) to gain insight from them: they reminded him of the loyal service of Mordecai and consequently allowed him to understand the evil of Haman. So Pope Innocent hopes that by reading this papal chronicle he too may gain insight and wisdom from history.

2 *seven years now*: Browning is being approximate. Innocent became Pope on 12 July 1691. He is imagined speaking on the evening of 21 Feb. 1698. See 2102 n.

3–6 *History... predecessors*: i.e. a comprehensive history of the popes. Browning probably did not have a particular work in mind; he knew a great deal about the diversity of histories of the popes from his father's researches: see Introduction and Appendix A.

7 *ancient*: elder, ancient author.

9 *of... end*: cf. Eccles. 12: 12.

From Peter first to Alexander last;
Can question each and take instruction so.
Have I to dare?—I ask, how dared this Pope?
To suffer?—Suchanone, how suffered he?
Being about to judge, as now, I seek
How judged once, well or ill, some other Pope;
Study some signal judgment that subsists
To blaze on, or else blot, the page which seals
The sum up of what gain or loss to God
Came of His one more Vicar in the world.
So, do I find example, rule of life;
So, square and set in order the next page,
Shall be stretched smooth o'er my own funeral cyst.

Eight hundred years exact before the year
I was made Pope, men made Formosus Pope,

12 *MS* I question 13 *MS 1868 1872* dare,— *MS* How 14 *1868 1872* suffer? *MS* How>Suchanone, *etc.* 15 *MS* judge as 16 *MS* Pope, 18 *MS* [ ]>which *MS* {no commas} 20 *MS* world: 21 *MS* So do *MS* life 22 So square *MS* my own>the next *MS* page. 23 *MS* Soon to>Shall *MS* ^own^ 24 *MS* {New paragraph indicated by 'New Par.' in left-hand margin} 25 *MS* pope,

11 *Alexander last*: Innocent's predecessor, Alexander VIII (6 Oct. 1689–1 Feb. 1691).

17 *subsists*: endures, continues.

18–19 *seals . . . up*: cf. Ezek. 28: 12.

23 *cyst*: receptacle, coffin. OED^2 gives the more normal spelling as 'cist'. These lines perhaps allude to one of the ceremonies at the funeral of a pope: 'The highest cardinal of his creation then covers the whole body [of the pope] with a red veil, and after placing beside it a tin tube, containing a parchment, on which all the acts of the Pope are registered, the coffin-lid is screwed down and sealed by the *camerlengo*': *Roba di Roma*, ii. 156. Cf. 2060–1 n.

25 *Formosus Pope*: the true story of Pope Formosus (b. *c.*816, elected pope 891, d. 896) and how his decaying corpse was exhumed and subjected to a macabre mock trial—the so-called 'cadaver synod' of Jan. 897—is one that Browning could have known about from many sources. It is mentioned briefly in Nathaniel Wanley's *Wonders of the Little World*, one of his favourite childhood books; it is repeated, again briefly, in his friend W. W. Story's *Roba di Roma* (1863). ii. 158–9. Browning's main source here, however, is his father's historical notebooks. Robert Browning Sen. became fascinated with the cadaver synod as a side-line to his researches into the history of the ruthless senatrix Marozia (*c.*892–*c.*937), which he conducted in the Paris libraries between 1862 and 1866. He had compiled and compared many different

Say Sigebert and other chroniclers.
Ere I confirm or quash the Trial here
Of Guido Franceschini and his friends,
Read,—how there was a ghastly Trial once
Of a dead man by a live man, and both, Popes:
Thus—in the antique penman's very phrase.

"Then Stephen, Pope and seventh of the name,
"Cried out, in synod as he sat in state,
"While choler quivered on his brow and beard,
"'Come into court, Formosus, thou lost wretch,
"'That claimedst to be late Pope as even I!'

[—]

26 *MS* Saith Sigebert with>Saith Sigebert, say 27 *MS* sentence>trial 28 *MS* On>Of *MS* gang,>friends, 29 *MS* Which>Read,—*etc.* **MS* *1868* how *1872 1888 1889* How *MS* trial 30 *MS* Of a dead man by a live man and both Popes:>Of dead man by live man and both men, Popes: 32–4 *MS* {no quotation marks at beginnings of lines} 32 *MS* {no commas} 33 *MS* {no commas} 34 *MS* {beginning of fo. 177} *MS* []>(While *MS* beard) 35 *MS* "Come 36–45 *MS* {no quotation marks at beginnings of lines} 36 *MS* late the Pope I am!" *1868 1872* the Pope as I!'

accounts of the cadaver synod, and sometime before his death (June 1866) he had specifically alerted Browning to the interest of this extraordinary story.

Various factors make the notebooks of Browning Sen. the certain source here: (1) the extent of correspondences between Browning's account and the notebooks; (2) Browning's careful understanding of the difficult pattern of events and of the ambiguous and sometimes contradictory nature of the historical record—again something that comes from the notebooks; and (3) Browning's emphasis on Stephen VII's pathological rage against Formosus, an emphasis probably taken over from his father's researches. For a more detailed account and for extracts, see Appendix A.

26 *Sigebert*: Sigebert of Gembloux (*c.*1035–1112), Benedictine historian.

31 *Thus . . . phrase*: Browning is not, in fact, following one chronicle account here, but drawing together a wide variety of sources: see Appendix A.

32 *Stephen . . . name*: also known as Stephen VI; his papacy was from May 896 to Aug. 897. The dual numbering now used for popes called Stephen arises because of Stephen II (752), who had a stroke three days after his election and was never consecrated. In referring to Stephen VII (i.e. in accepting Stephen II into the line of popes) Browning is simply following the official Roman Catholic listing of his day. 'The *Annuario Pontificio* (the official Vatican directory) included the original Stephen II in its official list of popes until 1960, but suppressed his name in 1961, giving all subsequent popes called Stephen a dual numbering': Richard P. McBrien, *Lives of the Popes* (1997), p. 121.

"And at the word, the great door of the church
"Flew wide, and in they brought Formosus' self,
"The body of him, dead, even as embalmed
"And buried duly in the Vatican
"Eight months before, exhumed thus for the nonce.
"They set it, that dead body of a Pope,
"Clothed in pontific vesture now again,
"Upright on Peter's chair as if alive.

"And Stephen, springing up, cried furiously
" 'Bishop of Porto, wherefore didst presume
" 'To leave that see and take this Roman see,
" 'Exchange the lesser for the greater see,
" '—A thing against the canons of the Church?'

"Then one—(a Deacon who, observing forms,
"Was placed by Stephen to repel the charge,
"Be advocate and mouthpiece of the corpse)—
"Spoke as he dared, set stammeringly forth
"With white lips and dry tongue,—as but a youth,
"For frightful was the corpse-face to behold,—
"How nowise lacked there precedent for this.

"But when, for his last precedent of all,
"Emboldened by the Spirit, out he blurts

37 *MS* {New paragraph indicated by 'New Par.' in left-hand margin} **1868 1872* word, *1888 1889* word 42 *MS* man>pope 44 *MS* Chair 45 *MS 1868* {no new paragraph} *MS* P[]>Stephen, *MS* up cried 46 *MS* "Bishop 47–58 *MS* {no quotation marks at beginnings of lines} 48 *MS* {line added later} 49 *MS* {no quotation mark at end of line} 50 *MS* he, the Deacon *1868* one, 51 *MS* the>this *MS* {no comma} 52 *MS* corpse, *1868* corpse) 57 *MS 1868* {no new paragraph. Paragraphing obscured in *1868* by this line's being at the head of the page} *MS* when for 58 *MS* spirit,> Spirit,

46 *Bishop of Porto*: Formosus had been appointed Cardinal-Bishop of Porto—in ancient times the chief harbour of Rome—in 864.

" 'And, Holy Father, didst not thou thyself
" 'Vacate the lesser for the greater see,
" 'Half a year since change Arago for Rome?'
" '—Ye have the sin's defence now, Synod mine!'
"Shrieks Stephen in a beastly froth of rage:
" 'Judge now betwixt him dead and me alive!
" 'Hath he intruded, or do I pretend?
" 'Judge, judge!'—breaks wavelike one whole foam of wrath.

"Whereupon they, being friends and followers,
"Said 'Ay, thou art Christ's Vicar, and not he!
" 'Away with what is frightful to behold!
" 'This act was uncanonic and a fault.'

"Then, swallowed up in rage, Stephen exclaimed
" 'So, guilty! So, remains I punish guilt!
" 'He is unpoped, and all he did I damn:
" 'The Bishop, that ordained him, I degrade:
" 'Depose to laics those he raised to priests:
" 'What they have wrought is mischief nor shall stand,
" 'It is confusion, let it vex no more!
" 'Since I revoke, annul and abrogate
" 'All his decrees in all kinds: they are void!
" 'In token whereof and warning to the world,
" 'Strip me yon miscreant of those robes usurped,

59 *MS* "And, 60, 61 *MS* {no quotation marks at beginnings of lines} 60 *MS* {no comma} 61 *MS* Rome?" 62 *MS* {beginning of fo. 178} *MS* "Ye *MS* synod mine!" *1868 1872* synod 63 *MS* {no quotation mark at beginning of line} *MS* rage 64 *MS* "Judge 65–71 *MS* {no quotation marks at beginnings of lines} 65 *MS* obtruded or *1868 1872* {no comma} 66 *MS* judge!"— *MS* white>whole 67 *MS* his friends and followers all, 68 *MS* "Ay, *MS* Vicar and not he: 70 *MS* uncanonic, null and void."> uncanonic, and a fault." 71 *MS* {no commas} 72 *MS* "So, *MS* guilt. 73–100 *MS* {no quotation marks at beginnings of lines} 73 *MS* {no comma} 74 *MS* {no commas} 77 *MS* []>It *MS* more 79 *MS* kinds, *MS* void. 81 *MS* {no comma}

75 *laics*: laymen.
78 *abrogate*: repeal, cancel.

"'And clothe him with vile serge befitting such!
"'Then hale the carrion to the market-place:
"'Let the town-hangman chop from his right hand
"'Those same three fingers which he blessed withal;
"'Next cut the head off once was crowned forsooth:
"'And last go fling them, fingers, head and trunk,
"'To Tiber that my Christian fish may sup!'
"—Either because of ΙΧΘΥΣ which means Fish
"And very aptly symbolizes Christ,
"Or else because the Pope is Fisherman,
"And seals with Fisher's-signet.

"Anyway,
"So said, so done: himself, to see it done,
"Followed the corpse they trailed from street to street
"Till into Tiber wave they threw the thing.
"The people, crowded on the banks to see,
"Were loud or mute, wept or laughed, cursed or jeered,

82 *MS* such, 83 *MS* market-place, *1868 1872* market-place; 85 *MS* withal, 86 *MS 1868 1872* off, *MS* forsooth, 87 *MS* then go fling all, fingers head and trunk *1868* fling all, 88 *MS* {beginning of fo. 179} *MS* In *1868* "'In *MS* the Christian *MS* [ ]>sup!" 89–93 {not found in *MS*} 91 *1868* {no comma} 92 *Yale 1* Fishers'>Fisher's 93 *1868* {no new paragraph} *1868* Anyway 94 *MS* {new paragraph} *MS* himself to *MS* done 95 *MS* Following *1868* "Following the corpse, 97 *MS* crowding *MS* {no commas} 98 *MS* ^Were loud or mute,^

82 *serge*: tough, woollen fabric (appropriate for a monk).

85 *three . . . withal*: the three fingers of the right hand, used to give the papal blessing.

89 ΙΧΘΥΣ: the initial letters of Ἰησοῦς Χριστὸς Θεοῦ Υἱὸς Σωτήρ (Jesus Christ, son of God, Saviour) make up the Greek word for 'fish'. Because of this, in the early centuries of the Christian era, a fish was a common symbol of Christ and of Christianity.

91 *Fisherman*: because of the saying of Christ to Peter and Andrew, 'I will make you fishers of men': Matt. 4: 19.

92 *Fisher's-signet*: the Pope's *anello pescatorio*, ring of the fisherman. 'The ring is so called from having engraved on its stone the figure of St. Peter drawing in his fisherman's net. According to Cancellieri, "Notizie sopra l'Origine e l'Uso dell'Anello Pescatorio, Rome, 1823," the earliest record of its use is of the year 1265. Originally it was nothing more than the Pope's private signet for his own correspondence. From the middle of the fifteenth century its use became reserved to the Pontifical utterances called Briefs, and has remained so ever since': *Conclaves*, 36. Cartwright also notes the ritual breaking of this ring at the first general meeting of Cardinals on the day after a pope's death.

"According as the deed addressed their sense;
"A scandal verily: and out spake a Jew
"'Wot ye your Christ had vexed our Herod thus?'

"Now when, Formosus being dead a year,
"His judge Pope Stephen tasted death in turn,
"Made captive by the mob and strangled straight,
"Romanus, his successor for a month,
"Did make protest Formosus was with God,
"Holy, just, true in thought and word and deed.
"Next Theodore, who reigned but twenty days,
"Therein convoked a synod, whose decree
"Did reinstate, repope the late unpoped,
"And do away with Stephen as accursed.
"So that when presently certain fisher-folk
"(As if the queasy river could not hold
"Its swallowed Jonas, but discharged the meal)
"Produced the timely product of their nets,
"The mutilated man, Formosus,—saved
"From putrefaction by the embalmer's spice,

99 *MS* sense, 100 *MS* verily, 101 *MS* "Wot ye that Christ *MS* King Herod thus?" 102–18 *MS* {no quotation marks at beginnings of lines} 102 *1868* {no new paragraph. Paragraphing obscured by this line's being at the head of the page} 104 *MS* Thrown into>Made captive and straight strangled by the mob,>Made captive by the mob and strangled straight, 105 *MS* Theodore,> Romanus, 114 *MS* {no comma} 115 *MS* {no comma} 116 *MS* Formosus, saved 117 *MS* {no comma}

101 *'Wot . . . thus?'*: 'Do you believe that Christ would have vexed Herod in this way?', i.e. Christ would not have acted like this even to Herod (a wicked Jew). This heavily ironic comment by the Jewish bystander is one of Browning's additions to the historical material: see Appendix A.

105 *Romanus*: 'Virtually nothing is known of his reign except that he was pro-Formosan': Kelly, 116. He is usually thought to have reigned from August to November 897.

108 *Theodore*: Theodore II reigned for only twenty days in November 897, the exact dates of which are unknown. Nonetheless, in that short time, he called a synod which effectively annulled the cadaver synod, and then arranged for Formosus' body to be reinterred, with honour, in its original grave in St Peter's.

112 *fisher-folk*: the detail, that Formosus' body was found by fishermen, is from Liutprand, *Antap.* i. 31: see 122 n.

"Or, as some said, by sanctity of flesh,—
"'Why, lay the body again,' bade Theodore,
"'Among his predecessors, in the church
"'And burial-place of Peter!' which was done.
"'And,' addeth Luitprand, 'many of repute,
"'Pious and still alive, avouch to me
"'That, as they bore the body up the aisle,
"'The saints in imaged row bowed each his head
"'For welcome to a brother-saint come back.'
"As for Romanus and this Theodore,
"These two Popes, through the brief reign granted each,
"Could but initiate what John came to close
"And give the final stamp to: he it was,
"Ninth of the name, (I follow the best guides)
"Who,—in full synod at Ravenna held
"With Bishops seventy-four, and present too
"Eude King of France with his Archbishopry,—
"Did condemn Stephen, anathematize
"The disinterment, and make all blots blank,

118 *MS* But much more by a 119 *MS* {beginning of fo. 180} *MS* "Why, *MS* again" bade Theodore *1868 1872* again' bade Theodore 120 *MS* "Among 121 *MS* {no quotation mark at beginning of line} *MS* Peter!" Which was done: 122 *MS* "And" *MS* "many *MS* {no commas} *1868 1872* "'And' addeth Luitprand 'many 123 *MS* "Pious *MS* {no comma} 124 *MS* "That *MS 1868* {no commas} 125 *MS* "The imaged saints in row 126 *MS* "In *MS* back." 127–36 *MS* {no quotation marks at beginnings of lines} 128 *MS* Popes through 129 *MS* had close by John>John came to close *130 *MS 1868* was, *1872 1888 1889* was 131 *MS* {line added later} *MS* name, I follow—{the best guides) not found in *MS*} 132 *MS* Who, in *MS* sat 133 *MS* seventy four, 134 *MS* Eudes *MS* Archbishopry, 136 *MS 1868* blank.

122 *Luitprand* [sic]: the chronicler Liutprand (*c.*920–72), bishop of Cremona, often gave credence to fable and idle report. The reference here is to his *Antapodosis*, often cited in the works used by Browning Sen. Browning here follows his father's spelling, 'ui' as opposed to 'iu'.

129 *John*: John IX, pope from January 898 to January 900.

132 *synod at Ravenna*: *c.*898.

"'For,' argueth here Auxilius in a place
"*De Ordinationibus*, 'precedents
"'Had been, no lack, before Formosus long,
"'Of Bishops so transferred from see to see,—
"'Marinus, for example:' read the tract.

"But, after John, came Sergius, reaffirmed
"The right of Stephen, cursed Formosus, nay
"Cast out, some say, his corpse a second time.
"And here,—because the matter went to ground,
"Fretted by new griefs, other cares of the age,—
"Here is the last pronouncing of the Church,
"Her sentence that subsists unto this day.
"Yet constantly opinion hath prevailed
"I' the Church, Formosus was a holy man."

Which of the judgments was infallible?
Which of my predecessors spoke for God?

137 *MS* "For," *MS* ^here^ 138–50 *MS* {no quotation marks at beginnings of lines} 138 *MS De ordinationibus Papæ*,—"precedents 139 *MS* [ ],>long, 140 *MS* thus 141 *MS* example": *1868* example': 142 But after John came 145 *MS* here, because *MS* ground 146 *MS* [ ] of>Fretted by *MS* age, 147 *MS* {beginning of fo. 181} *MS* {no comma} 148 *MS* And 150 *MS* In 151 {not found in *MS*} 152 *MS* the truth?>for God?

137 *Auxilius*: the pamphlets of the Frankish priest Auxilius (*c.*870–*c.*930) are a main source of historical information about the Formosan controversy. Auxilius defended Formosus and the validity of his ordinations.

142 *Sergius*: Sergius III (Jan. 904–Apr. 911). For convenience Browning here telescopes events: Sergius did not follow directly on John IX, who was in fact succeeded by Benedict IV (May 900–Aug. 903), about whom little is known, Leo V (Aug.–Sept. 903), and the antipope Christopher (Sept. 903–Jan. 904). These were all, however, pro-Formosan popes. As Browning indicates, Sergius was 'a violent hater of Formosus': Kelly, 119.

151 *Which . . . infallible*: a reference to the events of Browning's own time. The dogma of Papal Infallibility, the idea that, under certain circumstances, the Pope's teaching with regard to faith and morals was definitive and infallible, was being aired within the Roman Catholic Church in the 1860s. It was carefully defined and proclaimed at the First Vatican Council in 1870, to a storm of protest from outside the Church. As Browning portrays him, Innocent XII has no interest in the idea: he sees himself as only a frail person doing the best with the reason and intuition God has given him. Browning sometimes referred contemptuously to Papal Infallibility in his letters: see RB to Isabella Blagden, 19 Oct. 1870: *Letters*, 144.

And what availed Formosus that this cursed,
That blessed, and then this other cursed again?
"Fear ye not those whose power can kill the body
"And not the soul," saith Christ, "but rather those
"Can cast both soul and body into hell!"

John judged thus in Eight Hundred Ninety Eight,
Exact eight hundred years ago to-day
When, sitting in his stead, Vice-gerent here,
I must give judgment on my own behoof.
So worked the predecessor: now, my turn!

In God's name! Once more on this earth of God's,
While twilight lasts and time wherein to work,
I take His staff with my uncertain hand,
And stay my six and fourscore years, my due
Labour and sorrow, on His judgment-seat,
And forthwith think, speak, act, in place of Him—
The Pope for Christ. Once more appeal is made
From man's assize to mine: I sit and see
Another poor weak trembling human wretch
Pushed by his fellows, who pretend the right,
Up to the gulf which, where I gaze, begins
From this world to the next,—gives way and way,
Just on the edge over the awful dark:
With nothing to arrest him but my feet.

153, 154 {not found in *MS*} 156 *MS* soul, but>soul,"—saith Christ—"but *1868* Christ "but 159 *MS* Eight>Exact eight 160 *MS* and both for Christ,> and both for God,>Vice-gerent here, 163 *MS* his>God's, 165 *MS* his *MS* {no comma} 166 *MS* five 167 *MS* his 168 *MS* him 173 *MS* I [ ] he [?see]>I gaze, begins 175 *MS* {beginning of fo. 182} *MS* dark 176 *MS* feet—

155–7 "*Fear... hell!*": cf. Matt. 10: 28.

164 *While... work*: cf. John 9: 4.

166 *six... years*: actually the Pope was 82. A curious error given that Browning had written down the Pope's real date of birth so carefully in his chronology: 'Pope Innocent born at Spinazzola in the Neap. Territory, March 13. 1615': see Vol. VII, p. 324.

He catches at me with convulsive face,
Cries "Leave to live the natural minute more!"
While hollowly the avengers echo "Leave?
"None! So has he exceeded man's due share
"In man's fit licence, wrung by Adam's fall,
"To sin and yet not surely die,—that we,
"All of us sinful, all with need of grace,
"All chary of our life,—the minute more
"Or minute less of grace which saves a soul,—
"Bound to make common cause with who craves time,
"—We yet protest against the exorbitance
"Of sin in this one sinner, and demand
"That his poor sole remaining piece of time
"Be plucked from out his clutch: put him to death!
"Punish him now! As for the weal or woe
"Hereafter, God grant mercy! Man be just,
"Nor let the felon boast he went scot-free!"
And I am bound, the solitary judge,
To weigh the worth, decide upon the plea,
And either hold a hand out, or withdraw
A foot and let the wretch drift to the fall.
Ay, and while thus I dally, dare perchance
Put fancies for a comfort 'twixt this calm

177 *MS* Catches *MS* his convulsive 180–93 *MS* {no quotation marks at beginnings of lines} *181 *MS* licence *1868 1872* licence, *1888 1889* license, *MS* {no commas} 183 *MS* guilty and with>sinful and with 184 *MS* that grace the minute more, 185 {not found in *MS*} 186 *MS* Bound therefore> Bound 187 *MS* —[]>—We 188 *MS* Of this one sinner, and demand his sole 189 *MS* Remaining piece of time to purchase heaven 190 *MS* punish him now! 191 *MS* Put him to death! 192 *MS* was just, 193 *MS* scot-free. *MS* {no quotation mark at end of line} 194 *MS* the sole tribunal here, 195 *MS* its worth, *MS* such plea, 196 *MS* {no comma} 198 *MS* even thus>thus 199 *MS* fancy>fancies *MS* like *MS* twixt my face

182 *To . . . die*: cf. Gen. 3: 4.

191 *weal or woe*: i.e. happiness (in heaven) or torment (in hell).

197 *drift*: i.e. fall passively. Perhaps the image here is of drifting to a (water-)fall.

199–200 *this calm . . . bear*: i.e. this calm time (while musing over the murder-case) and that time of suffering (once he has had to announce his decision). The 'passion' here—with its clear association with Christ's passion—is the Pope's future sympathetic

And yonder passion that I have to bear,—
As if reprieve were possible for both
Prisoner and Pope,—how easy were reprieve!
A touch o' the hand-bell here, a hasty word
To those who wait, and wonder they wait long,
I' the passage there, and I should gain the life!—
Yea, though I flatter me with fancy thus,
I know it is but nature's craven-trick.
The case is over, judgment at an end,
And all things done now and irrevocable:
A mere dead man is Franceschini here,
Even as Formosus centuries ago.
I have worn through this sombre wintry day,
With winter in my soul beyond the world's,
Over these dismalest of documents
Which drew night down on me ere eve befell,—
Pleadings and counter-pleadings, figure of fact
Beside fact's self, these summaries to-wit,—

200 *MS* yon pale>yon black *MS* that it hates to bear, 201 *MS* How still reprieve is *MS* both,— 202 {not found in *MS*} 203 *MS* of 205 *MS* {beginning of fo. 183} *MS* In *Yale 1* In>I' *Yale 1* shall>shulld [sic] *MS* have gained the life! *Yale 1* life!>life!— 206 *MS* thus 207 *MS* craven-trick— 208 *MS* absolute,>at an end, 209 *MS* ended>done now *MS* irrevocable, 210 *MS* {no comma} 213 *MS* A winter 215 *MS* be come,—

suffering in Guido's suffering (once the death-sentence is known and imposed). The Pope presents himself as being in a 'calm' before this 'passion': a little like Christ in the garden of Gethsemane, he is partly tempted to walk away from something very difficult, and avoid finding Guido guilty, thus escaping responsibility for the death-sentence.

207 *craven-trick*: i.e. trick to make me a coward.

215 *Which . . . befell*: i.e. there was so much evil implicit in the legal documents they created their own 'night-time'.

216 *figure*: interpretation.

217 *summaries to-wit*: summaries namely. The Pope refers to the three pamphlets in OYB headed 'Summarium' (pams. 4, 7, and 11), 'fact's self' (as opposed to the lawyers' interpretations) because they give copies of the first-hand materials of the legal case: affidavits, witness statements, letters, etc. These 'summaries' contain some of the most vivid material of OYB: for example, the witness statement of the Franceschinis' servant; Pompilia's deposition concerning her flight from Arezzo; a statement by the priests who attended her death-bed; and copies of the much disputed love-letters between Pompilia and Caponsacchi.

How certain three were slain by certain five:
I read here why it was, and how it went,
And how the chief o' the five preferred excuse,
And how law rather chose defence should lie,—
What argument he urged by wary word
When free to play off wile, start subterfuge,
And what the unguarded groan told, torture's feat
When law grew brutal, outbroke, overbore
And glutted hunger on the truth, at last,—
No matter for the flesh and blood between.
All's a clear rede and no more riddle now.
Truth, nowhere, lies yet everywhere in these—
Not absolutely in a portion, yet
Evolvible from the whole: evolved at last
Painfully, held tenaciously by me.
Therefore there is not any doubt to clear
When I shall write the brief word presently
And chink the hand-bell, which I pause to do.

218 *MS* five, 219 *MS* {no commas} 220 *MS* of 222 *MS* Such 24 *MS* And here *MS* was torture's 226 *MS* on truth, blood and all,— 227 {not found in *MS*} 228 *MS* There's *MS* now— 229 *MS* no where, *MS* and>lies *MS* these 230 *MS* part, no less 231 *MS* *1868* Evolvable *MS* so held by me. 232 {not found in *MS*} 233 *MS* [ ]>clear 235 *MS* {beginning of fo. 184} *MS* handbell,

221 *defence . . . lie*: in Browning's version of events, both Guido and his lawyers initially wanted to plead complete innocence, but were then forced to change tack when, under torture, Guido admitted the basic facts of the murder.

222 *he*: i.e. Guido.

223 *play off*: act up (in an exaggerated way). This phrase occurs four other times in R&B, at II. 75, VIII. 1588, X. 414, and XI. 1324. Because it is not given in OED², we previously failed to identify its exact resonance, but now the EPD gives access to its meaning through various examples. 'To play off [an emotion]' appears originally to have been theatrical slang. The best comparable example is in Robert Southey: 'I am not one / Who can play off my smiles and courtesies / To every Lady of her lap-dog tired / Who wants a play-thing': 'To Margaret Hill', 23–6.

228 *rede*: story, interpretation; an unusual use; cf. *Prince Hohenstiel-Schwangau*, 9–11: 'Sphinx in wise old age, / Grown . . . jealous for her riddle's proper rede'.

231 *Evolvible*: deducible, educible (from OED² evolve *v.* 5—not from the Darwinian sense 7). It is a rare adjective, hence Browning's uncertainty about spelling it: in *MS* and *1868* he had 'evolvable'.

Irresolute? Not I, more than the mound
With the pine-trees on it yonder! Some surmise,
Perchance, that since man's wit is fallible,
Mine may fail here? Suppose it so,—what then?
Say,—Guido, I count guilty, there's no babe
So guiltless, for I misconceive the man!
What's in the chance should move me from my mind?
If, as I walk in a rough country-side,
Peasants of mine cry "Thou art he can help,
"Lord of the land and counted wise to boot:
"Look at our brother, strangling in his foam,
"He fell so where we find him,—prove thy worth!"
I may presume, pronounce, "A frenzy-fit,
"A falling-sickness or a fever-stroke!
"Breathe a vein, copiously let blood at once!"
So perishes the patient, and anon
I hear my peasants—"All was error, lord!
"Our story, thy prescription: for there crawled
"In due time from our hapless brother's breast
"The serpent which had stung him: bleeding slew
"Whom a prompt cordial had restored to health."
What other should I say than "God so willed:

236 *MS* Not I more the *1868* {no comma} 237 *MS* yonder. 238 *MS* Since the best wit of man is fallible, mine 239 *MS* Also may *MS* Why, suppose it so,— 240 *MS* Guido I doom as 241 *MS* Guiltless, so much I *MS* man: 242 *MS* Well, what is there should 243 *MS* {no commas} 244 *Yale 1* cry,>cry 245–50 *MS* {no quotation marks at beginnings of lines} 245 *MS* to-boot, 248 *MS* I might presume and say "A 249 *MS* fever-stroke— 250 *MS* {no quotation mark at end of line} 252 *MS* Reproach my 253–6 *MS* {no quotation marks at beginnings of lines} 253 *MS* prescription, 254 *MS* heart 255 *MS* him,— 256 *MS* When *MS* the sick." 257 *MS* willed—

236–7 *mound . . . yonder*: the Pope looks across to the Janiculum hill. Browning's later biographer, William Sharp, would notice how, in the wind, 'the tall pines / On the Janiculum heights / Sing their high song': *Sospiri di Roma* (1891), p. 23. There is one other reference in the monologue by which Browning tries to give us a sense of place: see 1011–13 n. Here the Pope finds a kinship between his own firmness and the Janiculum, often used as military strong-point in the defence of Rome.

246 *strangling . . . foam*: i.e. choking in his vomit.

250 *Breathe*: i.e. open, lance (a vein, in order to let out blood).

"Mankind is ignorant, a man am I:
"Call ignorance my sorrow, not my sin!"
So and not otherwise, in after-time,
If some acuter wit, fresh probing, sound
This multifarious mass of words and deeds
Deeper, and reach through guilt to innocence,
I shall face Guido's ghost nor blench a jot.
"God who set me to judge thee, meted out
"So much of judging faculty, no more:
"Ask Him if I was slack in use thereof!"
I hold a heavier fault imputable
Inasmuch as I changed a chaplain once,
For no cause,—no, if I must bare my heart,—
Save that he snuffled somewhat saying mass.
For I am ware it is the seed of act,
God holds appraising in His hollow palm,
Not act grown great thence on the world below,
Leafage and branchage, vulgar eyes admire.
Therefore I stand on my integrity,
Nor fear at all: and if I hesitate,
It is because I need to breathe awhile,
Rest, as the human right allows, review
Intent the little seeds of act, my tree,—
The thought, which, clothed in deed, I give the world
At chink of bell and push of arrased door.

[—]

258 *MS* Man is an ignorant, none other I, 259 *MS* sorrow and not *1868 1872* {no comma} 260 *MS* after time *MS* {no commas} 261 *MS* probe shall sound 263 *MS* {beginning of fo. 185} *MS* Deeper and 264 *MS* I would tell *MS* ghost, *MS* jot, 266, 267 *MS* {no quotation marks at beginnings of lines} 267 *MS* him 268 *MS* I think *MS* heaver 270 *MS* breast,— 272 *MS* seeds *MS* {no comma} 273 *MS* his 274 *MS* {no comma} 275 *MS* {no comma} 277 *MS* Fear not *MS* {no comma} 280 *MS* The little seed of *MS* fact>act *MS* the spreading tree, *1868* the tree,— 281 *MS* thought I clothe in *MS* [?f]>deed to give *1868* to clothe in deed, and give

272–3 *seed . . . palm*: perhaps an echo of the phrasing in the 'Essay on Shelley' (1851), where the subjective poet struggles to see 'the *Ideas* of Plato, seeds of creation lying burningly on the Divine Hand': see Vol. IV, p. 426.

282 *arrased*: i.e. curtained, covered with tapestry (for keeping out drafts and for quiet).

O pale departure, dim disgrace of day!
Winter's in wane, his vengeful worst art thou,
To dash the boldness of advancing March!
Thy chill persistent rain has purged our streets
Of gossipry; pert tongue and idle ear
By this, consort 'neath archway, portico.
But wheresoe'er Rome gathers in the grey,
Two names now snap and flash from mouth to mouth—
(Sparks, flint and steel strike) Guido and the Pope.
By this same hour to-morrow eve—aha,
How do they call him?—the sagacious Swede
Who finds by figures how the chances prove,
Why one comes rather than another thing,
As, say, such dots turn up by throw of dice,
Or, if we dip in Virgil here and there

283 *MS* departure of the ignoble day!>departure, dim disgrace of day, 284 *MS* Winter's in wane,—>Winter in wane, *Yale 1* Winter's>Winter 's *MS* sullen> vengeful *MS* thou!>thou, 286 *MS* dull>chill *MS* the place>our streets 287 *MS* gossipry, 288 *MS* Consort 'neath palace-archway,> House and consort 'neath archway, *MS* portico,— 289 *MS* And where> But wheresoe'er *MS* grey, two words>grey, 290 *MS* {beginning of fo. 186} 291 *MS* Sparks flint *MS* strike,— 292 *MS* to-morrow-eve— 293 *MS* we call him, the 294 *MS* chances go,>chance should go, 295 *MS* And>Why 296 *MS* in throw *MS* dice 297 *MS* you *Yale 1* you>we

284 *Winter's . . . wane*: i.e. winter is departing.

290 *snap and flash*: the image is clarified in the next line. The few people left outside this cold winter evening are warmed up (figuratively) by their lively discussions about whether the Pope should find Guido innocent or guilty: the names of Guido and the Pope are like sparks 'snapping' and 'flashing' 'from mouth to mouth'.

293 *sagacious Swede*: this has been thought to be a reference to Emanuel Swedenborg, the great Swedish mystic (1688–1772), who developed a theory of mathematical probability. As Rowena Fowler has shown, bearing in mind the full context, it is more likely to be an anachronistic reference to Pehr Wilhelm Wargentin (1717–83) and his pioneering work on demographic statistics. Wargentin was 'compiler of the "Swedish Life Tables", actuarial tables based on vital data from Sweden and used increasingly in the Registrar-General's reports in preference to the less accurate Northampton Tables. The *Biographie universelle* notes Wargentin's "sagacité"': Rowena Fowler, 'Blougram's Wager, Guido's Odds: Browning, Chance, and Probability', VP 41/1 (Spring 2003), 11–28.

297 *dip . . . there*: i.e. point with our finger at random in Virgil's *Aeneid*, supposedly a way of predicting the future; cf. v. 402 n.

And prick for such a verse, when such shall point.
Take this Swede, tell him, hiding name and rank,
Two men are in our city this dull eve;
One doomed to death,—but hundreds in such plight
Slip aside, clean escape by leave of law
Which leans to mercy in this latter time;
Moreover in the plenitude of life
Is he, with strength of limb and brain adroit,
Presumably of service here: beside,
The man is noble, backed by nobler friends:
Nay, they so wish him well, the city's self
Makes common cause with who—house-magistrate,
Patron of hearth and home, domestic lord—
But ruled his own, let aliens cavil. Die?
He'll bribe a gaoler or break prison first!
Nay, a sedition may be helpful, give
Hint to the mob to batter wall, burn gate,
And bid the favourite malefactor march.
Calculate now these chances of escape!
"It is not probable, but well may be."
Again, there is another man, weighed now
By twice eight years beyond the seven-times-ten,

300 *MS* eve 301 *MS* death, 305 *MS* adroit 306 *MS* {no comma} 307 *MS* friends, *Yale 1* friends,>friends: 308 *MS* And, for who *1868* Nay, for who *1872* Nay, so they 309 *MS 1868* with the house-magistrate, 310 *MS* Ruler of>Law of the *1868* The lord *MS* domestic right, *1868* domestic judge 311 *MS 1868* Who ruled his own and let men 312 *MS* Why, bribe *MS* goaler 313 *MS* once was *MS* gave 314 *MS* that battered *MS* down the>wall, burned *MS* gate 315 *MS* bade a favorite *Yale 1* bids>bid 316 *MS* escape,— 317 *MS* {no quotation marks} *Yale 1* {quotation marks added} *MS* certain, probable, but may be. 318 *MS* {beginning of fo. 187}

298 *prick . . . point*: i.e. aim for a particular verse, when it will be that the particular verse will be pointed at. This is another example of probability theory.

309 *house-magistrate*: i.e. lord or judge of his own household.

311 *let . . . cavil*: let strangers object. 'Aliens' would be people from outside Arezzo, or from outside Tuscany, i.e. people who do not know the local customs and sensibility.

318–20 *weighed . . . branch*: the Pope's life is like a branch weighed down by cold snow (his extreme age).

Appointed overweight to break our branch.
And this man's loaded branch lifts, more than snow,
All the world's cark and care, though a bird's nest
Were a superfluous burthen: notably
Hath he been pressed, as if his age were youth,
From to-day's dawn till now that day departs,
Trying one question with true sweat of soul
"Shall the said doomed man fitlier die or live?"
When a straw swallowed in his posset, stool
Stumbled on where his path lies, any puff
That's incident to such a smoking flax,
Hurries the natural end and quenches him!
Now calculate, thou sage, the chances here,
Say, which shall die the sooner, this or that?
"That, possibly, this in all likelihood."
I thought so: yet thou tripp'st, my foreign friend!
No, it will be quite otherwise,—to-day
Is Guido's last: my term is yet to run.

But say the Swede were right, and I forthwith
Acknowledge a prompt summons and lie dead:
Why, then I stand already in God's face
And hear "Since by its fruit a tree is judged,
"Show me thy fruit, the latest act of thine!
"For in the last is summed the first and all,—

320 *Yale 1* breaks>break *MS* branch,— 321 *MS* this same loaded *MS* bears,>lifts, 322 *MS* when 323 *MS* burthen,— 324 *MS* {no commas} 325 *MS* this day's *MS* it departs 326 *MS* such sweat 329 *MS* Tripped upon>Stumbled on 330 *MS* incidental to the>incident to such a 331 *MS* him. 332 *MS* calculate in turn *MS* these>the *MS* too,>here, 334 *MS* but this in>this in all 335 *MS* trippest, egregious *MS* [ ]>friend! 339 *MS* am>lie *MS* dead, 340 *MS* {no comma} 342–5 *MS* {no quotation marks at beginnings of lines} 342 *MS* thine, 343 *MS* all,

322 *cark*: distress, trouble (arch.), often as here coupled with 'care'.

328 *posset*: a warming milk drink, with added alcohol, sugar, and sometimes spices, often taken before going to bed.

330 *smoking flax*: i.e. guttering candle (one on the verge of going out). The phrasing is from Isa. 42: 3. Cf. VI. 148–9 n.

341–2 "*Since . . . fruit*: cf. Matt. 7: 17–20, etc.

"What thy life last put heart and soul into,
"There shall I taste thy product." I must plead
This condemnation of a man to-day.

Not so! Expect nor question nor reply
At what we figure as God's judgment-bar!
None of this vile way by the barren words
Which, more than any deed, characterize
Man as made subject to a curse: no speech—
That still bursts o'er some lie which lurks inside,
As the split skin across the coppery snake,
And most denotes man! since, in all beside,
In hate or lust or guile or unbelief,
Out of some core of truth the excrescence comes,
And, in the last resort, the man may urge
"So was I made, a weak thing that gave way
"To truth, to impulse only strong since true,
"And hated, lusted, used guile, forwent faith."
But when man walks the garden of this world
For his own solace, and, unchecked by law,
Speaks or keeps silence as himself sees fit,
Without the least incumbency to lie,
—Why, can he tell you what a rose is like,

345 *MS* {beginning of fo. 188} *MS* So 346 *MS* "This *MS* to-day." 347 *MS* Nor question nor reply expect 348 *MS* At that 349 *MS* the vile 350 *MS* That, 351 *MS* speech 352 *MS* the lie that *Yale 1* that>which *MS* {no comma} 353 *MS* his split 354 *MS* man since, 355 *MS* His *MS* disbelief, 356 *MS* shows>winds, 357 *MS* excuse may [ ]>excuse may be 358 *MS* the weak 359, 360 *MS* {no quotation marks at beginnings of lines} 359 *MS* an impulse *360 *MS* forewent *1868 1872* forwent *1888* forewent *DC BrU* forewent>forwent *1889* forwent 361 *MS* Man 362 *MS* and unchecked by law 363 *MS* is silent as he sees most fit 365 *MS* Why,

348 *figure*: imagine (through a picture or image).

351 *made . . . curse*: i.e. distanced from God through the Fall; cf. Gen. 3: 14–19.

352–3 *That . . . snake*: Browning repeats some elements of this image in *The Inn Album*, 2240–3: 'soul a-stir / Under its covert, as, beneath the dust, / A coppery sparkle all at once denotes / The hid snake has conceived a purpose.'

364 *incumbency*: pressure, obligation.

Or how the birds fly, and not slip to false
Though truth serve better? Man must tell his mate
Of you, me and himself, knowing he lies,
Knowing his fellow knows the same,—will think
"He lies, it is the method of a man!"
And yet will speak for answer "It is truth"
To him who shall rejoin "Again a lie!"
Therefore these filthy rags of speech, this coil
Of statement, comment, query and response,
Tatters all too contaminate for use,
Have no renewing: He, the Truth, is, too,
The Word. We men, in our degree, may know
There, simply, instantaneously, as here
After long time and amid many lies,
Whatever we dare think we know indeed
—That I am I, as He is He,—what else?
But be man's method for man's life at least!
Wherefore, Antonio Pignatelli, thou
My ancient self, who wast no Pope so long
But studiedst God and man, the many years
I' the school, i' the cloister, in the diocese
Domestic, legate-rule in foreign lands,—
Thou other force in those old busy days

366 *MS* slip[?;]>slip to false 367 *MS* better. 368 *MS* lies 369 *MS* And that his *MS* say 370 *MS* {no quotation marks} *MS* man, 371 *MS* And I shall fitly answer 372 *MS* {beginning of fo. 189} *MS* To one **1888 1889* lie!' 373 *MS* the>this filthy *etc. Yale 1* speak for>filthy *1868* this filthy 376 *MS* And past>Have no 377 *MS* And man, in due 379 {not found in *MS*} 382 *MS* {new paragraph} *MS* But the 384 *MS* {no comma} *385 *MS 1868 1872 1888* studied *DC BrU* studied>studiedst *1889* studiedst 386 *MS* In *MS* in the cloister, diocese 387 *MS* legate-life *MS* lands,

373 *filthy rags*: cf. Isa. 64: 6: 'But we are all as an unclean thing, and all our righteousnesses are as filthy rags.'

377–81 *We . . . else?*: the slight echo here is 1 Cor. 13: 12.

386–7 *diocese . . . lands*: Innocent had served both within Italy and abroad. He had been bishop of Lecce, then Faenza, and archbishop of Naples. Earlier popes had sent him as nuncio to Tuscany (1652), Poland (1660), and the imperial court at Vienna (1668).

Than this grey ultimate decrepitude,—
Yet sensible of fires that more and more
Visit a soul, in passage to the sky,
Left nakeder than when flesh-robe was new—
Thou, not Pope but the mere old man o' the world,
Supposed inquisitive and dispassionate,
Wilt thou, the one whose speech I somewhat trust,
Question the after-me, this self now Pope,
Hear his procedure, criticize his work?
Wise in its generation is the world.

This is why Guido is found reprobate.
I see him furnished forth for his career,
On starting for the life-chance in our world,
With nearly all we count sufficient help:
Body and mind in balance, a sound frame,
A solid intellect: the wit to seek,
Wisdom to choose, and courage wherewithal
To deal in whatsoever circumstance
Should minister to man, make life succeed.
Oh, and much drawback! what were earth without?
Is this our ultimate stage, or starting-place
To try man's foot, if it will creep or climb,
'Mid obstacles in seeming, points that prove
Advantage for who vaults from low to high

391 *MS* soul in 392 *MS* Nakeder than when fleshly robes were whole— 393 *MS* not the Pope but the old man of 394 *MS* Supposed sagacious 395 *MS* one speech I can 396 *MS* Speak to *MS* the self that's 399 *MS* {beginning of fo. 190} *MS* I call 400 *MS* I find *MS* {no comma} 401 *MS* {no comma} 402 *MS* God counts *MS* help; 403 the sound frame 404 *MS* The intellect its match>The solid intellect: *MS* [ ]> [ ]>seek 405 *MS* Judgment to choose, courage to *MS* form an>deal for good 406 *MS* Of both with what of earthly circumstance *1868* with whatsoever 407 *MS* success. 408 *MS* with>and *MS* drawback,>drawback! *MS* life exempt?>life without? 409 *MS* the ultimate 410 *MS* That tries the foot if *MS* {no commas} 411 *MS* mid 412 *MS* to who *MS* to to high

398 *Wise . . . world*: cf. Luke 16: 8.

411 *obstacles in seeming*: i.e. apparent obstacles.

And makes the stumbling-block a stepping-stone?
So, Guido, born with appetite, lacks food:
Is poor, who yet could deftly play-off wealth:
Straitened, whose limbs are restless till at large.
He, as he eyes each outlet of the cirque
And narrow penfold for probation, pines
After the good things just outside its grate,
With less monition, fainter conscience-twitch,
Rarer instinctive qualm at the first feel
Of greed unseemly, prompting grasp undue,
Than nature furnishes her main mankind,—
Making it harder to do wrong than right
The first time, careful lest the common ear
Break measure, miss the outstep of life's march.
Wherein I see a trial fair and fit
For one else too unfairly fenced about,
Set above sin, beyond his fellows here:
Guarded from the arch-tempter all must fight,
By a great birth, traditionary name,
Diligent culture, choice companionship,
Above all, conversancy with the faith

413 *MS* Turning>And makes *MS* stepping-stone. 414 *MS* So Guido with much appetite lacks food, *1868* food, 415 *MS* play off wealth, *Yale 1* play off>play-off *1868* wealth, 416 *MS* {no comma} *MS* large— *1868 1872* large: 417 *MS 1868* And, *1868* cirque, 418 *MS* His *1868* The 419 *MS 1868* the grate, 421 *MS* qualms>qualm *MS* [ ]>first *MS* sense 422 *MS* Of the unseemly, over>Of the unseemly *MS* greed and undue grasp,—>greed and grasp undue,— *1868* Of the unseemly greed and grasp undue, 423 *MS 1868* the main *MS* mankind 425 *MS* The first time, miss the outstep of life's march. 426 {not found in *MS*} 427 *MS* Herein 428 *MS* {beginning of fo. 191} *MS* Of 429 *MS* sin beyond *MS 1868* here, 430 *MS* arch-foe man needs *1868 1872* arch-tempter, *MS* {no comma}

413 *stumbling-block a stepping-stone*: i.e. the difficulty (in life or faith) a means to wisdom. Cf. 1 Cor. 1: 23.

415 *play-off*: act the part of, imitate: see 223 n.

420 *monition*: admonition, warning (from his conscience).

423 *her main mankind*: the mass of men, as 'the mainland' in l. 1608 means the bulk of a country contrasted with its mere frontier-fringe: Cook, 208.

425–6 *careful . . . measure*: i.e. careful lest people generally should miss the (correct) rhythm (of life).

426 *outstep*: i.e. the initial step.

432 *Diligent*: assiduous.

Which puts forth for its base of doctrine just
"Man is born nowise to content himself,
"But please God." He accepted such a rule,
Recognized man's obedience; and the Church,
Which simply is such rule's embodiment,
He clave to, he held on by,—nay, indeed,
Near pushed inside of, deep as layman durst,
Professed so much of priesthood as might sue
For priest's-exemption where the layman sinned,—
Got his arm frocked which, bare, the law would bruise.
Hence, at this moment, what's his last resource,
His extreme stay and utmost stretch of hope
But that,—convicted of such crime as law
Wipes not away save with a worldling's blood,—
Guido, the three-parts consecrate, may 'scape?
Nay, the portentous brothers of the man
Are veritably priests, protected each
May do his murder in the Church's pale,
Abate Paul, Canon Girolamo!
This is the man proves irreligiousest

434 *MS* doctrine this 435 *MS 1868 1872* {no comma} 436 *MS* {no quotation mark at beginning of line} *MS* God:" he 437 *MS* man obeys here,— *MS* took>and *MS* {no comma} 438 *MS* that rule's *Yale 1* - rules'>rule's 440 *MS* He pushed 441 *MS* plead>sue 442 *MS* As>For *MS* priest's exemption *MS* from the layman's sin>where the layman sinned,— 443 *MS* Thrust *MS* bruise: 444 *MS* Hence at this juncture what's>Hence at the moment what's *MS* []>one *etc.* 445 *MS* salutary> utmost stretch of 446 *MS* that, 447 *MS* the>a *MS* blood, 448 *MS* scape: 450 *MS* protectedly both>protected each 451 *MS* [ ]>his *MS* churches 453, 454 {not found in *MS*}

449 *portentous*: extraordinary, monstrous. The thought here—that had Paolo or Girolamo committed the murder they might, as priests, have been exempted from the death-penalty—clearly horrifies the Pope.

453 *This . . . man*: i.e. Guido. In the extended image that follows the Church is portrayed symbolically as a great bell-tower, from which the bell of Time tolls out its message, reminding people of life's brevity and the need for virtue: the bell 'sermonizes the world' (462). Guido is 'religion's parasite': he stays close to the Church (the bell-tower) not because he wants to help its mission, but simply as a way of being respectable, a cover and disguise for his own greed. He is like a sacristan who uses his position to rob people.

Of all mankind, religion's parasite!
This may forsooth plead dinned ear, jaded sense,
The vice o' the watcher who bides near the bell,
Sleeps sound because the clock is vigilant,
And cares not whether it be shade or shine,
Doling out day and night to all men else!
Why was the choice o' the man to niche himself
Perversely 'neath the tower where Time's own tongue
Thus undertakes to sermonize the world?
Why, but because the solemn is safe too,
The belfry proves a fortress of a sort,
Has other uses than to teach the hour:
Turns sunscreen, paravent and ombrifuge
To whoso seeks a shelter in its pale,
—Ay, and attractive to unwary folk
Who gaze at storied portal, statued spire,
And go home with full head but empty purse,
Nor dare suspect the sacristan the thief!
Shall Judas,—hard upon the donor's heel,

454 *Yale 1* religions'>religion's 455 *MS* This one forsooth would plead the>This forsooth would plead dulled sense, jaded ear,>This one forsooth pleads dinned sense>This one forsooth pleads dinned ear, jaded sense, 456 *MS* of *MS* {no comma} 457 *MS* wakes, beats his brain, 458 {not found in *MS*} 459 *MS* {beginning of fo. 192} 460 *MS* of 461 *MS* near>neath 462 *MS* Teaches the world,>Thus undertakes *etc.* 463 *MS* Because the solemn Belfry is 464 {not found in *MS*} 465 *MS 1868* hour, 466 *MS* Is 467 {not found in *MS*} 468 *MS* Ay, *MS* attraction>attractive *MS* a crowd of>unwary 469 *MS* gape>gaze *MS* at the>at *MS* splendid>statued 470 *MS* Go home with a>To go home with *MS* head and *MS* poke>purse *1868 1872* {no comma} 471 *MS* thief. 472 *MS* Judas, *MS* heel

457 *vigilant*: on the alert (on his behalf): see *MS* reading.

466 *paravent . . . ombrifuge*: wind shield and rain shield. These are both, in effect, coinages. *Paravent* is from French and Italian; its Italian etymology is 'para-' (protecting against) and 'vento' (wind); 'parasol' is a similar construction. 'Ombrifuge' is a more striking coinage, from Gk. ὄμβρος 'shower of rain' and L. *fugere* 'to flee'. One would have expected 'imbrifuge', formed from Latin elements; but perhaps there was interference from Italian 'ombrello'. It is sufficiently odd for C. S. Calverley to have used in his parody of Browning's style, 'The Cock and the Bull' (l. 41).

472–5 *Shall . . . company*: i.e. Judas could not claim his nearness to Christ as an excuse for his thieving, any more than Guido can claim his clericate (his nearness to the Church) as an excuse for his murder. The Pope conflates John 12: 6 (which

To filch the fragments of the basket,—plead
He was too near the preacher's mouth, nor sat
Attent with fifties in a company?
No,—closer to promulgated decree,
Clearer the censure of default. Proceed!

I find him bound, then, to begin life well;
Fortified by propitious circumstance,
Great birth, good breeding, with the Church for guide.
How lives he? Cased thus in a coat of proof,
Mailed like a man-at-arms, though all the while
A puny starveling,—does the breast pant big,
The limb swell to the limit, emptiness
Strive to become solidity indeed?
Rather, he shrinks up like the ambiguous fish,
Detaches flesh from shell and outside show,
And steals by moonlight (I have seen the thing)
In and out, now to prey and now to skulk.

473 *MS* [?Find]>To filch *Yale 1* fill>filch *MS* basket, 474 *MS* heard> sat 475 *MS* Seated>Attent 476 *MS* closest the promulgated 477 *MS* Clearest 478 *MS* {no new paragraph} *MS* {no commas} *MS* well 480 *MS* and the *MS 1868 1872 guide. *1888 1889* guide, 482 *MS* {no comma} 483 *MS* starveling, 484 *MS* The>Each *MS* up>to *etc.* 485 *MS* to be that solidity which seems? *Yale 1* which seems?> indeed? 486 *MS* {no commas} 487 *MS* show outside *Yale 1* show outside,>outside show, 489 *MS* {beginning of fo. 193} *MS* hide,

identifies Judas as a thief) with the accounts of the feeding of the five thousand, so producing an image of a greedy Judas trying to steal the baskets of fragments left over after the miracle. The 'donor' is the small boy who brought the loaves and fishes (John 6: 9). The crowd of five thousand was divided into 'fifties in a company' (Luke 9: 14), i.e. groups of fifty.

481 *coat of proof*: armour of proof, warranted armour. The image has religious overtones from Eph. 6: 13–17; cf. also Bunyan, *Pilgrim's Progress*, i. 173: 'I was cloathed with Armour of proof.'

486 *ambiguous fish*: not literally a fish, but some unspecified creature—at 497 it is called a 'slug'—that is ambiguous because it lives both in and out of the water, scavenging the smelly detritus of the shoreline. Cf. the use of 'ambiguous' in *Paradise Lost*, VII. 473, where the hippopotamus and crocodile are described as 'ambiguous between sea and land'. No actual creature fits the description here, and the image is rather a figurative expression of the Pope's intense disgust. Perhaps there is a half memory here of Caliban as 'a strange fish' in *The Tempest*: II. i. 27.

Armour he boasts when a wave breaks on beach,
Or bird stoops for the prize: with peril nigh,—
The man of rank, the much-befriended-man,
The man almost affiliate to the Church,
Such is to deal with, let the world beware!
Does the world recognize, pass prudently?
Do tides abate and sea-fowl hunt i' the deep?
Already is the slug from out its mew,
Ignobly faring with all loose and free,
Sand-fly and slush-worm at their garbage-feast,
A naked blotch no better than they all:
Guido has dropped nobility, slipped the Church,
Plays trickster if not cut-purse, body and soul
Prostrate among the filthy feeders—faugh!
And when Law takes him by surprise at last,
Catches the foul thing on its carrion-prey,
Behold, he points to shell left high and dry,
Pleads "But the case out yonder is myself!"
Nay, it is thou, Law prongs amid thy peers,
Congenial vermin; that was none of thee,
Thine outside,—give it to the soldier-crab!

[—]

490 *MS* {no comma} 491 *MS* A *MS* bird>hawk>bird *MS* [ ]>with *etc.* 492 *MS* much befriended man, *1868 1872* much-befriended man, 493 *MS* by 494 *MS* {no comma} 495 *MS* recognise, 496 *MS* hunt elsewhere? 497 *MS* the thing 498 *MS* fares *MS* all the loose *MS* {no comma} 499 *MS* [?o'er]>at 500 *MS* [ ]>blotch 503 *MS* [ ]> Prostrate 504 *MS* law *MS* steals up>takes him *etc.* 505 *MS* carrion-prey— 508 *MS* thou we prong

---

497 *mew*: cell, i.e. shell.

499 *slush-worm*: i.e. a worm that lives in slush or mud; an invented term.

509 *Congenial vermin*: i.e. wicked people he easily gets on with (presumably the four farm-hands who helped him with the murder).

510 *give . . . soldier-crab*: i.e. 'leave your clericate-casing for someone who will really do battle for the Church, some genuine soldier of Christ.' The soldier-crab (i.e. hermit-crab) 'carries its shell about with it and changes it for a larger one as it increases in size': Cook, 209.

For I find this black mark impinge the man,
That he believes in just the vile of life.
Low instinct, base pretension, are these truth?
Then, that aforesaid armour, probity
He figures in, is falsehood scale on scale;
Honour and faith,—a lie and a disguise,
Probably for all livers in this world,
Certainly for himself! All say good words
To who will hear, all do thereby bad deeds
To who must undergo; so thrive mankind!
See this habitual creed exemplified
Most in the last deliberate act; as last,
So, very sum and substance of the soul
Of him that planned and leaves one perfect piece,
The sin brought under jurisdiction now,
Even the marriage of the man: this act
I sever from his life as sample, show
For Guido's self, intend to test him by,
As, from a cup filled fairly at the fount,
By the components we decide enough
Or to let flow as late, or staunch the source.

[—]

511 *MS* it is denotes>black mark run through 512 *MS* life— 513 *MS* propension, *MS* these are>are these 514 *MS* Then that 515 *MS* figured in, was *MS* scale. 516 *MS* {beginning of fo. 194} *MS* Honor *MS* faith, 518 *MS* Past question for himself: one says 519 *MS* one does *MS* ill>bad 520 *MS* will>must *MS* [?lives]>thrive *MS* mankind. 521 *MS* trait 522 *MS* act of the man,>deliberate act, 523 *MS* [?his]>the 524 *MS* That planned *MS* [ ]>and *MS* this>one *MS* piece, the same 525 *MS* Which brings *MS* [ ]>him 528 *MS* [ ]>For *MS* Guido and intend 529 *MS* fairly from *MS* {no commas} 530 *MS* I 531 *MS* Shall I let flow or staunch the living source?>Shall I let flow as [ ]>Shall I let flow as late or staunch the source?

511 *impinge*: i.e. struck into, thrust upon; an unusual use. See *MS* readings: Browning originally tried 'run through the man' and 'denotes the man'. Maybe, as Cook suggests, Browning is coining a verb based on L. *pingere* (to paint). The meaning would then be simply 'paints', 'marks', 'dyes'.

530 *By*... *enough*: i.e. the mineral composition is sufficient for us to decide.

531 *Or*... *or*: Either... or.

He purposes this marriage, I remark,
On no one motive that should prompt thereto—
Farthest, by consequence, from ends alleged
Appropriate to the action; so they were:
The best, he knew and feigned, the worst he took.
Not one permissible impulse moves the man,
From the mere liking of the eye and ear,
To the true longing of the heart that loves,
No trace of these: but all to instigate,
Is what sinks man past level of the brute
Whose appetite if brutish is a truth.
All is the lust for money: to get gold,—
Why, lie, rob, if it must be, murder! Make
Body and soul wring gold out, lured within
The clutch of hate by love, the trap's pretence!
What good else get from bodies and from souls?
This got, there were some life to lead thereby,
—What, where or how, appreciate those who tell
How the toad lives: it lives,—enough for me!
To get this good,—with but a groan or so,
Then, silence of the victims,—were the feat.
He foresaw, made a picture in his mind,—

532 *MS* to marry,>a marriage, *MS* perceive,>remark, 533 *MS* the worst motives>no one motive 534 *MS* —Farthest, *MS* those>ends 535 *MS* were,— 536 *MS* He knew the best and took the worst of all>He knew and feigned the best and took the worst:>The best he knew and feigned the worst he took. 537 *MS* No 538 *MS* {no comma} 539 *MS* love>longing *etc.* *MS* that's love, 540 *MS* Not a trace: all that instigates,—and so 541 *MS* Sinks the man past the level *1868 1872* brute, 542 *MS* truth,— 543 *MS* {beginning of fo. 195} 544 *MS* Lie, rob, and, if it must be, murder—make 546 *MS* grasp>clutch 549 *MS* What, *MS* you who 550 *MS* he lives,— *MS* me: 551 *MS* And to get this with just a groan or so 552 *MS* Then silence of the victims were *MS* success:>the feat: 553 *MS* the picture *MS* [ ]>in *etc.* *MS* mind,

540–1 *but . . . brute*: i.e. 'but all that provokes him to action is that which makes man less than even the animals.'

543–4 *All . . . murder*: cf. 1 Tim. 6: 9–10.

549–50 *who . . . lives*: the life that Guido hopes to live, after treating Pompilia and her parents as a money-bag, is compared to the isolated, poisonous life of the toad. For the description of such a toad, see EBB to RB, 4 Jan. 1846: *Correspondence*, xi. 282.

Of father and mother stunned and echoless
To the blow, as they lie staring at fate's jaws
Their folly danced into, till the woe fell;
Edged in a month by strenuous cruelty
From even the poor nook whence they watched the wolf
Feast on their heart, the lamb-like child his prey;
Plundered to the last remnant of their wealth,
(What daily pittance pleased the plunderer dole)
Hunted forth to go hide head, starve and die,
And leave the pale awe-stricken wife, past hope
Of help i' the world now, mute and motionless,
His slave, his chattel, to first use, then destroy.
All this, he bent mind how to bring about,
Put plain in act and life, as painted plain,
So have success, reach crown of earthly good,
In this particular enterprise of man,
By marriage—undertaken in God's face
With all these lies so opposite God's truth,
For end so other than man's end.

Thus schemes
Guido, and thus would carry out his scheme:
But when an obstacle first blocks the path,

554 *MS* Father and 555 *MS* blow as stones lie, *MS* the fate>fate's jaws 556 *MS* into,— *MS* trap fell: 557 *MS* Chased>Edged *MS* villainy>cruelty 558 *MS* stand wherefrom>poor nook whence *MS* [ ]> wolf 559 *MS* [ ]>Feast *MS* his sport,>the lamb like *etc.* *MS* prey,— 560 *MS* Robbed so>Plundered 561 *MS* [ ]>The sorry pittance>What poor pittance>What daily pittance *MS* thief to dole,>thief to spare,> plunderer dole, 562 *MS* Hunted to Rome, <there> to hide head, starve and die,— 563 *MS* *1868* So 564 *MS* in 565 *MS* slave,— *MS* to use then destroy— *1868* to use and then destroy: *1872* destroy {broken sort} 567 *MS* This put in *1868* Put this in *MS* life as 568 *MS* [ ] were> Such were *1868* And have *MS* *1868* the crown *MS* good 570 *MS* *1868* A 571 *MS* {beginning of fo. 196} *MS* *1868* those *MS* the truth *Yale 1* the>God's 572 *MS* ends quite *1868* ends *MS* the end.>this end. *Yale 1* such>Man's 573 *MS* {no new paragraph} *MS* So 574 *MS* and so

554 *father and mother*: i.e. Pietro and Violante.

567 *Put . . . plain*: put into action, as previously exactly imagined.

When he finds none may boast monopoly
Of lies and trick i' the tricking lying world,—
That sorry timid natures, even this sort
O' the Comparini, want nor trick nor lie
Proper to the kind,—that as the gor-crow treats
The bramble-finch so treats the finch the moth,
And the great Guido is minutely matched
By this same couple,—whether true or false
The revelation of Pompilia's birth,
Which in a moment brings his scheme to nought,—
Then, he is piqued, advances yet a stage,
Leaves the low region to the finch and fly,
Soars to the zenith whence the fiercer fowl
May dare the inimitable swoop. I see.
He draws now on the curious crime, the fine
Felicity and flower of wickedness;
Determines, by the utmost exercise
Of violence, made safe and sure by craft,
To satiate malice, pluck one last arch-pang
From the parents, else would triumph out of reach,
By punishing their child, within reach yet,
Who, by thought, word or deed, could nowise wrong
I' the matter that now moves him. So plans he,

576 *MS* discovers none monopolise *1868* there is no 577 *MS* Lies *MS* in this 579 *MS* Of 581 *MS* finch>bramble finch *MS* butterf>moth, 582 *MS* matched,— 583–5 *MS* {lines added later} 583 *MS* story whether 584 *MS* This *MS* {no comma} 586 *MS* —Why, 588 *MS* nobler 589 *MS* swoop, I see: 591 *MS* wickedness, 592 *MS* {no comma} *Yale 1* {comma added} 593 *MS* {no commas} 594 *MS* [?win]>pluck 595 *MS* parents in their 596 *MS* child within 597 *MS* Who nowise wronged him, thought nor word nor deed, *1868* Who nowise could have wronged, thought, word or deed, 598 *MS* In *MS* him,—so

580 *gor-crow*: also spelt 'gore-crow': the carrion crow.

581 *bramble-finch*: probably the brambling, a winter visitor to England, here a type of the small, harmless bird.

590–1 *He . . . wickedness*: 'he proceeds to bring to fruition the subtle crime, the exquisite perfection of wickedness.' Guido's crime showed a 'curiosa felicitas', a phrase from Petronius' *Satyricon* (ch. 118) that has been echoed by other English authors: cf. Byron, *Don Juan*, XVI, st. 102, for example.

Always subordinating (note the point!)
Revenge, the manlier sin, to interest
The meaner,—would pluck pang forth, but unclench
No gripe in the act, let fall no money-piece.
Hence a plan for so plaguing, body and soul,
His wife, so putting, day by day, hour by hour,
The untried torture to the untouched place,
As must precipitate an end foreseen,
Goad her into some plain revolt, most like
Plunge upon patent suicidal shame,
Death to herself, damnation by rebound
To those whose hearts he, holding hers, holds still:
Such plan as, in its bad completeness, shall
Ruin the three together and alike,
Yet leave himself in luck and liberty,
No claim renounced, no right a forfeiture,
His person unendangered, his good fame
Without a flaw, his pristine worth intact,—
While they, with all their claims and rights that cling,
Shall forthwith crumble off him every side,
Scorched into dust, a plaything for the winds.
As when, in our Campagna, there is fired
The nest-like work that overruns a hut;

599 *MS* subordinating,—note the point, 601 *MS* meaner,—pluck the 602 *MS* money-piece! 603 *MS* {beginning of fo. 197} *MS* {no commas} 604 *MS* putting>trying>putting *MS 1868* day and hour *MS* hour 605 *MS* happy>novel *MS* on>to 606 *MS* a natural end>an end foreseen, 608 *MS* Some>Plunge upon 611 *MS 1868* a plan *MS* its completeness *1868* its completeness, *MS* should>shall 614 *MS* in forfeiture, 616 *MS* self intact 617 *MS* they and *MS* claims, *MS* ^and^ *MS* clung>cling 618 *MS* Should>Shall *MS* {no comma} 619 *MS* winds,— 620 *MS* {no commas} 621 *MS* lets some peasant house *1868 1872* that lets a peasant house;

602 *gripe*: cf. IX. 1007 n.

618 *crumble off*: fall off. The phrasing is explained in the following image where burning ivy or vine is imagined falling off 'some old malicious tower'.

620 *Campagna*: the *Campagna di Roma*, the rich countryside around Rome. Browning knew it well, and had often picnicked in it; 'Two in the Campagna' is one poem inspired by its landscape. In the image here he is probably thinking of some part of the southern portion. Story describes it as 'rolling like an inland sea whose waves have suddenly been checked and stiffened, green with grass, golden with grain,

And, as the thatch burns here, there, everywhere,
Even to the ivy and wild vine, that bound
And blessed the home where men were happy once,
There rises gradual, black amid the blaze,
Some grim and unscathed nucleus of the nest,—
Some old malicious tower, some obscene tomb
They thought a temple in their ignorance,
And clung about and thought to lean upon—
There laughs it o'er their ravage,—where are they?
So did his cruelty burn life about,
And lay the ruin bare in dreadfulness,
Try the persistency of torment so
Upon the wife, that, at extremity,
Some crisis brought about by fire and flame,
The patient frenzy-stung must needs break loose,
Fly anyhow, find refuge anywhere,
Even in the arms of who should front her first,
No monster but a man—while nature shrieked
"Or thus escape, or die!" The spasm arrived,

622 *MS* And as *MS* poor thatch>thatch *MS* blazes>burns 624 *MS 1868 1872* hut 626 *MS* The *MS* nest 627 *MS* The *MS* the 628 *MS* {line added later} 629 *MS* They>So *Yale 1* So>And 630 *MS* ravage and 631 *MS* So cold calm cruelty *MS* turned>turns *MS* winch and wheel, 632 {not found in *MS*} 633 *MS* {beginning of fo. 198} *MS* Tried> Tries *MS* slow>its 634 *MS* On the wife, harmless in thought, word and deed, *1868* O' the *1868* at some fierce *MS* {Between 634 and 635 extra line: <With> To this end that, at some extremity,} 635 *MS* by scrape of screw, 636 *MS 1868* stung to frenzy *MS* should>shall *1868* should 638 *MS* might>may *1868* might *MS* {no comma} 639 *MS* shrieked>shrieks 640 *MS* arrived—>arrives—

and gracious with myriads of wild flowers, . . . pendant vines shroud the picturesque ruins of antique villas, aqueducts and tombs, or droop from mediæval towers and fortresses': *Roba di Roma*, i. 313. The burning farm-house here is so vivid that it is probably taken from life. The peasants have built their hut against the ruins of what they thought was a temple; as the fire rages it becomes clear that the ruins are a 'malicious tower' or 'obscene tomb'.

626 *nucleus . . . nest*: centre of the tangle (of ivy, vine, and thatch).

627 *old malicious tower*: a recurring sinister image in Browning's poetry: see 'The Englishman in Italy', 219–20, 'Childe Roland', 181–4, and the discussion in Daniel Karlin, *Browning's Hatreds* (1985), 244–6.

obscene: loathsome, disgusting; cf. I. 581.

640 *Or . . . or*: Either . . . or.

spasm: convulsion, crisis. The image here is of Pompilia as a patient, so tortured by

Not the escape by way of sin,—O God,
Who shall pluck sheep Thou holdest, from Thy hand?
Therefore she lay resigned to die,—so far
The simple cruelty was foiled. Why then,
Craft to the rescue, let craft supplement
Cruelty and show hell a masterpiece!
Hence this consummate lie, this love-intrigue,
Unmanly simulation of a sin,
With place and time and circumstance to suit—
These letters false beyond all forgery—
Not just handwriting and mere authorship,
But false to body and soul they figure forth—
As though the man had cut out shape and shape
From fancies of that other Aretine,
To paste below—incorporate the filth
With cherub faces on a missal-page!

Whereby the man so far attains his end
That strange temptation is permitted,—see!

641 *MS* God 642 *MS* Who plucks that *MS* thou *MS* {no comma} *MS* thy 643 *MS* was>is 644 *MS* was>is>comes *MS* foiled: why 645 *MS* craft shall *1868* craft should 647 *MS* love-intrigue 648 *MS* The unmanly *MS* man, 649 *MS* A place, a time, a 652 *MS* [?that]>they *MS* forth 653 *MS* shape[ ]>shape 655 *MS* And pasted them as indivisible>To paste below—and>To paste below—incorporate the filth 656 *MS* From two pure>With cherub *MS* missal-page: 657 *MS* {no new paragraph} *MS* effects>attains *MS* [ ]>end 658 *MS* A

Guido that she reaches a convulsive nervous crisis in which she must either fulfil Guido's secret wish and escape with Caponsacchi as her lover, or she must face death.

641–2 *O . . . hand?*: cf. John 10: 28: 'And I give unto them [those who follow me] eternal life; and they shall never perish, neither shall any man pluck them out of my hand.'

647 *consummate*: complete, perfect. The stress is on the second syllable, as in Johnson and other older dictionaries.

654 *other Aretine*: cf. VI. 1947, IX. 1204 nn. The Pope believes that Guido's imagination, revealed in the forged love-letters, is as salacious as that of Pietro Aretino (1492–1556), the writer and dramatist. The phrasing at 653 suggests that Browning is not thinking of the cutting-out of Aretino's 'lewd sonnets', but rather of the cutting-out of the sexually explicit drawings, designed by Giulio Romano, that accompanied them. Like pornographic etchings pasted onto the page of an illuminated prayer-book ('missal-page'), so appear the forged love-letters when compared to the true natures of Pompilia and Caponsacchi.

Pompilia, wife, and Caponsacchi, priest,
Are brought together as nor priest nor wife
Should stand, and there is passion in the place,
Power in the air for evil as for good,
Promptings from heaven and hell, as if the stars
Fought in their courses for a fate to be.
Thus stand the wife and priest, a spectacle,
I doubt not, to unseen assemblage there.
No lamp will mark that window for a shrine,
No tablet signalize the terrace, teach
New generations which succeed the old
The pavement of the street is holy ground;
No bard describe in verse how Christ prevailed
And Satan fell like lightning! Why repine?
What does the world, told truth, but lie the more?

A second time the plot is foiled; nor, now,
By corresponding sin for countercheck,
No wile and trick that baffle trick and wile,—
The play o' the parents! Here the blot is blanched

*659 *MS 1868 1872* Pompilia, *1888 1889* Pompilia **MS 1868 1872* Caponsacchi, *1888 1889* Caponsacchi 660 *MS* {beginning of fo. 199} 661 *MS* be,>dare, 664 *MS* what fate should fall.>the fate to be.>a fate to be. 665 *MS* priest and wife,>wife and priest, 667 *MS* will light 668 *MS* Nor *MS* [ ]>signalize 669 *MS* that **MS 1868 1872 1888* old, *DC BrU* old,>old *1889* old 670 *MS* ground: 671 *MS* shall ever sing>shall put in verse 672 *MS* lightning. 673 *MS* [ ]>told 674 *MS* {no new paragraph} *MS* foiled, nor now 676 *MS* and wile, *1868* to baffle 677 *MS 1868* of *MS* parents,—here *MS* was

663–4 *stars . . . be*: cf. Judg. 5: 20: 'the stars in their courses fought against Sisera.'

665–6 *spectacle . . . there*: i.e. a spectacle for the angels and saints in heaven; cf. 1 Cor. 4: 9, and R&B I. 504 n.

668 *signalize*: distinguish, indicate the importance of.

671–2 *No bard . . . lightning*: i.e. 'no Milton-like poet will see into the religious dimension of these events'. Ironically, Browning himself is doing exactly this in *The Ring and the Book* as a whole. For 'Satan fell like lightning' cf. Luke 10: 18.

676–7 *No . . . parents*: the 'play o' the parents' is the way the Comparini matched Guido's 'trick and wile' with their own 'wile and trick': he had lied about his family's wealth; they now revealed the lie about Pompilia's parentage.

677 *blot is blanched*: the evil blot is whitened. The 'blot' is Guido's attempt to engineer adultery between Pompilia and Caponsacchi. Cf. I. 1398 n.

By God's gift of a purity of soul
That will not take pollution, ermine-like
Armed from dishonour by its own soft snow.
Such was this gift of God who showed for once
How He would have the world go white: it seems
As a new attribute were born of each
Champion of truth, the priest and wife I praise,—
As a new safeguard sprang up in defence
Of their new noble nature: so a thorn
Comes to the aid of and completes the rose—
Courage to-wit, no woman's gift nor priest's,
I' the crisis; might leaps vindicating right.
See how the strong aggressor, bad and bold,
With every vantage, preconcerts surprise,
Leaps of a sudden at his victim's throat
In a byeway,—how fares he when face to face
With Caponsacchi? Who fights, who fears now?
There quails Count Guido armed to the chattering teeth,
Cowers at the steadfast eye and quiet word
O' the Canon of the Pieve! There skulks crime
Behind law called in to back cowardice:
While out of the poor trampled worm the wife,
Springs up a serpent!

[—]

679 *MS* would 680 *MS* against all>from *MS* ^its own^ *MS* snow: 681 *MS* To say this is God's gift,—who showed sometimes>Such was this gift of God's,—who showed for once 682 *MS* he *MS* white,—there 684 *MS* this priest *MS* praise, 685 *MS* And 686 *MS* the new *MS* admirable>stainless *MS* nature; 687 *MS* rose: 688 *MS* {beginning of fo. 200} *MS* to wit, 689 *MS* In *Yale 1* In>I' *MS* crisis, *MS* right; 692 *MS 1868* Flies *695 *MS 1868 1872 1888* Guido, *DC BrU* Guido,>Guido *1889* Guido 697 *MS* Of the peaceful Canon at the Pieve!—skulks *1868 1872* at *698 *MS 1868 1872 1888* cowardice! *DC BrU* cowardice!>cowardice: *1889* cowardice: 700 *MS* Sprang *MS* serpent...

679 *ermine-like*: i.e. white and lovely, with the suggestion also of nobility and wisdom: ermine is worn by peers as a mark of rank and by judges. Cf. VIII. 224–6 n.

683 *As*: as if. Also in l. 685.

689 *might... right*: inverting the usual significance of the proverb 'Might is right': ODEP, 530.

691 *preconcerts*: pre-plans, devises.

But anon of these.
Him I judge now,—of him proceed to note,
Failing the first, a second chance befriends
Guido, gives pause ere punishment arrive.
The law he called, comes, hears, adjudicates,
Nor does amiss i' the main,—secludes the wife
From the husband, respites the oppressed one, grants
Probation to the oppressor, could he know
The mercy of a minute's fiery purge!
The furnace-coals alike of public scorn,
Private remorse, heaped glowing on his head,
What if,—the force and guile, the ore's alloy,
Eliminate, his baser soul refined—
The lost be saved even yet, so as by fire?
Let him, rebuked, go softly all his days
And, when no graver musings claim their due,
Meditate on a man's immense mistake
Who, fashioned to use feet and walk, deigns crawl—
Takes the unmanly means—ay, though to ends
Man scarce should make for, would but reach thro' wrong,—
May sin, but nowise needs shame manhood so:
Since fowlers hawk, shoot, nay and snare the game,

701 *MS* {no new paragraph} *MS* but **MS* these. *1868 1872 1888* these! *DC BrU* these!>these. *1889* these. 702 *MS* [?This]>Him *MS* and thus proceed 705 *MS* adjudicates— 706 *MS* in 708 *MS* Escape 711 *MS* head 712 *MS* if, 713 *MS* burnt clean, 715 *MS* Let the man but go 717 *MS* {beginning of fo. 201} 718 *MS* Who fashioned 719 *1868* end 720 *MS* shall *MS* wrong, 721 *MS 1868 1872* but must not needs *MS* so— 722 *MS* game—

707 *respites*: gives relief, or rest, to.

709 *minute's . . . purge*: as becomes clear in the next lines, this fiery purification of Guido's whole being could have been supplied by 'public scorn' and 'private remorse', if he had chosen to experience it.

713 *Eliminate*: burnt off, purified. An unusual use, but cf. IX. 1570, and 'Bishop Blougram's Apology', 732.

714 *lost . . . fire?*: cf. 1 Cor. 3: 15.

715 *go . . . days*: cf. Isa. 38: 15. A favourite quotation: cf. II. 457–8, VIII. 994 nn.

And yet eschew vile practice, nor find sport
In torch-light treachery or the luring owl.

But how hunts Guido? Why, the fraudful trap—
Late spurned to ruin by the indignant feet
Of fellows in the chase who loved fair play—
Here he picks up its fragments to the least,
Lades him and hies to the old lurking-place
Where haply he may patch again, refit
The mischief, file its blunted teeth anew,
Make sure, next time, first snap shall break the bone.
Craft, greed and violence complot revenge:
Craft, for its quota, schemes to bring about
And seize occasion and be safe withal:
Greed craves its act may work both far and near,
Crush the tree, branch and trunk and root, beside
Whichever twig or leaf arrests a streak
Of possible sunshine else would coin itself,
And drop down one more gold piece in the path:
Violence stipulates "Advantage proved

723 *MS* {no comma} 725 *MS* {no new paragraph} *MS* trap, 727 *MS* love *728 *MS 1868 1872 1888* the fragments *DC BrU* the fragments>its fragments *1889* its fragments *MS* {no comma} 731 *MS* old mischief, *MS* the blunted 732 *MS 1868* a snap 734 *MS* Craft for its quota schemes *MS* about, 735 *MS* Seize *MS* an>the 736 *MS* that one act may work far *MS* wide,>near, 737 *MS* Break *MS* {no commas} **MS* root beside *1868 1872* root beside, *1888* root beside. *DC* root beside.>root, beside. *BrU* root beside.>root, beside *1889* root, beside. 740 *1868* path. 741 *MS* stipulates,—advantage *Yale 1* stipulates,>stipulates— **1868 1872 1888* proved, *DC BrU* proved,>proved *1889* proved

724 *torch-light . . . luring owl*: i.e. unsporting ways of catching birds: at night-time, by sneaking up on them in their nests using torch-light, or by using a lure owl to trick them into exposure. For a description of how nineteenth-century Romans hunted by using a *civetta* (little owl) to entice larks to their death, see III. 338 n.

733 *complot*: plot together.

734 *for its quota*: to fulfil its part or share (in the plot).

736–40 *Greed . . . path*: 'The metaphor here employed is drawn from the bright spots with which sunshine chequers the ground under a tree. The branches, twigs, leaves of the tree, which intercept much of the sunshine, are Pietro and his family, who intercept a flow of revenue; they prevent the gold from falling upon the ground in a flood for Guido to scoop up. His greed therefore prompts him to destroy them; he will crush the tree, twigs, leaves and all': Cook, 211.

"And safety sure, be pain the overplus!
"Murder with jagged knife! Cut but tear too!
"Foiled oft, starved long, glut malice for amends!"
And what, craft's scheme? scheme sorrowful and strange
As though the elements, whom mercy checked,
Had mustered hate for one eruption more,
One final deluge to surprise the Ark
Cradled and sleeping on its mountain-top:
Their outbreak-signal—what but the dove's coo,
Back with the olive in her bill for news
Sorrow was over? 'T is an infant's birth,
Guido's first born, his son and heir, that gives
The occasion: other men cut free their souls
From care in such a case, fly up in thanks
To God, reach, recognize His love for once:
Guido cries "Soul, at last the mire is thine!
"Lie there in likeness of a money-bag
"My babe's birth so pins down past moving now,
"That I dare cut adrift the lives I late
"Scrupled to touch lest thou escape with them!

742–4 *MS* {no quotation marks at beginnings of lines} 742 *MS* my overplus— 743 *MS* knife,—cut 744 *MS* at this last! *Yale 1* at this last!">for amends!" *MS* {no quotation mark at end of line} 745 *MS* {beginning of fo. 202} *MS* And craft did seize the occasion sad>And craft does scheme,—sorrowful scheme *Yale 1* sorrowful scheme>scheme sorrowful *1868* And, last, craft schemes,— 746 *MS* {no commas} 748 *MS* Last and worst deluge, should>And last worst deluge should 750 *MS* The out-break's>The out-break *Yale 1* For>The *1868* The *MS* flight *Yale 1* flight>coo,— *1868* coos 752 *Yale 1* is>was *MS* over! 754 *MS* glad occasion:>occasion: 756 *MS* recognise his 757 *MS* cries, Soul, *Yale 1* cries,>cries 758–73 *MS* {no quotation marks at beginnings of lines} 759 *MS* This *1868* "This *MS* pins me>so pins *MS* {no comma} 760 *MS* away>adrift 761 *MS* them:

750 *dove's coo*: i.e. the gentle birth of a baby. Literally the reference is to Gen. 8: 4–11: as the dove with the olive leaf signalled joy to Noah, so the birth of his child *should* have signalled joy to Guido. For him, instead, it became the 'outbreak-signal' for the violence of the triple murder.

757–71 *Guido . . . knife*: 'If Guido killed Pompilia before she had given birth to an heir, the capital of which Pietro had the usufruct would go to his kinsmen, the "rightful heirs" of II. 580; he had therefore a strong motive for sparing her till after her confinement. This argument, borrowed from Bottini, has already been used in III. 1546–69 and in IV. 1102–6': Cook, 212.

761 *thou*: i.e. the money-bag, with which Guido's soul is identified.

"These parents and their child my wife,—touch one,
"Lose all! Their rights determined on a head
"I could but hate, not harm, since from each hair
"Dangled a hope for me: now—chance and change!
"No right was in their child but passes plain
"To that child's child and through such child to me.
"I am a father now,—come what, come will,
"I represent my child; he comes between—
"Cuts sudden off the sunshine of this life
"From those three: why, the gold is in his curls!
"Not with old Pietro's, Violante's head,
"Not his grey horror, her more hideous black—
"Go these, devoted to the knife!"
'T is done:
Wherefore should mind misgive, heart hesitate?
He calls to counsel, fashions certain four
Colourless natures counted clean till now,
—Rustic simplicity, uncorrupted youth,
Ignorant virtue! Here's the gold o' the prime
When Saturn ruled, shall shock our leaden day—
The clown abash the courtier! Mark it, bards!

762 *MS* Parents *MS* wife, *Yale 1* wife,>wife,— *MS 1868 1872* one 763 *MS* all,—their *MS* the head *Yale 1* her head>a head 765 *MS* of mine: 766 *MS* What *MS 1868 1872* passes now 767 *MS* me? 768 *MS 1868* the father 769 *MS* child, 771 *MS* why the *MS* curls, *Yale 1* curls> curls! 772 {not found in *MS*} 773 *MS* that grey *MS* that more 774 *MS* dark. 775 *MS* {beginning of fo. 203} 778 *MS* white 780 *MS* The clown's rude>Ignorant *MS* virtue: here's *MS* age o' 781 *MS* {no comma} *MS* shame>shock 782 *MS* Trow ye, bards?

774 *devoted to*: given over to, doomed to.

780–1 *gold . . . day*: the Pope mocks the idea that there was once a primitive world of goodness and love, where innocent rustics (like Guido's farm-hands) knew nothing of violence and greed. The Greek poet Hesiod first described the myth of a golden age; it was a kind of rural idyll, before towns, armies, and the ambiguities of civilization. This golden age (ruled by Saturn, not Jove) gave way to progressively lesser ages of silver, bronze, and finally lead (or iron), i.e. modern, debased times. The myth is referred to by the great Roman poets Horace, Virgil, and Ovid, the 'bards' the Pope is probably thinking of at l. 782: see, for example, Ovid, *Metamorphoses* 1. 89–150, a passage Browning has already alluded to.

782 *clown . . . courtier*: i.e. the farm-hand or peasant (by his goodness and simplicity) embarrasses the courtier or aristocrat.

The courtier tries his hand on clownship here,
Speaks a word, names a crime, appoints a price,—
Just breathes on what, suffused with all himself,
Is red-hot henceforth past distinction now
I' the common glow of hell. And thus they break
And blaze on us at Rome, Christ's birthnight-eve!
Oh angels that sang erst "On the earth, peace!
"To man, good will!"—such peace finds earth to-day!
After the seventeen hundred years, so man
Wills good to man, so Guido makes complete
His murder! what is it I said?—cuts loose
Three lives that hitherto he suffered cling,
Simply because each served to nail secure,
By a corner of the money-bag, his soul,—
Therefore, lives sacred till the babe's first breath
O'erweights them in the balance,—off they fly!

So is the murder managed, sin conceived
To the full: and why not crowned with triumph too?
Why must the sin, conceived thus, bring forth death?
I note how, within hair's-breadth of escape,
Impunity and the thing supposed success,
Guido is found when the check comes, the change,
The monitory touch o' the tether—felt

784 *MS* crime and notes the pay, 785 *MS* to suffuse 786 *MS* Red-heat henceforward 787 *MS* In *Yale 1* In>I' *MS* here>thus 788 *MS* Birth-night eve! *1868* Birthnight-eve! 789 *MS* peace— 790 *MS* {no quotation mark at beginning of line} *MS* to-day,— *Yale 1* to-day,—>today! 793 *MS* murder,— *MS* say? cuts 794 *MS* {no comma} 796 *MS* soul, 797 *MS* Therefore lives 798 *MS* O'erweighted *MS* fly. 799 *MS* {no new paragraph} *MS* was>is *MS* wickedness>sin conceived 800 *MS* why not a>why not perfect>and why not crowned with 801 *MS* the plan>must *etc.* 802 *MS* how within 803 *MS* {beginning of fo. 204} *MS* he calls>supposed *MS* {no comma} 804 *MS* Stands>Gets *MS* Guido when *MS* comes and the change, 805 *MS* That *MS* of

789–90 *angels . . . to-day*: cf. Luke 2: 13–14. Guido and his accomplices 'blaze' on Rome in a hellish parody of the angels lighting up the sky at Christ's birth.

801 *sin . . . death?*: i.e. why should Guido's sin (the murders) result in his death? echoing Jas. 1: 15: 'and sin, when it is finished, bringeth forth death.'

By few, not marked by many, named by none
At the moment, only recognized aright
I' the fulness of the days, for God's, lest sin
Exceed the service, leap the line: such check—
A secret which this life finds hard to keep,
And, often guessed, is never quite revealed—
Needs must trip Guido on a stumbling-block
Too vulgar, too absurdly plain i' the path!
Study this single oversight of care,
This hebetude that marred sagacity,
Forgetfulness of all the man best knew,—
How any stranger having need to fly,
Needs but to ask and have the means of flight.
Why, the first urchin tells you, to leave Rome,
Get horses, you must show the warrant, just
The banal scrap, clerk's scribble, a fair word buys,
Or foul one, if a ducat sweeten word,—
And straight authority will back demand,
Give you the pick o' the post-house!—how should he,
Then, resident at Rome for thirty years,
Guido, instruct a stranger! And himself

806 *MS* owned>named *MS* none[?,]>none 807 *MS 1868 1872* recognised 808 *MS* In *MS* [ ] sign lest sin>check lest sin *MS* {no commas} 809 *MS* limit here:>line traced here: *Yale 1* check,>check— 810 *MS* The *MS* of>which [ ]>finds 811 *MS* Yet, somehow *MS* shall never [?be]>is never quite *MS 1868* revealed. 812 *MS 1868* Guido must needs trip 813 *MS* all too>too absurdly *MS* in 814 *MS* This *MS* sagacity, 815 {not found in *MS*} *1868* mars 816 *MS 1868* of what *MS* knew *1868* knew! 817 {not found in *MS*} 817 *1868* Here is a stranger who, with need 818 *MS* One has to 819 *MS* stranger>urchin 821 *MS* scrap of>scrap, clerk's *MS* scribble a 822 *MS* a foul *MS* follow such,— >sweeten such,— *Yale 1* wood,—>word,— 823 *MS* there's authority *MS* to>will 824 *MS* of *MS* post-house: *MS* how I hear>in such wise *1868* in such wise, 825 {not found in *MS*} *1868* The resident 826 *MS* {no comma} *MS* instruct some>instructs a *1868* instructs a

---

812 *stumbling-block*: a biblical phrase: cf. Jer. 6: 21, Ezek. 14: 3, etc.

815 *hebetude*: dullness, obtuseness (from L. *hebetudo*).

820–4 *warrant . . . post-house*: SS 13 tells how Guido had demanded horses at an inn but failed to get them because he lacked 'l'ordine necessario' (the necessary warrant). Cf. III. 1628–30, V. 1722–5, XI. 1625–50.

Forgets just this poor paper scrap, wherewith
Armed, every door he knocks at opens wide
To save him: horsed and manned, with such advance
O' the hunt behind, why, 't were the easy task
Of hours told on the fingers of one hand,
To reach the Tuscan frontier, laugh at-home,
Light-hearted with his fellows of the place,—
Prepared by that strange shameful judgment, that
Satire upon a sentence just pronounced
By the Rota and confirmed by the Granduke,—
Ready in a circle to receive their peer,
Appreciate his good story how, when Rome,
The Pope-King and the populace of priests
Made common cause with their confederate
The other priestling who seduced his wife,
He, all unaided, wiped out the affront
With decent bloodshed and could face his friends,
Frolic it in the world's eye. Ay, such tale
Missed such applause, and by such oversight!
So, tired and footsore, those blood-flustered five
Went reeling on the road through dark and cold,

827 *MS* {no comma} 829 *MS* him, *MS* {no comma} 830 *MS* Of *MS* why 'tis *1868* why 'twere 831 *MS* {no comma} 832 *MS* Frontier **1868 1872 1888* at home, *DC BrU* at home,>at-home, *1889* at-home, 833 *MS* the best of the land, I see,— *Yale 1* land,—> place,— 834–6 *MS* {lines added later} 835 *MS* {beginning of fo. 205} 836 *MS* Grand Duke,— 837 *MS* salute>receive *MS* {no comma} 838 *MS* that good 839 *MS* Pope King 840 confederate,> confederate 843 *MS* the decent 845 *MS* applause by one such oversight; *1868* applause, all by 846 *MS* The>So, *MS* footsore and>foot-sore, those 847 *MS* {no comma}

832 *Tuscan frontier*: the frontier between the Papal States and Tuscany was only about 65–80 miles from Rome, depending on where Guido intended to cross.

835–6 *sentence . . . Granduke*: the original judgment of the Governor of Arezzo, finding Pompilia guilty of adultery and theft, had been ratified by the Ruota (the main criminal court) at Florence, and then approved by the Grand Duke Cosimo III on 24 Dec. 1697. This judgment is the first document in OYB: v–viii (5–7).

841 *priestling*: i.e. Caponsacchi. 'Priestling' is a contemptuous word for lower-ranked, young, or otherwise insignificant priest.

The few permissible miles, to sink at length,
Wallow and sleep in the first wayside straw,
As the other herd quenched, i' the wash o' the wave,
—Each swine, the devil inside him: so slept they,
And so were caught and caged—all through one trip,
One touch of fool in Guido the astute!
He curses the omission, I surmise,
More than the murder. Why, thou fool and blind,
It is the mercy-stroke that stops thy fate,
Hamstrings and holds thee to thy hurt,—but how?
On the edge o' the precipice! One minute more,
Thou hadst gone farther and fared worse, my son,
Fathoms down on the flint and fire beneath!
Thy comrades each and all were of one mind,
Thy murder done, to straightway murder thee
In turn, because of promised pay withheld.
So, to the last, greed found itself at odds
With craft in thee, and, proving conqueror,
Had sent thee, the same night that crowned thy hope,

848 *MS* [?last]>length *MS* {no commas} 849 *MS* {no comma} 850 *MS* ancient swine>other herd *MS* cooled>quenched *MS* in *MS* {no commas} 851 *MS* Each *MS* [?one] the>swine the 852 *MS* fault>trip, 853 *MS* Touch of forgetfulness in Guido! Fault *Yale 1* Guido!>Guido *1868* Touch of the fool 854 *MS* curses at this minute, 855 *MS* murder: why, 856 *MS* This *MS* was>is 857 *MS* in a trice,—>to thy hurt,— *MS* where? 858 *MS* of *MS* precipice: one *MS* {no comma} 859 *MS* {line added later} *MS* son 860 *MS* flint [ ]: for why?>flint beneath: for why? 861 *MS 1868* {no comma} 862 *MS* Straitway, *1868* Straightway, *MS 1868* thy murder done, to murder thee 863 *MS* withheld, 864 *MS* finds *MS* {no commas} 865 *MS* and proves craft's 866 *MS* {beginning of fo. 206} *MS* And sends *MS* [?this]>the *MS* of thy success>that crowns thy hope,

850–1 As . . . *him*: cf. Matt. 8: 28–34. As the herd of Gadarene swine quenched the fiery devils inside them by falling into the sea of Galilee, so Guido and his assassins fell exhausted into the straw of the hostelry. 'Quenched' is a slightly unusual intransitive use. Here Browning's original idea was of the devilish pigs 'cooled' by the water, just as the over-heated assassins were cooled by the 'dark and cold' and exhaustion of their journey: see *MS* variant.

859 *gone . . . worse*: proverbial: 'Go farther and fare worse': ODEP, 306. Cf. *Vanity Fair* (1848), ch. 4: 'She is just as rich as most of the girls who come out to India. I might go farther and fare worse, egad.'

860 *flint and fire*: hard rocks and fire (an image of hell).

Thither where, this same day, I see thee not,
Nor, through God's mercy, need, to-morrow, see.

Such I find Guido, midmost blotch of black
Discernible in this group of clustered crimes
Huddling together in the cave they call
Their palace, outraged day thus penetrates.
Around him ranged, now close and now remote,
Prominent or obscure to meet the needs
O' the mage and master, I detect each shape
Subsidiary i' the scene nor loathed the less,
All alike coloured, all descried akin
By one and the same pitchy furnace stirred
At the centre: see, they lick the master's hand,—
This fox-faced horrible priest, this brother-brute
The Abate,—why, mere wolfishness looks well,
Guido stands honest in the red o' the flame,
Beside this yellow that would pass for white,

869 *MS* {no new paragraph} *MS* central>midmost 870 group, these> group of 871 *MS* that>the *872 *MS* Arezzo;>Their palace, *1868 1872* palace, *1888 1889* {no comma} 873 *MS* Round him are *Yale 1* Round him are>Around him 875 *MS* Of *MS* Mage *MS* in the middle,>and master, *MS* those shapes>each shape 876 *MS* Subsidiaries>Subsidiary *MS* in *MS* [?since]> nor 878 *MS* flame, he>[ ]>furnace 879 *MS* foot,— 881 *MS* Abate, *MS* the>mere *MS* {no commas} 882 *MS* And Guido> Guido stands *MS* of *Yale 1* of>o' *MS* {no comma}

867 *Thither*: i.e. to hell. The Pope sees God's providence at work in Guido's arrest. Had he not been arrested, he would have been killed by his fellow assassins intent on getting the money he owed them. Dying in such a state of sin he would have risked going to hell, but now—the Pope implies—he has time for repentance. For the intention of Guido's farm-hands to murder him, see SS 18.

869–925 *Such . . . pleasure*: in this passage the macabre picture of the Franceschini family is similar in style to that at I. 544–82. Their palace at Arezzo becomes like a smoky, devilish cave in which Guido—both 'mage' and also 'wolf' (for his violence)—is surrounded by his semi-animal family: Abate Paolo (fox-like in his cunning), Girolamo, a hybrid of 'wolf' (violence) and 'fox' (cunning), and their mother, a 'nightmare' or cruel 'she-pard' (leopard).

880 *fox-faced*: cf. I. 549.

883 *yellow*: the particular soft brown of a wolf's fur could be described as yellow; Browning, at least, seems to have thought of it this way: cf. 'Artemis Prologizes', 7: 'each pregnant yellow wolf and fox-bitch sleek'.

Twice Guido, all craft but no violence,
This copier of the mien and gait and garb
Of Peter and Paul, that he may go disguised,
Rob halt and lame, sick folk i' the temple-porch!
Armed with religion, fortified by law,
A man of peace, who trims the midnight lamp
And turns the classic page—and all for craft,
All to work harm with, yet incur no scratch!
While Guido brings the struggle to a close,
Paul steps back the due distance, clear o' the trap
He builds and baits. Guido I catch and judge;
Paul is past reach in this world and my time:
That is a case reserved. Pass to the next,
The boy of the brood, the young Girolamo
Priest, Canon, and what more? nor wolf nor fox,
But hybrid, neither craft nor violence
Wholly, part violence part craft: such cross
Tempts speculation—will both blend one day,
And prove hell's better product? Or subside

884 *MS 1868* This *MS* and no *MS* {no commas} 885 *MS* gait and mien>mien and gait 886 *MS* our>and *etc.* *MS* disguised 887 *MS* lame and blind>lame, sick folk *MS* in *MS* temple-porch. 889 *MS* [?a]>who *etc.* 890 *MS* student's>antique *Yale 1* antique>classic 891 *MS* {no comma} *MS* scratch 892 *MS* [ ]>brings *MS* {no comma} 893 *MS* tempts no trap 894 *MS* {beginning of fo. 207} *MS* has found his fate,>I catch and judge. 895 *MS* Paul is past>But Paul, past *MS* time, 896 *MS* A>That is a *MS* {no comma} 899 *MS* A>But 900 *MS* craft, a 902 *MS* the better *Yale 1* the better>hell's better

885–7 *copier... temple-porch*: cf. Acts 3: 1–11, 5: 12–16, etc. Paolo 'copies' the apostles Peter and Paul because he is a man of God, a priest, and also because he shares Paul's name. Instead of curing sick people like the apostles, his priestly appearance is merely a vehicle for robbing them. The temple-porch was a prominent site of the apostles' healing miracles.

890 *turns... page*: i.e. reads the classics. The 'classic page' is a common phrase: EPD gives forty-six examples of its use.

893 *Paul... distance*: Abate Paolo negotiated the terms of Pompilia's house-arrest in Oct. 1697, then got permission from his Cardinal, sold his furniture and books, and left Rome, clearly permanently, some time before Gaetano's birth on 18 Dec. : see SS 9. For his after-history, see F. E. Faverty, 'The Absconded Abbot in *The Ring and the Book*', *Studies in Philology*, 36 (1939), 88–104.

And let the simple quality emerge,
Go on with Satan's service the old way?
Meanwhile, what promise,—what performance too!
For there's a new distinctive touch, I see,
Lust—lacking in the two—hell's own blue tint
That gives a character and marks the man
More than a match for yellow and red. Once more,
A case reserved: why should I doubt? Then comes
The gaunt grey nightmare in the furthest smoke,
The hag that gave these three abortions birth,
Unmotherly mother and unwomanly
Woman, that near turns motherhood to shame,
Womanliness to loathing: no one word,
No gesture to curb cruelty a whit
More than the she-pard thwarts her playsome whelps
Trying their milk-teeth on the soft o' the throat
O' the first fawn, flung, with those beseeching eyes,
Flat in the covert! How should she but couch,
Lick the dry lips, unsheathe the blunted claw,
Catch 'twixt her placid eyewinks at what chance
Old bloody half-forgotten dream may flit,
Born when herself was novice to the taste,
The while she lets youth take its pleasure. Last,
These God-abandoned wretched lumps of life,

903 *MS* {no comma} 905 *MS* too, 907 *MS* others—hell's>two—hell's own 909 *MS* [ ]>More 910 *MS* care? 913 *MS* mother, the *Yale 1* mother, the>mother and 914 *MS* Woman [?who] turns the>Woman, that turns the 915 *MS* The womanliness *MS* what, no word,>no one word, 917 *MS* wild beast>she-pard *MS* [ ]>her 918 *MS* of 919 *MS* Of *MS* ^flung,^ 920 *MS* Captured>Flat *MS* covert: what does>covert: how should *921 *MS* unsheathe the []>half unsheathe blunted *1868 1872* unsheathe *1888 1889* unsheath 922 *MS* {beginning of fo. 208} *MS* twixt *MS* placid winking eyelids>placid eyewinks *MS* [?an] old> what chance 923 *MS* Bloody and>Old bloody 924 {not found in *MS*} 925 *MS* And let youth take its pleasure. Last of all *Yale 1* which>while 926 *MS* {no comma}

911 *nightmare*: 'a spirit that, in the heathen mythology, was related to torment or suffocate sleepers': Johnson.

917 *she-pard*: female panther or leopard.

920 *covert*: thicket or hiding place (of the she-pard's young).

These four companions,—country-folk this time,
Not tainted by the unwholesome civic breath,
Much less the curse o' the Court! Mere striplings too,
Fit to do human nature justice still!
Surely when impudence in Guido's shape
Shall propose crime and proffer money's-worth
To these stout tall rough bright-eyed black-haired boys,
The blood shall bound in answer to each cheek
Before the indignant outcry break from lip!
Are these i' the mood to murder, hardly loosed
From healthy autumn-finish of ploughed glebe,
Grapes in the barrel, work at happy end,
And winter near with rest and Christmas play?
How greet they Guido with his final task—
(As if he but proposed "One vineyard more
"To dig, ere frost come, then relax indeed!")
"Anywhere, anyhow and anywhy,
"Murder me some three people, old and young,
"Ye never heard the names of,—and be paid
"So much!" And the whole four accede at once.
Demur? Do cattle bidden march or halt?
Is it some lingering habit, old fond faith
I' the lord o' the land, instructs them,—birthright-badge
Of feudal tenure claims its slaves again?

928 *MS* Untainted>Nor tainted 929 *MS* ^Much less^ *MS* of *MS* court. Just *1868 1872* court! 930 *MS* still— 931 *MS* And here goes impudence 932 *MS* [?To]>Shall *MS* murder for his>crime and proffer 933 *MS 1868 1872* tall bright-eyed and 934 *MS* With the blood>With blood 935 *MS* speach [*sic*] can break 936 *MS* Why, they are just in the mood, loose hardly yet 937 *MS* From the healthy Autumn labour, the *Yale 1* autumn labour,>autumn-finish, *1868 1872* autumn-finish, the 938 *MS* end 939 *MS 1868 1872* come with *MS* play! 941 *MS* said, one vineyard more to dig 942 *MS* {no quotation marks} *MS* Ere frost come, then relax with all my heart)— 943 *MS* {line added later} *MS* {no commas} 944–6 *MS* {no quotation marks at beginnings of lines} 944 *MS* {no commas} 945 *MS* You 946 *MS* once, 947 *MS* As cattle do bid *1868 1872* As cattle would, bid *MS* halt: *1868 1872* halt! 949 *MS* In *MS 1868* of *MS* comforts>instructs *MS* them, **MS* birthright badge *1868* birthright-badge *1872 1888 1889* birthright badge 950 the feudal

943 *anywhy*: for any or no reason.

Not so at all, thou noble human heart!
All is done purely for the pay,—which, earned,
And not forthcoming at the instant, makes
Religion heresy, and the lord o' the land
Fit subject for a murder in his turn.
The patron with cut throat and rifled purse,
Deposited i' the roadside-ditch, his due,
Nought hinders each good fellow trudging home,
The heavier by a piece or two in poke,
And so with new zest to the common life,
Mattock and spade, plough-tail and waggon-shaft,
Till some such other piece of luck betide,
Who knows? Since this is a mere start in life,
And none of them exceeds the twentieth year.

Nay, more i' the background yet? Unnoticed forms
Claim to be classed, subordinately vile?
Complacent lookers-on that laugh,—perchance
Shake head as their friend's horse-play grows too rough

952 *MS* {beginning of fo. 209} *MS* was 953 *MS* made 954 *MS* of 956 *MS* {no comma} 957 *MS* in the roadside ditch his *Yale 1* road-ditch>roadside-ditch, 958 *MS* What *Yale 1* What>Nought 959 *MS* the piece *Yale 1* the piece>a piece 960 *MS* And going back to common life again>And back with a new zest to the common life 961 *MS* or waggon-shaft, 962 *MS* befall>betide, 963 *MS* Since is 964 *MS* [ ]>exceeds *965 *1868* {new paragraph. Paragraphing obscured in *1872* by this line's being at the head of the page} *1888 1889* {no new paragraph} *MS* still more>more *MS* in *MS* background, still new forms>background yet, unnoticed forms 967 *MS* friends that stand and see,—>watchers on that see,— 968 *MS* Sigh on their comrade's horse-play, rough and rash,>Shake heads as their friend's horse-play, grows too rough *Yale 1* heads>head

961 *plough-tail*: 'the rear or handles of a plough. Symbolically, the following of the plough, the place of the farm-labourer, farm-labour': OED².

964 *exceeds . . . year*: cf. 2080–1. Perhaps deliberately, but probably inadvertently, Browning exaggerates the youth of the four assassins. What he remembers is that there are three occasions in OYB when the lawyers make some reference to two of the assassins, Gambassini and Pasquini, as potentially 'minors', and this as a mitigating factor: see OYB xxxix (37), cxxxviii (143), ccxxx (232). The age of minority in the England of Browning's day was 21. However, at OYB ccxxx (232) we learn that Pasquini's baptismal certificate was produced for the court, showing him to be 24 at the time of the murder, and that the age of 'minority' that the lawyers were thinking of was 25. Agostinelli and Baldeschi were almost certainly over 25.

With the mere child he manages amiss—
But would not interfere and make bad worse
For twice the fractious tears and prayers: thou know'st
Civility better, Marzi-Medici,
Governor for thy kinsman the Granduke!
Fit representative of law, man's lamp
I' the magistrate's grasp full-flare, no rushlight-end
Sputtering 'twixt thumb and finger of the priest!
Whose answer to the couple's cry for help
Is a threat,—whose remedy of Pompilia's wrong,
A shrug o' the shoulder, and facetious word
Or wink, traditional with Tuscan wits,
To Guido in the doorway. Laud to law!
The wife is pushed back to the husband, he
Who knows how these home-squabblings persecute

969 *MS* {line added later} *MS* child, 970 *MS* spoil the game>make bad worse 971 *MS* p[?l]>prayers: *MS* they>thou *MS* know>know'st 972 *MS* Their duty>Civility *MS* Marzi-Medici 973 *MS* Cousin *MS* Grand-Duke 974 *MS* This *MS* human law,>law, *MS* light>lamp 975 *MS* Magistrate's>I' the magistrate's *MS* [ ]>grasp *MS* [?twixt] of wax>rushlight-end 976 *MS* [ ]>Sputtering *MS* twixt *MS* priest,— *977 *MS* to these Comparinis' cry, *1868 1872* to these Comparini's cry *1888* couple's Comparini's *DC BrU* couple's Comparini's>couple's *1889* couple's 978 *MS* menace,—whose cure *MS 1868* wrong 979 *MS* of *1868* of>o' *MS 1868 1872* a facetious *MS* wor[ ]>word, 980 *MS* [ ]>The 981 *MS* {beginning of fo. 210} *MS* doorway; and you've law, 982 *MS* There's the wife pushed 983 *MS* That *MS* domestic squabblings>home squabblings *MS* plague>persecute

972 *Civility*: proper manners and behaviour, civilized conduct (used with high irony). Cf. I. 287 n.

Marzi-Medici: Vincenzo Marzi-Medici, Governor (*Commissario*) of Arezzo. His full name occurs in the letter he wrote to Abate Paolo, 2 Aug. 1694, supporting the Franceschini against the Comparini: OYB lxxxi f. (89–90). Marzi-Medici was not, however, as Browning supposes, kinsman to the Grand Duke of Florence, Cosimo III de' Medici.

975 *rushlight-end*: feeble bit of candle. A rushlight or rush-candle is the simplest form of candle, made by dipping the pith of a rush in tallow.

977–8 *answer . . . threat*: 'Accordingly when I saw that they [the Comparini] had become incorrigible, and were the talk of the town, . . . I availed myself of the authority vested in me by His Serene Highness, and threatened them with prison and punishment unless they behaved themselves': Marzi-Medici to Abate Paolo, 2 Aug. 1694: OYB lxxxii (90).

981 *Laud*: praise.

People who have the public good to mind,
And work best with a silence in the court!

Ah, but I save my word at least for thee,
Archbishop, who art under me, i' the Church,
As I am under God,—thou, chosen by both
To do the shepherd's office, feed the sheep—
How of this lamb that panted at thy foot
While the wolf pressed on her within crook's reach?
Wast thou the hireling that did turn and flee?
With thee at least anon the little word!

Such denizens o' the cave now cluster round
And heat the furnace sevenfold: time indeed
A bolt from heaven should cleave roof and clear place,
Transfix and show the world, suspiring flame,
The main offender, scar and brand the rest
Hurrying, each miscreant to his hole: then flood
And purify the scene with outside day—
Which yet, in the absolutest drench of dark,
Ne'er wants a witness, some stray beauty-beam
To the despair of hell.

[—]

984 *MS* mind,— 985 *MS* And what a lovely 986 *MS* {no new paragraph} *MS* have *MS* thee *987 *MS* under me as I>who art under me in the church *1868 1872* under me in *1888 1889* under, i' 988 *MS* thou placed>thou chosen 994 *MS* {no new paragraph} *MS* occupants>denizens *MS* of *Yale 1* of>o' *MS* cluster around>now cluster round 995 *MS* The cauldron and who feeds the furnace: time>Who heats the furnace sevenfold: time indeed 1000 *MS* ^outside^ 1002 *MS* beam of God's>beauty-beam 1003 *MS* Wrestling with>To the despair of

989 *feed . . . sheep*: i.e. spiritually nourish the Christians in his charge—from Christ's moving injunction to St Peter, in John 21: 15–17.

991–2 *wolf . . . hireling*: cf. John 10: 12–13.

995 *heat . . . sevenfold*: cf. Dan. 3: 19. The Franceschini family, the Governor, and the Archbishop—the 'denizens o' the cave'—persecute Pompilia just as Nebuchadnezzar persecuted Shadrach, Meshach, and Abednego: Nebuchadnezzar had the fiery furnace heated 'seven times more than it was wont to be heated' to receive them.

997 *suspiring flame*: by breathing out, sighing forth, flame (i.e. light). The sense is that, by suspiring flame, the lightning bolt reveals the 'main offender' (Guido).

First of the first,
Such I pronounce Pompilia, then as now
Perfect in whiteness: stoop thou down, my child,
Give one good moment to the poor old Pope
Heart-sick at having all his world to blame—
Let me look at thee in the flesh as erst,
Let me enjoy the old clean linen garb,
Not the new splendid vesture! Armed and crowned,
Would Michael, yonder, be, nor crowned nor armed,
The less pre-eminent angel? Everywhere
I see in the world the intellect of man,
That sword, the energy his subtle spear,
The knowledge which defends him like a shield—
Everywhere; but they make not up, I think,
The marvel of a soul like thine, earth's flower
She holds up to the softened gaze of God!
It was not given Pompilia to know much,
Speak much, to write a book, to move mankind,

1004 *MS* {New paragraph indicated by 'N. P.' in left-hand margin} 1006 *MS* Splendid of>Perfect in *MS 1868* whiteness— *MS* stand thou up,>look thou down, 1007 *MS* aged>poor old 1008 *MS* [ ]>his 1011 *MS* {beginning of fo. 211} *MS* Sword and shield—>Armed and crowned, 1012 *MS* Would not prince Michael stand, apart from these,>Would Michael, yonder, stand, nor crowned nor armed, 1013 *MS* [ ]>The *MS* preeminent 1016 *MS* that>which *MS* shield 1017 *MS* Everywhere, 1019 *MS* God. 1020 *MS* to this Pompilia>Pompilia to know much, 1021 *MS* rule a land,> move mankind,

1010–11 *old . . . vesture*: i.e. the vesture that symbolizes her earthly purity, not the more amazing vision of her as she is in heaven with her 'new splendid vesture' (her triumphant dress in Heaven). Cf. Rev. 19: 8, where 'fine linen, clean and white' symbolizes 'the righteousness of saints'.

1011–13 *Armed . . . angel?*: i.e. 'even without her heavenly apparel, Pompilia is clearly a saint'. The statue that the Pope refers to as 'yonder' is in fact some way away. It is the enormous bronze of the archangel Michael, sheathing his sword, on the top of the Castel Sant'Angelo, the fortress of Rome. The statue that Browning knew (the present one) was cast by the Flemish rococo sculptor Pieter Anton Verschaffelt (1710–93) for Benedict XIV, and set up in 1752. This replaced an earlier marble statue by Raffaele da Montelupo, which is the one that would have been standing in Innocent XII's day.

1015–16 *sword . . . shield*: these metaphors are suggested by Eph. 6: 14–17.

Be memorized by who records my time.
Yet if in purity and patience, if
In faith held fast despite the plucking fiend,
Safe like the signet stone with the new name
That saints are known by,—if in right returned
For wrong, most pardon for worst injury,
If there be any virtue, any praise,—
Then will this woman-child have proved—who knows?—
Just the one prize vouchsafed unworthy me,
Seven years a gardener of the untoward ground,
I till,—this earth, my sweat and blood manure
All the long day that barrenly grows dusk:
At least one blossom makes me proud at eve
Born 'mid the briers of my enclosure! Still
(Oh, here as elsewhere, nothingness of man!)
Those be the plants, imbedded yonder South
To mellow in the morning, those made fat
By the master's eye, that yield such timid leaf,
Uncertain bud, as product of his pains!

1024 *MS* kept firm>still firm *MS* {no comma} 1025 *MS* Like the white>Held like the *MS* signet-stone 1027 *MS* forgiveness>most pardon *etc.* *MS* most>worst 1029 *MS* well nigh>—who knows?— 1030 *MS* The one reward>Just the one prize *MS* [ ]>vouchsafed *MS* {no comma} 1031 *MS 1868* Ten *MS* the>a *MS* {no comma} 1032 *MS* This earth I till, *MS* which>my *MS* manure. 1033 {not found in *MS*} 1034 *MS* this *MS* blossom>beauty *MS* meets my hand at eve—>makes me proud at eve 1035 *MS* mid *MS* briars 1037 *MS* are *MS* set yonder in the South>embedded yonder South 1039 *MS* []>eye, *etc.* *MS* the timid *MS* leaf 1040 *MS* {beginning of fo. 212} *MS* The uncertain bud, product of all the pains—

1022 *memorized*: recorded (in the history books), perpetuated in the memory.

1024 *plucking*: clutching; suggested by John 10: 28–9. Cf. 641–2 n.

1025–6 *signet . . . by*: cf. Rev. 2: 17: 'To him that overcometh will I give to eat of the hidden manna, and will give him a white stone, and in the stone a new name written, which no man knoweth saving he that receiveth it.'

1028 *If . . . praise*: cf. Phil. 4: 8: 'if there be any virtue, and if there be any praise, think on these things.'

1031 *untoward*: intractable.

1037–9 *plants . . . eye*: cf. Ps. 92: 13–14.

While—see how this mere chance-sown cleft-nursed seed
That sprang up by the wayside 'neath the foot
Of the enemy, this breaks all into blaze,
Spreads itself, one wide glory of desire
To incorporate the whole great sun it loves
From the inch-height whence it looks and longs! My flower,
My rose, I gather for the breast of God,
This I praise most in thee, where all I praise,
That having been obedient to the end
According to the light allotted, law
Prescribed thy life, still tried, still standing test,—
Dutiful to the foolish parents first,
Submissive next to the bad husband,—nay,
Tolerant of those meaner miserable
That did his hests, eked out the dole of pain,—
Thou, patient thus, couldst rise from law to law,
The old to the new, promoted at one cry
O' the trump of God to the new service, not
To longer bear, but henceforth fight, be found
Sublime in new impatience with the foe!

1041 *MS* ^mere^ **MS 1868 1872 1888* chance-sown, *DC BrU* chance-sown,>chance-sown *1889* chance-sown *1868 1872 1888* seed, *DC BrU* seed,>seed *1889* seed 1042 *MS* This>This that *MS* [ ]>neath *MS* hoof>foot 1043 *MS* breaks out into *MS* one blaze,>a blaze, *Yale 1* a blaze,>blaze, 1044 *MS* [ ]>Spreads *MS* in a>one wide 1045 *MS* wide>great *MS* [ ]>loves 1046 *MS* longs. 1047 *MS* Perfect and true rose gathered for God's breast, 1048 *MS* all is 1050 *MS* [ ]>law 1051 *MS* And law of>Prescribed thy *MS* tried and standing test, 1056 *MS* to law 1058 *MS* Of 1059 *MS* Bear any more, but fight now, be sublime>Bear longer, but fight now, be found henceforth 1060 *MS* In all>Sublime in all *MS* foe.

1041–3 *chance-sown . . . enemy*: cf. Luke 8: 5, 12.

1046 *the inch-height*: i.e. the lowly position. The flower, only an inch off the ground, aspires to the sun.

1054 *miserable*: (pl.) wretched ones. The Pope is probably thinking of Girolamo, Guido's mother, and perhaps also Margherita, Guido's mistress-servant, whom he used to try and lure Pompilia into an affair with Caponsacchi.

1058 *trump of God*: in the Bible a 'trump of God' is often a sound raising people up, usually from earth to heaven, but here from one level of spirituality to another: from enduring the iniquities of man, to fighting positively on God's side against evil. Cf. 1 Cor. 15: 52, Thess. 4: 16, Rev. 4: 1.

Endure man and obey God: plant firm foot
On neck of man, tread man into the hell
Meet for him, and obey God all the more!
Oh child that didst despise thy life so much
When it seemed only thine to keep or lose,
How the fine ear felt fall the first low word
"Value life, and preserve life for My sake!"
Thou didst . . . how shall I say? . . . receive so long
The standing ordinance of God on earth,
What wonder if the novel claim had clashed
With old requirement, seemed to supersede
Too much the customary law? But, brave,
Thou at first prompting of what I call God,
And fools call Nature, didst hear, comprehend,
Accept the obligation laid on thee,
Mother elect, to save the unborn child,
As brute and bird do, reptile and the fly,
Ay and, I nothing doubt, even tree, shrub, plant
And flower o' the field, all in a common pact
To worthily defend the trust of trusts,
Life from the Ever Living:—didst resist—
Anticipate the office that is mine—
And with his own sword stay the upraised arm,

1061 *MS* Bear with>Endure *MS* plant a foot>set firm>plant firm foot 1062 *MS* the face>the neck *Yale 1* the neck>neck *MS* and tread him>tread man 1063 *MS* That helps>Meet for 1065 *MS* {no comma} 1066 *MS* Who gave thee the fine ear for the small word>Who gave thee the fine ear distinguished the low word>How felt the fine ear [ ] the first low word>How felt the fine ear prick the first low word 1067 *MS* my *MS* sake?" 1068 *MS* {beginning of fo. 213} *MS* hadst . . *1868 1872* didst . . *MS* say? . . received *1868 1872* say? . . 1070 *MS* should clash 1071 *MS* seem 1072 *MS* [ ]>brave! 1073 *MS* {no comma} 1074 *MS* nature, 1077 *MS* the brute>brute 1078 *MS* the>even *MS* the>shrub, 1079 *MS* of *MS* all>found>all 1080 *MS* To [ ]>To save the glory of that gift,>To [ ] the glory of that gift,>To worthily defend that trust of trusts *1868* that trust 1083 *MS* break>stay

1069 *standing . . . earth*: this refers back to 1061: 'Endure man and obey God.'

1083 *his own sword*: i.e. Guido's own sword. The Pope is referring to the incident in the inn at Castelnuovo where Pompilia snatched Guido's own sword to attack him. The Pope takes this incident as symbolic of the wider way in which she changed from patience and endurance under suffering, to *active* opposition to evil: cf. 1061–3.

The endeavour of the wicked, and defend
Him who,—again in my default,—was there
For visible providence: one less true than thou
To touch, i' the past, less practised in the right,
Approved less far in all docility
To all instruction,—how had such an one
Made scruple "Is this motion a decree?"
It was authentic to the experienced ear
O' the good and faithful servant. Go past me
And get thy praise,—and be not far to seek
Presently when I follow if I may!

And surely not so very much apart
Need I place thee, my warrior-priest,—in whom
What if I gain the other rose, the gold,
We grave to imitate God's miracle,
Greet monarchs with, good rose in its degree?
Irregular noble 'scapegrace—son the same!

1086 *MS* how had one>how might one>one *etc.* 1087 *MS* touch in *Yale 1* touch in>touch, i' 1088 *MS* in all docility so far *1868* so far 1089 *MS* such one straight 1090 *MS* scruple, *Yale 1* scruple,>scruple 1092 *MS* Of 1095 *MS* {beginning of fo. 214} 1096 *MS* warrior priest,— 1098 *MS* {no comma} *Yale 1* 'grave>grave 1099 *MS* And greet some monarchs, good in its degree?>Greet monarchs with, good rose in its degree? *1100 *MS 1868 1872 1888* scapegrace— *DC BrU* scapegrace—>'scapegrace— *1889* 'scapegrace—

1085 *Him*: i.e. Caponsacchi.

1089–90 *how . . . decree?*: i.e. 'how could such a one—a person practised in responding to God—have asked the doubting question "Is this prompting God's order?" ' Caponsacchi only hesitated in this way because he was less holy than Pompilia. A 'motion' here is an inward prompting or stirring of soul. Johnson cites South: 'Let a good man obey every good motion rising in his heart, knowing that every such motion proceeds from God.,'

1092 *good . . . servant*: cf. Matt. 25: 23.

1097–9 *other rose . . . degree*: at l. 1047, Pompilia is the first rose. The allusion is to the Golden Rose, exquisitely crafted in pure gold, given by the popes to outstanding Catholic kings and queens, princes and princesses, noblemen and generals, as a mark of esteem and affection. The rose is blessed on Laetare Sunday in Lent. Famous recipients have included Isabella I of Spain and Henry VIII of England. Browning's Pope is exactly right in saying that the rose is crafted 'to imitate God's miracle', i.e. to symbolize the incarnate Christ and his sacrifice: 'The golden flower and its shining splendour show forth Christ and His Kingly Majesty, who is heralded by the prophet as

Faulty—and peradventure ours the fault
Who still misteach, mislead, throw hook and line,
Thinking to land leviathan forsooth,
Tame the scaled neck, play with him as a bird,
And bind him for our maidens! Better bear
The King of Pride go wantoning awhile,
Unplagued by cord in nose and thorn in jaw,
Through deep to deep, followed by all that shine,
Churning the blackness hoary: He who made
The comely terror, He shall make the sword
To match that piece of netherstone his heart,
Ay, nor miss praise thereby; who else shut fire
I' the stone, to leap from mouth at sword's first stroke,
In lamps of love and faith, the chivalry
That dares the right and disregards alike
The yea and nay o' the world? Self-sacrifice,—
What if an idol took it? Ask the Church
Why she was wont to turn each Venus here,—

1102 *MS 1868 1872* line 1103 *MS* bring>land *etc.* 1105 *MS* Better leave 1111 *MS* {no comma} 1113 *MS* Fast in>In *MS* leap out, at>leap from mouth at sword's 1114 *MS* burning lamps>lamps 1116 *MS* smile and frown>yea and nay *MS* of the world,—self-sacrifice,— 1118 *MS* idol> Venus *MS* here *Yale 1* here,>here,—

"the flower of the field and lily of the valleys" . . . and the thorns and red tint tell of His Passion according to Isa. (lxiii, 2): "Why then is thy apparel red, and they garments like theirs that tread in the winepress?" ': *Catholic Encyclopedia*, vi. 629.

1103–11 *leviathan . . . heart*: the Pope makes creative use of the image of leviathan in Job ch. 41. In order, the references are to verses 15–16, 22–23 (for the impenetrable 'scaled neck'), 5, 34, 1–2, 32 (for the monster's shining wake as it passes through the water), 12 ('comely'), 26, 24. Here the monster leviathan stands for man's (specifically Caponsacchi's) unruly nature. It cannot, says the Pope, be simply trained or caught: mixed with Caponsacchi's pride and confusion, there is courage and virtue. See next n.

1111 *piece of netherstone*: cf. Job 41: 24: 'His heart is . . . as hard as a piece of the nether millstone.' Initially Caponsacchi (like leviathan) is hard-hearted, but God has the power to change this. See next n.

1113–14 *leap . . . faith*: cf. Job 41: 19: 'Out of his mouth go burning lamps, and sparks of fire leap out.' At the first stroke of God's sword, Caponsacchi's stone-like heart gives off 'lamps of love and faith' that burst out of him, just as 'lamps' and 'sparks' burst out of the mouth of leviathan.

1116–22 *Self-sacrifice . . . gratitude*: 'What if Caponsacchi's self-sacrifice was offered, primarily and directly, to an idol of his own (i.e. to Pompilia), and only indirectly to God and His saints, just as the love and gratitude of the half-Pagan, half-Christian

Poor Rome perversely lingered round, despite
Instruction, for the sake of purblind love,—
Into Madonna's shape, and waste no whit
Of aught so rare on earth as gratitude!
All this sweet savour was not ours but thine,
Nard of the rock, a natural wealth we name
Incense, and treasure up as food for saints,
When flung to us—whose function was to give
Not find the costly perfume. Do I smile?
Nay, Caponsacchi, much I find amiss,
Blameworthy, punishable in this freak
Of thine, this youth prolonged, though age was ripe,
This masquerade in sober day, with change
Of motley too,—now hypocrite's disguise,
Now fool's-costume: which lie was least like truth,

1120 *MS* love, *Yale 1* love,>love,— 1121 *MS* a God, and so>Madonna's shape, and 1123 *MS* {beginning of fo. 215} 1125 *MS* Incense and 1130 *MS 1868* prolonged though 1132 *1868* hypocrite's-disguise, 1133 *MS* fool's costume:

Roman were offered, primarily and directly, to the Venus whom the Church had changed into Madonna's shape, and only indirectly to Madonna herself? The self-sacrifice, like the love and gratitude, was there all the same': Cook, 217. Cook compares Pope, *The Dunciad*, III. 101–3: 'Till Peter's Keys some christen'd Jove adorn, / And Pan to Moses lends his Pagan horn; / See graceless Venus to a Virgin turn'd, . . . ' , and Pope's own note on these lines: 'After the Government of *Rome* devolved to the Popes, their zeal was for some time exerted in demolishing the Heathen Temples and Statues, so that the *Goths* scarce destroyed more Monuments of Antiquity out of Rage, than these out of Devotion. At length they spar'd some of the Temples by converting them to Churches, and some of the Statues, by modifying them into Images of Saints.'

1123 *sweet savour*: i.e. the sweet smell of Caponsacchi's virtue and self-sacrifice; cf. Eph. 5: 2, Phil. 4: 18.

not . . . thine: i.e. not the Church's, but Caponsacchi's own.

1124 *Nard . . . rock*: an image of Caponsacchi (and his virtue) as nard (i.e. spikenard, a sweet-smelling aromatic plant) growing wildly in a rock. The Pope can call this 'wild' virtue 'incense', i.e. holiness—drawing it within his Christian frame of reference—but he is aware that it is something that has grown up outside the Church's influence, even if now it can be drawn within the Church and 'treasured up as food for saints'.

1132 *motley*: i.e. foolish clothes. Motley is a cloth of mixed colours, and hence the parti-coloured costume worn by the professional fool or jester. First Caponsacchi was in 'hypocrite's disguise' in the period when he was an unbelieving, worldly canon, then he was in 'fool's-costume' when he dressed as a gentleman during his rescue of Pompilia.

Which the ungainlier, more discordant garb
With that symmetric soul inside my son,
The churchman's or the worldling's,—let him judge,
Our adversary who enjoys the task!
I rather chronicle the healthy rage,—
When the first moan broke from the martyr-maid
At that uncaging of the beasts,—made bare
My athlete on the instant, gave such good
Great undisguised leap over post and pale
Right into the mid-cirque, free fighting-place.
There may have been rash stripping—every rag
Went to the winds,—infringement manifold
Of laws prescribed pudicity, I fear,
In this impulsive and prompt self-display!
Ever such tax comes of the foolish youth;
Men mulct the wiser manhood, and suspect
No veritable star swims out of cloud.
Bear thou such imputation, undergo
The penalty I nowise dare relax,—
Conventional chastisement and rebuke.
But for the outcome, the brave starry birth
Conciliating earth with all that cloud,

1136 *MS* Churchman's *MS* Worldling's,— *1868 1872* worldling's,— *MS* judge 1137 *MS* Thine *1868* Adversary *MS* task: 1138 *Yale 2* the>what 1143 *MS* cirque's midst,>mid cirque, *MS* and>free 1144 *MS* {stripping— *interlined above undeleted* work when} 1145 *MS* infringement's, much I fear,>infringement manifold 1146 *MS* laws our time prescribes pudicity,>laws prescribed pudicity, I fear, 1147 *MS* self-display— 1148–50 *MS* {lines added later} 1148 *MS* Such is the fruit of the first foolish life,>Ever such tax comes of the foolish youth, 1149 *MS* Casting youth, my son>Men mulct the manhood, and suspect>Men mulct the [ ] manhood, and suspect>Men mulct the wiser manhood, and suspect 1150 *MS 1868 1872* cloud: *1888 1889* cloud. 1151 *MS* the>such 1152 *MS* must>dare 1153 *MS* Loving the son, I chastise>Conventional chastisement 1154 *MS* {beginning of fo. 216} *MS* brave bold>the brave 1155 *MS* {no comma}

1137 *Our adversary*: the Devil.

1139–43 *martyr-maid . . . fighting-place*: Caponsacchi is a gladiator defending an early Christian martyr (Pompilia) from wild beasts in the arena of the Coliseum.

1146 *pudicity*: modesty.

1149 *mulct*: reward.

Thank heaven as I do! Ay, such championship
Of God at first blush, such prompt cheery thud
Of glove on ground that answers ringingly
The challenge of the false knight,—watch we long
And wait we vainly for its gallant like
From those appointed to the service, sworn
His body-guard with pay and privilege—
White-cinct, because in white walks sanctity,
Red-socked, how else proclaim fine scorn of flesh,
Unchariness of blood when blood faith begs!
Where are the men-at-arms with cross on coat?
Aloof, bewraying their attire: whilst thou
In mask and motley, pledged to dance not fight,
Sprang'st forth the hero! In thought, word and deed,
How throughout all thy warfare thou wast pure,
I find it easy to believe: and if
At any fateful moment of the strange
Adventure, the strong passion of that strait,
Fear and surprise, may have revealed too much,—
As when a thundrous midnight, with black air
That burns, rain-drops that blister, breaks a spell,
Draws out the excessive virtue of some sheathed
Shut unsuspected flower that hoards and hides
Immensity of sweetness,—so, perchance,
Might the surprise and fear release too much
The perfect beauty of the body and soul

1159 *MS* look>watch **MS 1868 1872 1888* long, *DC BrU* long,>long *1889* long 1160 *MS* Exp>And *etc.* 1165 *MS 1868* begs? 1166 *MS* soldiery> men-at-arms 1168 *MS* the poor frippery,>mask and motley, 1169 *MS* Sprangst 1170 *MS* {no comma} 1172 *MS* that>the 1174 *MS* surprise may 1175 *MS* some>a 1177 *MS* flower>sheathed 1180 *MS* draw> release *etc.*

1156–9 *championship . . . knight*: cf. 'Count Gismond', 73–92.

1163 *White-cinct*: i.e. with white belt or girdle.

1164 *Red-socked*: as worn by cardinals and monsignors. As the Pope explains it, the red socks indicate 'fine scorn of flesh', 'unchariness of blood'. See next n.

1165 *Unchariness . . . begs*: i.e. a willingness to die or be wounded for a good cause, the willingness to be a martyr. The end of the sentence is an inversion: 'when faith begs blood'.

1173 *strait*: difficult time or situation.

Thou savedst in thy passion for God's sake,
He who is Pity. Was the trial sore?
Temptation sharp? Thank God a second time!
Why comes temptation but for man to meet
And master and make crouch beneath his foot,
And so be pedestaled in triumph? Pray
"Lead us into no such temptations, Lord!"
Yea, but, O Thou whose servants are the bold,
Lead such temptations by the head and hair,
Reluctant dragons, up to who dares fight,
That so he may do battle and have praise!
Do I not see the praise?—that while thy mates
Bound to deserve i' the matter, prove at need
Unprofitable through the very pains
We gave to train them well and start them fair,—
Are found too stiff, with standing ranked and ranged,
For onset in good earnest, too obtuse
Of ear, through iteration of command,
For catching quick the sense of the real cry,—
Thou, whose sword-hand was used to strike the lute,
Whose sentry-station graced some wanton's gate,
Thou didst push forward and show mettle, shame
The laggards, and retrieve the day. Well done!
Be glad thou hast let light into the world
Through that irregular breach o' the boundary,—see

1182 *MS* {beginning of fo. 217} *MS* borest>savedst *MS* on thy bosom for 1183 *MS 1868 1872* Pity: was 1187 *MS 1868 1872* pedestalled 1190 *MS* up to who dares fight>by the head and hair *MS* {no comma} 1191 *MS* {line added later} *MS* {no comma} 1194 *MS* in *MS* proved>prove 1196 *MS* up to>well and 1197 *MS* []>Are *MS* stiff with *MS* in the ranks,>ranked and ranged, 1200 *MS* To catch us the first breath of the battle-cry,—>To catch aright the sense of the real cry,—>For catching quick the sense of the real cry,— 1202 watch word>sentry station *etc.* 1205 *MS* sure>glad **1868 1872 1888* world, *DC BrU* world,>world *1889* world 1206 *MS* of

1185–7 *Why . . . triumph*: cf. 'Bishop Blougram's Apology', 666–8.

1188 "*Lead . . . temptations*: from the Lord's Prayer, the 'Our Father'.

1191 *Reluctant dragons*: echoing the *reluctantes dracones* (literally 'snakes fighting back') of Horace, *Odes*, IV. iv. 11.

The same upon thy path and march assured,
Learning anew the use of soldiership,
Self-abnegation, freedom from all fear,
Loyalty to the life's end! Ruminate,
Deserve the initiatory spasm,—once more
Work, be unhappy but bear life, my son!

And troop you, somewhere 'twixt the best and worst,
Where crowd the indifferent product, all too poor
Makeshift, starved samples of humanity!
Father and mother, huddle there and hide!
A gracious eye may find you! Foul and fair,
Sadly mixed natures: self-indulgent,—yet
Self-sacrificing too: how the love soars,
How the craft, avarice, vanity and spite
Sink again! So they keep the middle course,
Slide into silly crime at unaware,
Slip back upon the stupid virtue, stay
Nowhere enough for being classed, I hope
And fear. Accept the swift and rueful death,
Taught, somewhat sternlier than is wont, what waits
The ambiguous creature,—how the one black tuft
Steadies the aim of the arrow just as well
As the wide faultless white on the bird's breast!
Nay, you were punished in the very part
That looked most pure of speck,—'t was honest love
Betrayed you,—did love seem most worthy pains,

1210 *MS* end: ruminate, 1211 *MS* {beginning of fo. 218} 1213 *MS* twixt 1215 *MS* humanity, 1216 *MS* hide,— 1217 *MS* —A 1222 *MS* crime easy and half-aware,>silly crime at unaware, 1223 *MS* as readily into> upon the stupid 1225 *MS* sharp>swift *MS* piteous death,>rueful fate—>rueful death, 1226 *MS* sadlier>somewhat sternlier *MS* the rest>is wont *MS* doom betides>doom awaits>waits 1228 *Yale 1* Studies>Steadies 1229 *MS* broad>wide *MS* ^speckless^>^faultless^ *MS 1868* breast. 1231 *MS* speck,—the honest *1868* the honest 1232 *Yale 2* you,—>you: *MS* it>love

---

1211 *Deserve . . . spasm*: i.e. 'live up to the birth-pang that has begun the life of faith in you'.

1223 *stupid*: unknowing, naïve.

Challenge such purging, since ordained survive
When all the rest of you was done with? Go!
Never again elude the choice of tints!
White shall not neutralize the black, nor good
Compensate bad in man, absolve him so:
Life's business being just the terrible choice.

So do I see, pronounce on all and some
Grouped for my judgment now,—profess no doubt
While I pronounce: dark, difficult enough
The human sphere, yet eyes grow sharp by use,
I find the truth, dispart the shine from shade,
As a mere man may, with no special touch
O' the lynx-gift in each ordinary orb:
Nay, if the popular notion class me right,
One of well-nigh decayed intelligence,—
What of that? Through hard labour and good will,
And habitude that gives a blind man sight
At the practised finger-ends of him, I do
Discern, and dare decree in consequence,
Whatever prove the peril of mistake.
Whence, then, this quite new quick cold thrill,—cloud-like,
This keen dread creeping from a quarter scarce
Suspected in the skies I nightly scan?

1233 *MS* much *MS* as what should *Yale 1* as what should>as ordained *1868* as ordained 1234 *MS* Dare>Go! 1235 *MS* alternate black with white:> play>elude the choice of tints: 1236 *MS* Good>White *MS* bad,> black, *MS* yet>bad>good 1237 *MS* The bad compensated by good absolve the soul>Compensate bad in man, absolve him so: 1238 *MS* {line added later} 1239 *MS* {beginning of fo. 219} *MS* {no new paragraph. Paragraphing obscured by this line's being at the head of the page} *MS* class, declare of>see, pronounce on 1241 *MS* declare: 1243 [?see] the man>find the truth, 1244 *MS* I, a mere man, with no especial touch 1245 *MS* Of *MS* orb, 1246 *MS* shall decide,>weigh at all>class me right 1247 *MS* Obsolete, of>One well nigh of *1868 1872* well nigh 1248 *MS* {no comma} 1251 *MS* [?now] shall act>dare decree *MS* {no commas} 1252 *MS* mistake: 1253 *MS* Whence then this *MS* other>quite new *MS* thrill, cloud-like 1254 *MS* Dread>This keen dread *MS* what quarter?>a quarter scarce

1243 *dispart*: separate, sever.
1245 *lynx-gift*: lynxes are proverbially keen-sighted; cf. XI. 917, XII. 413.

What slacks the tense nerve, saps the wound-up spring
Of the act that should and shall be, sends the mount
And mass o' the whole man's-strength,—conglobed so late—
Shudderingly into dust, a moment's work?
While I stand firm, go fearless, in this world,
For this life recognize and arbitrate,
Touch and let stay, or else remove a thing,
Judge "This is right, this object out of place,"
Candle in hand that helps me and to spare,—
What if a voice deride me, "Perk and pry!
"Brighten each nook with thine intelligence!
"Play the good householder, ply man and maid
"With tasks prolonged into the midnight, test
"Their work and nowise stint of the due wage
"Each worthy worker: but with gyves and whip
"Pay thou misprision of a single point
"Plain to thy happy self who lift'st the light,
"Lament'st the darkling,—bold to all beneath!
"What if thyself adventure, now the place
"Is purged so well? Leave pavement and mount roof,
"Look round thee for the light of the upper sky,

1256 *MS* wound up *MS* [ ]>spring 1257 *MS* mount— 1258 *MS* Of>The pride>And mass *Yale 1* of>o' *MS* [?man confined in] [ ]>strength confirmed so late *Yale 1* strength,––>man's-strength,— 1259 *MS* in one moment to the dust?>into dust, one moment's work? 1260 *MS* fir[ ] [ ]>firm, go 1261 *MS* [ ]>For *MS 1868 1872* recognise *MS* arbitrate— 1263 *MS* Say *Yale 1* Say>Judge *MS* place" *Yale 2* place,">place,—" 1264 *Yale 2* me and to spare,—>sufficently,—[*sic*] 1265 *MS* pry— 1266–84 *MS* {no quotation marks at beginnings of lines} 1267 *MS* {beginning of fo. 220} 1268 night,> [?midnight] 1270 *MS* The well deserving,>Each worthy worker, *MS* spare> nor>with *MS* nor>and 1271 *MS* With whoso stumbles at>Spare whoso stumbles at>Pay thou misprision of a single point 1272 *MS* lift 1273 *MS* Look on>Lament *MS* beneath!" 1275 *MS* well, leave 1276 *MS* lights>light

1258 *conglobed*: focused, gathered together (in a single mass or ball).

1261 *recognize*: review, examine.

1265 *voice*: i.e. a voice of religious doubt.

Perk: thrust, peep (with your candle).

1271 *misprision*: misunderstanding, misapprehension. Cf. VIII. 428.

1273 *darkling*: i.e. ignorant person, person in the dark. Usually used, by Browning and others, as adj. or adv., only rarely (as here) as a noun.

bold . . . beneath! : i.e. 'to all upon whom the light of your candle falls': Cook, 218.

"The fire which lit thy fire which finds default
"In Guido Franceschini to his cost!
"What if, above in the domain of light,
"Thou miss the accustomed signs, remark eclipse?
"Shalt thou still gaze on ground nor lift a lid,—
"Steady in thy superb prerogative,
"Thy inch of inkling,—nor once face the doubt
"I' the sphere above thee, darkness to be felt?"

Yet my poor spark had for its source, the sun;
Thither I sent the great looks which compel
Light from its fount: all that I do and am
Comes from the truth, or seen or else surmised,
Remembered or divined, as mere man may:
I know just so, nor otherwise. As I know,
I speak,—what should I know, then, and how speak
Were there a wild mistake of eye or brain
As to recorded governance above?
If my own breath, only, blew coal alight
I styled celestial and the morning-star?

1277 *MS* the fire *Yale 1* the fire>thy fire *MS* [ ] [ ]>which finds 1278 *MS* the work of such an one as Guido here?>Guido Franceschini to his cost? *Yale 1* cost?>cost! 1279 *MS* {no commas} 1280 *MS* perceive>remark 1281 *MS* look steadily down>still gaze on ground 1282 *MS* Rejoice>Steady 1283 *MS* The 1284 *MS* In *MS* {no quotation mark at end} 1285 *MS* {no new paragraph} *MS* This poor>Yet this poor *MS* was first kindled at>had for its source, 1286 *MS* I>Thither I *MS* [?at]>compel 1289 *MS* may, 1291 *MS* know then and 1293 *MS 1868* In the recorded *MS* of>above?— 1294 *MS* My own *Yale 2* If my own breath, only,>If only my own breath *MS* the coal 1295 *MS* {beginning of fo. 221} *MS 1868* called *MS* [ ]>morning-star?

1277 *default*: failure, defect.

1283 *inkling*: understanding, intuition.

1284 *darkness . . . felt*: i.e. the darkness of religious doubt, something almost palpable. Browning is using metaphorically a phrase from Exod. 10: 21: 'And the Lord said unto Moses, Stretch out thine hand toward heaven, that there may be darkness over the land of Egypt, even darkness which may be felt.'

1289 *Remembered*: alluding to the Platonic doctrine of ἀνάμνησις ('recollection'): see Plato, *Phaedo* 72 E–78 B. Plato was Browning's favourite philosopher.

1294–5 *If . . . morning-star*: this particular religious doubt—the idea that God does not really exist, but that humankind creates him out of imaginative need and vision—derives from Ludwig Feuerbach, particularly his *Das Wesen des Christentums* (1841; 'The Essence of Christianity').

I, who in this world act resolvedly,
Dispose of men, their bodies and their souls,
As they acknowledge or gainsay the light
I show them,—shall I too lack courage?—leave
I, too, the post of me, like those I blame?
Refuse, with kindred inconsistency,
To grapple danger whereby souls grow strong?
I am near the end; but still not at the end;
All to the very end is trial in life:
At this stage is the trial of my soul
Danger to face, or danger to refuse?
Shall I dare try the doubt now, or not dare?

O Thou,—as represented here to me
In such conception as my soul allows,—
Under Thy measureless, my atom width!—
Man's mind, what is it but a convex glass
Wherein are gathered all the scattered points
Picked out of the immensity of sky,

1296 *MS* Shall I,>I, 1297 *MS 1868* the body and the soul, 1298 *MS 1868* this light 1299 *MS* [ ]>lack *MS* heart,—desert *Yale 1* courage,—>courage?— 1300 *MS* I too the *MS* blame, >blame? 1301 *MS* {no commas} *Yale 1* {commas inserted} *Yale 2* Refuse,>—Refuse, 1302 *MS* To grapple with the *Yale 1* To grapple with the>Grapple with *1868* Grapple with *MS* danger whereby souls grow? *Yale 1* ^strong^ 1304 *MS 1868* till 1305 *MS* peril to *Yale 1* to>of 1306 *MS* I face, *MS* refuse? 1308 *MS* [ ]>here *MS* to me>and now>to me 1309 *MS* In this conception, wide as life allows,—>In such conception as my life lets lie,—>In such conception as my life allows,— *Yale 1* conception,>conception 1310 *MS* {line added later} *MS* An atom width, under>Under the measureless an atom width, *1868* {no comma} 1311 *MS* (The mind of man, that little>(Our mind—what is it but the>(Our mind—what is it but a *1868* mind— 1312 *MS* ^[ ]>scattered^ 1313 *MS* Descried in> Picked out of *MS* heaven>sky

1302 *grapple danger*: i.e. struggle with the threat (of religious doubt). This is Browning's characteristic belief that a person grows through the process of intellectual and emotional struggle.

1308 *Thou*: i.e. God. The old forms, from AV and elsewhere, add grandeur in the following passage ('Thou', 'Thyself', 'Thee', 'madest', 'framedst', etc.).

1311 *convex glass*: rounded mirror, hence one that reflects the domed vault of the stars. Cf. *Red Cotton Night-Cap Country*, 706–9, where a 'bauble world / Of silvered glass' or 'ball-convexity' reflects in miniature the things around it.

To re-unite there, be our heaven for earth,
Our known unknown, our God revealed to man?
Existent somewhere, somehow, as a whole;
Here, as a whole proportioned to our sense,—
There, (which is nowhere, speech must babble thus!)
In the absolute immensity, the whole
Appreciable solely by Thyself,—
Here, by the little mind of man, reduced
To littleness that suits his faculty,
In the degree appreciable too;
Between Thee and ourselves—nay even, again,
Below us, to the extreme of the minute,
Appreciable by how many and what diverse
Modes of the life Thou madest be! (why live
Except for love,—how love unless they know?)
Each of them, only filling to the edge,
Insect or angel, his just length and breadth,
Due facet of reflection,—full, no less,
Angel or insect, as Thou framedst things.
I it is who have been appointed here
To represent Thee, in my turn, on earth,
Just as, if new philosophy know aught,
This one earth, out of all the multitude
Of peopled worlds, as stars are now supposed,—

1314 *MS* To reunite [ ], make man's heaven on earth>To reunite there, be our heaven on earth *1868* To reunite there, be our heaven on earth, 1315 *MS* His>Our *MS* Unknown, *MS* his>our *MS* Man,—) *Yale 1* man?—>man? 1316 *MS* [ ]>Existent *MS* whole, 1317 *MS* As here, *MS* sense, *Yale 1* sense,>sense,— 1318 *MS* There,—which *MS* we> speech *MS* thus,— 1319 *MS* {line added later} 1320 *MS* ^solely^ *MS* thyself,— 1321 *MS* in>by 1323 *MS 1868* Appreciable too in the *MS* degree,— *1868* degree; 1324 *MS* {beginning of fo. 222} *MS* {no commas} 1326 *MS* Apprecia-ble, *MS* ^how many and^ 1327 *MS* thou makest be,—why life *1868* makest 1328 *MS* know? 1329 *MS* brim>edge 1330 *MS* allotted space>just length and breadth 1331 *MS* [ ]>Due *MS* full no less 1332 *MS* insect as thou *MS 1868* things,— 1333 *MS* It is I 1334 *MS* thee in my turn on 1335 *MS* 'tis held by some philosophy,>if new philosophy knows aught, 1336 *MS* not>out of all 1337 *MS* worlds which>peopled worlds which

1323 *In . . . too*: i.e. understandable to the extent that man can understand.

Was chosen, and no sun-star of the swarm,
For stage and scene of Thy transcendent act
Beside which even the creation fades
Into a puny exercise of power.
Choice of the world, choice of the thing I am,
Both emanate alike from Thy dread play
Of operation outside this our sphere
Where things are classed and counted small or great,—
Incomprehensibly the choice is Thine!
I therefore bow my head and take Thy place.
There is, beside the works, a tale of Thee
In the world's mouth, which I find credible:
I love it with my heart: unsatisfied,
I try it with my reason, nor discept
From any point I probe and pronounce sound.
Mind is not matter nor from matter, but
Above,—leave matter then, proceed with mind!
Man's be the mind recognized at the height,—
Leave the inferior minds and look at man!

1338 *MS* sun of all>sun star of 1339 *MS* thy 1341 *MS* power: 1342 *MS* man>thing 1343 *MS* [ ]>Both *MS 1868* the dread 1346 *MS* thine— 1347 *MS* thy 1348 *MS* was,>is, *MS* thee 1349 *MS 1868* {no comma} *MS* found>find 1350 {not found in *MS*} 1352 *MS* sound: 1353 *MS* {beginning of fo. 223} 1354 *MS* and>then, *MS 1868* mind: 1355 *MS* Man is the *MS* recognised *MS* height, 1356 *MS* all the other>the inferior *MS* Man, *1868* man.

1339 *Thy transcendent act*: God's act of becoming a human being in Jesus, i.e. the Incarnation.

1348–9 *tale . . . mouth*: i.e. the story of Jesus, as told in the Gospels.

1351 *discept*: quarrel with, express disagreement.

1355 *at the height*: at the top of creation (i.e. above the minds of animals, etc.).

1356–72 *Leave . . . complete*: Cook summarizes the argument here: 'Of the minds of created beings that of man is the highest, but perfection is assuredly not there; it is present in none of the three spheres in which we seek for it, neither in his strength, nor in his intelligence, nor in his love (or "goodness"). Can it be found, in all the three, in God? That God's strength and intelligence are perfect Natural Religion amply attests, but evidence that His love is also perfect is wanting "to the human eye in the present state" (1365); the two corresponding sides of the triangle—God's perfect strength and perfect intelligence—are plain to us, but its base—"love without a limit"—we cannot see': Cook, 219–20. It is 'this tale', the Incarnation, which makes clear God's 'love without a limit'.

Is he the strong, intelligent and good
Up to his own conceivable height? Nowise.
Enough o' the low,—soar the conceivable height,
Find cause to match the effect in evidence,
The work i' the world, not man's but God's; leave man!
Conjecture of the worker by the work:
Is there strength there?—enough: intelligence?
Ample: but goodness in a like degree?
Not to the human eye in the present state,
An isoscele deficient in the base.
What lacks, then, of perfection fit for God
But just the instance which this tale supplies
Of love without a limit? So is strength,
So is intelligence; let love be so,
Unlimited in its self-sacrifice,
Then is the tale true and God shows complete.
Beyond the tale, I reach into the dark,
Feel what I cannot see, and still faith stands:
I can believe this dread machinery
Of sin and sorrow, would confound me else,
Devised,—all pain, at most expenditure

1357 *MS* [ ]>he 1358 *MS* No wise: 1359 *MS* Leave Man,—>Enough of the low, *MS* go on with the *MS* height. 1360 *MS* To match the [ ] in evidence, not Man's:>Find cause to match the effect in evidence: 1361 *MS* Not Man's, then God's: leave Man.>The work in the world not Man, then God: leave Man. *1868* Works in the world, not man's, then God's; leave man: 1362 *MS* workman *MS* work, 1363 *MS* there,—>there?— *MS* intelligence,>intelligence? 1364 *MS* [ ]>but *MS* degree[ ]>degree? 1365 *MS* world. 1366 *MS* {line added later} *MS 1868* This *MS* base— 1367 *MS* lacks of the perfection then of God 1369 *MS* limit, like the strength 1370 *MS* Like the intelligence, then love is so, *1868* then love is so, 1371 *MS* {line added later} *MS* selfsacrifice: *1868* self-sacrifice: 1372 *MS* that tale true nor God incomplete.>the world's tale true and God complete. 1376 *MS* that confounds 1377 *MS* pain at

1366 *isoscele . . . base*: an isosceles triangle, i.e. one with two equal sides, and one shorter or 'deficient' base. The equal sides represent God's strength and intelligence, evident from looking at the world. The shorter side is God's 'goodness' or love, which is less evident.

1369 *So*: i.e. without a limit.

1374 *stands*: holds up, maintains itself.

1377–8 *all . . . pain*: i.e. God, who devised the painful probation of earthly life, only did so at the cost of Christ's suffering on the cross.

Of pain by Who devised pain,—to evolve,
By new machinery in counterpart,
The moral qualities of man—how else?—
To make him love in turn and be beloved,
Creative and self-sacrificing too,
And thus eventually God-like, (ay,
"I have said ye are Gods,"—shall it be said for nought?)
Enable man to wring, from out all pain,
All pleasure for a common heritage
To all eternity: this may be surmised,
The other is revealed,—whether a fact,
Absolute, abstract, independent truth,
Historic, not reduced to suit man's mind,—
Or only truth reverberate, changed, made pass
A spectrum into mind, the narrow eye,—
The same and not the same, else unconceived—
Though quite conceivable to the next grade
Above it in intelligence,—as truth
Easy to man were blindness to the beast
By parity of procedure,—the same truth
In a new form, but changed in either case:

1378 *MS* to pain's deviser,— *MS* evolve 1379 *MS* counterpart,— 1380 *MS* man, to wit, 1381 *MS* Which make *MS* beloved,— 1383 *MS* God-like,—ay, *Yale 1* —ay,>(ay, 1384 *MS* {beginning of fo. 224} *MS* Ye are Gods,"—evolve thereby *Yale 1* nought?—>nought?) 1385 {not found in *MS*} 1386 *MS* as a 1389 *MS* Absolutely, abstractedly,>Absolute, abstract, 1390 *MS* and uncoloured by>and uncramped by>not reduced to suit 1391 *MS* truth>changed, 1385 *MS* Above, below it, in intelligence 1396 {not found in *MS*} 1398 *MS* still changed *MS* case.

1384 *"I . . . Gods,"*: cf. Ps. 82: 6; John 10: 34: 'Jesus answered them, Is it not written in your law, I said, Ye are gods?'

1387–8 *this . . . The other*: this idea—that earthly probation will lead to heaven—can be guessed at from looking at the world; the other matter, the Incarnation, is something 'revealed' (i.e. shown by God to humankind, *not* deducible by reason).

1388–92 *whether . . . eye*: Browning is thinking here of the so-called Higher Criticism, works like Ernest Renan's *Vie de Jésus* (1863) and David Friedrich Strauss's *New Life of Jesus* (1864), historical-critical works which contested simple or literalistic understandings of the Gospels. The Pope says that his point holds, whether the Gospels are understood as literal historical fact, or understood symbolically as a message attuned to the limits of man's finite intelligence, 'the narrow eye'.

1393 *else unconceived*: [a truth] otherwise inconceivable (by the human mind).

What matter so intelligence be filled?
To a child, the sea is angry, for it roars:
Frost bites, else why the tooth-like fret on face?
Man makes acoustics deal with the sea's wrath,
Explains the choppy cheek by chymic law,—
To man and child remains the same effect
On drum of ear and root of nose, change cause
Never so thoroughly: so my heart be struck,
What care I,—by God's gloved hand or the bare?
Nor do I much perplex me with aught hard,
Dubious in the transmitting of the tale,—
No, nor with certain riddles set to solve.
This life is training and a passage; pass,—
Still, we march over some flat obstacle
We made give way before us; solid truth
In front of it, what motion for the world?
The moral sense grows but by exercise.
'T is even as man grew probatively
Initiated in Godship, set to make
A fairer moral world than this he finds,
Guess now what shall be known hereafter. Deal
Thus with the present problem: as we see,

1399 *MS* matters so the *1868* so the 1400 *MS* angry— *MS* roars, 1401 *MS* the fret of tooth 1404 *MS* To both, one and the same effect remains *1868* To both, remains one and the same effect 1406 *MS* the>our *MS* [ ]>heart *1868* our heart *MS* is>be 1408 *MS* [ ]>perplex 1409 *MS* transmission>transmitting 1410 *MS* solve,— 1411 *MS* probation;>a passage; 1412 *MS* Why, you *MS* [?proud]>flat 1413 *MS* You *MS* you; 1414 *MS* In front, how then were motion possible?>In front, how then were motion for the world? *1868* it, were motion 1415 *MS* {beginning of fo. 225} 1416 *MS* Tis *MS* by probation here 1417 *MS* godship, 1418 *MS* than what 1419 *MS 1868* hereafter. Thus, 1420 *MS* Of the present problem,—as we men may speak, *1868* O' the present problem: as we see and speak,

1399 *filled*: satisfied.

1401 *fret*: pattern of jagged edges.

1403 *choppy*: chapped; cf. *Macbeth*, I. iii. 44.

chymic law: i.e. by chemistry.

1407 *God's . . . bare*: i.e. by truth revealed mythically or literally (in the Gospels).

1413–14 *solid . . . world?*: i.e. 'if religious truth were self-evident (like a "solid" object in front of us), what spiritual progress or "motion" could we make during our earthly life?'

A faultless creature is destroyed, and sin
Has had its way i' the world where God should rule.
Ay, but for this irrelevant circumstance
Of inquisition after blood, we see
Pompilia lost and Guido saved: how long?
For his whole life: how much is that whole life?
We are not babes, but know the minute's worth,
And feel that life is large and the world small,
So, wait till life have passed from out the world.

Neither does this astonish at the end,
That whereas I can so receive and trust,
Other men, made with hearts and souls the same,
Reject and disbelieve,—subordinate
The future to the present,—sin, nor fear.
This I refer still to the foremost fact,
Life is probation and the earth no goal
But starting-point of man: compel him strive,
Which means, in man, as good as reach the goal,—
Why institute that race, his life, at all?
But this does overwhelm me with surprise,

1422 *MS* in *MS* in God's despite.>where God should rule. 1424 *MS* we'll see 1425 *MS* saved and set 1426 *MS* Glorious for many a day:>Glorious for his whole life: *MS* that? 1427 *MS* babes: we *MS* worth[]> worth, 1428 *MS* Nor [ ] this world sufficient for our course.>Nor feel this world sufficient for our course.>And feel life large and the world small, so wait. 1429 {not found in *MS*} *Yale 1* So>So, *1430 *MS* {no new paragraph} *1868 1872* {new paragraph} *1888 1889* {paragraphing obscured by this line's being at the head of the page} *MS* [ ]>Neither 1431 *1868* That, 1432 *MS* Men made *1868* Men, made *MS* same as mine *1868* same as mine, 1435 *MS* leading>foremost 1436 *MS* probation: earth is not the goal>probation and this earth no goal *1868* this earth 1437 *MS* starting-[?line]>starting-point *MS* [?run],>strive, 1438 {not found in *MS*} 1439 *MS* his life, at all?>at all, his life? 1440 *MS* {no comma}

1421 *faultless creature*: i.e. Pompilia.

1424 *inquisition after blood*: the law case about or into (the deed of) blood.

1437–9 *compel . . . all?* : if God simply forced spiritual striving on man, man would inevitably reach the 'goal' of enlightenment and love. What then would be the point of the 'probation' of life on earth?

Touch me to terror,—not that faith, the pearl,
Should be let lie by fishers wanting food,—
Nor, seen and handled by a certain few
Critical and contemptuous, straight consigned
To shore and shingle for the pebble it proves,—
But that, when haply found and known and named
By the residue made rich for evermore,
These,—that these favoured ones, should in a trice
Turn, and with double zest go dredge for whelks,
Mud-worms that make the savoury soup! Enough
O' the disbelievers, see the faithful few!
How do the Christians here deport them, keep
Their robes of white unspotted by the world?
What is this Aretine Archbishop, this
Man under me as I am under God,
This champion of the faith, I armed and decked,
Pushed forward, put upon a pinnacle,
To show the enemy his victor,—see!
What's the best fighting when the couple close?

1441 *MS* terror, that the pearl of faith>terror,—not that faith the pearl 1442 *MS* the fishers *MS* [ ]>food,— 1445 *MS* {beginning of fo. 226} *MS* the shore *MS* stone *Yale 2* proves,—>seems,— 1446 *MS* {no comma} 1447 *MS* forevermore, 1448 *MS* ay these *Yale 1* ay these>ay, these *1868* ay, these 1449 *MS* wilks 1450 *MS* And mudworms to make soup of. Enough>Mud-worms that make the savoury soup: Enough *1868* soup. 1451 *MS* Of *Yale 1* Of>O' *MS* Disbelievers, 1456 *MS* I arm and deck *MS* {no commas} *Yale 1* decked>decked, 1457 *MS* Push 1458 *MS* show>scare *MS* his>with his *MS* see 1459 *MS* What his best fight amounts to,>Whats the best fighting in>Whats the best fighting when the couple close:

1441 *faith, the pearl*: cf. Matt. 13: 45–6. The following passage plays upon this parable. The pearl is a traditional symbol of religious faith.

1442–4 *fishers . . . contemptuous*: i.e. worldly people (only interested in eating, making a living, etc.) and sceptics: contemptuous, unbelieving intellectuals. Again, this is historically anachronistic. The sceptics the Pope is thinking of are clearly the Higher Critics, like Renan and Strauss: see 1388–92 n.

1445 *it proves*: i.e. in their mistaken judgment.

1447 *residue . . . evermore*: i.e. church people, who have the rich treasure of religious faith.

1453 *unspotted . . . world*: cf. Jas. 1: 27.

1459 *when . . . close*: i.e. when the Archbishop (as a soldier of faith) and 'the enemy' (the world, the flesh, and the devil) engage in combat.

Pompilia cries, "Protect me from the wolf!"
He—"No, thy Guido is rough, heady, strong,
"Dangerous to disquiet: let him bide!
"He needs some bone to mumble, help amuse
"The darkness of his den with: so, the fawn
"Which limps up bleeding to my foot and lies,
"—Come to me, daughter!—thus I throw him back!"
Have we misjudged here, over-armed our knight,
Given gold and silk where plain hard steel serves best,
Enfeebled whom we sought to fortify,
Made an archbishop and undone a saint?
Well, then, descend these heights, this pride of life,
Sit in the ashes with a barefoot monk
Who long ago stamped out the worldly sparks,
By fasting, watching, stone cell and wire scourge,
—No such indulgence as unknits the strength—
These breed the tight nerve and tough cuticle,
And the world's praise or blame runs rillet-wise
Off the broad back and brawny breast, we know!
He meets the first cold sprinkle of the world,
And shudders to the marrow. "Save this child?

1460 *MS* This poor girl cries, protect *MS* fiend! *1868* fiend!" 1461 *MS* "Ay, but this Guido is a heady, strong, *1868* "No, for thy Guido is one heady, strong, 1462–6 *MS* {no quotation marks at beginnings of lines} 1462 *MS* brute to deal with:>to disquiet: *MS* bide: 1463 *MS* prey>bone *MS* and> help 1464 *MS* with,—so this 1466 *MS*—[ ] []>—Look at *MS* *1868* daughter,— *MS* thee 1467 *MS* overarmed the *1868* the knight, 1468 *MS* silk to boot where plain steel serves *1868* the plain steel 1470 *MS* Made a saint>Made an archbishop *etc.* 1471 *MS 1868* Well then, 1472 *MS* *1868* the barefoot 1473 *MS* {beginning of fo. 227} *MS* Who has put out the greedy sparks, we boast,—>Who long ago stamped out the worldly sparks; *1868* sparks. 1474 *MS* Fasting and prayer, the>Fasting and watching, the *1868* Fasting and watching, *MS* the>wire 1475 *MS* nerve,>strength— 1476 *MS* [?tense]>tight 1477 *MS* {Let at beginning of line deleted but not replaced} *1868* Let *MS* run rillet wise *1868* run 1479 *MS* feels>meets *MS 1868* {no comma} 1480 *MS 1868* marrow, 1481–5 *MS* {no quotation marks at beginnings of lines}

1472 *barefoot monk*: the Augustinian friar, called 'the Roman', whose help Pompilia sought during confession; cf. III. 1017, IV. 809, and SS 7.

1476 *cuticle*: skin.

1477 *rillet-wise*: like a little stream.

"Oh, my superiors, oh, the Archbishop's self!
"Who was it dared lay hand upon the ark
"His betters saw fall nor put finger forth?
"Great ones could help yet help not: why should small?
"I break my promise: let her break her heart!"
These are the Christians not the worldlings, not
The sceptics, who thus battle for the faith!
If foolish virgins disobey and sleep,
What wonder? But, this time, the wise that watch,
Sell lamps and buy lutes, exchange oil for wine,
The mystic Spouse betrays the Bridegroom here.
To our last resource, then! Since all flesh is weak,
Bind weaknesses together, we get strength:
The individual weighed, found wanting, try
Some institution, honest artifice
Whereby the units grow compact and firm!
Each props the other, and so stand is made
By our embodied cowards that grow brave.
The Monastery called of Convertites,
Meant to help women because these helped Christ,—

1481 *MS* ^oh,^ *MS* the Archbishop here,— *1868* the Archbishop here! 1482 *MS* laid his>dared lay 1483 *MS* let>saw 1484 *MS* They all could help and will not:>Mine here could help yet help not: *MS* I? 1485 *MS* heart." 1486 *MS* not the infidel! 1487 {not found in *MS*} 1488 *MS* The 1489 *MS 1868* But the wise that watch, this time *Yale 2* watch,>watched, 1492 *MS* On to our last resource,—all *MS* weak 1493 *MS* together you get 1496 *MS 1868* firm: 1497 *MS* both stand>so stand *etc.* *MS* made: 1498 *MS* Embodied *MS* brave: to-wit, 1499 *MS* Convertites— 1500 *MS* {line added later} *MS* Christ

1482–3 *Who . . . forth?* : the presumptuous man, Uzzah, in 2 Sam. 6: 6–7. Cf. IV. 834 n.

1485 *I . . . promise*: to write a letter to Pompilia's parents, detailing her plight.

1488–90 *foolish virgins . . . wine*: cf. Matt. 25: 1–13. There should be no surprise if 'foolish virgins' (i.e. worldly people) failed Pompilia. The shock is that 'the wise that watch' (i.e. churchmen, the 'wise virgins' of the parable) have turned to worldliness ('lutes' and 'wine') and ignored Pompilia's need.

1491 *mystic Spouse . . . Bridegroom*: i.e. the Church betrays Christ. Cf. Rev. 19: 7.

1494 *weighed . . . wanting*: cf. Dan. 5: 27.

1499 *Monastery . . . Convertites*: in the following passage Browning conflates two separate convents, the one to which Pompilia was remanded after her flight with Caponsacchi, and the one that made a claim against her estate: see XII. 672–3 n.

A thing existent only while it acts,
Does as designed, else a nonentity,—
For what is an idea unrealized?—
Pompilia is consigned to these for help.
They do help: they are prompt to testify
To her pure life and saintly dying days.
She dies, and lo, who seemed so poor, proves rich.
What does the body that lives through helpfulness
To women for Christ's sake? The kiss turns bite,
The dove's note changes to the crow's cry: judge!
"Seeing that this our Convent claims of right
"What goods belong to those we succour, be
"The same proved women of dishonest life,—
"And seeing that this Trial made appear
"Pompilia was in such predicament,—
"The Convent hereupon pretends to said
"Succession of Pompilia, issues writ,
"And takes possession by the Fisc's advice."
Such is their attestation to the cause
Of Christ, who had one saint at least, they hoped:
But, is a title-deed to filch, a corpse
To slander, and an infant-heir to cheat?
Christ must give up his gains then! They unsay
All the fine speeches,—who was saint is whore.
Why, scripture yields no parallel for this!

1502 *MS* []>as *MS* nonentity. *1868* nonentity, 1503 *MS* unrealised? 1504 *MS* {beginning of fo. 228} *MS* This poor child *MS* []>these *MS* help: 1505 *MS* help,— *1868* help they {broken sort} *MS* it is who>are prompt to 1506 *MS* days: *1507 *MS* rich. *1868* rich *1872* rich! *1888* rich *DC BrU* rich>rich. *1889* rich. 1508 *MS* in 1509 *MS* [?dove] turns [?crow]>kiss turns bite 1510 *MS* Here is the dove's note changed to the crow's cry— 1511 *MS* "For seeing that the 1512–18 *MS* {no quotation marks at beginnings of lines} 1512 *MS* they *MS* grant>be 1513 *MS* same but women 1514 *MS* makes 1515 *MS* stood *MS* predicament 1517 *MS* Pompilia,— *MS* writ 1518 *MS* {no quotation mark at end of line} 1519 *MS* We have 1520 *MS* Christ,—he *MS* knew: 1521 *MS* There is *MS* [] [] to [],>title-deed to filch, 1522 *MS* cheat,— 1523 *MS* [?saint]>gains *MS* then,—they 1524 *MS* call the saint

1520 *one saint*: i.e. St Mary Magdalene, the patron saint of the order.

The soldiers only threw dice for Christ's coat;
We want another legend of the Twelve
Disputing if it was Christ's coat at all,
Claiming as prize the woof of price—for why?
The Master was a thief, purloined the same,
Or paid for it out of the common bag!
Can it be this is end and outcome, all
I take with me to show as stewardship's fruit,
The best yield of the latest time, this year
The seventeen-hundredth since God died for man?
Is such effect proportionate to cause?
And still the terror keeps on the increase
When I perceive... how can I blink the fact?
That the fault, the obduracy to good,
Lies not with the impracticable stuff
Whence man is made, his very nature's fault,
As if it were of ice the moon may gild
Not melt, or stone 't was meant the sun should warm
Not make bear flowers,—nor ice nor stone to blame:
But it can melt, that ice, can bloom, that stone,
Impassible to rule of day and night!
This terrifies me, thus compelled perceive,
Whatever love and faith we looked should spring

1528 *MS* that it 1529 *MS* it as a prize the woof of price 1531 *MS* bag. 1532 *MS* {beginning of fo. 229} 1535 *MS* seventeenth hundredth 1536 *MS* to such cause? 1538 *1868 1872* perceive . . 1539 *MS* this obduracy to good 1541 *MS* [ ] [ ]>Whence man 1542 *MS 1868 1872* ice, 1543 *MS* [ ]>Not *MS* or rock the sun was meant to warm *1868 1872* stone, 1544 *MS* bear grass,—>grass,—>bear flowers,— *MS* nor sun's nor moon's the blame: 1545 *MS* melt this ice, and bloom, this rock, *1868* and bloom, 1547 *MS* That

1526 *soldiers . . . coat*: cf. John 19: 23–4. Cf. VI. 52–6 n.

1529 *woof of price*: i.e. the valuable material (of Christ's coat).

1530–1 *thief . . . bag*: i.e. they claim Christ is like Judas; cf. John 12: 6.

1538 *blink*: avoid.

1539 *obduracy*: resistance.

1542–4 *As . . . flowers*: as if human nature were cold or insensitive, so that, if it were ice, the moon could only make it shine, not melt it, or, if it were stone, the sun could only warm it, not make it bear flowers.

1546 *Impassible . . . night*: i.e. exempt from such simple influences or external factors.

At advent of the authoritative star,
Which yet lie sluggish, curdled at the source,—
These have leapt forth profusely in old time,
These still respond with promptitude to-day,
At challenge of—what unacknowledged powers
O' the air, what uncommissioned meteors, warmth
By law, and light by rule should supersede?
For see this priest, this Caponsacchi, stung
At the first summons,—"Help for honour's sake,
"Play the man, pity the oppressed!"—no pause,
How does he lay about him in the midst,
Strike any foe, right wrong at any risk,
All blindness, bravery and obedience!—blind?
Ay, as a man would be inside the sun,
Delirious with the plenitude of light
Should interfuse him to the finger-ends—
Let him rush straight, and how shall he go wrong?
Where are the Christians in their panoply?
The loins we girt about with truth, the breasts
Righteousness plated round, the shield of faith,
The helmet of salvation, and that sword
O' the Spirit, even the word of God,—where these?
Slunk into corners! Oh, I hear at once
Hubbub of protestation! "What, we monks

1549 *MS* {no comma} 1550 *MS* And still>And yet *MS* source, 1552 *MS* {no comma} 1553 *MS* of what *MS* powers of the air,>powers, 1554 *MS* What>O' the air, what *MS* meteors, law 1555 *MS* And light by rule were sent to supersede? 1556 *MS* quick>stung 1558 *MS* {no quotation mark at beginning of line} *MS* oppressed,"— 1559 *MS* There does 1560 *MS* foe to right at 1561 *MS* {beginning of fo. 230} *MS* bravery,>bravery *MS* obedience,— *Yale 1* obedience,—>obedience!— 1563 *Yale 2* plentitude>plenitude 1564 *MS* Has interfused 1565 *MS* {line added later} *MS* go straight 1567–70 *MS* {lines added later} 1570 *MS* Of 1571 *MS* corners: oh, 1572 *MS* protestation,—what,

1549 *advent . . . star*: i.e. at the coming of Christ.

1566 *panoply*: complete armour (from Gk.). In Christian contexts, as here, the word is often used figuratively as meaning the 'complete armour for spiritual or mental warfare': OED² *sb.* 2.a.

1567–70 *loins . . . God*: cf. Eph. 6: 14–17.

"We friars, of such an order, such a rule,
"Have not we fought, bled, left our martyr-mark
"At every point along the boundary-line
" 'Twixt true and false, religion and the world,
"Where this or the other dogma of our Church
"Called for defence?" And I, despite myself,
How can I but speak loud what truth speaks low,
"Or better than the best, or nothing serves!
"What boots deed, I can cap and cover straight
"With such another doughtiness to match,
"Done at an instinct of the natural man?"
Immolate body, sacrifice soul too,—
Do not these publicans the same? Outstrip!
Or else stop race you boast runs neck and neck,
You with the wings, they with the feet,—for shame!
Oh, I remark your diligence and zeal!
Five years long, now, rounds faith into my ears,

1573–8 *MS* {no quotation marks at beginnings of lines} 1575 *MS* boundary line *Yale 1* boundary line>boundary-line 1576 *MS* world?> world, 1578 *MS* defence? And 1579 *MS* breathes low, 1580 *MS* serves: 1581–3 *MS* {no quotation marks at beginnings of lines} 1581 *MS* a deed I cap 1582 *MS* {no comma} 1583 *MS* Done for a vanity by *MS* {no quotation mark at end of line} 1584 *MS* the soul,— 1585 *MS* Outstrip 1586 *MS* Or [?run this]>Or stop the *1868 1872* race, 1587 *MS* wings,— 1589 *MS* long in my ears rings faith her peal,

1580 "*Or . . . or*: Either . . . or.

1581 *boots*: is the value of

cap and cover: i.e. trump (as in cards).

1585 *Do . . . same?*: cf. Matt. 5: 46: 'For if ye love them which love you, what reward have ye? do not even the publicans the same?'

1589–1604 *Five . . . difference!"* : this is a reasonable historical allusion to the argument over the Divine Names, an aspect of the famous 'Chinese rites' controversy, a matter which lasted from the early seventeenth through to the eighteenth century. The Jesuit Matteo Ricci (1552–1610), founder of the Catholic missions in China, responded to Chinese sensibilities by using the Chinese terms *T'ien* (heaven) and *Shang-ti* (Sovereign Lord) to designate God, though he preferred the more specific term *T'ien chu* (Lord of Heaven). After his death, controversy developed within the missionary community over the legitimacy of this accommodation, and in 1693 Charles Maigrot, Vicar Apostolic of Fukien (in southern China) forwarded for approval to the Pope an ordinance forbidding converts to use both *T'ien* and *Shang-ti*, and also forbidding them the veneration of Confucius and the ancestors. Innocent XII was annoyed, and referred the matter to a theological tribunal. He wrote to Maigrot

"Help thou, or Christendom is done to death!"
Five years since, in the Province of To-kien,
Which is in China as some people know,
Maigrot, my Vicar Apostolic there,
Having a great qualm, issues a decree.
Alack, the converts use as God's name, not
Tien-chu but plain *Tien* or else mere *Shang-ti*,
As Jesuits please to fancy politic,
While, say Dominicans, it calls down fire,—
For *Tien* means heaven, and *Shang-ti*, supreme prince,
While *Tien-chu* means the lord of heaven: all cry,
"There is no business urgent for despatch
"As that thou send a legate, specially
"Cardinal Tournon, straight to Pekin, there
"To settle and compose the difference!"
So have I seen a potentate all fume
For some infringement of his realm's just right,
Some menace to a mud-built straw-thatched farm
O' the frontier; while inside the mainland lie,
Quite undisputed-for in solitude,

1590 *MS* {no quotation marks} *MS* Help now, 1591 *MS* For whereas> Five years since in *etc.* 1592 *MS* as the whole world knows 1593 *MS* And Maigrot>Maigrot my 1594 *MS* Hath *MS* qualm and issues a decree— 1595 *MS* {beginning of fo. 231} *MS* It is observed they>For why? The converts 1596 *MS* *Tien* nor Shan-ti, as Jesuits recommend,>*Tien* nor Shang-ti, as Jesuits recommend,>*Tien-chu,* but plain Tien or else mere Shang-ti 1597 *MS* {line added later} *MS* As Jesuits recommend, as politic,>As Jesuits please to fancy politic, 1598 *MS* But Tien-chu, which should call down fire from heaven,—>While Dominicans say it calls down fire from heaven,— 1599, 1600 *MS* {lines added later} 1599 *MS* prince 1600 *MS* Heaven: you see, 1601–4 *MS* {no quotation marks at beginnings of lines} 1602 *MS* I send a legate,— 1603 *MS* Tournon straight 1604 *MS* difference. 1605 *MS* all-flame,>all-fume, 1607 *MS* some mud-built straw thatched 1608 *MS* On *MS 1868* frontier, *MS* lie 1609 {not found in *MS*}

---

emphasizing the importance of unity and urging him to live in peace with the other missionaries. Browning describes Maigrot as Vicar Apostolic of the Province of 'To-kien': this is a slip for 'Fu-kien'. In 1703, Innocent's successor, Clement XI, sent out Cardinal Tournon to deliver the theological verdict at Rome against the use of these terms. For a full account, see *Catholic Encyclopedia*, xiii. 37–9.

1589 *rounds*: dins; cf. IV. 600 n.

Whole cities plague may waste or famine sap:
What if the sun crumble, the sands encroach,
While he looks on sublimely at his ease?
How does their ruin touch the empire's bound?

And is this little all that was to be?
Where is the gloriously-decisive change,
Metamorphosis the immeasurable
Of human clay to divine gold, we looked
Should, in some poor sort, justify its price?
Had an adept of the mere Rosy Cross
Spent his life to consummate the Great Work,
Would not we start to see the stuff it touched
Yield not a grain more than the vulgar got
By the old smelting-process years ago?
If this were sad to see in just the sage
Who should profess so much, perform no more,
What is it when suspected in that Power
Who undertook to make and made the world,
Devised and did effect man, body and soul,
Ordained salvation for them both, and yet...
Well, is the thing we see, salvation?

1610 *MS* sap,— *Yale 1* sap,—>sap: 1611 *MS* {line added later} *MS* Lets the sun crumble and the 1612 *MS* [ ]>While *MS* ease: 1614 *MS* {no new paragraph} 1615 *Yale 1* gloriously decisive>gloriously-decisive 1616 *MS* *1868* The immeasurable metamorphosis 1618 *MS* {no commas} *Yale 1* {commas inserted} *MS* pay the awful price?>justify the price? *1868* the price? 1619 *MS* a [ ] [ ] of the>a mere adept of the *1868* a mere adept of the 1620 *MS* [ ]>Spent *MS* {no comma} 1621 *MS* not one *MS* [ ]> start 1622 *MS* not one 1624 *MS* [ ] [ ]>sad to *MS* the mere>just the 1625 *MS* more 1627 *MS* That that *MS* world,— 1628 *MS* soul,— 1629 *MS* {beginning of fo. 232} *MS* and... *1868 1872* yet . . 1630 {not found in *MS*}

1618 *its price*: human clay's price, i.e. Christ's sacrifice on the cross.

1619 *adept . . . Rosy Cross*: a member of the Rosicrucian sect, originally a seventeenth-century movement of esoteric wisdom. The 'Great Work' of the sect was alchemy, in particular the quest for 'the philosopher's stone', the substance that would transmute base metals into gold.

1621 *it*: (the result of) the Great Work, i.e. the philosopher's stone: see previous n.

I

Put no such dreadful question to myself,
Within whose circle of experience burns
The central truth, Power, Wisdom, Goodness,—God:
I must outlive a thing ere know it dead:
When I outlive the faith there is a sun,
When I lie, ashes to the very soul,—
Someone, not I, must wail above the heap,
"He died in dark whence never morn arose."
While I see day succeed the deepest night—
How can I speak but as I know?—my speech
Must be, throughout the darkness, "It will end:
"The light that did burn, will burn!" Clouds obscure—
But for which obscuration all were bright?
Too hastily concluded! Sun-suffused,
A cloud may soothe the eye made blind by blaze,—
Better the very clarity of heaven:
The soft streaks are the beautiful and dear.
What but the weakness in a faith supplies
The incentive to humanity, no strength
Absolute, irresistible, comports?
How can man love but what he yearns to help?
And that which men think weakness within strength,
But angels know for strength and stronger yet—

1635 *MS* One *MS* the thing one knows for dead: 1636 {not found in *MS*} 1637 *MS* soul, 1638 *MS* Something, *MS* me, 1639 *MS* {no quotation marks} *MS* arose; 1640 *MS* Now, *MS* deep[ ]>deepest 1641 *MS* know,— *MS* [ ]>speech 1642 {not found in *MS*} *1868 1872* end:" *Yale 2* end:">end: 1643 *MS* Is, that the light burn, therefore: clouds [ ]?>Is, the light did burn, will burn: clouds obscure? 1644 {not found in *MS*} 1645 *MS* I know not even that, all sun-suffused>Too hastily concluded: sun-suffused 1646 *MS* help>soothe *MS* blaze, 1647 *MS* heaven,— 1652 *MS* {line added later} *MS* when 1653, 1654 {not found in *MS*}

1634 *Power . . . Goodness*: this repeats the 'Trinity' of God's attributes from 1351–67: there God embodies 'strength', 'intelligence', and 'goodness' (or 'love without a limit').

1646 *made . . . blaze*: i.e. that would be blinded by a more direct view of God.

1647 *Better*: = may better (i.e. improve)—a verb, continuing the syntax of the previous line.

1651 *comports*: brings with it.

What were it else but the first things made new,
But repetition of the miracle,
The divine instance of self-sacrifice
That never ends and aye begins for man?
So, never I miss footing in the maze,
No,—I have light nor fear the dark at all.

But are mankind not real, who pace outside
My petty circle, world that's measured me?
And when they stumble even as I stand,
Have I a right to stop ear when they cry,
As they were phantoms who took clouds for crags,
Tripped and fell, where man's march might safely move?
Beside, the cry is other than a ghost's,
When out of the old time there pleads some bard,
Philosopher, or both, and—whispers not,
But words it boldly. "The inward work and worth

1655 *MS* is 1656 *MS* A 1659 {not found in *MS*} 1661 *MS* {no new paragraph} *MS* those men outside 1662 *MS* all the world to me, *1868 1872* the world measured me? *Yale 2* the world measured me?>measured world to me? 1663 {not found in *MS*} 1664 *MS 1868* ears *MS* cry? 1665–7 {not found in *MS*} 1665 *1868 1872* phantoms, took the clouds 1666 *1868* the march of man might move? *1872* the march of men might move? 1668 *MS* stoops some man 1669 *MS* Philosopher or bard and— *1868* both and 1670 *MS* {beginning of fo. 233} *MS* But thus pleads boldly.

1655 *first . . . new*: cf. Rev. 21: 5.

1665 *took . . . crags*: i.e. experienced soft things as hard difficulties.

1668–9 *bard . . . both*: initially this voice from 'out of the old time' (i.e. before Christ's birth) is unidentified, a generalized pagan writer. By l. 1701 it is clear that it is Euripides (*c*.484–406 BC), Browning's favourite Greek dramatist. Euripides' influence on Browning can be seen as early as 'Artemis Prologizes' (writ. 1841, pub. 1842), which was suggested by the *Hippolytus*. In the 1860s, though, Euripides came to have a particular significance for Browning. So, on holiday in France in Aug.–Sept. 1864, at a time when he was planning *The Ring and the Book*, Browning was also 'having a great read at Euripides—the one book I brought with me': RB to Isa Blagden, 19 Sept. 1864: *Dearest Isa*, 193. The extended treatment of Euripides here begins a period when the dramatist was much on Browning's mind: *Balaustion's Adventure* (1871) contains an adaptation of *Alcestis*; *Aristophanes' Apology* (1875)—centred on the artistic conflict between Aristophanes and Euripides—contains a 'transcript' of *Herakles*. The main edition of Euripides that Browning used was Frederick A. Paley, *Euripides: with an English Commentary*, 3 vols. (London, 1857–60).

"Of any mind, what other mind may judge
"Save God who only knows the thing He made,
"The veritable service He exacts?
"It is the outward product men appraise.
"Behold, an engine hoists a tower aloft:
" 'I looked that it should move the mountain too!'
"Or else 'Had just a turret toppled down,
" 'Success enough!'—may say the Machinist
"Who knows what less or more result might be:
"But we, who see that done we cannot do,
" 'A feat beyond man's force,' we men must say.
"Regard me and that shake I gave the world!
"I was born, not so long before Christ's birth
"As Christ's birth haply did precede thy day,—
"But many a watch before the star of dawn:
"Therefore I lived,—it is thy creed affirms,

1671–5 *MS* {no quotation marks at beginnings of lines} 1671 *MS* {no comma} 1672 *MS* God's *MS* what>the *MS* he *MS* {no comma} 1673 *MS* And how much service he exacts therefrom:>The veritable service he exacts: 1674 *MS* The outward product men may estimate>The outward product all may estimate>The outward product we may praise or blame>It is the outward product we appraise: 1675 *MS* aloft— 1676 *MS* 'I *MS* too" 1677–715 *MS* {no quotation marks at beginnings of lines} 1677 *MS* "Had 1678 *1868* "Success *MS* enough!"— *MS* Machinist: *Yale 1* Mac>Machinist 1679, 1680 {not found in *MS*} 1681 *MS* Man says "A>"A *MS* force," 1682 *MS* earth!>world! 1683 *MS* just>not *MS 1868 1872* birth, 1685 *MS* A poet or philosopher, or both.>But many a watch before the star of dawn. *1868 1872* watch, 1686 *MS* affirms,—

Euripides had a reputation (lacked by Aeschylus and Sophocles) as an artist who had rejected the pagan polytheism of his day in favour of a nebulously conceived monotheism. This is presumably why Browning has the Pope invoke him. The key text in this regard is *Herakles*, at the end of which the protagonist denies that there are 'gods' who lust after one another as the myths say, because 'God stands in need—/ If he is really God—of naught at all': (Browning's trans.) *Aristophanes' Apology*, 4981–2. This is the point of what the Pope makes him say at l.1724: 'How nearly did I guess at that Paul knew?' For more information about Browning's interest in Euripides, see the introductions in Vol. X of this edition.

1675 *engine . . . aloft*: 'a machine lifts up a tower', but given the echo of *Hamlet*, III. iv. 206–7, more probably 'a machine of war blows up a tower, lifting it into the sky'. The images of violent effect continue in 'toppled down' (1677) and 'shake' (1682).

1678 *Machinist*: engineer, the man who makes or operates the 'engine' of l. 1675.

1682 *shake*: blow, concussion (fig.). Euripides challenged older patterns of Greek thought.

"Pope Innocent, who art to answer me!—
"Under conditions, nowise to escape,
"Whereby salvation was impossible.
"Each impulse to achieve the good and fair,
"Each aspiration to the pure and true,
"Being without a warrant or an aim,
"Was just as sterile a felicity
"As if the insect, born to spend his life
"Soaring his circles, stopped them to describe
"(Painfully motionless in the mid-air)
"Some word of weighty counsel for man's sake,
"Some 'Know thyself' or 'Take the golden mean!'
"—Forwent his happy dance and the glad ray,
"Died half an hour the sooner and was dust.
"I, born to perish like the brutes, or worse,
"Why not live brutishly, obey brutes' law?
"But I, of body as of soul complete,
"A gymnast at the games, philosopher
"I' the schools, who painted, and made music,—all

1687 {not found in *MS*} 1689 *MS* proved 1690 *MS* aspiration>impulse to 1694 *MS* {no comma} *MS* [ ]>life 1696 {not found in *MS*} 1697 *MS* {no comma} 1698 *MS* []>Some *MS* "Know thyself" *MS* "Take *MS* mean," 1699 {not found in *MS*} 1701 *MS* brutes or 1702 *MS* *1868* *1872* my law? 1703 *MS* {beginning of fo. 234} 1705 *MS* In *MS* a painter, a musician, all

1698 *'Know... mean!'*: two well-known axioms of ancient Greek thought. 'Know thyself'—γνῶθι σεαυτόν—was written up on the wall of the temple of Apollo at Delphi. Plato's *Protagoras* 343 B attributes it to 'seven wise men'. 'The golden mean' is from Horace: *auream quisquis mediocritatem diligit*, 'one who loves the golden mean': *Odes*, II. x. 5.

1704–5 *gymnast... music*: these are early traditions about Euripides' life. Browning could have known them from a number of sources, but most probably simply from the 'Life of Euripides' in the Ambrosian Library, Milan, quoted in Paley: 'He practised at first wrestling or pugilism, his father having received an oracle that he was destined to conquer in the public games; and it is said that he was victorious at Athens. However, having subsequently changed his views, he betook himself to tragedy: and here he introduced several novelties, in natural philosophy, rhetoric, and the development of his plots, as having been a disciple of Anaxagoras, Prodicus, and Protagoras, and a companion of Socrates.... There are some who assert that Iophon or Timocrates of Argos composed for him lyric measures. They say likewise that he had been a painter, and that pictures of his were exhibited at Megara': Paley, vol. i, pp. lvii f. Greek drama was a musical drama, so any playwright was of necessity a musician.

"Glories that met upon the tragic stage
"When the Third Poet's tread surprised the Two,—
"Whose lot fell in a land where life was great
"And sense went free and beauty lay profuse,
"I, untouched by one adverse circumstance,
"Adopted virtue as my rule of life,
"Waived all reward, loved but for loving's sake,
"And, what my heart taught me, I taught the world,
"And have been teaching now two thousand years.
"Witness my work,—plays that should please, forsooth!
"'They might please, they may displease, they shall teach,
"'For truth's sake,' so I said, and did, and do.
"Five hundred years ere Paul spoke, Felix heard,—
"How much of temperance and righteousness,
"Judgment to come, did I find reason for,
"Corroborate with my strong style that spared
"No sin, nor swerved the more from branding brow
"Because the sinner was called Zeus and God?

1706 *MS* gathered on>met upon 1707 *MS* Poet stood there by>Poet's tread surprised 1709 *MS* was free *MS* was profuse, 1712 *MS 1868 1872* and loved for 1713 *MS* And what I saw fit, strove the world should see>And what I saw, I taught the world to see>And what I loved, I taught the world to love> And what my heart taught me, I taught the world 1714 *MS* these> now 1715 *MS* plays,—things meant to>work,—plays that should 1716 *MS* "They 1717 *MS* All for the truth's sake,">For truth's sake," *MS* so I said and did and do. 1718–90 *MS* {no quotation marks at beginnings of lines} 1718 *MS* {line added later} 1719 *MS* [ ]>temperance 1720 *MS* come do *MS* [ ]>find *MS* of>for, 1721 *MS* in that strong *MS* spares 1722 *MS* swerve> swerves *MS* ^the more^ 1723 *MS* was>is *MS* [ ]>Zeus

1707 *Third . . . Two*: Euripides himself is the 'Third Poet'—the third tragedian—after 'the Two': the earlier playwrights Aeschylus (525–456 BC) and Sophocles (495–406 BC).

1718–20 *Paul . . . come*: cf. Acts 24: 25: 'And as he [St Paul] reasoned of righteousness, temperance, and judgment to come, Felix trembled, and answered, Go thy way for this time.' St Paul preached before the Roman governor Felix, in Caesarea, in *c.* AD 55.

1721 *strong style*: (fig.) 'bold manner of expression', (lit.) 'powerful pen'. Browning is playing with the original meaning of 'style' (from L. *stilus*), the pointed iron or bone used as a writing instrument in the ancient world. Here the pointed iron can be used to brand the brow of the sinner. Cf. 1786 n.

"How nearly did I guess at that Paul knew?
"How closely come, in what I represent
"As duty, to his doctrine yet a blank?
"And as that limner not untruly limns
"Who draws an object round or square, which square
"Or round seems to the unassisted eye,
"Though Galileo's tube display the same
"Oval or oblong,—so, who controverts
"I rendered rightly what proves wrongly wrought
"Beside Paul's picture? Mine was true for me.
"I saw that there are, first and above all,
"The hidden forces, blind necessities,
"Named Nature, but the thing's self unconceived:
"Then follow,—how dependent upon these,
"We know not, how imposed above ourselves,
"We well know,—what I name the gods, a power

1724 *Yale 2* that>what *MS* he knew? 1725 *MS* As it is no untrue>How closely come, in what 1726 *MS* As>Man's *MS* the doctrine *MS* in blank? 1728 *MS* [ ] [ ]>Who draws 1730 *MS* {line added later} 1733 *MS* {beginning of fo. 235} 1735 *MS* force [ ]>forces, 1736 *MS* [ ]>Named *Yale 1* nature>Nature 1738 *MS* ourselves 1739 *MS* Gods,

1726 *his*: St Paul's.

1730 *Galileo's tube*: the telescope was probably invented, in simple form, in the Netherlands, but in 1609 the great Italian scientist and mathematician Galileo Galilei (1564–1642) took it over, improved it technically, and used it to revolutionize astronomy. Browning would have known his portrait, by Justus Sustermans, in the Uffizi Gallery.

1734–6 *I . . . unconceived*: i.e. 'I saw, as an absolute in the universe, hidden forces, which I named "Nature" .' These 'hidden forces' are Euripides' guess at the Christian God. For him this 'thing's self' is 'unconceived' because, of course, he has no exact doctrine of such a God.

1737–46 *Then . . . man*: i.e. 'Below the "hidden forces", but above humankind, I saw "a power / Various or one", which I embodied in the pagan gods and their actions.' As Euripides later explains, this is his symbolic embodiment of 'His [the Christian God's] operation manifold / And multiform' (1768–9). This is the 'one revealment possible' to humankind of the higher 'hidden forces' (i.e. God himself). In this passage Euripides shows his unease with the conception of the pagan gods available to him. They are a pagan prefiguring of the idea of God's action in the world. But they are a mixture of 'Wisdom and folly' (1742), and they do not therefore make up a real idea of God as Euripides can imagine him, yet—in his time—they seemed the only way for humankind to approach the higher 'hidden forces', '. . . what were unimagined else by man' (1746).

"Various or one: for great and strong and good
"Is there, and little, weak and bad there too,
"Wisdom and folly: say, these make no God,—
"What is it else that rules outside man's self?
"A fact then,—always, to the naked eye,—
"And so, the one revealment possible
"Of what were unimagined else by man.
"Therefore, what gods do, man may criticize,
"Applaud, condemn,—how should he fear the truth?—
"But likewise have in awe because of power,
"Venerate for the main munificence,
"And give the doubtful deed its due excuse
"From the acknowledged creature of a day
"To the Eternal and Divine. Thus, bold
"Yet self-mistrusting, should man bear himself,
"Most assured on what now concerns him most—
"The law of his own life, the path he prints,—
"Which law is virtue and not vice, I say,—
"And least inquisitive where search least skills,
"I' the nature we best give the clouds to keep.
"What could I paint beyond a scheme like this
"Out of the fragmentary truths where light
"Lay fitful in a tenebrific time?
"You have the sunrise now, joins truth to truth,

1740 *MS* one, *1868* one; 1741 *MS* weak, 1742 *MS* God, 1743 *MS* then that 1744 *MS* always to 1745 *MS* Therefore, as>And, so, *1868* And, 1746 *MS* man, 1747 *MS* —Therefore what Gods *MS 1868 1872* criticise, 1748 *MS* can>should *MS* but speak truth? *1868 1872* truth? 1749 *MS* and venerate>because of power, 1750 *MS* For the main mercy and>Superlative mercy and>Venerate for the main 1751 *MS* the due 1752 *MS* creatures 1753 *MS* Divine: so, 1754 *MS* self-mistrusting should 1756 *MS* life,— 1757 *MS* {line added later} 1758 *MS 1868 1872* least search skills, 1759 *MS* The 1760 *MS* What but a scheme like this behoved me paint *Yale 2* schene>scheme 1763 *MS* {beginning of fo. 236} *MS* sunrise,—which

1755–9 *Most . . . keep*: i.e. 'most certain about the moral law that should rule his earthly life, treading (*printing*) the path of virtue, and least curious about the nature of the "Eternal and Divine", leaving that mystery for "the clouds to keep", since this is where intellectual search is least effective'.

1762 *tenebrific*: shadowy, darkened; cf. III. 789 n.

"Shoots life and substance into death and void;
"Themselves compose the whole we made before:
"The forces and necessity grow God,—
"The beings so contrarious that seemed gods,
"Prove just His operation manifold
"And multiform, translated, as must be,
"Into intelligible shape so far
"As suits our sense and sets us free to feel.
"What if I let a child think, childhood-long,
"That lightning, I would have him spare his eye,
"Is a real arrow shot at naked orb?
"The man knows more, but shuts his lids the same:
"Lightning's cause comprehends nor man nor child.
"Why then, my scheme, your better knowledge broke,
"Presently re-adjusts itself, the small
"Proportioned largelier, parts and whole named new:
"So much, no more two thousand years have done!
"Pope, dost thou dare pretend to punish me,
"For not descrying sunshine at midnight,
"Me who crept all-fours, found my way so far—
"While thou rewardest teachers of the truth,
"Who miss the plain way in the blaze of noon,—
"Though just a word from that strong style of mine,
"Grasped honestly in hand as guiding-staff,
"Had pricked them a sure path across the bog,

1764 *MS* void, 1765 *MS* make now *MS* before. 1766 *MS* force and all necessity grows 1768 *MS* multiform>manifold 1771 *MS* right to feel: *1868 1872* feel: 1772 *MS* the child *MS* childhood long, 1773 *MS* The lightning I 1774 *MS* idle orb? 1776 *MS* The first cause 1777 *MS* then my 1778 *MS 1868* readjusts 1779 *Yale 1* larglier,>largelier, 1780 done. 1781 *MS* And do you 1782, 1783 *MS* {lines added later} 1783 *MS* Who crept on all fours, *MS* far, 1784 *MS* Reward your bishops, priests, and friars here 1785 *MS* path 1786 *MS* While *Yale 1* word>help>word 1787 *MS* guiding staff *Yale 1* guiding staff>guiding-staff *MS* {no comma} 1788 *MS* that bog *MS* {no comma}

1774 *naked orb*: i.e. naked eye.

1786 *strong style*: vigorous writing / strong pen: see 1721 n. Here the style (writing instrument) becomes a 'guiding-staff', one which—with its pointed end—can 'prick' or mark out a way across the 'bog' of worldliness.

"That mire of cowardice and slush of lies
"Wherein I find them wallow in wide day?"

How should I answer this Euripides?
Paul,—'t is a legend,—answered Seneca,
But that was in the day-spring; noon is now:
We have got too familiar with the light.
Shall I wish back once more that thrill of dawn?
When the whole truth-touched man burned up, one fire?
—Assured the trial, fiery, fierce, but fleet,
Would, from his little heap of ashes, lend
Wings to that conflagration of the world
Which Christ awaits ere He makes all things new:
So should the frail become the perfect, rapt
From glory of pain to glory of joy; and so,
Even in the end,—the act renouncing earth,
Lands, houses, husbands, wives and children here,—

1789 *MS* maze of lies   *1790 *MS 1868 1872* day?" *1888 1889* day!"   *1791 *MS* {no new paragraph} *1868 1872* {new paragraph} *1888 1889* {paragraphing obscured by this line's being at the head of the page}   1792 *MS* legend,   *MS* Seneca   1793 *MS* day spring,—   *MS 1868 1872* now *Yale 2* now>now: 1794 *MS* {beginning of fo. 237}   1796 *MS* up one fire *Yale 2* fire?>fire,   1797 *MS* Assured   *MS* fiery fierce and   1798 *MS* {no commas}   1799 *MS 1868* the conflagration   1800 *MS* [ ]>ere   *MS* he make   *MS 1868 1872* new— *Yale 2* new—>new?   1802 *MS* {no comma}   1804 *MS* husband wife> husbands wives   *MS* here,

---

1792 *Paul . . . Seneca*: the fourteen-letter correspondence between St Paul and the Roman Stoic philosopher Seneca (3 BC–AD 65) was regarded as genuine right down to the beginning of the Renaissance. In fact, it was probably written in the fourth century, being first mentioned by St Jerome in 392. The correspondence purports to be written in the period 58–64 AD, when both St Paul and Seneca were in Rome, during the first phase of Nero's reign. See M. R. James (trans.), *The Apocryphal New Testament* (Oxford, 1953), pp. 480–4.

1793 *day-spring*: i.e. the dawn of Christianity.

1797–800 *Assured . . . new*: i.e. 'assured that his individual martyrdom would contribute to bring on the purifying fire at the end of time, after which Christ will make the new, uncorrupted Kingdom'. Cf. Rev. 21: 5. The Pope is thinking of the spiritual intensity of the martyrs of the early Church, and how they gave their lives as witness to their faith.

1801 *rapt*: i.e. 'swept up into heaven' (Ohio).

1803–8 *act . . . life*: cf. Mark 10: 29–30: 'And Jesus answered and said, Verily I say unto you, There is no man that hath left house, or brethren, or sisters, or father, or mother, or wife, or children, or lands, for my sake, and the gospel's, but he shall

Begin that other act which finds all, lost,
Regained, in this time even, a hundredfold,
And, in the next time, feels the finite love
Blent and embalmed with the eternal life.
So does the sun ghastlily seem to sink
In those north parts, lean all but out of life,
Desist a dread mere breathing-stop, then slow
Re-assert day, begin the endless rise.
Was this too easy for our after-stage?
Was such a lighting-up of faith, in life,
Only allowed initiate, set man's step
In the true way by help of the great glow?
A way wherein it is ordained he walk,
Bearing to see the light from heaven still more
And more encroached on by the light of earth,
Tentatives earth puts forth to rival heaven,
Earthly incitements that mankind serve God
For man's sole sake, not God's and therefore man's.
Till at last, who distinguishes the sun
From a mere Druid fire on a far mount?

1805 *MS* [ ]>all *MS* {no commas} 1806 *MS* An hundred fold in this time and the next 1807 {not found in *MS*} 1808 *MS* Blends and embalms *MS 1868 1872* its eternal 1809 *MS* sink, say who live>steadily seem to die 1810 *MS* dip 1811 *MS* breathing-while, 1812 *MS 1868* Reassert 1813 *MS* Was not>Was *MS* the after-stage,—>the after-stage?— 1814 {not found in *MS*} 1816 *MS* glow, 1817 *MS* The way he walks in,—'tis the trial's gist,— 1819 *MS* [ ]>lights 1820, 1821 *MS* {line added later} 1820 *MS* Earth's tentatives put 1821 *MS* Earth's motives for doing God's work for man 1822 {not found in *MS*} *1868* man's, 1823 *MS* {no comma} *MS* [ ]>sun 1824 *MS* the mere *MS* the far hill?

receive an hundredfold now in this time . . . and in the world to come eternal life.' 'In this time' = in this earthly life; 'in the next time' = in heaven. 'embalmed' (1808) = preserved sweetly.

1809 *ghastlily*: not as unusual an adverb as one might suppose; it is also used by EBB in *A Drama of Exile* (1844), l. 2139.

1820 *Tentatives*: attempts, experiments (a French use); cf. 'Easter-Day', 793.

1824 *From . . . mount?*: i.e. from a simple earthly fire. The Druids were ancient Celtic priests. The point here is that this Druid fire (earthly ways of illumination and insight) is simply lit by men, an act generated by their own superstition; it is 'the world's gross torch' (1831), not the true illumination of God.

More praise to him who with his subtle prism
Shall decompose both beams and name the true.
In such sense, who is last proves first indeed;
For how could saints and martyrs fail see truth
Streak the night's blackness? Who is faithful now?
Who untwists heaven's white from the yellow flare
O' the world's gross torch, without night's foil that helped
Produce the Christian act so possible
When in the way stood Nero's cross and stake,—
So hard now when the world smiles "Right and wise!
"Faith points the politic, the thrifty way,
"Will make who plods it in the end returns
"Beyond mere fool's-sport and improvidence.
"We fools dance thro' the cornfield of this life,
"Pluck ears to left and right and swallow raw,
"—Nay, tread, at pleasure, a sheaf underfoot,
"To get the better at some poppy-flower,—
"Well aware we shall have so much less wheat
"In the eventual harvest: you meantime

1825 *MS* new-found prism 1827 *MS* {beginning of fo. 238} *MS* indeed, *1868 1872* indeed; *1888 1889* {; is broken and looks like :} 1828 *MS* For saints and martyrs cannot but see truth 1829 *MS* blackness,—who *MS* now *1868 1872* now, 1830 *MS* Untwists the pure white *1868 1872* Untwists heaven's pure white 1831 *MS* Of *MS 1868 1872* without a foil to help. 1832 *MS* O splendid Christian *1868 1872* act, 1834 *MS* So hard when all the world smiles, "Rightly done, *1868 1872* now that *1868 1872* "Rightly done! 1835–47 *MS* {no quotation marks at beginnings of lines} 1835 *MS* It is the *1868 1872* "It is the 1836 *MS* Will clearly make you in *1868 1872* "Will clearly make you in 1837 *MS* Beyond our fool's play and improvidence,— *1868 1872* "Beyond our fool's-sport and improvidence: 1838 *MS 1868 1872* go thro' *MS* {no comma} 1840 *MS* Nay, tread at 1842 *MS 1868 1872* wheat less 1843 *MS* harvest,—you meanwhile

1826 *decompose both beams*: analyse into their constituent parts the two light-sources (i.e. the fire of the sun and the earthly Druid fire).

1827 *last . . . first*: cf. Matt. 19: 30, etc. People of the seventeenth or nineteenth centuries have a harder and nobler job to discern faith than the first Christians.

1833 *Nero's . . . stake*: i.e. the means by which Nero tortured the early Christians. The Roman emperor Nero (AD 37–68) was reputedly one of the cruellest persecutors of the early Christians, crucifying some and burning others at the stake. Tradition says that both St Peter and St Paul were martyred in Rome in his persecutions of the 60s AD. Cf. VI. 1788–9, 1790 nn.

"Waste not a spike,—the richlier will you reap!
"What then? There will be always garnered meal
"Sufficient for our comfortable loaf,
"While you enjoy the undiminished sack!"
Is it not this ignoble confidence,
Cowardly hardihood, that dulls and damps,
Makes the old heroism impossible?

Unless . . . what whispers me of times to come?
What if it be the mission of that age
My death will usher into life, to shake
This torpor of assurance from our creed,
Re-introduce the doubt discarded, bring
That formidable danger back, we drove
Long ago to the distance and the dark?
No wild beast now prowls round the infant camp:
We have built wall and sleep in city safe:
But if some earthquake try the towers that laugh
To think they once saw lions rule outside,
And man stand out again, pale, resolute,
Prepared to die,—which means, alive at last?
As we broke up that old faith of the world,
Have we, next age, to break up this the new—

1844 *MS* and rich reward will reap: 1846 *MS* Enough to make a>Enough to make our 1847 *MS* Why you go feast on the undiminished prize. *1868 1872* prize!" *MS* {no quotation mark at end of line} 1849 *MS* {no commas} 1850 *MS* impossible . . unless 1851 *MS* {no new paragraph} *MS* . . What is it whispers *1868 1872* Unless . . 1852 *MS* of next age *1868 1872* age, 1853 *MS* Waiting my death to begin life, to shake 1854 *MS* {no comma} 1855 *MS* {beginning of fo. 239} 1856 *MS 1868* The 1857 *MS* dark. 1858 *MS* camp, *1868* Camp; 1860 *MS 1868* the earthquake *1868 1872* towers, 1862 *MS 1868* Till man 1863 *MS 1868 1872* that is, alive 1864 *MS* {no comma}

1852–3 *that age . . . life*: i.e. the age of religious doubt that will follow his death: the eighteenth and nineteenth centuries, periods when scepticism became stronger, when religious faith seemed undermined by scientific and philosophical advance.

1858 *infant camp*: newly created camp (a characterization of the early Church). The 'wild beast' may allude again to Nero: see 1833 n.

Faith, in the thing, grown faith in the report—
Whence need to bravely disbelieve report
Through increased faith i' the thing reports belie?
Must we deny,—do they, these Molinists,
At peril of their body and their soul,—
Recognized truths, obedient to some truth
Unrecognized yet, but perceptible?—
Correct the portrait by the living face,
Man's God, by God's God in the mind of man?
Then, for the few that rise to the new height,
The many that must sink to the old depth,
The multitude found fall away! A few,
E'en ere new law speak clear, may keep the old,
Preserve the Christian level, call good good
And evil evil, (even though razed and blank
The old titles,) helped by custom, habitude,
And all else they mistake for finer sense
O' the fact than reason warrants,—as before,
They hope perhaps, fear not impossibly.

1866 *MS* {no commas} 1868 *MS* in things *1868* in thing 1870 *MS* {line added later} *MS* soul, 1871 *MS* Received *MS* in obedience 1872 *MS* perceptible, 1873 *MS* {line added later} 1874 *MS* {no comma} *MS* Man? 1876 *MS* that sink to the old depth again, 1877 *MS* that falls 1878 *MS* the new law speaks clear, keep *1868* the new law speak clear, keep 1880 *MS* evil, even 1881 *MS* titles stand,—thro' *1868* titles stand,) thro' custom 1882 *MS* all they would *1868* all they may 1883 *MS* Of *Yale 1* Of>O' **MS 1868 1872* fact than *1888 1889* fact that *MS* warrants:>warrants,— 1884 *MS* Would hope

1866–8 *Faith . . . belie*: i.e. 'faith in the actual symbolic significance of Christ, grown faith in something less—something second-hand, a rather literalistic reading of the Gospels—whence the need to bravely disbelieve the literal "report" of the Gospels through an increased faith in the symbolic significance of Christ, something that the Gospels (read in too simple a way) seem to "belie" or misrepresent'. Browning again lets his Pope speak in a way that is historically anachronistic. The Pope is really addressing nineteenth-century problems of religious doubt, particularly the way in which the Higher Criticism was developing a historical-critical understanding of the Gospels, and so undermining a literalistic way of reading the 'report' of Christ's life. As elsewhere, Browning is arguing that a historicist understanding of the Gospels does not invalidate Christian faith; rather the Higher Criticism requires Christians to understand their faith in new ways.

1869 *Molinists*: cf. IX. 33 n.

At least some one Pompilia left the world
Will say "I know the right place by foot's feel,
"I took it and tread firm there; wherefore change?"
But what a multitude will surely fall
Quite through the crumbling truth, late subjacent,
Sink to the next discoverable base,
Rest upon human nature, settle there
On what is firm, the lust and pride of life!
A mass of men, whose very souls even now
Seem to need re-creating,—so they slink
Worm-like into the mud, light now lays bare,—
Whose future we dispose of with shut eyes
And whisper—"They are grafted, barren twigs,
"Into the living stock of Christ: may bear
"One day, till when they lie death-like, not dead,"—
Those who with all the aid of Christ succumb,
How, without Christ, shall they, unaided, sink?
Whither but to this gulf before my eyes?
Do not we end, the century and I?

1885 *MS* {beginning of fo. 240} *MS 1868* Surely some one Pompilia in 1886 *MS* Would *MS* [ ]>place *MS* the f[ ]>the foot>the foot's feel, 1887 *MS* {no quotation mark at beginning of line} *MS* I tread *MS* it; wherefore> firm; wherefore 1888 *MS* would fall forthwith *1868* will fall, perchance, 1889 *MS* truth subjacent late *1868* truth subjacent late, *MS* {no commas} 1891 *MS 1868* take their stand 1892 *MS* fact, the lusts and prides *1868* fact, 1893 *MS 1868* The 1894 *MS* recreating,— 1895 *MS* depths light *1868* mud light 1897 *MS* "They are baptised,—grafted, the barren twigs *1868* "They are baptized,—grafted, the barren twigs 1898, 1899 *MS* {no quotation marks at beginnings of lines} 1898 *MS* will bear 1899 *MS* death-like not 1900 *MS* {line added later} *MS 1868* lie thus, 1901 *MS* What will they do, whither, *1868* How, without Christ, whither, 1902 *MS* What but this here rehearsed before my eyes— *1868* What but to this rehearsed before my eyes? 1903 {not found in *MS*}

1886 *by foot's feel*: i.e. by instinct.

1889 *subjacent*: lying underneath, below, stressed on the first syllable here; cf. 'circumjacent' XI. 2158 (contrast *MS 1868*, and 'adjacent').

1892 *lust . . . life*: cf. 1 John 2: 16.

1897–9 "*They . . . dead,"*: based on John 15: 1–8, particularly 15: 5: 'I am the vine, ye are the branches: he that abideth in me, and I in him, the same bringeth forth much fruit: for without me ye can do nothing.'

1902 *this gulf*: i.e. this gulf of unbelief and immorality.

The impatient antimasque treads close on kibe
O' the very masque's self it will mock,—on me,
Last lingering personage, the impatient mime
Pushes already,—will I block the way?
Will my slow trail of garments ne'er leave space
For pantaloon, sock, plume and castanet?
Here comes the first experimentalist
In the new order of things,—he plays a priest;
Does he take inspiration from the Church,
Directly make her rule his law of life?
Not he: his own mere impulse guides the man—
Happily sometimes, since ourselves allow
He has danced, in gaiety of heart, i' the main
The right step through the maze we bade him foot.

1904 *MS* ^impatient^ *MS* even on the heel>close on kibe 1905 *MS* Of *MS* ^very^ *MS* me 1906 *MS* Of the last lingering masquer whom it mocks>Last lingering personage, they press; then>Last lingering personage, the first mime—>Last lingering personage, the first pushing mime— 1907 {not found in *MS*} 1908 *MS* that>my *MS* slow-trail *Yale 1* slow-trail>slow trail *MS* give place>leave space 1909 *MS* For the new mime and mirthful interlude?> For the new mime that mirthful interlude?>For pantaloon, sock, plume and castanet? 1912 *MS* [ ] [ ]>Does he take 1914 *MS* his course— 1915 *MS* *1868* admit 1917 *MS* {beginning of fo. 241} *MS 1868* in the *MS* had bade

1904–5 *impatient . . . masque's self*: i.e. the gross, confused behaviour of the world without religious faith. A masque was a theatrical entertainment of the seventeenth century that acted out a pageant of moral, political, and religious order. The antimasque, which usually preceded it, was its symbolic opposite, an enactment of the forces of evil, ugliness, and chaos, usually involving witches, clowns, or other grotesques. While the atmosphere of the masque was serene, decorative, and ordered, the antimasque was burlesque and farcical: see Stephen Orgel, *The Jonsonian Masque* (Cambridge, Mass., 1965). Here the Pope sees his own age, the seventeenth century, as the last age of religious order and vision, hence symbolized by the pageantry of the masque. It will be followed, he fears, by an antimasque of confusion and subjectivism, in which each person has to find his or her own individual way to truth. The phrase 'treads close on kibe' = 'comes closely on the heels'.

1909 *pantaloon*: comic breeches or trousers, as worn by the foolish old man figure of *commedia dell'arte*.

sock: 'a light shoe worn by comic actors on the ancient Greek and Roman stage; hence used allusively to denote comedy or the comic muse': OED[2]. Cf. 'Jonson's learned sock': Milton, 'L'Allegro', 132; and 'The Two Poets of Croisic', st. cxxx. The list of 'pantaloon, sock, plume, and castanet' suggests the farcical costume and props for the performers of the antimasque, representing the religious confusion the Pope sees about to be unleashed on the world.

1914 *mere*: i.e. sole, unaided.

But if his heart had prompted him break loose
And mar the measure? Why, we must submit,
And thank the chance that brought him safe so far.
Will he repeat the prodigy? Perhaps.
Can he teach others how to quit themselves,
Show why this step was right while that were wrong?
How should he? "Ask your hearts as I asked mine,
"And get discreetly through the morrice too;
"If your hearts misdirect you,—quit the stage,
"And make amends,—be there amends to make!"
Such is, for the Augustin that was once,
This Canon Caponsacchi we see now.
"But my heart answers to another tune,"
Puts in the Abate, second in the suite,
"I have my taste too, and tread no such step!
"You choose the glorious life, and may, for me!
"I like the lowest of life's appetites,—
"So you judge,—but the very truth of joy
"To my own apprehension which decides.

1918 *MS 1868* What if *MS 1868 1872* prompted to 1919 *MS* figure? *MS 1868* submit 1920 *MS 1868* safely through. 1921 *MS* Can>Will *MS* Perhaps: 1923 *MS 1868* Prove *MS 1868* right, 1924 *MS* []>How *MS* {no quotation mark} *MS* {no comma} 1925–7 {not found in *MS*} 1925 *1868* so; 1927 *Yale 2* be there>suppose *1868* make," 1928 *MS* This *MS* that Saint Bernard *Yale 1* Saint Bernard>Augustine *1868* Augustine *MS* once 1929 *MS* The 1930 *MS 1868* "And *MS* {no comma} *Yale 1* {comma inserted} 1932 *MS* for the opposite>and choose no such *MS* step: *Yale 1* step:>step! 1933–41 *MS* {no quotation marks at beginnings of lines} 1933 *MS* You live *MS* may for me *1868* me, 1934 *MS* Who *1868* "Who 1935 *MS* What you call,—and *1868* "What 1936 *MS* must judge,— *1868* must judge.

1921 *prodigy*: unlikely, amazing act.

1925 *morrice*: i.e. complex dance. The morris dance was the traditional English folk dance. OED[2] defines it as 'a grotesque dance performed by persons in fancy costume', an emphasis appropriate here.

1928–9 *Augustin . . . now*: i.e. 'Instead of St Augustine, a strong man of faith believing in and guided by the Church's institutional structure, now we have Caponsacchi, a man dancing the dance of virtue only through his own instinct.' St Augustine of Hippo (354–430) was one of the greatest and most solemn thinkers and theologians of the early Church.

1931 *the Abate*: i.e. Guido's brother, Abate Paolo; cf. I. 553 n.

1933 *glorious life*: cf. Rom. 8: 21: 'the glorious liberty of the children of God'.

"Call me knave and you get yourself called fool!
"I live for greed, ambition, lust, revenge;
"Attain these ends by force, guile: hypocrite,
"To-day, perchance to-morrow recognized
"The rational man, the type of common sense."
There's Loyola adapted to our time!
Under such guidance Guido plays his part,
He also influencing in the due turn
These last clods where I track intelligence
By any glimmer, these four at his beck
Ready to murder any, and, at their own,
As ready to murder him,—such make the world!
And, first effect of the new cause of things,
There they lie also duly,—the old pair
Of the weak head and not so wicked heart,
With the one Christian mother, wife and girl,
—Which three gifts seem to make an angel up,—
The world's first foot o' the dance is on their heads!

Still, I stand here, not off the stage though close
On the exit: and my last act, as my first,
I owe the scene, and Him who armed me thus

1937 *MS* fool. 1938 *MS* revenge, 1939 *MS* ^ends^ *MS* guile,—hypocrite 1940 *MS* To-day,— 1941 *MS* sense" 1942 *MS* Lola>Loyola 1943 *MS* his guidance 1944 *MS 1868* in due 1946 *MS 1868* those 1948 *MS* {beginning of fo. 242} *MS* these are the world: *1868* these are 1949 *MS* the first *MS* [ ]>effect *MS* state>cause 1950 *MS* duly: *Yale 1* duly:>duly,— 1952 *MS 1868* And 1953 *MS* Which *MS* gifts make *MS* up, 1954 *MS 1868* The first foot of *MS* heads. *1955 *MS 1868* {new paragraph. Paragraphing obscured in *1872* by this line's being at the head of the page} *1888 1889* {no new paragraph} 1956 *MS* {no commas}

1942 *Loyola . . . time!*: i.e. 'there's a kind of Ignatius Loyola, but practising an even more devious kind of reasoning'. St Ignatius Loyola (1491–1556), founder of the Jesuits, was often regarded by Protestants in the nineteenth century as the originator of the casuistic processes of reasoning that they saw as typical of the Jesuit Order.

1945 *clods*: (lit.) 'idiots', (fig.) 'lumps of earth': the four farm-hands who helped Guido with the murders.

1947 *at their own*: i.e. at their own [beck].

1949 *new . . . things*: cf. 'new order of things', l. 1911.

1954 *world's . . . heads*: i.e. the grotesque dance of the antimasque (predicted at ll. 1904–9) has the Comparini and Pompilia as its first victims.

With Paul's sword as with Peter's key. I smite
With my whole strength once more, ere end my part,
Ending, so far as man may, this offence.
And when I raise my arm, who plucks my sleeve?
Who stops me in the righteous function,—foe
Or friend? Oh, still as ever, friends are they
Who, in the interest of outraged truth
Deprecate such rough handling of a lie!
The facts being proved and incontestable,
What is the last word I must listen to?
Perchance—"Spare yet a term this barren stock
"We pray thee dig about and dung and dress
"Till he repent and bring forth fruit even yet!"
Perchance—"So poor and swift a punishment
"Shall throw him out of life with all that sin:
"Let mercy rather pile up pain on pain
"Till the flesh expiate what the soul pays else!"
Nowise! Remonstrants on each side commence
Instructing, there's a new tribunal now

1958 *MS* keys,—I *Yale 1* key,—I>key. I 1959 *MS* more then *1868* more, then 1961 *MS 1868* what 1962 *MS* What *MS* foes 1963 *MS* friends? O, *1868* O, 1964 *MS* the outraged 1966 *MS* are>being *MS* here incontestably *Yale 1* here>and *MS* {no comma} 1968 *MS 1868* Is it "Spare *MS* tree *1868 1872* stock, 1969, 1970 *MS* {no quotation marks at beginnings of lines} 1969 *MS* We mean to 1970 *MS* yet? *MS* {no quotation mark at end of line} *1868* yet?" 1971 *MS* Or else "So>Is it "So *1868* Is it "So *MS* punishment? 1972–4 *MS* {no quotation marks at beginnings of lines} 1972 *MS* You *MS 1868* sin? 1974 *MS 1868* else?" 1975 *MS* {beginning of fo. 243} *MS* Nowise: remonstrance on all sides begins *1868* Nowise! Remonstrance on all sides begins 1976 *MS* Instruct me *1868* Instruct me,

---

1958 *Paul's . . . key*: i.e. with Paul's sword of justice as with Peter's key of spiritual authority. The Pope refers to the traditional attributes of the two apostles, St Paul's sword (with which he was executed), and St Peter's key (the key to heaven, from Matt. 16: 19). Browning, however, is thinking of the sword in terms of Eph. 6: 17: 'the sword of the Spirit, which is the word of God'. He might be remembering the colossal statues of the two saints at the bottom of the flight of steps up to St Peter's. These statues, St Peter with his key by Giuseppe de Fabris, and St Paul with his sword by Adamo Tadolini, were erected in the mid-nineteenth century by Pius IX.

1968–70 "*Spare . . . yet!*": cf. Luke 13: 8–9: 'Lord, let it [the fig tree] alone this year also, till I shall dig about it, and dung it.'

1974 *expiate*: atone for.

1975 *Remonstrants*: objectors, protesters; cf. I. 362.

Higher than God's—the educated man's!
Nice sense of honour in the human breast
Supersedes here the old coarse oracle—
Confirming none the less a point or so
Wherein blind predecessors worked aright
By rule of thumb: as when Christ said,—when, where?
Enough, I find it pleaded in a place,—
"All other wrongs done, patiently I take:
"But touch my honour and the case is changed!
"I feel the due resentment,—*nemini*
"*Honorem trado* is my quick retort."
Right of Him, just as if pronounced to-day!
Still, should the old authority be mute,
Or doubtful, or in speaking clash with new,
The younger takes permission to decide.
At last we have the instinct of the world
Ruling its household without tutelage:
And while the two laws, human and divine,
Have busied finger with this tangled case,
In pushes the brisk junior, cuts the knot,
Pronounces for acquittal. How it trips

1977 *MS 1868* God's,— *MS* man's,— 1980 *MS 1868* Confirming handsomely a 1981 *MS 1868* the predecessor 1983 *MS* Enough we find it in a pleading here,— *Yale 1* Enough>Enough, *1868* Enough, I find it in a pleading here,— 1985–7 *MS* {no quotation marks at beginnings of lines} 1985 *MS* changed, 1987 *MS 1868 1872 trado,* 1988 *MS* Right, just as right as *1989 *MS 1868 1872* mute, *1888 1889* mute *1990 *MS 1868 1872* doubtful, *1888 1889* doubtful 1991 *MS* takes it on him 1993 *MS 1868* tutelage, 1995 *MS* busied noddle *MS* knotty>tangled 1996 *MS* The brisk youth pushes in and cuts the knot,>The brisk junior pushes in and cuts knot,>In the brisk junior pushes, cuts the knot, *1868* In the brisk junior pushes, cuts the knot,

---

1978 *Nice*: exact, fastidious.

1986–7 : *nemini / Honorem trado*: 'I will not give my honour to another' (L.). Here the Pope is simply reading from Arcangeli's speech, one of the documents he has in front of him, and so following Arcangeli into error: cf. VIII. 663–66. Christ, of course, never said anything like this. (The biblical quotations which come nearest to fitting are Isa. 42: 8, 48: 11, but even these, in the Vulgate, are not close.) This is one of many small touches of realism in Browning's portrait of the Pope: the frail, old man makes a mistake with the Bible, even though he is otherwise wise and saintly.

1996 *brisk junior*: i.e. the 'new', 'younger', worldly authority (of ll. 1989–91).

Silverly o'er the tongue! "Remit the death!
"Forgive, . . . well, in the old way, if thou please,
"Decency and the relics of routine
"Respected,—let the Count go free as air!
"Since he may plead a priest's immunity,—
"The minor orders help enough for that,
"With Farinacci's licence,—who decides
"That the mere implication of such man,
"So privileged, in any cause, before
"Whatever Court except the Spiritual,
"Straight quashes law-procedure,—quash it, then!
"Remains a pretty loophole of escape
"Moreover, that, beside the patent fact
"O' the law's allowance, there's involved the weal
"O' the Popedom: a son's privilege at stake,
"Thou wilt pretend the Church's interest,
"Ignore all finer reasons to forgive!
"But herein lies the crowning cogency—
"(Let thy friends teach thee while thou tellest beads)
"That in this case the spirit of culture speaks,
"Civilization is imperative.

1998 *MS* O'er the silver tongue "You will remit the death;>Silverly o'er the tongue "Remit the death; 1999–2061 *MS* {no quotation marks at beginnings of lines} 1999 *MS* Forgive, . . *1868 1872* "Forgive, . . *MS* you please— 2000 *MS* Decency's sake, 2001 *MS* Respected, *MS* air 2002 *MS* immunity, 2003 *MS* {beginning of fo. 244} *MS* {no comma} 2004 *MS* Farinaccio's *MS* he decides 2005 *MS* {no comma} 2007 *1868 1872* court 2008 *MS 1868* the procedure,— *Yale 2* law-procedure,—>law-procedure: *MS* it then; 2009 *MS* It proves *1868* "It proves 2011 *MS* Of 2012 *MS* Of *MS* Popedom,— *MS* [ ]>privilege 2013 *MS* You may *Yale 1* Thou may'st>Thou wilt *MS* Churche's *MS* dignity, 2014 *MS* forgive: 2015 *MS* proper cogency *1868* proper cogency— 2016 *MS* (Let us but teach you while you tell your beads) *Yale 1* your beads)>beads)

1998 *Remit*: cancel, forego.

2004 *Farinacci's*: Prospero Farinacci (1544–1616), the important Italian jurist: see VIII. 148 n.

2005 *implication*: involvement, connection.

2011 *weal*: prestige, well-being.

2018 *Civilization*: i.e. the civilized ideal. Browning's use is ironic and double-edged: too smooth an ideal of culture, honour, and the deference due to rank obscures larger truths of morality and religion. Cf. I. 287 n.

"To her shall we remand all delicate points
"Henceforth, nor take irregular advice
"O' the sly, as heretofore: she used to hint
"Remonstrances, when law was out of sorts
"Because a saucy tongue was put to rest,
"An eye that roved was cured of arrogance:
"But why be forced to mumble under breath
"What soon shall be acknowledged as plain fact,
"Outspoken, say, in thy successor's time?
"Methinks we see the golden age return!
"Civilization and the Emperor
"Succeed to Christianity and Pope.
"One Emperor then, as one Pope now: meanwhile,
"Anticipate a little! We tell thee 'Take
"'Guido's life, sapped society shall crash,
"'Whereof the main prop was, is, and shall be
"'—Supremacy of husband over wife!'
"Does the man rule i' the house, and may his mate
"Because of any plea dispute the same?
"Oh, pleas of all sorts shall abound, be sure,
"One but allowed validity,—for, harsh
"And savage, for, inept and silly-sooth,

2021 *MS* On *MS* heretofore,— 2022 *MS* Apologies when law was difficult *1868* "Apologies when 2024 *MS* was>that *MS* impudence, *Yale 1* impudence:>arrogance: 2026 *MS* all acknowledge to be>soon shall be acknowledged *MS* the plain truth *Yale 1* truth,>fact, *1868 1872* the plain fact, 2027 *MS* your 2028 *MS* I see *MS* return,— 2030 *MS* the Christianity *1868* thy Christianity 2031 *MS* {beginning of fo. 245} *MS* now. Meanwhile, 2032 *MS* She anticipates a little and tells you, *Yale 1* and tells>to tell *1868* "She anticipates a little to tell thee *MS* [ ]>Take 2033 *MS* Count Guido's life you sap society, *1868* "'Count Guido's life, and sap society, 2034 *MS 1868* shall prove 2035 *MS* wife. *MS* {no quotation mark at end of line} 2036 *MS* Shall *1868* "Shall *MS* in *MS* or shall *1868* or may 2037 *MS* same— 2038 *MS* For pleas *Yale 1* "For pleas>"Oh, pleas 2039 *MS* If once *1868* "If once *MS* for harsh 2040 *MS* for inept

---

2022 *Remonstrances*: grievances, objections.

2033 *sapped society . . . crash*: i.e. demoralized society will collapse.

2039–42 *for . . . slave*: i.e. 'women ("the ingenious sex") will prove the best master in the world to be either harsh and savage, inept and naïve, or something or other'. For 'silly-sooth' cf. III. 805–6 n.

"For, this and that, will the ingenious sex
"Demonstrate the best master e'er graced slave:
"And there's but one short way to end the coil,—
"Acknowledge right and reason steadily
"I' the man and master: then the wife submits
"To plain truth broadly stated. Does the time
"Advise we shift—a pillar? nay, a stake
"Out of its place i' the social tenement?
"One touch may send a shudder through the heap
"And bring it toppling on our children's heads!
"Moreover, if ours breed a qualm in thee,
"Give thine own better feeling play for once!
"Thou, whose own life winks o'er the socket-edge,
"Wouldst thou it went out in such ugly snuff
"As dooming sons dead, e'en though justice prompt?
"Why, on a certain feast, Barabbas' self
"Was set free, not to cloud the general cheer:
"Neither shalt thou pollute thy Sabbath close!

2041 *MS* {no commas} 2042 *MS* ere *MS* slave, 2044 *MS 1868* By giving 2045 *MS* To *1868* "To *MS* submits: 2046 *MS* There *1868* "There *MS 1868* it is broadly stated,—nor the time 2047 *MS* Admits *1868* "Admits *MS* Nay, 2048 *MS* in *1868* i' *MS 1868* the tenement, one touch 2049 *MS* Whereto *MS* ma[ ]>may *1868* "Whereto may 2050 *MS 1868* our heads perchance. 2051 *MS* Moreover if this breed *Yale 1* Moreover>Moreover, *1868* Moreover, if this breed *MS* you, 2052 *MS* [ ]>Give *MS* [ ]>your *MS 1868* own feelings play for once,—deal death? 2053 *MS* You, *MS* socket-edge 2054 *MS* Would you *1868 1872* "Would'st thou 2055 *MS* sons to death though justice were? *1868* sons to death, though justice bade? 2056 *MS* feast Barabbas' 2057 *MS 1868* {no comma} *MS* cheer; *1868* cheer. 2058 *MS* Trouble not your own sabbath close!>Nor trouble nor pollute your sabbath close!

2043 *coil*: complexity, confusion.

2053 *winks . . . socket-edge*: i.e. 'is near to extinction'. The socket is the part of the candlestick that holds the candle, and a candle 'burnt to the socket' is one burnt right down. Browning is producing a variant of this well-used figure and applying it to the life of man; OED[2] cites Walter Scott, *Chronicles of the Canongate* (1827), vol. i, ch. 1: 'The light of life . . . was trembling in the socket.'

2056 *Barabbas' self*: see Matt. 27: 15–26.

2058 *pollute . . . close*: pollute the ending of your holy day, i.e. your reign as Pope. Christ's body was taken down from the cross to avoid polluting the Sabbath: cf. John 19: 31.

"Mercy is safe and graceful. How one hears
"The howl begin, scarce the three little taps
"O' the silver mallet silent on thy brow,—
"'His last act was to sacrifice a Count
"'And thereby screen a scandal of the Church!
"'Guido condemned, the Canon justified
"'Of course,—delinquents of his cloth go free!'
"And so the Luthers chuckle, Calvins scowl,
"So thy hand helps Molinos to the chair
"Whence he may hold forth till doom's day on just
"These *petit-maître* priestlings,—in the choir
"*Sanctus et Benedictus*, with a brush
"Of soft guitar-strings that obey the thumb,
"Touched by the bedside, for accompaniment!
"Does this give umbrage to a husband? Death
"To the fool, and to the priest impunity!
"But no impunity to any friend
"So simply over-loyal as these four
"Who made religion of their patron's cause,

2059 *MS* {beginning of fo. 246} 2061 *MS* Of *MS* ended on your *1868* ended on thy 2062 *MS* "His *MS* man 2063–98 *MS* {no quotation marks at beginnings of lines} 2063 *MS* Church: 2065 *MS* free, 2066 *MS* your Luthers and your Calvins come, *1868* the Luthers and the Calvins come, 2067 *MS* your 2069 *MS* *petit-maitre*-priestlings,— *MS* Choir *1868 1872* choir, 2070 *MS* *Benedictus*,— 2072 *MS* accompaniment. 2075 *MS* This husband too>But no impunity *etc.* 2076 *MS* As 2077 *MS* Patron's

2060–1 *three . . . brow*: a detail of the ceremonies attending the death of a Pope which Browning read about in W. W. Story: 'As soon as he [the Pope] has breathed his last, the cardinal *camerlengo*, dressed in his *paonazzo* robes, with the *chierici* of the reverend chamber, clothed in black without lace, enter the room, and cover the face of the dead Pope with a white handkerchief. The cardinal, after making a brief prayer, rises, the face of the Pope is uncovered, and approaching the bed, he strikes three times with a silver hammer on the forehead of the corpse, calling him as many times by name to answer. As the corpse remains speechless, he turns to his companions, and formally announces that "*Il papa è realmente morto*" ': *Roba di Roma*, ii. 152.

2065 *of his cloth*: i.e. of his kind (a priest).

2067 *Molinos*: cf. IX. 33 n.

2069 *petit-maître*: foppish.

2069–72 *in . . . accompaniment*: i.e. 'in church they sing the Sanctus and Benedictus (parts of the Mass) as required, but this is accompanied (as it were) by their sensual "strumming" on the guitar, by the bedside (as they woo their lovers)'.

"Believed in him and did his bidding straight,
"Asked not one question but laid down the lives
"This Pope took,—all four lives together made
"Just his own length of days,—so, dead they lie,
"As these were times when loyalty's a drug,
"And zeal in a subordinate too cheap
"And common to be saved when we spend life!
"Come, 't is too much good breath we waste in words:
"The pardon, Holy Father! Spare grimace,
"Shrugs and reluctance! Are not we the world,
"Art not thou Priam? Let soft culture plead
"Hecuba-like, '*non tali*' (Virgil serves)
"'*Auxilio*,' and the rest! Enough, it works!
"The Pope relaxes, and the Prince is loth,
"The father's bowels yearn, the man's will bends,
"Reply is apt. Our tears on tremble, hearts
"Big with a benediction, wait the word
"Shall circulate thro' the city in a trice,
"Set every window flaring, give each man

2078 *MS* {no comma} 2079 *MS* their lives ⋆2080 *MS 1868* made *1872 1888 1889* make 2081 *MS* so dead they are, 2082 *MS* These being the times 2084 *MS* life. *Yale 1* life.>life! 2085 *MS* breathe *Yale 2* words:> words. 2086 *MS* spare 2087 *MS* {beginning of fo. 247} *MS* reluctance. 2088 *MS* Bid you, our Priam, let *1868* "Bid thee, our Priam, let 2089 *MS* "Non tali" ⋆2090 *MS* Auxilio, *1868 1872* "'*Auxilio*,' *1888 1889* " '*Auxilio* ' {? broken sort} *MS* rest: enough, *MS* works: 2092 *MS* The Man's will bends, the Father's heart flows o'er.>The Father's bowels yearn, the Man's will bends. 2093 *MS* Speak the apt word; our tears are trembling, hearts>Reply is apt: our tears on tremble, hearts 2094 *MS* {no comma} 2096 *MS* every house-face

---

2080–1 *all . . . days*: cf. 964 n.

2088–90 *Priam . . . rest*: see *Aeneid*, II. 521–2. When Troy was overrun by the Greeks and their victory inevitable, Priam, King of Troy, old and withered, nonetheless put on his youthful armour to make a last heroic gesture of defence. His wife Hecuba pleaded with him that this was useless: *non tali auxilio nec defensoribus istis / tempus eget* ('Not such help as this, not such defenders, the time demands'). The Pope too, ancient as Priam, should now (says the voice of the protester) give way quietly.

2091 *Prince is loth*: i.e. the Pope (as an earthly ruler) is reluctant.

2092 *bowels yearn*: i.e. he feels compassion; cf. Gen. 43: 30, 1 Kgs. 3: 26. The Pope, as a spiritual father to one of the 'sons' of the Church (Guido), will feel compassion for him.

"O' the mob his torch to wave for gratitude.
"Pronounce then, for our breath and patience fail!"

I will, Sirs: but a voice other than yours
Quickens my spirit. "*Quis pro Domino?*
"Who is upon the Lord's side?" asked the Count.
I, who write—
"On receipt of this command,
"Acquaint Count Guido and his fellows four
"They die to-morrow: could it be to-night,
"The better, but the work to do, takes time.
"Set with all diligence a scaffold up,
"Not in the customary place, by Bridge
"Saint Angelo, where die the common sort;
"But since the man is noble, and his peers
"By predilection haunt the People's Square,
"There let him be beheaded in the midst,
"And his companions hanged on either side:
"So shall the quality see, fear and learn.
"All which work takes time: till to-morrow, then,
"Let there be prayer incessant for the five!"

[—]

2097 *MS* Of 2098 *MS* Pronounce it, *1868* "Pronounce it, *MS* {no quotation mark at end of line} 2099 *MS 1868* for a 2100 *MS* "Quis pro Domino? 2101 {not found in *MS*} 2102 *MS* I am,>I, 2103–116 *MS* {no quotation marks at beginnings of lines} 2103 *MS* our>this *MS* {no comma} 2106 *MS* but I want work done 2107 *MS* {no comma} 2108 *MS* the Bridge 2109 *MS* Angelo where *MS* sort, 2111 *MS* haunt Del Popolo, 2112 *MS* {no comma} 2113 *MS* side,— 2114 *MS* Quality *Yale 2* see, fear>see, and fear 2115 *MS* {beginning of fo. 248} *MS* {no commas} 2116 *MS* Five."

2100–1 "*Quis . . . Count*: 'Who is for the Lord' (L.): the words of Moses in Exod. 32: 26. Guido boldly used these words at v. 1549; the Pope now throws them back at him.

2102 *I, who write*: Browning makes up the wording of the *chirograph* (special writ) with which the Pope condemned Guido, but he did know, from OYB ccxxxix (238), that the Pope signed it *alle due di notte* (at the second hour of the night), i.e. at approximately 7 p.m., a fact he noted in his chronologies, and which shapes the evening setting of this monologue: see Vol. VII, pp. 323, 325.

2108–11 *Bridge . . . People's Square*: cf. I. 350, 355 nn.

2114 *quality*: aristocracy, upper echelons of society. Cf. I. 276 n.

For the main criminal I have no hope
Except in such a suddenness of fate.
I stood at Naples once, a night so dark
I could have scarce conjectured there was earth
Anywhere, sky or sea or world at all:
But the night's black was burst through by a blaze—
Thunder struck blow on blow, earth groaned and bore,
Through her whole length of mountain visible:
There lay the city thick and plain with spires,
And, like a ghost disshrouded, white the sea.
So may the truth be flashed out by one blow,
And Guido see, one instant, and be saved.
Else I avert my face, nor follow him
Into that sad obscure sequestered state
Where God unmakes but to remake the soul
He else made first in vain; which must not be.
Enough, for I may die this very night
And how should I dare die, this man let live?

Carry this forthwith to the Governor!

2117 *MS* {New paragraph indicated by 'New P.' in left-hand margin} 2120 *MS* have conjectured 2123 *MS* blow earth 2124 *MS* visible, 2125 *MS* City *MS* [ ]>plain 2126 *MS* dis-shrouded,

2126 *disshrouded*: deprived of a shroud; fig. unveiled, exposed. OED^2 says it is 'very rare' and gives only one other use.

2130–1 *sad . . . soul*: i.e. Purgatory, where the soul is purged of its sins in order to enter Heaven.

INTRODUCTION TO BOOK XI
GUIDO

BOOK XI, the second monologue of Count Guido Franceschini, is the climax of *The Ring and the Book* as a whole, the cornerstone (to use a Browningesque metaphor) that gives shape to the work. Here is a daring artistic decision: to revisit the psychology of Guido for a second time. He is the only character in the poem who has the honour of two monologues devoted to him. The circumstances of the Book are gothic, though, as we shall see, its psychology is perhaps the most realistic in the poem.

Browning is now rounding his drama to its close. 'Half-Rome' (Book II) was imagined speaking just one or two days after the murders, on 3 or 4 January 1698. Now it is the early hours of 22 February. Guido Franceschini is in his prison cell, and two priests of aristocratic origin, the Cardinal Acciaiuoli and the Abate Panciatichi, his friends in early life, have come to hear his confession and prepare him for death. Browning learnt this detail from the Secondary Source (para. 19), and it is the only real fact grounding the monologue.

As the different titles of Books V and XI make clear, we are now seeing Guido in a new guise. In Book V he was the lofty 'Count Guido Franceschini', hopeful that he might get off, cunning in argument, and in his self-presentation to the court: 'I am representative of a great line, / One of the first of the old families / In Arezzo, ancientest of Tuscan towns' (v. 140–2). Now he is stripped down, just plain 'Guido'. He is still trying all the ruses he can to justify himself and to escape death, but there is more panic and confusion underlying his whole position. Evasive and wheedling, he has fewer means of escape: 'the very gripe / O' the jaws of death's gigantic skull' is one of the ominous notes in the monologue (1035–6).

The *mise en scène* is not recalled here, but the claustrophobic intensity of the speech reminds us where we are: 'in a close fetid cell, / Where the hot vapour of an agony, / Struck into drops on the cold wall, runs down—/ Horrible worms made out of sweat and tears' (I. 1286–9). This is Guido's agony as he faces up to the way the Pope has rejected his appeal on the grounds of the clericate, and to the fact he will now be executed. It is a parodic version of Christ's agony in the Garden of Gethesmane, with nothing good or virtuous to redeem it. Guido fails in his task of confessing his sins and making his peace with God and the world; instead he continues with the business of self-exculpation, casuistic excuses for the whole course of his behaviour, demands and pleas for a last-minute reprieve. At times he is even philosophical, utilitarian at one point, neopagan at another (515–34, 1911–2003). The priests are horrified. Abate Panciatichi keeps thrusting the crucifix in Guido's face. (Traditionally a man facing execution was expected to kiss the crucifix as a sign of his repentance.) Guido, in 'wolf-like' fashion, eventually threatens to bite off the Abate's hand (2222).

As was evident in Book V, though there was a historical Guido Franceschini who participated in the real series of events comprising the murder and trial, the character and psychology of the evil monster Browning conjures up were his own invention. This is reinforced here. There is nothing in the sources guiding or constraining the way in which the poet conceived Guido in these hours of stress. Operating within this freedom, and having already established the framework of the character in Book V, Browning produces an eerie *tour de force* of psychological exploration as the high-point of his whole work.

Here (more than in Book V) it is clearly unhelpful to call Guido 'evil' without knowing what we mean by that term (or by related terms, repentance and grace). His character is in many respects fascinating and charismatic: we enjoy some of his arguments, a lot of his vivid phrase-making, and so we are lead into complex reactions of sympathy and distaste in relation to some of the things he says. Cook makes the point well:

> Browning's Guido, like his other scoundrels, . . . is highly intellectualized; his thoughts, like theirs, often hit the truth, they are sometimes profound, sometimes almost noble; he is a master of irony, satire, and invective; many of his descriptions, some of his vilest imaginings, are of amazing power and brilliancy.[1]

In these circumstances, it seems worthwhile to spell out some of the ways in which our sympathy is most obviously engaged.

First, the fear of death. Guido gives a powerful, eerie description of the *mannaia* (guillotine) that will eventually kill him (181–258), which Browning based on his own shocked recollection of seeing a just-used guillotine.[2] As Guido imagines it, the young men of the town lounge

[1] Cook, 236. [2] See ll. 214–41 n.

round it, discussing its workings as modern loafers might discuss a car (242–6). As its wooden rafters shake in the wind, the guillotine is like a famished 'old skeleton bat', after long hibernation eager for its next meal (451–3). Later Guido will try to say that he is sick of the whole atrocious, tedious thing called Life, but fear obtrudes. Everyone moves inexorably to the grave like waves to a rock. This rock (of Death) is 'the boundary whereon I break to mist' (2357). It is the partly lyrical nature of this passage that makes it so haunting: death comes 'Spite of the blue tranquillity above, / Spite of the breadth before of lapsing peace / Where broods the halcyon and the fish leaps free' (2360–2).

Second, Guido has an impressive sense of the vanity of things, of 'the world' (in St John's sense of it). He brilliantly evokes the social machine of church and state, its disorientations and alienations, where people struggle for wealth and position, where some are 'up' and others 'down'—on this he casts a cold eye. The pageantry of Catholicism in Rome seems to him a sham; all religion indeed seems mincing and unmasculine (he yearns for the amoral vigour, as he sees it, of paganism, 1911–2003). And he picks out ludicrous stories and ludicrous instances of costume and position to back his attack on worldliness: there is the 'wasp-like black and yellow foolery' worn by the Swiss Guards, for instance, and 'His Altitude the Referendary', in correct robes, waiting for an audience with the Pope (627, 638). Under this, and partly endorsing it, is Browning's Protestant sensibility: 'Who has ever heard of a "Referendary"?' he might seem to ask. The elaborate institutional machine, with all its nuances, laws, and rituals: what has this really to do with the religion of Christ?

Guido's attack on religious hypocrisy is particularly effective, the fact that (as he sees it) most people are no more than 'Born-baptized-and-bred Christian-atheists' (709). This seems a palpable hit from most points of view. He seems to echo the Pope in the way he contrasts Christianity's first age with the long age of worldly religious compromise that has since followed (1975–2003). Guido wants 'Entire faith, or else complete unbelief!' (730) He is rather like the Misfit, in Flannery O'Connor's 'A Good Man is Hard to Find', who, having rejected the possibility of a supernatural dimension, sees 'no pleasure but meanness'.[3] Like the Misfit, Guido, in the face of nihilism, has chosen to satisfy his deepest sadistic urges. None the less, his perverse choice of unbelief is (in his case) a dark inversion of the longing for coherent religious vision.

[3] Flannery O'Connor, *A Good Man is Hard to Find* (Faber, 1968), p. 22.

Finally, there is his self-presentation as a middle-aged man, envious of youth, but attracted to its beauty and energy. He is the sexually experienced man: Pompilia (at his first sight of her) appears insipid, 'with milk for blood', a pathetic 'dog-rose bell' with no aroma (965, 1098). He wants really to enjoy sexuality: the 'beads' of 'froth' on top of the 'black o' the wine' of life (1080–2). He wants a woman who is a 'hundred-petalled Provence prodigy' 'breathing spice' (1099–1100). I am still 'juicy', I am full of 'sap', 'young still', he insists (like a million middle-aged men before him): 'I'd live /And die conceding age no right of youth! / It is the will runs the renewing nerve / Through flaccid flesh that faints before the time' (148, 152, 1897–1901).

So, he celebrates himself as being like Titian—a sombre, sensuous, worldly genius, and Pompilia's 'chalky' virtue as being like the monkish imaginings of Fra Angelico (2114–24). Implicitly, he holds up his robust temperament, against this lack of virility and push; and, again, from one perspective, he is thoroughly Protestant in doing so.[4] The height of his sexual fantasy is the depiction of the wife he would really have liked, a hyper-sensuous Delilah, a passionate, independent, amoral, highly sexed woman, who would, none the less, be the slave of his wishes and commands (2182–2205). One critic is particularly indignant: 'It . . . is a kind of climax, a climax of rottenness at the core of a drab, deprived, menopausal monster desirous only of glutting himself on evil and teasing himself into a state of solitary sexual frenzy by imagining himself . . . dominant over the indomitable.'[5] This may be the case, but these passages resonate with common experience, and we enjoy their vividly realized mindset.

Aspects of Guido's evil, however, are clearly on the surface. Long before 'sexism' was thought of, Browning was exploring something of what it meant. 'Manly', 'man', and 'manliness' are some of Guido's most insistent terms (43, 799, 987, 2252, 2412), and his idea here is mixed up with his sense of hierarchy and aristocratic privilege—and with his sadism. Browning, a political liberal, draws together the worst excesses of what could be imagined of an aristocrat of the *ancien régime*, jealous of his own privileges, contemptuous of those under him, with the expectation that the world revolve around him. Guido looks down from above, and controls (or fantasizes control over) all that is beneath.

[4] For nineteenth-century reactions to the 'monkish' aspect of Fra Angelico's paintings, see D. J. DeLaura, 'The Context of Browning's Painter Poems', *PMLA* 95 (1980), 367–88.

[5] Buckler, 265.

First we notice the 'virile' energy of his contempt. Old men, without passion, are 'shrunk-shanked, . . . windlestraws that stare while purblind death / Mows here, mows there' (145–8). The middle-class Comparini are 'abominable nondescripts', 'ambiguous insects' (1116, 1263). The Cardinal and the Abate display 'swine-like snuffling greed and grunting lust' (1502). His fellow assassins will swing on the gallows 'like scarecrows in a hemp-field' (1753). Examples could be multiplied.

Then, there is his sadism. Guido remembers the multiple wounds he inflicted on Pietro Comparini, how he 'cut away' his life 'morsel by morsel' (472–3). Before her parents abandoned her at his palace, he recalls how Pompilia 'could play off her sex's armoury, . . . Try all the shrieking doubles of the hare': she is the panicked hare desperately seeking to preserve her life, he is the huntsman, or perhaps the blood-smelling hound (1330). When he caught the 'lovers' at the inn at Castelnuovo he wishes he had 'pinned them each to other partridge-wise' (1542). He boasts of how his knowledge of anatomy (learnt as a young man from his fencing-master) allowed him to stab Pompilia more effectively (1679). Some critics point out that a lot of this has the air of macho fantasy, brag, and bravura: underneath Guido is more sneaking and frightened, with neither the courage nor dash to live up to this self-image. None the less, our fantasies are part of our deepest reality, and his fantasies are insistently ugly. When the teenage Pompilia is first brought before him, Guido remembers how she had to be kept away from her toys, and he sees her 'loose' at last of her mother, 'Held only by the mother's finger-tip' (975). The relish in this phrase, and the doubly ironic presentation, cast Guido as a kind of child molester, and Pompilia as his next victim.

The real source of the monologue's impressiveness, however, comes from another, larger aspect: the way in which it depicts Guido completely locked within the world of his own thinking, the world of his own prejudices and presuppositions, the way he cannot see out of this. Several times he is disturbed by deep recollections of Pompilia. Once, indeed, her image is so insistent that it seems like a hallucination (2076–7). In one part of his mind he is disturbed by the fact that he *knows* that she intended nothing but good to him. She was profoundly virtuous; even now she would beg God for his forgiveness, and weep at the thought of him in hell: 'There was no touch in her of hate' (2089). This kind of recognition haunts him in a perverse way, but he can make nothing of it. His thoughts of Pompilia—like any thoughts he might have of God—never reach home, never reveal their true meaning to him, though sometimes they come close to doing so.

Browning's skill here is to create the closed-up mind of the truly wretched man. There are realms of goodness, intimacy, virtue, kindness, and joy that Guido has deliberately chosen not to access. He has not accessed them because he has preferred to maintain the insecure fantasy of his own dominance. He looks back with nostalgia to the good old days, when a lord could kill a peasant with impunity (103–6). In this context, he constructs himself as a 'manly' aristocrat, within a hierarchical society that validates his own importance, and that should allow him to prey on whom he pleases.

Debate has arisen about whether Guido's final lines constitute a moment of 'salvation' or 'redemption', or whether they are only a moment of sheer panic.[6] Certainly they are deeply satisfying in dramatic terms. As he has been unwinding the long coil of his complex nature through his speech, the dawn has been gradually coming up, so that now it penetrates even his fetid cell. The *Compagnia della Morte e della Misericordia* arrive, the volunteers with their black hats and hoods with eye-slits, whose job it is to accompany him to the place of execution. Guido sees their lights flickering on the other side of his death cell, and hears their chanting of the psalm. Now he is frantic. He begs to be simply treated as a madman, chained forever to the floor of the cell (but not executed) (2422–3). And then his last words: 'Pompilia, will you let them murder me?' (2427)

It is hard to conceive that this breathless question entails self-knowledge. As one critic argues persuasively, if Guido could 'see the stark truth [of all he has done], admit his complicity in it, and face the consequence with a degree of moral grandeur', then we should be dealing with his 'tragic redemption', and this is not at all the feel of this 'pathetic' ending.[7] But Guido knows that Pompilia would not condemn him, and she stands therefore as an image of God's mercy, or at least (in his own harsher terms) 'the terrible patience of God' (1380). And what do we make of his claim that 'God takes his own part in each thing He made' (2301)? Is it a real theological intuition, or the worst delusion? In his final moment, Guido seems to revert to the hallucination of Pompilia that he has at 2076–7. His appeal to her can certainly be seen as bogus, simply marking out the depths of his depravity. Yet, if it shows nothing as large or certain as 'redemption', it does show his mind touching for a moment on higher things, the realms of compassion and

[6] See ll. 2426–7 n. [7] Buckler, 269.

love that he has spent his life radically excluding from view. So, we have a genuine ambivalence here, something inconclusive and open-ended, that returns us again to the whole mystery of his wickedness: how did he ever manage to construct his world? how did he ever manage so comprehensively to misread reality?

XI.

GUIDO.

YOU are the Cardinal Acciaiuoli, and you,
Abate Panciatichi—two good Tuscan names:
Acciaiuoli—ah, your ancestor it was
Built the huge battlemented convent-block
Over the little forky flashing Greve
That takes the quick turn at the foot o' the hill
Just as one first sees Florence: oh those days!
'T is Ema, though, the other rivulet,
The one-arched brown brick bridge yawns over,—yes,

MS {fo. 249. At the head of the page is the title '11. Guido. <[ ]>' in RB's hand}
1 *MS* you   3 *1868 1872* was,   8 *MS* rivulet   9 *MS* yes

---

1–2 *Acciaiuoli . . . Panciatichi*: see SS 19: 'At the 8th hour, the death-sentence was communicated to Franceschini and his companions, and they were placed in the Consorteria: there, with the aid of Signor Abate Panciatici [*sic*] and Cardinal Acciaiuoli, they prepared themselves, without difficulty, to make a good death.' Browning would also have come upon these names in his researches into Innocent XII. Both, he realized, were old Florentine families, and he makes Guido appeal to the priests on this account as fellow Tuscan aristocrats. Niccolò Acciaiuoli (b. 1630) was made a cardinal by Clement IX. He was a serious contender for the papacy in the conclaves of both 1691 and 1700, but was blocked by the Austrian interest, a fact that Browning knew: see 2346–7 n. Abate Panciatichi, an obscure figure, was harder to characterize, and Browning did so via his relative, Cardinal Bandino Panciatichi (b. 1629). This Cardinal was also considered as a potential pope in the conclave that elected Innocent, and was subsequently one of his closest advisers: he is referred to in ll. 1243–56.

4 *battlemented convent-block*: the fortress-like, Carthusian monastery complex, Certosa di Galluzzo, which rises on the summit of a hill to the south of Florence, about 2½ miles from 'the Roman Gate' (11). In its day, it was one of the most powerful monasteries in Europe. 'The building crowns the pleasant height, a beautiful and regularly formed hill, covered with olives and vines; and its first aspect, with its fine Gothic windows, battlements, and tower-like masses, is entirely like that of a castle': Murray's *Handbook for Travellers in Northern Italy* (4th ed., 1852), p. 547. As Guido

Gallop and go five minutes, and you gain
The Roman Gate from where the Ema's bridged:
Kingfishers fly there: how I see the bend
O'erturreted by Certosa which he built,
That Senescal (we styled him) of your House!
I do adjure you, help me, Sirs! My blood
Comes from as far a source: ought it to end
This way, by leakage through their scaffold-planks
Into Rome's sink where her red refuse runs?
Sirs, I beseech you by blood-sympathy,
If there be any vile experiment
In the air,—if this your visit simply prove,
When all's done, just a well-intentioned trick
That tries for truth truer than truth itself,
By startling up a man, ere break of day,
To tell him he must die at sunset,—pshaw!
That man's a Franceschini; feel his pulse,
Laugh at your folly, and let's all go sleep!
You have my last word,—innocent am I
As Innocent my Pope and murderer,
Innocent as a babe, as Mary's own,

10 *MS* {no comma} 13 *MS* {no comma} 14 *MS* House. 16 *MS* source,— 17 *MS* {no comma} 21 *MS* air, *Yale 1* air,>air,— *22 *1868 1872 1888* trick, *DC BrU* trick,>trick *1889* trick 23 *MS* {no comma} 24 *MS* {no commas} 29 *MS* {beginning of fo. 250}

asserts, its construction was begun in 1341 at the behest of Niccolò Acciaiuoli (1310–68), from the wealthy Florentine family. Niccolò settled at Naples as a trader, made a large fortune, and, *c.* 1348, became Grand Seneschal of Queen Giovanna (see next n.). He is buried in an elaborate tomb in the monastery. Outside the monastic buildings rises the battlemented Acciaiuoli Palace, a fact Browning presumably knows. His evocation of the scene, and the meeting of the rivers Greve and Ema, is drawn from memory.

14 *Senescal*: an important official to a sovereign, dealing with the administration of justice and domestic arrangements: see previous n.

16–18 *ought . . . runs?*: i.e. ought my aristocratic blood to end up in the sewer of the shambles, mixing with that of the slaughtered animals?

24–5 *ere . . . sunset*: Guido was informed of the death-sentence 'at the 8th hour', approximately 1 a.m.: see SS 19. Browning assumes that Panciatici and Acciaiuoli arrived some time afterwards, but 'ere cock-crow' (XII. 124). Guido's execution took place the following afternoon.

As Mary's self,—I said, say and repeat,—
And why, then, should I die twelve hours hence? I—
Whom, not twelve hours ago, the gaoler bade
Turn to my straw-truss, settle and sleep sound
That I might wake the sooner, promptlier pay
His due of meat-and-drink-indulgence, cross
His palm with fee of the good-hand, beside,
As gallants use who go at large again!
For why? All honest Rome approved my part;
Whoever owned wife, sister, daughter,—nay,
Mistress,—had any shadow of any right
That looks like right, and, all the more resolved,
Held it with tooth and nail,—these manly men
Approved! I being for Rome, Rome was for me.
Then, there's the point reserved, the subterfuge
My lawyers held by, kept for last resource,
Firm should all else,—the impossible fancy!—fail,
And sneaking burgess-spirit win the day:
The knaves! One plea at least would hold,—they laughed,—
One grappling-iron scratch the bottom-rock
Even should the middle mud let anchor go!
I hooked my cause on to the Clergy's,—plea
Which, even if law tipped off my hat and plume,
Revealed my priestly tonsure, saved me so.
The Pope moreover, this old Innocent,

31 *MS* self, *MS* repeat, 32 *MS* {no commas} 36 *MS 1868* dues 38 *MS* again: 39 *MS* part, 41 *MS* the mere>any 42 *MS* and all *MS* resolved 44 *MS* Approved,— *1868 1872* me! 46 *MS* resource 47 *MS* fancy!,—drop— *1868* fail,— ⋆48 *MS 1868 1872* day: *1888 1889* day. 49 *MS* ^The knaves!^ *MS* hold, they said, *1868* hold, they laughed, 50 *MS* grappling iron *Yale 1* grappling iron>grappling-iron *MS* bottom rock 51 *MS* slide— *1868* go— 52 *MS 1868* And hook 53 *MS* should law tip off hat 54 *MS* Showed the Pope my priest's-tonsure, saved me so,— *1868* Would show *1868* so,—

34 *straw-truss*: a bundle of straw (used as a bed).
37 *fee . . . good-hand*: i.e. tip, Anglicizing *buonamano* (It.).
48 *burgess-spirit*: i.e. the spirit of the middle classes.
53 *hat and plume*: i.e. his status as gentleman and aristocrat.

Being so meek and mild and merciful,
So fond o' the poor and so fatigued of earth,
So . . . fifty thousand devils in deepest hell!
Why must he cure us of our strange conceit
Of the angel in man's likeness, that we loved
And looked should help us at a pinch? He help?
He pardon? Here's his mind and message—death!
Thank the good Pope! Now, is he good in this,
Never mind, Christian,—no such stuff's extant,—
But will my death do credit to his reign,
Show he both lived and let live, so was good?
Cannot I live if he but like? "The law!"
Why, just the law gives him the very chance,
The precise leave to let my life alone,
Which the archangelic soul of him (he says)
Yearns after! Here they drop it in his palm,
My lawyers, capital o' the cursed kind,—
Drop life to take and hold and keep: but no!
He sighs, shakes head, refuses to shut hand,
Motions away the gift they bid him grasp,
And of the coyness comes—that off I run
And down I go, he best knows whither! mind,
He knows, who sets me rolling all the same!
Disinterested Vicar of our Lord,
This way he abrogates and disallows,

57 *MS* {beginning of fo. 251} *MS* of 58 *MS 1868 1872* So . . 60 *MS* {no comma} 61 *MS* pinch. 62 *MS 1868* death, 65 *MS* ?>, 66 *MS* {no comma} 68 *MS* Why just 69 *MS* {no comma} 70 *MS 1868* angelic *MS* him, he says, 71 *MS* after,—here 72 *MS* T>My *MS* of *Yale 1* of>o' *MS* kind, 73 *MS 1868* A life *MS* save: no>keep: but 76 *MS 1868* comes that *MS* roll>run 77 *MS* well>best *MS 1868* whither,— *MS* blame>mind 78 *MS* Who>He *MS* {no comma} *MS* [ ] sets>and sets *1868* and sets *MS* while>same! 80 *MS* {no comma}

72 *capital . . . kind*: i.e. wealth (the wealth that is Guido's life) now under sentence of death.

80 *abrogates*: annuls, cancels. In the phrasing 'abrogates and disallows, / Nullifies and ignores' Guido is parodying what he regards as the mincing legal language of the Pope's formal sentence disallowing his claim to the clericate.

Nullifies and ignores,—reverts in fine
To the good and right, in detriment of me!
Talk away! Will you have the naked truth?
He's sick of his life's supper,—swallowed lies:
So, hobbling bedward, needs must ease his maw
Just where I sit o' the door-sill. Sir Abate,
Can you do nothing? Friends, we used to frisk:
What of this sudden slash in a friend's face,
This cut across our good companionship
That showed its front so gay when both were young?
Were not we put into a beaten path,
Bid pace the world, we nobles born and bred,
We body of friends with each his scutcheon full
Of old achievement and impunity,—
Taking the laugh of morn and Sol's salute
As forth we fared, pricked on to breathe our steeds
And take equestrian sport over the green
Under the blue, across the crop,—what care?
If we went prancing up hill and down dale,
In and out of the level and the straight,
By the bit of pleasant byeway, where was harm?
Still Sol salutes me and the morning laughs:
I see my grandsire's hoof-prints,—point the spot
Where he drew rein, slipped saddle, and stabbed knave

82 *MS* {no comma} 83 *MS* away, will 85 *MS* {beginning of fo. 252} 86 *MS* on 87 *MS* {no comma} 90 *MS* Showing its gay front when we both 91 *MS* Were not we not put 93 *MS 1868* The 94 {not found in *MS*} *Yale 1* achievent>achievement 98 *MS* corn,—>crop,— 99 *MS* So we go *1868* So we went *MS* {no comma} 100 *MS* {no comma} 101 *MS* bye way, where's the harm? 102 {not found in *MS*}

85 *ease his maw*: i.e. vomit.
87 *frisk*: play together, frolic. Cf. 'Pied Piper of Hamelin', 113: 'gay young friskers'.
95 *Sol's salute*: the sun's greeting.
96 *pricked ... breathe*: spurred on to exercise.
100 *In ... straight*: i.e. dipping in and out of good, often misbehaving themselves.
104 *knave*: peasant, yokel.

For daring throw gibe—much less, stone—from pale:
Then back, and on, and up with the cavalcade.
Just so wend we, now canter, now converse,
Till, 'mid the jauncing pride and jaunty port,
Something of a sudden jerks at somebody—
A dagger is out, a flashing cut and thrust,
Because I play some prank my grandsire played,
And here I sprawl: where is the company? Gone!
A trot and a trample! only I lie trapped,
Writhe in a certain novel springe just set
By the good old Pope: I'm first prize. Warn me? Why?
Apprise me that the law o' the game is changed?
Enough that I'm a warning, as I writhe,
To all and each my fellows of the file,
And make law plain henceforward past mistake,
"For such a prank, death is the penalty!"
Pope the Five Hundredth (what do I know or care?)
Deputes your Eminency and Abateship

105 *MS* Who dared throw stone from pale, then vaulted back>Who dared throw gibe from pale, then back and on *1868* pale, 106 *MS* And up with the cavalcade; just so wend we *1868* cavalcade; 107 {not found in *MS*} 108 *MS* mid mid>mid *MS* sportive mirth>jauncing pride *MS* grace 110 *MS* thrust 111 *MS* [ ]>Because 112 *MS* Gone, 113 *MS* A-trot *MS* trample,— *MS* {no comma} 116 {not found in *MS*} *1868 1872* Apprize 117 *MS* {beginning of fo. 253} *MS* lie *MS* {no commas} 118 *MS* {no comma} 119 *MS* And the law's 120 *MS* penalty." 121 *MS 1868* Hundredth . . what *MS 1868* care? 122 *MS 1868* Eminence

---

105 *pale*: fence. The word would be used of a simple fence, the kind that goes round a sheepfold, which the peasant may be guarding.

108 *jauncing*: prancing, curvetting (of the movement of horses). OED[2] cites Cotgrave: '*Iancer un cheval*, to stirre a horse in the stable till hee sweat withall; or (as our) to iaunt; (an old word)'. Here, though, the motion is clearly through the countryside. Cf. also *Richard II*, v. v. 94, *Romeo and Juliet*, II. v. 52.

port: deportment, bearing (referring to the confident way in which the young aristocrats hold themselves).

114 *springe*: trap.

121 *Five Hundredth*: Innocent XII is the 239th pope, by the current Vatican reckoning. Guido makes no attempt at accuracy, and is wilfully wrong, in order to indicate that he cares nothing for the ancientness of the institution that condemns him.

To announce that, twelve hours from this time, he needs
I just essay upon my body and soul
The virtue of his brand-new engine, prove
Represser of the pranksome! I'm the first!
Thanks. Do you know what teeth you mean to try
The sharpness of, on this soft neck and throat?
I know it,—I have seen and hate it,—ay,
As you shall, while I tell you! Let me talk,
Or leave me, at your pleasure! talk I must:
What is your visit but my lure to talk?
Nay, you have something to disclose?—a smile,
At end of the forced sternness, means to mock
The heart-beats here? I call your two hearts stone!
Is your charge to stay with me till I die?
Be tacit as your bench, then! Use your ears,
I use my tongue: how glibly yours will run
At pleasant supper-time . . . God's curse! . . . to-night
When all the guests jump up, begin so brisk
"Welcome, his Eminence who shrived the wretch!
"Now we shall have the Abate's story!"

Life!
How I could spill this overplus of mine
Among those hoar-haired, shrunk-shanked odds and ends
Of body and soul old age is chewing dry!

123 *MS* {no commas} 124 *MS* I shall essay 125 *MS 1868* bran-new *MS* engine, brave 126 *MS* I make proof 127 *MS* First . . do *MS* guess> know *MS* bid me try 128 *MS* {no comma} 129 *MS* hate the same, 130 *MS 1868* you: let *MS* talk! 131 *MS* pleasure: *MS* must, 133 *MS 1868* You have a *MS* disclose,— *MS* smile 134 *MS* {no comma} *Yale 1* {comma added} 135 *MS* here: *MS* stone: 139 *MS 1868 1872* supper-time . . *MS 1868 1872* curse! . . 142 *MS* story!—" 143 *MS* {no new paragraph} 145 *MS 1868 1872* shrunk-shanked, 146 *MS* {beginning of fo. 254} *MS 1868 1872* soul, *MS* dry,

125 *engine*: machine, device: i.e. the guillotine.

126 *pranksome*: i.e. people given to mischief or crime.

133 *a smile*: i.e. a smile of forgiveness (which the priests would expect to give after the 'sternness' of confession).

141 *shrived*: absolved, after hearing the confession of.

145 *shrunk-shanked*: thin-legged (as a sign of old age); cf. *As You Like It*, II. vii. 161.

Those windlestraws that stare while purblind death
Mows here, mows there, makes hay of juicy me,
And misses just the bunch of withered weed
Would brighten hell and streak its smoke with flame!
How the life I could shed yet never shrink,
Would drench their stalks with sap like grass in May!
Is it not terrible, I entreat you, Sirs?—
With manifold and plenitudinous life,
Prompt at death's menace to give blow for threat,
Answer his "Be thou not!" by "Thus I am!"—
Terrible so to be alive yet die?

How I live, how I see! so,—how I speak!
Lucidity of soul unlocks the lips:
I never had the words at will before.
How I see all my folly at a glance!
"A man requires a woman and a wife:"
There was my folly; I believed the saw.
I knew that just myself concerned myself,
Yet needs must look for what I seemed to lack,
In a woman,—why, the woman's in the man!
Fools we are, how we learn things when too late!
Overmuch life turns round my woman-side:
The male and female in me, mixed before,

147 *1868 1872* windle-straws 148 *MS* and misses, all the same,>and misses just the bunch 149 {not found in *MS*} *1868* misses, *1868 1872* weed, 150 *MS* flame. 151 *1872* life, *MS* never miss 153 *MS 1868 1872* Sirs? 154 *MS 1868 1872* Such *MS* {no comma} 156 *MS* "Be not!" *MS* "Thus feel I am!" 157 {not found in *MS*} 158 *MS* {no new paragraph} *MS* Therefore I speak— 161 {not found in *MS*} 162 *MS* {no quotation marks} *MS* f> and *etc.* *MS* wife. 163 *MS* my bane, I was born man and strong: *1868 1872* saw: 168 *MS* Much *MS* the woman side of me, *1868 1872* woman-side;

147 *windlestraws*: dried up stalks of grass, here used fig. for 'dried up old men'. Browning uses the word literally in *Fifine at the Fair*, l. 90, where birds use 'thistle-fluffs and bearded windlestraws' to make their nests.

163 *saw*: proverb.

166 *woman's . . . man*: i.e. we're self-sufficient: man already has a 'female' side. This is perhaps a reference to Gen. 2: 21–2, where the rib from which Eve is made is literally within Adam.

Settle of a sudden: I'm my wife outright
In this unmanly appetite for truth,
This careless courage as to consequence,
This instantaneous sight through things and through,
This voluble rhetoric, if you please,—'t is she!
Here you have that Pompilia whom I slew,
Also the folly for which I slew her!
Fool!
And, fool-like, what is it I wander from?
What did I say of your sharp iron tooth?
Ah,—that I know the hateful thing! this way.
I chanced to stroll forth, many a good year gone,
One warm Spring eve in Rome, and unaware
Looking, mayhap, to count what stars were out,
Came on your fine axe in a frame, that falls
And so cuts off a man's head underneath,
Mannaia,—thus we made acquaintance first:
Out of the way, in a by-part o' the town,
At the Mouth-of-Truth o' the river-side, you know:

170 *MS* settles *MS* sudden, 172 *MS* {no comma} 174 *MS* rhetoric if *MS* she, 176 *MS* her,—I . 177 {not found in *MS*} 178 *MS* {beginning of fo. 255} *MS* {no new paragraph} *MS* Am a fool, what 179 {not found in *MS*} *1868* What, of the sharpness of your iron tooth 180 *MS 1868* thing: 183 *MS* out 184 *MS 1868* huge axe 186 *MS* Mannaja,— *MS 1868* first, 187 *1868 1872* bye-part *MS* of 188 *MS* Mouth of Truth on

179 *sharp . . . tooth*: referring again to the *mannaia.*

186 *Mannaia*: (It.) 'axe', 'blade', i.e. the guillotine. Such guillotines in seventeenth-century Italy were broadly similar to those perfected in 1792, though less sophisticated. Browning takes the term from SS 19, keeping its strangeness for the English reader as part of his wider imaginative purpose. See 214–41 n. for details of the machine.

188 *Mouth-of-Truth . . . river-side*: the Piazza Bocca della Verità, near the 'river-side' of the Tiber, opposite the Ponte Palatino. This quiet square (now surrounded by noisy traffic) is named after the Bocca della Verità ('Mouth of Truth'), a flat, round marble disc, over a metre across, incorporated in the portico of the nearby church of Santa Maria in Cosmedin. On the disc (or mascaron) is carved a large, grotesque face, with shaggy hair, strong nose, and incised holes for mouth and eyes. Legend has it that if a perjurer put his hand inside the marble mouth, it would close on it. Browning has presumably chosen this location ironically for the anecdote that follows; it is certainly ironic that Guido should mention a 'Mouth-of-Truth' at all. For a photograph, see Thomas, 328.

One goes by the Capitol: and wherefore coy,
Retiring out of crowded noisy Rome?
Because a very little time ago
It had done service, chopped off head from trunk
Belonging to a fellow whose poor house
The thing must make a point to stand before—
Felice Whatsoever-was-the-name
Who stabled buffaloes and so gained bread,
(Our clowns unyoke them in the ground hard by)
And, after use of much improper speech,
Had struck at Duke Some-title-or-other's face,
Because he kidnapped, carried away and kept
Felice's sister who would sit and sing
I' the filthy doorway while she plaited fringe
To deck the brutes with,—on their gear it goes,—
The good girl with the velvet in her voice.
So did the Duke, so did Felice, so
Did Justice, intervening with her axe.
There the man-mutilating engine stood
At ease, both gay and grim, like a Swiss guard
Off duty,—purified itself as well,
Getting dry, sweet and proper for next week,—
And doing incidental good, 't was hoped,
To the rough lesson-lacking populace

190 *MS* middle>crowded 192 *MS 1868 1872* trunk, 194 *MS 1868* had made *MS 1868 1872* before. 197 *MS* (People 199 *MS* spat in *MS* [ ]->Some- *MS* {no comma} 201 *MS 1868* that would 202 *MS* On>In 204 *MS* voice 205 *MS* Felice>the Duke, *etc.* 206 *MS* justice>Justice 207 *MS* {beginning of fo. 256} *MS* business>engine 208 *MS* as>both *MS* grim as>grim like *Yale 1* grim>grim, *MS* Guard 209 *MS* being purified 211 *MS* good, belike, **1868 1872 1888* hoped *DC BrU* hoped>hoped, *1889* hoped, 212 *MS* gross>rough *MS* multitude>populace

189 *Capitol*: the southern summit of the Capitoline hill.

wherefore coy: i.e. why was the guillotine shy or reserved, in this out of the way location?

196–7 *buffaloes . . . by*: buffaloes were still around Rome in Browning's day; they were used for farming and for meat. From *Roba di Roma* Browning would have known that it was only in the 1820s that a law was passed prohibiting them from being driven into the city for sale and for slaughter: *Roba di Roma*, ii. 2.

Who now and then, forsooth, must right their wrongs!
There stood the twelve-foot-square of scaffold, railed
Considerately round to elbow-height,
For fear an officer should tumble thence
And sprain his ankle and be lame a month
Through starting when the axe fell and head too!
Railed likewise were the steps whereby 't was reached.
All of it painted red: red, in the midst,
Ran up two narrow tall beams barred across,
Since from the summit, some twelve feet to reach,
The iron plate with the sharp shearing edge
Had slammed, jerked, shot, slid,—I shall soon find which!—
And so lay quiet, fast in its fit place,
The wooden half-moon collar, now eclipsed
By the blade which blocked its curvature: apart,

215 *MS* {no comma} *1868* elbow-height: 216 *MS* —Suppose *1868* (Suppose 217 *MS* ancle *MS* week **1868 1872 1888* month, *DC BrU* month,>month *1889* month 218 *MS* falls *MS* too? *1868* too?) 220 *MS* {no commas} 223 *MS* sharb 224 *MS 1868* Had . . slammed, jerked, shot or slid,—I shall find *MS* which. *1868 1872* which! 225 *MS 1868* There it lay 227 *MS* {no comma}

214–41 *twelve-foot-square . . . duty done*: the following description of the guillotine is very detailed, particularly in the way it notes the means used to clean up after execution: a 'pitcher' of water (238), a 'broad dish' or 'platter' of sawdust (239, 243), a 'broom' (239), and a 'scraper-rake' (240). It draws on Browning's own shocked witness of a guillotine in the aftermath of an execution, in May 1860, in Rome. This incident is not recorded in the standard biographies, but is described by Henry Adams, in *The Education of Henry Adams*: 'One morning, Adams happened to be chatting in the studio of Hamilton Wilde, when a middle-aged Englishman came in, evidently excited, and told of the shock he had just received, when riding near the Circus Maximus, at coming unexpectedly on the guillotine, where some criminal had been put to death an hour or two before. The sudden surprise had quite overcome him; and Adams, who seldom saw the point of a story till time had blunted it, listened sympathetically to learn what new form of grim horror had for the moment wiped out the memory of two thousand years of Roman bloodshed, or the consolation, derived from history and statistics, that most citizens of Rome seemed to be the better for guillotining. Only by slow degrees, he grappled the conviction that the victim of the shock was Robert Browning; and, on the background of the Circus Maximus, the Christian martyrs flaming as torches, and the morning's murderer on the block, Browning seemed rather in place, as a middle-aged gentlemanly English Pippa Passes; while afterwards, in the light of Belgravia dinner-tables, he never made part of his background except by effacement': *The Education of Henry Adams*, ed. Ernest Samuels (Boston, 1973), pp. 92–3.

The other half,—the under half-moon board
Which, helped by this, completes a neck's embrace,—
Joined to a sort of desk that wheels aside
Out of the way when done with,—down you kneel,
In you're pushed, over you the other drops,
Tight you're clipped, whiz, there's the blade cleaves its best,
Out trundles body, down flops head on floor,
And where's your soul gone? That, too, I shall find!
This kneeling-place was red, red, never fear!
But only slimy-like with paint, not blood,
For why? a decent pitcher stood at hand,
A broad dish to hold sawdust, and a broom
By some unnamed utensil,—scraper-rake,—
Each with a conscious air of duty done.
Underneath, loungers,—boys and some few men,—
Discoursed this platter, named the other tool,
Just as, when grooms tie up and dress a steed,
Boys lounge and look on, and elucubrate
What the round brush is used for, what the square,—
So was explained—to me the skill-less then—
The manner of the grooming for next world
Undergone by Felice What's-his-name.
There's no such lovely month in Rome as May—
May's crescent is no half-moon of red plank,

229 *MS* That, 232 *MS 1868* wheeled, 233 *MS 1868* you are *MS 1868* the blade on you, 235 *MS* {beginning of fo. 257} *MS* find. *236 *1888* kneeling place *DC BrU* kneeling place>kneeling-place *1889* kneeling-place 238 *MS* A decent 240 *MS* With>By *MS* utensil, scraper-rake, 242 *MS* Underneath loungers, boys *MS* men, 243 *MS 1868* platter and the 244 *MS* {no commas} 245 *MS* and men>lounge and *MS* lucubrate aloud 247 *MS* explained to *MS* skilless man *1868* skill-less man— 251 *MS* {no comma}

243 *Discoursed . . . platter*: i.e. spoke knowledgeably about this platter—referring back to the 'broad dish' for holding the sawdust (239).

245 *elucubrate*: or 'lucubrate' = explain learnedly or pompously. Strictly speaking, it means 'to compare or write by lamplight, by the expenditure of "midnight oil" ', but its more modern sense is as here. Cf. Byron, 'The Curse of Minerva', 183–4: 'Round the thronged gate shall sauntering coxcombs creep / To lounge and lucubrate, to prate and peep.'

251 *May's . . . plank*: i.e. the crescent moon is beautiful, not like the grotesque, red-painted 'half-moon collar' of the guillotine. The reference is to l. 226.

And came now tilting o'er the wave i' the west,
One greenish-golden sea, right 'twixt those bars
Of the engine—I began acquaintance with,
Understood, hated, hurried from before,
To have it out of sight and cleanse my soul!
Here it is all again, conserved for use:
Twelve hours hence, I may know more, not hate worse.

That young May-moon-month! Devils of the deep!
Was not a Pope then Pope as much as now?
Used not he chirrup o'er the Merry Tales,
Chuckle,—his nephew so exact the wag
To play a jealous cullion such a trick
As wins the wife i' the pleasant story! Well?
Why do things change? Wherefore is Rome un-Romed?
I tell you, ere Felice's corpse was cold,
The Duke, that night, threw wide his palace-doors,
Received the compliments o' the quality
For justice done him,—bowed and smirked his best,
And in return passed round a pretty thing,
A portrait of Felice's sister's self,
Florid old rogue Albano's masterpiece,

252 *MS* wave, the West 253 *MS* twixt 254 *MS* engine I 255 before 256 *MS* soul: 257 *MS* use, 258 *MS 1868* hence I 259 *MS* {no new paragraph} 260 *MS* the Pope 261 *MS* {no comma} 263 *MS* {beginning of fo. 258} *MS* Would play the 264 *MS* his wife in *MS* story: well? 266 *MS* cold 267 *MS* palace doors, 268 *MS* of *1868 1872* quality, 269 *MS* On the justice 270 *MS* masterpiece,>pretty thing, 271 *MS* Miniature>A portrait

259 *May-moon-month*: i.e. the month of spring and love.

261 *Merry Tales*: probably Franco Sacchetti's *Trecentonovelle* (1392), cf. v. 559–60 n., but maybe Boccaccio's *Decameron* (1358), cf. III. 1446 n. In either case, Guido means bawdy medieval tales of love, adultery, and sexual farce.

262 *nephew*: this could be read literally, or perhaps as signifying the 'cardinal nephew', a position at the papal court, but it could be a euphemism for 'son': cf. 'The Bishop Orders His Tomb', 3.

263 *cullion*: scoundrel, rogue—here the jealous husband who is to be outwitted. The earlier pope Guido has in mind (it is not clear which one) would not be averse to his own nephew seducing a married woman.

268 *the quality*: the upper classes. Cf. X. 2114 n.

272–4 *Albano's . . . bull*: the Bolognese painter Francesco Albano (or Albani) (1578–1660) was famous for his mythological scenes and his light-hearted style. Griffin and

As—better than virginity in rags—
Bouncing Europa on the back o' the bull:
They laughed and took their road the safelier home.
Ah, but times change, there's quite another Pope,
I do the Duke's deed, take Felice's place,
And, being no Felice, lout and clout,
Stomach but ill the phrase "I lose my head!"
How euphemistic! Lose what? Lose your ring,
Your snuff-box, tablets, kerchief!—but, your head?
I learnt the process at an early age;
'T was useful knowledge, in those same old days,
To know the way a head is set on neck.
My fencing-master urged "Would you excel?
"Rest not content with mere bold give-and-guard,
"Nor pink the antagonist somehow-anyhow!
"See me dissect a little, and know your game!
"Only anatomy makes a thrust the thing."
Oh Cardinal, those lithe live necks of ours!

273 *Yale 1* thanvirginity>than virginity 274 *MS* bull,— 275 *MS* [ ]>their 278 *MS* Who, *MS* Felice lout 279 *MS* phrase, **1888* lost *DC BrU* lost>lose *1889* lose *MS* head." 281 *MS* kerchief,—but your head! *Yale 1* kerchief,—but your head!>kerchief!—but, your head? 282 *MS* age, 283 *MS 1868* knowledge in 284 {not found in *MS*} 285 *MS 1868* fencing master 286–9 *MS* {no quotation marks at beginnings of lines} 286 *MS* bald *MS* cut and thrust>give and guard 287 *MS* somehow anyhow,— *1868* somehow-anyhow,— 288 *MS* game, 289 *MS* {no quotation mark at end of line}

Minchin suggest that Browning saw this particular painting, 'The Rape of Europa' (1645), at the Hermitage, during his 1834 trip to St Petersburg, though this seems unlikely given that it is a relatively obscure painting in that great collection: see Griffin and Minchin, p. 63. Probably he is remembering the copy of it in the Uffizi, Florence. The painting shows Jove, in the form of a bull, galloping off with a full-figured Europa on his back. She clutches his horns to steady herself, and looks desperately backwards to a group of friends. The painting is more decorous than lubricious, but Europa's legs and left breast are exposed as she bounces along. To the Duke (and Guido), this image is more appealing than 'virginity in rags', Felice's sister as she really was before she was raped: see ll. 201–3.

278 *clout*: coarse thing, clod, good-for-nothing, here essentially a rhyming synonym for 'lout': an uncouth person.

281 *tablets*: notebook.

287 *pink*: strike, prick.

Here go the vertebræ, here's *Atlas*, here
Axis, and here the symphyses stop short,
So wisely and well,—as, o'er a corpse, we cant,—
And here's the silver cord which... what's our word?
Depends from the gold bowl, which loosed (not "lost")
Lets us from heaven to hell,—one chop, we're loose!
"And not much pain i' the process," quoth a sage:
Who told him? Not Felice's ghost, I think!
Such "losing" is scarce Mother Nature's mode.
She fain would have cord ease itself away,
Worn to a thread by threescore years and ten,
Snap while we slumber: that seems bearable.
I'm told one clot of blood extravasate
Ends one as certainly as Roland's sword,—
One drop of lymph suffused proves Oliver's mace,—
Intruding, either of the pleasant pair,
On the arachnoid tunic of my brain.
That's Nature's way of loosing cord!—but Art,

291 *MS atlas,* 293 *MS* {beginning of fo. 259} *MS* well, as *MS* corpse we 294 *MS* which . . *MS* the word? 296 *MS* Lets you *MS* you're 297 *MS* in *MS 1868 1872* the sage: 299 *MS* {no quotation marks} *MS* way>mode. 300 *MS* {no comma} 302 *MS* you slumber: *MS 1868 1872* bearable: 304 *MS* Ends you *MS* sword, 305 *MS* One ounce *MS* mace 307 *MS* the brain. 308 *MS* cord,—

291–2 *Atlas . . . symphyses*: *Atlas* and *Axis* are the first and second neck bones, supporting the skull. The symphyses are the cartilaginous joints between them. The reference here originates in Browning's study of anatomy in relation to art. EBB mentions this in the winter of 1860–1, at Rome, in describing his hours of clay-modelling at the studio of W. W. Story: 'He has given a great deal of time to anatomy with reference to the expression of form, and the clay is only the new medium which takes the place of drawing'; 'Robert has taken to modelling under Mr. Story (at his studio) and is making extraordinary progress, turning to account his studies in anatomy': EBB to Sarianna Browning, 19 Jan. 1861; EBB to E. F. Haworth, 1 Feb. 1861: *Letters of EBB*, ii. 434, 411. This also accounts for his use of 'omoplat': see v. 118 n.

294–5 *silver cord . . . gold bowl*: cf. Eccles. 12: 6. Here silver cord = spine, gold bowl = brain. The spine 'depends from' (is suspended from) the brain.

303 *extravasate*: out of place, out of its appropriate blood vessel.

305 *lymph suffused*: lymph is a colourless fluid, similar to blood, but containing no red corpuscles. Here it is imagined 'suffused', overspread, i.e. out of its proper place.

307 *arachnoid tunic*: web-like covering. OED^2 defines the arachnoid (tunic) as 'the delicate serous membrane or membranous sac lining the *dura mater*, and enveloping the brain and spinal cord'.

How of Art's process with the engine here,
When bowl and cord alike are crushed across,
Bored between, bruised through? Why, if Fagon's self,
The French Court's pride, that famed practitioner,
Would pass his cold pale lightning of a knife,
Pistoja-ware, adroit 'twixt joint and joint,
With just a "See how facile, gentlefolk!"—
The thing were not so bad to bear! Brute force
Cuts as he comes, breaks in, breaks on, breaks out
O' the hard and soft of you: is that the same?
A lithe snake thrids the hedge, makes throb no leaf:
A heavy ox sets chest to brier and branch,
Bursts somehow through, and leaves one hideous hole
Behind him!

And why, why must this needs be?
Oh, if men were but good! They are not good,
Nowise like Peter: people called him rough,
But if, as I left Rome, I spoke the Saint,
—"*Petrus, quo vadis?*"—doubtless, I should hear,
"To free the prisoner and forgive his fault!

309 *MS 1868* here? 310 *MS* {no comma} 311 *MS* {no comma} 312 *MS* That famed practitioner the French Court pays, 314 *MS* joint *Yale 1* joint>joint, 315 *MS* gentlefolks!" *1868 1872* gentlefolks!"— 316 *MS* Not so bad were the thing to bear: brute force 318 *MS* Of hard 319 *MS* nor throbs one leaf— *Yale 1* leaf—>leaf: 320 *MS* briar *MS* bough, 321 *MS* {beginning of fo. 260} *MS* Burst 322 *MS* Behind him: and why, why must this needs be? 323 {not found in *MS*} 324 *MS* {no new paragraph} 325 *MS* call 326 *MS* met the 327 *MS* —"Petrus, quo vadis?" "Guido", I should hear, 328 *MS* fault!"

311 *Fagon's self*: Guy Crescent Fagon (1638–1718), Louis XIV's chief physician from 1693 until the king's death in 1715. His skill at surgery, suggested here, is Browning's invention. The extensive entry in the *Biographie universelle*, xiv. 99–100, makes no mention of it.

314 *Pistoja-ware*: made in Pistoia (about 18 miles north-west of Florence), i.e. of the highest quality.

317 *Cuts . . . comes*: i.e. cuts at random.

327–30 "*Petrus . . . thee?*": Guido parodies the words exchanged between Christ and St Peter, in the famous legend, casting himself as Christ and Pope Innocent as Peter. In the legend, first recorded in the *Acta Petri* in the third century, when St Peter fled Rome along the Appian way to escape Nero's persecution, he saw a vision of Christ

"I plucked the absolute dead from God's own bar,
"And raised up Dorcas,—why not rescue thee?"
What would cost one such nullifying word?
If Innocent succeeds to Peter's place,
Let him think Peter's thought, speak Peter's speech!
I say, he is bound to it: friends, how say you?
Concede I be all one bloodguiltiness
And mystery of murder in the flesh,
Why should that fact keep the Pope's mouth shut fast?
He execrates my crime,—good!—sees hell yawn
One inch from the red plank's end which I press,—
Nothing is better! What's the consequence?
How should a Pope proceed that knows his cue?
Why, leave me linger out my minute here,
Since close on death comes judgment and comes doom,
Not crib at dawn its pittance from a sheep
Destined ere dewfall to be butcher's-meat!
Think, Sirs, if I have done you any harm,
And you require the natural revenge,
Suppose, and so intend to poison me,
—Just as you take and slip into my draught
The paperful of powder that clears scores,

330 *MS* "Raised up Jairus daughter,—why not thee?" 332 *MS* {no comma} 333 *MS* speech. 341 *1868* How does 342 *1868* leaves *MS* moment>minute 343 *MS* [?comes] doom,>such doom, *1868* the doom, 344 *MS 1868 1872* Nor *MS* cribs>crib *1868* cribs 345 *MS* Because>Destined *MS* destined>to be *MS* butcher's meat. 346 *MS 1868* had *MS* harm 347 *MS* required 348 {not found in *MS*} 349 *MS* take it, slip 350 *MS* paper full>paperful

travelling in the other direction, about two miles outside the city. Struck with amazement, Peter exclaimed *Domine, quo vadis*? ('Lord, where are you going?), to which Christ replied *Venio iterum crucifigi* ('I go to be crucified a second time'). The vision then vanished. St Peter realized that he must return to the city and face martyrdom. The Church of *Domine Quo Vadis* (officially S. Maria in Palmis) is built on the supposed site of the legend. The other allusion here is to Acts 9: 36–41, where St Peter raises from death the woman disciple Tabitha, or Dorcas, a scene depicted by Masolino on the walls of the Brancacci Chapel in the Carmine, which Browning would have seen.

336 *mystery* . . . *flesh*: 'the very embodiment of the art of murder': Altick.
344 *crib* . . . *its pittance*: steal . . . its small remainder (of life).

You notice on my brow a certain blue:
How you both overset the wine at once!
How you both smile! "Our enemy has the plague!
"Twelve hours hence he'll be scraping his bones bare
"Of that intolerable flesh, and die,
"Frenzied with pain: no need for poison here!
"Step aside and enjoy the spectacle!"
Tender for souls are you, Pope Innocent!
Christ's maxim is—one soul outweighs the world:
Respite me, save a soul, then, curse the world!
"No," venerable sire, I hear you smirk,
"No: for Christ's gospel changes names, not things,
"Renews the obsolete, does nothing more!
"Our fire-new gospel is re-tinkered law,
"Our mercy, justice,—Jove's rechristened God,—
"Nay, whereas, in the popular conceit,
" 'T is pity that old harsh Law somehow limps,
"Lingers on earth, although Law's day be done,
"Else would benignant Gospel interpose,
"Not furtively as now, but bold and frank
"O'erflutter us with healing in her wings,

351 *MS* {beginning of fo. 261} 352 {not found in *MS*} 353 *MS* pause, *MS* plague— 354–7 *MS* {no quotation marks at beginnings of lines} 355 *MS* so die, 357 *MS* Put powder up, step aside and enjoy!">Step aside and enjoy the spectacle! 359 *MS* Christ lays it down— 360 *MS* soul, let the world wag! 361 *MS* "No," verily I think *MS* smirk 362 *MS* "No, 363–80 *MS* {no quotation marks at beginnings of lines} 363 *MS* and>does *MS* else,>more, 364 *MS 1868* retinkered 365 *MS* mercy's justice,— *MS* Jove's>Jove 367 *MS* Tis pity the old law still *Yale 1* that the old law>that harsh old Law 368 *MS* its day *Yale 1* law's>Law's *1868* done,— *1872* "Although Law's day be done, lingers on earth,— 369 *MS* gospel *Yale 1* gospel>Gospel *MS* {no comma} 371 *MS* wings—

351 *certain blue*: i.e. the sign of plague.

352 *overset*: knock over.

359 *one . . . world*: cf. Matt. 16: 26, Mark 8: 36.

364 *fire-new*: cf. v. 529 n.

law: in this passage law is firstly the Judaic law, but then, by association, simply legal law strictly applied.

365 *Jove's . . . God*: i.e. a pagan ideal is simply co-opted into Christianity.

371 *O'erflutter . . . wings*: cf. Malachi 4: 2.

"Law being harshness, Gospel only love—
"We tell the people, on the contrary,
"Gospel takes up the rod which Law lets fall;
"Mercy is vigilant when justice sleeps!
"Does Law permit a taste of Gospel-grace?
"The secular arm allow the spiritual power
"To act for once?—no compliment so fine
"As that our Gospel handsomely turn harsh,
"Thrust victim back on Law the nice and coy!"
Yes, you do say so, else you would forgive
Me whom Law does not touch but tosses you!
Don't think to put on the professional face!
You know what I know: casuists as you are,
Each nerve must creep, each hair start, sting and stand,
At such illogical inconsequence!
Dear my friends, do but see! A murder's tried,
There are two parties to the cause: I'm one,
—Defend myself, as somebody must do:
I have the best o' the battle: that's a fact,
Simple fact,—fancies find no place just now.
What though half Rome condemned me? Half approved:
And, none disputes, the luck is mine at last,
All Rome, i' the main, acquitting me: whereon,
What has the Pope to ask but "How finds Law?"

372 {not found in *MS*} *1868* "Law is all harshness, Gospel were all love!— 373 *MS 1868* We like to put it, *1868 1872* contrary,— 374 *Yale 1* law>Law *MS* fall, 375 *MS* sleeps— *1868* sleeps; 376 {not found in *MS*} *1868* let Guido taste the 377 *MS* allows 378 *MS* once,—what compliment so fit *1868* what compliment 379 *MS* As doing just the harsh deed whence law shrunk, *MS* ^harsh^ *1868* the Gospel *1868* be harsh 380 *MS* Pressing a>Urging a *1868* "Thrust back Law's *MS 1868* victim on the nice and coy?" 381 *MS 1868 1872* so,— 382 *MS* {beginning of fo. 262} *1868 1872* Me, *MS* law dares *1868* Law dares 383 *MS* face— 384 *MS* know,—being casuists both; *1868 1872* know,— 385 *MS* stand 387 {not found in *MS*} 388 *MS* a cause: 389 *MS*—[ ]>—Defend 390 *MS* of *MS* battle,— 391 *MS* [ ]>Simple *MS* fact fancies *MS* beside; *1868* beside: 392 *MS* Suppose *MS* me,—half approved, 393 *MS* And none 394 *MS* All Rome acquits me in the main,—and now *1868* acquits me: whereupon

380 *nice and coy*: exacting and reserved.

"I find," replies Law, "I have erred this while:
"Guilty or guiltless, Guido proves a priest,
"No layman: he is therefore yours, not mine:
"I bound him: loose him, you whose will is Christ's!"
And now what does this Vicar of our Lord,
Shepherd o' the flock,—one of whose charge bleats sore
For crook's help from the quag wherein it drowns?
Law suffers him employ the crumpled end:
His pleasure is to turn staff, use the point,
And thrust the shuddering sheep, he calls a wolf,
Back and back, down and down to where hell gapes!
"Guiltless," cries Law—"Guilty" corrects the Pope!
"Guilty," for the whim's sake! "Guilty," he somehow thinks,
And anyhow says: 't is truth; he dares not lie!

Others should do the lying. That's the cause
Brings you both here: I ought in decency
Confess to you that I deserve my fate,
Am guilty, as the Pope thinks,—ay, to the end,
Keep up the jest, lie on, lie ever, lie
I' the latest gasp of me! What reason, Sirs?
Because to-morrow will succeed to-day
For you, though not for me: and if I stick
Still to the truth, declare with my last breath,
I die an innocent and murdered man,—
Why, there's the tongue of Rome will wag apace

396 *MS* Law "I *MS* through haste,>this while: 397–9 *MS* {no quotation marks at beginnings of lines} 397 *MS* priest 398 *MS* layman,— *MS* he is yours not mine: I bound—>therefore he is yours not mine: 399 *MS* Loose>I bound him, loose *MS* you; your will 400 *MS 1868* the Lord, 401 *MS* of *MS* Flock,— 403 *MS 1868* put forth *MS 1868 1872* end,— 405 *MS* [ ], he calls wolf,>sheep he calls a wolf, *1868* sheep he 406 *MS* Back and down to damnation . . there it gapes!>Back and back, down and down to . . there it gapes! 407 *MS* "Guiltless" quoth *MS* Pope, 408 *MS* thinks 409 *MS* speaks: 410 *MS 1868* {no new paragraph} *MS* 'Tis I 411 *MS* {beginning of fo. 263} *MS* here,— 412 *MS* I>to 414 *MS* Carry 415 *MS* In *MS* me,—your 416 *MS* to-day, 417 *MS* you if not 418 *MS* last cry, 420 *MS* talk of *MS* Rome [ ]>Rome *MS* will treat the truth *MS* case>truth *1868 1872* a-pace

403 *crumpled end*: the curved end (of the shepherd's crook).

This time to-morrow: don't I hear the talk!
"So, to the last he proved impenitent?
"Pagans have said as much of martyred saints!
"Law demurred, washed her hands of the whole case.
"Prince Somebody said this, Duke Something, that.
"Doubtless the man's dead, dead enough, don't fear!
"But, hang it, what if there have been a spice,
"A touch of... eh? You see, the Pope's so old,
"Some of us add, obtuse: age never slips
"The chance of shoving youth to face death first!"
And so on. Therefore to suppress such talk
You two come here, entreat I tell you lies,
And end, the edifying way. I end,
Telling the truth! Your self-styled shepherd thieves!
A thief—and how thieves hate the wolves we know:
Damage to theft, damage to thrift, all's one!
The red hand is sworn foe of the black jaw.
That's only natural, that's right enough:
But why the wolf should compliment the thief
With shepherd's title, bark out life in thanks,
And, spiteless, lick the prong that spits him,—eh,
Cardinal? My Abate, scarcely thus!
There, let my sheepskin-garb, a curse on't, go—

421 *MS 1868 1872* to-morrow,— *MS* them talk! 423–30 *MS* {no quotation marks at beginnings of lines emended to quotation marks at beginnings of lines} 423 *MS* saints: 425 *MS* Something that,— 426 *MS* fear, 428 *MS 1868 1872* of . . *MS* you see, 429 *MS 1868 1872* obtuse,— 430 *MS* first," 432 *MS* the lies, 433 *MS* {no commas} 434 *MS* truth: your *MS* shepherd is *Yale 1* is>thieves! 435 *MS* that thieves hate wolves 436 *MS* theft or thrift, all's one—red hand 437 *MS* Is sworn foe of black jaw: that's right enough: *1868 1872* jaw! 438 {not found in *MS*} 439 *MS* But that 440 *MS* {beginning of fo. 264} *MS* the shepherd's *MS* breath in 441 *MS* And dying, look the point that spits him,—why, *MS* ^dying,^ *Yale 1* And>And, 442 *MS* Cardinal, no! Abate, 443 *MS* sheepskin garb,

427–8 *a spice . . . eh?*: 'the suppressed word probably is "doubt": see below, l. 721, "a spice of doubt"': Altick.

435 *A thief . . . know*: i.e. thieves hate wolves because the latter steal the sheep first.

437 *red hand*: i.e. the guilty hand of the thief. Cf. 'Muckle-Mouth Meg', 1.

Leave my teeth free if I must show my shag!
Repent? What good shall follow? If I pass
Twelve hours repenting, will that fact hold fast
The thirteenth at the horrid dozen's end?
If I fall forthwith at your feet, gnash, tear,
Foam, rave, to give your story the due grace,
Will that assist the engine half-way back
Into its hiding-house?—boards, shaking now,
Bone against bone, like some old skeleton bat
That wants, at winter's end, to wake and prey!
Will howling put the spectre back to sleep?
Ah, but I misconceive your object, Sirs!
Since I want new life like the creature,—life,
Being done with here, begins i' the world away:
I shall next have "Come, mortals, and be judged!"
There's but a minute betwixt this and then:
So, quick, be sorry since it saves my soul!
Sirs, truth shall save it, since no lies assist!
Hear the truth, you, whatever you style yourselves,
Civilization and society!
Come, one good grapple, I with all the world!
Dying in cold blood is the desperate thing;
The angry heart explodes, bears off in blaze

446 *MS* hook fast 451 *MS* hiding-house, that's shaking now 452 *MS* {no comma} 453 *MS* now winter's done, *MS* live?>live; 454 *MS* that>howling *456 *MS* I want life like the creature,—life being done *1868 1872* creature,—life *1888* life *DC BrU* life>life, *1889* life, 457 {not found in *MS*} 458 *MS* And the world away: come, mortals, and be judged! 459 *MS* then, 460 *MS* I should be *MS* [ ]>should *MS* soul. 461 *MS* do good.>assist. 462 *MS* Come, all of you,>Hear []>Hear the truth, you, 463 *MS* society,— 465 *MS* thing, 466 *MS* But angry hearts explode, bear

444 *shag*: rough hide (of the wolf).

450 *engine*: guillotine; cf. l. 125 n.

451 *hiding-house*: the building where the guillotine is kept.

boards: i.e. the wooden boards of the guillotine.

452–3 *like . . . prey!*: i.e. the guillotine is like a bat, emaciated after long hibernation, and therefore eager to eat its next victim. A wonderfully grotesque image. The guillotine is simply shaking in the wind.

456 *like the creature*: i.e. like the bat (cf. 452).

The indignant soul, and I'm combustion-ripe.
Why, you intend to do your worst with me!
That's in your eyes! You dare no more than death,
And mean no less. I must make up my mind.
So Pietro,—when I chased him here and there,
Morsel by morsel cut away the life
I loathed,—cried for just respite to confess
And save his soul: much respite did I grant!
Why grant me respite who deserve my doom?
Me—who engaged to play a prize, fight you,
Knowing your arms, and foil you, trick for trick,
At rapier-fence, your match and, maybe, more.
I knew that if I chose sin certain sins,
Solace my lusts out of the regular way
Prescribed me, I should find you in the path,
Have to try skill with a redoubted foe;
You would lunge, I would parry, and make end.
At last, occasion of a murder comes:
We cross blades, I, for all my brag, break guard,
And in goes the cold iron at my breast,
Out at my back, and end is made of me.
You stand confessed the adroiter swordsman,—ay,
But on your triumph you increase, it seems,
Want more of me than lying flat on face:
I ought to raise my ruined head, allege
Not simply I pushed worse blade o' the pair,
But my antagonist dispensed with steel!

468 *MS* me, 469 *MS* {beginning of fo. 265} *MS* eyes,—you *MS* death 470 *MS* less,—I *1868 1872* mind! 471 *MS* Pietro when 473 *MS* loathed, cried 476 *MS* you 477 *MS* you trick for trick 478 *MS* rapier fence, *1868 1872* may be, 480 *MS* heart>lusts 482 *MS* cross swords>try skill 483 *MS* Let him>You would *MS* so>make 484 {not found in *MS*} 485 *MS* guard 492 *MS* of *Yale 1* of>o' 493 *MS* steel:

469–70 *You . . . mind*: 'You are determined, says Guido, that I shall die, but you don't dare to condemn me to hell afterwards; you therefore want me to show penitence': Cook, 242.

476 *to play a prize*: 'to engage in a contest or match, esp. a fencing-match': OED².

485 *break guard*: i.e. fail to maintain the correct defensive posture.

489 *increase*: i.e. raise your demands.

There was no passage of arms, you looked me low,
With brow and eye abolished cut-and-thrust
Nor used the vulgar weapon! This chance scratch,
This incidental hurt, this sort of hole
I' the heart of me? I stumbled, got it so!
Fell on my own sword as a bungler may!
Yourself proscribe such heathen tools, and trust
To the naked virtue: it was virtue stood
Unarmed and awed me,—on my brow there burned
Crime out so plainly intolerably red,
That I was fain to cry—"Down to the dust
"With me, and bury there brow, brand and all!"
Law had essayed the adventure,—but what's Law?
Morality exposed the Gorgon-shield!
Morality and Religion conquer me.
If Law sufficed would you come here, entreat
I supplement law, and confess forsooth?
Did not the Trial show things plain enough?
"Ah, but a word of the man's very self
"Would somehow put the keystone in its place
"And crown the arch!" Then take the word you want!

[—]

*495 *MS 1868 1872* cut-and-thrust *1888 1889* cut and thrust 496 *MS* weapon: this 498 *MS* {beginning of fo. 266} *MS* In *MS* head>heart *MS* so, 499 *MS* may, 503 *MS 1872* plainly, *1868* plainly, intolerably, 504 *MS* "down 505 *MS* {no quotation mark at beginning of line} *507 *MS* must bare the Gorgon-shield, *Yale 1* must bear>exposed *1868 1872* Gorgon-shield! *1888 1889* Gorgon shield! 509 *MS* Unless you say so, why>If law sufficed, would you 510 *MS* the law, confess 512–14 *MS* {no quotation marks at beginnings of lines} 514 *MS* arch: then

494 *you . . . low*: i.e. cowered me into submission simply by the way you looked at me.

500 *proscribe*: forbid, prohibit.

506 *the adventure*: i.e. the passage of arms with me, the fight.

507 *Gorgon-shield*: i.e. Pallas Athene's shield that could terrify people, or even turn them to stone. It had on it an image of the Gorgon Medusa's severed head. Browning would have known Caravaggio's painting of it, glued to a circular wooden shield, in the Uffizi. Commissioned by Cardinal Del Monte, the picture was presented by him to the Second Duke Ferdinand.

514 *Then . . . want!*: 'You want a word from me', says Guido, 'and you shall have it.' But the word they get will not be the word that they would like to get: Cook, 242.

I say that, long ago, when things began,
All the world made agreement, such and such
Were pleasure-giving profit-bearing acts,
But henceforth extra-legal, nor to be:
You must not kill the man whose death would please
And profit you, unless his life stop yours
Plainly, and need so be put aside:
Get the thing by a public course, by law,
Only no private bloodshed as of old!
All of us, for the good of every one,
Renounced such licence and conformed to law:
Who breaks law, breaks pact therefore, helps himself
To pleasure and profit over and above the due,
And must pay forfeit,—pain beyond his share:
For, pleasure being the sole good in the world,
Anyone's pleasure turns to someone's pain,
So, law must watch for everyone,—say we,
Who call things wicked that give too much joy,
And nickname mere reprisal, envy makes,
Punishment: quite right! thus the world goes round.
I, being well aware such pact there was,
I, in my time who found advantage come
Of law's observance and crime's penalty,—

515 *MS* {no new paragraph} 517 *MS* {no comma} 518 *MS* extralegal, 520 *MS* stopped 521 *MS* needed 522 *MS* The same thing 523 *MS* old: 524 *MS* {no commas} 525 *MS* law, 526 *MS* {beginning of fo. 267} *MS 1868 1872* pact, 529 *MS 1868* For pleasure is 531 *MS 1868* let law watch *MS* everyone, say 532 *MS* Calling>Who call 533 *MS* the reprisal envy *1868* the reprisal, 534 *MS* right,— 536 *MS 1868* Who in *MS 1868* have found *MS 1868* too 537 *MS 1868* In

515–34. In the following lines Guido articulates a version of utilitarian philosophy, which Browning, from a Christian perspective, clearly finds abhorrent: 'Guido's first excursus into the broad field of modern ethical and political theory is his reconstruction and endorsement of the theory of the "social contract" as developed by Hobbes and popularly known as utilitarianism, a theory that was given its peculiar nineteenth-century orientation by Jeremy Bentham and its most popular exposition by John Stuart Mill': Buckler, 274.

518 *extra-legal*: outside the law; illegal.

533–4 *nickname . . . Punishment*: i.e. we nickname 'Punishment' what is really simple reprisal made on account of envy.

Who, but for wholesome fear law bred in friends,
Had doubtless given example long ago,
Furnished forth some friend's pleasure with my pain,
And, by my death, pieced out his scanty life,—
I could not, for that foolish life of me,
Help risking law's infringement,—I broke bond,
And needs must pay price,—wherefore, here's my head,
Flung with a flourish! But, repentance too?
But pure and simple sorrow for law's breach
Rather than blunderer's-ineptitude?
Cardinal, no! Abate, scarcely thus!
'T is the fault, not that I dared try a fall
With Law and straightway am found undermost,
But that I failed to see, above man's law,
God's precept you, the Christians, recognize?
Colly my cow! Don't fidget, Cardinal!
Abate, cross your breast and count your beads
And exorcize the devil, for here he stands
And stiffens in the bristly nape of neck,
Daring you drive him hence! You, Christians both?
I say, if ever was such faith at all

538 *MS* [?I]>Who, *MS* this bred 540 *MS* friends 541 *MS* And by my death pieced *MS* life, 542 *MS* I, could not for *MS* me 544 *MS* wherefore here's 545 *MS* []>Flung 546 *MS* []>law's 547 *MS* blunderer's ineptitude? 548 {not found in *MS*} 549 *MS* The fault is not that *MS* I try fall with Law>I trying a fall>I dared try a fall 550 *MS* am>and straightway am 551 *MS 1868* fail *MS* Man's *MS* {no commas} 552 *MS* will which you>precept you, *MS 1868* Christians recognize? 554 *MS* self>breast 555 *MS* {beginning of fo. 268} 556 *MS* neck of him>nape of neck 557 *MS* hence. What, Christians

549 *fall*: bout at wrestling.

553 *Colly my cow!*: 'Ridiculous, ludicrous!'—an exasperated expletive. This phrase has baffled commentators. For some odd explanations see Cook, 242–3. In fact it is from the old broadside ballad 'Colly my Cow', also called 'The Countryman's Lamentation for the Death of his Cow', which originated in the seventeenth century. The first verse runs: 'Little Tom Dogget, what dost thou mean, / To kill thy poor Colly, / now she's so lean: [Refrain] *Sing, Oh poor* Colly; / Colly *my Cow*; / *For* Colly *will give me / no more milk now.*' Browning's use of the phrase is nonetheless unusual: we have been unable to trace another use of it separate from the ballad like this. For the full text, see *The Euing Collection of English Broadside Ballads*, with an introduction by John Holloway (Glasgow, 1971), pp. 42–5.

Born in the world, by your community
Suffered to live its little tick of time,
'T is dead of age, now, ludicrously dead;
Honour its ashes, if you be discreet,
In epitaph only! For, concede its death,
Allow extinction, you may boast unchecked
What feats the thing did in a crazy land
At a fabulous epoch,—treat your faith, that way,
Just as you treat your relics: "Here's a shred
"Of saintly flesh, a scrap of blessed bone,
"Raised King Cophetua, who was dead, to life
"In Mesopotamy twelve centuries since,
"Such was its virtue!"—twangs the Sacristan,
Holding the shrine-box up, with hands like feet
Because of gout in every finger joint:
Does he bethink him to reduce one knob,
Allay one twinge by touching what he vaunts?
I think he half uncrooks fist to catch fee,
But, for the grace, the quality of cure,—
Cophetua was the man put that to proof!
Not otherwise, your faith is shrined and shown
And shamed at once: you banter while you bow!

559 *MS* world and your 560 *MS* [ ]>Suffered to *MS* minute> tick 561 *MS 1868* age now, 563 *MS* us death, 566 *MS* epoch: *MS* faith, I say, 567 *MS* "here's 568 *MS* bone 569 *MS* Cophetua up to life again 571 *MS* virtue",—quoth 577 *Yale 1* But,>—But, *MS* ^grace, the^ *MS* cure, *Yale 1* cure,>cure,— 579 *MS* otherwise your faith, 580 [ ]>you *etc.*

565–6 *in . . . epoch*: i.e. in a mad country (Israel), long ago (when people still believed in miracles).

569 *King Cophetua*: legendary Ethiopian king, known for falling in love with a beggar girl, an event celebrated in the old ballad 'A Song of a Beggar and a King'. The ballad is mentioned several times by Shakespeare, and is the basis of Tennyson's reworking 'The Beggar Maid'. Guido simply grabs the first ancient name that comes to hand, and makes up a story about it, in order to show his contempt for the idea of relics, and his conviction that miracles are impossible.

571 *twangs*: i.e. speaking in a nasal, unctuous manner.

580 *you . . . bow*: i.e. treat it in a light-hearted, joking way, while apparently showing it reverence.

Do you dispute this? Come, a monster-laugh,
A madman's laugh, allowed his Carnival
Later ten days than when all Rome, but he,
Laughed at the candle-contest: mine's alight,
'T is just it sputter till the puff o' the Pope
End it to-morrow and the world turn Ash.
Come, thus I wave a wand and bring to pass
In a moment, in the twinkle of an eye,
What but that—feigning everywhere grows fact,
Professors turn possessors, realize

581 *MS* monster laugh, 582 *MS* mad man's 583 *MS* {beginning of fo. 269} *MS* me, 584 *MS* I'm alight, 585 *MS* I sputter *MS* of 586 *MS* End me 588 *MS* [?the]>a 589 *MS* that feigning *MS* suddenly>everywhere

581–4 *Come . . . candle-contest*: i.e. 'allow me a little Carnival freedom and fun'. Guido is speaking on the night of 21–2 February (i.e. well into Lent). He is imagining himself back, ten days earlier, on 11 February, Shrove Tuesday, the last joyous day of Carnival. Browning's calculations about the times of Carnival and Lent in 1698 can be seen in the chronology he drew up to help him organize precisely this kind of detail: see our Vol. VII, p. 323.

The 'candle-contest', on the evening of Shrove Tuesday, was the riotous end of Carnival, a symbolic snuffing out of Carnival's joy, and something Browning had witnessed on several occasions. There are good accounts of it in Dickens's *Pictures from Italy* (1846), the section on 'Rome', and in Alexandre Dumas's *The Count of Monte Cristo* (1844–5), ch. 36. Here is another description: 'Only think of a hundred thousand wax tapers no larger than so many candle-ends, lighted simultaneously in the hands of this vast mass of human beings, half frantic with frolicsome glee. They display them triumphantly, pelt each other with them, and snatch them out of each other's hands . . . The whole Corso seems alive with fire-flies of a giant growth. Those who are riding, as well as those who are stationed at their doors, are all brandishing the indispensable *moccolo* [little candle]. Then the fun consists in puffing out one's neighbour's taper, and struggling to light one's own again; for woe to the unhappy wight who would set himself above such a symbol of equality! . . . People in England or France can have no idea of the burlesque joy, the hurly-burly and wild buffoonery, that runs, like an electric spark, throughout the whole town on the evening in question. . . . No sooner has the great bell of the capitol rung the knell intended to exorcise the spirit of frolic, than the noise ceases as if by magic, all hilarity vanishes, the *moccoli* are extinguished . . . the Corso, so thronged with human beings but a moment before, is now become a desert; that bell has tolled the last agonies of the joyous carnival, who gives up the ghost to make way for Lent': Chevalier de Chatelain, *Rambles Through Rome* (London, 1851), p. 290.

586 *Ash*: i.e. Ash Wednesday (hence the capital letter); figuratively, Guido's death.

588 *In . . . eye*: cf. 1 Cor. 15: 52: 'In a moment, in the twinkling of an eye, at the last trump'.

The faith they play with as a fancy now,
And bid it operate, have full effect
On every circumstance of life, to-day,
In Rome,—faith's flow set free at fountain-head!
Now, you'll own, at this present, when I speak,
Before I work the wonder, there's no man
Woman or child in Rome, faith's fountain-head,
But might, if each were minded, realize
Conversely unbelief, faith's opposite—
Set it to work on life unflinchingly,
Yet give no symptom of an outward change:
Why should things change because men disbelieve?
What's incompatible, in the whited tomb,
With bones and rottenness one inch below?
What saintly act is done in Rome to-day
But might be prompted by the devil,—"is"
I say not,—"has been, and again may be,—"
I do say, full i' the face o' the crucifix
You try to stop my mouth with! Off with it!
Look in your own heart, if your soul have eyes!
You shall see reason why, though faith were fled,
Unbelief still might work the wires and move
Man, the machine, to play a faithful part.
Preside your college, Cardinal, in your cape,

594 *MS* fountain-head: 595 *MS 1868 1872* present when 598 *MS* {no commas} 600 *MS* Let it go work *MS* {no comma} 602 *MS* life>things **MS* you disbelieve? *1868 1872* men disbelieve? *1888 1889* disbelieve 603 *MS* {no commas} 604 *MS* [?And]>With *MS* the dead men's bones>bones and rottenness 607 *MS* {no quotation marks} *1868 1872* be,"— 608, 609 {not found in *MS*} 610 *MS* into *MS* heart if you *Yale 1* heart>heart, 611 *MS* [?is]>were *MS* {no commas} 612 *MS* may 613 *MS* {beginning of fo. 270} *MS* {no commas} *MS* part— 614 *MS* {line added later} *MS* College, *MS* cape,—

603–4 *whited . . . below*: cf. Matt. 23: 27.

608–9 *full . . . it!*: the Abate is trying to persuade Guido to kiss the crucifix as a sign of his repentance and his devotion to Christ. This was still a normal practice in Browning's day, and continued as prisoners approached the scaffold. Cf. Dumas, *The Count of Monte Cristo*, ch. 35 (trans.): 'From time to time each of them [the condemned men] would kiss the crucifix that a confessor held out to him.' Cf. 2222 n.

614 *Preside*: be head of, control. Cf. Carlyle, *French Revolution*, I. III. iii: 'He . . . sits there, since he must sit, presiding that Bureau of his.'

Or,—having got above his head, grown Pope,—
Abate, gird your loins and wash my feet!
Do you suppose I am at loss at all
Why you crook, why you cringe, why fast or feast?
Praise, blame, sit, stand, lie or go!—all of it,
In each of you, purest unbelief may prompt,
And wit explain to who has eyes to see.
But, lo, I wave wand, make the false the true!
Here's Rome believes in Christianity!
What an explosion, how the fragments fly
Of what was surface, mask and make-believe!
Begin now,—look at this Pope's-halberdier
In wasp-like black and yellow foolery!
He, doing duty at the corridor,
Wakes from a muse and stands convinced of sin!
Down he flings halbert, leaps the passage-length,
Pushes into the presence, pantingly

615 {not found in *MS*} 616 *MS* {line added later} *MS* feet,— 617 {not found in *MS*} 618 *MS* feast, 619 *MS* or go, or live, or die,>lie or go, live, die, all of it 620 *MS* All of it>In each of you purest 621 *MS* Explain>[?And] so explain *622 *MS* *1868* *1872* make *1888* *1889* made 624 *MS* fall>fly 625 *MS* []>surface *MS* a mere lie!>make believe! 626 *MS* Look at this fellow,—the>Begin now,—look at this 627 *MS* Wasp-like in>In wasp-like 628 *MS* golden door,>corridor 629 *MS* [ ]>Wakes *MS* and stands>to stand 630 *MS* halberd,>halbert, *MS* passage length,

616 *gird . . . feet*: i.e. re-enact Christ's washing of his disciples' feet at the Last Supper, something the Pope does every Holy Thursday.

618 *crook*: genuflect, bow obsequiously. Cf. *Colombe's Birthday*, I. 177, and also Jonson, *Sejanus*, I. 204: 'With sacrifice of knees, of crookes, and cringe'.

626–7 *Pope's-halberdier . . . foolery!*: a member of the Pope's Swiss guard, whose first duty is to protect the pope's own person. 'The privates of the Swiss guard carry halberds 8 feet long, with fine damaskeened steel blades. . . . The peculiar dress of the Swiss guard is said to be the ancient doublet and hose of the Swiss national costume, modified by the designs of Michael Angelo. It consists of full breeches to the knee of alternate wide stripes of red yellow and black. The stockings are striped yellow and black . . . Their doublets, padded at the shoulder and drawn in at the waist with a belt, are of smaller stripes of red yellow and black, and they wear black helmets with white horsehair plumes': M. A. R. Tuker and Hope Malleson, *Handbook to Christian and Ecclesiastical Rome*, 4 parts (London, 1897–1900), iv. 356.

629 *convinced of sin*: cf. John 8: 46.

630 *halbert*: a weapon that is a combination of an axe and spear.

Submits the extreme peril of the case
To the Pope's self,—whom in the world beside?—
And the Pope breaks talk with ambassador,
Bids aside bishop, wills the whole world wait
Till he secure that prize, outweighs the world,
A soul, relieve the sentry of his qualm!
His Altitude the Referendary,—
Robed right, and ready for the usher's word
To pay devoir,—is, of all times, just then
'Ware of a master-stroke of argument
Will cut the spinal cord . . . ugh, ugh! . . . I mean,
Paralyse Molinism for evermore!
Straight he leaves lobby, trundles, two and two,
Down steps to reach home, write, if but a word
Shall end the impudence: he leaves who likes
Go pacify the Pope: there's Christ to serve!
How otherwise would men display their zeal?
If the same sentry had the least surmise
A powder-barrel 'neath the pavement lay
In neighbourhood with what might prove a match,

634 *MS* ambassadors, 635 *MS* bishops, 636 *MS* {no commas} 637 *MS* human soul,>soul, *MS* qualm. 638 *MS* Referendary 639 *MS* world>word 640 *MS* devoir, 641 *MS* Ware *MS* subtle piece> masterstroke 642 *MS 1868 1872* cord . . *MS 1868 1872* ugh! . . 643 *MS* forevermore: 644 *MS* trundles two and two *Yale 1* trundles two and two> trundles, two and two, 645 *MS* {beginning of fo. 271} *MS* staircase, to *1868* steps, to *MS 1868* write if 646 *MS* impudence,— 648 *MS* do men 649 *MS* that same 650 *MS* []>Some *Yale 1* That>A *MS* neath 651 *MS* be>prove *MS* {no comma}

636 *prize . . . world*: i.e. prize, *which* outweighs the world. Cf. 359 n.

638 *His . . . Referendary*: i.e. a very important Cardinal. 'His Altitude' translates It. *Sua Altezza*, though in English it has a sarcastic effect (which is what Guido intends); cf. 'Her Eminence', IV. 55 n. A referendary was an important official within the Papal Curia, with the duty of examining and reporting on petitions, requests, use of the seal, and other matters. 'In the Papal Curia the office of "referendarii Apostolici" originated in the Middle Ages; their duty was to receive all petitions directed to the Holy See, to report on them to the pope, and to tender him advice. . . . The *referendarii* were entrusted with all arrangements for these papal decisions, which they had to prepare for the pope's signature': *The Catholic Encyclopaedia*, xii. 700. After the loss of the Papal States, this office became less important, and was abolished by Pius X in 1908.

646 *impudence*: i.e. the heresy (of Molinism).

Meant to blow sky-high Pope and presence both—
Would he not break through courtiers, rank and file,
Bundle up, bear off and save body so,
The Pope, no matter for his priceless soul?
There's no fool's-freak here, nought to soundly swinge,
Only a man in earnest, you'll so praise
And pay and prate about, that earth shall ring!
Had thought possessed the Referendary
His jewel-case at home was left ajar,
What would be wrong in running, robes awry,
To be beforehand with the pilferer?
What talk then of indecent haste? Which means,
That both these, each in his degree, would do
Just that,—for a comparative nothing's sake,
And thereby gain approval and reward,—
Which, done for what Christ says is worth the world,
Procures the doer curses, cuffs and kicks.
I call such difference 'twixt act and act
Sheer lunacy unless your truth on lip
Be recognized a lie in heart of you!
How do you all act, promptly or in doubt,
When there's a guest poisoned at supper-time
And he sits chatting on with spot on cheek?
"Pluck him by the skirt, and round him in the ears,

653 *MS* courtiers rank 654 *MS* up and bear *MS* {no commas} 655 *MS* Of the *1868* O' the 656 *MS* fool's freak *Yale 1* there>here 657 *MS* {no comma} 658 *MS* {no comma} *Yale 1* {comma added} *MS* ring. *Yale 1* ring.>ring! 660 *MS* A jewelcase 661 *MS* [ ]>Where 662 *MS* pilferer, 663 *MS* Who *MS* {no comma} 665 *MS* that, 666 *MS* reward, 667 *MS* {no commas} 668 *MS* kicks,>kicks. 669 {not found in *MS*} **1868 1872 1888 1889* act, 670 *MS* [ ]>Its lunacy *etc.* 671 *MS* ^in^ 674 *MS* {beginning of fo. 272} *MS* brow? *Yale 1* brow?> cheek? 675 *MS* {no quotation mark at beginning of line} *MS* Round him in the ears, have at him by the beard,>Pluck him by the skirt, and round him in the ears,

662 *To . . . pilferer*: i.e. to get there before the thief.
667 *what . . . world*: i.e. saving one's soul, getting to heaven: cf. 636 n.
675 *skirt*: edge of his robe or coat.
round . . . ears: i.e. shout at him; cf. IV. 600 n.

"Have at him by the beard, warn anyhow!"
Good, and this other friend that's cheat and thief
And dissolute,—go stop the devil's feast,
Withdraw him from the imminent hell-fire!
Why, for your life, you dare not tell your friend
"You lie, and I admonish you for Christ!"
Who yet dare seek that same man at the Mass
To warn him—on his knees, and tinkle near,—
He left a cask a-tilt, a tap unturned,
The Trebbian running: what a grateful jump
Out of the Church rewards your vigilance!
Perform that self-same service just a thought
More maladroitly,—since a bishop sits
At function!—and he budges not, bites lip,—
"You see my case: how can I quit my post?
"He has an eye to any such default.
"See to it, neighbour, I beseech your love!"
He and you know the relative worth of things,
What is permissible or inopportune.
Contort your brows! You know I speak the truth:
Gold is called gold, and dross called dross, i' the Book:
Gold you let lie and dross pick up and prize!

676 *MS* {no quotation marks} *MS* have>Have 678 *MS* dissolute, *MS* [ ]>the *MS* [ ],>feast, 682 *MS* out at mass 683 *MS* the tinkle 687 *MS* selfsame 688 *MS* [ ]>since *MS* Bishop 689 *MS* function,—why *MS* not,— 695 *MS* brows,—you 696 *MS* dross,—what then? 697 *MS* prize

681 *admonish . . . Christ*: cf. Rom. 15: 14, Col. 3: 16, etc.

683 *tinkle near*: i.e. the high-point of the Mass approaching. A bell is rung before the consecration, the most solemn moment of the Mass.

685 *Trebbian*: i.e. wine made from the Trebbiano grape, now considered a mediocre grape for white wine, but in the nineteenth century—as Browning would have known it—better thought of: 'The *Montepulciano* wine, termed by an Italian poet *d'ogni vino il rè* ("the king of all wines"), was a product of the Tuscan State. The *Aleatico*, the *Columbano*, the *Trebbiano*, the *Vernaccia*, also enjoyed a high repute': Mabel Sharman Crawford, *Life in Tuscany* (1859), p. 167.

696 *Gold . . . Book*: 'dross' is used on several occasions in the Bible for evil or evildoers: see Ps. 119: 119: 'Thou puttest away all the wicked of the earth like dross'; see also Isa. 1: 22, 25, Ezek. 22: 18–19. Less often, 'gold' is used as an image of goodness and purity: cf. Job 23: 10.

—Despite your muster of some fifty monks
And nuns a-maundering here and mumping there,
Who could, and on occasion would, spurn dross,
Clutch gold, and prove their faith a fact so far,—
I grant you! Fifty times the number squeak
And gibber in the madhouse—firm of faith,
This fellow, that his nose supports the moon;
The other, that his straw hat crowns him Pope:
Does that prove all the world outside insane?
Do fifty miracle-mongers match the mob
That acts on the frank faithless principle,
Born-baptized-and-bred Christian-atheists, each
With just as much a right to judge as you,—
As many senses in his soul, and nerves
I' neck of him as I,—whom, soul and sense,
Neck and nerve, you abolish presently,—
I being the unit in creation now
Who pay the Maker, in this speech of mine,
A creature's duty, spend my last of breath
In bearing witness, even by my worst fault,
To the creature's obligation, absolute,

698 *MS* Despite 699 *MS* {no comma} 700 *MS* [ ]>Who *MS* {no commas} 701 *MS* gold and 702 *MS* {beginning of fo. 273} 703 *MS* madhouse firm 704 *MS* fellow that *MS 1868 1872* moon, 705 *MS* That worthy, his old *MS* Pope,— 709 *MS* Born, bred and baptized>Born, baptized and bred 710 *MS* we,—>you,— 711 *MS* and>or *1868* or 712 *MS* In *MS* whose nerves and>whom, soul and sense, 713 *MS* present-ly *MS* {no commas} 715 *MS* Who at this moment pay the Maker thus> Who pay the Maker in this speech of mine *Yale 1* Maker>Maker, *Yale 1* mine> mine, 716 *MS* dying>last of 717 *MS 1868* fault

699 *a-maundering . . . mumping*: rambling (physically or mentally) and muttering (or grinning inanely); cf. *Aristophanes' Apology*, 1880, 'A Pillar at Sebzevar', 40. These rather vague words are usually associated with daydreaming, idleness, beggary, or senility. OED^2, for example, cites Bulwer-Lytton (1841): 'A day-dreamer who has wasted away his life in dawdling and maundering over Simple Poetry'; and for 'mumping' as an adj., Thomas Hood (1826): 'But the beggar man made a mumping face, / And knocked at every gate.' At l. 1895 Browning uses 'mumping' as an adj. to mean 'sentimental'. Here Guido despises what he sees as the near-imbecilic unworldliness of monks and nuns who actually believe their faith.

718 *the creature's obligation*: to be absolutely sincere towards his Creator: Cook, 244.

Perpetual: my worst fault protests, "The faith
"Claims all of me: I would give all she claims,
"But for a spice of doubt: the risk's too rash:
"Double or quits, I play, but, all or nought,
"Exceeds my courage: therefore, I descend
"To the next faith with no dubiety—
"Faith in the present life, made last as long
"And prove as full of pleasure as may hap,
"Whatever pain it cause the world." I'm wrong?
I've had my life, whate'er I lose: I'm right?
I've got the single good there was to gain.
Entire faith, or else complete unbelief!
Aught between has my loathing and contempt,
Mine and God's also, doubtless: ask yourself,
Cardinal, where and how you like a man!
Why, either with your feet upon his head,
Confessed your caudatory, or, at large,
The stranger in the crowd who caps to you
But keeps his distance,—why should he presume?
You want no hanger-on and dropper-off,
Now yours, and now not yours but quite his own,
According as the sky looks black or bright.

719 *MS* "the>"The 720–7 *MS* {no quotation marks at beginnings of lines} 720 *MS* acquit just>give all she *MS* {no comma} 722 *MS* but all or nought 723 *MS* this descent 726 *MS* be *Yale 1* be,>hap, 727 *MS* I cause the world: 730 *MS* {beginning of fo. 274} *MS 1868* unbelief,— 732 *MS* And God's too, I feel certain:>As mine, so God's too, I feel:>Mine and God's also, doubtless, *MS* yourself 733 *MS* ^where and^ *MS* the>a man, 734 *MS* {no commas} 735 *MS 1868* or at large 736 *MS* gallant>stranger *MS* never caps>caps to you 737 *MS* distance, *MS* what is he to you?>why should he presume? 738 *MS* {no comma} 739 *MS* {no commas}

721 *a spice of doubt*: a slight touch, or trace, of doubt. OED[2] gives many examples of this formula: (1790) 'The Flemings have a spice of obstinacy in their character'; (1835) 'The horse had a considerable spice of devil in his composition'; etc.

735 *caudatory*: servant, lackey. This Englishes It. *caudatario*, a person who bears up the train of a bishop. Not recorded in OED[2], it is almost certainly Browning's coinage from the Italian.

736 *caps*: i.e. takes his hat off, as a mark of respect.

Just so I capped to and kept off from faith—
You promised trudge behind through fair and foul,
Yet leave i' the lurch at the first spit of rain.
Who holds to faith whenever rain begins?
What does the father when his son lies dead,
The merchant when his money-bags take wing,
The politician whom a rival ousts?
No case but has its conduct, faith prescribes:
Where's the obedience that shall edify?
Why, they laugh frankly in the face of faith
And take the natural course,—this rends his hair
Because his child is taken to God's breast,
That gnashes teeth and raves at loss of trash
Which rust corrupts and thieves break through and steal,
And this, enabled to inherit earth
Through meekness, curses till your blood runs cold!
Down they all drop to my low level, rest
Heart upon dungy earth that's warm and soft,
And let who please attempt the altitudes.
Each playing prodigal son of heavenly sire,

741 *MS* [?declared] the>kept off from *MS* faith *MS* {Between 741 and 742 deleted extra line: You and the rest are bound to take up cross} 742 *MS* And trudge>You promised trudge 743 *MS* [ ]>Yet *MS* in *MS* cloud that comes.> spit of rain: 744 *MS* faith's skirt now that 745 *MS* says>does 748 *MS* {no comma} 749 *MS* Wants but of>Now for obedience *etc.* *MS* edify! 750 *MS* spit *MS* faith of face>face of faith 751 *MS* one rends 753 *MS* The other gnashes teeth at loss of trash *MS* gold>trash *Yale 1* teeth,>teeth 754 *MS* That *MS* {no comma} 756 *MS* cold: 757 *MS* {beginning of fo. 275} *MS* slip>drop *MS 1868 1872* level, ease 758 *MS* on the dungy *MS* {no comma} 759 *MS* who will go try the altitudes: *1868 1872* who will, *Yale 1* altitudes:>altitudes. 760 *MS* We have the prodigal son and heir of heavenly sire>We have the prodigal son of heavenly sire *1868* We have the *1872* Each is the

742 *trudge behind*: i.e. as a caudatory, bearing up faith's train: see 735 n.

749 *Where's . . . edify*: cf. 1 Cor. 8: 1.

754 *Which . . . steal*: cf. Matt. 6: 19.

755–6 *inherit . . . meekness*: cf. Matt. 5: 5. See previous two nn.: Guido is mocking these biblical texts and their aspirations, almost putting them in quotation marks.

758 *dungy earth*: cf. *Antony and Cleopatra*, I. i. 35, *Winter's Tale*, II. i. 157.

760–3 *prodigal . . . taste!*: adapting the Parable of the Prodigal Son, Luke 15: 11–32. 'Fain' = glad or content (under the circumstances), an archaism directly from (AV) Luke 15: 16.

Turning his nose up at the fatted calf,
Fain to fill belly with the husks, we swine
Did eat by born depravity of taste!

Enough of the hypocrites. But you, Sirs, you—
Who never budged from litter where I lay,
And buried snout i' the draff-box while I fed,
Cried amen to my creed's one article—
"Get pleasure, 'scape pain,—give your preference
"To the immediate good, for time is brief,
"And death ends good and ill and everything!
"What's got is gained, what's gained soon is gained twice,
"And,—inasmuch as faith gains most,—feign faith!"
So did we brother-like pass word about:
—You, now,—like bloody drunkards but half-drunk,
Who fool men yet perceive men find them fools,—
Vexed that a titter gains the gravest mouth,—
O' the sudden you must needs re-introduce
Solemnity, straight sober undue mirth
By a blow dealt me your boon companion here
Who, using the old licence, dreamed of harm
No more than snow in harvest: yet it falls!
You check the merriment effectually

761 {not found in *MS*} 762 *MS* Gl>Fain *MS 1868* {no comma} 763 *MS* with>by *MS* such depravity>some depravity 764 *MS* {no new paragraph} *MS* hypocrites: but *MS* you 766 {not found in *MS*} 767 *MS* Said 768-72 *MS* {no quotation marks at beginnings of lines} 768 *MS* giving preference 769 *MS* good,— *MS* brief 770 *MS* everything, *1868* everything: 772 *MS* And inasmuch *MS* {no quotation mark at end of line} 773 *MS* about— 774 *MS* Till now, 775 *MS* and perceive *MS* fools *1868* fools, 776 *MS 1868* And that *MS* face,>mouth, 777 *MS* You on 778 *MS* and sober *1868* must sober 779 *MS 1868 1872* dealt your 781 *MS* falls—

766 *draff-box*: i.e. pig trough, containing draff (waste, refuse).

774 *bloody drunkards*: i.e. people so drunk they are liable to fight.

776 *gains*: i.e. comes upon.

778 *sober*: make sober.

780–1 *dreamed . . . harvest*: i.e. thought any kind of harm completely unlikely. This adapts the proverbial 'As welcome as snow in harvest', itself derived from Prov. 25: 13: see ODEP, 748.

By pushing your abrupt machine i' the midst,
Making me Rome's example: blood for wine!
The general good needs that you chop and change!
I may dislike the hocus-pocus,—Rome,
The laughter-loving people, won't they stare
Chap-fallen!—while serious natures sermonize
"The magistrate, he beareth not the sword
"In vain; who sins may taste its edge, we see!"
Why my sin, drunkards? Where have I abused
Liberty, scandalized you all so much?
Who called me, who crooked finger till I came,
Fool that I was, to join companionship?
I knew my own mind, meant to live my life,
Elude your envy, or else make a stand,
Take my own part and sell you my life dear.
But it was "Fie! No prejudice in the world
"To the proper manly instinct! Cast your lot
"Into our lap, one genius ruled our births,
"We'll compass joy by concert; take with us
"The regular irregular way i' the wood;
"You'll miss no game through riding breast by breast,
"In this preserve, the Church's park and pale,
"Rather than outside where the world lies waste!"
Come, if you said not that, did you say this?
Give plain and terrible warning, "Live, enjoy?

785 {not found in *MS*} 786 *MS* hocus pocus,— 787 *MS* laughter-loving of them, 788 *MS* {beginning of fo. 276} *MS* Chap-fallen, 790 *MS* "Vainly, *MS* laughs>sins *MS* see[ ]>see!" 793 *MS* came 794 *MS* {'join' interlined above undeleted 'make'} *MS* companionship,>companionship? 795 *MS* Cast in my lot, and feast at Rome with you?>I knew my own mind, meant to take my way 797 *MS* dear *1868* dear: 799–805 *MS* {no quotation marks at beginnings of lines} 802 *MS* wood, 804 *MS* Churches 805 *MS 1868* is 806 *MS* that did *MS* this— 807 *MS* Plain>Give plain

784 *blood for wine*: i.e. execution instead of merry-making. A terrifying change of reds, the blood of execution replacing the wine of drunkenness and fun.

789–90 *he . . . vain*: cf. Rom. 13: 4.

800 *one . . . births*: i.e. 'we're aristocrats like you'.

801 *We'll . . . concert*: i.e. 'we'll have our fun together'.

803 *no game*: i.e. no worldly enjoyment.

"Such life begins in death and ends in hell!
"Dare you bid us assist your sins, us priests
"Who hurry sin and sinners from the earth?
"No such delight for us, why then for you?
"Leave earth, seek heaven or find its opposite!"
Had you so warned me, not in lying words
But veritable deeds with tongues of flame,
That had been fair, that might have struck a man,
Silenced the squabble between soul and sense,
Compelled him to make mind up, take one course
Or the other, peradventure!—wrong or right,
Foolish or wise, you would have been at least
Sincere, no question,—forced me choose, indulge
Or else renounce my instincts, still play wolf
Or find my way submissive to your fold,
Be red-crossed on my fleece, one sheep the more.
But you as good as bade me wear sheep's wool
Over wolf's skin, suck blood and hide the noise
By mimicry of something like a bleat,—
Whence it comes that because, despite my care,
Because I smack my tongue too loud for once,
Drop baaing, here's the village up in arms!
Have at the wolf's throat, you who hate the breed!
Oh, were it only open yet to choose—
One little time more—whether I'd be free

808–12 *MS* {no quotation marks at beginnings of lines} 808 *MS* hell: 809 *MS 1868* assist you to your sins 811 *MS* delights 812 *MS* Leave them, 814 *MS* {no comma} 816 *MS* {beginning of fo. 277} 817 *MS 1868* him make his 818 *MS* peradventure,— *MS* right 821 *MS* My instincts,>Or else renounce my instincts, 822 *MS* drop>find my way *MS* the fold, 823 *MS* red crossed on the fleece one *1868* the fleece, 825 *MS* wolf's shag, *MS* [ ]>suck 829 *MS* arms, *830 *1888 1889* wolf s {broken sort} *MS* we who 831 *MS* {no comma} *MS* choose 832 *MS* more whether

814 *But . . . flame*: i.e. but by good deeds (and holy lives) inspired by the Holy Spirit. Cf. Acts 2: 3–4.

823 *Be red-crossed*: be marked with the sign of the cross, i.e. be a true Christian within the Church's fold.

832–3 *whether . . . forsooth!*: i.e. whether I'd be your open enemy, or drawn into alliance with you through gain (or the hope of gain). Guido is thinking of the 'minor orders' he has taken in the Church.

Your foe, or subsidized your friend forsooth!
Should not you get a growl through the white fangs
In answer to your beckoning! Cardinal,
Abate, managers o' the multitude,
I'd turn your gloved hands to account, be sure!
You should manipulate the coarse rough mob:
'T is you I'd deal directly with, not them,—
Using your fears: why touch the thing myself
When I could see you hunt, and then cry "Shares!
"Quarter the carcase or we quarrel; come,
"Here's the world ready to see justice done!"
Oh, it had been a desperate game, but game
Wherein the winner's chance were worth the pains!
We'd try conclusions!—at the worst, what worse
Than this Mannaia-machine, each minute's talk
Helps push an inch the nearer me? Fool, fool!

You understand me and forgive, sweet Sirs?
I blame you, tear my hair and tell my woe—
All's but a flourish, figure of rhetoric!
One must try each expedient to save life.

836 *MS* of 838 *MS* [ ]>You *MS* mob, 839 *MS* they>them, *Yale 1* them,>them,— 840 *MS* [ ]>your 841 *MS 1868* {no comma} 842, 843 *MS* {no quotation marks at beginnings of lines} 842 *MS 1868* carcass 844 *MS* {beginning of fo. 278} 845 *MS* is worth the pains, *Yale 1* is>were *Yale 1* pains.>pains *1868 1872* pains 846 *MS* So, try conclusions,— *Yale 1* Ride, try conclusions,—>To try conclusions!— *1868* To try *MS* what's worse 847 *MS* this the red machine, *Yale 1* Mannaia machine>Mannaia-machine *MS 1868* talk, 848 *MS* a little>an inch the *MS* nearer,—oh, fool, fool! 851 *MS* rhetoric,

---

837 *gloved hands*: these indicate the high status of the priests, but also Guido is continuing the hunting image: see ll. 803–5. The Cardinal and Abate's hands are apparently 'clean', removed from the crimes and manipulation in which they engage—like the huntsman's gloved hands, not directly covered in blood.

840 *Using your fears*: using your fears of being exposed as hypocrites, the 'justice' referred to in 843. Guido would be like a mafioso, letting the Cardinal and Abate rob the people, and then ruthlessly demanding his share.

846 *try conclusions*: i.e. be in open conflict. Cf. v. 1125 n.

849–51 *You . . . rhetoric!*: Guido changes tone abruptly. He realizes that he has overdone his argument. He backs off, fawning, claiming that the argument was only a 'figure of rhetoric'.

One makes fools look foolisher fifty-fold
By putting in their place men wise like you,
To take the full force of an argument
Would buffet their stolidity in vain.
If you should feel aggrieved by the mere wind
O' the blow that means to miss you and maul them,
That's my success! Is it not folly, now,
To say with folk, "A plausible defence—
"We see through notwithstanding, and reject?"
Reject the plausible they do, these fools,
Who never even make pretence to show
One point beyond its plausibility
In favour of the best belief they hold!
"Saint Somebody-or-other raised the dead:"
Did he? How do you come to know as much?
"Know it, what need? The story's plausible,
"Avouched for by a martyrologist,
"And why should good men sup on cheese and leeks
"On such a saint's day, if there were no saint?"
I praise the wisdom of these fools, and straight
Tell them my story—"plausible, but false!"
False, to be sure! What else can story be
That runs—a young wife tired of an old spouse,
Found a priest whom she fled away with,—both
Took their full pleasure in the two-days' flight,

853 *MS* I make *MS* fifty fold 854 *MS 1868* place the wise *MS 1868* {no comma} 856 *MS* That buffets *MS* vain— 858 *MS* Of *MS* that ought 859 *MS* success. 860 *MS 1868 1872* folks, 861 *MS* {no quotation mark at beginning of line} *MS* {no comma} *MS* reject." 862 *MS* fools 863 *MS* made 866 *MS* {no quotation marks} *MS* Somebody or other 868–71 *MS* {no quotation marks at beginnings of lines} 871 *MS* {beginning of fo. 279} *MS* was *MS* {no quotation mark at end of line} 872 {not found in *MS*} 873 *MS* I tell my 877 *MS* Taking their pleasure *MS* two-days

853–9 *One . . . success!*: i.e. 'People like you really show up how foolish most men are. The exaggerated argument I've just been guilty of would have had little effect on such people, whereas you are distressed even by a hint of it.'

869 *martyrologist*: an expert in saints and martyrs.

870 *sup . . . leeks*: i.e. fast (not eat meat).

Which a grey-headed greyer-hearted pair,
(Whose best boast was, their life had been a lie)
Helped for the love they bore all liars. Oh,
Here incredulity begins! Indeed?
Allow then, were no one point strictly true,
There's that i' the tale might seem like truth at least
To the unlucky husband,—jaundiced patch,—
Jealousy maddens people, why not him?
Say, he was maddened, so forgivable!
Humanity pleads that though the wife were true,
The priest true, and the pair of liars true,
They might seem false to one man in the world!
A thousand gnats make up a serpent's sting,
And many sly soft stimulants to wrath
Compose a formidable wrong at last
That gets called easily by some one name
Not applicable to the single parts,
And so draws down a general revenge,
Excessive if you take crime, fault by fault.
Jealousy! I have known a score of plays,
Were listened to and laughed at in my time
As like the everyday-life on all sides,
Wherein the husband, mad as a March hare,
Suspected all the world contrived his shame.

878 *MS* Helped by>Which a grey headed greyer hearted pair 879 *MS* Whose *Yale 1* Whose>(Whose *MS* was *Yale 1* was>was, *MS* lie, *Yale 1* lie,> lie) 880 *MS* liars— 883 *MS* in *884 *MS 1868 1872* patch,— *1888 1889* patch —{broken sort} 886 *MS* maddened and forgiveable! *1868* so, 888 *MS* And the *MS* and the pair>the pair 891 *MS* As 892 *1868 1872* last, 894 *MS* thousand 895 *MS* draw 896 *MS* [ ]>Excessive *MS* take them fault 897 *MS* {no comma} 899 *MS* everyday life 900 *MS* {beginning of fo. 280} *MS* march 901 *MS* [ ] [ ]>all the *MS 1868* shame;

---

878 *grey-headed . . . pair*: i.e. the Comparini.

884 *jaundiced patch*: jealous fool. Literally 'jaundiced' refers to the yellow appearance of a person suffering from the disease jaundice; here it has its figurative sense: 'disordered by envy, jealousy, spleen, etc.' OED² cites Garth (1699): 'Here jealousy with jaundic'd look appears.'

900 *mad . . . hare*: proverbial, i.e. as lunatic in behaviour as a hare in the mating season: see ODEP, 497.

What did the wife? The wife kissed both eyes blind,
Explained away ambiguous circumstance,
And while she held him captive by the hand,
Crowned his head,—you know what's the mockery,—
By half her body behind the curtain. That's
Nature now! That's the subject of a piece
I saw in Vallombrosa Convent, made
Expressly to teach men what marriage was!
But say "Just so did I misapprehend,
"Imagine she deceived me to my face,"
And that's pretence too easily seen through!
All those eyes of all husbands in all plays,
At stare like one expanded peacock-tail,
Are laughed at for pretending to be keen
While horn-blind: but the moment I step forth—
Oh, I must needs o' the sudden prove a lynx

902 *MS* On the other hand,>What did the wife? *MS* the wife 905 *MS* Made his head, *MS* mockery, 908 *MS* Val[ ]>Vallombrosa 909 *MS* was. 910 *MS* But say—and just so I misapprehend— *1868* misapprehend!" 911 *MS* {no quotation marks} *MS* Or just so she *1868* Or "Just so she *MS* face *1868 1872* face!" 912 *MS* That's a 913 *MS* {no comma} 914 *MS* {no comma} 915 *MS* You laugh at 916 *MS* horn-blind,— *MS* forth 917 *MS* the lynx

902 *kissed . . . blind*: i.e. 'showed excessive affection, so the husband did not suspect what she was up to'. The scenario here is reminiscent of Chaucer's Merchant's Tale.

905 *Crowned his head*: i.e. made him a cuckold. Here the wife holds her husband's hand tenderly while, behind a curtain, having sex with her lover.

907–8 *piece . . . Convent*: as the context makes clear, 'the piece' is a play or playlet, not a painting. The Brownings had visited the monastery of Vallombrosa in July 1847, staying at the guesthouse, though EBB, as a woman, was not allowed into the main monastic building. The monks had a tradition of plays going back to the seventeenth century, and they were still acting them in the middle of the nineteenth century; Browning could have heard about them, though he would not have seen one, as they were for the community only. Browning, therefore, gives this statement to Guido, from a memory he had from 1847, although the scene is likely to have come from a secular play he may have seen elsewhere. It is unlikely that the real Guido would have gained admittance to a play at Vallombrosa, though Browning could have thought that, as a minor cleric, he might have seen one. The plays, of course, were written by the monks themselves and were on biblical and moral subjects.

916 *horn-blind*: i.e. blind to their cuckolds' horns.

917 *prove a lynx*: i.e. prove an especially sharp-eyed person: cf. X. 1245 n.

And look the heart, that stone-wall, through and through!
Such an eye, God's may be,—not yours nor mine.

Yes, presently . . . what hour is fleeting now?
When you cut earth away from under me,
I shall be left alone with, pushed beneath
Some such an apparitional dread orb
As the eye of God, since such an eye there glares:
I fancy it go filling up the void
Above my mote-self it devours, or what
Proves—wrath, immensity wreaks on nothingness.
Just how I felt once, couching through the dark,
Hard by Vittiano; young I was, and gay,
And wanting to trap fieldfares: first a spark
Tipped a bent, as a mere dew-globule might
Any stiff grass-stalk on the meadow,—this
Grew fiercer, flamed out full, and proved the sun.
What do I want with proverbs, precepts here?
Away with man! What shall I say to God?
This, if I find the tongue and keep the mind—

918 *MS* That looks the stone wall through and through,—read hearts. 920 *MS* {no new paragraph} **MS* in the next . .>presently . . *1868 1872* presently . . *1888 1889* presently . . {broken sort} 921 *MS* {no comma} 923 *MS* eye>orb *1868* orb; 924 {not found in *MS 1868*} 925 *MS* fancy may go *MS* sky>void 927 *MS* Immensity may do for nothingness>Immensity may wreak on nothingness *Yale 1* please to>please *1868* Immensity please wreak on nothingness. *1872* Proves wrath, 928 *MS 1868* Just so *MS* [ ]>felt *MS* dark 929 *MS* Vittiano, *MS* young and gay I was,>young I was, and gay, 930 *MS* watched to catch>watched to trap the>wanting to trap *MS* feldfares; 931 *MS* like>as *MS* dew globule 934 *MS* {line added later} 935 *MS* with you.

923 *apparitional*: like an apparition, i.e. supernatural, strange; cf. *Aristophanes' Apology*, 231.

925–7 *I . . . nothingness*: i.e. 'I imagine the eye of God getting bigger and bigger, "filling up" the whole space above me, so that I am like a floating speck of dust "devoured" by its huge, glaring presence; or I imagine it like the wrath that immensity naturally inflicts on nothingness.'

929 *Vittiano*: the Franceschini's country estate: cf. v. 364. But see the Afterword, in this volume, for the truth of this matter.

930 *fieldfares*: a species of thrush (*Turdus pilaris*), good to eat.

931 *bent*: stalk of grass.

"Do Thou wipe out the being of me, and smear
"This soul from off Thy white of things, I blot!
"I am one huge and sheer mistake,—whose fault?
"Not mine at least, who did not make myself!"
Someone declares my wife excused me so!
Perhaps she knew what argument to use.
Grind your teeth, Cardinal: Abate, writhe!
What else am I to cry out in my rage,
Unable to repent one particle
O' the past? Oh, how I wish some cold wise man
Would dig beneath the surface which you scrape,
Deal with the depths, pronounce on my desert
Groundedly! I want simple sober sense,
That asks, before it finishes with a dog,
Who taught the dog that trick you hang him for?
You both persist to call that act a crime,
Which sense would call . . . yes, I maintain it, Sirs, . . .
A blunder! At the worst, I stood in doubt
On cross-road, took one path of many paths:
It leads to the red thing, we all see now,
But nobody saw at first: one primrose-patch

937–40 *MS* {no quotation marks at beginnings of lines} 937 *MS* Wipe out the being of me, smear this soul>Do thou wipe out the being of me, and smear 938 *MS* From off the white of things, it blots,—whose fault?>This soul from off the white of things, it blots,— 939 *MS* {line added later} 940 *MS* mine, 941, 942 {not found in *MS*} 941 *Yale 1* Some one>Someone *Yale 1* said that>declares 942 *Yale 1* use:>use. 943 *MS* Gnash your teeth, Cardinal, contort your brow,— *1868 1872* Cardinal, 944 *MS* {no comma} 949 *MS* Groundedly,— *Yale 1* Groundedly—>Groundedly! 950 *MS* says,>asks, 952 *MS* {no comma} *Yale 1* {comma added} 953 *MS* He *Yale 1* He>Sense *1868 1872* Sense *MS 1868 1872* would call . . yes, I do assure you, Sirs, . . 954 *MS* blunder,—at 955 *MS* cross road, *MS* paths,— *Yale 1* paths:—>paths: 957 *MS 1868* But nobody at first saw one primrose *1872* But nobody at first saw: one primrose

940–1 *who . . . so!*: 'So he was made; he nowise made himself' (Pompilia's words): VII. 1731.

956 *the red thing*: i.e. the guillotine: see ll. 220–36 for Guido's description of its redness.

957–9 *one . . . wayfare*: i.e. this particular path did not look any less pleasing than the others.

In bank, one singing-bird in bush, the less,
Had warned me from such wayfare: let me prove!
Put me back to the cross-road, start afresh!
Advise me when I take the first false step!
Give me my wife: how should I use my wife,
Love her or hate her? Prompt my action now!
There she is, there she stands alive and pale,
The thirteen-years'-old child, with milk for blood,
Pompilia Comparini, as at first,
Which first is only four brief years ago!
I stand too in the little ground-floor room
O' the father's house at Via Vittoria: see!
Her so-called mother,—one arm round the waist
O' the child to keep her from the toys, let fall
At wonder I can live yet look so grim,—
Ushers her in, with deprecating wave
Of the other,—and she fronts me loose at last,
Held only by the mother's finger-tip.
Struck dumb,—for she was white enough before!—
She eyes me with those frightened balls of black,
As heifer—the old simile comes pat—
Eyes tremblingly the altar and the priest.

958 *MS* The less in bank one singing-bird in bush,>In bank or singing-bird in bush, the less *Yale 1* or singing-bird>one singing-bird 959 *MS* To warn of the>To warn wayfarer: let me prove you that!>To warn from wayfare: let me prove you that! *1868* To warn from wayfare: let me prove you that! *1872* wayfare, 960 *MS* [?on]>at *MS* afresh,— *Yale 1* afresh!—>afresh! 961 *MS* {beginning of fo. 282} 962 *MS* I have a wife: *MS* this wife, 964 *MS 1868* she stands, there she is 965 *1889* thirteen-years' old {broken sort} 967 *MS* ago. 968 *MS* groundfloor room, 969 *MS* At Via Vittoria, of the father's house: see—>Of the father's house at Via Vittoria: see— 970 *MS* mother, 971 *MS* Of *MS* toys let fall, *1868* toys—let fall, 972 {not found in *MS*} *Yale 1* At the>At 973 *MS* {no comma} 974 *MS 1868* there she *MS 1868* loose, at large, 975 *MS* finger-tip: *1868* finger-tip— 976 *MS* dumb— *1868 1872* dumb, *MS* before— *1868 1872* before! 977 *MS* black— *Yale 1* black> black, 978 *MS* pat 979 *MS* priest— *1868* priest:

964–1021. Compare Pompilia's account of the incident at VII. 389–409.

978–9 *heifer . . . priest*: probably recalling the image on the Parthenon frieze (British Museum), also alluded to in Keats's 'Ode on a Grecian Urn', 31–3, or perhaps recalling the innocent Iphigenia sacrificed by her father.

The amazed look, all one insuppressive prayer,—
Might she but breathe, set free as heretofore,
Have this cup leave her lips unblistered, bear
Any cross anywhither anyhow,
So but alone, so but apart from me!
You are touched? So am I, quite otherwise,
If 't is with pity. I resent my wrong,
Being a man: I only show man's soul
Through man's flesh: she sees mine, it strikes her thus!
Is that attractive? To a youth perhaps—
Calf-creature, one-part boy to three-parts girl,
To whom it is a flattering novelty
That he, men use to motion from their path,
Can thus impose, thus terrify in turn
A chit whose terror shall be changed apace
To bliss unbearable when grace and glow,
Prowess and pride descend the throne and touch
Esther in all that pretty tremble, cured
By the dove o' the sceptre! But myself am old,

980 *MS* {no commas} *MS* prayer 981 *MS 1868 1872* she but be set free 983 *MS* {no comma} 984 *MS* Only alone, only 985 *MS* touched,—so *MS* but>quite 986 *MS* pity: 987 *MS 1868* we only 988 *MS 1868* flesh, *MS* thus: *Yale 1* thus:>thus! 989 *MS* perhaps 990 *MS* {beginning of fo. 283} *MS* {no commas} *MS* three parts girl to one part boy:>one part boy to three parts girl: 995 *MS 1868 1872* when, 998 *MS* on *MS* sceptre: but

980 *insuppressive*: insuppressible, that cannot be suppressed. Perhaps this word is not as 'rare' as OED[2] supposes: it occurs, for example, in *Julius Caesar* (II. i. 134), Edward Young's *Night Thoughts*, and some nineteenth-century dramas, as well as four times elsewhere in Browning.

982 *Have . . . unblistered*: cf. Matt. 26: 39.

990 *Calf-creature*: i.e. callow young man. The implicit bull–calf opposition here, and the effeminacy of the imagined young man, are reminiscent of Horace, *Odes*, II. v.

994 *chit*: young girl.

995 *glow*: almost certainly Browning is recalling the glittering gold and jewels on King Ahasuerus' robes: see next n.

997–8 *Esther . . . sceptre*: Guido is sardonic about how glorious the young man will appear to the trembling adolescent girl. The allusion is to the Book of Esther, chap. 5, where Esther appears unsummoned before the mighty King Ahasuerus, so risking death, and then is favourably received by him. Browning, however, alludes to the fuller version of events in the Greek text (in the English Apocrypha, 'The rest of the chapters of the Book of Esther'), ch. 15. King Artaxerxes (Ahasuerus) appears terrify-

O' the wane at least, in all things: what do you say
To her who frankly thus confirms my doubt?
I am past the prime, I scare the woman-world,
Done-with that way: you like this piece of news?
A little saucy rose-bud minx can strike
Death-damp into the breast of doughty king
Though 't were French Louis,—soul I understand,—
Saying, by gesture of repugnance, just
"Sire, you are regal, puissant and so forth,
"But—young you have been, are not, nor will be!"
In vain the mother nods, winks, bustles up,
"Count, girls incline to mature worth like you!
"As for Pompilia, what's flesh, fish, or fowl
"To one who apprehends no difference,
"And would accept you even were you old
"As you are . . . youngish by her father's side?
"Trim but your beard a little, thin your bush

999 *MS* On *MS* {no comma} 1000 *MS* doubt, 1001 *MS* []>the 1002 *MS* Done with *Yale 1* Done with>Done-with *MS* [?that]>this 1003 *MS* Sweet air, a little saucy minx>A little saucy rose-bud minx 1006 *MS* []>by *MS* the gesture *Yale 1* the gesture>gesture 1008 *MS* But []>But young— *MS* be." 1009 *MS 1868 1872* up 1011–17 *MS* {no quotation marks at beginnings of lines} 1011 *MS* show>what's *MS 1868 1872* fish or 1014 *MS 1868 1872* are . . *MS* side,

---

ing, 'clothed with all his robes of majesty, all glittering with gold and precious stones'. Esther faints: 'Then God changed the spirit of the king into mildness, who in a fear leaped from his throne, and took her in his arms, till she came to herself again, and comforted her with loving words. . . . And so he held up his golden sceptre, and laid it upon her neck, and embraced her, and said, Speak unto me': ch. 15: 6–12. In Guido's phrasing, Esther is 'cured' of her 'tremble' by the 'dove o' the sceptre' because this is a sign of peace, a sign that the king will not kill her: as Esther explains earlier, it is well known that 'whosoever, whether man or woman, shall come unto the king into the inner court, who is not called, there is one law of his to put him to death, except such to whom the king shall hold out the golden sceptre, that he may live': ch. 4: 11.

1002 *Done-with*: exhausted, used up.

1004 *Death-damp*: a collocation used by a few poets before Browning; cf. W. E. Aytoun, 'Poland' (1832), ll. 501–4: 'Seest thou that dying soldier on the ground . . . No friend to wipe the death-damp from his brow.'

1005 *French Louis*: Louis XIV of France (1638–1715) was notorious for his sexual affairs. Even the all-powerful Louis XIV, when ageing, discovered in the gesture of repugnance of a young girl the fact of his own loss of sexual attractiveness. Guido's point is that Pompilia's flinching from him reinforces his own fear he is 'past his prime'.

"Of eyebrow; and for presence, portliness,
"And decent gravity, you beat a boy!"
Deceive yourself one minute, if you may,
In presence of the child that so loves age,
Whose neck writhes, cords itself against your kiss,
Whose hand you wring stark, rigid with despair!
Well, I resent this; I am young in soul,
Nor old in body,—thews and sinews here,—
Though the vile surface be not smooth as once,—
Far beyond that first wheelwork which went wrong
Through the untempered iron ere 't was proof:
I am the wrought man worth ten times the crude,
Would woman see what this declines to see,
Declines to say "I see,"—the officious word
That makes the thing, pricks on the soul to shoot
New fire into the half-used cinder, flesh!
Therefore 't is she begins with wronging me,
Who cannot but begin with hating her.

1016 *MS* eyebrow, *MS 1868 1872* portliness 1017 *MS* {no comma} 1018 *MS* {beginning of fo. 284} *MS 1868 1872* Deceive you for a *MS* second *Yale 1* second>second, *1868 1872* second, *MS* {no commas} *Yale 1* may>may, 1019 *MS* of Pompilia that loves age 1021 *MS* Stark, rigid with despair at what shall>Whose hand you wring stark, rigid with despair. 1023 *MS* there,— 1025 *MS* Worth ten times the old>Far beyond the first *1868* the first *MS* []>that went *1868* that went 1027 *MS* I am worth ten times the man I was before>I am the steel man worth ten times the crude,—and>I am the steel man worth ten times the crude,— *1868 1872* steel man *1868 1872* crude,— 1028 *MS* If a woman saw 1029 *MS* "'Tis there," 1031 *MS* coal> cinder, *MS* flesh. *Yale 1* flesh.>flesh!

1020 *cords itself*: i.e. twists so much, that the muscles stand out (like cords). This use antedates the earliest comparable use in OED^2, from Stevenson's *Dr Jekyll and Mr Hyde*, x. 121: 'The hand . . . was lean, corded, knuckly.'

1025 *wheelwork*: wheels (within a machine). Cf. *Sordello*, III. 844, where the soul is compared to an 'engine' with 'strange wheelwork'.

1026 *untempered*: unhardened.

proof: proved, tested.

1027 *wrought*: fashioned, fully formed; but also, from the previous line, punning on the idea of 'wrought iron' (properly worked, strong iron) as opposed to 'untempered iron'.

1029 *officious*: kind, efficacious—not the common modern sense. Cf. *Paradise Lost*, VIII. 99.

Our marriage follows: there she stands again!
Why do I laugh? Why, in the very gripe
O' the jaws of death's gigantic skull, do I
Grin back his grin, make sport of my own pangs?
Why from each clashing of his molars, ground
To make the devil bread from out my grist,
Leaps out a spark of mirth, a hellish toy?
Take notice we are lovers in a church,
Waiting the sacrament to make us one
And happy! Just as bid, she bears herself,
Comes and kneels, rises, speaks, is silent,—goes:
So have I brought my horse, by word and blow,
To stand stock-still and front the fire he dreads.
How can I other than remember this,
Resent the very obedience? Gain thereby?
Yes, I do gain my end and have my will,—
Thanks to whom? When the mother speaks the word,
She obeys it—even to enduring me!
There had been compensation in revolt—
Revolt's to quell: but martyrdom rehearsed,
But predetermined saintship for the sake
O' the mother?—"Go!" thought I, "we meet again!"
Pass the next weeks of dumb contented death,
She lives,—wakes up, installed in house and home,
Is mine, mine all day-long, all night-long mine.
Good folk begin at me with open mouth
"Now, at least, reconcile the child to life!

1034 *MS 1868* we stand 1036 *MS* Of *MS 1868* {no comma} *MS* does he—>do I 1037 *MS* Do I grin>Grin 1038 *MS* ^each^ 1041 *MS* {no comma} *Yale 1* {comma added} 1044 *MS* Rises,>Sits, rises>Comes and sits, rises *Yale 1* sits,>kneels, 1046 *MS* {beginning of fo. 285} *MS* stock still 1050 *MS* {no comma} 1051 *MS* obeys—even to supporting 1053 *MS* Left me to 1055 *MS* Of the mother!— 1057 *MS* wakes up, is>lives,—wakes up 1058 *MS* day long, all night long mine *Yale 1* day long>day-long *Yale 1* night long>night-long 1059 *MS 1868 1872* folks 1060 *MS* life, *Yale 1* life,>life!

1040 *toy*: trifle, fancy.
1046 *front*: face, confront.

"Study and make her love . . . that is, endure
"The . . . hem! the . . . all of you though somewhat old,
"Till it amount to something, in her eye,
"As good as love, better a thousand times,—
"Since nature helps the woman in such strait,
"Makes passiveness her pleasure: failing which,
"What if you give up boy-and-girl-fools'-play
"And go on to wise friendship all at once?
"Those boys and girls kiss themselves cold, you know,
"Toy themselves tired and slink aside full soon
"To friendship, as they name satiety:
"Thither go you and wait their coming!" Thanks,
Considerate advisers,—but, fair play!
Had you and I, friends, started fair at first,
We, keeping fair, might reach it, neck by neck,
This blessed goal, whenever fate so please:
But why am I to miss the daisied mile
The course begins with, why obtain the dust
Of the end precisely at the starting-point?
Why quaff life's cup blown free of all the beads,
The bright red froth wherein our beard should steep
Before our mouth essay the black o' the wine?
Foolish, the love-fit? Let me prove it such
Like you, before like you I puff things clear!

1061–72 *MS* {no quotation marks at beginnings of lines} 1061 *MS 1868 1872* love . . 1062 *MS 1868 1872* The . . *MS 1868 1872* the . . *MS* {no comma} 1067 *MS* boys'-and girls'-fools' play *1868* boys' and girls' fools'-play *1872* boy and girl fools'-play 1071 *MS* satiety, 1072 *MS* And there 1074 *MS* {beginning of fo. 286} *MS* Had she *Yale 1* she>you **MS 1868 1872* and I but started fair at first, *1888 1889* first 1080 *MS* [ ]>blown *MS* {no comma} 1081 *MS* That *MS* [ ]>our

1061–2 *endure / The . . . hem!*: 'endure the [sexual intercourse, sexual side of marriage]'. The good folk hesitate here, then use polite euphemism: 'the . . . all of you though somewhat old', i.e. your whole person, in sexual terms.

1067 *boy-and-girl-fools'-play*: i.e. sexual intercourse. Another polite euphemism: see previous n.

1070 *Toy*: play, dally sexually.

1080 *beads*: i.e. bubbles (on top of the wine). Cf. Keats, 'Ode to a Nightingale', 17.

1084 *puff things clear*: blow off the bubbles from the wine, i.e. forgo sexual intercourse with Pompilia.

"The best's to come, no rapture but content!
"Not love's first glory but a sober glow,
"Not a spontaneous outburst in pure boon,
"So much as, gained by patience, care and toil,
"Proper appreciation and esteem!"
Go preach that to your nephews, not to me
Who, tired i' the midway of my life, would stop
And take my first refreshment, pluck a rose:
What's this coarse woolly hip, worn smooth of leaf,
You counsel I go plant in garden-plot,
Water with tears, manure with sweat and blood,
In confidence the seed shall germinate
And, for its very best, some far-off day,
Grow big, and blow me out a dog-rose bell?
Why must your nephews begin breathing spice
O' the hundred-petalled Provence prodigy?

1085–8 *MS* {no quotation marks at beginnings of lines} 1085 *MS* content— 1086 *MS 1868 1872* the first 1087 *MS* Nor *1868 1872* "Nor *MS* {no comma} 1088 *MS* as gained *MS* toil,— *1868* toil!" 1089 {not found in *MS 1868*} 1090 *MS* nephew, *Yale 1* nephew,>nephews, 1091 *MS* in 1092 *MS 1868 1872* refreshment in 1093 *MS* without a>worn smooth of *MS* {no commas} 1094 *MS* garden-pot *1868 1872* garden-pot, 1097 *MS* {line added later} *MS* And for *MS* far off 1098 *MS* Grow, great in, *Yale 1* great in>big, and *MS* bell— 1099 *MS* nephew *Yale 1* nephew>nephews *MS* only>begin *MS* breathe the *Yale 1* breathe the>breathing 1100 *MS* []>Of

1087 *boon*: gift, blessing.

1090 *nephews*: perhaps used euphemistically for 'sons': cf. 262 n.

1093 *hip*: the round fruit of the rose, which appears after all the rose flowers have gone, i.e. when the rose is 'worn smooth of leaf'.

1095 *Water... tears*: cf. Isa. 16: 9.

manure... blood: cf. x. 1032–3.

1098 *dog-rose bell*: a wild-rose flower, i.e. the simple wild rose, only faintly perfumed, with a few white (or sometimes pink) petals. Usually it has five petals: at l. 1103 Guido says just 'three leaves' for exaggeration. This simple rose is contrasted with the magnificent Provence rose: see next n.

1100 *hundred-petalled... prodigy*: i.e. the wonderfully full flower of the Provence rose (here an image of the nephews' sexual fulfilment). Variously known as *Rosa centifolia*, the Hundred-Petalled Rose, or the Cabbage rose, it has a beautiful medium pink colour, a strong fragrance, and a 'very double' bloom form. Cf. the *Roman de la Rose*, where smelling luscious roses is equated with desire, and plucking them with sexual fulfilment.

Nay, more and worse,—would such my root bear rose—
Prove really flower and favourite, not the kind
That's queen, but those three leaves that make one cup
And hold the hedge-bird's breakfast,—then indeed
The prize though poor would pay the care and toil!
Respect we Nature that makes least as most,
Marvellous in the minim! But this bud,
Bit through and burned black by the tempter's tooth,
This bloom whose best grace was the slug outside
And the wasp inside its bosom,—call you "rose"?
Claim no immunity from a weed's fate
For the horrible present! What you call my wife
I call a nullity in female shape,
Vapid disgust, soon to be pungent plague,
When mixed with, made confusion and a curse
By two abominable nondescripts,
That father and that mother: think you see
The dreadful bronze our boast, we Aretines,
The Etruscan monster, the three-headed thing,
Bellerophon's foe! How name you the whole beast?
You choose to name the body from one head,
That of the simple kid which droops the eye,

1102 *MS* Really the *MS* favorite, 1104 *MS* {beginning of fo. 287} 1105 *MS* toil— 1106 *MS* nature *MS* an>as 1107 *MS* Marvelous *MS* this frowzy bud, 1109 *MS* ^bloom^ *MS* in the>the 1110 *MS* bosom, call no rose, *1868 1872* "rose?" 1112 *MS* they gave f>you call my 1114 *MS* disgust, made pungent and a>disgust,—soon to be a pungent 1116 *MS* {no comma} 1119 *MS* and three headed *MS* {no commas} 1120 *MS* Bellerophon slew:>Bellerophon's foe: *MS* how 1121 *MS* chose *MS* ^to^ *MS* {no comma} 1122 *MS* eyes

1107 *minim*: smallest creature—from the phrase 'minim of nature' (one of the smallest forms of animal life). Browning uses it of a tiny insect in *Red Cotton Night-Cap Country*, 3422. The ultimate source of the phrase is the Vulgate, Prov. 30: 24: *Quattuor sunt minima terrae, et ipsa sunt sapientiora sapientibus*. Cf. *Paradise Lost*, VII. 482.

1108 *by... tooth*: i.e. by frost, here the bite of the devil.

1113 *nullity*: nonentity.

1117 *think*: imagine.

1118–22 *dreadful... eye*: in Greek mythology the Chimaera was a fire-breathing monster, part lion, part she-goat, part snake; as ll. 1121–2 make clear, it is named from the she-goat (*chimaira*), extended by synecdoche to the whole monster. It was killed by the Corinthian hero Bellerophon, riding on the winged horse Pegasus. Homer refers

Hangs the neck and dies tenderly enough:
I rather see the griesly lion belch
Flame out i' the midst, the serpent writhe her rings,
Grafted into the common stock for tail,
And name the brute, Chimæra which I slew!
How was there ever more to be—(concede
My wife's insipid harmless nullity)—
Dissociation from that pair of plagues—
That mother with her cunning and her cant—
The eyes with first their twinkle of conceit,
Then, dropped to earth in mock-demureness,—now,
The smile self-satisfied from ear to ear,
Now, the prim pursed-up mouth's protruded lips,
With deferential duck, slow swing of head,
Tempting the sudden fist of man too much,—
That owl-like screw of lid and rock of ruff!
As for the father,—Cardinal, you know,
The kind of idiot!—such are rife in Rome,

1123 *MS* head 1125 *MS* and where the serpent writhes,>the serpent writhe her wings, 1127 *MS* {no comma} *MS* slew. 1128 *MS* be . . concede 1129 *MS* nullity . . 1132 *MS* {beginning of fo. 288} 1133 *MS* Then the>Then dropped *MS* now 1135 *MS* {no commas} 1136 *MS* head,— 1137 *MS* much, *Yale 1* much,>much,— 1139 *MS* know 1140 *MS* ideot,— rife are such *Yale 1* idiot,—>idiot!— *1868* rife are such

to the incident in *Iliad*, VI. 180–3: 'Of divine birth was she [the Chimaera] and not of men, in front a lion, and behind a serpent, and in the midst a goat; and she breathed dread fierceness of blazing fire.'

Guido refers to an Etruscan bronze statue of the Chimaera, first dug up at Arezzo by Cosimo di Medici's workmen in 1553. It is particularly vivid: the main body is that of a lion, with its front legs down, crouching, and its mouth open in a roar. Halfway along its back sticks up the head of a goat with horns, and the lion's tail curves back on itself, ending in a snake's head. The bronze dates from about the fifth century BC. Browning had seen it in the Uffizi, in the 'Hall of Niobe', one of the rooms off the western corridor. It is now in the Museo Archeologico. For a photograph, see Nigel Spivey, *Etruscan Art* (London, 1997), pp. 184–5, or Thomas, 330.

1125 *rings*: coils.

1138 *owl-like . . . ruff*: i.e. screwing up her eyes like an owl, and swaying her ruff like an owl turning its collar of feathers. The image suggests Violante's stupidity: to be 'owl-like' here means to have the 'appearance of gravity and wisdom . . . with implication of underlying stupidity': OED^2. Cf. 'Christmas-Eve', 180–1: 'Gave his eyelids yet another screwing / And rocked himself as the woman was doing.'

But they wear velvet commonly; good fools,
At the end of life, to furnish forth young folk
Who grin and bear with imbecility:
Since the stalled ass, the joker, sheds from jaw
Corn, in the joke, for those who laugh or starve.
But what say we to the same solemn beast
Wagging his ears and wishful of our pat,
When turned, with holes in hide and bones laid bare,
To forage for himself i' the waste o' the world,
Sir Dignity i' the dumps? Pat him? We drub
Self-knowledge, rather, into frowzy pate,
Teach Pietro to get trappings or go hang!
Fancy this quondam oracle in vogue
At Via Vittoria, this personified
Authority when time was,—Pantaloon
Flaunting his tom-fool tawdry just the same
As if Ash-Wednesday were mid-Carnival!
That's the extreme and unforgiveable
Of sins, as I account such. Have you stooped
For your own ends to bestialize yourself

1141 *MS* commonly, rich fools *1868* commonly, such 1142 *MS* fit to help poor young *1868* can furnish 1143 *MS* imbecility *1868* imbecility, 1144 *MS* [ ]>Since *MS* thereby>from jaw 1145 *MS* and starve: *1868* starve 1147 *MS* [ ]>our *MS* {no comma} *Yale 1* {comma added} 1148 *MS 1868* hide in holes 1150 *MS* Dumps! 1152 *MS* Teach him>And teach this Pietro *etc.* *Yale 1* And teach the>Teach *MS* to go trapped or hang. *Yale 1* trapped or hang!> trappings or go hang! 1155 *MS* this Pantaloon 1156 *MS* [ ]>Flaunting *MS* [ ]>just 1157 *MS* Ash Wednesday 1158 *MS* Thats 1159 *MS* {no comma} *MS* such; have *Yale 1* such; have>such. Have 1160 *MS* {beginning of fo. 289} *MS* [ ]>For

1141 *wear velvet*: i.e. are wealthy.

1144–5 *stalled ass . . . starve*: i.e. the young relations have to patronize the old wealthy fool to get his money at death.

1150 *Sir . . . dumps*: i.e. the formerly lordly man, depressed by his present poverty. Cf. v. 1147, 'Sir Jealousy'. Shakespeare has similar examples of this sardonic formula: 'Sir Valour' (*Troilus and Cressida*, I. iii. 176), 'Sir Oracle' (*Merchant of Venice*, I. i. 93).

1151 *frowzy*: unkempt, dirty.

1152 *trappings*: (lit.) the decorative coverings (appropriate to a beast of burden), (fig.) wealth.

1153 *quondam*: former.

1155 *Pantaloon*: the foolish old-man figure of the *commedia dell'arte*; cf. x. 1909.

1156 *tom-fool tawdry*: i.e. his ridiculous, tasteless costume.

By flattery of a fellow of this stamp?
The ends obtained or else shown out of reach,
He goes on, takes the flattery for pure truth,—
"You love, and honour me, of course: what next?"
What, but the trifle of the stabbing, friend?—
Which taught you how one worships when the shrine
Has lost the relic that we bent before.
Angry! And how could I be otherwise?
'T is plain: this pair of old pretentious fools
Meant to fool me: it happens, I fooled them.
Why could not these who sought to buy and sell
Me,—when they found themselves were bought and sold,
Make up their mind to the proved rule of right,
Be chattel and not chapman any more?
Miscalculation has its consequence;
But when the shepherd crooks a sheep-like thing
And meaning to get wool, dislodges fleece
And finds the veritable wolf beneath,
(How that staunch image serves at every turn!)
Does he, by way of being politic,
Pluck the first whisker grimly visible?
Or rather grow in a trice all gratitude,
Protest this sort-of-what-one-might-name sheep
Beats the old other curly-coated kind,
And shall share board and bed, if so it deign,
With its discoverer, like a royal ram?
Ay, thus, with chattering teeth and knocking knees,
Would wisdom treat the adventure! these, forsooth,
Tried whisker-plucking, and so found what trap

1162 *MS* obtained, or else clear out *1868 1872* obtained, 1164 *MS 1868* love and 1165 *MS* What but *MS* friend, 1166 *MS* That *Yale 1* That>Which 1167 *MS* L[]>Has 1168 *MS* Angry? 1172 *MS* sold 1173 *MS* {no comma} 1177 *MS* pluck>get *MS* []>dislodges 1179 *MS* still that>that staunch 1181 *MS 1868* visible?— 1187 *MS* thus with *MS* knees 1188 *MS* {beginning of fo. 290} *MS 1868* adventure:

1174 *chattel . . . chapman*: i.e. the bought item and not the seller.
1176–8 *shepherd . . . beneath*: cf. Matt. 7: 15.

The whisker kept perdue, two rows of teeth—
Sharp, as too late the prying fingers felt.
What would you have? The fools transgress, the fools
Forthwith receive appropriate punishment:
They first insult me, I return the blow,
There follows noise enough: four hubbub months,
Now hue and cry, now whimpering and wail—
A perfect goose-yard cackle of complaint
Because I do not gild the geese their oats,—
I have enough of noise, ope wicket wide,
Sweep out the couple to go whine elsewhere,
Frightened a little, hurt in no respect,
And am just taking thought to breathe again,
Taste the sweet sudden silence all about,
When, there they raise it, the old noise I know,
At Rome i' the distance! "What, begun once more?
"Whine on, wail ever, 't is the loser's right!"
But eh, what sort of voice grows on the wind?
Triumph it sounds and no complaint at all!
And triumph it is. My boast was premature:
The creatures, I turned forth, clapped wing and crew
Fighting-cock-fashion,—they had filched a pearl
From dung-heap, and might boast with cause enough!
I was defrauded of all bargained for:
You know, the Pope knows, not a soul but knows

1191 *MS* the prying fingers felt too late.>too late the prying fingers felt. 1195 *MS* ^hubbub^ 1197 *MS* gooseyard 1198 *MS* did>do 1199 *MS* had>have *MS* oped>ope *MS* wide *Yale 1* wide>wide, 1200 *MS* Swept>Sweep 1202 *MS* was>am *MS* breathe once more, 1204 *MS 1868* there they are at it, *MS* know 1205 *MS* in *Yale 1* in>i' *MS* again? 1206 *MS* {no quotation mark at beginning of line} *MS* losers' *MS* right!">right! 1209 *MS* was! *1868* is! 1210 *MS* {no commas} 1212 *MS* the dungheap *MS* before the w>with cause enough. 1213 *MS 1868* for,— 1214 *MS* soul disputes

---

1190 *perdue*: hidden, concealed.

1198 *gild*: supply. This is a mixed metaphor. The fig. sense of 'gild' is 'to supply with gold or money', i.e. to cover someone's hand with a thin layer of gold (the money itself): see OED^2 *v.*^{1} 3. This is the primary meaning here. It is combined, however, with the image of the Comparini as quarrelsome geese demanding to be fed their oats, i.e. demanding to live in a comfortable way in Guido's house. Perhaps Browning is thinking of the oats as golden in colour.

My dowry was derision, my gain—muck,
My wife, (the Church declared my flesh and blood)
The nameless bastard of a common whore:
My old name turned henceforth to . . . shall I say
"He that received the ordure in his face"?
And they who planned this wrong, performed this wrong,
And then revealed this wrong to the wide world,
Rounded myself in the ears with my own wrong,—
Why, these were (note hell's lucky malice, now!)
These were just they who, they alone, could act
And publish and proclaim their infamy,
Secure that men would in a breath believe,
Compassionate and pardon them,—for why?
They plainly were too stupid to invent,
Too simple to distinguish wrong from right,—
Inconscious agents they, the silly-sooth,
Of heaven's retributive justice on the strong
Proud cunning violent oppressor—me!
Follow them to their fate and help your best,
You Rome, Arezzo, foes called friends of me,
They gave the good long laugh to, at my cost!
Defray your share o' the cost, since you partook
The entertainment! Do!—assured the while,
That not one stab, I dealt to right and left,
But went the deeper for a fancy—this—
That each might do me two-fold service, find

1216 *MS* {line added later} *MS* {beginning of fo. 291} *MS* wife, the *MS* blood, *Yale 1* blood,)>blood) 1217 *MS* {line added later} *MS* nam[ ]>nameless 1218 *MS 1868 1872* to . . *1219 *MS* face"? *1868 1872 1888 1889* face?" 1223 *MS 1868* were . . note *MS 1868* now! . . 1224 *MS 1868* they, and they 1225 *MS 1868* publish in this wise *MS* {no comma} *Yale 1* {comma added} *1226 *MS 1868 1872 1888 1889* believe 1230 *MS* Mere passive>Inconscious 1233 *MS* —Follow *Yale 1* —Follow>Follow 1234 *MS 1868 1872* mine, 1235 *MS 1868* {no comma} 1236 *MS* of *MS* {no comma} 1237 *MS* entertainment!>entertainment— *MS* Do! Assured 1238 *MS* stab that I dealt right *MS* {no commas}

1219 "*He . . . face*": cf. v. 1491.
1222 *Rounded*: dinned, shouted; see 675 n.
1230 *silly-sooth*: naïve, unwitting: cf. III. 805–6, X. 2039–42 nn.

A friend's face at the bottom of each wound,
And scratch its smirk a little!
Panciatichi!
There's a report at Florence,—is it true?—
That when your relative the Cardinal
Built, only the other day, that barrack-bulk,
The palace in Via Larga, someone picked
From out the street a saucy quip enough
That fell there from its day's flight through the town,
About the flat front and the windows wide
And bulging heap of cornice,—hitched the joke
Into a sonnet, signed his name thereto,
And forthwith pinned on post the pleasantry:
For which he's at the galleys, rowing now
Up to his waist in water,—just because
Panciatic and *lymphatic* rhymed so pat!
I hope, Sir, those who passed this joke on me
Were not unduly punished? What say you,
Prince of the Church, my patron? Nay, indeed,
I shall not dare insult your wits so much
As think this problem difficult to solve.
This Pietro and Violante then, I say,

1242 *MS* little. 1246 *MS* {beginning of fo. 292} 1249 *MS* days 1251 *MS 1868* ugly heap *1872* bulgeing heap 1252 *MS* thereto 1253 *MS* pleasantry, *1868* pleasantry. 1254 *MS* gallies,>galleys, 1256 *MS* Panciatic *MS* lymphatic *MS 1868* pat: 1258 *MS* {no comma} 1259 *MS* No indeed! *1868* indeed! 1261 *MS 1868 1872* solve! 1262 *MS* his Violante, then, *1868* Violante,

1245–53 *Cardinal . . . pleasantry*: Palazzo Panciatichi, built at the southern end of Via Cavour (in Browning's day, Via Larga) at the corner with Via de' Pucci, and opposite the Palazzo Medici-Riccardi. Browning knew about the witty attacks on the palace's ugly façade from his main guidebook to Florence, Federigo Fantozzi's *Nuova guida ovvero descrizione storico-artistico-critica della città contorni di Firenze* (Florence, 1851), p. 461: 'Lo stile architettonico di questo vasto e grandioso palazzo non è commendevole; le finestre sono male spaziate, e profilate senza grazia e leggiadria; ed il cornicione è tozzo, pesante e senza carattere. Allorchè rimase compito, il popolo fiorentino, sempre arguto e pungente nei suoi frizzi, vedendolo privo di bozze e di quella maschia decorazione con la quale si erano fino a quel giorno abbellite le fabbriche della città, lo andava chiamando il *Palazzo di basso rilievo*.'

1256 *lymphatic*: dull, sluggish. The jesting sonnet implies that the Panciatichi are as uninspired as their palace.

These two ambiguous insects, changing name
And nature with the season's warmth or chill,—
Now, grovelled, grubbing toiling moiling ants,
A very synonym of thrift and peace,—
Anon, with lusty June to prick their heart,
Soared i' the air, winged flies for more offence,
Circled me, buzzed me deaf and stung me blind,
And stunk me dead with fetor in the face
Until I stopped the nuisance: there's my crime!
Pity I did not suffer them subside
Into some further shape and final form
Of execrable life? My masters, no!
I, by one blow, wisely cut short at once
Them and their transformations of disgust,
In the snug little Villa out of hand.
"Grant me confession, give bare time for that!"—
Shouted the sinner till his mouth was stopped.
His life confessed!—that was enough for me,
Who came to see that he did penance. 'S death!
Here's a coil raised, a pother and for what?
Because strength, being provoked by weakness, fought
And conquered,—the world never heard the like!
Pah, how I spend my breath on them, as if

1263 *MS* Were *MS* {no comma} 1264 *MS* chill, 1265 *MS* grovelling>grovelled *MS* [ ]>, *MS* ants 1266 *MS* metaphor>synonym *MS* peace:>peace,— 1269 *MS* [ ]>me *MS* f>buzzed *etc.* 1270 *MS* [ ]>stunk 1274 *MS* {beginning of fo. 293} 1275 *MS* {no comma} 1276 *MS 1868* {no comma} 1277 *MS* snug 1278 *MS* confession, the bare *MS* that!" 1279 *MS* stopped: 1280 *MS* I had not waited>His life confessed: *etc.* *MS* {no comma}

1265 *moiling*: hard labouring, drudging, 'sometimes with some trace of the etymological sense . . To work in wet and mire': OED². It is often paired with 'toil', in Browning and elsewhere.

1270 *fetor*: an offensive smell.

1276 *transformations of disgust*: disgusting transformations, changes of nature.

1277 *out of hand*: without hesitation, ruthlessly.

1278–9 "*Grant . . . stopped*: this detail, of Pietro crying out for Confession, is from SS 11.

1281 *'S death!* : 'God's (Christ's) death', an oath.

1282 *coil*: tumult, fuss.

'T was their fate troubled me, too hard to range
Among the right and fit and proper things!

Ay, but Pompilia,—I await your word,—
She, unimpeached of crime, unimplicate
In folly, one of alien blood to these
I punish, why extend my claim, exact
Her portion of the penalty? Yes, friends,
I go too fast: the orator's at fault:
Yes, ere I lay her, with your leave, by them
As she was laid at San Lorenzo late,
I ought to step back, lead you by degrees,
Recounting at each step some fresh offence,
Up to the red bed,—never fear, I will!
Gaze at her, where I place her, to begin,
Confound me with her gentleness and worth!
The horrible pair have fled and left her now,
She has her husband for her sole concern:
His wife, the woman fashioned for his help,
Flesh of his flesh, bone of his bone, the bride
To groom as is the Church and Spouse to Christ:
There she stands in his presence: "Thy desire
"Shall be to the husband, o'er thee shall he rule!"
—"Pompilia, who declare that you love God,
"You know who said that: then, desire my love,

1286 *MS* was hard 1290 *MS* []>In 1299 *MS 1868* you place *MS* {no commas} 1300 *MS* worth: 1301 *MS* {beginning of fo. 294} 1302 *MS 1868* concern, 1304 *MS* []>bride 1305 *MS* the groom *Yale 1* the groom>groom *MS* Church, the Spouse, to *1868 1872* Spouse, 1306 *MS 1868* presence,— *MS* "her>"Thy 1307–9 *MS* {no quotation marks at beginnings of lines} 1307 *MS* rule" 1308 {not found in *MS*}

1289 *unimplicate*: = unimplicated (participial adj.); OED² gives only this instance.

1298 *the red bed*: i.e. her red (bloody) death-bed.

1303–4 *woman . . . bone*: cf. Gen. 2: 20, 23.

1304–5 *the bride . . . Christ*: cf. Eph. 5: 23–5.

1306–7 "*Thy . . . rule!*": cf. Gen. 3: 16: 'Unto the woman he [God] said . . . thy desire shall be to thy husband, and he shall rule over thee.' See previous two nn.: Guido backs up his viewpoint with three biblical quotations in succession.

1309 *You . . . that*: i.e. God said it, in the Book of Genesis: see previous n.

"Yield me contentment and be ruled aright!"
She sits up, she lies down, she comes and goes,
Kneels at the couch-side, overleans the sill
O' the window, cold and pale and mute as stone,
Strong as stone also. "Well, are they not fled?
"Am I not left, am I not one for all?
"Speak a word, drop a tear, detach a glance,
"Bless me or curse me of your own accord!
"Is it the ceiling only wants your soul,
"Is worth your eyes?" And then the eyes descend,
And do look at me. Is it at the meal?
"Speak!" she obeys, "Be silent!" she obeys,
Counting the minutes till I cry "Depart,"
As brood-bird when you saunter past her eggs.
Departs she? just the same through door and wall
I see the same stone strength of white despair.
And all this will be never otherwise!
Before, the parents' presence lent her life:
She could play off her sex's armoury,
Entreat, reproach, be female to my male,
Try all the shrieking doubles of the hare,
Go clamour to the Commissary, bid

1310 *MS* {no quotation marks} 1313 *MS* Of 1314 *MS* also: well, *MS* not they *Yale 1* not they>they not 1315–18 *MS* {no quotation marks at beginnings of lines} 1318 *MS* [ ]>ceiling 1319 *MS* {no quotation marks} *MS 1868* {no comma} 1320 *MS* me: is>me. Is 1321 *MS* "be 1322 *MS* I bid depart, 1323 *MS* the partridge>the brood bird *Yale 1* the brood-bird>brood-bird *MS* eggs: 1324 *MS* "Go thou!"—why, *MS* all> just *1868 1872* Departed, just 1328 *MS* sexes' 1329 *1868 1872* Intreat, 1330 *MS* {beginning of fo. 295}

1315 *one for all*: i.e. one person who replaces, and is more valuable than, her parents who have left. This is Guido's fantasy of his part pathetic, part sardonic speech to Pompilia.

1323 *As . . . eggs*: i.e. as a nervous, nesting bird, longing for you to go away.

1328 *play off*: show off, act up: cf. x. 223 n.

1330 *doubles*: evasion manoeuvres, sharp turns in running (made by a hunted hare in order to escape capture). Cf. Shakespeare, *Venus and Adonis*, 681–2: 'How he [the hare] outruns the wind, and with what care / He cranks and crosses with a thousand doubles.'

1331 *Commissary*: Governor (of Arezzo).

The Archbishop hold my hands and stop my tongue,
And yield fair sport so: but the tactics change,
The hare stands stock-still to enrage the hound!
Since that day when she learned she was no child
Of those she thought her parents,—that their trick
Had tricked me whom she thought sole trickster late,—
Why, I suppose she said within herself
"Then, no more struggle for my parents' sake!
"And, for my own sake, why needs struggle be?"
But is there no third party to the pact?
What of her husband's relish or dislike
For this new game of giving up the game,
This worst offence of not offending more?
I'll not believe but instinct wrought in this,
Set her on to conceive and execute
The preferable plague: how sure they probe—
These jades, the sensitivest soft of man!
The long black hair was wound now in a wisp,
Crowned sorrow better than the wild web late:
No more soiled dress, 't is trimness triumphs now,
For how should malice go with negligence?
The frayed silk looked the fresher for her spite!
There was an end to springing out of bed,
Praying me, with face buried on my feet,

1333 *MS* {no comma} 1334 *MS* hound. 1336 *MS* trick of theirs>that their trick 1337 *MS* Tricking me she supposed>Had tricked me whom she thought 1339 *MS 1868* sake, 1340 *MS* {no quotation mark at beginning of line} 1342 *MS* liking>relish *MS* [?f]>or 1347 *MS 1868* plague... *MS* well>sure *MS* probe *Yale 1* probe>probe,— *1868 1872* probe,— 1348 *Yale 1* jades,>jades,— 1349 *MS 1868* wisp,— 1351 *MS* a triumph day by day, 1354 *MS* {no comma}

1348 *jades*: (lit.) ill-tempered, or otherwise inferior, horses; (fig.) naughty women. In this second sense, Johnson defines a jade as 'a sorry woman. A word of contempt noting sometimes age, but generally vice.' Guido's mind is running much on this image of woman as a horse that may be unruly and that needs dominating: cf. ll. 1364, 1397–9.

soft: soft part.

1349 *a wisp*: a neat band or plait. (The word is usually used of a band of straw or hay, but here of hair.)

1350 *wild web late*: i.e. her previously dishevelled hair.

Be hindered of my pastime,—so an end
To my rejoinder, "What, on the ground at last?
"Vanquished in fight, a supplicant for life?
"What if I raise you? 'Ware the casting down
"When next you fight me!" Then, she lay there, mine:
Now, mine she is if I please wring her neck,—
A moment of disquiet, working eyes,
Protruding tongue, a long sigh, then no more,—
As if one killed the horse one could not ride!
Had I enjoined "Cut off the hair!"—why, snap
The scissors, and at once a yard or so
Had fluttered in black serpents to the floor:
But till I did enjoin it, how she combs,
Uncurls and draws out to the complete length,
Plaits, places the insulting rope on head
To be an eyesore past dishevelment!
Is all done? Then sit still again and stare!
I advise—no one think to bear that look
Of steady wrong, endured as steadily
—Through what sustainment of deluding hope?
Who is the friend i' the background that notes all?
Who may come presently and close accounts?
This self-possession to the uttermost,
How does it differ in aught, save degree,

1358–60 *MS* {no quotation marks at beginnings of lines} 1358 *MS* {beginning of fo. 296} **1888 1889* 'Vanquished {broken sort} 1359 *MS* Why, then I'll>What if I 1360 *MS* {no commas} *MS* mine. 1361 *MS* neck, 1363 *MS 1868* more— 1365 *MS* hair!" why, 1368 *MS* did>do 1369 *MS* {no comma} 1371 *MS* dishevelment[ ]>dishevelment! 1374 *MS* {no comma} *1868 1872* steadily, 1375 *MS* Through 1376 *MS* in *MS* back ground 1378 *MS* {no comma} 1379 *MS* {no commas}

1371 *eyesore . . . dishevelment!*: to Guido, Pompilia's put-up hair seems an insult, a conscious withdrawal of sexual favour. Browning often makes much of the sexual attractiveness of hair: see 'Soliloquy of the Spanish Cloister', 'Andrea del Sarto', 'Gold Hair'.

1375 *Through . . . hope?* : i.e. 'what unreal hope allowed Pompilia to maintain "that look of steady wrong", her dignified (not abased) bearing?' As Guido partly implies in the following lines, Christ (God) is 'the friend' who sustains Pompilia through her sufferings.

From the terrible patience of God?
                                        "All which just means,
"She did not love you!" Again the word is launched
And the fact fronts me! What, you try the wards
With the true key and the dead lock flies ope?
No, it sticks fast and leaves you fumbling still!
You have some fifty servants, Cardinal,—
Which of them loves you? Which subordinate
But makes parade of such officiousness
That,—if there's no love prompts it,—love, the sham,
Does twice the service done by love, the true?
God bless us liars, where's one touch of truth
In what we tell the world, or world tells us,
Of how we love each other? All the same,
We calculate on word and deed, nor err,—
Bid such a man do such a loving act,
Sure of effect and negligent of cause,
Just as we bid a horse, with cluck of tongue,
Stretch his legs arch-wise, crouch his saddled back
To foot-reach of the stirrup—all for love,
And some for memory of the smart of switch
On the inside of the foreleg—what care we?
Yet where's the bond obliges horse to man
Like that which binds fast wife to husband? God
Laid down the law: gave man the brawny arm
And ball of fist—woman the beardless cheek
And proper place to suffer in the side:
Since it is he can strike, let her obey!

1382 *MS* {no quotation mark at beginning of line} *MS* Now the 1383 *MS* me: now you 1384 *MS* ope! 1386 *MS* {beginning of fo. 297} 1389 *MS* That if *MS* it, love the *MS* truth>sham 1390 *MS* {no comma} ★*MS 1868 1872 1888* true. *DC BrU* true.>true? *1889* true? 1392 *MS* [ ]>In *MS* world, the world 1393 *MS 1868* like *MS* {no comma} 1394 *MS* err, 1395 *MS* {line added later} *MS* an>a loving 1397 *MS* one bids>you bid *MS* {no commas} 1399 *MS* love?>love, 1400 *MS* [?And]>Or 1401 *MS* you?

1380 *terrible patience of God*: cf. Ps. 7: 11–12.

1398–9 *crouch . . . stirrup*: i.e. lowers his back, so he can more easily be mounted.

Can she feel no love? Let her show the more,
Sham the worse, damn herself praiseworthily!
Who's that soprano Rome went mad about
Last week while I lay rotting in my straw?
The very jailer gossiped in his praise—
How,—dressed up like Armida, though a man;
And painted to look pretty, though a fright,—
He still made love so that the ladies swooned,
Being an eunuch. "Ah, Rinaldo mine!
"But to breathe by thee while Jove slays us both!"
All the poor bloodless creature never felt,
Si, do, re, mi, fa, squeak and squall—for what?
Two gold zecchines the evening. Here's my slave,
Whose body and soul depend upon my nod,
Can't falter out the first note in the scale
For her life! Why blame me if I take the life?
All women cannot give men love, forsooth!
No, nor all pullets lay the henwife eggs—

1408 *MS* love, let 1409 *MS* her self>her-self *MS* praiseworthily. *1410 *MS* *1868* soprano *1872* *1888* *1889* soprano, 1412 *1868* *1872* jailor 1414 *MS* pretty though a fright, 1415 *MS* {beginning of fo. 298} 1417 *MS* {no quotation mark at beginning of line} **MS* *1868* *1872* both!" *1888* *1889* both! 1418 *MS* {no comma} *Yale 1* {comma added} 1419 *1868* Si, do, re, mi, fa, *MS* what 1420 *MS* *1868* evening! *MS* wife, 1422 *MS* faulter 1424 *MS* it seems:>forsooth:

1409 *Sham . . . praiseworthily*: i.e. pretend as badly as she can (even without feeling), and so prove herself a good wife by the extent of the pretence (even if technically she is damning herself by lying).

1410–17 *soprano . . . both!"*: an accurate historical allusion, since the fashion for castrato singing in opera was at its height in the late-seventeenth through to the mid-eighteenth century. A castrato was 'a type of high-voiced male singer, brought about by castrating young boys with promising voices before they reached puberty, that was central to Italian opera in the 17th and 18th centuries' (Grove). The part imagined here is that of Armida, the Arab sorceress, who falls in love with the Christian hero Rinaldo, in the story orginally derived from Torquato Tasso's *Gerusalemme liberata* (1581). Various Italian operas of the seventeenth century used this story, with its vivid setting in the First Crusade. Later operas based on it are Handel's *Rinaldo* (1711), Haydn's *Armida* (1784), and Rossini's *Armida* (1817). In Rome, in public opera, women were not allowed to appear on the stage until 1798, a rule which naturally led to prominent use of castrati in the women's parts.

1418 *bloodless*: passionless, without sexual desire.

1420 *zecchines*: gold coins (of modest value).

Whereat she bids them remedy the fault,
Brood on a chalk-ball: soon the nest is stocked—
Otherwise, to the plucking and the spit!
This wife of mine was of another mood—
Would not begin the lie that ends with truth,
Nor feign the love that brings real love about:
Wherefore I judged, sentenced and punished her.
But why particularize, defend the deed?
Say that I hated her for no one cause
Beyond my pleasure so to do,—what then?
Just on as much incitement acts the world,
All of you! Look and like! You favour one,
Browbeat another, leave alone a third,—
Why should you master natural caprice?
Pure nature! Try: plant elm by ash in file;
Both unexceptionable trees enough,
They ought to overlean each other, pair
At top, and arch across the avenue
The whole path to the pleasaunce: do they so—
Or loathe, lie off abhorrent each from each?
Lay the fault elsewhere: since we must have faults,
Mine shall have been,—seeing there's ill in the end

*1432 *MS 1868 1872* her. *1888* her *DC BrU* her>her. *1889* her. 1436 *MS* [?so]>as *1437 *MS 1868 1872* one, *1888* one *BrU* one>one, *1889* one, *1440 *MS 1868 1872* nature! *1888* nature *DC BrU* nature>nature! *1889* nature! *MS* Plant>Try—plant *1868* Try—plant 1443 *MS 1868* {no comma} *MS* [ ]> arch 1444 *MS* {beginning of fo. 299} *MS* so[ ]>so— 1446 *MS 1868* elsewhere, *MS 1868* faults:

1427 *Brood . . . chalk-ball*: i.e. sit on an imitation white egg made of chalk. This will encourage the pullets to lay real eggs.

1433 *But . . . deed?*: the injured, self-justifying question is reminiscent of the manner of the Duke in 'My Last Duchess', 34–5, 44–5.

1440 *elm by ash*: the idea that elm and ash planted side by side will grow away from each other, and refuse to form a shaded arcade, is clearly a popular superstition, but we have been unable to trace it.

1444 *pleasaunce*: the specially secluded and beautiful part of a garden, in medieval poetry a place of pleasure and dalliance. Perhaps Guido alludes to this idea: the path to sexual pleasure is destroyed by his unavoidable aversion to Pompilia, just as the contrariness of the trees here destroys the avenue leading to the beautiful place. The more usual spelling is 'pleasance'.

Come of my course,—that I fare somehow worse
For the way I took: my fault... as God's my judge,
I see not where my fault lies, that's the truth!
I ought... oh, ought in my own interest
Have let the whole adventure go untried,
This chance by marriage: or else, trying it,
Ought to have turned it to account, some one
O' the hundred otherwises? Ay, my friend,
Easy to say, easy to do: step right
Now you've stepped left and stumbled on the thing,
—The red thing! Doubt I any more than you
That practice makes man perfect? Give again
The chance,—same marriage and no other wife,
Be sure I'll edify you! That's because
I'm practised, grown fit guide for Guido's self.
You proffered guidance,—I know, none so well,—
You laid down law and rolled decorum out,
From pulpit-corner on the gospel-side,—
Wanted to make your great experience mine,
Save me the personal search and pains so: thanks!
Take your word on life's use? When I take his—
The muzzled ox that treadeth out the corn,

1449 *MS 1868 1872* took,— *1868 1872* fault .... *MS 1868* judge 1450 *MS 1868* the fault 1451 *MS 1868 1872* ought . . 1453 *MS 1868 1872* marriage,— 1454 *MS 1868* {no comma} 1455 *MS* Of *MS* otherwises. *Yale 1* otherwises.> otherwises! 1456 *MS 1868* do,— 1458 *MS* The *MS* thing: doubt 1461 *MS* you: that's 1462 *MS* self: 1464 *MS* [ ]>laid 1465 *MS* the pulpit-corner 1467 *MS* [ ]>Save 1469 *MS* ^muzzled^

1451–2 *ought... Have let*: Cook notes that Browning often omits 'to' between 'ought' and an infinitive, as here and at 411.

1455 *otherwises*: = other ways. OED[2] gives this as a nonce-use.

1458 *The red thing!*: i.e. the guillotine. Cf. 214 n.

1465 *on the gospel-side*: i.e. on the left-hand side of the church, as you face the altar. The distinction between the 'epistle side' of a church (i.e. the right-hand side, as you face the altar) and the 'gospel side' goes back to early times when the priest read the epistle and then the gospel from different sides of the altar. (Browning knew the distinction: cf. 'The Bishop Orders His Tomb', 21: 'One sees the pulpit o' the epistle-side'.) Here the phrase is clearly backing up the (false) sense of decorum evoked in the previous line.

1469 *muzzled ox... corn*: cf. Deut. 25: 4: 'Thou shalt not muzzle the ox when he treadeth out the corn'. Cf. 1 Cor. 9: 9, 1 Tim. 5: 18.

Gone blind in padding round and round one path,—
As to the taste of green grass in the field!
What do you know o' the world that's trodden flat
And salted sterile with your daily dung,
Leavened into a lump of loathsomeness?
Take your opinion of the modes of life,
The aims of life, life's triumph or defeat,
How to feel, how to scheme, and how to do
Or else leave undone? You preached long and loud
On high-days, "Take our doctrine upon trust!
"Into the mill-house with you! Grind our corn,
"Relish our chaff, and let the green grass grow!"
I tried chaff, found I famished on such fare,
So made this mad rush at the mill-house-door,
Buried my head up to the ears in dew,
Browsed on the best: for which you brain me, Sirs!
Be it so. I conceived of life that way,
And still declare—life, without absolute use
Of the actual sweet therein, is death, not life.
Give me,—pay down,—not promise, which is air,—
Something that's out of life and better still,
Make sure reward, make certain punishment,
Entice me, scare me,—I'll forgo this life;
Otherwise, no!—the less that words, mere wind,

1470 *MS* path, 1471 *MS* field. 1472 *MS* {beginning of fo. 300} *MS* of *MS* thats 1477 *MS 1868 1872* scheme and 1478 *MS* You shall lesson me— 1480, 1481 *MS* {no quotation marks at beginnings of lines} 1481 *MS* [ ]>Relish 1483 *MS* made one mad *MS* millhouse door *MS* {no comma} 1485 *MS 1868 1872* Browzed *MS 1868* best, 1486 *1868* so! 1487 *MS* maintain—>declare— *MS* {no comma} 1488 *MS* therein is 1489 *MS* down not 1491 *MS* Secure 1492 *MS* me, I 1493 *MS* for words,

1474 *Leavened*: fermented, transformed (by the dung). For the collocation of 'leaven' and 'lump' cf. 1 Cor. 5: 6, 7.

1479 *high-days*: important holy days.

1489 *promise . . . air*: cf. 'I eat the air, promise-cramm'd': *Hamlet*, III. ii. 94.

1492 *Entice . . . me*: i.e. entice me with a certain heaven, scare me with a certain hell.

1493–5 *the less . . . here*: i.e. the less so because words will annoyingly waste time and frustrate my full revenge.

Would cheat me of some minutes while they plague,
Baulk fulness of revenge here,—blame yourselves
For this eruption of the pent-up soul
You prisoned first and played with afterward!
"Deny myself" meant simply pleasure you,
The sacred and superior, save the mark!
You,—whose stupidity and insolence
I must defer to, soothe at every turn,—
Whose swine-like snuffling greed and grunting lust
I had to wink at or help gratify,—
While the same passions,—dared they perk in me,
Me, the immeasurably marked, by God,
Master of the whole world of such as you,—
I, boast such passions? 'T was "Suppress them straight!
"Or stay, we'll pick and choose before destroy.
"Here's wrath in you, a serviceable sword,—
"Beat it into a ploughshare! What's this long
"Lance-like ambition? Forge a pruning-hook,

1494 *MS* Which cheat us *MS* all the while. *1868 1872* plague. 1495 *MS 1868 1872* The *MS* blame such words 1496 *MS* self 1497 *MS* They ⋆*MS* afterward—>afterward *1868 1872* afterward! *1888* afterward *DC* afterward>afterward. *BrU* afterward>afterward! *1889* afterward! 1500 *MS* {beginning of fo. 301} 1503 *MS* must>have *etc. Yale 1* have>had 1504 *MS* passions . . dare *Yale 1* dare>dared 1505 *MS* marked by God 1507 *MS* to boast passions? 1508–14 *MS* {no quotation marks at beginnings of lines} 1508 *MS* best pick *MS* [ ]>destroy: *1868* destroy: 1509 *MS 1868* you,— 1510 *MS* ploughshare: 1511 *MS* {no comma}

1498 "*Deny myself*": 'control myself, exercise self-discipline': the traditional Christian injunction. Cf. Matt. 16: 24.

1499 *save the mark*: = 'God help us!'—an apologetic or impatient exclamation. It is usually used after something horrible, disgusting, or ridiculous has been said. Here, clearly, it undercuts 'sacred and superior', since Guido does *not* believe the priests are holy at all. The full form of the phrase is 'God save the mark' or 'God bless the mark', where 'save' = avert, and 'mark' = ? sign or omen. It is used five times in Shakespeare, notably *Romeo and Juliet*, III. ii. 53 and *Othello*, I. i. 33. Its origin is unknown.

1503 *wink at*: ignore, turn a blind eye to.

1504 *perk*: jump up, arise.

1505 *immeasurably marked*: i.e. marked out as superior (as an aristocrat).

1509–12 *wrath . . . tall!*: i.e. 'if you feel the natural anger that might make you a good fighter, suppress it; if you feel the ambition that might make you thrust ahead in life, refocus it onto farming.' The phrasing is suggested by Isa. 2: 4.

“May be of service when our vines grow tall!
“But—sword use swordwise, spear thrust out as spear?
“Anathema! Suppression is the word!”
My nature, when the outrage was too gross,
Widened itself an outlet over-wide
By way of answer, sought its own relief
With more of fire and brimstone than you wished.
All your own doing: preachers, blame yourselves!

’T is I preach while the hour-glass runs and runs!
God keep me patient! All I say just means—
My wife proved, whether by her fault or mine,—
That’s immaterial,—a true stumbling-block
I’ the way of me her husband. I but plied
The hatchet yourselves use to clear a path,
Was politic, played the game you warrant wins,
Plucked at law’s robe a-rustle through the courts,
Bowed down to kiss divinity’s buckled shoe
Cushioned i’ the church: efforts all wide the aim!
Procedures to no purpose! Then flashed truth.
The letter kills, the spirit keeps alive
In law and gospel: there be nods and winks
Instruct a wise man to assist himself
In certain matters, nor seek aid at all.
“Ask money of me,”—quoth the clownish saw,—

1512 *MS* Shall *MS* the vines *MS* tall. 1513 *MS* But sword used *1868 1872* used *MS* spear, 1517 *1868* answer?— 1518 *MS* was wished: *1868* wished? 1520 *MS* I preach while here’s the hourglass *1868* hourglass 1521 *MS* means 1522 *MS* mine 1524 *MS* In *MS 1868* husband: *MS* plyed>plied 1527 *MS* {beginning of fo. 302} *MS* a rustle 1529 *MS* in *MS* aim, 1530 *MS* purpose: then>purpose. Then *MS* quoth I, *1868 1872* truth! 1531 *MS* “The letter kills, the letter keeps alive 1534 *1868* {no comma} *MS* all: 1535 *MS* me”,—says

1514 *Anathema*: i.e. Curse it!

1527–9 *Plucked . . . church*: i.e. sought law’s advice, fawned to the Church’s authority.

1531 *The letter . . . alive*: cf. 2 Cor. 3: 6.

1535–8 “*Ask . . . himself!*”: i.e. some things you can ask for; some things you must do for yourself.

"And take my purse! But,—speaking with respect,—
"Need you a solace for the troubled nose?
"Let everybody wipe his own himself!"
Sirs, tell me free and fair! Had things gone well
At the wayside inn: had I surprised asleep
The runaways, as was so probable,
And pinned them each to other partridge-wise,
Through back and breast to breast and back, then bade
Bystanders witness if the spit, my sword,
Were loaded with unlawful game for once—
Would you have interposed to damp the glow
Applauding me on every husband's cheek?
Would you have checked the cry "A judgment, see!
"A warning, note! Be henceforth chaste, ye wives,
"Nor stray beyond your proper precinct, priests!"
If you had, then your house against itself
Divides, nor stands your kingdom any more.
Oh why, why was it not ordained just so?
Why fell not things out so nor otherwise?
Ask that particular devil whose task it is
To trip the all-but-at perfection,—slur
The line o' the painter just where paint leaves off
And life begins,—put ice into the ode
O' the poet while he cries "Next stanza—fire!"
Inscribe all human effort with one word,
Artistry's haunting curse, the Incomplete!

1536 *MS* purse; but, *MS* respect, 1537 *MS* "[?Find]>"Need 1544 *MS* [ ]>sword, 1549, 1550 *MS* {no quotation marks at beginnings of lines} 1551 *MS* did, 1553 *MS* Oh, 1555 *MS* {beginning of fo. 303} 1556 *MS* perfection[ ]>perfection, *MS* [ ]>slur 1557 *MS* of 1558 *MS* *1868 1872* puts 1559 *MS* Of *MS* "next *MS* verse—and>stanza— 1560 *MS 1868 1872* Inscribes 1561 *MS* The artist's>Artistry's

1551–2 *your house . . . more*: cf. Matt. 12: 25, etc.

1556 *slur*: blur, spoil.

1561 *Artistry's . . . Incomplete!*: this line also occurs in 'Beatrice Signorini': 'would love's success defeat / Artistry's haunting curse—the Incomplete' (37–8). 'Beatrice Signorini' was probably written in 1853, and then carefully revised for publication in *Asolando* (1889). Here, in other words, Browning is recalling a poem he had already composed but not yet published. For these datings, see Michael Meredith, 'Foot over the Threshold: Browning at Work', BSN 26 (2000), 48–54.

Being incomplete, my act escaped success.
Easy to blame now! Every fool can swear
To hole in net that held and slipped the fish.
But, treat my act with fair unjaundiced eye,
What was there wanting to a masterpiece
Except the luck that lies beyond a man?
My way with the woman, now proved grossly wrong,
Just missed of being gravely grandly right
And making mouths laugh on the other side.
Do, for the poor obstructed artist's sake,
Go with him over that spoiled work once more!
Take only its first flower, the ended act
Now in the dusty pod, dry and defunct!
I march to the Villa, and my men with me,
That evening, and we reach the door and stand.
I say... no, it shoots through me lightning-like
While I pause, breathe, my hand upon the latch,
"Let me forebode! Thus far, too much success:
"I want the natural failure—find it where?
"Which thread will have to break and leave a loop
"I' the meshy combination, my brain's loom
"Wove this long while, and now next minute tests?
"Of three that are to catch, two should go free,
"One must: all three surprised,—impossible!
"Beside, I seek three and may chance on six,—

1562 *MS* incomplete the *1868 1872* the act *MS* success, 1563 *MS* now: every 1564 *MS* [?f]>and *MS* fish: 1565 *MS* {no commas} 1566 *MS* seems there 1570 *MS 1868* critics laugh o' *1872* critics laugh on 1571 *MS* sake 1572 *MS* more. 1573 *MS* that ended 1575 *MS* the men *MS* {no comma} 1576 *MS* gate>door 1577 *MS 1868 1872* say . . 1579 *MS* forbode: *Yale 1* forbode!>forebode! *MS* too much success thus far:>thus far too much success: 1580–1601 *MS* {no quotation marks at beginnings of lines} 1582 *MS* In 1583 *MS* {beginning of fo. 304} *1868* {no comma} 1585 *MS* surprised, *Yale 1* surprised,>surprised,— 1586 *MS* {no commas} *Yale 1* Beside>Beside, *MS* six

1570 *making... side*: i.e. disconcerting my enemies. The phrase is proverbial: ODEP, 445.

1571 *obstructed*: i.e. frustrated.

1579 *forebode*: forecast, conjecture.

1580 *want*: lack.

"This neighbour, t'other gossip,—the babe's birth
"Brings such to fireside, and folks give them wine,—
" 'T is late: but when I break in presently
"One will be found outlingering the rest
"For promise of a posset,—one whose shout
"Would raise the dead down in the catacombs,
"Much more the city-watch that goes its round.
"When did I ever turn adroitly up
"To sun some brick embedded in the soil,
"And with one blow crush all three scorpions there?
"Or Pietro or Violante shambles off—
"It cannot be but I surprise my wife—
"If only she is stopped and stamped on, good!
"That shall suffice: more is improbable.
"Now I may knock!" And this once for my sake
The impossible was effected: I called king,
Queen and knave in a sequence, and cards came,
All three, three only! So, I had my way,
Did my deed: so, unbrokenly lay bare
Each tænia that had sucked me dry of juice,
At last outside me, not an inch of ring
Left now to writhe about and root itself
I' the heart all powerless for revenge! Henceforth
I might thrive: these were drawn and dead and damned.
Oh Cardinal, the deep long sigh you heave
When the load's off you, ringing as it runs

1588 *MS 1868* fireside and 1589 *MS* Tis 1590 *Yale 1* fonnd>found 1592 *MS* {no comma} 1593 *MS* city watch 1595 *MS* {no comma} *Yale 1* {comma added} 1597 *MS* []>Violante 1599 *MS* And, so but she 1600 {not found in *MS*} 1601 *MS* []>Now *MS* will>may 1603 *MS* came 1604 *MS* only: so I 1606 *MS* [ ]>Each 1608 *MS* Was left within>Left now 1609 *MS* In 1610 *MS* die: ⋆*MS* drawn, and dead, and damned! *1868 1872* damned. *1888* damned *DC BrU* damned>damned. *1889* damned. 1612 *MS* {beginning of fo. 305}

1591 *posset*: a warming, bed-time drink.
1593 *city-watch*: night-time patrol, law officers.
1597 *Or*... *or*: Either... or.
1606 *tænia*: tape-worm, intestinal worm (from L.).

All the way down the serpent-stair to hell!
No doubt the fine delirium flustered me,
Turned my brain with the influx of success
As if the sole need now were to wave wand
And find doors fly wide,—wish and have my will,—
The rest o' the scheme would care for itself: escape?
Easy enough were that, and poor beside!
It all but proved so,—ought to quite have proved,
Since, half the chances had sufficed, set free
Anyone, with his senses at command,
From thrice the danger of my flight. But, drunk,
Redundantly triumphant,—some reverse
Was sure to follow! There's no other way
Accounts for such prompt perfect failure then
And there on the instant. Any day o' the week,
A ducat slid discreetly into palm
O' the mute post-master, while you whisper him—
How you the Count and certain four your knaves,
Have just been mauling who was malapert,
Suspect the kindred may prove troublesome,
Therefore, want horses in a hurry,—that
And nothing more secures you any day
The pick o' the stable! Yet I try the trick,
Double the bribe, call myself Duke for Count,
And say the dead man only was a Jew,
And for my pains find I am dealing just
With the one scrupulous fellow in all Rome—

1617 *MS* [ ]>find 1618 *MS* of *Yale 1* of>o' **MS 1868 1872* escape? *1888 1889* escape 1620 *MS* ought to so have proved 1621 *MS* Since half 1622 *MS* {no commas} 1623 *MS* the flight: but drunk, 1625 *MS* follow: there's 1626 *MS* ^such^ 1627 *MS* instant: any *MS* {no comma} 1629 *MS* Of the post-master, *MS* him 1630 *MS* {no comma} 1631 *MS* Having been *MS* {no comma} 1632 *MS* his kindred may be *MS* {no comma} 1633 *MS* And so want 1635 *MS* of 1636 *MS* Count 1638 *MS* And find, for once, that>And, for my pains, find

1631 *malapert*: impudent, insolent.
1637 *And . . . Jew*: Guido tries to exploit the standard anti-Semitism of his day.

Just this immaculate official stares,
Sees I want hat on head and sword in sheath,
Am splashed with other sort of wet than wine,
Shrugs shoulder, puts my hand by, gold and all,
Stands on the strictness of the rule o' the road!
"Where's the Permission?" Where's the wretched rag
With the due seal and sign of Rome's Police,
To be had for asking, half-an-hour ago?
"Gone? Get another, or no horses hence!"
He dares not stop me, we five glare too grim,
But hinders,—hacks and hamstrings sure enough,
Gives me some twenty miles of miry road
More to march in the middle of that night
Whereof the rough beginning taxed the strength
O' the youngsters, much more mine, both soul and flesh,
Who had to think as well as act: dead-beat,
We gave in ere we reached the boundary
And safe spot out of this irrational Rome,—
Where, on dismounting from our steeds next day,
We had snapped our fingers at you, safe and sound,
Tuscans once more in blessed Tuscany,
Where laws make wise allowance, understand
Civilized life and do its champions right!

1640 *MS* {beginning of fo. 306} 1641 *MS* have no hat on head nor sword *Yale 1* have no>want *Yale 1* nor>and *MS* {no comma} 1642 *MS* And cloak with 1644 *MS* road 1647 *MS* asking half an hour 1649 *MS* They> He *MS* don't dare 1652 *MS* [?H]>More 1654 *MS* Of *MS 1868 1872* mine, such as you see, 1655 *MS* {no comma} 1656 *MS* boundary, 1657 *MS* The *MS* Rome, 1659 *MS* you safe 1661 *MS 1868 1872* the laws make allowance, 1662 *MS* right—

1640 *immaculate*: sinless, incorruptible. A sardonic use, partially alluding to the Roman Catholic doctrine of the Immaculate Conception of the Virgin Mary.

1641 *Sees . . . head*: a detail suggested by SS 12: 'in their haste, one assassin forgot his cloak, and Franceschini left behind his hat, articles that would later incriminate them'.

1650 *hacks and hamstrings*: i.e. 'slows us down, lames us, by injuring the back of our knees' (in a fig. sense). 'To hamstring' is literally 'to cut the hamstrings, the tendons of the knees'. In 'hacks' Browning may be remembering 'houghs', which essentially means the same as 'hamstrings'.

1662 *Civilized*: Browning has already accrued a significant amount of irony around ideas of 'civilization' and 'civility': cf. for example I. 287, II. 1473, X. 2018 nn.

Witness the sentence of the Rota there,
Arezzo uttered, the Granduke confirmed,
One week before I acted on its hint,—
Giving friend Guillichini, for his love,
The galleys, and my wife your saint, Rome's saint,—
Rome manufactures saints enough to know,—
Seclusion at the Stinche for her life.
All this, that all but was, might all have been,
Yet was not! baulked by just a scrupulous knave
Whose palm was horn through handling horses' hoofs
And could not close upon my proffered gold!
What say you to the spite of fortune? Well,
The worst's in store: thus hindered, haled this way
To Rome again by hangdogs, whom find I
Here, still to fight with, but my pale frail wife?
—Riddled with wounds by one not like to waste
The blows he dealt,—knowing anatomy,—
(I think I told you) bound to pick and choose
The vital parts! 'T was learning all in vain!
She too must shimmer through the gloom o' the grave,
Come and confront me—not at judgment-seat
Where I could twist her soul, as erst her flesh,
And turn her truth into a lie,—but there,

1664 *MS* uttered and the Duke *MS* {no commas} 1666 *MS* {no commas} 1667 *MS* gallies, *MS* saint 1668 *MS* {beginning of fo. 307} *MS* That manufactures *MS* know, 1669 *MS* life: 1670 *MS* been 1671 *MS* And was not— 1677 *MS* Is still *MS* {no commas} 1679 *MS* anatomy, 1680 *MS* I *MS* you,— *MS* who could>one to *1868 1872* one to 1681 *MS* parts: twas *MS* in pure wa>all in vain. 1682 *MS* {no comma} 1683 *MS* me at the judgment seat *Yale 1* at the>at 1684–7 {not found in *MS*}

1663–5 *Witness . . . hint*: the sentence of the Ruota (Criminal Court) of Florence, following the judgment of the Commissary or Governor of Arezzo, was confirmed by the Grand Duke on 24 Dec. 1697. This is the first document in OYB: v–viii (5–7).

1669 *Stinche*: the Florence prison.

1672 *horn*: i.e. hard, insensitive.

1676 *hangdogs*: i.e. despicable people: the law officers who escorted him to Rome. Cf. 'Fra Lippo Lippi', 27, where the members of the night-watch are so called.

1679–80 *knowing anatomy . . . you*: at 282–96 Guido boasts of how he learnt about anatomy in connection with fencing: see ll. 291–2 n.

1685 *turn . . . lie*: cf. Rom. 1: 25.

O' the death-bed, with God's hand between us both,
Striking me dumb, and helping her to speak,
Tell her own story her own way, and turn
My plausibility to nothingness!
Four whole days did Pompilia keep alive,
With the best surgery of Rome agape
At the miracle,—this cut, the other slash,
And yet the life refusing to dislodge,
Four whole extravagant impossible days,
Till she had time to finish and persuade
Every man, every woman, every child
In Rome, of what she would: the selfsame she
Who, but a year ago, had wrung her hands,
Reddened her eyes and beat her breasts, rehearsed
The whole game at Arezzo, nor availed
Thereby to move one heart or raise one hand!
When destiny intends you cards like these,
What good of skill and preconcerted play?
Had she been found dead, as I left her dead,
I should have told a tale brooked no reply:
You scarcely will suppose me found at fault
With that advantage! "What brings me to Rome?
"Necessity to claim and take my wife:
"Better, to claim and take my new-born babe,—
"Strong in paternity a fortnight old,
"When 't is at strongest: warily I work,
"Knowing the machinations of my foe;
"I have companionship and use the night:

1689 *MS* nothingness: 1690 *MS* [ ]>Pompilia *MS* {no comma} 1692 *MS* cut the 1693 *MS* {no comma} 1694 *MS* {no comma} 1695 *MS* has 1697 *MS 1868* {no comma} 1700 *MS* {beginning of fo. 308} *MS* {no comma} 1702 *MS* {no comma} 1704 *MS* {no commas} 1707 *MS* advantage: *MS* why I come>what brings me 1708–24 *MS* {no quotation marks at beginnings of lines} 1709 *MS* newborn *MS* babe 1710 *MS* {no comma} 1711 *MS* {no comma} 1712 *MS* the>my *MS* foe,

1691 *surgery*: i.e. doctors.

1698–1701 *had . . . hand!*: referring to when Pompilia fled for aid to the Archbishop and then to the Governor of Arezzo.

1703 *preconcerted*: pre-planned, premeditated.

"I seek my wife and child,—I find—no child
"But wife, in the embraces of that priest
"Who caused her to elope from me. These two,
"Backed by the pander-pair who watch the while,
"Spring on me like so many tiger-cats,
"Glad of the chance to end the intruder. I—
"What should I do but stand on my defence,
"Strike right, strike left, strike thick and threefold, slay,
"Not all—because the coward priest escapes.
"Last, I escape, in fear of evil tongues,
"And having had my taste of Roman law."
What's disputable, refutable here?—
Save by just this one ghost-thing half on earth,
Half out of it,—as if she held God's hand
While she leant back and looked her last at me,
Forgiving me (here monks begin to weep)
Oh, from her very soul, commending mine
To heavenly mercies which are infinite,—
While fixing fast my head beneath your knife!
'T is fate not fortune. All is of a piece!
When was it chance informed me of my youths?
My rustic four o' the family, soft swains,
What sweet surprise had they in store for me,
Those of my very household,—what did Law
Twist with her rack-and-cord-contrivance late
From out their bones and marrow? What but this—
Had no one of these several stumbling-blocks
Stopped me, they yet were cherishing a scheme,

1714 *MS* find the priest>find no child— 1715 *MS* My 1716 *MS* The pair,>These two, 1721 *MS* slay 1723 *MS* {no commas} 1725 *MS* here 1726 *MS* {no comma} 1728 *MS* {beginning of fo. 309} *MS* leans *Yale 1* leans>leant *MS* looks *Yale 1* looks>looked *MS* {no comma} 1729 *MS* me . . here *MS* weep . . 1731 *MS* infinite 1733 *MS 1868 1872* fortune! 1734 *MS 1868* What was it you informed *MS* friends? 1735 {not found in *MS*} 1737 *MS* law 1740 *MS* not one 1741 *MS* had> were *etc.*

1726 *ghost-thing*: i.e. Pompilia (on her deathbed).

1729–31 *Forgiving . . . infinite*: the account of Pompilia's death by the Augustinian friar who attended her is full of pathos: OYB lvii f. (57–8).

All of their honest country homespun wit,
To quietly next day at crow of cock
Cut my own throat too, for their own behoof,
Seeing I had forgot to clear accounts
O' the instant, nowise slackened speed for that,—
And somehow never might find memory,
Once safe back in Arezzo, where things change,
And a court-lord needs mind no country lout.
Well, being the arch-offender, I die last,—
May, ere my head falls, have my eyesight free,
Nor miss them dangling high on either hand,
Like scarecrows in a hemp-field, for their pains!

And then my Trial,—'t is my Trial that bites
Like a corrosive, so the cards are packed,
Dice loaded, and my life-stake tricked away!
Look at my lawyers, lacked they grace of law,
Latin or logic? Were not they fools to the height,
Fools to the depth, fools to the level between,
O' the foolishness set to decide the case?
They feign, they flatter; nowise does it skill,

1742 *MS* All their own>All of their 1743 *MS* quietly, *MS* morn>day *MS 1868 1872* cock, 1744 *MS* ^own^ *MS* too for 1746 *MS* On *MS* that, 1747 *MS* {no comma} 1749 *MS* fear>mind 1750 *MS* arch-offender I die last, 1751 *MS* And ere *MS* falls have 1752 *MS* []>miss 1753 *MS* hempfield *MS* {no comma} *MS* pains. 1755 *MS* any corrosive, the 1756 *MS* {beginning of fo. 310} *MS* away. 1759 *MS* between 1760 *MS* Of 1761 *MS* flatter,

1744 *behoof*: advantage, benefit.

1747 *find memory*: i.e. remember to pay them.

1750 *I die last*: Guido was indeed executed last, a detail that Browning takes from SS 22.

1753 *scarecrows . . . hemp-field*: a bitter, sardonic image. Hemp, an annual herbaceous plant, was used to make strong ropes, and so is synonymous with the ropes for hanging and with hanging itself. A 'stretchhemp', for example, is a person who deserves to be hanged; 'to wag hemp' means 'to be hanged'. There is the saying 'Hemp for your hanging begins to bud.' See also *Henry V*, III. vi. 43. Here, all the hemp ropes make the gallows look like a hemp-field; Guido's accomplices—hanging in awkward and angular ways—look like scarecrows within it.

1755 *packed*: fixed or shuffled (so as to cheat me).

1761 *skill*: matter, make a difference.

Everything goes against me: deal each judge
His dole of flattery and feigning,—why,
He turns and tries and snuffs and savours it,
As some old fly the sugar-grain, your gift;
Then eyes your thumb and finger, brushes clean
The absurd old head of him, and whisks away,
Leaving your thumb and finger dirty. Faugh!

And finally, after this long-drawn range
Of affront and failure, failure and affront,—
This path, 'twixt crosses leading to a skull,
Paced by me barefoot, bloodied by my palms
From the entry to the end,—there's light at length,
A cranny of escape: appeal may be
To the old man, to the father, to the Pope,
For a little life—from one whose life is spent,
A little pity—from pity's source and seat,
A little indulgence to rank, privilege,
From one who is the thing personified,
Rank, privilege, indulgence, grown beyond

1762 *MS* All>Everything 1764 *MS* {no comma} 1765 *MS 1868* an old *MS* sugar-grain your gift, 1767 *MS* away 1770 *MS* affront, *1868 1872* affront, failure, 1771 *MS* twixt *MS* {no commas} 1774 *MS 1868* escape,— 1775 *MS* our father, to this Pope, 1778 *MS* rank and *MS* {no commas} 1779 *MS* For 1780 *MS* privilege and indulgence grown

1769 *range*: row, line (fig.).

1771 *leading . . . skull*: i.e. leading to a place of execution, a Golgotha; the allusion is to Christ's passion. Christ was executed on a hill called Golgotha (Hebrew for 'skull': see Matt. 27: 33). The 'crosses' are, figuratively speaking, the 'affront and failure' that line Guido's path.

1772 *palms*: feet, soles of the feet. OED² describes this sense as 'rare', but Browning had already used it in *The Return of the Druses*, III. 116, and there are three prominent uses in Shelley, his favourite poet. The most interesting is in *Adonais*, st. xxiv, which also describes palms being wounded and bloodied, and so has something of the pathetic resonance intended here: 'Out of her secret Paradise she [Urania] sped, / Through camps and cities rough with stone, and steel, / And human hearts, which to her aery tread / Yielding not, wounded the invisible / Palms of her tender feet where'er they fell.'

1780–1 *Rank . . . Jansenius else*: Cornelius Jansen (1585–1638), Bishop of Ypres, whose teachings were condemned as heretical by several popes, might well consider the Papacy the epitome of 'rank, privilege, indulgence'. The historical reference here is

Earth's bearing, even, ask Jansenius else!
Still the same answer, still no other tune
From the cicala perched at the tree-top
Than crickets noisy round the root: 't is "Die!"
Bids Law—"Be damned!" adds Gospel,—nay,
No word so frank,—'t is rather, "Save yourself!"
The Pope subjoins—"Confess and be absolved!
"So shall my credit countervail your shame,
"And the world see I have not lost the knack
"Of trying all the spirits: yours, my son,
"Wants but a fiery washing to emerge
"In clarity! Come, cleanse you, ease the ache
"Of these old bones, refresh our bowels, boy!"
Do I mistake your mission from the Pope?
Then, bear his Holiness the mind of me!
I do get strength from being thrust to wall,
Successively wrenched from pillar and from post
By this tenacious hate of fortune, hate

1781 *MS* bearing even, 1782 *MS* []>no 1783 *MS* {beginning of fo. 311} 1784 *MS* And *MS* root,—tis "Die"— *1868 1872* root,— 1785 *MS* Quoth *MS* quoth 1786 *MS* tis *MS* yourself"— 1787 *MS* "confess 1788–93 *MS* {no quotation marks at beginnings of lines} 1788 *MS* {no comma} 1789 we have 1790 *MS* spirits,—yours, we know, *1868* spirits,— 1791 *Yale 1* emerge!"> emerge 1792 *MS* clarity: come, *Yale 1* clarity: come> clarity! Come 1793 *MS* Son!" 1794 {not found in *MS*} 1795 *MS* Cardinal, bear him>bear his Holiness *MS* me: 1797 *MS* From post and pillar wrenched successively>Successively wrenched from pillar and from post 1798 *MS* say>hate

a loose one, however, for Jansen himself lived in many ways an exemplary life and did not come under papal scrutiny. It was only after his death that his posthumously published work *Augustinus* (1640) generated followers of different kinds for its rigorist, quasi-Calvinistic version of Catholicism, and it was this book and these followers who came under sustained papal attack. Three popes in the seventeenth century explicitly condemned aspects of the *Augustinus*: Urban VIII in 1642, Innocent X in 1653, and Alexander VII in 1656.

1788 *countervail*: offset, compensate for.

1790 *Of . . . spirits*: of testing out the spirits (that are in people). The phrasing comes from 1 John 4: 1: 'Beloved, believe not every spirit, but try the spirits whether they are of God: because many false prophets are gone out into the world.'

1793 *refresh our bowels*: i.e. lift our spirits. The phrasing is biblical: see Philem. 7, and 20: 'Yea, brother, let me have joy of thee in the Lord: refresh my bowels in the Lord.'

Of all things in, under, and above earth.
Warfare, begun this mean unmanly mode,
Does best to end so,—gives earth spectacle
Of a brave fighter who succumbs to odds
That turn defeat to victory. Stab, I fold
My mantle round me! Rome approves my act:
Applauds the blow which costs me life but keeps
My honour spotless: Rome would praise no more
Had I fallen, say, some fifteen years ago,
Helping Vienna when our Aretines
Flocked to Duke Charles and fought Turk Mustafa;
Nor would you two be trembling o'er my corpse
With all this exquisite solicitude.
Why is it that I make such suit to live?
The popular sympathy that's round me now
Would break like bubble that o'er-domes a fly:
Solid enough while he lies quiet there,
But let him want the air and ply the wing,
Why, it breaks and bespatters him, what else?
Cardinal, if the Pope had pardoned me,

1799 *MS* Hate of>Of all 1800 *MS* {no commas} 1801 *MS* give the spectacle 1803 *MS* victory: come, 1804 *MS* applauds>approves 1806 *MS* had done no>would praise no 1808 *MS* those>our 1812 *MS* {beginning of fo. 312} 1814 *MS* [ ]>like *MS* foam bell>bubble *MS 1868 1872* fly— 1815 *MS 1868 1872* Pretty

1801 *gives . . . spectacle*: cf. 1 Cor. 4: 9. Compare also R&B, I. 504, and X. 665–6 nn.

1803–4 *I . . . me!*: a half allusion whereby Guido compares himself to the dying Julius Caesar: cf. *Julius Caesar*, III. ii. 170, 187.

1807–9 *Had . . . Mustafa*: i.e. 'had I died a hero fighting against the Turks to protect Christendom'. The allusion is to the Siege of Vienna in the summer of 1683, a famous turning-point in history, where the advance of Islam and the Turkish empire into Europe was halted. The Grand Vizier, Kara Mustafa, had besieged the capital of the Holy Roman Empire with a force of 200,000 men. Charles V, duke of Lorraine, who was in the service of the Holy Roman Emperor, Leopold II, joined with the Polish king, Jan Sobieski, and broke the siege on 12 September. The Medici rulers of Tuscany were allied to the Habsburgs both by marriage and formal treaty, hence the Aretines' going to fight for the Christian cause. Browning would have known this detail from his researches into the history of Arezzo: see our Vol. VII, p. xxiv.

1813–17 *The . . . else?*: i.e. while he appears a passive victim, the mob will sympathize with him; if he shows a lust for life, and wants to get out of prison, the mob will soon be reviling him.

And I walked out of prison through the crowd,
It would not be your arm I should dare press!
Then, if I got safe to my place again,
How sad and sapless were the years to come!
I go my old ways and find things grown grey;
You priests leer at me, old friends look askance,
The mob's in love, I'll wager, to a man,
With my poor young good beauteous murdered wife:
For hearts require instruction how to beat,
And eyes, on warrant of the story, wax
Wanton at portraiture in white and black
Of dead Pompilia gracing ballad-sheet,
Which eyes, lived she unmurdered and unsung,
Would never turn though she paced street as bare
As the mad penitent ladies do in France.
My brothers quietly would edge me out
Of use and management of things called mine;
Do I command? "You stretched command before!"
Show anger? "Anger little helped you once!"
Advise? "How managed you affairs of old?"
My very mother, all the while they gird,
Turns eye up, gives confirmatory groan;
For unsuccess, explain it how you will,

1820 *MS* ^not^ *MS* hold! 1821 *MS* again,— *Yale 1* again,—>again, 1822 *MS* 'Tis doubtful>How sad and *etc.* *MS* come,— 1823 *MS* all>things *MS* grey— *1824 *MS* askance,— *1868 1872* askance; *1888* askance *DC BrU* askance>askance, *1889* askance, 1825 *MS* mob [ ]>mob's *MS* man 1831 *MS* Who, had she died *1868* Which, had she died unmurdered *1836 *MS* before"! *1868 1872* before!" *1888* before! *DC BrU* before!>before!" *1889* before!" 1838 *MS* old?"— 1840 *MS* Giving, belike, the confirmatory groan,— *1868* groan,— 1841 *MS* {beginning of fo. 313} *MS* will

1820 *It . . . press!*: i.e. 'I should be a pariah. I shouldn't dare hold on to a respectable arm, like yours.'

1828–9 *wax / Wanton*: grow lustful.

1833 *penitent . . . France*: this is not an obvious historical allusion. Browning certainly associates France with 'penance-sheets', and he may be thinking of women so dressed, rather than of complete nakedness: cf. 'Count Gismond', 55–6.

1839 *gird*: sneer, gibe, taunt.

Disqualifies you, makes you doubt yourself,
—Much more, is found decisive by your friends.
Beside, am I not fifty years of age?
What new leap would a life take, checked like mine
I' the spring at outset? Where's my second chance?
Ay, but the babe . . . I had forgot my son,
My heir! Now for a burst of gratitude!
There's some appropriate service to intone,
Some *gaudeamus* and thanksgiving-psalm!
Old, I renew my youth in him, and poor
Possess a treasure,—is not that the phrase?
Only I must wait patient twenty years—
Nourishing all the while, as father ought,
The excrescence with my daily blood of life.
Does it respond to hope, such sacrifice,—
Grows the wen plump while I myself grow lean?
Why, here's my son and heir in evidence,
Who stronger, wiser, handsomer than I
By fifty years, relieves me of each load,—
Tames my hot horse, carries my heavy gun,
Courts my coy mistress,—has his apt advice
On house-economy, expenditure,
And what not. All which good gifts and great growth

1843 *MS* Much 1845 *MS* baulked 1846 *MS* In 1847 *MS 1868 1872* babe . . 1850 *MS* gaudeamus *MS* thanksgiving psalm! 1856 *MS* this sacrifice, 1862 *MS* word to say>apt advice 1863 *MS* house,>house oeconomy, *1864 *MS 1868 1872 1888* not? *DC BrU* not?>not. *1889* not. *MS* these good gifts, over growth>which good gifts and much growth

1850 *gaudeamus*: i.e. joyous song (secular or religious); from L. 'Let us rejoice.'

1851–2 *poor*. . . *phrase?*: this is not directly a proverbial phrase, but presumably either a memory of Matt. 19: 21, or Matt. 13: 45–6.

1855 *excrescence*: unnatural growth or swelling, anticipating the image of the wen (l. 1857). More abstractly, an excrescence is 'somewhat growing out of another without use, and contrary to the common order of production' (Johnson).

1857 *wen*: wart, fleshy protuberance. The disgusting image here is of a son growing up like an enlarging wart or tumour, at this father's expense, sucking up his father's life-blood as he expands.

1862 *my coy mistress*: echoing the title of Andrew Marvell's poem 'To His Coy Mistress': Guido is being highly sarcastic about how a grown-up son will take over his life.

Because of my decline, he brings to bear
On Guido, but half apprehensive how
He cumbers earth, crosses the brisk young Count,
Who civilly would thrust him from the scene.
Contrariwise, does the blood-offering fail?
There's an ineptitude, one blank the more
Added to earth in semblance of my child?
Then, this has been a costly piece of work,
My life exchanged for his!—why he, not I,
Enjoy the world, if no more grace accrue?
Dwarf me, what giant have you made of him?
I do not dread the disobedient son:
I know how to suppress rebellion there,
Being not quite the fool my father was.
But grant the medium measure of a man,
The usual compromise 'twixt fool and sage,
—You know—the tolerably-obstinate,
The not-so-much-perverse but you may train,
The true son-servant that, when parent bids
"Go work, son, in my vineyard!" makes reply
"I go, Sir!"—Why, what profit in your son
Beyond the drudges you might subsidize,

1865 *MS* Through my decline, he brings forthwith to bear>Through my decline, he justly brings to bear>Because of my decline, he brings to bear 1866 *MS* only half aware how shamefully>hardly apprehensive how 1867 *MS* makes wait> crosses *MS* [?son]>Count, 1868 *MS* Fit civilly to 1869 *MS* {beginning of fo. 314} 1870 *MS* one ineptitude>this ineptitude *MS* and blank> one blank 1871 *MS* fashion of a son?>semblance of my child? 1872 *MS* Why, 1873 *MS* his,— 1876 *MS* *1868* *1872* son— 1879 *MS* []>a 1880 *MS* Usual compromise—between>The usual compromise 'twixt 1881 *MS* tolerably obstinate, 1882 *MS* not so much perverse *MS* guide,>train, 1884 *MS* Son, 1886 *MS* {no comma}

1869 *Contrariwise . . . fail?*: i.e. 'what happens if, on the other hand, my life-blood, poured into the growth of a son, produces not a "brisk young Count" but a weakling or idiot?'

1870 *ineptitude*: less perhaps 'an instance of incompetence' than 'a person lacking competence, a person foolish or silly'. Cf. *Aristophanes' Apology*, 2592.

1883–5 *son-servant . . . Sir!"*: cf. Matt. 21: 28–32, the parable of the two sons. In the parable, the son who says obediently 'I go, sir' does *not* in fact go to the vineyard: Guido is being ironical, or there is a small irony at his expense.

Have the same work from, at a paul the head?
Look at those four young precious olive-plants
Reared at Vittiano,—not on flesh and blood,
These twenty years, but black bread and sour wine!
I bade them put forth tender branch, hook, hold,
And hurt three enemies I had in Rome:
They did my hest as unreluctantly,
At promise of a dollar, as a son
Adjured by mumping memories of the past.
No, nothing repays youth expended so—
Youth, I say, who am young still: grant but leave
To live my life out, to the last I'd live
And die conceding age no right of youth!
It is the will runs the renewing nerve
Through flaccid flesh that faints before the time.
Therefore no sort of use for son have I—
Sick, not of life's feast but of steps to climb
To the house where life prepares her feast,—of means
To the end: for make the end attainable
Without the means,—my relish were like yours.
A man may have an appetite enough

1887 *MS* To do the same work at *1868* {no comma} 1888 *MS* young fellows, olive plants *Yale 1* previous>precious 1889 *MS* blood 1890 *MS* wine,— 1891 *MS* I bade put forth the tender branch and hook *1868 1872* and hook 1892 *MS* hang 1893 *MS* {no comma} 1895 *MS* by all [ ]>by all sweet memories *etc. 1868 1872* past! 1897 *MS* {beginning of fo. 315} *MS 1868* still,—give *1872* still: give 1898 *MS* I live *MS* I live 1899 *MS* youth; 1901 *1868* flesh, would faint 1903 *MS* life, but of the weary way>life's feast but the steps to climb 1904 *MS* [ ]>house *MS* ^means^ 1905 *MS* end,—and make 1906 *MS* mean,— *MS* were as keen 1907 {not found in *MS*}

1887 *paul*: small coin, of little value.

1888 *four . . . olive-plants*: cf. Ps. 128: 3: 'thy children like olive plants round about thy table', an allusion confirming that his farm-hands are quite as good to him as any real son.

1895 *Adjured*: charged.

mumping: 'foolishly or excessively sentimental', strictly speaking a nonce use; cf. l. 699 n. The usual sense of 'mumping' is 'grimacing'. Browning seems to have shifted the sense to suit his own ends: these memories are, perhaps, the kind that make you 'mump' or grimace.

1899 *conceding . . . youth*: i.e. not giving up any of the rights of youth as I get older.

For a whole dish of robins ready cooked,
And yet lack courage to face sleet, pad snow,
And snare sufficiently for supper.

Thus
The time's arrived when, ancient Roman-like,
I am bound to fall on my own sword: why not
Say—Tuscan-like, more ancient, better still?
Will you hear truth can do no harm nor good?
I think I never was at any time
A Christian, as you nickname all the world,
Me among others: truce to nonsense now!
Name me, a primitive religionist—
As should the aboriginary be
I boast myself, Etruscan, Aretine,
One sprung,—your frigid Virgil's fieriest word,—
From fauns and nymphs, trunks and the heart of oak,
With,—for a visible divinity,—
The portent of a Jove Ægiochus

1908 *MS* As for a dish *MS* cooked— 1909 *MS* Though of no mind f>Though of no mind to face sleet and pad snow 1910 *MS* To snare sufficiency of mornings. Thus *MS* {no new paragraph} 1911 {not found in *MS*} 1912 *Yale 1* time s>time's *MS* ancient-Roman-like, 1913 *MS 1868 1872* sword,— 1914 *MS* Tuscan-like, which is older,>Die Tuscan-like, more ancient, 1918 *MS* now: 1919 *MS* religionist *MS* {no comma} 1920 *MS* an>the 1924 *MS* divinity

---

1914 *Tuscan-like . . . still?*: see next n.

1919–21 *primitive religionist . . . Aretine*: Guido paints himself as a religious aborigine, an adherent of an older pagan religion that has deeper roots than this new-fangled Christianity. The Etruscan civilization of central Italy, which flourished from *c.*700 to *c.*500 BC, did indeed precede Roman civilization: Browning was, of course, well aware of some of its most impressive products: the ring of *The Ring and the Book* itself, and the wonderful bronze Chimaera: see 1118–19 n.

1922–3 *sprung . . . oak*: the allusion is to King Evander's speech in *Aeneid*, VIII (313–15), where he describes the very earliest inhabitants of Rome: *tum rex Euandrus Romanae conditor arcis: / 'haec nemora indigenae Fauni Nymphaeque tenebant / gensque virum truncis et duro robore nata'*: 'Then spoke King Evander, founder of Rome's citadel: "In these woodlands the native Fauns and Nymphs once dwelt, and a race of men sprung from trunks of trees and hardy oak." '

1925 *portent*: wondrous (or ominous) sign.

Jove Ægiochus: Jove the aegis-bearer. The aegis is Jove's shield, with a storm-cloud on it: when he brandished it it was supposed to create thunder and lightning. Cf. *Iliad*, IV. 166–8, and next n.

Descried 'mid clouds, lightning and thunder, couched
On topmost crag of your Capitoline:
'T is in the Seventh Æneid,—what, the Eighth?
Right,—thanks, Abate,—though the Christian's dumb,
The Latinist's vivacious in you yet!
I know my grandsire had our tapestry
Marked with the motto, 'neath a certain shield,
Whereto his grandson presently will give gules
To vary azure. First we fight for faiths,
But get to shake hands at the last of all:
Mine's your faith too,—in Jove Ægiochus!
Nor do Greek gods, that serve as supplement,
Jar with the simpler scheme, if understood.
We want such intermediary race
To make communication possible;
The real thing were too lofty, we too low,
Midway hang these: we feel their use so plain
In linking height to depth, that we doff hat
And put no question nor pry narrowly

1926 *MS* mid 1927 *MS* the top crag *MS 1868 1872* Capitoline— 1928 *MS* {beginning of fo. 316} 1929 *MS* dumb 1932 *MS 1868* shield 1933 *MS 1868 1872* His grandson presently will give some gules 1934 *MS* argent. 1936 *MS* Ægiochus; 1937 *MS* [] the>Nor the *MS* Gods, *Yale 1* Gods>gods 1938 *MS* understood— 1940 *MS* possible,— 1942 *MS* these; 1943 *MS* we doff our 1944 *MS* ask>put *MS* questions

1926–8 *Descried . . . Eighth?*: another allusion to King Evander's speech: see 1922–3 n. Evander describes how his Arcadians, looking up to the top of the Capitoline hill—the most sacred hill of Rome—sometimes thought they saw Jove shaking out lightning: *'hoc nemus, hunc' inquit 'frondoso vertice collem / (quis deus incertum est) habitat deus; Arcades ipsum / credunt se vidisse Iovem, cum saepe nigrantem / aegida concuteret dextra nimbosque cieret'*: 'Some god,' he said, 'it is not sure what god, lives in this grove, this hilltop thick with leaves. My Arcadians think they have seen great Jove himself, when, as often, with his right hand he brandishes his black aegis, summoning the storm-clouds': *Aeneid*, VIII. 351–4. Guido adapts these lines with vivid energy, even if, in his haste, he assumes they are from Book VII of the *Aeneid*, rather than Book VIII.

1932 *the motto*: presumably the phrase from line 1923 'From fauns and nymphs, trunks and the heart of oak', though obviously in Latin.

1933–4 *grandson . . . azure*: 'his grandson' refers to Guido himself. He means that when he suffers his bloody execution he will add 'gules' (i.e. the colour red, in heraldic terminology) to the blue of the family coat of arms.

1936 *Mine's . . . Ægiochus*: Guido insists that his faith in a supreme pagan god is no different from his interlocutors' faith in a supreme Christian God.

Into the nature hid behind the names.
We grudge no rite the fancy may demand;
But never, more than needs, invent, refine,
Improve upon requirement, idly wise
Beyond the letter, teaching gods their trade,
Which is to teach us: we'll obey when taught.
Why should we do our duty past the need?
When the sky darkens, Jove is wroth,—say prayer!
When the sun shines and Jove is glad,—sing psalm!
But wherefore pass prescription and devise
Blood-offering for sweat-service, lend the rod
A pungency through pickle of our own?
Learned Abate,—no one teaches you
What Venus means and who's Apollo here!
I spare you, Cardinal,—but, though you wince,
You know me, I know you, and both know that!
So, if Apollo bids us fast, we fast:
But where does Venus order we stop sense
When Master Pietro rhymes a pleasantry?
Give alms prescribed on Friday: but, hold hand
Because your foe lies prostrate,—where's the word
Explicit in the book debars revenge?

1945 *MS* natures 1946 *MS* require—>demand— 1947 *MS* But do not, *MS* refine 1948 *MS* wise>idly wise 1950 *MS* we obey 1951 *MS* I>we *MS* my>our *MS* *1868* *1872* due? 1952 *MS* [ ]> say 1953 *MS* shines, sing psalm, for Jove is glad!>shines, and Jove is glad sing psalm! 1956 *MS* novel smart>pungency *MS* your 1957 *MS* {beginning of fo. 317} *MS* Abate, 1958 *MS* here: 1959 *MS* [ ]>Cardinal,— *MS* enough, you wince: 1960 *MS* we both know that. 1961 *MS* So if *MS* me *MS* I 1962 *MS* I 1964 *MS* the poor alms on Friday,—but hold *1868* *1872* Friday,— 1965 *MS* When there 1966 *MS* prevents

1954 *pass prescription*: i.e. exceed the ordinary duties.

1954–5 *devise . . . sweat-service*: i.e. plan a blood sacrifice when all that is required is hard work.

1955–6 *lend . . . own?*: i.e. give the stick of punishment an extra sting from having soaked it in brine or vinegar. This adapts the proverbial phrase 'a rod in pickle', or 'to have a rod in pickle', i.e. to have punishment in store: cf. II. 1541–2 n.

1962–3 *we . . . pleasantry?*: i.e. we refuse to listen to a sexually explicit or indecent poem by Pietro Aretino: see X. 654 n.

The rationale of your scheme is just
"Pay toll here, there pursue your pleasure free!"
So do you turn to use the medium-powers,
Mars and Minerva, Bacchus and the rest,
And so are saved propitiating—whom?
What all-good, all-wise and all-potent Jove
Vexed by the very sins in man, himself
Made life's necessity when man he made?
Irrational bunglers! So, the living truth
Revealed to strike Pan dead, ducks low at last,
Prays leave to hold its own and live good days
Provided it go masque grotesquely, called
Christian not Pagan. Oh, you purged the sky
Of all gods save the One, the great and good,
Clapped hands and triumphed! But the change came fast:
The inexorable need in man for life—
(Life, you may mulct and minish to a grain
Out of the lump, so that the grain but live)
Laughed at your substituting death for life,
And bade you do your worst: which worst was done
In just that age styled primitive and pure

1969 *MS* your *MS* {no comma} 1970 {not found in *MS*} 1971 *MS* *1868* what? 1972 *MS 1868* What all good, all wise and all potent *MS* God 1974 *MS* man's>life's *MS* made. 1975 *MS* What, the 1977 *MS* Prays that he hold his *Yale 1* Prays that it>Prays leave to 1978 *MS* he go 1979 *MS 1868* Pagan? 1981 *MS* is come,>came fast: 1983 *MS* Life *1868* Life,— *MS* {no comma} 1984 *MS 1868* so the grain left but *1872* grain left *MS* live— *1868* live,— 1985 *MS* {no comma} 1986 *MS* *1868* worst,— 1987 *MS* {beginning of fo. 318} *MS* In that age styled the primitive *1868* —Pass that age styled the primitive

1970 *Mars . . . Bacchus*: the gods (respectively) of war, crafts, and drink.

1975–6 *living . . . dead*: i.e. the vital truth of Christianity that was revealed to humankind to kill off paganism. The allusion is to a legend first told by Plutarch in *De Oraculorum Defectu*, 17: at the hour of the Crucifixion, certain Greek sailors heard a mysterious voice proclaiming 'Pan is dead' and were told to report this. The suggestion lies behind EBB's 'The Dead Pan'.

1977 *live good days*: cf. Ps. 34:12, 1 Pet. 3: 10.

1978 *masque*: i.e. in disguise.

1983 *mulct and minish*: penalize and diminish. The usual meaning of 'to mulct' is 'to punish with fine or forfeiture': Johnson.

1987 *age . . . pure*: i.e. the early centuries AD—when many Christians died for their faith under Roman persecution.

When Saint this, Saint that, dutifully starved,
Froze, fought with beasts, was beaten and abused
And finally ridded of his flesh by fire:
He kept life-long unspotted from the world!
Next age, how goes the game, what mortal gives
His life and emulates Saint that, Saint this?
Men mutter, make excuse or mutiny,
In fine are minded all to leave the new,
Stick to the old,—enjoy old liberty,
No prejudice in enjoyment, if you please,
To the new profession: sin o' the sly, henceforth!
The law stands though the letter kills: what then?
The spirit saves as unmistakeably.
Omniscience sees, Omnipotence could stop,
Omnibenevolence pardons: it must be,
Frown law its fiercest, there's a wink somewhere!

Such was the logic in this head of mine:
I, like the rest, wrote "poison" on my bread,

1990 *MS* rid *MS 1868 1872* fire, 1991 *MS* Kept all the while *Yale 1* world!> world!— *1868* Keeping the while unspotted from the world!— *1872* world!— 1992 *MS 1868* Good: but next age, how goes the game, who gives 1993 *MS 1868* that and this? 1994 *MS* They boggle, *1868* They mutiny, *MS 1868* mutter who knows what excuse? *1872* excuse, 1995 *MS 1868* make up their minds to *MS* {no comma} 1996 *MS* the liberty, 1997 *MS 1868* No prejudice, all the same, if so it please, 1998 *MS* late profession: *MS* henceforth,— 1999 *MS 1868* Let the law stand: the letter kills, what then? 2001 *MS* omnipotence 2002 *MS* All mericulness [*sic*] pardons,— *1868* All-mercifulness pardons,— 2003 *MS* somewhere. 2004 *MS* {no new paragraph} *MS* []>Such *MS* mine,— 2005 *MS* bread *1868* bread;

1991 *He . . . world!*: i.e. 'he [the early Christian saint] kept himself unspotted from the world'. The phrasing alludes to Jas. 1: 27: 'Pure religion . . . is this, to visit the fatherless and widows in their affliction, and to keep himself unspotted from the world.'

1995–6 *leave . . . old*: i.e. abandon Christianity, and stick to paganism.

1998 *new profession*: i.e. new (hypocritical) profession of Christianity.

1999–2000 *law . . . saves*: cf. Matt. 5: 17, 'Think not that I come to destroy the law', and 2 Cor. 3: 6, 'for the letter killeth, but the spirit giveth life'. Guido's use of these texts is ironical: he means that men find a lax, semi-pagan interpretation of Christianity that suits their true natures.

2003 *wink*: i.e. a gesture of forgiveness or condonation. The word is not exclusively biblical, but it does have biblical precedent: cf. Acts 17: 30.

But broke and ate:—said "Those that use the sword
"Shall perish by the same;" then stabbed my foe.
I stand on solid earth, not empty air:
Dislodge me, let your Pope's crook hale me hence!
Not he, nor you! And I so pity both,
I'll make the true charge you want wit to make:
"Count Guido, who reveal our mystery,
"And trace all issues to the love of life:
"We having life to love and guard, like you,
"Why did you put us upon self-defence?
"You well knew what prompt pass-word would appease
"The sentry's ire when folk infringed his bounds,
"And yet kept mouth shut: do you wonder then
"If, in mere decency, he shot you dead?
"He can't have people play such pranks as yours
"Beneath his nose at noonday: you disdained
"To give him an excuse before the world
"By crying 'I break rule to save our camp!'
"Under the old rule, such offence were death;
"And you had heard the Pontifex pronounce

2006 *MS* ate, *MS 1868 1872* "those *MS* [ ]>that *etc.* 2007 *MS* {no quotation mark at beginning of line} *MS* same,' *Yale 1* same,">same;" 2008 *MS* Stand therefore on the solid earth, not air— *Yale 1* air—>air: 2009 *MS* logic pluck>Pope's crook hale *MS* thence!>hence! 2010 *MS* End welcome!> Not he, nor you! *MS* both 2011 *MS 1868* the speech you want the 2012 *MS* you have bared>who reveal *MS* []>, 2013–44 *MS* {no quotation marks at beginnings of lines} 2013 *MS* You bring all issues from *1868* "You **MS 1868 1872* life: *1888 1889* life. 2014 *MS 1868* have a *MS 1868* you. 2016 *MS* know what's the 2017 *MS* you>folk *MS 1868 1872* infringe 2018 *MS* keep *MS* silence,—where's the>mouth shut—do you 2019 *MS* shoots 2020 *MS* [ ]>play *MS 1868 1872* you 2021 *MS 1868 1872* noonday, who disdain 2022 *MS 1868 1872* world, 2023 *MS* "I do this *MS* Camp." 2025 *MS* Just so had you heard Pontifex pronounce *1868* so had you heard

2006–7 "*Those . . . same;*": cf. Matt. 26: 52.

2012 *reveal our mystery*: i.e. expose our professional practice.

2023 '*I break rule*: i.e. 'I do wrong (in this case, break the formality of giving the password) in order to save our whole camp.' Cf. 2036–44, where Guido is urged to justify the illegality of his murders on the higher ground of his hurried zeal against heresy.

2025 *Pontifex*: High Priest, i.e. the Pope.

"'Since you slay foe and violate the form,
"'Slaying turns murder, which were sacrifice
"'Had you, while, say, law-suiting foe to death,
"'But raised an altar to the Unknown God,
"'Or else the Genius of the Vatican.'
"Why then this pother?—all because the Pope,
"Doing his duty, cried 'A foreigner,
"'You scandalize the natives: here at Rome
"'*Romano vivitur more:* wise men, here,
"'Put the Church forward and efface themselves.
"'The fit defence had been,—you stamped on wheat,
"'Intending all the time to trample tares,—
"'Were fain extirpate, then, the heretic,
"'You now find, in your haste was slain a fool:
"'Nor Pietro, nor Violante, nor your wife
"'Meant to breed up your babe a Molinist!
"'Whence you are duly contrite. Not one word
"'Of all this wisdom did you urge: which slip

2026 *MS* "Here *MS* want the proper form: 2027 *MS* That is now *1868* "'That turns to 2028 {not found in *MS*} *1868* law-suiting him 2029 *MS* Had you raised altar **1868 1872* God, *1888 1889* God 2030 *MS* Vatican." 2031 *MS* pother all *MS 1868* {no comma} 2032 *MS* cries "You foreigner *1868* cries 2033 *MS* Scandalize natives wantonly: at Rome 2034 *MS* Romano vivitur more: *MS* {no commas} 2035 *MS* themselves: 2036 *MS* Had it been hard to urge, you *MS* wheat 2037 *MS* root out 2038 *MS* to extirpate the *Yale 1* to extirpate the>extirpate, then, the *MS* {no commas} 2039 *MS* And, in>And *MS* {no comma} *1868* "'And *MS 1868* you slew 2041 *MS* Molinist— 2042 *MS* 'Tis this slip 2043 {not found in *MS*} *1868* urge!—

2029–30 *raised . . . Vatican*: i.e. made gesture of deference and respect to religious authority, so pretending a religious nature and motivation. How Guido might have done this is explained in the following lines: he might have pretended that he only killed Pompilia, Pietro, and Violante because he mistakenly believed that were going to bring up his son as a heretic. 'The Unknown God' is from Acts 17: 23. 'Genius' = guardian spirit or god.

2034 *Romano vivitur more*: 'one does as Rome does' (L.).

2036–7 *you . . . tares*: i.e. 'I killed good people by accident, when I only really intended to put down "weeds", i.e. heretics'. The imagery comes from Matt. 13: 24–30.

2038 *extirpate*: pluck up (by the roots), destroy—continuing the plant images from the preceding lines.

2041 *Molinist*: i.e. a heretic. See IX. 33 n.

"'Death must atone for.'"
So, let death atone!
So ends mistake, so end mistakers!—end
Perhaps to recommence,—how should I know?
Only, be sure, no punishment, no pain
Childish, preposterous, impossible,
But some such fate as Ovid could foresee,—
Byblis in fluvium, let the weak soul end
In water, *sed Lycaon in lupum*, but
The strong become a wolf for evermore!
Change that Pompilia to a puny stream
Fit to reflect the daisies on its bank!
Let me turn wolf, be whole, and sate, for once,—
Wallow in what is now a wolfishness
Coerced too much by the humanity
That's half of me as well! Grow out of man,
Glut the wolf-nature,—what remains but grow

2044 *MS* for!" *1868* for!'" 2045 *MS* {no comma} 2046 *MS* End *Yale 1* End>end 2047 *MS* {beginning of fo. 320} 2048 *MS* Only be sure no *MS* pains 2049 *MS* impossible,— *Yale 1* impossible,—>impossible, 2050 *MS* s[?uc]>some *MS* end 2051 *MS* Byblis in fluvium, Lycaon in lupum,—ay— 2052, 2053 {not found in *MS*} 2055 *MS* bank,— 2056 *MS* whole and sate for 2057 *MS* the wolfishness 2058 *MS* Coërced *MS* through life>too much *MS* this 2059 *MS* well: grow

---

2048–9 *Only . . . impossible*: the traditional Christian notion of Hell is ludicrous, thinks Guido.

2050–3 *Ovid . . . evermore!*: 'Byblis into a river', 'But Lycaon into a wolf' (L.). The references are to Byblis and Lycaon in Ovid's *Metamorphoses*, bks. 1 and 9 respectively. In some accounts Lycaon, the savage Arcadian king, turns into a werewolf after eating human flesh. In *Metamorphoses* he tries to kill Jupiter, when the latter comes to his house disguised as a human. When this plan fails, Lycaon kills a Molossian hostage in cold blood, and attempts to have the flesh served up to Jupiter for his supper. In his rage, Jupiter destroys Lycaon's house by lightning, and transforms Lycaon into a wolf (a symbol of his savagery): 'His clothes changed into fur, his arms to legs; he became a wolf but keeps traces of his old appearance; his grey head is the same, the same violence of his face, the same eyes gleam, there is the same wild look': *Met.* I. 236–9 (trans. D. E. Hill). By contrast, the weak nymph Byblis falls in love with her twin brother Caunus and only declares her illicit feelings after much hesitation and confusion. When her brother flees, she makes an attempt to follow him, then breaks down completely, and by her perpetual weeping turns into a spring: *sic lacrimis consumpta suis Phoebeia Byblis / vertitur in fontem* ('so was Phoebean Byblis consumed by her own tears / and turned into a spring'): *Met.* IX. 663–4.

2060 *what remains*: i.e. what will be left to happen after that.

Into the man again, be man indeed
And all man? Do I ring the changes right?
Deformed, transformed, reformed, informed, conformed!
The honest instinct, pent and crossed through life,
Let surge by death into a visible flow
Of rapture: as the strangled thread of flame
Painfully winds, annoying and annoyed,
Malignant and maligned, thro' stone and ore,
Till earth exclude the stranger: vented once,
It finds full play, is recognized a-top
Some mountain as no such abnormal birth,
Fire for the mount, not streamlet for the vale!
Ay, of the water was that wife of mine—
Be it for good, be it for ill, no run
O' the red thread through that insignificance!
Again, how she is at me with those eyes!
Away with the empty stare! Be holy still,
And stupid ever! Occupy your patch
Of private snow that's somewhere in what world
May now be growing icy round your head,
And aguish at your foot-print,—freeze not me,
Dare follow not another step I take,
Not with so much as those detested eyes,
No, though they follow but to pray me pause
On the incline, earth's edge that's next to hell!

2062 *MS* man; do 2063 *MS* conformed>informed, conformed: 2064 *MS* [ ]>pent and 2068 *MS* earth>stone 2069 *MS* Till earth>Till angry earth *MS* creature: *2071 *MS 1868 1872* birth. *1888* birth *DC BrU* birth> birth, *1889* birth, *2072 *MS 1868 1872 1888* the streamlet *DC BrU* the streamlet>not streamlet *1889* not streamlet 2075 *MS* Of 2076 *MS* How she is ever>Again, how she is *MS* eyes— *Yale 1* eyes—>eyes! 2077 *MS* {beginning of fo. 321} 2078 *MS* ever: occupy 2079 *MS* April snow 2080 {not found in *MS*} 2081 *MS* Is 2085 *MS* the>earth's *MS* Hell!

2063 *Deformed . . . conformed*: i.e. turned into a werewolf, as a cathartic experience, and then back into a reasonable man. 'Conformed' and 'transformed' make a slight ironic echo with Rom. 12: 2.

2064 *pent and crossed*: confined and frustrated.

2069 *exclude*: throw out, expel.

2075 *red thread*: i.e. the red thread of fire, from l. 2066.

None of your abnegation of revenge!
Fly at me frank, tug while I tear again!
There's God, go tell Him, testify your worst!
Not she! There was no touch in her of hate:
And it would prove her hell, if I reached mine!
To know I suffered, would still sadden her,
Do what the angels might to make amends!
Therefore there's either no such place as hell,
Or thence shall I be thrust forth, for her sake,
And thereby undergo three hells, not one—
I who, with outlet for escape to heaven,
Would tarry if such flight allowed my foe
To raise his head, relieved of that firm foot
Had pinned him to the fiery pavement else!
So am I made, "who did not make myself:"
(How dared she rob my own lip of the word?)
Beware me in what other world may be!—
Pompilia, who have brought me to this pass!
All I know here, will I say there, and go
Beyond the saying with the deed. Some use
There cannot but be for a mood like mine,
Implacable, persistent in revenge.
She maundered "All is over and at end:
"I go my own road, go you where God will!

2087 *MS* ^at me^ 2088 *MS* tell and testify 2090 *MS* mine,— *Yale 1* mine!—>mine! 2091 *MS* her 2092 *MS* amends— 2094 *MS* I [?be]>I have respite for *etc.* *MS* {no commas} 2099 *MS* Late *MS* there. 2100 *MS* {no quotation marks} 2101 {not found in *MS*} 2102 *MS* Before>Beware *MS* be! 2103 {not found in *MS*} 2106 *MS* {no comma} *Yale 1* {comma added} 2108 *MS* {beginning of fo. 322} *MS* She would say 2109, 2110 *MS* {no quotation marks at beginnings of lines} 2109 *MS* will:

2086 *abnegation*: renunciation. Pompilia is reported to have forgiven Guido on her deathbed: OYB lvii (57–8). One of her reported sayings is 'May God pardon him in heaven as I pardon him on earth': OYB lviii (59).

2095 *three hells*: Guido exaggerates for effect: to escape hell because of Pompilia's forgiveness would be, for him, like enduring three hells.

2099 *fiery pavement*: i.e. the bottom of hell. cf. *Paradise Lost*, I. 682, 726.

2100 "*who . . . myself:*": cf. 940–1 n.

2108 *maundered*: murmured, spoke dreamily; cf. 699 n.

"Forgive you? I forget you!" There's the saint
That takes your taste, you other kind of men!
How you had loved her! Guido wanted skill
To value such a woman at her worth!
Properly the instructed criticize
"What's here, you simpleton have tossed to take
"Its chance i' the gutter? This a daub, indeed?
"Why, 't is a Rafael that you kicked to rags!"
Perhaps so: some prefer the pure design:
Give me my gorge of colour, glut of gold
In a glory round the Virgin made for me!
Titian's the man, not Monk Angelico
Who traces you some timid chalky ghost
That turns the church into a charnel: ay,
Just such a pencil might depict my wife!
She,—since she, also, would not change herself,—
Why could not she come in some heart-shaped cloud,
Rainbowed about with riches, royalty
Rimming her round, as round the tintless lawn

2112 *MS* 'Tis I wanted skill>'Tis myself want skill 2113 *MS* worth,— 2114 *MS* [ ]>Myself, you the 2115 *MS* the>you 2116, 2117 *MS* {no quotation marks at beginnings of lines} 2116 *MS* It's *MS* in *MS* This he calls a daub?>Dirty a daub indeed? 2117 *MS* he has kicked>this you kick 2118 *MS* design 2122 *MS* tintless chalky 2124 *MS* should> might 2125 {not found in *MS*} 2126 *MS* {no comma} 2128 *MS* Round her, as runs a selvage, cloth of gold,—>Rimming her round, as round the feeble lawn

2117 *Rafael*: i.e. a great masterpiece by the famous Renaissance painter Raphael (1483–1520); in particular one of his beautiful Madonnas, whose purity and grace are like Pompilia's. Cf. VI. 406 n. The violence of the image is extraordinary: the canvas of the beautiful painting kicked to pieces.

2120 *glory*: partly with the sense 'aureole, halo'; cf. II. 398.

2121 *Titian's . . . Monk Angelico*: Guido prefers the complex, worldly, richly-coloured sensuousness of Titian (1477–1576) to the idealized, highly religious style of the Dominican monk Fra Angelico (1387–1455). This contrast anticipates that between the *femme fatale* Lucrezia Borgia, whom Guido would like as his wife, and the saintly Pompilia, whom he says he loathes. Browning himself rejected what he saw as overvaluations of Fra Angelico's work by critics like Alexis François Rio, and often preferred the later to the earlier Renaissance: see 'Fra Lippo Lippi', and David J. DeLaura, 'The Context of Browning's Painter Poems', PMLA 95 (1980), 367–88.

2128 *tintless lawn*: colourless fine linen.

Guardingly runs the selvage cloth of gold?
I would have left the faint fine gauze untouched,
Needle-worked over with its lily and rose,
Let her bleach unmolested in the midst,
Chill that selected solitary spot
Of quietude she pleased to think was life:
Purity, pallor grace the lawn no doubt
When there's the costly bordure to unthread
And make again an ingot: but what's grace
When you want meat and drink and clothes and fire?
A tale comes to my mind that's apposite—
Possibly true, probably false, a truth
Such as all truths we live by, Cardinal!
'T is said, a certain ancestor of mine
Followed—whoever was the potentate,
To Paynimrie, and in some battle, broke
Through more than due allowance of the foe,
And, risking much his own life, saved the lord's.
Battered and bruised, the Emperor scrambles up,

2129 *MS* Runs for a guard>Guardingly runs 2130 *MS* [?ores ?rose] *MS* alone,>untouched, 2131 {not found in *MS*} 2132 *MS* stand 2133 *MS* Keep *2134 *MS 1868 1872* life: *1888 1889* life. 2136 *MS* the bordure> beside the bordure *MS* one unthreads 2137 *MS* makes 2138 *MS* {beginning of fo. 323} 2143 *MS* Followed whoever 2145 *MS 1868* {no comma} 2146 *MS* And saved the lord's life, risking much his own. *MS* his>the 2147 *MS* bruised the

2129 *selvage . . . gold*: border, edging, made of gold cloth. Johnson defines selvage as 'the edge of cloth where it is closed by complicating the threads'; its etymology is from 'self' + 'edge', after the equivalent early mod. Dutch *selfegghe*: OED². 'Cloth of gold' echoes *Antony and Cleopatra*, II. ii. 199 (cf. V. 407 n.), and is an image of the wealth Guido hoped to get with Pompilia.

2130 *faint fine gauze*: thin white material—a synonym for 'tintless lawn' (2128).

2131 *its . . . rose*: i.e. its tedious symbols of purity and beauty; also a poetic cliché, both Latin and Italian, for the colour-combination of white and read, e.g. a beauty's cheeks and lips.

2132 *bleach*: turn white, become colourless and pure.

2136 *bordure*: = border; repeating the image of the selvage cloth of gold (2129). Strictly a 'bordure' is the heraldic term for the edging of a shield or an escutcheon.

2144 *Paynimrie*: i.e. the land of the paynims (pagans), i.e. the Holy Land. A generalized term used to refer to those lands in dispute between Christians and Saracens at the time of the Crusades.

Rubs his eyes and looks round and sees my sire,
Picks a furze-sprig from out his hauberk-joint,
(Token how near the ground went majesty)
And says "Take this, and if thou get safe home,
"Plant the same in thy garden-ground to grow:
"Run thence an hour in a straight line, and stop:
"Describe a circle round (for central point)
"The furze aforesaid, reaching every way
"The length of that hour's run: I give it thee,—
"The central point, to build a castle there,
"The space circumjacent, for fit demesne,
"The whole to be thy children's heritage,—
"Whom, for thy sake, bid thou wear furze on cap!"
Those are my arms: we turned the furze a tree
To show more, and the greyhound tied thereto,
Straining to start, means swift and greedy both;
He stands upon a triple mount of gold—
By Jove, then, he's escaping from true gold

2149 *MS* Then picks>Picks *MS* ^out^ 2150 *MS* (Witness>(Token *MS* ^near^ *MS* was 2151 *MS* says, *1868* and, *MS* []>get *MS* safe home again, 2152–60 *MS* {no quotation marks at beginnings of lines} 2152 *MS* gardenground 2153 *MS* stop, 2154 *MS* round, for *MS* point, 2157 *MS* on>there, 2158 *MS* With the surrounding>The circumjacent *1868* The circumjacent *MS 1868* space, for 2160 *MS* my 2161–7 {not found in *MS*} 2163 *Yale 1* both,>both;

2149 *furze-sprig*: a piece of gorse.

hauberk-joint: i.e. a gap in his chain mail, his armour.

2161–4 *Those . . . gold*: Browning acquired these details from a small watercolour drawing of the Franceschini coat of arms made by his friend Seymour Kirkup and subsequently sent to him. The sketch is annotated in Kirkup's hand *Arme Franceschini Famiglia Aretina*, and *Da un MS Priorista Aretino esistente presso la famiglia Albergotti* ('from a manuscript record of the Priori of Arezzo preserved by the Albergotti family'). It is dated July 1868, which suggests how late in the process of composition it had come into Browning's hands: see our Vol. VII, p. xxxiii. Browning pasted the drawing on the front inside cover of OYB.

The drawing shows 'a triple mount of gold'—a conventional mountain, comprised of three small rounded shapes—on top of which is a straight-stemmed tree with bushy foliage at the top. The dog tied to the tree is leaping and straining to get away from it, its front paws off the ground, its neck secured to the tree by a leash. The interpretation of the design's significance given here is, of course, Browning's invention. In connection with this coat of arms, see also XII. 784, 822–4 nn.

And trying to arrive at empty air!
Aha! the fancy never crossed my mind!
My father used to tell me, and subjoin
"As for the castle, that took wings and flew:
"The broad lands,—why, to traverse them to-day
"Scarce tasks my gouty feet, and in my prime
"I doubt not I could stand and spit so far:
"But for the furze, boy, fear no lack of that,
"So long as fortune leaves one field to grub!
"Wherefore, hurra for furze and loyalty!"
What may I mean, where may the lesson lurk?
"Do not bestow on man, by way of gift,
"Furze without land for framework,—vaunt no grace
"Of purity, no furze-sprig of a wife,
"To me, i' the thick of battle for my bread,
"Without some better dowry,—gold will do!"
No better gift than sordid muck? Yes, Sirs!
Many more gifts much better. Give them me!
O those Olimpias bold, those Biancas brave,

2170–5 *MS* {no quotation marks at beginnings of lines} 2171 *MS 1868* Would task *MS 1868* though in 2173 *MS* that,>that *Yale 1* that>that, 2174 *MS* {beginning of fo. 324} *MS* grub, 2175 *MS 1868* {no comma} 2176 *MS* do>may 2177 *MS 1868* {no commas} 2178–81 *MS* {no quotation marks at beginnings of lines} 2178 *MS 1868* some substantial framework,—grace 2179 *MS 1868* a furze-sprig 2181 *MS 1868* house and land!" *MS* []>house 2182, 2183 *MS* {lines added later} 2182 *MS 1868* other gift *MS* [ ]?>muck? *MS 1868 1872* Sir! 2183 *MS 1868* more and much 2184 *MS* Olimpias,>Olimpias bold, *MS* brave

2173–4 *But . . . grub*: i.e. 'but so long as we have even one field to grub (dig), we'll have plenty of furze'. A sardonic comment: furze or gorse is worthless, and grows on poor-quality land. The Franceschini family, loyal to their superiors, are left with their aristocratic symbol and pitifully little else.

2180 *i' . . . bread*: i.e. struggling to earn a living.

2182–3 *No . . . me!*: i.e. 'I don't just want a submissive wife with a good dowry ("sordid muck"); I want much more.' As he goes on to explain in the following lines, he wants a passionate, amoral, highly sexual woman, submissive to his desires, but his match in cruelty and ruthlessness.

2184 *Olimpias . . . Biancas*: Guido is probably thinking of Olympia Pamfili (1594–1656)—already mentioned at IV. 1236–7—the sister-in-law of Pope Innocent X, who is supposed to have been beautiful, avaricious, and power-hungry. She is reputed to have engineered Innocent X's rise to the papacy, and to have been his mistress. The

That brought a husband power worth Ormuz' wealth!
Cried "Thou being mine, why, what but thine am I?
"Be thou to me law, right, wrong, heaven and hell!
"Let us blend souls, blent, thou in me, to bid
"Two bodies work one pleasure! What are these
"Called king, priest, father, mother, stranger, friend?
"They fret thee or they frustrate? Give the word—
"Be certain they shall frustrate nothing more!
"And who is this young florid foolishness
"That holds thy fortune in his pigmy clutch,
"—Being a prince and potency, forsooth!—
"He hesitates to let the trifle go?
"Let me but seal up eye, sing ear to sleep
"Sounder than Samson,—pounce thou on the prize

2185 *MS* [ ]>wills *1868* will *MS* Ormuz *MS* [ ]>wealth! 2186 *MS* why what *Yale 1* why what>why, what *MS* am I but thine?>but thine am I? 2187–205 *MS* {no quotation marks at beginnings of lines} 2188 *MS 1868* souls, be thou in me to 2190 *MS* king and priest, called stranger or called friend?>king priest, father mother, stranger friend? *2194 *1888* ortune *DC BrU* ortune>fortune *1889* fortune 2196 *MS* And hesitates *1868 1872* "And hesitates 2198 *MS* Sampson,—

---

other woman he may have in mind is the even more notorious Bianca Cappello (1548–89), the long-term mistress of the Grand Duke Francesco. She is supposed to have connived in her first husband's murder, to have faked the birth of a son, to have been a practitioner of the dark arts, and to have been the perpetrator of any other amount of treachery, craft, and crime. There are biographies of both women in T. A. Trollope's *A Decade of Italian Women*, 2 vols. (London, 1859), which may be one of Browning's sources for his knowledge here, though Bianca Cappello is notorious from other retellings of her story.

2185 *Ormuz'*: in the seventeenth century, Ormuz (near the entrance to the Persian gulf) was famous for its wealth.

2186–205 "*Thou . . . indeed!*": this sexual fantasy is one of the high points of the monologue. Guido imagines himself in thrall to some young prince ('this young florid foolishness', 'a prince and potency'), who holds his 'fortune' (metaphorically speaking, his future or fate) in his hands. The wife Guido fantasizes will act like Delilah for him: she will seduce the young prince, until he has surrendered the 'fortune' or 'prize' to her. She will then let the 'fortune' 'slip from off' her breast, in the room where, in the shadows, Guido waits to snatch it up. In voyeuristic mode, Guido will also wait to see what else 'Delilah dares do' (2202): i.e. how far she will go sexually with the young prince. The resounding answer is that she will go no further: she will prefer the mature Guido in middle age to the callow prince, for her only wish is to act as her husband's 'call-bird', i.e. his decoy-bird, leading lesser birds (lesser men) into her husband's power. 'Délilah' here is stressed on the first syllable, like Milton's Dálila in *Samson Agonistes*; cf. spelling in *MS*.

"Shall slip from off my breast, and down couch-side,
"And on to floor, and far as my lord's feet—
"Where he stands in the shadow with the knife,
"Waiting to see what Delilah dares do!
"Is the youth fair? What is a man to me
"Who am thy call-bird? Twist his neck—my dupe's,—
"Then take the breast shall turn a breast indeed!"
Such women are there; and they marry whom?
Why, when a man has gone and hanged himself
Because of what he calls a wicked wife,—
See, if the very turpitude bemoaned
Prove not mere excellence the fool ignores!
His monster is perfection,—Circe, sent
Straight from the sun, with wand the idiot blames
As not an honest distaff to spin wool!
O thou Lucrezia, is it long to wait
Yonder where all the gloom is in a glow
With thy suspected presence?—virgin yet,
Virtuous again, in face of what's to teach—

2199 *MS* breasts *MS 1868 1872* couch-side 2201 *MS 1868* sword 2202 *MS* Dalila *MS* do: 2204 *MS* neck,— *MS* dupe,— 2205 *MS* {beginning of fo. 325} *MS* breasts *MS* to breasts 2207 *MS* [ ]>Why, 2208 *MS* Because he had, he says, a worthless wife,—>Because of what he calls a wicked wife,— 2209 *MS* this monster that he howls about>the turpitude he makes his moan *1868* the turpitude, he makes his moan, 2210 *MS 1868* Be *MS* ignores,— 2211 *MS* perfection, Circe sent *Yale 1* Circe>Circe, *1868* perfection, 2212 *MS 1868* rod 2216 *MS* presence,— 2217 *MS 1868* {no comma} *MS* what shall be—>what must be—

2209 *turpitude*: wickedness, depravity.

2211 *Circe*: the witch or sorceress Circe lived on the island of Aeaea. She is 'sent straight from the sun' because she is the child of the sun-god Helios. In the *Odyssey*, bk. X, when she encounters Odysseus' men, she first gives them a potion to drink, and then (in Pope's translation) 'Instant her circling wand the Goddess waves, / To hogs transforms 'em, and the Sty receives'—they have become pigs with the minds of men: see *Odyssey*, X. 238–41.

2214–20 *Lucrezia . . . be!*: though seen as a relatively innocent figure by modern historians, Lucrezia Borgia (1480–1519) is traditionally one of the most notorious figures of the Renaissance, infamous for wickedness and licentiousness, and for sharing in the plots and murders instigated by her father, Pope Alexander VI, and her brother Cesare Borgia. She is alleged to have committed incest with both father and brother, and this is the 'sin unimagined, unimaginable' that excites Guido here. Guido wants to be Lucrezia's new 'burning bridegroom', replacing her brother ('thy Borgia's self'), because he

Sin unimagined, unimaginable,—
I come to claim my bride,—thy Borgia's self
Not half the burning bridegroom I shall be!
Cardinal, take away your crucifix!
Abate, leave my lips alone,—they bite!
Vainly you try to change what should not change,
And shall not. I have bared, you bathe my heart—
It grows the stonier for your saving dew!
You steep the substance, you would lubricate,
In waters that but touch to petrify!

You too are petrifactions of a kind:
Move not a muscle that shows mercy. Rave
Another twelve hours, every word were waste!
I thought you would not slay impenitence,
But teased, from men you slew, contrition first,—
I thought you had a conscience. Cardinal,
You know I am wronged!—wronged, say, and wronged, maintain.
Was this strict inquisition made for blood

2219 *MS* My bride I come to claim thy>I come to claim my bride thy 2220 *MS* Bridegroom 2222 *MS 1868* alone, 2223 *MS* 'Tis no use trying to change, what *1868* 'Tis vain you change, what 2224 *MS 1868 1872* cannot. *MS* bared the heart, you bathe— *MS* steep—>bathe— 2229 *MS* mercy,—rave *1868 1872* mercy; rave 2230 *MS* word's in waste. 2231 impenitence,— 2232 *MS 1868* Teazed first contrition from the man you slew,— 2233 *MS* {beginning of fo. 326} 2234 *MS 1868* wronged maintain. 2235 *MS* there this>this strict

feels that he is an even more appropriate match for her wicked nature. Browning's sense of the evil of the Borgia family would have started with his childhood reading of Nathaniel Lee's *Caesar Borgia*, the first play he ever read: see II. 939–40 n.

2222 *Abate . . . bite!*: cf. 608–9 n. In true wolf-like fashion, Guido threatens to bite the Abate's hand if he persists in trying to make him kiss the crucifix.

2225 *saving dew*: i.e. the 'saving dew' of grace and Christian teaching. As Ohio points out, dew is a common image in the Old Testament of the Lord's favour: cf. Hos. 14: 5. The allusion might also be to the 'saving dew' of manna in Exod. 16, when God provides for his people, but their hearts still grow hard against him.

2226 *lubricate*: make soft.

2234 *wronged . . . maintain*: wronged, I say, and wronged, I maintain.

2235–7 *Was . . . College?*: i.e. 'Were you so strict in enquiring into spilt blood when you were first made a cardinal?' Cf. Ps. 9: 12: 'When he [God] maketh inquisition for blood, he remembereth them: he forgetteth not the cry of the humble'.

When first you showed us scarlet on your back,
Called to the College? Your straightforward way
To your legitimate end,—I think it passed
Over a scantling of heads brained, hearts broke,
Lives trodden into dust! How otherwise?
Such was the way o' the world, and so you walked.
Does memory haunt your pillow? Not a whit.
God wills you never pace your garden-path,
One appetizing hour ere dinner-time,
But your intrusion there treads out of life
A universe of happy innocent things:
Feel you remorse about that damsel-fly
Which buzzed so near your mouth and flapped your face?
You blotted it from being at a blow:
It was a fly, you were a man, and more,
Lord of created things, so took your course.
Manliness, mind,—these are things fit to save,
Fit to brush fly from: why, because I take
My course, must needs the Pope kill me?—kill you!
You! for this instrument, he throws away,
Is strong to serve a master, and were yours
To have and hold and get much good from out!
The Pope who dooms me needs must die next year;

2236 *MS* red upon 2237 *MS 1868* That straightforward 2238 *MS 1868* that legitimate 2240 *MS 1868* dust,—how 2241 *MS 1868* is *MS* of *MS 1868* walk: 2243 *MS 1868* {no comma} 2244 *MS 1868* {no comma} 2246 *MS* An 2248 *MS 1868* face, 2249 *MS 1868* blow? 2252 *MS* save;>save, 2253 *MS* To brush the *MS* {no comma} 2254 *MS* me? Kill you? *Yale 1* me? Kill you!—>me?! kill you— {RB probably intended to transpose the dash and not the exclamation mark, which would have given: me? Kill you!—>me?—kill you! 2255 *MS 1868* Because this *MS 1868* {no commas} 2256 *MS 1868* master: it 2257 *1868* such good 2258 *1868 1872* me,

2239 *a scantling of*: i.e. a few, a modicum.

2247 *damsel-fly*: a lovely blue or green fly, similar to a dragonfly, but more slender and with a slower speed of flight. Cf. the description in *Sordello*, I. 908–10: 'before him, aye aloof, / Flittered in the cool some azure damsel-fly, / Born of the simmering quiet, there to die'.

2254 *kill you!*: i.e. in effect, kill you also: see next n.

2255 *for . . . away*: i.e. this instrument (Guido himself) that he (the Pope) throws away.

I'll tell you how the chances are supposed
For his successor: first the Chamberlain,
Old San Cesario,—Colloredo, next,—
Then, one, two, three, four, I refuse to name;
After these, comes Altieri; then come you—
Seventh on the list you come, unless . . . ha, ha,
How can a dead hand give a friend a lift?
Are you the person to despise the help
O' the head shall drop in pannier presently?
So a child seesaws on or kicks away
The fulcrum-stone that's all the sage requires
To fit his lever to and move the world.
Cardinal, I adjure you in God's name,
Save my life, fall at the Pope's feet, set forth
Things your own fashion, not in words like these
Made for a sense like yours who apprehend!
Translate into the Court-conventional
"Count Guido must not die, is innocent!

2260 *MS* Chamberlain— *Yale 1* Chamberlain—>Chamberlain, 2262 *MS* {beginning of fo. 327} *MS 1868* name, 2263 *MS* After these, Altieri,— 2264 *MS 1868* are, unless . . *1872* unless . . 2265 *MS* man> hand 2267 *MS* Of *MS* panier 2268 *MS* child kicks away the leverage>child seesaws on or kicks away 2269 *MS* {line added later} 2270 *MS* Wherewith the sage's lever moves>To fit f[ ]>To fit his lever with and move 2271 *MS* name 2275 *MS* [ ]>court- *1868 1872* court-conventional *2276 *1888* Count *DC BrU* Count>"Count *1889* "Count *MS* innocent,

2261–5 *San Cesario . . . lift?*: Leonardo Colloredo and Paluzzi degli Albertoni (who took the name Altieri) were prominent cardinals, very different in character, but both potential popes. Colloredo, a devout and learned Oratorian, was made a cardinal in 1686 by Innocent XI; at the conclave of 1691 he played an important role in the election of Innocent XII and subsequently became one of his close advisers. Altieri was made a cardinal earlier, in 1664, by Alexander VII. Under Clement X (1670–6) he was in charge of all ecclesiastical affairs of state, and is often accused of accumulating offices and riches for himself and his family. San Cesario is one of the *tituli* to which cardinals are named; incumbents include Baronius and John Paul II. The natural reading is that 'Old San Cesario' is the Chamberlain, but at XII. 47 Browning seems to take it as an actual name. How exactly, we might wonder, is Guido proposing to help Cardinal Acciaiuoli to the papacy. Simply through influence? Or is he actually proposing some murders to clear away opponents?

2269–70 *sage . . . world*: alluding to the famous saying of the Greek inventor and mathematician Archimedes: 'Give me a place to stand and I will move the earth.'

2275 *Court-conventional*: i.e. the correct idiom of the Papal Court.

"Fair, be assured! But what an he were foul,
"Blood-drenched and murder-crusted head to foot?
"Spare one whose death insults the Emperor,
"Nay, outrages the Louis you so love!
"He has friends who will avenge him; enemies
"Who will hate God now with impunity,
"Missing the old coercive: would you send
"A soul straight to perdition, dying frank
"An atheist?" Go and say this, for God's sake!
—Why, you don't think I hope you'll say one word?
Neither shall I persuade you from your stand
Nor you persuade me from my station: take
Your crucifix away, I tell you twice!

Come, I am tired of silence! Pause enough!
You have prayed: I have gone inside my soul
And shut its door behind me: 't is your torch
Makes the place dark: the darkness let alone
Grows tolerable twilight: one may grope
And get to guess at length and breadth and depth.
What is this fact I feel persuaded of—
This something like a foothold in the sea,
Although Saint Peter's bark scuds, billow-borne,

2277–85 *MS* {no quotation marks at beginnings of lines} 2279 *MS* Save 2280 *MS* And outrages *1868* "And outrages 2281 *MS* him,— 2282 *MS* Who *1868* "Who *MS 1868* hate the church now *MS 1868* {no comma} 2283 *MS* then you send 2285 *MS* atheist." 2287 *MS* Nor I>Neither shall I *MS* stand—nor you>stand 2288 *MS* Me from my station—take it from my mouth>Nor you persuade me from my station—take *Yale 1* station—> station: 2289 *MS* ^away,^ 2290 *MS* {no new paragraph} 2292 *MS* {beginning of fo. 328} 2293 *MS 1868* dark,— 2294 *MS 1868* twilight,— 2296 *MS* of

2279–80 *Emperor . . . Louis*: i.e. the major Catholic powers: the Holy Roman Emperor, Leopold I, and the King of France, Louis XIV.

2283 *Missing . . . coercive*: missing the restraint (that stops them being atheists and murderers): the sense that the Church is on their side.

2290 *Come . . . enough!*: a long silence precedes this line, a break in the monologue: the Cardinal and the Abate have been praying; Guido has gone inside himself. Browning manages the monologue's climax in highly theatrical terms.

2298–9 *Although . . . first?*: i.e. 'although the Church (the "boat" captained by the Pope—St Peter) refuses to rescue me from the death-sentence'. Cf. Matt. 14: 24–33.

Leaves me to founder where it flung me first?
Spite of your splashing, I am high and dry!
God takes his own part in each thing He made;
Made for a reason, He conserves his work,
Gives each its proper instinct of defence.
My lamblike wife could neither bark nor bite,
She bleated, bleated, till for pity pure
The village roused up, ran with pole and prong
To the rescue, and behold the wolf's at bay!
Shall he try bleating?—or take turn or two,
Since the wolf owns some kinship with the fox,
And, failing to escape the foe by craft,
Give up attempt, die fighting quietly?
The last bad blow that strikes fire in at eye
And on to brain, and so out, life and all,
How can it but be cheated of a pang
If, fighting quietly, the jaws enjoy
One re-embrace in mid back-bone they break,
After their weary work thro' the foe's flesh?
That's the wolf-nature. Don't mistake my trope!
A Cardinal so qualmish? Eminence,
My fight is figurative, blows i' the air,
Brain-war with powers and principalities,
Spirit-bravado, no real fisticuffs!

2299 *MS* Bidding me founder>Leaves me to founder 2301 *MS 1868 1872* he 2302 *MS 1868 1872* he *MS* work[?:]>work, 2305 *MS* 'till *MS* pity's sake,>pity pure, *1868 1872* pure, 2306 *MS 1868 1872* roused it, *MS* staff>pole 2307 *MS* wolf 2309 *MS 1868 1872* to kinship 2310 *MS 1868* And failing *MS 1868 1872* by these, 2312 *MS* ^last^ 2314 *MS* []>How 2315 *MS 1868* While, 2316 *MS 1868* Their *MS* backbone *MS* {no comma} 2317 *1868* foes' *MS* flesh. 2319 *MS 1868* The Cardinal is qualmish! 2321 *MS* {beginning of fo. 329} 2322 *MS* not>no *MS* fisticuffs.

2308 *turn*: i.e. an evasive turn.

2312 *last bad blow*: i.e. the death blow (dealt by the person killing the wolf).

2316 *re-embrace*: i.e. joining together.

2319 *qualmish*: i.e. nervous. Acciaiuoli has started back, assuming that Guido is literally going to attack him.

2321 *powers and principalities*: i.e. spiritual forces. A phrase in the Pauline epistles: cf. Rom. 8: 38, Eph. 6: 12, etc.

I shall not presently, when the knock comes,
Cling to this bench nor claw the hangman's face,
No, trust me! I conceive worse lots than mine.
Whether it be, the old contagious fit
And plague o' the prison have surprised me too,
The appropriate drunkenness of the death-hour
Crept on my sense, kind work o' the wine and myrrh,—
I know not,—I begin to taste my strength,
Careless, gay even. What's the worth of life?
The Pope's dead now, my murderous old man,
For Tozzi told me so: and you, forsooth—
Why, you don't think, Abate, do your best,
You'll live a year more with that hacking cough
And blotch of crimson where the cheek's a pit?
Tozzi has got you also down in book!
Cardinal, only seventh of seventy near,
Is not one called Albano in the lot?
Go eat your heart, you'll never be a Pope!
Inform me, is it true you left your love,
A Pucci, for promotion in the church?
She's more than in the church,—in the churchyard!
Plautilla Pucci, your affianced bride,

2324 *MS* flea *1868* flee 2326 *MS 1868* {no comma} 2327 *MS* of 2329 *1868* Creep *MS 1868* the work *MS* myrrh, 2331 *MS 1868* even: what's 2332 *MS* pope is dead, my *1868* Pope is dead, my 2335 *MS* three years *Yale 1* three years>a year 2337 *MS 1868* book. 2338 *MS* seventy two, 2339 {not found in *MS*} 2341 *MS* me if 'tis 2342 *MS* Church? 2343 *MS* Church,— *MS* churchyard; 2344 *MS* {no commas}

2329 *wine and myrrh*: i.e. a sedative given to those being executed. The allusion is to Mark 15: 23, where Jesus is offered 'wine mingled with myrrh' before being crucified. Presumably Guido speaks metaphorically here, aligning himself with the suffering Christ.

2332 *dead now*: i.e. as good as dead.

2333 *Tozzi*: the Pope's physician: cf. IX. 1268 n.

2338 *seventy near*: ideally there were seventy cardinals in the Sacred College that elected the new pope. At the time of Innocent XII's death in 1700, there were sixty-six cardinals to elect his successor.

2339 *Albano*: Guido is prophetic: Cardinal Giovanni Francesco Albani was elected as the next pope in November 1700, taking the name Clement XI.

2344 *Plautilla Pucci*: Plautilla Pucci is Browning's (or Guido's) invention. There is no mention of such a fiancée in the brief biographies of Acciaiuoli we have been able to consult.

Has dust now in the eyes that held the love,—
And Martinez, suppose they make you Pope,
Stops that with *veto*,—so, enjoy yourself!
I see you all reel to the rock, you waves—
Some forthright, some describe a sinuous track,
Some, crested brilliantly, with heads above,
Some in a strangled swirl sunk who knows how,
But all bound whither the main-current sets,
Rockward, an end in foam for all of you!
What if I be o'ertaken, pushed to the front
By all you crowding smoother souls behind,
And reach, a minute sooner than was meant,
The boundary whereon I break to mist?
Go to! the smoothest safest of you all,
Most perfect and compact wave in my train,
Spite of the blue tranquillity above,
Spite of the breadth before of lapsing peace

2345 *MS* eyes, 2347 *MS* veto,— *MS* so enjoy 2350 *MS 1868* Some crested, brilliantly with 2351 *MS* {beginning of fo. 330} 2353 *MS* you. 2354 *MS* It happens I am oertaken, *1868* am 2355 *MS* By you, the crowd of 2357 *MS 1868* boundary, *MS* mist. 2358 *MS* my train,>you all, 2359 *MS* ^wave^ 2360 *MS* tranquility 2361 *MS* ^of the^ **MS* breadth of peacefulness before>breadth of lapsing peace before *1868 1872* peace *1888* peace, *DC BrU* peace,>peace *1889* peace

2346–7 *Martinez . . . veto*: in 1694 George Adam Count von Martinitz was appointed as the Emperor Leopold I's representative in Rome. He was devoted to his master and to absolutist ideas of his powers, and these factors, combined with his arrogance and an aggressive attitude towards protocol, made him the most hated ambassador in Rome: 'In the end this strange diplomatist allowed himself in his blindness to be betrayed into adopting an unbecoming and offensive attitude even towards the person of the Pope himself. After that he was no longer received in audience': Pastor, xxxii (1940), 671. Browning's historical research inspires Guido's remark here. At the conclave to elect the new pope in 1700, the Emperor tried to have Cardinal Acciaiuoli excluded, and later, when he was proposed for pope, Empire-inclined cardinals opposed his elevation. By then, however, Martinitz had been replaced as ambassador by Count Leopold von Lamberg. Had he still been in Rome, he would undoubtedly have acted against Acciaiuoli as best he could, though he had no formal power of veto.

2361 *breadth . . . peace*: the expanse of peaceful ocean, i.e. the long years ahead, apparently untroubled. 'Lapsing' is used of water to mean 'gliding, smooth-flowing, dropping'; cf. *Roba di Roma*, ii. 94: 'Rome is the city of fountains. Wherever one goes he hears the pleasant sound of lapsing water.'

Where broods the halcyon and the fish leaps free,
Will presently begin to feel the prick
At lazy heart, the push at torpid brain,
Will rock vertiginously in turn, and reel,
And, emulative, rush to death like me.
Later or sooner by a minute then,
So much for the untimeliness of death!
And, as regards the manner that offends,
The rude and rough, I count the same for gain.
Be the act harsh and quick! Undoubtedly
The soul's condensed and, twice itself, expands
To burst thro' life, by alternation due,
Into the other state whate'er it prove.
You never know what life means till you die:
Even throughout life, 't is death that makes life live,
Gives it whatever the significance.
For see, on your own ground and argument,
Suppose life had no death to fear, how find
A possibility of nobleness
In man, prevented daring any more?
What's love, what's faith without a worst to dread?
Lack-lustre jewelry! but faith and love
With death behind them bidding do or die—
Put such a foil at back, the sparkle's born!

2362 *MS* halcyon, 2365 *MS* Vertiginously rock *MS* {no commas} 2366 *MS 1868* me: 2368 *MS 1868* death,— 2369 *MS* his>regards the 2370 *MS 1868* gain— 2373 *MS* Bursts right>To burst *MS 1868 1872* in alternation 2376 *MS* through *Yale 1* through our>throughout 2379 *MS* {beginning of fo. 331} 2381 *MS* {no comma} *Yale 1* {comma added} 2382 *MS* the>a 2383 *MS 1868* jewelry;

2362 *halcyon*: kingfisher.

2369–70 *manner*. . . *rough*: i.e. the rough execution by guillotine.

2385 *foil*: 'a thin leaf of some metal placed under a precious stone to increase its brilliancy': OED[2]. With the image here, cf. Marlowe, *Jew of Malta*, II. iii. 55: 'What sparkle does it [the diamond] give without a foil?' Cf. also *Richard II*, I. iii. 265–7.

From out myself how the strange colours come!
Is there a new rule in another world?
Be sure I shall resign myself: as here
I recognized no law I could not see,
There, what I see, I shall acknowledge too:
On earth I never took the Pope for God,
In heaven I shall scarce take God for the Pope.
Unmanned, remanned: I hold it probable—
With something changeless at the heart of me
To know me by, some nucleus that's myself:
Accretions did it wrong? Away with them—
You soon shall see the use of fire!

Till when,
All that was, is; and must forever be.
Nor is it in me to unhate my hates,—
I use up my last strength to strike once more
Old Pietro in the wine-house-gossip-face,
To trample underfoot the whine and wile
Of beast Violante,—and I grow one gorge
To loathingly reject Pompilia's pale
Poison my hasty hunger took for food.
A strong tree wants no wreaths about its trunk,
No cloying cups, no sickly sweet of scent,

2391 *MS* In>On 2393 *Yale 1* Unmanned,>Unmade, *MS 1868* remade: 2397 *MS* fire,—till when *MS* {no new paragraph} 2398 {not found in *MS*} 2399 *MS* is, *1868* for ever *MS* be— 2400 *MS* un[ ]>unhate 2403 *MS* out of life,>underfoot 2404 *MS* That>Of that *1868* Of that 2407 *MS* wreathes *MS* root>trunk *MS* {no comma} 2408 *MS* {beginning of fo. 332} *MS* [ ]>No *etc.* *MS* stars,

2386 *strange colours*: see previous n.. 'Faith and love', backed by the 'foil' of death, shine all the more brightly. Guido's character is partly composed of their opposite, unbelief and hate: backed by the 'foil' of death these create 'strange colours'—Titian-like splendours perhaps, or at least lurid, strange tones. For commentary on this, and the ending generally, see Daniel Karlin, *Browning's Hatreds* (Oxford, 1993), 235–8.

2407 *wreaths*: i.e. tangles of ivy.

2408 *cups*: i.e. flowers (of the ivy). Here Guido presents the traditional image of the tree (the man) with the good woman curled about him (like ivy). He rejects its sentimentalism.

But sustenance at root, a bucketful.
How else lived that Athenian who died so,
Drinking hot bull's blood, fit for men like me?
I lived and died a man, and take man's chance,
Honest and bold: right will be done to such.

Who are these you have let descend my stair?
Ha, their accursed psalm! Lights at the sill!
Is it "Open" they dare bid you? Treachery!
Sirs, have I spoken one word all this while
Out of the world of words I had to say?
Not one word! All was folly—I laughed and mocked!
Sirs, my first true word, all truth and no lie,
Is—save me notwithstanding! Life is all!
I was just stark mad,—let the madman live
Pressed by as many chains as you please pile!
Don't open! Hold me from them! I am yours,
I am the Granduke's—no, I am the Pope's!

2409 *MS* bucket-ful— 2410 *MS* [ ]>How *MS* {no comma} 2411 *MS* *1868* bull's-blood, 2413 *MS* the bold.>to such: 2414 *MS* {no new paragraph} *MS* Whom *MS* ascend *MS* the>my 2415 *MS* door sill 2416 *MS* "open" *MS* [ ]>Treachery! 2417 *MS* Judge,>Sirs, 2418 *MS* Of words a world to say? I laughed and mocked.>Out of the world of words I had to say? 2419 *MS* {line added later} *MS* word,—all *MS* mocked. 2420 *MS* Cardinal,>Sirs, *MS* ^true^ *MS* word all *MS* lie 2421 *MS* all— 2422 *MS* mad, 2423 *MS* Under>Pressed by *MS* can 2424 *MS* open—hold *MS* them, 2425 *MS* The Pope's, God's,>Am the Pope's! Cardinal,—Abate,—God,—>I am the Granduke's—no, I am the Pope's!

2410–11 *Athenian . . . blood*: Themistocles (*c*.524–459 BC), the Athenian hero, one of the greatest men of his time, played a crucial role in defeating the Persian invaders of Greece. Probably he died naturally, but a popular legend says that he committed suicide by drinking bull's blood in order to trick the Persian king into not invading Greece a second time: see Diodorus Siculus, XI. 58; Aristophanes, *Knights*, 83–4. The image here is the apogee of Guido's cult of manliness.

2414 *Who . . . stair?* : the *Compagnia della Morte e della Misericordia* ('the Company of Death and Mercy') are arriving at the cell to escort Guido to his execution: see SS 19.

2425 *Granduke's . . . Pope's*: as Cook points out, Guido hesitates because he is finally acknowledging the Pope's legal jurisdiction: prior to this, he has kept insisting on the importance of the decision of the Florence court.

Abate,—Cardinal,—Christ,—Maria,—God, . . .
Pompilia, will you let them murder me?

2426 *MS* {line added later} *MS* Abate, Cardinal, Christ, Maria, God,—

2426–7 *Abate . . . me?*: the sheer panic of these last lines compares most obviously with the dying moments of Marlowe's Dr Faustus, but much debate has arisen as to whether the invocation to Pompilia signals a 'saving illumination' or just a spasm of fear. Early critics took the former view, restated by Langbaum: 'I see in [the invocation] Guido's recognition of Pompilia's goodness and his own evil, which suggests his moral regeneration': 'Is Guido Saved?', VP 10 (1972), 289–305 (289). This seems only sentimentalism to critics like A. K. Cook, William Buckler, and W. C. DeVane: 'I am inclined to believe . . . that no spark but abject terror disturbs the clod which is Guido': *Handbook*, 336. Browning's only known comment bypasses this debate. Discussing the relationship between history and imagination in the making of the poem, he says: 'For instance—in the last speech to which you refer [Book XI]—the *fact* is that the two ecclesiastics passed the night preceding his execution with Guido: and, knowing as he did the innocence of his wife, what so likely as that, in his last utterance of despair, *her* name, with an appeal to it, should suggest itself?': RB to F. J. Furnivall, 20 Feb. 1883: *Trumpeter*, 67.

INTRODUCTION TO BOOK XII

THE BOOK AND THE RING

IN the Old Yellow Book (Browning's major source), apart from the formal printed pleadings for and against Guido's innocence, there are three handwritten letters, all dated 22 February 1698, the day of Guido's execution. All three are addressed to Francesco Cencini, a lawyer in Florence. The first is by a person we already know, Giacinto Arcangeli, 'Procurator of the Poor', the speaker of Book VIII. The other two are also from Roman lawyers, Gaspero del Torto and Carlo Antonio Ugolinucci (neither mentioned elsewhere in OYB). All three men, however, seem to see Cencini as their 'patron' (Arcangeli and Ugolinucci refer to him explicitly as such). And each letter covers essentially the same ground: they inform Cencini of the Roman court's guilty verdict on Guido on Tuesday 18 February; they tell how Arcangeli appealed against this and sought for delay to prove Guido's 'clericate' (minor orders); and then how the Pope overruled any further delay on the evening of 21 February, by *Chirografo particulare* (special writ). All three lawyers are saddened by Guido's execution. Arcangeli laments his own shortcomings, 'my inability in offering the valid grounds'; del Torto notes that Franceschini was 'pitied by all gallant men, and his house has lost nothing in the matter of reputation'; Ugolinucci comments 'I will not tell your Excellency my own grief, because you yourself will be able to be a true witness of it.'[1] These three letters gave Browning a significant amount of information about the last week of the legal case, but they also suggested to him the format for his own ending: the three worldly epistles of Book XII.

The first epistle of Book XII (31–208) is spoken by a new minor character, the Venetian 'man of rank' who just happens to be in Rome for the Carnival. In this epistle Browning deploys the detailed information in the Secondary Source, paragraphs 19–23, about Guido's execution (information not available to him in OYB itself).[2] The account of the Venetian 'man of rank', in other words, serves to round off the basic plot. It gives us a vivid picture of the Piazza del Popolo decked out with

[1] OYB ccxxxv–ccxl (235–8). [2] See our Vol. VII, pp. 317–19.

palchetti (miniature grandstands), the crowds jostling at windows, Guido's procession to the place of execution, his demeanour on the scaffold, and his last speech to the crowd. At the same time, Browning advances his larger meaning through his depiction of this new character. The Venetian 'man of rank' recalls the Italian 'person of quality' who spoke 'Up at a Villa—Down in the City', or (within the poem) 'Tertium Quid'. He is essentially an aristocratic fop, obsessed with fun and gossip, the latest joke, his next bet. Browning gets a lot of humour out of sending up his character, but on the more serious side we notice that he is a sycophant of power and social hierarchy, a friend of Austria, a despiser of 'the mob', and nonchalant in his religious attitudes. He regards the Pope's decision to move the place of Guido's execution from the usual location, by Ponte Sant'Angelo, to the Piazza del Popolo, as a 'left-wing' gesture (147–8). Emphatically this man of mode is one of Browning's worldlings in the way he moves with airy indifference within the political and social status quo.

The second of the epistles, Arcangeli's to Cencini (239–88), is Browning's direct translation from the original Italian letter in the OYB. He makes a few small changes and additions to the original Italian, and ever so slightly (and mischievously) alters the phrasing in order to exaggerate its deferential tone, so tipping it over into the oily and unctuous. Then, however, he invents a secret codicil. The 'official' letter is for clients and fellow lawyers. In the racy second half of Arcangeli's letter (291–390) we meet again, in all his vivid rush and eloquence, the speaker of Book VIII. Arcangeli is maddened to have lost the legal case, annoyed at the Pope, envious of Cencini (who lives outside the papal jurisdiction), full of pride for a witticism of his son, and hoping against hope that losing the legal case will somehow ingratiate him with the Pope and advance his son's career. He is ever the optimist, but (as usual) he shows not a shred of feeling for the pity and pathos of the drama on which he has been professionally engaged.

The final epistle of Book XII (406–58, 647–750) is by the other lawyer, Giovanni Battista Bottini, who we know well from Book IX. Again, a strong worldly tone prevails. Bottini won the case, proved Guido's guilt, and so should be rejoicing in his victory, but in fact he is just as annoyed as Arcangeli. He feels that the case he had to prove was too simple, like 'shooting fish in a barrel' (a simile on which he produces his own variant—410–13). There was no room to show his own cleverness, and all he can do is look forward to his next case: suing Pompilia's estate on behalf of the Convent of St Mary Magdalene of the Convertites. Bottini was on Pompilia's side, now he will act against her—at last he will have a chance to show his virtuosity. As with Arcangeli's epistle, Browning is again following historical fact from OYB, but changing it to suit his own ends. It was Francesco Gambi (and not Bottini) who prosecuted this case, but they were lawyers with similar titles and similar roles—so this was perhaps a minor licence. In what was most probably a slip he conflates two Roman convents.[3] However, the essential fact that Browning has latched onto here was true, and clearly shocked him to some extent: shortly after Pompilia's death a Roman convent made a play to secure all her wealth on the grounds that she was a fallen woman. It seems highly appropriate that, at the head of their case, he should put his own unscrupulous Bottini.

It is at this point that the essential pattern becomes clear. Book XII is the epilogue to the whole work, the ending in which Browning draws together its larger themes, and then delivers his own abrupt verdict on the world and a brief explanation of the role of art. But the Book is primarily ironic, its irony grounded in the profundity of Browning's Protestant religious sensibility.

The three letter writers here, each in their way, show the heartlessness of worldly mentalities. To the Venetian 'man of rank', an idle visitor at Rome, the Franceschini case is a passing tourist diversion, nothing of significance. Arcangeli and Bottini are both, in different ways, annoyed at the case's outcome, have various sarcastic things to say about it, and about the Pope's verdict, but quickly turn back to the advance of their own careers. In fact their minds, like mice in a wheel, only move within the circle of their professional concerns and ambitions. For them the whole matter is either just a small triumph or minor set-back in the course of their careers, nothing like a religious drama of good and evil.

Browning brings out his essential ironic pattern by the extract from the sermon of Fra Celestino which he inserts into Bottini's letter (459–646). Fra Celestino, as we remember, was the Augustinian friar who attended at Pompilia's death-bed and who wrote a moving testimony of her 'good death' for the court (OYB lvii–f.). The sermon, however—quoted by Bottini with disgust—is entirely Browning's invention, his own development of a tone of voice he gleaned from OYB. Even late in the day, Browning seems to have conceived of a longer Book XII, in which, therefore, this sermon would have been less prominent. On 19 November 1868 he told Julia Wedgwood that the last Book would contain (as it

[3] See XII. 672–3 n.

does) 'the Augustinian' preaching 'a sermon', and also: 'the Priest has a final word to add in his old age. "I can no more"—as dying operatic heroes sing.'[4] In other words, he intended to have a final word from Caponsacchi, reviewing his encounter with Pompilia from the perspective of old age. This speech, had it been included, would have directed attention back to the 'love' between Caponsacchi and Pompilia, and so turned the ending sentiment towards pathos and romance. Instead, the sermon of Fra Celestino takes us in a different direction.

Its text is Romans 3: 4: 'Let God be true, but every man a liar'—hardly an innocent choice. The Epistle to the Romans is the central Pauline epistle from many perspectives, but particularly from a Protestant one.[5] In relation to the early chapters of Romans Luther developed his conviction of the truth of justification by faith. Chapter 3 is one of the places where St Paul begins to set up his profound antimony between the Law and the crooked human heart, on the one hand, and the saving grace of God and true freedom of the spirit, on the other. This antimony is reflected in Book XII as a whole, in Browning's contrast between the complete failure of law and lawyers—and the complete failure of the corrupt human heart—to discern the truth and goodness of Pompilia. Browning has been variously seen as liberal and heterodox in his religious perspective, but in Fra Celestino's sermon, movingly, he seems to latch on to the substance of the Epistle to the Romans (at least as that substance is reflected and refracted through a hundred real sermons) in order to contrast human evil and inhumanity with the transcendence of the spirit.

Browning's Fra Celestino is old, in some respects hesitant, but unlike the Pope of Book X, he is firmly prophetic in his manner of speaking. As one critic notes, 'Celestino's basic purpose is far different from Innocent's self-reflexive and soul-searching journey.'[6] 'The world', he says, makes terrible mistakes. It has (for the most part) completely misjudged Pompilia, just as the Romans misjudged the first Christians. Human speech, our truth-telling ability, is corrupted at its core by our devious hearts. Fra Celestino's sermon is marked all over by a mood taken over from the Epistle to the Romans, or at least that mood as interpreted within the particular tradition of which Browning was a part. So we have phrases like 'the world's calumny, / Stupidity, simplicity' (490–1), 'a man born blind like all his mates' (499), 'procuration of the powers / Of darkness'

[4] *Wedgwood*, 161. See our Vol. VII, p. xxxiii.

[5] Luther called it 'the principal and most excellent part of the new testament, and pure evangelion' (trans. Tyndale).

[6] P. D. Rigg, *Robert Browning's Romantic Irony in 'The Ring and the Book'* (1999), 96.

(569–70), the 'marvellous perversity of man' (575), 'earth's prerogative of lies' (607). Our society is somehow corrupted at its heart, systemically corrupted, and it takes a profound reorientation of the human spirit to discern the truth.

This is the ironic contrast on which Browning ends his epic: the three worldlings, the Venetian 'man of rank', Arcangeli, and Bottini, think they see everything, but really see nothing. And this links into the essential problem of all language and art. Humankind does not see, prophetically, the larger truth of its situation: 'For this people's heart is waxed gross, and their ears are dull of hearing, and their eyes they have closed' (Matt. 13: 15), and yet—told this in direct terms—they do not recognize it as a truth (XII. 845–7). Sullivan paraphrases well the thought of XII. 835–66: 'The creative process ... does not involve a presentation of truth directly to man, but a gradual revelation, indirectly, by the poet-agent working through the medium of other human voices. In the process, through his special gifts of insight and "outsight" and extraordinary will-power, the poet gives to the final revelation a spiritual and eternal value: this poem will "Suffice the eye and save the soul beside" (867).'[7] And so, it is through art, and, in this particular case, through the complex indirect method of the monologues, that humankind's eyes *may* be opened to the larger prophetic truth.

[7] Sullivan, 172–3.

XII.

THE BOOK AND THE RING.

HERE were the end, had anything an end:
Thus, lit and launched, up and up roared and soared
A rocket, till the key o' the vault was reached
And wide heaven held, a breathless minute-space,
In brilliant usurpature: thus caught spark,
Rushed to the height, and hung at full of fame
Over men's upturned faces, ghastly thence,
Our glaring Guido: now decline must be.
In its explosion, you have seen his act,
By my power—may-be, judged it by your own,—
Or composite as good orbs prove, or crammed
With worse ingredients than the Wormwood Star.
The act, over and ended, falls and fades:
What was once seen, grows what is now described,
Then talked of, told about, a tinge the less
In every fresh transmission; till it melts,
Trickles in silent orange or wan grey
Across our memory, dies and leaves all dark,

MS {fo. 333. At the head of the page is the title 'The Book and the Ring. 12.' in RB's hand} 3 *MS* th[] key>the key **MS 1868 1872 1888* reached, *DC BrU* reached,>reached *1889* reached 6 *MS* {no comma} 7 *MS* mens' 9 *MS* act

---

3 *key . . . vault*: i.e. the keystone of the arch (of the sky).

11 *Or . . . or*: Either . . . or.

composite: knit together (from various elements).

11–12 *crammed . . . Wormwood Star*: filled with worse ingredients than the poisonous meteor of Rev. 8: 10–11: 'And the name of the star is called Wormwood: and the third part of the waters became wormwood; and many men died of the waters, because they were made bitter.'

And presently we find the stars again.
Follow the main streaks, meditate the mode
Of brightness, how it hastes to blend with black!

After that February Twenty-Two,
Since our salvation, Sixteen-Ninety-Eight,
Of all reports that were, or may have been,
Concerning those the day killed or let live,
Four I count only. Take the first that comes.
A letter from a stranger, man of rank,
Venetian visitor at Rome,—who knows,
On what pretence of busy idleness?
Thus he begins on evening of that day.

"Here are we at our end of Carnival;
"Prodigious gaiety and monstrous mirth,
"And constant shift of entertaining show:
"With influx, from each quarter of the globe,
"Of strangers nowise wishful to be last
"I' the struggle for a good place presently
"When that befalls fate cannot long defer.

21 *MS* brightness— 22 *MS* Twenty Two, 23 *MS* Sixteen Ninety Eight, 28 *MS* {beginning of fo. 334} *MS* Venitian 31–208 *MS* {quotation marks at beginnings of lines added later} 31 *MS* Carnival: 33 *MS* show— 34 *MS* {no commas} 37 *MS* befalls— *1868 1872* befalls,

19 *And . . . again*: i.e. we see again the normal, natural, God-given world.

20 *main streaks*: main streaks of light, as the firework dies away, i.e. the last accounts of the murder and its aftermath (which are now to follow).

28 *Venetian visitor*: in choosing to make the first speaker of Book XII the anonymous Venetian 'man of rank' Browning may have been influenced by Leopold von Ranke's *History of the Popes* (1834–6). The appendix to this work gives extended quotation from the original sources, including, for the seventeenth century, several reports by Venetian ambassadors to Rome. One in particular, that of the Venetian ambassador Domenico Contarini, of 5 July 1696, is almost certainly a document that was important to Browning because of its detail concerning Innocent XII's character: see Leopold von Ranke, *The History of the Popes*, trans. by Mrs. E. Foster, 3 vols. (1847–8), iii. 463–66. Cf. 117 n.

29 *busy idleness*: the standard translation of Horace's 'strenua inertia': *Epistles*, I. xi. 28. Cf. *Aurora Leigh*, v. 350.

"The old Pope totters on the verge o' the grave:
"You see, Malpichi understood far more
"Than Tozzi how to treat the ailments: age,
"No question, renders these inveterate.
"Cardinal Spada, actual Minister,
"Is possible Pope; I wager on his head,
"Since those four entertainments of his niece
"Which set all Rome a-stare: Pope probably—
"Though Colloredo has his backers too,
"And San Cesario makes one doubt at times:
"Altieri will be Chamberlain at most.

"A week ago the sun was warm like May,
"And the old man took daily exercise
"Along the river-side; he loves to see
"That Custom-house he built upon the bank,
"For, Naples-born, his tastes are maritime:
"But yesterday he had to keep in-doors
"Because of the outrageous rain that fell.
"On such days the good soul has fainting-fits,

40 *MS* ailments— 41 *MS* renders now 42 *MS* minister, 46 *MS* Coloredo 47 *Yale 2* times:>times, 49 *MS* {no new paragraph} 52 *MS* Customhouse *53 *MS 1868 1872* Naples-born, *1888 1889* Naples born, 56 *MS* {beginning of fo. 335}

39 *Malpichi*: Marcello Malpighi of Bologna, the first of Innocent XII's chief physicians; cf. VII. 423. His name occurs prominently in the historical records because of the bad fall suffered by Innocent XII soon after taking office. For over a year and a half the Pope was unable to say mass. Malpighi is credited with gradually restoring him to health.

40 *Tozzi*: cf. IX. 1268, XI. 2333 nn.

42–3 *Spada . . . Pope*: Cardinal Fabrizio Spada, a former French nuncio, was Secretary of State under Innocent XII, but was not the future pope. Guido prophesies better than the Venetian visitor: see XI. 2339 n.

46–8 *Colloredo . . . Chamberlain*: see XI. 2261–5 n.

52–3 Custom-house . . . maritime: Innocent had the *Dogana di Mare* (Maritime Customs House) built on the Ripa Grande (the large bank) of the Tiber to deal with sea-borne goods, hence Browning's coinage of the mixed name for it, 'Dogana-by-the-Bank' (89). It was near to the hospice of St Michael, one of Innocent's favourite projects, which he made into a huge orphanage. The hospice building survives today, but the Customs House has long been demolished. Browning's knowledge is exact here, and Cook, rarely for him, is wrong on this point.

"Or lies in stupor, scarcely makes believe
"Of minding business, fumbles at his beads.
"They say, the trust that keeps his heart alive
"Is that, by lasting till December next,
"He may hold Jubilee a second time,
"And, twice in one reign, ope the Holy Doors.
"By the way, somebody responsible
"Assures me that the King of France has writ
"Fresh orders: Fénelon will be condemned:
"The Cardinal makes a wry face enough,
"Having a love for the delinquent: still,
"He's the ambassador, must press the point.
"Have you a wager too, dependent here?

"Now, from such matters to divert awhile,
"Hear of to-day's event which crowns the week,
"Casts all the other wagers into shade.
"Tell Dandolo I owe him fifty drops
"Of heart's blood in the shape of gold zecchines!

58 *MS* beads; 65 *MS 1868 1872* Fenelon 66 *MS* []>enough, 68 *MS* Ambassador, 69 *MS 1868* {no comma} 70 *MS* {New paragraph indicated by 'New Par.' in left-hand margin} 74 *MS* zecchines:

60–1 *December . . . time*: i.e. by surviving till December 1699, Innocent would be able (as he did) to commence the Jubilee of the Holy Year of 1700. He had already celebrated such a special year in 1694.

62 *Holy Doors*: the special opening of these bricked-up doors into St Peter's marked the symbolic commencement of a Jubilee year, and was a symbol of the forgiveness of sins: see III. 567 n.

64–7 *King . . . delinquent*: the semi-Quietistic teachings of François Fénelon (1651–1715), from 1695 Archbishop of Cambrai, had caused theological controversy in France from about 1694. In April 1697 Fénelon himself submitted his theological teachings to Rome for the Pope's judgement. In an autograph letter of July 1697, Louis XIV requested the Pope to give a speedy verdict (Louis was against Fénelon). Between October 1697 and October 1698 there were sixty-four sittings of an expert theological committee to adjudicate the matter. Finally, in March 1699, twenty-three propositions extracted from Fénelon's work were condemned by the papal judgement *Cum alias*. Fénelon submitted. 'The Cardinal' here is Cardinal Bouillon who, in July 1697, took over from Cardinal Forbin as Louis XIV's representative at the papal court. Bouillon worked zealously on Fénelon's side, trying to prevent a condemnation of his work, something that annoyed Louis. Cf. VI. 323 n.

74 *zecchines*: gold coins.

"The Pope has done his worst: I have to pay
"For the execution of the Count, by Jove!
"Two days since, I reported him as safe,
"Re-echoing the conviction of all Rome:
"Who could suspect its one deaf ear—the Pope's?
"But prejudices grow insuperable,
"And that old enmity to Austria, that
"Passion for France and France's pageant-king
"(Of which, why pause to multiply the proofs
"Now scandalously rife in Europe's mouth?)
"These fairly got the better in our man
"Of justice, prudence, and *esprit de corps*,
"And he persisted in the butchery.
"Also, 't is said that in his latest walk
"To that Dogana-by-the-Bank he built,
"The crowd,—he suffers question, unrebuked,—
"Asked, 'Whether murder was a privilege
"'Only reserved for nobles like the Count?'
"And he was ever mindful of the mob.
"Martinez, the Cæsarian Minister,
"—Who used his best endeavours to spare blood,

75 *MS* worst,— 79 *MS 1868* the one 83 *MS* proofs?)>proofs 84 *MS* {line added later} 85 *MS* {beginning of fo. 336} *MS 1868 1872* the man 89 *MS 1868 1872* Dogana-by-the-Bank, 91 *MS* "Asked "whether>"Asked 'whether 92 *MS* "Only>"'Only *MS* Count?"> Count?' 95 *MS* "Who>"—Who *MS* {no comma}

81–4 *enmity . . . mouth?*: not a just accusation, but certainly the kind that was made in the heated politics of this period. Till 1697 France and Austria were at war, and it was hard for Innocent XII to appear impartial. At the beginning of his pontificate, relations with Austria were good, but they deteriorated rapidly. To the Austrians Innocent's rapprochement with Louis XIV over ecclesiastical matters in 1693 looked like some kind of favouritism, and suspicions deepened. The aggressive attitudes of the imperial ambassadors, first Liechenstein and then Martinitz, worsened matters: see XI. 2346–7 n.

86 *esprit de corps*: i.e. aristocratic fellow feeling.

89 *Dogana-by-the-Bank*: Maritime Customs House: cf. 52–3 n.

94–9 *Martinez . . . you!*: Martinitz, the imperial minister (i.e. the ambassador of Leopold I): see XI. 2346–7 n. It is not known that Martinitz was really so opposed to the execution, but Browning is developing a hint in OYB ccxxxvii (237), in the letter of Gaspero del Torto to Francesco Cencini, 22 Feb. 1698: 'and there have not

"And strongly pleaded for the life 'of one,'
"Urged he, 'I may have dined at table with!'—
"He will not soon forget the Pope's rebuff,
"—Feels the slight sensibly, I promise you!
"And but for the dissuasion of two eyes
"That make with him foul weather or fine day,
"He had abstained, nor graced the spectacle:
"As it was, barely would he condescend
"Look forth from the *palchetto* where he sat
"Under the Pincian: we shall hear of this.
"The substituting, too, the People's Square
"For the out-o'-the-way old quarter by the Bridge,
"Was meant as a conciliatory sop
"To the mob; it gave one holiday the more.
"But the French Embassy might unfurl flag,—
"Still the good luck of France to fling a foe!
"Cardinal Bouillon triumphs properly.
"*Palchetti* were erected in the Place,
"And houses, at the edge of the Three Streets,
"Let their front windows at six dollars each:

96 *MS* "of one">'of one' *MS* {no comma} 97 *MS* "[?Quoth]>"Urged *MS* {no comma} *MS* "I>'I *MS* with!"—>with!'— 98 *MS* []>will 99 *MS* "Feels 102 *Yale 2* spectacle:>spectacle, 105 *MS 1868 1872* this! 112 *MS 1868 1872* properly! 113 *MS* "Palchetti 114 *MS* houses at 115 []>six

been lacking admonitions of greatest consequence, since the Ambassador of the Emperor spoke of that point on Tuesday, as he himself told me the day before yesterday'.

100 *two eyes*: i.e. the eyes of a woman he is in love with.

104 *palchetto*: miniature grandstand, from SS 19.

105 *Pincian*: the Monte Pincio, or Pincian hill, rising to the east of the Piazza del Popolo.

106–9 *People's Square . . . mob*: cf. I. 350 n.

110–11 *But . . . foe*: that the French were against Guido is merely Browning's deduction from the fact that the Austrians may have been for him: see ll. 94–9 n.

112 *Cardinal Bouillon*: cf. 64–7 n.

114 *Three Streets*: the three streets leading into Piazza del Popolo from the south: Via del Babuino, the Corso, and Via di Ripetta.

115 *Let . . . each*: a detail from SS 19: 'Crowds were so pressing that the views from some windows were let for as much as six scudi.'

"Anguisciola, that patron of the arts,
"Hired one; our Envoy Contarini too.

"Now for the thing; no sooner the decree
"Gone forth,—'t is four-and-twenty hours ago,—
"Than Acciaiuoli and Panciatichi,
"Old friends, indeed compatriots of the man,
"Being pitched on as the couple properest
"To intimate the sentence yesternight,
"Were closeted ere cock-crow with the Count.
"They both report their efforts to dispose
"The unhappy nobleman for ending well,
"Despite the natural sense of injury,
"Were crowned at last with a complete success.
"And when the Company of Death arrived
"At twenty-hours,—the way they reckon here,—
"We say, at sunset, after dinner-time,—
"The Count was led down, hoisted up on car,
"Last of the five, as heinousest, you know:
"Yet they allowed one whole car to each man.
"His intrepidity, nay, nonchalance,

*118 *1868 1872* {new paragraph. Paragraphing obscured in *1888* and *1889* by this line's being at the head of the page} *MS* the Count; 119 *MS* four and twenty 120 *MS 1868 1872* Acciaioli 121 *MS* Count, 122 *MS* "Were *Yale 2* "Being> ("Being 123 *MS* yestereven>yesternight,—>yesternight, *Yale 2* yesternight,>yesternight) 124 *MS* "[]>"And 128 *MS 1868* success: 130 *MS* twenty-hours, *MS* count time>reckon *MS* here, 131 *MS* past>at *MS* after-dinner-time, 133 *MS* know, 134 *MS* "(Yet *MS* man.) 135 *MS* nonchalance

117 *Contarini*: Browning handles history impressionistically. Domenico Contarini (b. 1642) was nominated as Venetian ambassador in 1689, and, after serving, died in 1696. See *Dizionario biografico degli italiani*, 59 vols. to date (1960–), xxviii. 147–50.

122 *pitched on*: picked out, selected.

130–1 *twenty-hours . . . dinner-time*: Browning seems to have confused his timings here. In Book I, he has the Company of Death arrive in the early dawn light: I. 1308. Here he follows SS 19, which describes it as 'alle ore 20 giunta', but understands the phrase not in strict seventeenth-century mode (cf. Vol. VII, 323, 325) but in modern Italian idiom as 'at 8 p.m.' The phrase *dopo il pranzo*, which he translates 'after dinner-time', is from OYB ccxxxix (238).

132 *car*: cart, tumbril.

135–7 *intrepidity . . . saw*: following the It. of SS 20: 'Franceschini, che mostrò più degli altri intrepidezza e sangue freddo, con meraviglia universale'.

"As up he stood and down he sat himself,
"Struck admiration into those who saw.
"Then the procession started, took the way
"From the New Prisons by the Pilgrim's Street,
"The street of the Governo, Pasquin's Street,
"(Where was stuck up, 'mid other epigrams,
"A quatrain . . . but of all that, presently!)
"The Place Navona, the Pantheon's Place,
"Place of the Column, last the Corso's length,
"And so debouched thence at Mannaia's foot
"I' the Place o' the People. As is evident,
"(Despite the malice,—plainly meant, I fear,
"By this abrupt change of locality,—
"The Square's no such bad place to head and hang)
"We had the titillation as we sat
"Assembled, (quality in conclave, ha?)
"Of, minute after minute, some report
"How the slow show was winding on its way.
"Now did a car run over, kill a man,
"Just opposite a pork-shop numbered Twelve:
"And bitter were the outcries of the mob
"Against the Pope: for, but that he forbids
"The Lottery, why, Twelve were Tern Quatern!

139 *MS* to>by 140 *MS* "The Street *MS* Pasquin's Street *141 *MS* mid *1868* 'mid *1872 1888 1889* mid 142 *MS* {beginning of fo. 338} *MS 1868 1872* quatrain . . 145 *MS* the Mannaia>Mannaia's foot[ ]>Mannaia's foot 147–9 {not found in *MS*} 152 *MS* each report 153 *MS* "Of how the show **MS* way: *1868 1872* way. *1888* way *DC BrU* way>way. *1889* way. 155 *MS* Twelve— 156 *MS* crowd 158 *MS* why twelve>why Twelve *MS* Quatern:

139–44 *New Prisons . . . length*: this route is from SS 21. At I. 1325 Browning describes it as 'the longest way'. In fact it is a relatively direct route, simply going via the widest streets and squares: first east, via Piazza Navona and the Pantheon, to Piazza Colonna, and then north along the Corso.

145 *debouched*: issued, emerged (from a narrower into a wider space).

151 *quality . . . conclave*: the upper classes, sitting like the college of Cardinals selecting a pope: cf. X. 2114 n.

157–8 *forbids / The Lottery*: 'In Italy the lottery was proscribed by Innocent XII., Benedict XIII., and Clement XII. But it was soon revived': *Roba di Roma*, i. 124.

158 *Tern Quatern*: 'a three bet, a four bet', i.e. a huge win. Browning knew about the Roman lottery from seeing it—it was very popular in the Rome of his day—and

"Now did a beggar by Saint Agnes, lame
"From his youth up, recover use of leg,
"Through prayer of Guido as he glanced that way:
"So that the crowd near crammed his hat with coin.
"Thus was kept up excitement to the last,
"—Not an abrupt out-bolting, as of yore,
"From Castle, over Bridge and on to block,
"And so all ended ere you well could wink!

"To mount the scaffold-steps, Guido was last
"Here also, as atrociousest in crime.
"We hardly noticed how the peasants died,
"They dangled somehow soon to right and left,
"And we remained all ears and eyes, could give
"Ourselves to Guido undividedly,
"As he harangued the multitude beneath.
"He begged forgiveness on the part of God,
"And fair construction of his act from men,
"Whose suffrage he entreated for his soul,

159 *MS* st>lame 161 *MS* way,— 162 *MS* coin: 164 *MS* []>as *etc.* 165 *MS* block 167 *MS* {no new paragraph} *MS 1868* "Guido was last to mount the scaffold-steps 168 *MS* "There *MS* crime: 173 *MS* addressed>harangued *MS* beneath,>beneath. 174 *MS* {beginning of fo. 339} *MS* "Entreated pardon>"He begged forgiveness *MS* {no comma} 175 *MS* {no comma}

also perhaps from reading the discussions of it in books by two of his friends, Story's *Roba di Roma* (i. 121–45) and W. C. Cartwright's *Papal Conclaves*, 56–7. The Roman lottery was a five-number draw, a one-number ticket producing a modest return, a three- or four-number ticket (a *terno* or *quaterno*), a huge prize. As Cartwright notes, 'It is proverbial that in Italy nothing is saved from conversion into some reduction into numbers that are made available for the lottery.' He cites the ludicrous example of a cardinal, locked in conclave, betting on 17 and 25 because 'in the morning's balloting [for the next Pope] another Cardinal, occupying apartment 25, had 17 votes': *Conclaves*, 57.

159 *Saint Agnes*: the Church of S. Agnese, on the west side of the Piazza Navona: see 139–44 n. The Venetian man-of-rank reports this miracle with worldly-wise nonchalance, too blasé to be concerned whether it is fake or real. For him, it is simply the kind of thing to be expected on such an occasion.

174–81 "*He . . . decency*: with the exception of l. 175, this follows closely the Italian of SS 22. 'Suffrage' = intercessory prayer, is suggested by 'e pregò a suffragargli l'anima'.

"Suggesting that we should forthwith repeat
"A *Pater* and an *Ave*, with the hymn
"*Salve Regina Cœli*, for his sake.
"Which said, he turned to the confessor, crossed
"And reconciled himself, with decency,
"Oft glancing at Saint Mary's opposite,
"Where they possess, and showed in shrine to-day,
"The blessed *Umbilicus* of our Lord,
"(A relic 't is believed no other church
"In Rome can boast of)—then rose up, as brisk
"Knelt down again, bent head, adapted neck,
"And, with the name of Jesus on his lips,
"Received the fatal blow.

"The headsman showed
"The head to the populace. Must I avouch
"We strangers own to disappointment here?
"Report pronounced him fully six feet high,
"Youngish, considering his fifty years,

178 *MS* Ave, 180 *MS* Confessor there 182 *MS* "Then knelt down, bent head and adapted neck,>"Oft glancing at Saint Mary's opposite, *MS 1868 1872* {no comma} 183 *MS* possess the *Umbilicum* of our Lord, 184 {not found in *MS*} *1868 1872* Blessed 188 *MS* lips 189 *MS* blow: the headsman showed 190 {not found in *MS*, no new paragraph} 194 *MS* "Youngish considering

182–4 *Saint Mary's . . . Umbilicus*: the Rome of Browning's day was full of extraordinary alleged relics: the finger of St Thomas, with which he is said to have touched Jesus' wounded side (in Santa Croce in Gerusalemme); the *Santa Culla*, or Holy Manger (in S. Maria Maggiore); half of the Sacred Pillar of Flagellation, to which Jesus was fastened and scourged (in S. Prassede); etc. Nonetheless, here the reader may wonder if this is an invented relic, a high Protestant joke, or a real alleged relic. In fact it is the last (and it is not a detail that Browning takes from SS). Innocent III refers to the holy *umbilicus* or navel in his treatise *De sacro altaris mysterio* in *c.*1198, but it was known long before this: see Migne, *Patrologia Latina* 217, 876 D–877 A. At one time, at least two churches claimed to have it: 'The Virgin Mary is said to have picked up her son's navel after his birth and guarded the precious relic all her life. It greatly comforted her after his death. . . . Eventually the navel fell into the hands of Charlemagne, who cut it in two and gave one half to Rome, as a gift to Pope Leo III, and the other to the church of Notre-Dame-en-Vaux, Châlons-sur-Marne': James Bentley, *Restless Bones: The Story of Relics* (1985), 134. Browning shows a sly Protestant wit in making the Venetian man-of-rank refer to the *umbilicus* in a largely matter-of-fact way. This reference sets up Arcangeli's joke at 746: see n.

"And, if not handsome, dignified at least.
"Indeed, it was no face to please a wife!
"His friends say, this was caused by the costume:
"He wore the dress he did the murder in,
"That is, a *just-a-corps* of russet serge,
"Black camisole, coarse cloak of baracan
"(So they style here the garb of goat's-hair cloth)
"White hat and cotton cap beneath, poor Count,
"Preservative against the evening dews
"During the journey from Arezzo. Well,
"So died the man, and so his end was peace;
"Whence many a moral were to meditate.
"Spada,—you may bet Dandolo,—is Pope!
"Now for the quatrain!"

No, friend, this will do!
You've sputtered into sparks. What streak comes next?
A letter: Don Giacinto Arcangeli,
Doctor and Proctor, him I made you mark
Buckle to business in his study late,
The virtuous sire, the valiant for the truth,
Acquaints his correspondent,—Florentine,
By name Cencini, advocate as well,

196 {not found in *MS*} 199 *MS* is a 201 *MS* goats-hair 205, 206 {not found in *MS*} 207 *MS* Spada, you may bet Dandolo, is Pope. 208 *MS* {beginning of fo. 340} 209–30 *MS* {quotation marks at beginnings of lines deleted and '[Am]end' written in left-hand margin} 209 *MS* {New paragraph indicated by 'New Paragr.' with line —— between this & the above} *MS* do, 211 *MS* letter of Don 212 *MS* hear 213 *MS* late.

198–202 *He ... beneath*: translating, and explaining, SS 23. 'Giustacore di panno bigio' becomes 'a *just-a-corps* of russet serge': strictly 'bigio' is 'grey' rather than 'russet'. A *just-a-corps* is a close-fitting coat or doublet (from F. *juste* close-fitting + *au corps* to the body). 'Camiciuola nera' becomes 'black camisole', in other words, some simple form of undershirt.

207 *Spada*: cf. 42–3 n.

211–16 *A letter ... Cencini*: this is an actual letter in OYB, hence Browning's emphasis on its reality: see ll. 239–88 n.

Socius and brother-in-the-devil to match,—
A friend of Franceschini, anyhow,
And knit up with the bowels of the case,—
Acquaints him, (in this paper that I touch)
How their joint effort to obtain reprieve
For Guido had so nearly nicked the nine
And ninety and one over,—folk would say
At Tarocs,—or succeeded,—in our phrase.
To this Cencini's care I owe the Book,
The yellow thing I take and toss once more,—
How will it be, my four-years'-intimate,
When thou and I part company anon?—
'T was he, the "whole position of the case,"
Pleading and summary, were put before;
Discreetly in my Book he bound them all,
Adding some three epistles to the point.
Here is the first of these, part fresh as penned,
The sand, that dried the ink, not rubbed away,
Though penned the day whereof it tells the deed:
Part—extant just as plainly, you know where,
Whence came the other stuff, went, you know how,
To make the Ring that's all but round and done.

---

217 *MS* match, 220 *MS* him,—in *MS* touch,— 222 *MS* []>nearly 223 *MS* over, he would say, *1868 1872* he would say, 224 *MS* tarocs, or succeeded, in 225 *MS* book *MS* {no comma} 226 *MS 1868* more 227 *MS 1868* —How 229 *MS* the whose *MS* case, 230 *MS* summary were *MS* before, 231 *MS* a book 234 *MS* sand that *MS* ink not 238 *MS 1868 1872* ring

217 *Socius*: colleague (L.).

219 *knit . . . case*: i.e. involved emotionally with the case.

222 *nicked*: hit, made.

224 *Tarocs*: the complex Italian card game: cf. VI. 349 n.

225 *Cencini's . . . Book*: cf. I. 694 n.

226 *yellow . . . more*: recalling I. 33–5.

227 *four-years'-intimate*: 1864–8, the period when Browning wrote the poem: see our Vol. VII, pp. xxii–xxix.

229 "*whole . . . case,*": translating the opening words of the hand-written title-page of OYB: 'Posizione di tutta la causa criminale . . . ' Cf. I. 122.

236–8 *Part . . . done*: i.e. the other part, extant in Browning's imagination: referring to ll. 291–390.

"Late they arrived, too late, egregious Sir,
"Those same justificative points you urge
"Might benefit His Blessed Memory
"Count Guido Franceschini now with God:
"Since the Court,—to state things succinctly,—styled
"The Congregation of the Governor,
"Having resolved on Tuesday last our cause
"I' the guilty sense, with death for punishment,
"Spite of all pleas by me deducible
"In favour of said Blessed Memory,—
"I, with expenditure of pains enough,
"Obtained a respite, leave to claim and prove
"Exemption from the law's award,—alleged
"The power and privilege o' the Clericate:
"To which effect a courier was despatched.
"But ere an answer from Arezzo came,
"The Holiness of our Lord the Pope (prepare!)
"Judging it inexpedient to postpone
"The execution of such sentence passed,
"Saw fit, by his particular cheirograph,

239–88 *MS* {quotation marks at beginnings of lines added later} 239 *MS* {beginning of fo. 341} *MS* {New paragraph indicated by 'New Par.' in left-hand margin and —— (line between paragraphs. at head of page} 241 *MS* [?the]>His 245 *MS* Cause 248 *MS* [ ]>said *MS* Memory 258 *MS 1868 1872* chirograph,

239–88 Here Browning is translating the Italian of the actual letter from Arcangeli to Monsignor Francesco Cencini, 22 Feb. 1698 (the day of the executions). It is the first of three hand-written letters bound in with the other documents of OYB: ccxxxv (235–6). Browning translates the letter with only a few rephrasings and small additions: see following nn.

egregious: excellent, distinguished.

252 *Clericate*: translating *clericato* (minor orders).

258 *particular cheirograph*: 'handwritten document', rendering the term *Chirografo particolare* from the letter. The *1868* and *1872* texts—and indeed I. 346—have the usual spelling 'chirograph'. Here, in his last text, Browning opts for the scholarly (or pedantic) 'cheirograph', from the Gr. original χειρόγραφον. It is not clear, either from here, or I. 346, that he knew precisely what it was. His friend, W. C. Cartwright, however, carefully explains the nature of the chirograph, contrasting it with more formal documents, like the Bull and the Brief: 'There is yet a third form of Papal expression in writing, called a Chirograph, the exact nature of which is difficult to define. It appears indeed to have no binding force except what it may derive from

"To derogate, dispense with privilege,
"And wink at any hurt accruing thence
"To Mother Church through damage of her son:
"Also, to overpass and set aside
"That other plea on score of tender age,
"Put forth by me to do Pasquini good,
"One of the four in trouble with our friend.
"So that all five, to-day, have suffered death
"With no distinction save in dying,—he,
"Decollate by mere due of privilege,
"The rest hanged decently and in order. Thus
"Came the Count to his end of gallant man,
"Defunct in faith and exemplarity:
"Nor shall the shield of his great House lose shine
"Thereby, nor its blue banner blush to red.
"This, too, should yield sustainment to our hearts—
"He had commiseration and respect
"In his decease from universal Rome,
"*Quantum est hominum venustiorum*,
"The nice and cultivated everywhere:
"Though, in respect of me his advocate,

261 *MS 1868* son; 262 *MS* [ ]>overpass 263 *MS* {no comma} 265 *MS* friend: 268 *MS* {beginning of fo. 342} *MS 1868* "Decollated by way of *MS* {no comma} 272 *MS 1868* shine, 273 *MS 1868* "Nor its blue banner blush to red thereby. 279 *MS* to me

personal respect for its author, and resembles in authority somewhat the minutes which at times are drawn up in our offices, or the peculiar expression of Royal wishes formerly in use in Prussia, and termed Cabinets-order': *Conclaves*, 37.

259 *derogate*: take away, lessen—translating *derogaro*.

268 *Decollate*: beheaded, translating *Decollazione*.

269 *decently . . . order*: cf. 1 Cor. 14: 40.

269–73 *Thus . . . red*: Browning takes this sentiment from the second letter (Gaspero del Torto to Francesco Cencini, 22 Feb. 1698) and adds it in to Arcangeli's letter: 'For aside from the fact that he has died with exemplary courage, he has also been pitied by all gallant men, and his house has lost nothing in the matter of reputation': OYB ccxxxvii (237).

277 *Quantum . . . venustiorum*: 'All persons of sensitivity there are', from Catullus 3. 2. This is Browning's addition to the original. By this small touch he recalls to our minds the full character of Arcangeli from Book VIII: Arcangeli loves fine Latin, and reaches naturally for this elegant, mock-heroic flourish.

"Needs must I groan o'er my debility,
"Attribute the untoward event o' the strife
"To nothing but my own crass ignorance
"Which failed to set the valid reasons forth,
"Find fit excuse: such is the fate of war!
"May God compensate us the direful blow
"By future blessings on his family,
"Whereof I lowly beg the next commands;
"—Whereto, as humbly, I confirm myself. . . "

And so forth,—follow name and place and date.
On next leaf—
"*Hactenus senioribus!*
"There, old fox, show the clients t'other side
"And keep this corner sacred, I beseech!
"You and your pleas and proofs were what folk call
"Pisan assistance, aid that comes too late,
"Saves a man dead as nail in post of door.
"Had I but time and space for narrative!
"What was the good of twenty Clericates
"When Somebody's thick headpiece once was bent
"On seeing Guido's drop into the bag?
"How these old men like giving youth a push!
"So much the better: next push goes to him,

281 *MS* event of things 284 *MS* "The fit 285 *1872* blow, 286 *MS* *1868* *1872* {no comma} 288 *MS* {no quotation mark at end of line} 289 *MS* {no new paragraph} *MS* (And *MS* date)>date: *1868* date: 290 *MS* There, on>On *MS* *1868* the next *MS* leaf—) 292–390 *MS* {quotation marks at beginnings of lines added later} 293 *MS* {no comma} 294 *MS* *1868* *1872* folks 297 *MS* {beginning of fo. 343} 298 *MS* clericates 299 *MS* headpiece was once fairly>thick headpiece once was bent 302 *MS* {no comma}

291 "*Hactenus senioribus!*: 'Thus far (i.e. what I've written so far) for the elders!'—Arcangeli means clients or fellow lawyers. From now on his letter is private (and also all Browning's invention).

295 *Pisan assistance*: 'soccorso di Pisa' is proverbial for 'aid that comes too late'. During the siege of Jerusalem in the First Crusade the Genoese, who managed the besieging machines, wanted help from the Pisans; but the Pisan fleet was delayed by contrary winds and they did not appear till after the victory had been won (July 1099): Cook, 267.

"And a new Pope begins the century.
"Much good I get by my superb defence!
"But argument is solid and subsists,
"While obstinacy and ineptitude
"Accompany the owner to his tomb—
"What do I care how soon? Beside, folk see!
"Rome will have relished heartily the show,
"Yet understood the motives, never fear,
"Which caused the indecent change o' the People's Place
"To the People's Playground,—stigmatize the spite
"Which in a trice precipitated things!
"As oft the moribund will give a kick
"To show they are not absolutely dead,
"So feebleness i' the socket shoots its last,
"A spirt of violence for energy!

"But thou, Cencini, brother of my breast,
"O fox whose home is 'mid the tender grape,
"Whose couch in Tuscany by Themis' throne,
"Subject to no such . . . best I shut my mouth

307 *MS 1868 1872* tomb; 308 *MS 1868 1872* folks *MS* see: 312 *MS* playground,—whence the spite had birth 313 *MS* "That *318 *1868 1872* {new paragraph. Paragraphing obscured in *1888* and *1889* by this line's being at the head of the page} 319 *MS 1868 1872* fox, *MS* mid 321 *MS 1868 1872* but I

305 *subsists*: lasts, endures.

311–12 *indecent . . . Playground*: cf. ll. 106–9, and I. 350 n.

314 *moribund*: dying person.

316 *feebleness . . . socket*: the feeble flame in the socket of the candle-holder, i.e. the Pope in his dotage. Cf. X. 2053 n.

319 *fox . . . grape*: 'O cunning fellow, whose home is amid the rich vineyards of Tuscany, i.e. amid rich pickings for lawyers'. Cf. S. of S. 2: 15: 'Take us the foxes, the little foxes, that spoil the vines: for our vines have tender grapes.' The love of foxes for grapes was proverbial: see Theocritus V, 112–13. In S. of S. the woman tells her lover to catch the foxes to stop them consuming the 'tender' (i.e. ripe) grapes. Here Arcangeli wittily misapplies the image. At l. 321 he is hinting that, in Tuscany, Cencini also has the advantage of being free of the Papal jurisdiction.

320 *by Themis' throne*: by the throne of Themis, Greek goddess of justice. Arcangeli elegantly characterizes Tuscany (by contrast with Rome) as the very seat of law and order. Themis' throne is next to Zeus; her children are the Rule of Law (Eunomia), Justice, and Peace (Pindar, *Olympians* 9. 21–2, 13. 6–8); Browning knows his Pindar.

"Or only open it again to say,
"This pother and confusion fairly laid,
"My hands are empty and my satchel lank.
"Now then for both the Matrimonial Cause
"And the Case of Gomez! Serve them hot and hot!

"*Reliqua differamus in crastinum!*
"The impatient estafette cracks whip outside:
"Still, though the earth should swallow him who swears
"And me who make the mischief, in must slip—
"My boy, your godson, fat-chaps Hyacinth,
"Enjoyed the sight while Papa plodded here.
"I promised him, the rogue, a month ago,
"The day his birthday was, of all the days,
"That if I failed to save Count Guido's head,
"Cinuccio should at least go see it chopped
"From trunk—'So, latinize your thanks!' quoth I.
" 'That I prefer, *hoc malim*,' raps me out
"The rogue: you notice the subjunctive? Ah!
"Accordingly he sat there, bold in box,

324 *MS* [?b]lank;>lank. 325 *MS* {beginning of fo. 344} 326 *MS 1868 1872* case 327 *MS* {no new paragraph} *MS crastinu[ ]!>crastinum!* 328 *MS* cra[ ]>cracks 330 *MS 1868* slip 331 *MS 1868* "—My 336 *MS* "Cintino>"Cinuccio *337 *MS* so latinize your thanks, quoth I: *1868 1872* thanks!' *1888 1889* thanks! *1868* I: *1872* I 338 *MS* "Hoc>" 'That

325–6 *Matrimonial . . . Gomez*: new legal cases that Arcangeli looks forward to. These are mentioned in passing in OYB ccxxxix f. (238), from where Browning takes the names. In fact, it is Browning's invention that these cases concerned Arcangeli, or indeed later Bottini: see 657 n.

327 "*Reliqua . . . crastinum!*: 'Leave the rest till tomorrow' (L.), from Scipio's closing words in Cicero, *De Re Publica*, II, 70. Arcangeli again shows off his Latin: cf. 277 n.

328 *estafette*: mounted courier.

331 *fat-chaps Hyacinth*: Arcangeli's beloved son, already slightly fat round the jaws (taking after his father in this respect): see VIII. 1 n. It is Browning's invention that Cencini is Hyacinth's godson.

336 *Cinuccio*: a playful diminutive for Hyacinth: see VIII. 2 n. Variants occur at 346, 352, 389.

338–9 *hoc malim . . . subjunctive?*: 'That I would prefer' (L.). Hyacinth uses the subjunctive mood correctly, so delighting his father: see VIII. 7 n.

“Proud as the Pope behind the peacock-fans:
“Whereon a certain lady-patroness
“For whom I manage things (my boy in front,
“Her Marquis sat the third in evidence;
“Boys have no eyes nor ears save for the show)
“‘This time, Cintino,’ was her sportive word,
“When whiz and thump went axe and mowed lay man,
“And folk could fall to the suspended chat,
“‘This time, you see, Bottini rules the roast,
“‘Nor can Papa with all his eloquence
“‘Be reckoned on to help as heretofore!’
“Whereat Cinone pouts; then, sparkishly—
“‘Papa knew better than aggrieve his Pope,
“‘And baulk him of his grudge against our Count,
“‘Else he'd have argued-off Bottini's’ . . what?
“‘His nose,’—the rogue! well parried of the boy!
“He's long since out of Cæsar (eight years old)
“And as for tripping in Eutropius . . . well,
“Reason the more that we strain every nerve
“To do him justice, mould a model-mouth,
“A Bartolus-cum-Baldo for next age:
“For that I purse the pieces, work the brain,
“And want both Gomez and the marriage-case,

343 *MS* stretch a point>manage things 344 *MS* “The *MS* evidence, 346 *MS* Cinto,’>Cintino,’ 348 *MS 1868 1872* folks 349 *MS* time Bottini,>time, you see, Bottini 351 *MS* for>to 353 *MS* {beginning of fo. 345} 356 *MS* rogue: 358 *MS 1868 1872* Eutropius . . *MS* Well,

341 *Pope . . . peacock-fans*: i.e. Arcangeli's little son sits as proud as the Pope on ceremonial occasions, when fans of peacock feathers were held in front of him. This detail is again from the papacy of Browning's own day; EBB notices it in her ‘Christmas Gifts’, 43–8.

357 *Cæsar*: the writings of Julius Caesar, often given to beginners in Latin because of their lucid, unrhetorical style.

358 *tripping . . . Eutropius*: i.e. making mistakes in reading the Latin of Eutropius. This fourth-century historian published a complete compendium of Roman history in ten books, from Romulus through to his own times. Its style was clear and simple, so that it ‘was for a long time a favourite elementary school-book’: *Encyclopædia Britannica*, 11th ed.

361 *Bartolus-cum-Baldo*: i.e. an excellent lawyer. Bartolus and Baldo were famous fourteenth-century jurists: see I. 224 n.

"Success with which shall plaster aught of pate
"That's broken in me by Bottini's flail,
"And bruise his own, belike, that wags and brags.
"*Adverti supplico humiliter*
"*Quod*, don't the fungus see, the fop divine
"That one hand drives two horses, left and right?
"With this rein did I rescue from the ditch
"The fortune of our Franceschini, keep
"Unsplashed the credit of a noble House,
"And set the fashionable cause at Rome
"A-prancing till bystanders shouted ''ware!'
"The other rein's judicious management
"Suffered old Somebody to keep the pace,
"Hobblingly play the roadster: who but he
"Had his opinion, was not led by the nose
"In leash of quibbles strung to look like law!
"You'll soon see,—when I go to pay devoir
"And compliment him on confuting me,—
"If, by a back-swing of the pendulum,
"Grace be not, thick and threefold, consequent.
"'I must decide as I see proper, Don!
"'I'm Pope, I have my inward lights for guide.
"'Had learning been the matter in dispute,
"'Could eloquence avail to gainsay fact,
"'Yours were the victory, be comforted!'

*368 *MS 1868 1872* "Quod, *1888 1889* "Quod   371 *MS* your   373 *MS 1868* of Rome   379 *MS* a leash   381 *MS* [ ]>on *etc.*   382 *MS* {beginning of fo. 346}   *MS* pendulum   383 *1868 1872* consequent!   384 *MS* "I> "'I   385 *MS* "'Being Pope, *1868 1872* "'The Pope, *Yale 2* "'The>"'A

367–8 *Adverti . . . Quod*: 'I humbly beg that it may be noticed' (L.). A turn of phrase used by the real Arcangeli: OYB xii (13).

368 *fungus*: upstart.

376 *old Somebody*: i.e. the Pope.

377 *roadster*: 'a horse for riding (or driving) on the road': OED².

379 *leash*: bridle, leather thong (used to control a horse). Arcangeli is claiming he has deliberately strung the Pope along, by constructing a pleading that appeared insubstantial, so that the Pope, in seeing through it, could congratulate himself on his own cleverness.

"Cinuzzo will be gainer by it all.
"Quick then with Gomez, hot and hot next case!"

Follows, a letter, takes the other side.
Tall blue-eyed Fisc whose head is capped with cloud,
Doctor Bottini,—to no matter who,
Writes on the Monday two days afterward.
Now shall the honest championship of right,
Crowned with success, enjoy at last, unblamed,
Moderate triumph! Now shall eloquence
Poured forth in fancied floods for virtue's sake,
(The print is sorrowfully dyked and dammed,
But shows where fain the unbridled force would flow,
Finding a channel)—now shall this refresh
The thirsty donor with a drop or two!
Here has been truth at issue with a lie:
Let who gained truth the day have handsome pride
In his own prowess! Eh? What ails the man?

"Well, it is over, ends as I foresaw:
"Easily proved, Pompilia's innocence!
"Catch them entrusting Guido's guilt to me
"Who had, as usual, the plain truth to plead.
"I always knew the clearness of the stream
"Would show the fish so thoroughly, child might prong
"The clumsy monster: with no mud to splash,

391 *MS* letter— *MS* side 393 *MS* whom,>who, 395 *MS* confidence in>honest championship of 397 *MS* triumph: now 400 *MS* fain, *MS* without>the unbridled *etc.* 402 *MS* two:>two. *405 *MS 1868 1872* Eh? *1888 1889* Eh! 406, 408 *MS* {quotation marks at beginnings of lines added later, with note in left-hand margin '[ ]otes to [ ]d'} 407 {not found in *MS*} 408 *MS* [?Cath]>Catch *MS* cause to me! *1868 1872* me! 409 {not found in *MS*} *1868 1872* "I had, 410–646 *MS* {no quotation marks at beginnings of lines} 410 *MS* {beginning of fo. 347} 411 *MS* so plain, a

394 *Monday . . . afterward*: Browning had calculated that the day of execution, 22 Feb., was a Saturday: see our Vol. VII, p. 325.

404 *the day*: i.e. the victory.

410–12 *I . . . monster*: cf. IX. 1419–20, where Bottini employs a similar metaphor.

412 *splash*: i.e. stir up from the river-bed.

"Small credit to lynx-eye and lightning-spear!
"This Guido,—(much sport he contrived to make,
"Who at first twist, preamble of the cord,
"Turned white, told all, like the poltroon he was!)—
"Finished, as you expect, a penitent,
"Fully confessed his crime, and made amends,
"And, edifying Rome last Saturday,
"Died like a saint, poor devil! That's the man
"The gods still give to my antagonist:
"Imagine how Arcangeli claps wing
"And crows! 'Such formidable facts to face,
"'So naked to attack, my client here,
"'And yet I kept a month the Fisc at bay,
"'And in the end had foiled him of the prize
"'By this arch-stroke, this plea of privilege,
"'But that the Pope must gratify his whim,
"'Put in his word, poor old man,—let it pass!'
"—Such is the cue to which all Rome responds.
"What with the plain truth given me to uphold,
"And, should I let truth slip, the Pope at hand
"To pick up, steady her on legs again,
"My office turns a pleasantry indeed!
"Not that the burly boaster did one jot
"O' the little was to do—young Spreti's work!
"But for him,—mannikin and dandiprat,

413 *MS* What>Where>Small credit *etc.* 414 *MS* was he fit to>he contrived to 416 *MS* white and told—like 418 *MS* made all 421 *MS* antagonist— 422 *MS 1868 1872* wing, 423 *MS* "Such 424 "So 425 *MS* "And 426 *MS* "And 427 *MS* "By 428 *MS* "But 429 *MS* "Put *MS* word— *MS* pass!" 430 *MS* responds: 431 *MS* def>uphold, 436 *MS* {'[]9.426' written in left-hand margin}

---

413 *lynx-eye*: cf. X. 1245 n.

415 *cord*: torture. Cf. I. 979–80 n.

427 *plea of privilege*: i.e. the plea of the clericate: see 252 n.

434 *pleasantry*: joke, amusement.

436 *Spreti*: Arcangeli's assistant lawyer: see I. 200 n.

437 *mannikin*: 'little man; dwarf': Johnson. Gulliver is called a 'mannikin' in Brobdingnag.

dandiprat: 'little fellow; urchin': Johnson.

"Mere candle-end and inch of cleverness
"Stuck on Arcangeli's save-all,—but for him
"The spruce young Spreti, what is bad were worse!

"I looked that Rome should have the natural gird
"At advocate with case that proves itself;
"I knew Arcangeli would grin and brag:
"But what say you to one impertinence
"Might move a stone? That monk, you are to know,
"That barefoot Augustinian whose report
"O' the dying woman's words did detriment
"To my best points it took the freshness from,
"—That meddler preached to purpose yesterday
"At San Lorenzo as a winding-up
"O' the show which proved a treasure to the church.
"Out comes his sermon smoking from the press:
"Its text—'Let God be true, and every man
"'A liar'—and its application, this
"The longest-winded of the paragraphs,
"I straight unstitch, tear out and treat you with:
"'T is piping hot and posts through Rome to-day.
"Remember it, as I engage to do!"

---

438 *MS* {beginning of fo. 348} *MS* The 441 *MS* {New paragraph indicated by 'New Par:' in left-hand margin} 443 {not found in *MS*} 445 *MS* *1868* man? *1872* stoic? *Yale 2* you are>please 448 *MS* speech>points *MS* skimmed>took 449 *MS* —This 451 *MS* shows have proved *1868* shows, have proved 452 *MS* his>the 453 *MS* It is>Its *etc.* *MS* "Let 454 *MS* "A liar"— *1868* *1872* this, 455 *MS* {no comma} 457 *MS* Rome by this. *458 *MS* *1868* *1872* *1888* *1889* {no quotation mark at end of line}

439 *save-all*: the small metal pan, with projecting pin, stuck into the base of a candle; it allowed the candle to burn right to the very bottom. The insulting image here is of Spreti as a tiny candle, shedding just a little bit of illumination on the case, held up on a 'save-all' by Arcangeli.

446 *barefoot Augustinian*: Fra Celestino, who attended Pompilia's death-bed: cf. III. 4, 18 nn., XI. 1729–31 n.

453–4 '*Let . . . liar*': cf. Rom. 3: 4: 'yea, let God be true, but every man a liar'.

457 *posts*: hurries.

"But if you rather be disposed to see
"In the result of the long trial here,—
"This dealing doom to guilt and doling praise
"To innocency,—any proof that truth
"May look for vindication from the world,
"Much will you have misread the signs, I say.
"God, who seems acquiescent in the main
"With those who add 'So will he ever sleep'—
"Flutters their foolishness from time to time,
"Puts forth His right-hand recognizably;
"Even as, to fools who deem He needs must right
"Wrong on the instant, as if earth were heaven,
"He wakes remonstrance—'Passive, Lord, how long?'
"Because Pompilia's purity prevails,
"Conclude you, all truth triumphs in the end?
"So might those old inhabitants of the ark,
"Witnessing haply their dove's safe return,
"Pronounce there was no danger, all the while
"O' the deluge, to the creature's counterparts,
"Aught that beat wing i' the world, was white or soft,—
"And that the lark, the thrush, the culver too,
"Might equally have traversed air, found earth,
"And brought back olive-branch in unharmed bill.

460 *MS* Trial 466 *MS* {beginning of fo. 349} *MS* "And so will ever be"— *1872* "Will *Yale 2* "Will>"With *1868* He 467 *MS* D[]>Flutters *etc. MS* that foolishness 468 *MS 1872* his 469 *1872* he 471 *MS* remonstrance: "passive, *MS* long?" 472 *MS* is plain, 473 *MS* I>Conclude *etc. MS* you truth must triumph 475 *MS* the dove's 476 *MS 1868 1872* {no comma} 477 *MS* deluge to 478 *MS* and soft,— 479 *MS* lark, the thrush, the nightingale,

459–646. Fra Celestino's homily is entirely Browning's invention.

466 *who add*: i.e. to some such words as 'God sleeps': Cook, 269.

468 *His right-hand*: in the Psalms God's right hand is a frequent image of his saving power: see Ps. 60: 5, 74: 11, 138: 7, etc.

471 '*Passive . . . long?*': a frequent biblical cry, most famously in Ps. 94: 3: 'Lord, how long shall the wicked, how long shall the wicked triumph?', but see also Jer. 12: 1–4, Ps. 35: 17, 82: 2, etc.

474–81 *So . . . bill*: the scenario is from Gen. 8: 8–11.

Culver: pigeon.

"Methinks I hear the Patriarch's warning voice—
" 'Though this one breast, by miracle, return,
" 'No wave rolls by, in all the waste, but bears
" 'Within it some dead dove-like thing as dear,
" 'Beauty made blank and harmlessness destroyed!'
"How many chaste and noble sister-fames
"Wanted the extricating hand, so lie
"Strangled, for one Pompilia proud above
"The welter, plucked from the world's calumny,
"Stupidity, simplicity,—who cares?

"Romans! An elder race possessed your land
"Long ago, and a false faith lingered still,
"As shades do, though the morning-star be out.
"Doubtless some pagan of the twilight-day
"Has often pointed to a cavern-mouth
"Obnoxious to beholders, hard by Rome,
"And said,—nor he a bad man, no, nor fool,
"Only a man born blind like all his mates,—
" 'Here skulk in safety, lurk, defying law,

483 *MS* 'Though *MS* breast return by miracle, 484 *MS* 'No 485 *MS* 'Within 486 *MS* 'Beauty *MS* [ ]>made 488 *MS 1868 1872* and lie *492 *MS* {no new paragraph} *1868 1872* {new paragraph. Paragraphing obscured in *1888* and *1889* by this line's being at the head of the page} *MS* Romans, the elder race,>Romans! The elder race, 493 *MS* while the false 494 *MS* {beginning of fo. 350} **MS 1868 1872* do, though *1888* do though {broken sort} *MS* out: 495 *MS* Doubtless, *1868* "Doubtless, *MS* twilight-day, 496 *MS* cavern's mouth *1868 1872* cavern-mouth, 498 *MS* no nor fool,— *1868 1872* fool,— 499 *MS* and blind *1868 1872* man, so, blind 500 *MS* 'Here *MS* skulked>skulk *MS* died,>lurked,>lurk,

482 *Patriarch's*: i.e. Noah's.

490 *welter*: the heaving sea.

494 *though . . . out*: though dawn has come, i.e. though the Christian faith has been revealed.

496 *cavern-mouth*: the entrance to one of the underground catacombs, the great labyrinth of passages under and near Rome, excavated by the early Christians to bury their dead. In Browning's day the catacombs were topical because of the ongoing work of the great archaeologist Giovanni Battista de Rossi (1822–94), who set study of them (the tombs, paintings, inscriptions, etc.) on a scientific basis.

497 *Obnoxious*: offensive, objectionable.

"'The devotees to execrable creed,
"'Adoring—with what culture . . . Jove, avert
"'Thy vengeance from us worshippers of thee! . . .
"'What rites obscene—their idol-god, an Ass!'
"So went the word forth, so acceptance found,
"So century re-echoed century,
"Cursed the accursed,—and so, from sire to son,
"You Romans cried 'The offscourings of our race
"'Corrupt within the depths there: fitly fiends
"'Perform a temple-service o'er the dead:
"'Child, gather garment round thee, pass nor pry!'
"Thus groaned your generations: till the time
"Grew ripe, and lightning had revealed, belike,—
"Thro' crevice peeped into by curious fear,—
"Some object even fear could recognize
"I' the place of spectres; on the illumined wall,
"To-wit, some nook, tradition talks about,
"Narrow and short, a corpse's length, no more:
"And by it, in the due receptacle,
"The little rude brown lamp of earthenware,
"The cruse, was meant for flowers but now held blood,

501 *MS* 'The *MS* of>to *etc.* 502 *MS* 'Adorers— *MS 1868 1872* culture . . 503 *MS* 'Thy *MS 1868 1872* thee! . . 504 *MS* 'What rites obscene their idol-god—an Ass! *1872* {no comma} 506 *MS* {no comma} 507 *MS* [ ]>Cursed *MS* accursed,—so, 508 *MS* "The>'The *1872* race, 509 *MS* 'Corrupt *MS 1868 1872* fitly, 510 *MS* 'Perform *MS* there>a *MS* temple service 511 *MS* 'Child, 512 *MS* So *1868 1872* "So 513 *MS* ripe,— *MS* hath revealed,—belike, 515 *MS* you could 516 *MS* shadows— 518 *1872* length no *MS* more, 521 *MS* flowers, that held the blood, *1868 1872* flowers, but held the blood,

504 *idol-god, an Ass*: this was a common misunderstanding or insult foisted by the pagans on the early Christians.

508 *offscourings*: dregs, disreputable people. Cf. 1 Cor. 4: 13.

517–18 *nook . . . length*: in the catacombs 'the graves, or *loculi*, are cut out of the rock sides of the galleries, so that the length of the bodies can be judged from the length of the graves': *Catholic Encyclopedia*, iii. 417.

521 *cruse*: small earthen pot or phial. Many of these small pots or ampullae have been found secured to the outer surface of the mortar seals of the catacomb graves, containing, on their insides, a deposit of a reddish-brown tinge. In Browning's day it was believed that the pots had held blood, and that they indicated the graves of martyrs.

"The rough-scratched palm-branch, and the legend left
"*Pro Christo*. Then the mystery lay clear:
"The abhorred one was a martyr all the time,
"Heaven's saint whereof earth was not worthy. What?
"Do you continue in the old belief?
"Where blackness bides unbroke, must devils brood?
"Is it so certain not another cell
"O' the myriad that make up the catacomb
"Contains some saint a second flash would show?
"Will you ascend into the light of day
"And, having recognized a martyr's shrine,
"Go join the votaries that gape around
"Each vulgar god that awes the market-place?
"Are these the objects of your praising? See!
"In the outstretched right hand of Apollo, there,
"Lies screened a scorpion: housed amid the folds
"Of Juno's mantle lurks a centipede!
"Each statue of a god were fitlier styled
"Demon and devil. Glorify no brass
"That shines like burnished gold in noonday glare,
"For fools! Be otherwise instructed, you!
"And preferably ponder, ere ye judge,
"Each incident of this strange human play

522 *MS* {beginning of fo. 351} 523 *MS Christo*: then *MS* was>lay *MS* clear. 524 *MS* ones were the martyrs all the while,>one was a martyr all the time, 525 *MS* The saints>A saint *1868 1872* "A saint *MS* Well?> What? 526 *MS* belief— 527 *MS* {no comma} *MS 1868 1872* be? 528 *MS* The certainty that *1868 1872* certain, 529 *MS 1868 1872* catacomb, 530 *MS* a>some *MS* show 533 *MS* the>join *etc.* 534 *MS* Each god that [ ] the>Each god that [ ] the>Each vulgar god that awes the 535 *MS* Be *1868 1872* "Be *MS* Praise>See! 536 *MS* outstretched hand *MS* Apollo,>the Apollo, 537 *MS* [ ]>Is screened *1868 1872* "Is 538 *MS* mantle, lo a cockatrice! *1868 1872* mantle, lo, a cockatrice! 540 *MS* devil: glorify 541 *MS* burnished like> shines like burnished *Yale 2* shines>shines, *MS* noon-day 542 *MS* Say fools: be 543 *MS* ye pass *1868 1872* ye pass,

522 *palm-branch*: a symbol of the triumph of the martyrs: cf. Rev. 7: 9.

523 *Pro Christo*: 'For Christ' (L.).

525 *whereof . . . worthy*: cf. Heb. 11: 38.

538 *centipede*: this worm-like insect can be poisonous in hot countries. In the end, insists Fra Celestino, worship of the pagan gods can be deadly to the soul.

"Privily acted on a theatre
"That seemed secure from every gaze but God's,—
"Till, of a sudden, earthquake laid wall low
"And let the world perceive wild work inside
"And how, in petrifaction of surprise,
"The actors stood,—raised arm and planted foot,—
"Mouth as it made, eye as it evidenced,
"Despairing shriek, triumphant hate,—transfixed,
"Both he who takes and she who yields the life.

"As ye become spectators of this scene,
"Watch obscuration of a pearl-pure fame
"By vapoury films, enwoven circumstance,
"—A soul made weak by its pathetic want
"Of just the first apprenticeship to sin
"Which thenceforth makes the sinning soul secure
"From all foes save itself, souls' truliest foe,—
"Since egg turned snake needs fear no serpentry,—
"As ye behold this web of circumstance
"Deepen the more for every thrill and throe,

545 *1868 1872* theatre, 546 *MS* Was deemed *1868 1872* "Was deemed 547 *MS* Where[?on]>Whereof *MS* a sudden earthquake lays *1868 1872* lays 548 *MS 1868 1872* lets *MS 1868 1872* see the *MS 1868 1872* inside, 550 *MS* {beginning of fo. 352} *MS 1868 1872* stand,— *MS* foot, 551 *MS* ^Mouth as it made,^ 552 *MS* hat[?red],>hate, *MS* transfixed 553 *MS* life,— 554 *MS* {no new paragraph} *MS 1868 1872* scene— 555 *MS 1868 1872* a fame pearl-pure 556 *MS* In *1868 1872* "In *MS* films of>films, 558 *1868 1872* sin, 559 *MS* Would thenceforth make *1868 1872* "Would thenceforth make 560 *MS* that's truest *1868 1872* that's truliest 561 *MS* Egg that turns *1868 1872* "For

551–2 *Mouth . . . hate*: i.e. mouth as it made despairing shriek (Pompilia's cry), eye (Guido's) as it evidenced triumphant hate. This rhetorical flourish anticipates the startling rhetoric of ll. 554–609, the climax of Fra Celestino's homily, which is just one extended sentence.

555 *pearl-pure fame*: in the following extended sentence Pompilia's pure fame is like a 'star' (571), 'orb' (579), or 'disc' (587) which the powers of evil try to cover with webs and meshes, or otherwise darken. Evidently, however, through the Pope's judgement, the star 'culminates' at the top of the sky, shining in its true splendour.

557–61 *A . . . serpentry*: i.e. a person who knows sin, knows how to deal with the world on its own terms; Pompilia is so pure that only her own soul challenges her, to take her to deeper levels of virtue—hence she is vulnerable to the world's vicious ways.

"Convulsive effort to disperse the films
"And disenmesh the fame o' the martyr,—mark
"How all those means, the unfriended one pursues,
"To keep the treasure trusted to her breast,
"Each struggle in the flight from death to life,
"How all, by procuration of the powers
"Of darkness, are transformed,—no single ray,
"Shot forth to show and save the inmost star,
"But, passed as through hell's prism, proceeding black
"To the world that hates white: as ye watch, I say,
"Till dusk and such defacement grow eclipse
"By,—marvellous perversity of man!—
"The inadequacy and inaptitude
"Of that self-same machine, that very law
"Man vaunts, devised to dissipate the gloom,
"Rescue the drowning orb from calumny,
"—Hear law, appointed to defend the just,
"Submit, for best defence, that wickedness
"Was bred of flesh and innate with the bone
"Borne by Pompilia's spirit for a space,
"And no mere chance fault, passionate and brief:
"Finally, when ye find,—after this touch
"Of man's protection which intends to mar
"The last pin-point of light and damn the disc,—
"One wave of the hand of God amid the worlds

566 *MS* pursued *MS* {no commas} 567 *MS* breast— 568 *MS* life— 570 *MS* darkness were 571 *MS* {no comma} 572 *MS* proceeded 573 *MS* []>white: *MS* watched, 574 *MS* grew 575 *MS* man,— 576 *MS* ineptitude 578 *MS* {beginning of fo. 353} 579 *MS* []>Rescue *MS* of innocence,— 580 *MS* —And 581 *MS* Submitted for defence that 583 {not found in *MS*} 585 *MS* Last,>Finally, *MS* happy touch>touch 588 *MS* world

565 *disenmesh*: extricate, free. OED[2] gives only this instance, and describes it as 'very rare'. We have been unable to trace any other use.

576 *inaptitude*: i.e. uselessness.

577 *machine . . . law*: cf. I. 1108–10 n.

580–4 *Hear . . . brief*: i.e. Bottini's supposed defence of Pompilia did not see the impropriety of her escape with Caponsacchi as a 'mere chance fault', but as the outcome of deep-seated wickedness.

588 *hand of God*: cf. 468 n.

"Bid vapour vanish, darkness flee away,
"And let the vexed star culminate in peace
"Approachable no more by earthly mist—
"What I call God's hand,—you, perhaps,—mere chance
"Of the true instinct of an old good man
"Who happens to hate darkness and love light,—
"In whom too was the eye that saw, not dim,
"The natural force to do the thing he saw,
"Nowise abated,—both by miracle,—
"All this well pondered,—I demand assent
"To the enunciation of my text
"In face of one proof more that 'God is true
" 'And every man a liar'—that who trusts
"To human testimony for a fact
"Gets this sole fact—himself is proved a fool;
"Man's speech being false, if but by consequence
"That only strength is true: while man is weak,
"And, since truth seems reserved for heaven not earth,
"Plagued here by earth's prerogative of lies,
"Should learn to love and long for what, one day,
"Approved by life's probation, he may speak.

[—]

590 *MS 1868 1872* leave 592 *MS* hand; and the world,—this chance *1868 1872* this chance *Yale 2* this>call 595 *MS* eye, *MS* dim 596 *MS* {no comma} 598 *MS* [ ]>All *MS* why refuse assent 600 *MS* that God 601 *MS* {no quotation marks at beginning of line} *MS* liar— 603 *MS* fool, 605 *MS* true, *1868* true; *1872* true! 607 {not found in *MS 1868*} 608 *MS* Learns to love now *1872* Now learns *MS 1868* what he may speak one day. 609 {not found in *MS 1868*}

590 *culminate*: (astron.) reach its zenith, reach its high point in the sky. This is a curious, perhaps accidental, echo of the use in Tennyson's *The Princess*, II. 326–7: ' "Be it so" the other, "that we still may lead / The new light up, and culminate in peace . . . '

594 *hate . . . light*: cf. John 3: 20–1.

595–7 *In . . . abated*: a beautiful comparison of the ageing Pope to the ageing Moses; cf. Deut. 34: 7: 'And Moses was an hundred and twenty years old when he died: his eye was not dim, nor his natural force abated.'

600–1 '*God . . . liar*': cf. ll. 453–4 n.

602 *human testimony*: cf. l. 839 n.

605 *strength*: integrity, hardihood of virtue.

605–9 *while . . . speak*: the main clause here is: 'while man is weak, And . . . Should learn to love and long for what, one day, . . . he may speak', viz. the truth he will be able to utter in heaven.

"For me, the weary and worn, who haply prompt
"To mirth or pity, as I move the mood,—
"A friar who glides unnoticed to the grave,
"With these bare feet, coarse robe and rope-girt waist,—
"I have long since renounced your world, ye know:
"Yet what forbids I weigh the prize forgone,
"The worldly worth? I dare, as I were dead,
"Disinterestedly judge this and that
"Good ye account good: but God tries the heart.
"Still, if you question me of my content
"At having put each human pleasure by,
"I answer, at the urgency of truth:
"As this world seems, I dare not say I know
"—Apart from Christ's assurance which decides—
"Whether I have not failed to taste much joy.
"For many a doubt will fain perturb my choice—
"Many a dream of life spent otherwise—
"How human love, in varied shapes, might work
"As glory, or as rapture, or as grace:
"How conversancy with the books that teach,

610 *MS* {beginning of fo. 354} *MS* {no new paragraph indicated. Paragraphing obscured in *MS* by this line's being at the head of the page} *MS 1868 1872* the worn, who prompt *MS* [ ]>who 611 *MS* pity as may move the mood 612 {not found in *MS*} *1868* glide 613 *MS* Bare *1868* "Bare *MS 1868* feet, coarse robe and rope-girt waist of *MS* mine, *1868* mine,— 614 *MS* know[ ]> know, 615 *MS* Yet *MS 1868* weigh the worth of worldly prize *MS* put by:>foregone: 616 {not found in *MS 1868*} 617 *MS* pronounce on 620 the human 621 *MS 1868* truth, 622 *MS* 'As 624 *MS* joy: *1868* some joy. 625 *MS 1868* dream would *1872* would 626 {not found in *MS 1868*} 627 *MS 1868* How love, in those the varied shapes, might show 628 *MS* glory, as>glory, or 629 *MS* And

618 *God . . . heart*: cf. 1 Chr. 29: 17: 'I know also, my God, that thou triest the heart, and hast pleasure in uprightness.'

621 *urgency*: urging.

622–4 *I . . . joy*: 'I cannot say for certain that I haven't missed out on a lot of joy—I only know this through Christ's assurance.' 'Christ's assurance' is that given in Mark 10: 29–30: see x. 1803–8 n.

627–8 *human . . . grace*: i.e. married love might be a glorious pathway to heaven.

629–33 *conversancy . . . there*: as a monk, Fra Celestino has renounced learning and scholarship. Here he wonders if he had become an intellectual whether he might then have spread goodness further.

"The arts that help,—how, to grow good and great,
"Rather than simply good, and bring thereby
"Goodness to breathe and live, nor, born i' the brain,
"Die there,—how these and many another gift
"Of life are precious though abjured by me.
"But, for one prize, best meed of mightiest man,
"Arch-object of ambition,—earthly praise,
"Repute o' the world, the flourish of loud trump,
"The softer social fluting,—Oh, for these,
"—No, my friends! Fame,—that bubble which, world-wide
"Each blows and bids his neighbour lend a breath,
"That so he haply may behold thereon
"One more enlarged distorted false fool's-face,
"Until some glassy nothing grown as big
"Send by a touch the imperishable to suds,—
"No, in renouncing fame, my loss was light,
"Choosing obscurity, my chance was well!"

"Didst ever touch such ampollosity
"As the monk's own bubble, let alone its spite?
"What's his speech for, but just the fame he flouts?
"How he dares reprehend both high and low,
"Nor stoops to turn the sentence 'God is true

630 *MS* that to grow great, in fine, *1868* how, to grow great, in fine, 633 *MS* there: all 634 *MS 1868* May well be precious 635 *MS* But for *MS* mighty 637 *MS* of>o' *MS* fame's trump, 638 {not found in *MS*} 639 *MS* for that *MS* world-[ ]>world-wide 640 *MS* Ye blow and bid your>Each blows and bids his *MS* his breath,>the breath, 642 *MS* dis>en-larged 643 *MS* {beginning of fo. 355} 645 *MS 1868* the loss 646 *MS* I have not erred! *1868* the chance *647–51 *MS 1868 1872 1888 1889* {no quotation marks at beginnings of lines} 648 *MS 1868 1872* man's *MS* [ ]>fool's-speech, *etc.* 649, 650 {not found in *MS*} 649 *1868* flouts— 650 *1868* low? 651 *MS* He might have round period>He might have turned the sentence *etc. 1868* Else had he turned

635 *meed*: reward.

639 *Fame . . . bubble*: cf. III. 1353–4 n., and 'Karshish', 4 n.

643 *some . . . big*: i.e. someone else's gross 'bubble' of fame.

647 *ampollosity*: pomposity, exaggeration, inflatedness. Browning's coinage from the It. *ampollosità*.

649 *flouts*: denigrates.

651–4 *Nor. . . period*: i.e. he does not even make the Pope an exception to his text 'God is true and every man a liar.'

"'And every man a liar—save the Pope
"'Happily reigning—my respects to him!'
"And so round off the period. Molinism
"Simple and pure! To what pitch get we next?
"I find that, for first pleasant consequence,
"Gomez, who had intended to appeal
"From the absurd decision of the Court,
"Declines, though plain enough his privilege,
"To call on help from lawyers any more—
"Resolves earth's liars may possess the world
"Till God have had sufficiency of both:
"So may I whistle for my job and fee!

"But, for this virulent and rabid monk,—
"If law be an inadequate machine,
"And advocacy, froth and impotence,
"We shall soon see, my blatant brother! That's
"Exactly what I hope to show your sort!
"For, by a veritable piece of luck,
"The providence, you monks round period with,
"All may be gloriously retrieved. Perpend!

[—]

*652 *MS 1868 1872 1888 1889* "And *653 *MS 1868 1872 1888 1889* "Happily *MS 1868 1872 1888 1889* him!" *654–734 *MS 1868 1872 1888 1889* {no quotation marks at beginnings of lines} 654 *MS* And—so round>—So rounded *1868* —So, rounded *1872* —So, rounding 655 *MS* pure—to *MS* this>what 659 *MS* plainly on his [ ]>plain enough his privilege, 660 *MS* have to do with>call on help from 661 *MS 1868 1872* the liars *MS* persuade>harangue **MS 1868 1872 1888* world, *DC BrU* world,>world *1889* world 662 *MS* both,— 664 *MS* {no new paragraph} 666 *MS* And advocates—superfluous impotence, *1868* so much impotence, 667 *MS* There's 668 *MS* sort— 670 *MS* providence you

654 *Molinism*: i.e. heresy.

657 *Gomez*: the case already mentioned at ll. 325–6: see n. In the following lines, it would appear that Gomez has been influenced by Fra Celestino's sermon, and given up the idea of pursuing his case further in the courts—much to Bottini's annoyance. Both Bottini's potential involvement in this case, and this detail of Gomez's withdrawal from the legal process, are Browning's invention.

665 *inadequate machine*: Bottini refers angrily to Fra Celestino's characterization of the law at l. 577: see n.

667 *blatant*: vulgar, pushy, noisy.

670 *round period with*: i.e. piously mention at the end of every sentence.

671 *Perpend*: ponder, consider.

"That Monastery of the Convertites
"Whereto the Court consigned Pompilia first,
"—Observe, if convertite, why, sinner then,
"Or what's the pertinency of award?—
"And whither she was late returned to die,
"—Still in their jurisdiction, mark again!—
"That thrifty Sisterhood, for perquisite,
"Claims every piece whereof may die possessed
"Each sinner in the circuit of its walls.
"Now, this Pompilia seeing that, by death
"O' the couple, all their wealth devolved on her,
"Straight utilized the respite ere decease,
"By regular conveyance of the goods
"She thought her own, to will and to devise,—

672 *MS* {beginning of fo. 356} **1868* {new paragraph. Paragraphing obscured in *1872*, *1888* and *1889* by this line's being at the head of the page} 674 *MS* then 675 *MS 1868* Or where the 679 *MS 1868 1872* every paul 681 *MS 1868* Pompilia, *MS 1868* that by 683 *MS* Had utilized *MS 1868* {no comma} 684 *MS* all good 685 *MS* [ ]>She *MS* devise

672–3 *Monastery...first*: here, and in what follows, Browning draws on the last document of OYB, the *Instrumentum Sententiæ Definitivæ* ('Instrument of Final Judgement') of 9 Sept. 1698: cclix–cclxii (252–6). This shows that, after Pompilia's death and Guido's execution, the Convent of St Mary Magdalene of the Convertites, in the Corso (founded 1520 *pro mulieribus ab inhonesta vita ad honestam se convertentibus*) laid claim to the whole of Pompilia's property on the ground of their privilege of receiving the property of women of evil life who died in Rome: they argued that, at least implicitly, she had been caught in adultery, therefore she was a 'fallen woman', so they should be her major heir. Eventually, as the 'Instrument of Final Judgement' shows, Marcantonio Venturini, the 'Most Illustrious Governor in criminal cases', ruled against this claim.

Browning was baffled, perhaps shocked, by this piece of fast-dealing by a religious institution trying to snap up available wealth, and he weaves this final document on the Franceschini case into his story. He does, however, make certain changes, probably with poetic licence, perhaps in error. After her flight with Caponsacchi from Arezzo in April 1697, Pompilia was remanded into the care of a convent on the Via della Lungara, the Conservatory of the Holy Cross of the Penitents, also known as the *Scalette*: see OYB cxlvii (151), ccxxii (223). Here, as at x. 1499–1500, Browning conflates this with the Convent of St Mary Magdalene, which did indeed make the claim on her estate: see OYB cxlvii (151), ccxxii (223). For other changes, see the following nn.

674 *convertite*: i.e. reformed woman, penitent.

676 *whither... die*: Browning was uncertain where she had died: cf. II. 4 n. In actual fact, Pompilia died in her parents' house.

"Gave all to friends, Tighetti and the like,
"In trust for him she held her son and heir,
"Gaetano,—trust which ends with infancy:
"So willing and devising, since assured
"The justice of the Court would presently
"Confirm her in her rights and exculpate,
"Re-integrate and rehabilitate—
"Place her as, through my pleading, now she stands.
"But here's the capital mistake: the Court
"Found Guido guilty,—but pronounced no word
"About the innocency of his wife:
"I grounded charge on broader base, I hope!
"No matter whether wife be true or false,
"The husband must not push aside the law,
"And punish of a sudden: that's the point:
"Gather from out my speech the contrary!
"It follows that Pompilia, unrelieved
"By formal sentence from imputed fault,
"Remains unfit to have and to dispose
"Of property which law provides shall lapse.
"Wherefore the Monastery claims its due:
"And whose, pray, whose the office, but the Fisc's?
"Who but I institute procedure next

686 *MS* To certain friends, *MS* rest, 687 *MS* for whom 688 *MS* *1868 1872* to end 689 *MS* Willing, devising, as assured, no doubt, 690 *MS* pending>justice 691 *MS* rights as exculpate, 693 *MS* [ ]>Just *MS* as, thro' my endeavour, *1868* Station as, 697 *MS* warily>grounded 699 *MS* [ ]>The *MS* [?punish with his hands]>push aside the law, 700 *MS* {beginning of fo. 357} *MS* point— *1868 1872* point! 701 *Yale 2* Gather from out> Who gathers from *Yale 2* contrary!>contrary? 705 *MS* property, such fault *1868 1872* property, *MS 1868 1872* lapse: 706 *MS* due— *1868 1872* due. 707 *MS* pray,— *MS* Fisc's, 708 *MS* procedure now

686–8 *Tighetti . . . Gaetano*: Domenico Tighetti is named as Pompilia's *hæres beneficiatus* ('heir beneficiary') throughout the 'Instrument of Final Judgement'. The detail that Gaetano was the proper heir is from OYB cxiii (121).

691 *exculpate*: find free from guilt.

692 *Re-integrate*: restore, renew. This word is taken straight from the first phrase of the 'Instrument of Final Judgement': 'Latæ pro reintegratione famæ'. Cf. IX. 1471 n.

705 *lapse*: (a legal sense), i.e. cease to be hers or her heirs.

708 *Who but I*: in fact it was Francesco Gambi, Procurator General of the Fisc, who pursued this case, not Bottini: see OYB cclx (253). Browning takes poetic licence here.

"Against the person of dishonest life,
"Pompilia, whom last week I sainted so?
"I it is teach the monk what scripture means,
"And that the tongue should prove a two-edged sword,
"No axe sharp one side, blunt the other way,
"Like what amused the town at Guido's cost!
"*Astræa redux!* I've a second chance
"Before the self-same Court o' the Governor
"Who soon shall see volte-face and chop, change sides.
"Accordingly, I charge you on your life,
"Send me with all despatch the judgment late
"O' the Florence Rota Court, confirmative
"O' the prior judgment at Arezzo, clenched
"Again by the Granducal signature,
"Wherein Pompilia is convicted, doomed,
"And only destined to escape through flight
"The proper punishment. Send me the piece,—
"I'll work it! And this foul-mouthed friar shall find
"His Noah's-dove that brought the olive back
"Turn into quite the other sooty scout,
"The raven, Noah first put forth the ark,
"Which never came back but ate carcasses!

*710 *MS 1868 1872* Pompilia, *1888 1889* Pompilia 711 *MS* I'll>I, *1868 1872* I, *MS 1868 1872* is, 712 *MS* should be 715 *MS* Astræa redux, 717 *MS 1868 1872* sides! 719 *MS* sentence>judgement 720 *MS* and>Court, 721 *MS* Of>O' 722 *MS* Ganduke's [*sic*] signature and seal— 725 *1872* peace,— 727 *MS* this>the *MS 1868 1872* back, 728 *MS* {beginning of fo. 358} *MS 1868* Is turned into the 729 *MS* raven Noah first of all *MS* [ ]> put *1868 1872* first of all put 730 *MS* That *1868* And *MS 1868 1872* back,

709 *dishonest*: dishonorable, wicked.

712 *tongue . . . two-edged sword*: cf. Heb. 4: 12: 'For the word of God is quick, and powerful, and sharper than any two-edged sword.' In his annoyance, Bottini makes witty, ironic use of the text: it is his own tongue (not the word of God, scripture) that is the sword, and it is 'two-edged' because he has the skill to argue both for and against Pompilia.

715 *Astræa redux!*: 'Justice brought back' (L.).

720–2 *Florence . . . signature*: cf. XI. 1663–5 n.

727–30 *His . . . carcasses!*: i.e. his beautiful dove (Pompilia) turned into a disgusting bird; cf. Gen. 8: 7. Bottini is referring contemptuously to Fra Celestino's use of Genesis at ll. 474–91.

"No adequate machinery in law?
"No power of life and death i' the learned tongue?
"Methinks I am already at my speech,
"Startle the world with 'Thou, Pompilia, thus?
" 'How is the fine gold of the Temple dim!'
"And so forth. But the courier bids me close,
"And clip away one joke that runs through Rome,
"Side by side with the sermon which I send.
"How like the heartlessness of the old hunks
"Arcangeli! His Count is hardly cold,
"The client whom his blunders sacrificed,
"When somebody must needs describe the scene—
"How the procession ended at the church
"That boasts the famous relic: quoth our brute,
" 'Why, that's just Martial's phrase for 'make an end'—
" '*Ad umbilicum sic perventum est!*'
"The callous dog,—let who will cut off head,
"He cuts a joke and cares no more than so!

732 {not found in *MS*} 734 *MS* Start the exordium>Startle the world with **MS 1868 1872 1888 1889* "Thou 735 *MS 1868 1872 1888 1889* "How **MS* dim," *1868 1872 1888 1889* dim!" **736–44 *MS 1868 1872 1888 1889* {no quotation marks at beginnings of lines} 737–50 {not found in *MS*} 738 *1868* send— 741 *1868* His *745 *MS 1868 1872 1888 1889* "Why *746 *MS 1868 1872 1888 1889* "*Ad* **MS 1868 1872 1888 1889* *est!*" *747–9 *MS 1868 1872 1888 1889* {no quotation marks at beginnings of lines} 748 *1868 1872* joke,

732 *No . . . tongue?*: cf. Prov. 18: 21: 'Death and life are in the power of the tongue.'

735 *How . . . dim!*: cf. Lam. 4: 1: 'How is the gold become dim! how is the most fine gold changed!'

737 *clip away*: tell quickly.

739 *hunks*: 'a covetous, sordid wretch; a miser; a curmudgeon': Johnson.

746 *Ad . . . est!*: 'thus is the *umbilicus* (i.e. the end) reached', adapting Martial, *Epigrams*, 11. 89. 2. Bottini reports this bad joke by Arcangeli, a pun on two senses of *umbilicus* (the end of a book, and the umbilical cord): Arcangeli is referring to the information given us at ll. 182–4: see n. In the first sense, in the ancient world, the *umbilicus* was either the rod on which a papyrus was wound, or an ornamental knob attached to the end of that rod; hence the phrase *ad umbilicum*, 'to the end (of the book)'.

748 *cuts*: makes. This is a nonce use, simply taking up 'cut off' in the preceding line: while the executioner cuts off a head, Arcangeli cuts language to make a smart joke.

"I think my speech shall modify his mirth.
" 'How is the fine gold dim!'—but send the piece!"

Alack, Bottini, what is my next word
But death to all that hope? The Instrument
Is plain before me, print that ends my Book
With the definitive verdict of the Court,
Dated September, six months afterward,
(Such trouble and so long the old Pope gave!)
"In restitution of the perfect fame
"Of dead Pompilia, *quondam* Guido's wife,
"And warrant to her representative
"Domenico Tighetti, barred hereby,
"While doing duty in his guardianship,
"From all molesting, all disquietude,
"Each perturbation and vexation brought
"Or threatened to be brought against the heir
"By the Most Venerable Convent called
"Saint Mary Magdalen o' the Convertites
"I' the Corso."
Justice done a second time!
Well judged, Marc Antony, *Locum-tenens*

749 *1868 1872* mirth: 750 *MS 1868 1872 1888 1889* "How *MS 1868 1872 1888 1889* dim!"— *MS 1868 1872 1888 1889* piece! 753 *MS* Book,> Book 754 *MS* jud>verdict *etc.* *MS* {no comma} 755 *MS* afterward 756 *MS 1868 1872* long, *MS* {brackets added later} 757 *MS* [?"To]>"In 760 *MS* thereby, 762 *MS* molestings,>molesting 764 *MS* the same 765 *MS* most>Most *767 *MS 1868 1872* "I' *1888 1889* 'I' {broken sort} 768 *MS* {New paragraph indicated by 'New Par/' in right-hand margin} *MS* time— 769 *MS locumtenens>Locumtenens*

---

752 *The Instrument*: the 'Instrument of Final Judgment': see 672–3 n.

757–67 *"In . . . Corso."*: a fairly exact translation of the opening sentence of the 'Instrument': OYB cclix (252).

769–70 *Marc Antony . . . too*: the detail here is suggested by the phrasing at OYB cclx, that Marcus Antonius Venturinus (Marcantonio Venturini) 'holds the judicial bench on behalf of the Most Illustrious and Most Reverend Governor of our dear city'. It is Browning's poetic licence that the Governor was also a Venturini. *locum-tenens* = substitute or deputy.

O' the Governor, a Venturini too!
For which I save thy name,—last of the list!

Next year but one, completing his nine years
Of rule in Rome, died Innocent my Pope
—By some accounts, on his accession-day.
If he thought doubt would do the next age good,
'T is pity he died unapprised what birth
His reign may boast of, be remembered by—
Terrible Pope, too, of a kind,—Voltaire.

And so an end of all i' the story. Strain
Never so much my eyes, I miss the mark
If lived or died that Gaetano, child
Of Guido and Pompilia: only find,
Immediately upon his father's death,
A record, in the annals of the town—
That Porzia, sister of our Guido, moved

770 *MS* and Venturini 771 *MS* name: *MS* list. 772 *MS* {beginning of fo. 359} *MS* {New paragraph indicated by 'New Par.' in left-hand margin} *774 *MS 1868* accounts, *1872 1888 1889* account, 776 *MS* Tis 777 *MS* boast and be 779 *MS* {New paragraph indicated by 'New Par.' in left-hand margin} 780 *MS* aught marks 781 *MS 1868* There lived *MS* Gaetano-child 782 *MS* {no comma} 783 *MS* {no comma} 784 *MS 1868* {no comma} *MS 1868* town 785 *MS* our worthy,

774 *By . . . accession day*: Innocent was voted into office on 12 July 1691 and died on 27 Sept. 1700. The coincidence of dates in 'some accounts' may come from his later official inauguration in 1691, but we have been unable to determine the date of this.

778 *Voltaire*: the great French intellectual (1694–1778), but certainly someone whose wit and general attitude laid the ground for religious scepticism. He is 'Pope, too, of a kind' because he was a leader of the Enlightenment, with a wide authority and influence. He often savagely attacked revealed religion and the Catholic Church, insisting on a broad humanitarianism, a simple deism in matters of faith, and the importance of rationality and of religious tolerance. Browning's attitude towards him was admiring but ambivalent. In 'The Two Poets of Croisic' (1878) Voltaire is made to think of himself as 'the Iconoclast, / The Poet, the Philosopher, the Rod / Of iron for imposture' (1086–8), but is then shown as the dupe of a simple literary fraud. In 'La Saisiaz' (1878) he is 'wit's self', a man in whom 'Laughter . . . bejewels Learning', but he is also a strange snake twisted round the Tree of Knowledge (583–6, 596).

784 *record . . . town*: in what follows here, Browning draws on a real document, still in the civic archives of Arezzo. Dated Dec. 1701, it is a short, lavishly-worded proclamation of the premier position and worth in Arezzo of the Conti di Bivignano

The Priors of Arezzo and their head
Its Gonfalonier to give loyally
A public attestation of the right
O' the Franceschini to all reverence—
Apparently because of the incident
O' the murder,—there's no mention made o' the crime,
But what else could have caused such urgency
To cure the mob, just then, of greediness
For scandal, love of lying vanity,
And appetite to swallow crude reports
That bring annoyance to their betters?—bane
Which, here, was promptly met by antidote.
I like and shall translate the eloquence
Of nearly the worst Latin ever writ:
"Since antique time whereof the memory

788 *MS* to the 789 *MS 1868* to men's 791 *MS* made of that, *1868* made of crime, 792 *MS 1868* caused such urgency to cure 793 *MS* [?There]> The *MS* common people of their qualms—so prompt>mob, just then, of chronic qualmishness? *1868* The mob, just then, of chronic greediness 794 {not found in *MS*} 795 *MS* To swallow crude report so it>Do not folks ever swallow crude report 796 *MS* brings *MS 1868* Bane 797 *MS* f>here, 798 *MS* I have read and shall repeat you word for word>I read and shall translate the eloquence

---

family, the family into which Guido's sister, Porzia, had married. (It mentions Porzia, as 'formerly of the Franceschini'.) Browning twists the document to apply directly to the Franceschini family, though really it shows the widow Porzia dei Conti di Bivignano seeking to clear her name of the slur of the murder-case. Browning, of course, knew nothing about the Conti di Bivignano family from the sources available to him, and they formed no part of his story, so—if he wanted to draw on the document at all—his sleight of hand was sensible in imaginative terms. The proclamation is in the civic archives of Arezzo, *Registri di lettere*, vol. 32, fols. 207^{v}–208^{r}. (It was discovered in 2001 by Simonetta Berbeglia, in connection with the research presented in the Afterword of this volume.) Contrary to the belief of Cook and others, Browning could not have discovered this document himself in his very brief passages through Arezzo in 1860 and 1861. We conjecture that it was found in Arezzo by Seymour Kirkup in the summer of 1868, copied by him, and sent to Browning along with his watercolour drawing of the Franceschini coat of arms: see XI. 2161–4 n. This would explain why the references both to the coat of arms and to this 'public attestation . . . to all reverence' occur so late in the poem.

786–7 *Priors . . . Gonfalonier*: the *Priori*, the ruling council of Arezzo, had eight members, four of whom were noblemen, with at its head the *Gonfaloniere* or Chief Magistrate. *Gonfaloniere* = lit. 'bearer of the *gonfalone*' (It. banner, flag). See Franco Cristelli, *Storia civile e religiosa di Arezzo in età medicea* (Arezzo, 1982), pp. 13–16.

"Holds the beginning, to this present hour,
"The Franceschini ever shone, and shine
"Still i' the primary rank, supreme amid
"The lustres of Arezzo, proud to own
"In this great family, the flag-bearer,
"Guide of her steps and guardian against foe,—
"As in the first beginning, so to-day!"
There, would you disbelieve the annalist,
Go rather by the babble of a bard?
I thought, Arezzo, thou hadst fitter souls,
Petrarch,—nay, Buonarroti at a pinch,
To do thee credit as *vexillifer!*
Was it mere mirth the Patavinian meant,
Making thee out, in his veracious page,
Founded by Janus of the Double Face?

Well, proving of such perfect parentage,
Our Gaetano, born of love and hate,

801 *MS* {beginning of fo. 360} *MS* "Preserves>"Holds the 802 *1868* "Our *MS 1868 1872* shine, 803 *MS* "I' the *MS* supreme their lustre mid 804 *MS* "The light of our 805 *MS 1868* family—her 807 *MS* {no quotation mark at end of line} 808 *MS 1868* stern History, 809 *MS 1868* Trust rather to 810–12 {not found in *MS*} 813 *MS* Ah, City, was it mirth *MS* that Livius meant>the Paduan meant 816 *MS* {no new paragraph} *MS* this perfect 817 {not found in *MS*}

808–9 *There . . . bard?*: an ironic question: 'Are you really going to disbelieve a serious historian, as against me, a mere poet?'

811 *Petrarch*: because his father was in exile from Florence, the great Italian poet Petrarch (1304–74) was born in Arezzo. However, he spent only a few years here, since his father subsequently took the family to Avignon, in southern France.

811 *Buonarroti . . . pinch*: Michelangelo Buonarroti (1475–1564) can only just be claimed for Arezzo because he was born at Chiusi-e-Caprese, within the diocese of Arezzo. Browning is probably remembering Michelangelo's joke to Vasari (recorded near the beginning of Vasari's life of him): 'Giorgio, if I have anything good in me, that comes from my birth in the pure air of your country of Arezzo': Vasari, v. 229. In 1529 Michelangelo was expected in Arezzo to plan improvements in the town fortifications, but it is not certain whether he arrived.

812 *vexillifer*: flagbearer (giving the original Latin for the word in l. 805).

813–15 *Was . . . Face?*: the sense is: 'If the annals of Arezzo can celebrate the Franceschini as a glorious family, at the moment when the Aretines must know the family's viciousness, then perhaps the historian Livy intended more than a joke

Did the babe live or die? I fain would find!
What were his fancies if he grew a man?
Was he proud,—a true scion of the stock
Which bore the blazon, shall make bright my page—
Shield, Azure, on a Triple Mountain, Or,
A Palm-tree, Proper, whereunto is tied
A Greyhound, Rampant, striving in the slips?
Or did he love his mother, the base-born,
And fight i' the ranks, unnoticed by the world?

Such, then, the final state o' the story. So
Did the Star Wormwood in a blazing fall
Frighten awhile the waters and lie lost.
So did this old woe fade from memory:
Till after, in the fulness of the days,
I needs must find an ember yet unquenched,

818 *MS 1868* die?—one *1872* die?—I *MS* know: *819 *1888* ancies *DC BrU* ancies>fancies *1889* fancies 820 *MS* chip of the old block,—>scion of the stock, *1868* stock,— 821 *MS* [?A]>Of *MS* bearing blason, still makes bright my book— *1868* Of bearing blason, *1868* Book— 822 *MS* azure,>Azure *MS* triple mountain>Triple Mountain, 823 *MS* palm-tree, proper,>Palm-tree, Proper, 824 greyhound,>Greyhound, 825 *MS* low-born, *1872* base born, 826 *MS* And get to her, 827 *MS* Such were the final flash 828 *MS* star wormwood>Star Wormwood 829 *MS 1868 1872* lost: 830 *MS 1868* memory, *1872* memory. 832 *MS* {beginning of fo. 361}

when he said the town was founded by Janus Bifrons, the god whose symbol is a double-faced head looking in opposite directions, i.e. the Aretines must be hypocrites.' Livy (59 BC–AD 17) is 'the Patavinian' because he was born in *Patavium* (Padua), but the title comes to him because of Pollio's criticism of him for 'Patavinitas' (see Quintilian, I, 5, 56; 8, I, 3), though what exactly Pollio meant by this has been the subject of dispute. In his history Livy does not say directly that Janus founded Arezzo. He does, however, note the rather two-faced behaviour of the Aretines during the Second Punic War (XXVII. 24), and Browning exaggerates this hint to make his point here.

821 *blazon*: coat of arms.

822–4 *Shield . . . Rampant*: cf. XI. 2161–4 n. The heraldic terms are 'Or' = gold, 'Proper' = in its natural colouring, 'Rampant' = standing on its left hind-leg, with both forelegs elevated, i.e. bounding.

824 *slips*: leash; this line recalls *Henry V*, III. i. 31–2: 'I see you stand like greyhounds in the slips, / Straining upon the start.'

828–9 *Star . . . lost*: cf. ll. 11–12 n.

831 *in . . . days*: cf. Gal. 4: 4.

And, breathing, blow the spark to flame. It lives,
If precious be the soul of man to man.

So, British Public, who may like me yet,
(Marry and amen!) learn one lesson hence
Of many which whatever lives should teach:
This lesson, that our human speech is naught,
Our human testimony false, our fame
And human estimation words and wind.
Why take the artistic way to prove so much?
Because, it is the glory and good of Art,
That Art remains the one way possible
Of speaking truth, to mouths like mine at least.
How look a brother in the face and say
"Thy right is wrong, eyes hast thou yet art blind,
"Thine ears are stuffed and stopped, despite their length:
"And, oh, the foolishness thou countest faith!"
Say this as silverly as tongue can troll—
The anger of the man may be endured,

835 *MS* {New paragraph indicated by 'New Par.' in left-hand margin} *MS* yet 836 *MS* (Marry, 837 *MS* the many whatsoever>many anything that 838 *MS* This one, that our best 839 *MS* false—and, oh, 840 *MS* Our human estimate, our fame, how false! 841 *MS* to tell 842 *MS* Because,— *Yale 2* Because,>Because *MS* art,—>Art,— 843 *MS* Art still remains 844 *MS 1872* mine, at least: *1868* mine, 847 *MS* for all their length, *1868* length, 848 *MS* "And what a 850 {not found in *MS*}

835 *So . . . yet*: a witty recollection, and adaptation, of the direct address to the British public in Book I: 410, 1379. See our Vol. VII, p. xxxiii.

839 *human testimony*: repeating the phrase from Fra Celestino's homily, l. 602. There is an implicit contrast here with 'God's testimony', which is true and pure, while human testimony or speech is distorted by sinfulness. In the AV 'testimony' is used of the preaching of the Gospel; more importantly it is used of the Ten Commandments, God's words of friendship to humankind: cf. Exod. 31: 18, 32: 15, etc.

846–7 *eyes . . . length*: cf. Isa. 6: 9–10, Matt. 13: 13–17. 'Despite their length', i.e. you have long ass's ears, is a mischievous addition to the biblical allusion.

848 *foolishness . . . faith!*: cf. 1 Cor. 3: 19: 'For the wisdom of this world is foolishness with God.'

849 *troll*: roll it out, utter melodiously.

The shrug, the disappointed eyes of him
Are not so bad to bear—but here's the plague
That all this trouble comes of telling truth,
Which truth, by when it reaches him, looks false,
Seems to be just the thing it would supplant,
Nor recognizable by whom it left:
While falsehood would have done the work of truth.
But Art,—wherein man nowise speaks to men,
Only to mankind,—Art may tell a truth
Obliquely, do the thing shall breed the thought,
Nor wrong the thought, missing the mediate word.
So may you paint your picture, twice show truth,
Beyond mere imagery on the wall,—
So, note by note, bring music from your mind,
Deeper than ever e'en Beethoven dived,—
So write a book shall mean beyond the facts,
Suffice the eye and save the soul beside.

And save the soul! If this intent save mine,—
If the rough ore be rounded to a ring,

852 *MS* Were *MS* bane 853 {not found in *MS*} 854 *MS* That 856 {not found in *MS*} *1868* left— 857 *MS* comes in aid of truth that fails. 858 *MS* men 860 *MS* that breeds the thought. 861 *MS* by the immediate>missing the immediate 862 *MS* picture and show truth 863 *MS* {beginning of fo. 362} *MS* that imagery 864 *MS* Or, *MS* soul>mind 865 *MS 1868 1872* ever the Andante *MS* [ ]>dived 866 *MS 1868 1872* mean, 867 {not found in *MS*} *868 *1868 1872* {new paragraph. Paragraphing obscured in *1888* and *1889* by this line's being at the head of the page} *MS* your soul. *MS* [ ]>mine,

861 *missing . . . word*: not having the intermediary word, i.e. because it does not express the thought in words. The sense here is perhaps more easily understood if the syntax is rearranged: 'Art may tell a truth obliquely, missing the mediate word, do the thing shall breed the thought, nor wrong the thought.' Art (including literature) works by suggestion, creating thoughts, moods, and views; it does not hammer out 'meaning' in the literalistic manner of ll. 846–8.

865 *ever . . . dived*: the MS reading is interesting: 'ever the Andante dived'. It suggests that at first Browning was thinking of a specific work by Beethoven, perhaps one of the late piano sonatas or quartets.

Render all duty which good ring should do,
And, failing grace, succeed in guardianship,—
Might mine but lie outside thine, Lyric Love,
Thy rare gold ring of verse (the poet praised)
Linking our England to his Italy!

870 *MS* And serve as symbol, as *MS* a ring>good ring 871 {not found in *MS*} 872 *MS* May it go *MS* [ ]>O Lyric Love, 873 *MS* Thy ring of verse, rare gold,— *MS* [ ]>her *MS* poet praised,— 874 *MS* their Italy? {At end of poem L.D.I.E. [Laus Deo Inscriptum Est] in RB's hand}

871 *failing . . . guardianship*: (lit.) failing in beauty, nonetheless succeed in the lesser function of acting as a guard-ring; (fig.) failing to bring holiness (the saved soul), nonetheless succeed in the lesser function of being a kind of guardian angel.

872–4 *Might . . . Italy*: i.e. 'might my completed work of art (the "ring" that is *The Ring and the Book*) simply act as a guard ring to the "gold ring of verse" that is EBB's poetry'.

'Lyric love' is both 'love that is like lyric poetry' and a name for EBB: see I. 1391 n. In these closing lines Browning alludes to the inscription on the plaque set up on the wall of Casa Guidi in 1862 by the city of Florence. The poet Niccolò Tommaseo (1802–1874) composed its wording: (in trans.) 'Here wrote and died Elizabeth Barrett Browning, who in the heart of a woman united the learning of a scholar and the spirit of a poet and made with her verse a golden ring between Italy and England. Grateful Florence places this memorial 1861': for the original Italian text, see Vol. VII, p. 335. Here, in a loving act of deference to EBB, Browning sees his own completed poem as only a 'guard ring' protecting the more graceful and wonderful 'ring' that is her work. The function of a 'guard ring' is well illustrated from this use cited in OED[2], from Maria Edgeworth's *Harrington* (1817): 'She never wore Sir Josceline's ring, without putting on . . . another, . . . which she called her guard ring, a ring which being tighter than Sir Josceline's, kept it safe on her finger.' Browning sees *The Ring and the Book*, set in Italy, as a kind of small complement to EBB's work, celebrating Italy and the Risorgimento, because *both* their works point towards religious truth, EBB's lyrically and directly, his own by more oblique dramatic means.

APPENDIX A

THE CADAVER SYNOD

THE sources for x. 1–150—Pope Innocent's discussion of the cadaver synod and the Formosan controversy—have not been satisfactorily established in previous editions.[1] As I have demonstrated elsewhere,[2] Browning's main source was not recondite, though it was of an unusual nature. Between 1862 and 1866, in the Paris libraries, Browning's father researched the history of the Roman senatrix Marozia (*c*.892–*c*.937) and her family, the house of Theophylact, which dominated the papacy during part of the tenth century. As an offshoot of this research, he investigated the cadaver synod and its aftermath (897–*c*.910), partly for its intrinsic interest, partly because it could act as an introduction to the corruptions of late ninth and early tenth-century Rome, the background to Marozia's life. He had collected together as many references to the event as he could find, and had already developed significant writing of his own about it, all to be used in a book about Marozia that never came to fruition. This material, both about Marozia and about the synod, is now in the Brighton Public Library: it is a large work, in manuscript, running to over forty short notebooks.[3] The library's index lists it as the *Marozia Manuscript* (the title used here) and describes it as being concerned with Marozia, 'a Roman lady notorious for her profligacy and for the influence she exercised over the Papal Court'. Browning's interest in at least part of this material suggests temperamental and intellectual affinities with his father. More importantly, the *Marozia Manuscript* is a good instance of the poet's use of historical sources and of his attitude in shaping them.

Robert Browning Sen. speaks of beginning his work on Marozia in a letter to his daughter of 24 May 1862.[4] This research was one of his primary occupations in the last years of his life. There are three later letters concerning this research, from Browning Sen. to Browning, which

[1] See e.g. Ohio, vol. ix, p. 308.

[2] Stefan Hawlin, 'A New Source for *The Ring and the Book*, Book X', BSN 23 (1996), 27–34.

[3] The manuscript is part of the Bloomfield Collection, index number BC 945.02/B82. It is listed as J90 in Kelley and Coley. I should like to thank Vanessa Hayward and her colleagues at the Brighton Public Library for their help in examining it.

[4] Fitzwilliam Museum, Cambridge, 'E. B. Browning Letters', no. 224 c.

can be reliably dated to 1865 or 1866.[5] They all cover the same ground. Browning Sen. tries to interest his son, or someone his son may recommend, in the Marozia material. His researches, he says, have now reached in bulk as much 'as a man might carry'. The inefficiencies and inadequacies of the Paris libraries have been a problem in his work. And he tries to demonstrate the interest of the material: in particular, as one of 'many interesting narratives connected with the History of Marozia' he draws his son's attention to 'the remarkable trial of the dead body of Formosus'.[6] He senses his inability to carry the research through to a finished book, and so: 'I wish you knew of any young man who would wish to try his hand on Marozia', since, from the material gathered 'an entertaining as well as useful biography might be made'.[7]

Another letter that should probably be considered in relation to the *Marozia Manuscript* is from Browning to Seymour Kirkup, 19 Feb. 1867. Here Browning is speaking of the last months of his father's life (i.e. April–June 1866):

> The intellect [of my father], always very extraordinarily active, was quite unaffected: he continued his studies to the very last—and, on my requesting him to investigate the history of one of the Popes—(I did it to interest him, mainly) he sent me, a few weeks before the end, a regular book of researches, and a narrative of his own, exhausting the subject.[8]

This is potentially a reference to elements of the *Marozia Manuscript*, for there are notebooks that closely correspond to this description of 'a regular book of researches' and 'a narrative of his own'. The part of the manuscript that best fits the description of 'a regular book of researches' (extract 1 below) has small pencil ticks in the margin in material closely relating to X. 23–150, as though someone (perhaps Browning) had been carefully noting particular facts.

From the letters above, and from other fragmentary references, it is possible to conjecture various scenarios. When Browning was on holiday with his father in Pornic in August 1865, or when he visited him in April

[5] The letters are nos. 229, 230, and 231 in 'E. B. Browning Letters': see previous n. Letters 230 and 229 speak of the research taking 'the last five years'; letter 231 speaks of 'the last four years'. The letters are datable by these references in connection with the letter cited in note 4. Mary Ellis Gibson hypothesized a connection between Book X and Browning Sen.'s historical researches on the basis of these letters, though she was unaware of the existence of the *Marozia Manuscript*: see 'The Manuscripts of Robert Browning, Sr.: A Source for *The Ring and the Book*', SBHC 13 (1985), 11–19.

[6] No. 229.

[7] No. 230.

[8] *Letters*, pp. 105–6.

1866 in Paris, they might easily have spoken about Formosus and the cadaver synod, given that Browning Sen.'s mind was full of these matters. Alternatively, it may have been Browning Sen.'s direct reference to 'the remarkable trial of the dead body of Formosus' that sparked Browning's interest. He was himself contemplating Pope Innocent XII and trying to gather historical background; perhaps he requested more information (even though Formosus was from a very different period of the papacy) and hence his father sent him the cadaver synod material. These are only surmises, but the evidence of the manuscript itself, taken with the poem, and with the letters referred to above, are sufficient to establish the following: (i) many correspondences between Browning's account of the cadaver synod and its aftermath and his father's account of the same events; (ii) that both Browning and his father were fascinated by the ambiguities and contradictions in the historical record—something manifest both in Book X and the accounts in the *Marozia Manuscript*; and (iii) that both Browning and his father were particularly interested in the grotesqueness of the events and in the pathological anger of Stephen VII. The evidence suggests that Browning had studied *all* the research that his father had done on the cadaver synod. If this assumption is correct, then this part of Book X was probably written some time after his father's death in June 1866, when he was able to review the whole of the research.

The *Marozia Manuscript*, now bound in six volumes, originally comprised over forty separate notebooks.[9] In these Robert Browning Sen. transcribes, translates, and cross-references a mass of information on Marozia, the house of Theophylact, and the historical background of Rome in the late ninth and early tenth centuries. The bulk of the research consists of extracts from sources, from chronicles, editions of chronicles, modern histories covering the medieval period, ecclesiastical histories, and other reference works. There are also genealogies, tables, and chronologies (laid out in Browning Sen.'s customary lively style), jottings, queries, blank pages, and brief notes, as well as the beginnings of more formal drafts of material clearly intended for a book. There are sections dealing with crucial events in Marozia's life, and also biographies of people connected to her story. Within all this, there are a group of notebooks concerned with the popes of Marozia's lifetime and with the cadaver synod, as well as important 'extracts' concerning Formosus elsewhere in the notebooks.

[9] Browning Sen. gives titles to all the notebooks in a large, bold script, and paginates them. All references here give his titles and page numbers.

In Volume 2 of the *Marozia Manuscript*, in a group of three notebooks, Browning Sen. begins to develop his understanding of the cadaver synod and its aftermath. The notebook titled 'Marozia. The 10 Popes From ( ) to ( )' is an attempt to grapple with the basic chronological record of the popes of the 890s and 900s, one often confused in terms of dates and events. Relatively speaking, it is a small and sketchy notebook. The next notebook—titled 'Marozia. Popes (ii), & Authors'—adds considerable detail to the lives of the popes, and begins to show a focused interest in the synod and its aftermath. The third notebook, 'Marozia. Popes (iii)', develops more detail and has a special section headed 'The trial of *Formosus* from various writers'. This is the section that has received marginal pencil ticks. The method of this section is to cite an authority (in brackets, abbreviated), and then to transcribe or translate material from it, with only occasional interjections of Browning Sen.'s own. The following text of it expands some of Browning Sen.'s contractions, but retains his spellings, omission marks | |, some oddities of syntax and phrasing, and some mistakes and mistranscriptions.

Extract 1: from the notebook 'Marozia. Popes (iii)', pp. 17–21

The trial of *Formosus* from various writers

(Ricaut)[10] He ordered the Body of *Formosus* to be taken out of the Grave, & divested of his Pontifical habit. Cut off the *2* fingers of his right hand (used in consecration) which were then thrown into the Tiber.

[10] It is difficult to identify all the sources cited. Using occasional mentions or allusions elsewhere in the manuscript, it is possible to compile the following provisional list:
Paul Rycaut, *The Lives of the Popes, from the time of our Saviour Jesus Christ to the reign of Sixtus IV. Written originally in Latine by Baptista Platina Native of Cremona, and translated into English. And the same History continued from the year 1471 to this present time* (London, 1685), p. 174; François Dantine, *L'Art de vérifier les dates* (Paris, 1770, and editions thereafter); Voltaire, *Abregé de l'Histoire universelle, depuis Charlemagne, jusques à Charlequint*, 2 vols. (London, 1753), i. 227–8; the other *Abregé* has not been identified: elsewhere in the manuscript Browning Sen. cites P. A. Alletz, *Histoire abrégée des papes, depuis Saint Pierre jusqu'à Clement XIV*, 2 vols. (Amsterdam, 1776), which contains similar material but is not the *Abregé* quoted here; James Craigie Robertson, *History of the Christian Church, Volume II*, 2 Parts (London, 1862), ii. 412–13; *Hist. Chron. des Papes* is probably the *Histoire Chronologique des Papes* (1684) referred to elsewhere in the manuscript, but it has not been possible to identify it further; Nathaniel Wanley, *The Wonders of the Little World* (London, 1678), Book IV, Chap. XI: 'Of the bitter Revenges that some have taken upon their Enemies'; *Ligue* is unidentified; William Derby, *Mnemonika* (Philadelphia, 1812); Claude Fleury, *Histoire Ecclesiastique*, 35 vols. (Paris, 1719–58).

(l'art de Vérifier dates) he brought the dead body into the Council, clothed in his Pontifical vestments, seated him in the chair, & even appointed him an advocate to plead his cause as if he had been living. Convicted, condemned & degraded him. He then cut off &c.—

(Voltaire) Having all his lifetime hated *Formosus*, he caused his body &c.—Produced it in the Council assembled to "Judge his Memory". They gave the corps an advocate, that the proceedings might be conducted with due regularity. The dead body was pronounced guilty of having changed his Bishoprick & quitted the see of Porto for that of Rome. Its head was then cut off by the common hangman. The *3* fingers were then cut off, & the body thrown into the Tiber.

(Abregé) *Stephen* immediately proceeded to one of the most horrible scandals the Church had ever been guilty of. He called a Council composed of the principal Bishops of his faction. | | Those whom he charged with the execution of this decree (viz. exhuming the body) pillaged the treasure of the Lateran. | | When the body was brought in, *Stephen* questioned him, as if he had been still alive—"Bishop of Porto, how dared your ambition to usurp the chair of St. Peter?" | | Stripped of his sacred vestments & clothed in a laic Habit.

(Robertson Hist. Christian Ch) *Stephen* in the contentions of rival pretenders to the Empire, had taken an opposite side to *Formosus*; & it should seem that this political enmity was the motive of the extraordinary outrage which followed. | | The charge that he had been uncanonically translated from a lesser See to Rome, a charge which, as there had been such a translation in the case of *Marinus*, it was thought necessary to aggravate by a false addition that *Formosus* had submitted to a 2[d] consecration. *Auxilius* argues that even if *Formosus* had submitted to a new imposition of hands, it would only have been analogous to the consecration of a Bishop. | | A Deacon was assigned to the dead Pope for an advocate; but it was useless to attempt a defence. *Formosus* was condemned, & the ordinations conferred by him were annulled. [Luitprand represents the outrages upon the body of *Formosus* as having taken place under *Sergius*. It has been commonly supposed that he mistook *Sergius* for *Stephen* (Baronius. 897.2) But Mr *Scudamore* argues that *Stephen* had allowed the corpse of *Formosus* to be re-enterred, & that *Sergius* & his party again tore it from the grave & cast it into the river. That *Luitprand's* error would be that of referring these acts to the Papacy of *Sergius* instead of to an earlier part of his life (England & Rome, 445). It would seem however that *Luitprand* supposed that *Sergius* was the immediate successor of *Boniface* vi.] But the river (it is said) repeatedly cast it out; & after the murder of *Stephen* (897) it was taken up & again laid in St. Peters, when it was carried into the Church, some statues of Saints inclined towards it with reverence in attestation of the Sanctity of *Formosus*.

(l'art &c) But *Stephen* did not stop here. He deposed all who had been consecrated by *Formosus* (*but who could not have been many) & ordered that they should be consecrated anew. Never had the Church seen a Pontiff in such a fury. But he was justly punished for these violences, being seized, bound, loaded with chains, & confined in a dark Dungeon where he was strangled.—(897)

(*One writer, anxious for the honour of the Holy See, says, "he condemned the memory of *Formosus* from an Excess of Rigour." (Hist. Chron. des Papes).

(Voltaire) This farce, as horrible as it was ridiculous, rendered the Pope so hateful, that the friends of *Formosus* having risen against *Stephen*, loaded him with chains & strangled him in prison, *Stephen*'s enemies caused the body of *Formosus* to be taken up again, & buried a second time in his Pontifical robes. This quarrel heated the minds of many.

(Abregé) After this infamous farce he cancelled all the acts of *Formosus*; degraded the Bishops who had consecrated him; & made void all his Ecclesiastical Preferments. After that, he acknowledged *Arnoul* for Emperor, not allowing the consecration of *Formosus* to have been valid. If it is true (as *Sigonius* affirms) that *Stephen* had himself been Bishop of Arago, it is strange that he should have served *Formosus* thus, for the same crime. But in this *Sigonius* is evidently mistaken.

Muratori assures us, that this affair greatly scandalized all classes in Rome. A conspiracy was immediately entered into against the Pope, who was seized & consigned to a prison, where he died a few days afterwards.

(Wanley) *Stephen* caused the Body of *Formosus* to be taken out of the Sepulchre, stripped of the Pontificial ornaments, clothed in secular garments, & *buried without the church*, & his 3 fingers, only, to be cast into the Tiber. *Sergius iii* caused his body to be brought out of this 2^d^ Burial place, to be beheaded in the Public Forum & cast into the Tiber. (Wier. oper. p. 829. lib. de Irâ. Heyl. Cosm. p. 107; Gruter p.1162). [*this if correct is the only means of reconciling the actions of *Stephen* with those recorded of *Sergius*. But still there are difficulties].

(Ligue) The factions of Spoleto & Frioul came to blows ("en viennent encore aux mains) about giving a head to the Church. The people would have chosen a venerable prelate, but the nobles elected (sword in hand) a scoundrel unworthy of the name of man. This was *Stephen* vii. Scarcely was this monster installed, than with unpitiable rage, he caused *Formosus* to be exhumed, & his body to be carried before a Synod, assembled for the purpose of degrading & condemning the acts of this Pope. They re-clothed this carcase, which was in a state of decomposition, with the Pontifical vestments; and *Stephen* himself interrogated him, who even gave the (pretended) reply, & then condemned & excommunicated him. Then he caused him to be stripped of his marks of dignity, cut off the 3 fingers, with which he used to give the benediction, & then ordered his head to be cut off. The mutilated carcase was then thrown into the Tyber. [Annals of *Fulde*, *Sigonius*, *Luitprand*]. This infamous Pontiff died, strangled.

(Mnemonica. Philadelphia, 1812) Stephen *vi*, a Roman, abrogated all the acts of *Formosus* his predecessor, which afterwards became customary, from his example, the following Popes infringing, if not fully cancelling, all the acts of their immediate predecessors. He died 901 (3.yrs).

(Hist. Ecclesiastique) After the Death of Formosus, the popular faction elected *Boniface*, who died 15 days afterwards. *Stephen* succeeded 2^d May (897). He had no sooner been consecrated than he called a Council at Rome for the condemnation of *Formosus* who had died the preceding year. *Stephen* caused the body to be disenterred. . . . Stephen did not expect after his death, that the same indignities would be offered to his carcase, which he had shewn to *Formosus*, yet he was chased away a short time afterwards, cast into prison, where he was strangled in the month of august. *Romanus* succeeded him 17 September.

After the three notebooks previously described, there are two important developments in the manuscript. In a later notebook—titled 'Marozia, Family, 2'—Browning Sen. works up his research into a sustained narrative covering the synod and the ensuing Formosan controversy through the reigns of Romanus, Theodore II, John IX, and Sergius III: this narrative follows the pattern of events described in X. 24–150, ending—like Browning's account—with Sergius III's possible responses to Formosus. Another notebook, titled 'Marozia, 16', reworks this material into a version aiming at literary polish and completeness, where the emphasis shifts from the Formosan controversy itself to its significance in the light of Marozia's life: that is to say, it becomes an introduction to the corrupt times and actions of Marozia. This account emphasizes the anger of Stephen against Formosus (something also evident in Browning's version).

These two full accounts of the Formosan controversy, covering the cadaver synod through to the judgements of Sergius III, are similar to each other in many respects, and it is unnecessary to reproduce both in full. The following extracts give the account of the cadaver synod from the notebook 'Marozia, 16' and then, immediately following, the account of its aftermath from the notebook 'Marozia, Family, 2'. The extracts should be read together, and then compared with the poem.

Extract 2: from the notebook 'Marozia, 16', pp. 27–40

Formosus

We shall only enter upon so much of the history of Formosus as will be necessary to elucidate the proceedings which were afterwards put in practice against him in succeeding pontificates; otherwise a more particular account of him would be scarcely worth noticing in the History of Marozia. [...]

Stephen vii—

However alert the popular faction might have been at the time of the death of Formosus the still more sudden death of *Boniface* found them unprepared to take advantage of it. And the faction inimical to the popular party placed Stephen vii triumphantly in St. Peter's chair. Formosus & himself had ever been bitter enemies & now that *Stephen* was advanced to the papacy with full power to crush this enemy, that enemy was no longer in existence.

The trial of Formosus.—

The accounts that have come down to us, of this remarkable trial, are in some instances so irreconcilible with each other, that we must strictly adhere to our plan, of confining ourselves to the popular account of it;—& only discarding those circumstances which appear inconsistent with probability. In perusing the few particulars we have of it—(& which no historian has had the assurance to deny) we are so much struck with the extreme folly of the contrivers of it, as we can possibly be with the malice & fury with which it was carried out.

Scarcely was Stephen vii seated in the Pontific chair than a Council, as was usual upon such occasions, was summoned. These had naturally made up their minds upon the subjects which they expected would have occasioned the object of their meeting—some affair of the greatest importance—so what must have been their surprize, when informed, that they were convened for the trial of the late Pope—*Formosus*! However a wretcheder set of men could not have been well collected, none but the basest of characters would have attended such an unjustifiable meeting. They were then informed that a most serious and awful charge was about to be exhibited against the late successor & representative of St. Peter. In order, however, that strict justice should be administered to the accused, no less a person than a Deacon was appointed for his advocate,—& all the forms of proceeding in a regular court of law were to be as strictly adhered to, as if the party were alive and sensible of what was going forward. We have no word in English corresponding with the legal terms of his accusation. It is technically called "testing the Memory". The accused, as was usual, was not present, as it was not customary to have him produced till after the trial was over.

The trial proceeded. The chief, & indeed only charge against *Formosus* was, that he had in defiance of the express canon removed from the Bishopric of Porto to that of Rome. We are not informed what were the arguments used by the deacon but much could have been urged in favour of the accused. Pope *Marin* had been a Bishop, before he was removed to the Papacy, & if tradition might have been allowed to pass for evidence, St. Peter himself had formerly been in possession of the see of Antioch. But supposing it really criminal, the man was now beyond all human jurisdiction, & if found guilty, no adequate punishment could have been awarded to him. But he was unanimously found guilty, & the disgusting spectacle of a dead body, brought into a court of Justice to receive sentence, was immediately carried into execution. The corpse had been removed from its grave. It was then clothed in the Pontifical vestments, placed in the Ecclesiastical chair, & with the most ridiculous solemnity, brought in & placed before the council. It no sooner caught the eye of *Stephen* (whose ebullition of rage is thus recorded by several historians) than he exclaimed, addressing the corpse as if it had been still alive, "Why hast thou—ambitious mortal!—quitted your See of Porto, to invade the throne of St. Peter". Of course no reply was given, & he was accordingly condemned for contumacy. The sentence was then recorded, & the carrying out of which was as singular and disgraceful an affair as the trial itself. As there was no precedent upon record, they were obliged to invent one. His pontifical ornaments were taken from him. He was clad in the garments of a laic. His head was ordered to be cut off by the hands of the common executioner. The three fingers of his right hand, displayed always by his holiness when conferring a blessing upon the people, were ordered to be cut off, & his body, after having been ignominiously dragged through the streets of Rome, was then thrown into the Tiber. There are circumstances attending this part of the story, which we shall have afterwards occasion to notice & which make it very uncertain whether the whole of the sentence was carried into execution. There had been an instance when a similar sentence had been prevented by a rescue from the populace, & we must recollect, that Formosus had at one period been their idol. But of this we shall have more to say. It seems that revenge alone did not prompt the Pope & his cabal to these shocking enormities. The sentence extended not only to every Bishop who had been consecrated by the late Pope, but to every ecclesiastic who had been ordained by him. And as these were only restored to their former position by means of pecuniary, or other emoluments, we see what a golden hand was likely to repay the friends of the Pope for the trouble & expense they had been at in securing his Election.

Extract 3: from the notebook 'Marozia, Family, 2.', pp. 12–19

He [Stephen] moreover made void all ecclesiastical preferments which had been granted by Formosus, & as *Platina* remarks, all this proved a precedent of very evil consequences afterwards, succeeding Popes making it a custom either to break or entirely to abrogate the acts of their immediate predecessors. This was not only contrary to the practice of all former Popes but was a great objection to their claim to Infallibility. Never had the church seen the Pontiff exhibit such an implacable & revengeful spirit. But (says the historian) he was justly punished for these violences, being seized, loaded with chains, & confined in a dark dungeon, where he was strangled (897). But the Formosan controversy was not yet over. The opposite faction appear to have gained a temporary advantage, & *Romanus* was seated in St. Peter's chair. Though his pontificate lasted so short a period, that by many he is not considered as a legally consecrated Pope, it was employed in restoring the Decrees of Formosus, & cancelling all the proceedings which had been recently taken against him. But between the interval of his death & the appointment of a successor a long interval elapsed, occasioned by the absence of the Emperor *Lambert*'s deputies, in whose presence the ordination was to have been made. Theodore ii was appointed, & though he possessed the Tiara but 20 days, endeavoured in that short period to restore Unity to the church & reestablish the ordinances of Formosus—whose body, having been recovered by some fishermen (& not cast up by the river itself) was restored with great solemnity to a tomb in St. Peter's.

[A section follows describing the election of John IX, then:]

He [John IX] had at least the credit of repairing the scandal caused by Stephen's behaviour to the dead body of Formosus;—for, the first act of his Pontifical career was to call a council at Rome, & afterwards a second one at Ravenna, at which the Emperor Lambert presided in person & at which 74 Bishops attended. There the Pope annulled all the proceedings instituted against Formosus, & made void all the acts which Stephen had ordered contrary to law; & forbid the plundering of the Palace & several other crimes which in that age had been customary on the death of the Pope. John died in (905).

[Mention is made of the brief pontificates of Benedict IV, Leo V, and Christopher, then:]

Sergius iii succeeded, a man whose private character had always been accounted disreputable. His animosity against Formosus continued unabated, & glad would he have been to have had the opportunity of revenging what he considered his grievances even upon the dead body of his former antagonist. But the conduct of Stephen had created such a disgust in the majority of the people of Rome, although they were not friends to Formosus, that he dared not to repeat so violent & unbecoming an outrage.

And here we have a fresh opportunity of observing into what inconsistencies the wretched historians of those times have caused the more intelligent modern ones to fall. Sigonius (a valuable historian) says, & he is followed by several writers, that Sergius disenterred the body of Formosus a second time, & annulled his decrees. Both these charges are proved to have been false. Platina says, that at the instigation of King Lothaire, Sergius abolished all the acts of Formosus, took his carcase out of the grave, cut off his head & threw it into the Tyber. And assigns the reason of the French king's hatred to the memory of Formosus, which was that he had been the means of translating the Empire from the French race to that of the Lombards.

And even Voltaire mentions his throwing the body into the Tyber. This is not improbable, but what regards the decapitation & cutting off of the fingers, that had been done already. But Fleury says that Sergius had the body (Wanley says from his second burial place) taken up & honorably interred. Yet several writers persist in adhering to the improbable (not to say impossible) story, that the ridiculous proceedings of Stephen were acted over again by Sergius. The same inconsistency may be observed in the lives of several other Popes & Persons of distinction of that period, & we are often surprized in reading word for word in the account of one Pope, what we had just before been reading in the history of another.

In such an unsatisfactory statement ends the celebrated controversy of Formosus.

There are two points of fact in X. 24–150 that have not emerged in the extracts so far: the first is the detail that King Eudes of France was present at John IX's Ravenna synod (l. 134); the second is the name of the tract in which Auxilius proves the legitimacy of Formosus' election: *De Ordinationibus* (l. 138). In extract 3 above, it is the Emperor Lambert who is associated with the Ravenna synod. The detail of the presence of King Eudes probably comes from the account of the Formosan controversy in John Foxe's *Acts and Monuments of the Martyrs*. Browning Sen. copies out this account in a notebook titled 'Marozia, Extracts xiii'.[11] The detail of *De Ordinationibus* might have come from James Craigie Robertson's *History of the Christian Church* (1862). In the part of this work transcribed in extract 1, Browning Sen. does not give the whole of the relevant footnote. Elsewhere, in 'Marozia, Extracts (3)', he copies out a fuller if still abbreviated version:

Auxilius, de Ordinationibus *Formosi* 26 (Patrol. cxxix) argues that even if *Formosus* had submitted to a new imposition of hands, it would only have been analogous to the consecration of a Bishop insomuch as the Priesthood & the Episcopate are one order, & a priest on being consecrated receives but the "augmentum ministerii." *Marinus* had been Bishop of Caere, & *Photius* now objected to him on the ground of his translation.[12]

Various generalizations can be made about this material. As the above makes clear, Browning could have gleaned almost everything he required for Book X. 49–150 from his father's historical notebooks. A difficult and obscure piece of history had already been sorted and sifted for him. He

[11] In the standard edition of *The Acts and Monuments*, ed. Josiah Pratt (London, 1877) the passage about the Ravenna Synod can be found at Vol. II, pp. 34–5. Browning Sen.'s transcription of this passage, and other material, is in the notebook 'Marozia, Extracts xiii', pp. 3–15.

[12] 'Marozia, Extracts (3)', pp. 10–11. For the original, see James Craigie Robertson, *History of the Christian Church, Volume II*, 2 Parts (London, 1862), ii. 412.

had not engaged in careful research of his own, but had intelligently taken over his father's material. There may be a few instances where he went back to the original sources, but where he did so his father's work provided him with easy references. So, for example, when, in relation to Auxilius' *de Ordinationibus*, Browning tells the reader to 'read the tract' (l. 141), it may be that he himself had done so, following up the reference to J. P. Migne's *Patrologiæ Cursus Completus*, vol. cxxix (1853) supplied in his father's transcription of Robertson (see above). This was simply the turning up of an easily available book. Early sources were not, perhaps, his mainstay. Of all the accounts quoted by Browning Sen. that in Robertson's *History of the Christian Church* is one of the clearest and best.

His father had already given a certain dramatic shape to the material, and Browning took over and elaborated on this. His emphasis, for example, on Stephen VII's pathological anger (ll. 34, 45, 63, 66) is something that Browning Sen. had already used to dramatic effect (as in extract 2 above). The dramatic moment where the deacon responds for the corpse (ll. 50–61) is also anticipated there: 'We are not informed what were the arguments used by the deacon but much could have been urged in favour of the accused.'

The source material gives us a clear instance of how Browning uses history, and his sense of the relationship between 'fact' and 'fancy'. Browning does not simply take over any one account provided by his father; rather, following his father's example, he continues to evaluate the conflicting accounts. He is concerned with a kind of fidelity and accuracy (something in keeping with the character of the man he is imagining speaking about these events). For example: Did Sergius III follow the example of Stephen VII and also order that the body of Formosus be thrown in the river? Browning does not attempt to resolve the difficulty. Liutprand is an authority that supports this event; clearly though, as Browning Sen. surmises, the incident may easily be a mistaken transfer of events from the reign of Stephen; and, from his father's collations, he knows there are other and confusing views of the matter (see extract 1). So, Browning tactfully asserts that 'some say' this happened (144), and avoids melodrama. Similarly, he knows from elsewhere in his father's notes about the potential confusion in the numbering of popes called John, and signals this: 'Ninth of the name, (I follow the best guides)' (131). Such hints of restraint also add to the voice of Pope Innocent, contributing to our sense that he is maintaining a sober, balanced viewpoint.

In several places Browning adds a flourish or detail of his own to the source material. The most obvious additions are: the picture of the young, stammering deacon revolted by the face of Formosus' corpse (53–5); the words of Stephen in a 'beastly froth of rage' (62–6); the jibe about 'Christian fish' and the ironic explanation for the throwing of the corpse into the Tiber (88–92); and the sardonic comment of the Jewish bystander, horrified at the cruelty of those who call themselves Christians (100–1). In these instances Browning is shaping the material to be dramatic in itself, and to develop his characterization of the Pope. These additions show Pope Innocent's fine sense of the horror and futility of the events, and so help to enhance our sense of his humility in facing up to them, and the reality of his own sense of human fallibility.

Within the nature of this shaping, Browning's concern for faithfulness to the historical record remains: he refuses to indulge the melodrama of the story, or to make an aggressive or simplistic anti-Catholic statement. The reins of his imagination are held tight. The extraordinary incidents become part of the musings of his Pope Innocent XII, a very old, thoughtful, and wise man.

APPENDIX B

YALE VARIANTS

THE revisions unique to *Yale 2* made in Books IX, X, and XII (there are none in Book XI) are equally balanced between accidentals and substantives (fourteen of the former, fifteen of the latter). In the case of the accidentals the effect is preponderantly to strengthen the punctuation. In one case comma becomes comma long dash, and in two others comma long dash becomes colon. Colon itself becomes full stop in one instance, and in another exclamation mark. In XII. 541, a comma is inserted, which has the effect of strengthening the contrast between the brass and the burnished gold for which fools take it. The addition of a long dash before 'Refuse' in X. 1301 makes lines 1301 and 1302 clearly part of the sentence which begins in line 1296, thus creating a triple question '—shall I too lack courage?—leave I, too, the post of me...?—Refuse...to grapple danger...?' which powerfully conveys the Pope's passionate indignation. In X. 1796 and 1800, Browning moves the question mark from the end of 1796, where it makes for somewhat curious syntax, and places it at the end of 1800, where it strengthens the contrast between the questions posed in 1795 to 1800 and the resolution which begins with 1801. The insertion of brackets in XII. 122 and 123 not only improves the sense of the passage but also points up the flavour of the Venetian visitor's letter. There are only three places where Browning has weakened the punctuation, all in Book XII. In lines 47 and 102 he changes colon to comma in order to make the passage run on without so marked a pause, thus reflecting the somewhat breathless and frivolous tone of the Venetian visitor. In line 842 he suppresses the comma at the end of the line, thereby improving both the flow and the sense of the passage.

The substantive revisions are for the most part either designed to improve the rhythm (X. 1294, If my own breath, only,>If only my own breath, and XII. 701, Gather from out my sense the contrary!>Who gathers from my speech the contrary?, where not only the rhythm is improved but also the sense), or to strengthen the sense (IX. 526, Enough in the escape from death, I hope,>Enough is in escape from death, I trust; and X. 1445, proves,—>seems,—, where logically, not to say, theologically, faith, the pearl, can only seem a pebble, not prove to be a pebble). In X. 1724, that>what is better sense and closer to everyday speech, while in l. 2114 see, fear>see, and fear is more impressive and more menacing. In some cases the revision in *Yale 2* is either not an improvement or else is less effective than the later revision made for *1888*. In IX. 393, I is changed to he, but as long as the quotation marks remain this does not work syntactically. In X. 1662, the world measured me?>measured world to me? improves the rhythm, but *1888's* world that's measured me? not only improves the rhythm but is also better sense. Similarly, XII. 385 "'The>"'A is intended to strengthen the line, but *1888* "'I'm is more effective. Another case is XII. 592, where this>call strengthens the phrase but *1888* mere does so even better.

Revisions in *Yale 2* and *1888* compared

Line	In *Yale 2* only	In *Yale 2* and *1888* (* = corrected literal)	In *1888* conflicting with *Yale 2*
Book IX			
393	I>he		
526	Enough in the escape from death, I hope,>Enough is in escape from death, I trust,		Enough was found in mere escape from death,
807		let>lest*	
1428	remonstrance: snake,> remonstrance! Snake,		
Book X			
1138	the>what		
1232	you,—>you:		
1263	place,">place,—"		
1264	me and to spare,—> sufficently,—[*sic*]		
1294	If my own breath, only,>If only my own breath,		
1301	Refuse,>—Refuse,		
1445	proves,—>seems,—		
1489	watch,>watched,		
1563		plentitude>plenitude*	
1642		end:">end:	
1662	the world measured me?>measured world to me?		world that's measured me?

Revisions in *Yale 2* and *1888* compared (*cont.*)

1724	that>what		
1760		schene>scheme*	
1793		now>now:	
1796	fire?>fire,		
1800	new—>new?		new:
1927	be there>suppose		
2008	law-procedure,—>law-procedure:		
2085	words:>words.		
2114	see, fear>see, and fear		
Book XI			
None			
Book XII			
47	times:>times,		
102	spectacle:>spectacle,		
122	“Being>(“Being		
123	yesternight,>yesternight)		
385	“‘The>“‘A		“‘I’m
445	you are>please		
466		“Will>“With*	
541	shines>shines,		
592	this>call		mere
701	Gather from out my speech the contrary!>Who gathers from my speech the contrary?		
842	Because,>Because		

APPENDIX C

COMPOSITORS

IX.

1–133	[ ]
134–247	Barsham
248–364	Hales
365–489	Barsham
490–989	Broadhead[1]
990–1051	Hales
1052–1178	[Strange?]
1179–1296	Barsham
1297–1416	[B. Sutherland?]
1417–76	Hales
1477–end	Barsham

X.

1–118	Broadhead
119–234	Barsham
235–344	Malcolm
345–457	Jenkins
459–570	Hales
571–631	[ ]
633–744	Jenkins
745–61	Broadhead
762–865	Barsham
866–1094	Hales
1095–1210	Plumb
1211–1323	Barsham
1324–1444	Jenkins
1445–1560	Barsham
1561–1628	B. Sutherland
1629–1702	[Ker?]
1703–1947	[Strange?][1]
1948–end	Hales

XI.

1–115	Jenkins
117–234	Hales
235–350	Graham
351–468	Ker
469–582	Strange
583–701	Barsham
702–815	[Graham?]
816–928	B. Sutherland
929–1045	Ker
1046–1159	Malcolm
1160–1273	[ ]
1274–1385	Jenkins
1386–1499	Graham
1500–1611	Jenkins
1612–1727	B. Sutherland
1728–1840	Barsham
1841–1956	Graham
1957–2076	Jenkins
2077–204	Barsham
2205–end	Broadhead

XII.

1–55	Barsham
56–238	Ker[1]
239–96	Barsham
297–352	Jenkins

353–408	Ker	578–771	Ker
410–65	Broadhead	772–831	B. Sutherland
466–521	Hales	832–end	Barsham
522–77	Jenkins		

[1] At IX. 745, 869, X. 1827 and XII. 174, there is a pencil mark such as usually indicates the beginning of a compositor's stint, but no name.

AFTERWORD

THE TRUTH BEHIND THE FRANCESCHINI MURDER CASE

by Michael Meredith and Simonetta Berbeglia

THE people whose lives Robert Browning explored in *The Ring and the Book* were, in reality, simpler, and rougher than the men and women depicted in the poem. Browning's different versions of the story create a sophistication of character, a complexity of motive, quite alien to the thrustful events played out in the houses and streets of Arezzo and Rome. *The Ring and the Book* elevates a provincial scandal and its brutal consequence into a psychological masterpiece.

Browning's knowledge of Count Guido Franceschini, Pompilia Comparini, and Giuseppe Caponsacchi was limited to the facts he read in the legal proceedings outlined in the Old Yellow Book and the Secondary Source. These dealt almost exclusively with events from 1693, when Guido married Pompilia, until the murders of 1698 and his execution. Apart from these, only Violante's deception over the circumstances of Pompilia's birth was described. The legal documents were not concerned with family histories or the social scene to which the main characters belonged.

While a lack of constricting historical detail was an advantage to Browning in creating his fictional characters, it did cause him to make some basic factual errors in his telling of the story. For example, Guido was not the eldest son of the Franceschini and thus head of the family on the death of his father; nor was he as old as Browning made him, being just 40 at the time of his execution. Caponsacchi in the poem is a strongly independent character, unencumbered by family ties, although in real life he had been badly influenced by a rapscallion of an elder brother. As for the enigma of Pompilia, Browning's intuition was to make her innocent and to suggest that she was illiterate and the love-letters were forgeries. In fact she had attended an infants' school in Rome, so had at least the rudiments of reading and writing.[1] We now know that her husband loved poetry, so it is likely that her unexpected knowledge of *Il Pastor Fido,* and similar works glanced at in the love-letters, came from books he owned.[2]

Browning's inability, or reluctance, to research the backgrounds of his characters beyond their depiction in the Old Yellow Book led him to conclusions completely at odds with historical fact. Caponsacchi and Pompilia were lovers and their flight to Rome was made on the discovery of her pregnancy. Gregorio Guillichini played a larger part in their story than Browning realized, and was thought by many in Arezzo to be Pompilia's lover too. Guido Franceschini was not a monster, but a weak, ineffective man, well suited to play the part of helpless cuckold. The revenge he took on his guilty wife, and the methods he used, were in keeping with his response to an earlier amatory misfortune.

To separate fact from fiction, our researches in the church and state archives of Arezzo now allow us to give a more realistic and detailed account of the Franceschini murder case, the personalities involved, and the family histories that lie behind the tragedy. Census returns, registers of births, marriages, and deaths, as well as parish records, enable us to recreate accurately the factual background of the drama, while the proceedings of the criminal court give an insight into the daily life of Arezzo. Had the quarrelsome

[1] Beatrice Corrigan (ed.), *Curious Annals: New Documents Relating to Browning's Roman Murder Story* (Toronto, 1956), 35. Professor Corrigan's book is the only serious attempt until now to unravel the complexities of the Franceschini–Comparini–Caponsacchi affair. A preliminary account of our researches may be found in Michael Meredith, 'Flight from Arezzo: Fact and Fictions in *The Ring and the Book*', SBHC 25 (2003) 101–116.

[2] Guido proclaimed his love of poetry in the Arezzo court on 2 July 1691 (Arezzo State Archives, *Atti criminali*, vol. 872, fo. 2422). It is likely that, early in their marriage, Guido and Pompilia read poetry together, particularly once it is recognized that much of their discordant married life, as described by Browning, is a fallacy. It is possible that later she read poetry with Caponsacchi, as Corrigan believes. Poetry was fashionable among the Aretine upper classes at this time. In 1683 the Accademia dei Forzati, later degli Arcadi, was founded to promote poetry. Its members, who in 1714 included Paolo Franceschini, were expected to write their own poems, keeping to strict forms and metres. See V. Gazzola Stacchini and G. Bianchini, *Le accademie dell'Aretino nel XVII e XVIII secolo* (Florence, 1978), 216–28.

Franceschini and Caponsacchi families not been brought before the law-courts so often, there would be less evidence to work from. That in itself is an ominous anticipation of the bloody events of 1698.

THE FRANCESCHINI FAMILY

Five of the Franceschini feature in *The Ring and the Book*: the widow Beatrice (née Romani), and her four children Porzia, Paolo, Girolamo, and Guido. They came from a well-established but impoverished Aretine family, one of the second rank of nobility, and had lived for several generations (unknown to Browning) in a modest town-house in the unfashionable Borgo de' Cenci. Descriptions in the poem of the faded grandeur of a vast gloomy Franceschini Palace are, therefore, well wide of the mark.

The family consisted of the two parents:

Tommaso	1617–81
Beatrice	1631–1701

and their five children:

Paolo	1650–1718
Porzia	1652–1738
Girolamo	1654–1724
Guido	1657–98
Anton Maria	1660–1730

Three other children—a girl and two boys—had died in infancy. The family owned farms and vineyards outside Arezzo, like most noble Aretine families, but the proceeds from these were insufficient to provide a comfortable existence. Their chief estates were vineyards and chestnut groves at Monistero and S. Formena,[3] five miles south of Arezzo, and olive and chestnut groves at San Severo and Peneto on the mountain-side to the north-east. Browning wrongly refers throughout *The Ring and the Book* to their villa at Vittiano, from where Guido hired some of his ruffians, but, if this

[3] Both villages exist today, although now called Monastero and S. Firmina. They are situated on hillsides, and, therefore, are not as rich and fertile as the estates on the plain, like those owned by the Caponsacchi family. San Severo and Peneto are higher up, suitable only for planting olive groves and chestnut trees.

ever existed, it belonged to another branch of the family, with whom Guido and his family had no communication.[4]

When Tommaso Franceschini died, his financial situation was sufficiently serious for Girolamo and Guido, both minors, to renounce their paltry inheritance and thus, presumably, avoid a number of lawsuits. Luckily Porzia made a good marriage to Aldobrandino dei Conti di Bivignano (1651–96) and led a prosperous and respectable life as wife and widow. She bore Aldobrandino twelve children. After Guido's execution, she petitioned the Priori in Arezzo for the restitution of her family's good name, which they granted in 1701.

The four Franceschini brothers, encouraged by their mother, whose family, the Romani, possessed powerful church patronage, looked to the priesthood for advancement. Paolo, the eldest and brightest, went to Rome, where he made a good career for himself as secretary to Cardinal Lauria, until his progress was blighted by Guido's behaviour, as recounted in *The Ring and the Book*. Selling up and leaving Rome in 1697, he spent a long wandering exile in Prague, Spain, Venice, and Milan, without ever finding satisfactory employment. He returned to Arezzo around 1712 and lived in the house in Borgo de' Cenci which had been left empty following the death of his mother and the imprisonment of brother Girolamo. For the rest of his life he assisted at the Pieve Church, his ambitions

[4] Vittiano (modern Vitiano) presents a problem. Browning obtained the name from OYB cxxviii (136), where Guido refers to the man who recommended two of the thugs who murdered Pompilia and her parents as 'Santi . . . a labourer of mine at my villa in Vittiano' [Santi . . . era mio lavoratore nella mia Villa di Vittiano]. However, this is false. Contemporary land records show that Guido's family did not own lands at Vittiano; any Franceschinis living in the village were not related to him. Had Guido owned a villa there, he and his family would surely have spent summers there, and Pompilia would have been sent there during the time she was reputed to be having an affair with Caponsacchi. How then may we explain the comment in OYB?

It is likely that there was a misunderstanding in the transcription of the legal argument in Pamphlet 9. Vittiano was usually called Villa Vittiano in the seventeenth and eighteenth centuries (a usage similar to the French 'ville', and common throughout Italy, e.g. Bagni di Lucca Villa). Guido employed a man from Vittiano, called Rossi, as a farm-labourer and bodyguard. The church records of Vittiano reveal a Santi Rossi at this time, and it almost certainly was he who recommended Alessandro Baldeschi and Biagio Agostinelli to Guido as potential murderers. The passage in OYB would, therefore, have been more accurate as 'Santi . . . a labourer of mine from Villa Vittiano'.

sadly curtailed. As a young man he had published a poem to his patron Cardinal Lauria, 'Presagio di prosperità all'armi cristiane nel presente assedio di Vienna', and, on his return, he was elected to the prestigious Accademia degli Arcadi in Arezzo. Paolo was among the academicians who presented their poems to Princess Violante Beatrice di Toscana on her visit to the city on 8 June 1714. This grand occasion, when Paolo recited his long adulatory ode to the princess, must have awakened memories of his time in Rome, when the world seemed at his feet. He died, unfulfilled, aged 68 in 1718.

Girolamo, the second brother, is described by Browning as fox-faced, vicious, lusting after his sister-in-law Pompilia. During Guido's marriage he certainly lived at home with his mother and the married couple, but there is no evidence that he was especially licentious. He was, however, a quarrelsome fellow, and in 1681 had been badly injured in a street brawl with the Caponsacchi family.[5] Later, in 1705, he was involved in another fight with more serious consequences. By then he was a canon of the Pieve, and on 1 September he attacked a fellow canon, Angiolo Lambardi, in the street with a knife, wounding him in the kidneys and chest. The cause of the quarrel was trivial—the withholding of twelve bushels of corn from Girolamo for failing to say a specific number of masses—but Lambardi died of his wounds, and Girolamo was charged with murder. He escaped the death-penalty, but was sentenced instead to life imprisonment.[6] Girolamo was released from prison in 1711 on the grounds of ill-health, and allowed by the bishop to return to his estate at Monistero, within sight of Arezzo, on the condition he did not return to the city.[7] He lived there in exile until his death in 1724, when he was buried in the local church.

[5] *Atti criminali*, 853. 148–9.

[6] Arezzo Diocesan Archives, *Curia vescovile, Atti criminali*, 2123.

[7] The Bishop's edict of 29 July 1711 concludes 'He has also promised and promises to keep at a two-mile distance from the town of Arezzo, not to go further than one mile from the above-said villa at Monistero. He can make an exception and go towards the town when he wants to go and stay in his villa at Santa Formena.' Both 'villas' were little more than farmhouses.

A more successful career was enjoyed by Anton Maria, the youngest brother. He became the priest at Pieve a Sovara in the diocese of Sansepolcro from 1692 to 1730.[8] There he exercised considerable influence, as Sovara had twelve dependent churches, with thirty priests under Anton Maria's jurisdiction. As the leading cleric he received substantial church taxes, often in the form of wheat and oil, which he stored in the barns behind his church. He was thus able to supply provisions for his family back in Arezzo. Guido made regular trips over the mountains to Sovara for this purpose, staying the night either with his brother or at the parish guest-house beside the Pieve. It was during some of these trips that Pompilia entertained Caponsacchi in Borgo de' Cenci. (One such assignation is recorded in the love-letters which passed between them.[9]) After Aldobrandino's death, Anton Maria also helped his sister Porzia's family in a similar way. Guido's later notoriety had less impact on him than on other members of the family, because Anton Maria had severed close ties with Arezzo, and his parishioners in Sovara would have been unaware of murders happening in Rome, however sensational their nature.

GUIDO FRANCESCHINI

Guido was the least clever and least decisive of the four brothers. Like his siblings he sought preferment in the church, but not as a priest. He was instead a cleric, that is a man with limited church duties who had taken no vows and could, therefore, doff his cassock, whenever he wished, for a secular post or for marriage. As such, Guido was in a good position to look after the family estates for his mother, leading a more domestic life than his brothers. Many of his late father's duties, therefore, devolved on Guido, not because he wished to take them on, but because there was no one else to do so. He remained at home in Borgo de' Cenci, sharing the house with his elder brother Canon Girolamo and his mother.

[8] A number of registers in his meticulous hand, recording births, marriages, and deaths, survive today in the vestry of the church at Pieve a Sovara.

[9] OYB xcvi (103).

He found his job, which included meeting his tenant farmers and negotiating the sale of produce, dull and routine. Guido lacked the ambition or the intelligence to make a success of it, and he began to drift. In 1686, when he was 28, Guido was before the Arezzo court accused of card-sharping.[10] He had joined a gambling circle in the city who used to meet at Father Fondati's; on this occasion it was claimed that they used fake cards and cheated while playing *minchiate*. Guido was acquitted on a technicality, but the case showed what company he was keeping.

Five years later Guido was arrested for being involved in a brawl over his mistress Annina di Minchione, nicknamed 'Minchioncina' ('The Little Fool').[11] Annina was a known prostitute, but Guido had been keeping her as his mistress for over a year and was fiercely possessive of her. When he discovered that he had a rival in Pietro Paolo Betti, a guard at the Porta Santo Spirito, near where Annina lived, Guido angrily forbade him to see the girl. Learning that his threats had been ineffective, Guido collected together a group of young thugs one night in July 1691 with the intention of punishing Betti, but unfortunately in the dark they mistook another man for the guard and beat him up instead.

The result of the case was inconclusive and Guido escaped punishment—after the indignity of a fortnight in the police cells—but his reputation was seriously damaged, because his choice of sexual companion was laughably inappropriate for a man of his rank. Clearly Guido found sexual relations easiest when the woman was either by profession or by age submissive, so his marriage to the 13-year-old Pompilia two years later was entirely in character. Also Guido's employment of ruffians to assist him set a precedent for his brutal revenge against Pompilia and her foster-parents in 1698. His failure to deal with Betti man-to-man anticipated his feebleness towards Caponsacchi in the inn at Castelnuovo.

After this debacle, Beatrice suggested that Guido should go to Rome to find a job in the church like brother Paolo. An appointment with the eminent Cardinal Nerli (formerly Archbishop of

10 *Atti criminali*, 867. 1077^{v}–1078^{r}.

11 Ibid. 872. 2364–67.

Florence) came to nothing, presumably because Guido lacked the ability or perseverance for the work, so he toyed with the idea of finding a rich wife. One day, when ordering a wig for a Florentine lady friend, he told the wig-maker, Antonia Scarduelli, that if she knew of a lady with a dowry of 8,000–10,000 scudi, he would marry her. Antonia, with the promise of money, effected the meeting with the Comparini which led to the marriage settlement between Guido and Pompilia recounted in the Old Yellow Book, and by Browning in his poem.

How accurate was Browning's depiction of Guido and of his married life in Arezzo? The man himself was neither as old nor as ugly as he was described. The beak nose, the bushy beard, the black hair, the pallid expression, came from the only physical description Browning could find, when, exhausted by torture and imprisonment, Guido was being led to execution—hardly the best circumstances in which to portray anyone. Earlier references to him, unknown to Browning, show him to have been a short man, looking younger than his years ('giovane' is a common appellation of him in Arezzo documents of 1697), a fine gentleman, wearing the fashionable long wig of the late seventeenth century. Pompilia, too, moved through the streets of Arezzo dressed in clothes and jewels appropriate to a count's wife ('andava vestita al pari d'ogni altra gentildonna di veste e di gioie conforme l'altre').[12] Witnesses after her escape remember her wearing beautiful silk dresses, with all sorts of pearl jewellery and rings. She was very pretty, but with a generous waist-line—'donna di bello aspetto . . . alquanto grassa che piuttosto li dava bellezza'.[13] Such descriptions do not suggest the ill-fed, well-guarded wife of Browning's poem.

These glimpses of the married couple call into question the accusation of domestic disharmony and unhappiness produced at Guido's trial and reported in the Old Yellow Book. Clearly there was friction for the first six months between Beatrice Franceschini and the Comparini, with the blame shared equally, as each family tried to assert its dominance over the other in the town house in Borgo de' Cenci. After her foster-parents departed back to Rome,

[12] *Atti criminali,* 884. 458^{v}.
[13] Ibid. 885. 1624^{v}.

the little girl Pompilia, still only thirteen, panicked and sought help from the Bishop and the Governor. Significantly both men returned her to her husband, so presumably they knew of nothing specially amiss with the marital home. We know that after his marriage Guido took his administrative responsibilities seriously and worked hard to raise money from his estates, and as Pompilia grew from girl to woman it seems that she was given a greater independence, which, with the advent of Giuseppe Caponsacchi, she abused. Food and drink were more plentiful than the testimony of a dismissed servant, Angelica from Castelluccio, suggested, and Guido kept a full cellar.

An incident in July 1696 revealing his vulnerability, happened in the Borgo di Seteria, next to the Pieve church, when Guido was manhandled by a local farmer, Onofrio Roselli, a tall man with chestnut-brown hair and beard, who punched him, banged his head against the church wall, and tore off his wig and neckerchief. The argument was about money Roselli claimed he was owed and which Guido denied. Luckily one of Guido's farm-labourers[14] who was with him helped to restore order, and Roselli was arrested and charged with assault.

This public humiliation, the lack of respect shown to Guido's rank, and the resulting gossip that went through the city was further exacerbated the following February, when rumours flew round Arezzo that Pompilia was unfaithful to him. As so often before Guido felt helpless. He did nothing in public, but confronted his wife privately, who denied everything, before mocking him as 'the Jealous One' in letters to her lover. Far from being tyrannical and domineering, Guido was well-intentioned but passive, irresolute and feeble. When he was put upon, he was slow to anger, but after further provocation his anger would boil over, and he would behave impetuously and spitefully. He was, therefore, no match for the clever and charismatic Caponsacchi.

[14] The farm-labourer was Santi Rossi (see n. 4). Rossi, who seems to have accompanied Guido as a protector, lifted Roselli off the ground ['mi prese di peso'] and stopped his assault. For the court cross-examination of Roselli, see *Atti criminali*, 881 [27 July 1696].

THE CAPONSACCHI FAMILY

The Caponsacchi led an affluent life in their large house in Canto de' Bacci on the main street a hundred yards down from the Romanesque church of Santa Maria della Pieve. They owned larger and more fertile farms than the Franceschini, and were one of the leading aristocratic families of Arezzo.

Giuseppe Maria Caponsacchi was the fifteenth of twenty-one children, and it is, therefore, unlikely he had a close relationship with his parents; instead he would have been brought up by family servants and his older siblings. Eight of his brothers and sisters died before he was eleven, and he lost his father when he was eighteen. His family consisted of his parents:

Ludovico	died 1690
Maddalena (née Guazzesi)	1637–1714

and the following children, many of whom Giuseppe never knew:

Margherita	1655–66
Francesco	1657–78
Lisabetta	1658
Maria Maddalena	1659–1729
Orsola Maria	1660
Pietro Paolo	1662–1735
Orsola	1663
Maria Anna	1664
Cristofano Donato	1665–89
Alessandro	1666–76
Margherita	1668
Tommaso	1669–*post* 1728
Anton Simone	1670
Maria Vittoria	1671–6
Giuseppe Maria	1672–1728
Maria Anna	1674
Maria Alloisia	1675–83
Maria Vittoria	1676–83
Alessandro	1678
Pier Francesco	1683
Francesca Giustina	1683–4

The impressionable young Giuseppe took as his role-model his elder brother Pietro Paolo, ten years his senior and constantly in trouble. He was a swaggerer, proud of his machismo, a street-brawler who enjoyed carrying illegal weapons. In 1681 he was arrested for attacking Girolamo Franceschini and cutting him on the face and head with his dagger,[15] while his brutality with prostitutes led to a six-month exile in 1683, after he stabbed a girl called Angiola in the stomach, having first raped her in the public street.[16]

Not all Giuseppe's brothers behaved in this way. Two, both sadly short-lived, had been priests, and it is possible that the death of the younger of these, Cristofano Donato (as well as Giuseppe's first appearance in front of the magistrates at the age of 18 on an assault charge), led his family to suggest that he, too, might like to make a career for himself in the church. Giuseppe became a cleric in November 1693, took minor orders in September 1694, was made a subdeacon the following December, and soon became a Canon of the Pieve, his local church. At no time was he a full priest able to celebrate Mass, but he wore clerical clothes, assumed the tonsure, and had regular full-time duties at the Pieve. Had things turned out differently, he would have taken the final step and committed his life to Christ.

THE AREZZO 'BOYS'

Some time during the early 1690s Giuseppe Caponsacchi joined a group of upper-class youths and young men who, bored with their comfortable and aimless lives, sought excitement at night under cover of darkness. This group had no leader and no organization; its escapades were usually improvised rather than planned. Its members participated irregularly, and left altogether when they married.

[15] Ibid. 853. 4355–6; 855. 148–9. This episode, which is discussed further in Meredith, op. cit., p. 107, reveals the Caponsacchi and Franceschini families brawling in the streets of Arezzo like the Montagues and Capulets in *Romeo and Juliet*.

[16] *Atti criminali*, 858. 2289–90; 861. 4463^{v}.

The two most common activities were fighting and fornicating. All the group possessed illegal guns, swords, and daggers, which they carried for bravado, to spite the heavy police presence in the streets. They sometimes turned these on each other, or on citizens of Arezzo against whom they had a grudge. Injuries were common (and occasionally there were fatalities) in the fighting and brawling that ensued. Sometimes aggression was shown towards women, particularly prostitutes, as the young men sought sexual satisfaction without having to pay the usual price for their pleasures.

There were, however, differences between this unsavoury crowd and the riff-raff of most cities. They were nearly all from aristocratic or well-to-do families, and therefore were not frequenters of the many inns and taverns in Arezzo, which had a more working-class clientele. Alcohol and drunkenness appeared to play little part in their activities; if they drank, it was with each other in their own houses.

When they were arrested, which happened very frequently, it was common practice for this group of young men to lie on oath and to pretend they were elsewhere when the offence occurred. 'Character' witnesses were called to assert their nobility and good name. Mocking the law and its representatives, usually in the shape of some fairly unintelligent guards or policemen, became part of the game. The young men actively enjoyed outwitting the magistrates, most times escaping scot-free even when guilty. On the few times they were convicted, the fines were so paltry that they were easily paid, while tougher sentences were always subject to appeal.

Giuseppe Caponsacchi's particular friends were Gasparri Massi and the Guillichini brothers, Gregorio, Marcello, and Pietro Paolo. He also knew members of the distinguished Romani and Conti families. All were of the same age, in their early twenties, though Massi was slightly older, thirty-two, at the time of Pompilia's escape.

Gasparri Massi had the reputation of being the most successful womanizer of the group, and led his younger friends towards the Arezzo red-light district near the Porta Santo Spirito, where he was well known. There could be found in her untidy two-roomed house Elizabetta Lanzini (called Lanzina), known to many of the young idle rich. Massi's particular favourite was her 23-year-old daughter Caterina, with whom he was sleeping on the night of Pompilia and Caponsacchi's flight, and which he used as an acceptable alibi when he was arrested. At that time, however, Massi's attention was all towards Lanzina's other daughter, the beautiful Maria, unexpectedly still a virgin. Using the help of a bawd, Anna Bembo, who lived next door, he importuned her hotly. A meeting was arranged for 27 March 1697 when Maria held him off, but on Maundy Thursday she succumbed. From then on Massi paid her a retainer on a daily basis.[17] When he discovered she was five months pregnant, he arranged for her to be married to a 45-year-old vagrant, and himself attended the wedding breakfast. Thereafter he slept with both sisters at will. It was Gasparri Massi who on occasions stood sentinel when Giuseppe Caponsacchi paid surreptitious visits to Pompilia in Borgo de' Cenci.

With this man as friend, it was not surprising that Caponsacchi, even though he was a subdeacon, had sexual encounters himself. One unsuccessful venture was a visit on consecutive nights in May 1696 to two girls who lived in a house adjacent to San Domenico church. Caponsacchi and four friends knocked at the door and were refused entry. One of his friends climbed in through an upstairs window to let in the others, taking the door off its hinges in the process. The girls claimed 'they touched our breasts, kissed us, and abused us in other ways'.[18] The following night the men broke in again and took the girls for a forced walk to a grassy hill, where some indecent behaviour took place, for which, the girls reported, they were given nothing—presumably because they denied the men full intercourse.

Caponsacchi and the others were arrested for their lewd behaviour and brought to trial. Before sentencing, Caponsacchi took sanctuary in the church of Sant'Adriano, where his friend Urbano Romani was priest. He stayed there a month, during which time he improved his pistol shooting in the garden, before he was arrested on another count. Foolishly he had left the safety of the priest's house and was taking the air with Urbano and some friends,

[17] *Atti criminali*, 884. 667 ff.
[18] Ibid. 886. 315 ff.

including one who had abused the women with him, when they were accosted by two policemen. Caponsacchi fired his flint-lock rifle at them, but the bullet ricocheted off a wall and accidentally hit Urbano in the leg. A second shot pierced a policeman's jerkin.[19]

Caponsacchi was described after his affair with Pompilia as 'persona arbitriaria',[20] which can best be translated in these circumstances as 'headstrong'. His dubious reputation was known throughout Arezzo, and it was stated at his trial that 'he was imprisoned and tried for his low morals more than once'.[21] The picture Browning draws of him as the young priest, attracted to a secular life, at ease in high society, yet ultimately loyal to his calling, is, therefore, completely false. Instead, Caponsacchi was a hedonist and a hypocrite, participating in the services at the Pieve by day, and then seeking out cheap thrills by night, while openly flouting the law. As a member of Arezzo's privileged young, he could always depend on the support of his rich friends to help him out of a fix. For example, among those signing an affidavit alleging Guido's 'cruelty' towards Pompilia, used by the prosecution in Franceschini's trial for murder, were Marco Romani, Urbano Romani, and Francesco Jacopo Conti, all of whom were complicit with Caponsacchi in disreputable practices, and whose word was worth absolutely nothing. Yet the testimony of such men contributed to Guido's downfall.[22]

THE LOVE AFFAIR

Soon after Caponsacchi extricated himself from the shooting drama, he became aware of the plump, blossoming Pompilia—more desirable and yet potentially more dangerous than his previous conquests. Undaunted, he was soon parading down Borgo de'

[19] *Atti criminali*, 884. 265^{v}.

[20] Ibid. 885. 1609^{r}.

[21] Ibid.

[22] OYB liii (53–4). It is surprising that Guido's defence counsel did not make this point at the murder trial. Either he was badly briefed or incompetent. At no time did he cite Caponsacchi's reputation for womanizing. On the other hand the prosecution made much of a partial and inaccurate account of the conditions Pompilia was forced to endure in her husband's house.

Cenci, glancing up at her windows, accompanied by his best friends Gregorio Guillichini and Gasparri Massi. At first he merely raised his hat, but later tried to speak to her.[23] Love letters passed between the two of them, some of which were carried by Canon Conti, a friend of Caponsacchi's who had easy entry into the Franceschini home as Porzia's brother-in-law.

To begin with, it was little more than a light flirtation, Caponsacchi writing her poems and she hunting for suitable passages in Tasso among her husband's books. The impetuous Caponsacchi and his world was a completely new experience for the young girl on the threshold of womanhood, and she fell deeply in love with the priest, the first time in her short life she had experienced strong passion for anyone. She required something more than the devotion accorded to a courtly lady, which he was giving her. The game needed to become real.

Caponsacchi, who had always seen her as a desirable conquest, took advantage of her infatuation and they devised times to meet when Guido and Girolamo were out of town. Beatrice proved a stumbling-block, as the lovers could never be sure of her movements. On one occasion she returned when Caponsacchi was with Pompilia: within minutes Pompilia, lantern in hand, was seen by neighbours slowly opening the door to allow Caponsacchi to slip into the street and escape.

By February 1697 their secret was out. Canon Conti no longer agreed to act as go-between, and may have told Guido what was happening. On Caponsacchi's orders, Gregorio Guillichini was sent to various houses to silence the more voluble gossips by threatening them with beatings.[24] Guido became more and more suspicious. As Pompilia was now being watched, the lovers had to be even more careful.

Events were forced when, in early April, Pompilia became pregnant. The young wife, only too aware that the baby was not her husband's, pleaded to be taken away from Arezzo, so Caponsacchi had to devise a plan. On Palm Sunday he sent two

[23] *Atti criminali*, 884. 454–5.

[24] Ibid. 884. 456; 885. 1614–15. One of the witnesses, Margherita Bacci, claimed she saw Caponsacchi lurking in the doorway when Guillichini threatened her.

illiterate young Aretines, Paolo and Luca, to Rome with a letter to Pietro Comparini, Pompilia's foster-father, and told Luca he expected letters to be brought back. Pietro read the letter but informed Luca that there was no reply, an answer that so enraged Caponsacchi that he refused to pay the boys the money he had promised them.

What exactly was the Caponsacchi plan? He clearly wished to restore Pompilia to the Comparini in Rome, but what then? Would he have given up his orders and married her, after she had obtained a judicial separation from Guido? Such a suggestion was unthinkable in the late seventeenth century, even though Pompilia in one of the love-letters had stated that, if it could be accomplished, she would 'more willingly be your wife than your servant'.[25] Did he hope merely to carry on a relationship with her away from Arezzo, or thankfully rid himself of a girl who was becoming a liability? The latter solution would be in character. Reading between the lines of the carefully worded but false statement he made to the Rome court, it would seem this is what he intended.

He had first to get her to Rome. He would hire a carriage for them both, ask the driver to park it outside the northern San Clemente gate by a quiet farmhouse owned by the nuns of St Catherine (the former Horse Inn). Near there was a dilapidated part of the high walls over which the lovers might scramble at night when the city gates were shut. He alerted his friends to help him, and then set a date: 28 April at midnight. All Pompilia had to do was to drug the family's wine, so they would be soundly asleep when she escaped.

Both Pompilia's and Caponsacchi's accounts of what happened next survive. Both are fabrications, in the case of Pompilia through fear of telling the truth, in the case of Caponsacchi through cunning. The truth and the exact order of events on 27–9 April 1697, in which Gregorio Guillichini and one of his brothers had an important part to play, and which Gasparri Massi was privy to, can be accurately reconstructed from the contemporary police files.

[25] OYB xcvi (103).

THE ESCAPE

27 April

Afternoon	At the Canal Inn opposite the Pieve, Caponsacchi ordered a *calèche* (a two-wheeled light carriage, capable of travelling at fast speeds) for the following day. He told the inn-keeper Agostino Chimenti he wished to go to Camoscia on business late at night. The driver should wait for him by the former Horse Inn outside the walls. He would be late, nearly midnight, as he had to go home to change from his cassock, and then go to his villa at Patrignone 'to collect a few trifles he wanted to carry with him'.[26]

28 April

Midday	Pompilia went to the Pieve church with Porzia, where Caponsacchi was assisting at the Mass. This meant they could communicate, at least by looks. The sight of him stiffened her resolve for the evening's adventure.
8.00 p.m.	Francesco Bossi (known as Venerino), just after sunset and before the San Clemente gate was closed for the night, drove the *calèche* to the Horse Inn farmhouse. He persuaded Mattio, the deaf old farmer, to allow him to park it out of sight at the entrance to a barn. He then made himself and his two horses comfortable for the long wait.
8.45 p.m.	Pompilia took her mother-in-law supper on a tray in her bedroom. (Beatrice had been ill for a fortnight with a fever and was still not well enough to come downstairs.) The old lady took one look at the cloudy red wine Pompilia had doctored, and refused to drink it. Luckily Guido had just returned and he poured his

[26] This, of course, was a lie, to explain away the long gap of time between sunset and the midnight assignation and escape with Pompilia. Camoscia is today known as Camucia.

	mother a carafe of fresh white wine from a cask in the cellar. Pompilia, therefore, knew that later that evening she would have to be very careful, as Beatrice might be woken by any noise.
9.30 p.m.	At dinner (which Pompilia did not eat on the pretext she had dined earlier) Guido and Girolamo drank the drugged wine rejected by Beatrice, as well as some laid out for them by Pompilia.
9.45 p.m.	Caponsacchi arrived at Guillichini's house next to San Vito church, where he sat at the open window with Gregorio and his brother Pietro Paolo. Stuffed in his pockets were Pompilia's recent letters to him.
10.00 p.m.	Guido and Pompilia went to bed, where Guido quickly fell into a drugged sleep.
10.15 p.m.	Pompilia dressed herself and began to collect together clothes and jewellery for the journey. She had keys for most of the chests and cases, but had to force one jewel-box.
11.00 p.m.	Pietro Paolo Guillichini left his home to take up his position as look-out on the Via Sacra, the route the lovers would use. On his way he was stopped by two guards and asked what he was doing. His reply satisfied them, and he was able to divert them to another part of the city.
11.45 p.m.	Caponsacchi and Gregorio Guillichini, heavily armed, entered the Franceschini house through a neighbouring building to avoid being seen. They clambered through a store-room which Pompilia had unlocked, and found her waiting for them with the pile of clothes and jewels ready.

29 April

Midnight	Pompilia, dressed in a black bonnet and a rich blue cloak trimmed with gold, left the house with Caponsacchi and Guillichini, carrying between them an arquebus, two rifles, a short sword, and a dagger, as

well as Pompilia's loot which included a suit of Guido's, presumably intended for her father. Caponsacchi was wearing a black jacket, a black hat with a silver border, and a neckerchief.

12.15 a.m. The police battered on Lanzina's door, and discovered Gasparri Massi *in flagrante delicto* with her elder daughter. Knowing of Caponsacchi's escapade, Massi had deliberately chosen to go to Lanzina's to provide himself with an alibi when questioned next day.

12.30 a.m. The lovers and Guillichini reached the San Clemente gate, having made slow careful progress along the Via Sacra, specially chosen for its lack of night travellers, as it was bordered by churches and monasteries.

12.45 a.m. They clambered over the wall at Il Torrione, no easy feat with all their luggage, and made their way towards the *calèche*, using the high walls as cover from the bright moonlight. Guillichini waved the lovers goodbye, as Venerino set off towards Camoscia.

1.15 a.m. Gregorio Guillichini, on his way to Borgo de' Cenci to make sure all was quiet, was stopped by two guards at La Chiavica, a crossing in the Borgo Maestro, only a few yards from Franceschini's house. He had difficulty in throwing them off, and was relieved to find all was well in Borgo de' Cenci. Beatrice had not woken up.

1.30 a.m. Nearing Camoscia, the *calèche* was passed by Donna Costanza's carriage going in the opposite direction.[27] She noted its great speed, but was able to recognize Caponsacchi with a lady. Just before this Venerino claimed he saw the lovers kissing.

1.40 a.m. The lovers reached Camoscia.

2.10 a.m. Caponsacchi and Pompilia changed carriages, waiting impatiently half an hour for the new horses to be fed at Pietro Sandini's inn. They left nearly all their

[27] Donna Costanza was the widow of Domenico Santi of Arezzo. She lived in the Sant'Adriano district, very close to the Franceschini, and therefore would have known Pompilia and Caponsacchi by sight. She gave evidence on 3 June 1697 before the Aretine court that on 29 April, as she was returning home from Cortona in the early hours, she recognized the lovers travelling in the opposite direction.

	weapons at Camoscia, and set out for Perugia en route for Rome.
c.8.00 a.m.	Guido woke and discovered his wife missing. A quick search of the house with his mother revealed what had happened.
c.10.30 a.m.	Guido began the pursuit, accompanied by a posse of police officers. At Foligno the Chief of Police and one of his men, Anton Francesco Bartoli, turned back, leaving the pursuit to the rest.

THE AFTERMATH

Once Caponsacchi and Pompilia had been arrested at Castelnuovo, Guido engrossed himself in legal matters and moved to Florence to be near the best advocates. He immediately brought a suit of *processus fugae* against the lovers in Rome, where they were correctly found guilty of carnal intercourse, in spite of their denials. The leniency of their sentences must have disappointed Guido, especially the sequestration of Caponsacchi in the monastery at Civitavecchia for three years.

Simultaneously Guido prosecuted his wife, Guillichini, and Venerino in Arezzo. (Caponsacchi, being a cleric, could not be tried in a civil court.) Guillichini, recognizing that the game was up, took refuge in San Vito, the church next door to his mother's house, when the police came to arrest him. As they entered the church, he made his way to the roof and was then chased through Arezzo until he reached the monastery of San Bernardo, where he took sanctuary for several months.[28] In December the court sentenced him to five years in the galleys at Portoferraio for his part in helping Pompilia to escape. It is highly unlikely that he served any of his sentence, for he died, probably of a fever, in Arezzo in October 1698 at the age of 24. He took to the grave the secret of whether or not he was, like Caponsacchi, Pompilia's lover.

Pompilia was herself found guilty by the Arezzo court, but, as she was already under the jurisdiction of the Rome court and in the

[28] *Atti Criminali*, 885. 1618–19.

Scalette convent, sentence was suspended. (She had just begun a suit of her own against Guido for a legal separation, which was never concluded owing to both their deaths.) The hapless Venerino, after a number of cross-examinations during which he became befuddled and contradicted himself, was found not guilty and acquitted.

The release of Pompilia from prison into the care of her foster-parents, and the birth of her son in December, incensed Guido. He felt that he had been humiliated and the guilty had escaped their rightful punishment. Taking the law into his own hands, he and his four hired men travelled to Rome where they murdered Pompilia and her parents in a bloody action, which was both clumsy and inept. Not only was Pompilia left alive for a few days to testify against them and to attract enormous sympathy to herself, but the murderers had no sensible escape plan and so were quickly apprehended and imprisoned.

Their trial, which forms the central issue of *The Ring and the Book*, could just as easily have ended in acquittal as condemnation. The defence arguments were as strong as, if not stronger than, those used by the prosecution, so that Guido was unlucky in the sentence and in the Pope's refusal of mercy. As with the Thane of Cawdor, nothing in Guido's wretched life became him like the leaving of it: he behaved with calm dignity on the scaffold and during the preliminary gruesome religious rites.

Pompilia's lingering death and the confessions she made to the Augustinian priests were well advertised through Rome. Such statements as 'she died as an innocent martyr', 'she was the most exemplary and edifying Christian I have ever seen', and 'the bystanders blessed her as a saint'[29] influenced the Rome court, just as later they influenced Robert Browning. They may well also have contributed towards the severity of Guido's sentence. In September 1698, six months after his execution, the same Rome court formally confirmed Pompilia's good name.

This last judgment was plainly wrong. However sympathetic one may feel towards Pompilia as a victim caught up in circumstances that bewildered and terrified her, she was guilty of adultery.

[29] OYB lvii–lx (58–61).

She had lied again and again: about the love-letters and her alleged illiteracy, about her relationship with Caponsacchi, about her escape from Arezzo, about her arrival at Castelnuovo, and finally on her death-bed. Sold first by her prostitute mother, then forced to marry an unsuitable husband by her foster-parents, she was seduced by Caponsacchi into a relationship that could only end in disaster for her, if not for him.

Caponsacchi, of course, survived. After serving his three years at Civitavecchia, he returned to Arezzo, where he resigned his canonship of the Pieve in 1702, though he still remained a subdeacon. He was little changed by his experiences. As late as 1724 he was before the courts for drawing a knife in a brawl after being accused of cheating at cards in the casino. His accuser, Leonetto Lauri, threw a candlestick at him; he retaliated by throwing another and the brawl ensued.[30] Yet again in this trial Caponsacchi appears to have lied on oath. He died, having received the last rites, on 17 August 1728 and was buried the same day in the church of the Augustinians. He was 56 years old.

Beatrice Franceschini outlived Guido by three years, loyal to the end. She was lucky not to have to endure the trial of a second son for murder. After Girolamo's imprisonment the house in Borgo de' Cenci became empty. It was looked after by a maid-servant Marzia and a friend of Guido's, Carlo Santoli, until Paolo returned from his wanderings in 1712. He lived there until his death, when Porzia, by now a widow, moved in with some of her family. On her own death in 1732, memories of Guido and his misfortunes faded. Soon they were relegated to a few lines or a footnote in the histories of Arezzo—until Robert Browning found the Old Yellow Book on the stall beside the Church of San Lorenzo in Florence in 1860, and began to write his poem. It is through his account that Guido, Pompilia, and Caponsacchi are remembered today, in a compelling fiction which bears little relation to the truth.

[30] *Atti criminali*, 921. 1293; 924. 341–3; 925. 3333.